W9-DCO-390

Fodor's 2000

Switzerland

by Nancy Coons

The complete guide, thoroughly up-to-date

Packed with details that will make your trip

The must-see sights, off and on the beaten path

What to see, what to skip

Mix-and-match vacation itineraries

City strolls, countryside adventures

Smart lodging and dining options

Essential local do's and taboos

Transportation tips, distances and directions

Key contacts, savvy travel tips

When to go, what to pack

Clear, accurate, easy-to-use maps

Books to read, videos to watch, background essay

Fodor's Travel Publications, Inc. • New York, Toronto, London, Sydney, Auckland
www.fodors.com/switzerland

Fodor's Switzerland

EDITOR: Jennifer J. Paull

Editorial Contributors: Katrin Gygax, Jennifer McDermott, Kara Misenheimer, Ian Plenderleith, Helayne Schiff, Lito Tejada-Flores, Susan Rose, Susan Tuttle-Laube, Kay Winzenried

Editorial Production: Linda K. Schmidt

Maps: David Lindroth, *cartographer*; Bob Blake, *map editor*

Design: Fabrizio La Rocca, *creative director;* Guido Caroti, *art director;* Jolie Novak, *photo editor*

Cover Design: Pentagram

Production/Manufacturing: Mike Costa

Cover Photograph: Peter Guttman

Copyright

Copyright © 1999 by Fodor's Travel Publications, Inc.

Fodor's is a registered trademark of Random House, Inc.

All rights reserved under International and Pan-American Copyright Conventions. Published in the United States by Fodor's Travel Publications, Inc., a division of Random House, Inc., New York, and simultaneously in Canada by Random House of Canada Limited, Toronto. Distributed by Random House, Inc., New York.

No maps, illustrations, or other portions of this book may be reproduced in any form without written permission from the publisher.

ISBN 0–679–00345–2

ISSN 0071–6553

Special Sales

Fodor's Travel Publications are available at special discounts for bulk purchases for sales promotions or premiums. Special editions, including personalized covers, excerpts of existing guides, and corporate imprints, can be created in large quantities for special needs. For more information, contact your local bookseller or write to Special Markets, Fodor's Travel Publications, 201 East 50th Street, New York, NY 10022. Inquiries from Canada should be directed to your local Canadian bookseller or sent to Random House of Canada, Ltd., Marketing Department, 2775 Matheson Boulevard East, Mississauga, Ontario L4W 4P7. Inquiries from the United Kingdom should be sent to Fodor's Travel Publications, 20 Vauxhall Bridge Road, London SW1V 2SA, England.

PRINTED IN THE UNITED STATES OF AMERICA

10 9 8 7 6 5 4 3 2 1

Important Tip

Although all prices, opening times, and other details in this book are based on information supplied to us at press time, changes occur all the time in the travel world, and Fodor's cannot accept responsibility for facts that become outdated or for inadvertent errors or omissions. So **always confirm information when it matters,** especially if you're making a detour to visit a specific place.

CONTENTS

Maps and Charts

ON THE ROAD WITH FODOR'S

EVERY Y2K TRIP is a significant trip. So if there was ever a time you needed excellent travel information, it's now. Acutely aware of that fact, we've pulled out all stops in preparing *Fodor's Switzerland 2000*. To guide you in putting together your Swiss experience, we've created multiday itineraries and neighborhood walks. And to direct you to the places that are truly worth your time and money in this important year, we've rallied the team of endearingly picky know-it-alls we're pleased to call our writers. Having seen all corners of the regions they cover for us, they're real experts. If you knew them, you'd poll them for tips yourself.

About Our Writers

Nancy Coons has been tracing ancestral trails in Switzerland since moving to Europe in 1987, when she also began covering Luxembourg, Belgium, and much of northeastern France for Fodor's. Based in her 300-year-old farmhouse in Lorraine, she has written on European culture and food for the *Wall Street Journal, European Travel & Life, Opera News,* and *National Geographic Traveler.*

Katrin Gygax was born in Zürich. She moved to California when she was four, Vancouver when she was six, and didn't stop traveling for the next 28 years. Now based in Zürich with her own translating business, she also writes movie reviews for a Swiss fashion magazine, is working on a mystery-novel series, and sings whenever possible. For this edition she updated the Eastern Switzerland and Luzern and Central Switzerland chapters.

Geneva updater **Jennifer McDermott** arrived in the city at age 11 and can't quite imagine living anywhere else. Her career as a freelance writer and editor began in 1997 with the editorship of *The Illustrated Greek Wine Guide* (Olive Press, 1999), and she is a member of the Geneva Writers Group. She also writes poetry, monitors Geneva's cultural scene for a local radio station, and teaches theater to young people.

The first flight **Kara Misenheimer** took *anywhere* was to Switzerland. After more than a decade of constant contact with the country, she still sits in awe on train trips through its Alpine splendor, searching out a window seat on even the most familiar routes. A writer/producer and musician, she hasn't yet tried her hand at penning her Heidi-like adventures, but she has published a number of CD-ROMs, collaborated on European Union information projects, and performed with the Basel Opera. Her current work in film, publishing, and international media spans cities on several continents—from Helvetia to Hollywood. For this edition she updated the Graubünden and Basel chapters.

Zürich and Valais updater **Ian Plenderleith** is a freelance journalist and writer whose time is chiefly devoted to looking after his two young daughters. In the summer of 1999 he moved with his family to Washington, D.C., leaving behind his twin Swiss loves of Lake Zürich and the soccer team FC Zürich.

Susan Rose, a writer, translator, and editor, is a native of California. She speaks French, German, and several animal languages including Sheep—many of which came in handy during the update of the Fribourg, Neuchâtel, and the Jura chapter. She holds advanced degrees in linguistics and documentary film, as well as a certificate in motherhood and intercultural family life. She lives next to a cow pasture near Fribourg.

Susan Tuttle-Laube has been showing Switzerland to family and friends since moving there in 1981. As an "outsider living on the inside," she enjoys discovering the details that make the difference between a good trip and a great one; in this edition, the Bern, Berner Oberland, and Ticino chapters benefited from her perspective. Her book *Inside Outlandish* (Bergli Books, Basel, Switzerland 1997) recounts her mostly humorous experiences as a foreigner living abroad.

Vaud updater **Kay Winzenried** made her first visit to Switzerland in 1980 and has returned every year since. Now a dual citizen by marriage, she has lived in both the French- and German-speaking regions. She's used the centrally located country as

On the Road with Fodor's

a base for travels throughout Europe and a solo trip around the world, and as a training site for high-altitude trekking. Hiking with friends, exploring vineyards, and dining—be it rustic or haute cuisine—are her pleasures.

We'd also like to thank the staff of the Swiss regional tourist offices, as well as Erika Lieben and Evelyne Mock of the Switzerland Tourism office in New York, for their help with questions big and small.

Don't Forget to Write

Keeping a travel guide fresh and up-to-date is a big job. So we love your feedback— positive and negative—and follow up on all suggestions. Contact the Switzerland editor at editors@fodors.com or c/o Fodor's, 201 East 50th Street, New York, New York 10022. And have a wonderful trip!

Karen Cure
Editorial Director

Switzerland (Suisse, Schweiz, Svizzera)

Cantons of Switzerland

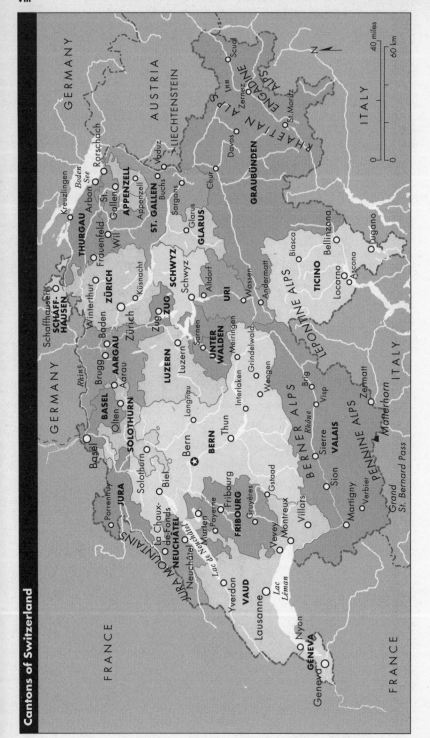

SMART TRAVEL TIPS A TO Z

Basic Information on Traveling in Switzerland,
Savvy Tips to Make Your Trip a Breeze, and
Companies and Organizations to Contact

AIR TRAVEL

BOOKING YOUR FLIGHT

When you book **look for nonstop flights** and **remember that "direct" flights stop at least once.** Try to avoid connecting flights, which require a change of plane.

CARRIERS

When flying internationally, you must usually choose among a domestic carrier, the national flag carrier of the country you are visiting, and a foreign carrier from a third country. You may, for example, choose to fly Swissair to Switzerland. National flag carriers have the greatest number of nonstops. Domestic carriers may have better connections to your hometown and serve a greater number of gateway cities. Third-party carriers may have a price advantage.

➤ MAJOR AIRLINES: **Air Canada** (☎ 800/776–3000) to Geneva, Zürich. **American Airlines** (☎ 800/433–7300) to Zürich. **Delta** (☎ 800/221–1212) to Zürich. **Swissair** (☎ 800/221–4750) to Geneva, Zürich and Basel.

➤ FROM THE U.K.: **British Airways** (☎ 0345/222–111) flies directly to Zürich from London's Heathrow or Gatwick airports, as does **Swissair** (☎ 020/7434–7300). There are nine flights daily. **Crossair** (☎ 020/7439–4144) offers direct service from London City, **Swissair** and **Aer Lingus** (☎ 020/8899–4747) from Manchester. **EasyJet** (☎ 0870/600–0000) flies direct between London Luton and Zürich. Service to Geneva has greatly improved. There are now five nonstop flights daily by BA and four by Swissair from Heathrow. The flying time is 1 hour 35 minutes. There are three daily BA flights from Gatwick, and Crossair has three daily flights from London City Airport. Basel's airport (Euro Airport) has two BA flights from Heathrow daily, while Crossair offers three flights daily from Heathrow. Crossair also offers a weekly flight from Gatwick to Sion. EasyJet has three daily flights between London Luton and Geneva, plus a daily flight from Liverpool to Geneva.

➤ SMALLER AIRLINES: **Air Engiadina** (☎ 0848/848328 for reservations), a regional airline, uses small planes to make short-hop flights within Switzerland and to other European cities. **Crossair** (☎ 0848/852000 for reservations), based in Basel's EuroAirport, has direct routes between several Swiss cities, as well as international flights.

CHECK-IN & BOARDING

Assuming that not everyone with a ticket will show up, airlines routinely overbook planes. When that happens, airlines ask for volunteers to give up their seats. In return these volunteers usually get a certificate for a free flight and are rebooked on the next flight out. If there are not enough volunteers, the airline must choose who will be denied boarding. The first to get bumped are passengers who checked in late and those flying on discounted tickets, so **get to the gate and check in as early as possible,** especially during peak periods.

Always **bring a government-issued photo ID to the airport.** You may be asked to show it before you are allowed to check in.

CUTTING COSTS

The least-expensive airfares to Switzerland must usually be purchased in advance and are nonrefundable. It's smart to **call a number of airlines, and when you are quoted a good price, book it on the spot**—the same fare may not be available the next day. Always **check different routings** and look into

SMART TRAVEL TIPS A TO Z

using different airports. Travel agents, especially low-fare specialists (☞ Discounts & Deals, *below*), are helpful.

Consolidators are another good source. They buy tickets for scheduled international flights at reduced rates from the airlines, then sell them at prices that beat the best fare available directly from the airlines, usually without restrictions. Sometimes you can even get your money back if you need to return the ticket. Carefully read the fine print detailing penalties for changes and cancellations, and **confirm your consolidator reservation with the airline.**

When you **fly as a courier** you trade your checked-luggage space for a ticket deeply subsidized by a courier service. There are restrictions on when you can book and how long you can stay.

➤ CONSOLIDATORS: **Cheap Tickets** (☎ 800/377–1000). **Up & Away Travel** (☎ 212/889–2345). **Discount Airline Ticket Service** (☎ 800/576–1600). **Unitravel** (☎ 800/325–2222). **World Travel Network** (☎ 800/409–6753).

➤ COURIERS: **Air Courier Association** (✉ 15000 W. 6th Ave., Suite 203, Golden, CO 80401, ☎ 800/282–1202, www.aircourier.org).

International Association of Air Travel Couriers (✉ 220 S. Dixie Hwy. no. 3, P.O. Box 1349, Lake Worth, FL 33460, ☎ 561/582–8320, FAX 561/582–1581, www.courier.org).

Now Voyager Travel (✉ 74 Varick St., Suite 307, New York, NY 10013 ☎ 212/431–1616, FAX 212/219–1753 or 212/334–5243, www.nowvoyager-travel.com).

DOMESTIC FLIGHTS

The entire country of Switzerland is smaller in area than the state of West Virginia, so flying from one region to another is a luxury that, considering the efficiency of the trains, few travelers require—unless there's a convenient connection from your intercontinental arrival point (Geneva, Zürich) to a lesser airport (Basel, Bern, Lugano, St. Moritz). Crossair (☞ Smaller Airlines, *above*)

is Switzerland's domestic airline, servicing local airports and various Continental cities as well: Brussels, Düsseldorf, Florence, Nice, Paris, London, and Venice.

For 20 SF per bag round-trip, air travelers on Swissair and partner airlines holding tickets or passes on Swiss Federal Railways can forward their luggage to their final destination, allowing them to make stops on the way unencumbered; the baggage is retrieved from the train station of the final destination. Baggage check-in and issuance of boarding passes is also possible at 116 train stations in Switzerland. A "Fly–Rail Baggage" brochure is available free of charge, in English, from the Swiss Federal Railways (☎ 1572222; 1.19 SF/min).

ENJOYING THE FLIGHT

For more legroom **request an emergency-aisle seat.** Don't sit in the row in front of the emergency aisle or in front of a bulkhead, where seats may not recline. If you have dietary concerns, **ask for special meals when booking.** These can be vegetarian, low-cholesterol, or kosher, for example. On long flights, try to maintain a normal routine, to help fight jet lag. At night **get some sleep.** By day **eat light meals, drink water** (not alcohol), and **move around the cabin** to stretch your legs.

Many carriers have prohibited smoking on all their international flights; others allow smoking only on certain routes or certain departures, so **contact your carrier regarding its smoking policy.** Swissair, which does not allow smoking, stocks Nicorette gum.

FLYING TIMES

Flying time is just under two hours from London, seven hours from New York, 10 hours from Chicago, and 14 hours from Los Angeles.

HOW TO COMPLAIN

If your baggage goes astray or your flight goes awry, complain right away. Most carriers require that you **file a claim immediately.**

➤ AIRLINE COMPLAINTS: U.S. Department of Transportation **Aviation**

Consumer Protection Division (✉ C-75, Room 4107, Washington, DC 20590, ☎ 202/366–2220). **Federal Aviation Administration Consumer Hotline** (☎ 800/322–7873).

AIRPORTS

The major gateways are Zürich and Geneva.

➤ MAJOR AIRPORTS: Zürich: **Kloten Airport** (☎ 01/8121212 or 1571060 at.86 SF/min.). Geneva: **Cointrin International Airport** (☎ 022/7177111).

➤ OTHER AIRPORTS: Lugano: **Aeroporto Lugano-Agno** (☎ 091/6101212). Basel: **EuroAirport** (✉ Just across the border in France, ☎ 061/3253111). **Upper Engadine:** (✉ Samedan, ☎ 081/8525433). Bern: **Belpmoos** (☎ 031/9602121). **Sion:** (✉ Rte. de Aeroport, ☎ 027/3222480).

BIKE TRAVEL

BIKES IN FLIGHT

Most airlines accommodate bikes as luggage, provided they are dismantled and boxed. For bike boxes, often free at bike shops, you'll pay about $5 (at least $100 for bike bags) from airlines. International travelers can sometimes substitute a bike for a piece of checked luggage at no charge; otherwise, the cost is about $100. Domestic and Canadian airlines charge $25–$50.

➤ BIKE MAPS: Local tourist offices are the best places to get cycling maps for specific areas; you can also contact **Cartes Cyclistes** (✉ VCS/ATE, Velokarten, Postfach, CH-3360 Herzogenbuchsee, ☎ 062/9565656, FAX 062/9565699).

BIKE RENTALS

Bikes can be rented at all train stations and returned to any station (but with a 6 SF service charge for drop-off at a different station than its pickup). Rates for standard bikes are 20 SF per half day, 26 SF per day, and 100 SF per week. Mountain bikes are 25 SF per half day, 32 SF per day, or 128 SF per week. Groups get reductions according to the number of bikes. Individuals must make a reservation by 6 PM the day before they plan to use the bike, groups a week in advance. A daily train pass for a bike costs 15 SF.

BOAT & FERRY TRAVEL

All of Switzerland's larger lakes are crisscrossed by elegant steamers, some of them restored paddle steamers. Their café-restaurants serve drinks, snacks, and hot food at standard mealtimes; toilet facilities are provided. Service continues year-round but is reduced in winter. Unlimited travel is free to holders of the Swiss Pass. If you are not traveling by train, **consider the Swiss Boat Pass,** which for 35 SF allows half-fare travel on all lake steamers (January 1–December 31). The Swiss Half-Fare Travel card (☞ Train Travel, *below*) may also be used for boat travel.

BUS TRAVEL

Switzerland's famous yellow postbuses, with their stentorian tritone horns, link main cities with villages off the beaten track and even crawl over the highest mountain passes. Both postbuses and city buses follow posted schedules to the minute: You can set your watch by them. Free timetables can be picked up in post offices, where the buses usually depart. Watch for the yellow sign with the picture of a hunting horn. Postbuses cater especially to hikers: Good walking itineraries are available at postbus stops.

DISCOUNT PASSES

The Swiss Pass (☞ Train Travel, *below*) gives unlimited travel on the postbuses.

BUSINESS HOURS

BANKS & OFFICES

Businesses still close for lunch in Switzerland, generally from 12:30 to 2, but this is changing, especially in larger cities. All remain closed on Sunday, and many stay closed through Monday morning. Banks are open weekdays from 8:30 to 4:30.

MUSEUMS & SIGHTS

Museums generally close on Monday. There is, however, an increasing trend toward staying open late one night a week, usually on Thursday or Friday evening.

SHOPS

Shops are generally open every day but Sunday, with an hour or two lunch break; some stay closed through Monday morning. Stores in train stations often stay open until 9 PM; in Geneva and Zürich airports, shops are open on Sunday.

CAMERAS & PHOTOGRAPHY

➤ PHOTO HELP: **Kodak Information Center** (☏ 800/242–2424). *Kodak Guide to Shooting Great Travel Pictures,* available in bookstores or from Fodor's Travel Publications (☏ 800/533–6478; $16.50 plus $4 shipping).

EQUIPMENT PRECAUTIONS

Always **keep your film and tape out of the sun.** Carry an extra supply of batteries, and **be prepared to turn on your camera or camcorder** to prove to security personnel that the device is real. Always **ask for hand inspection of film,** which becomes clouded after successive exposures to airport X-ray machines, and **keep videotapes away from metal detectors.**

CAR RENTAL

If booked from overseas, rates in Zürich and Geneva begin at $45 a day and $178 a week for an economy car with air-conditioning, a manual transmission, and unlimited mileage. This does not include the 6.5% tax on car rentals. Try to arrange for a rental before you go; rentals booked in Switzerland are considerably more expensive.

➤ MAJOR AGENCIES: **Alamo** (☏ 800/522–9696; 020/8759–6200 in the U.K.). **Avis** (☏ 800/331–1084; 800/879–2847 in Canada; 02/9353–9000 in Australia; 09/525–1982 in New Zealand). **Budget** (☏ 800/527–0700; 0144/227–6266 in the U.K.). **Dollar** (☏ 800/800–6000; 020/8897–0811 in the U.K., where it is known as Eurodollar, 02/9223–1444 in Australia). **Hertz** (☏ 800/654–3001; 800/263–0600 in Canada; 020/8897–2072 in the U.K.; 02/9669–2444 in Australia; 03/358–6777 in New Zealand). **National InterRent** (☏ 800/227–3876; 0345/222525 in the U.K., where it is known as Europcar InterRent).

CUTTING COSTS

To get the best deal **book through a travel agent who will shop around.** Do **look into wholesalers,** companies that do not own fleets but rent in bulk from those that do and often offer better rates than traditional car-rental operations. Payment must be made before you leave home.

➤ WHOLESALERS: **Auto Europe** (☏ 207/842–2000 or 800/223–5555, FAX 800–235–6321). **Europe by Car** (☏ 212/581–3040 or 800/223–1516, FAX 212/246–1458). **DER Travel Services** (✉ 9501 W. Devon Ave., Rosemont, IL 60018, ☏ 800/782–2424, FAX 800/282–7474 for information; 800/860–9944 for brochures). **Kemwel Holiday Autos** (☏ 914/835–3000 or 800/678–0678, FAX 914/835–5126).

INSURANCE

When driving a rented car you are generally responsible for any damage to or loss of the vehicle. Before you rent see what coverage your personal auto-insurance policy and credit cards already provide.

Collision policies that car-rental companies sell for European rentals usually do not include stolen-vehicle coverage. Before you buy it, check your existing policies—you may already be covered.

REQUIREMENTS & RESTRICTIONS

In Switzerland your own driver's license is acceptable. However, an International Driver's Permit is a good idea; it's available from the American or Canadian automobile association, and, in the United Kingdom, from the Automobile Association or Royal Automobile Club. These international permits are universally recognized, and having one in your wallet may save you a problem with the local authorities.

SURCHARGES

Before you pick up a car in one city and leave it in another **ask about**

drop-off charges or one-way service fees, which can be substantial. Note, too, that some rental agencies charge extra if you return the car before the time specified in your contract. To avoid a hefty refueling fee **fill the tank just before you turn in the car,** but be aware that gas stations near the rental outlet may overcharge.

CAR TRAVEL

AUTO CLUBS

➤ IN AUSTRALIA: **Australian Automobile Association** (☎ 02/6247–7311).

➤ IN CANADA: **Canadian Automobile Association** (CAA, ☎ 613/247–0117).

➤ IN NEW ZEALAND: **New Zealand Automobile Association** (☎ 09/377–4660).

➤ IN THE U.K.: **Automobile Association** (AA, ☎ 0990/500–600). **Royal Automobile Club** (RAC, ☎ 0990/722–722 for membership; 0345/121–345 for insurance).

➤ IN THE U.S.: **American Automobile Association** (☎ 800/564–6222).

EMERGENCIES

All road **breakdowns** should be called in to the central Swiss-wide emergency number, 140. If you are on the autoroute, pull over to the shoulder and look for arrows pointing you to the nearest orange radio-telephone, called Bornes SOS; use these phones instead of a mobile phone, as police can locate you instantly and send help. There are SOS phones every km (½ mi), on alternate sides of the autoroute.

FROM THE U.K. BY FERRY

In addition to the relatively swift (and expensive) Channel Tunnel (Chunnel), on which cars piggyback trains to cross the channel from Dover to Boulogne, there are many drive-on/drive-off car ferry services across the Channel, but only a few are suitable as a means of getting to Switzerland. The situation is complicated by the different pricing systems operated by ferry companies and the many off-peak fares, and by the tolls charged by France on some of its motorways; these add up, particularly if you drive long distances. To avoid the tolls, **take a northerly route through Belgium or the Netherlands and Germany,** where motorways are free. The crossings for this route are Felixstowe or Dover to Zeebrugge; Sheerness to Vlissingen; and Ramsgate to Dunkirk. All these Continental ports have good road connections, and Switzerland can be reached in a day of hard driving.

GASOLINE

Unleaded (*sans plomb* or *bleifrei*) gas costs around 1.11 SF per liter, and super costs around 1.21 SF per liter. Leaded regular is no longer available. Prices are slightly higher in mountain areas. **Have some 10 SF and 20 SF notes available,** as many gas stations (especially in the mountains) offer vending-machine gas even when they're closed. Simply slide in a bill and fill your tank. Many of these machines also now accept major credit cards with pre-coded pin codes (☞ Money, *below*). You can get a receipt if you ask the machine for it.

PARKING

Parking areas are clearly marked. Blue or red zones indicate free parking for a limited period of time. Note that when parking in a blue or red zone, a "disque" (provided in rental cars or available free from banks or police stations) must be placed clearly in the front window noting the time of arrival; this will automatically tell you how long you may use the space. Parking in public lots normally costs 2 SF for the first hour, increasing by 1 SF every half hour thereafter.

ROAD CONDITIONS

Swiss roads are usually well surfaced but wind around considerably—especially in the mountains—so **don't plan on achieving high average speeds.** When estimating likely travel times, look carefully at the map: There may be only 32 km (20 mi) between one point and another—but there may be an Alpine pass in the way. There is a well-developed highway network, though some notable gaps still exist in the south along an east–west line, roughly between

Lugano and Sion. A combination of steep or winding routes and hazardous weather means that some roads will be closed in winter. Signs are posted at the beginning of the climb.

To find out about road conditions, traffic jams, itineraries, etc., there are two places to turn: The **Swiss Automobile Club** has a number (☎ 031/3283111, FAX 031/3110310) with operators standing by 24 hours a day to provide information in all languages. Dues-paying members of the **Touring Club of Switzerland** may call ☎ 022/4172424, FAX 022/4172020 for similar information. Note that neither of these numbers gets you breakdown service (☞ *below*). For frequent and precise information in Swiss languages, you can dial 163, or tune in to local radio stations.

RULES OF THE ROAD

Driving is on the right. In built-up areas, the speed limit is 50 kph (30 mph); on main highways, it's 80 kph (50 mph); on expressways, the limit is 120 kph (75 mph). It is not legal to make a right-hand turn on a red light. The blood-alcohol limit is .08.

Children under 12 are not permitted to sit in the front seat. **Use headlights** in heavy rain or poor visibility and in road tunnels—they are compulsory. Always **carry your valid license and car-registration papers;** there are occasional roadblocks to check them. **Wear seat belts** in the front and back seats—they are required.

To use the main highways, you must display a sticker, or *vignette,* in the lower left-hand corner of the windshield. You can buy it at the border (cash only; neighboring foreign currencies can be changed). It costs 40 SF and can also be purchased from any post office and from most gas stations; it's valid to the end of the year. Cars rented within Switzerland already have these stickers; if you rent a car elsewhere in Europe, **ask if the company will provide the vignette for you.**

Traffic going up a mountain has priority except for postbuses coming down. A sign with a yellow post horn on a blue background means that postbuses have priority.

In winter, **use snow chains,** compulsory in some areas and advisable in all. Snow-chain service stations have signs marked SERVICE DE CHAÎNES À NEIGE or SCHNEEKETTENDIENST; snow chains are available for rent.

If you have an accident, even a minor one, you must call the police.

CHILDREN IN SWITZERLAND

If you are renting a car don't forget to **arrange for a car seat** when you reserve.

➤ BABY-SITTING: Supervised playrooms are available in some of the better Swiss hotels, and many winter resorts also provide lists of reliable baby-sitters. For recommended local sitters, **check with your hotel desk.**

CHILDREN'S CAMPS & HOLIDAY COURSES

Every summer, some 120 private schools in Switzerland offer leisurely language study and recreation courses for primary and secondary school-age children from around the world. Summer camps similar to those in the United States are also available. Ask Switzerland Tourism (☞ Visitor Information, *below*) for a copy of "Holiday and Language Courses," a list of camps and summer programs in Switzerland.

FLYING

If your children are two or older **ask about children's airfares.** As a general rule, infants under two not occupying a seat fly at greatly reduced fares or even for free. When booking **confirm carry-on allowances** if you're traveling with infants. In general, for babies charged 10% of the adult fare, you are allowed one carry-on bag and a collapsible stroller; if the flight is full the stroller may have to be checked or you may be limited to less.

Experts agree that it's a good idea to use safety seats aloft for children weighing less than 40 pounds. Airlines set their own policies: U.S. carriers usually require that the child be ticketed, even if he or she is young enough to ride free, since the seats

must be strapped into regular seats.
Do **check your airline's policy about
using safety seats during takeoff and
landing.** And since safety seats are not
allowed just everywhere in the plane,
get your seat assignments early.

When reserving, **request children's
meals or a freestanding bassinet** if
you need them. But note that bulkhead seats, where you must sit to use
the bassinet, may lack an overhead
bin or storage space on the floor.

GETTING AROUND

Families traveling together in Switzerland should **buy a Family Card,** a
special pass (20 SF if purchased in
Switzerland or free with the purchase
of a Swiss Pass or Europass) that
allows children under 16 to travel free
on trains, postbuses (☞ Bus Travel,
above), and boats when accompanied
by ticket-holding parents or
guardians. The pass is valid for one
year. Adults must hold a valid Swiss
Pass, Swiss Card, Swiss Transfer
Ticket, or Eurail tariff ticket to obtain
the Family Card, available at any
Swiss train station, for their children
(☞ Train Travel, *below*).

➤ ORGANIZATIONS: For listings of
family hotels throughout the country,
contact the **Swiss Hotel Association**
(✉ Monbijoustr. 130, Postfach, CH-
3001 Bern, ☎ 031/3704111, FAX 031/
3704444) or **Switzerland Tourism** (☞
Visitor Information, *below*).

SIGHTS & ATTRACTIONS

Places that are especially good for
children are indicated by a rubber
duckie icon in the margin. The "Adult
Plus" version of the **Swiss Museum
Passport** (☞ Discounts & Deals,
below) gives up to five children age
16 and under free entrance to participating museums.

CONSUMER PROTECTION

Whenever shopping or buying travel
services in Switzerland, **pay with a
major credit card** so you can cancel
payment or get reimbursed if there's a
problem. If you're doing business
with a particular company for the
first time, **contact your local Better
Business Bureau and the attorney
general's offices** in your state and the

company's home state, as well. Have
any complaints been filed? Finally, if
you're buying a package or tour,
always **consider travel insurance** that
includes default coverage (☞ Insurance, *below*).

➤ LOCAL BBBs: **Council of Better
Business Bureaus** (✉ 4200 Wilson
Blvd., Suite 800, Arlington, VA
22203, ☎ 703/276–0100, FAX 703/
525–8277).

CUSTOMS & DUTIES

When shopping, **keep receipts** for all
purchases. Upon reentering the country, **be ready to show customs officials
what you've bought.** If you feel a
duty is incorrect or object to the way
your clearance was handled, note the
inspector's badge number and ask to
see a supervisor. If the problem isn't
resolved, write to the appropriate
authorities, beginning with the port
director at your point of entry.

IN AUSTRALIA

Australia residents who are 18 or
older may bring home $A400 worth
of souvenirs and gifts (including
jewelry), 250 cigarettes or 250 grams
of tobacco, and 1,125 ml of alcohol
(including wine, beer, and spirits).
Residents under 18 may bring back
$A200 worth of goods. Prohibited
items include meat products. Seeds,
plants, and fruits need to be declared
upon arrival.

➤ INFORMATION: **Australian Customs
Service** (Regional Director, ✉ Box 8,
Sydney, NSW 2001, ☎ 02/9213–
2000, FAX 02/9213–4000).

IN CANADA

Canadian residents who have been
out of Canada for at least 7 days may
bring home C$500 worth of goods
duty-free. If you've been away less
than 7 days but more than 48 hours,
the duty-free allowance drops to
C$200; if your trip lasts 24–48 hours,
the allowance is C$50. You may not
pool allowances with family members. Goods claimed under the C$500
exemption may follow you by mail;
those claimed under the lesser exemptions must accompany you. Alcohol
and tobacco products may be included in the 7-day and 48-hour

SMART TRAVEL TIPS A TO Z

exemptions but not in the 24-hour exemption. If you meet the age requirements of the province or territory through which you reenter Canada, you may bring in, duty-free, 1.14 liters (40 imperial ounces) of wine or liquor *or* 24 12-ounce cans or bottles of beer or ale. If you are 16 or older you may bring in, duty-free, 200 cigarettes and 50 cigars. Check ahead of time with Revenue Canada or the Department of Agriculture for policies regarding meat products, seeds, plants, and fruits.

You may send an unlimited number of gifts worth up to C$60 each duty-free to Canada. Label the package UNSOLICITED GIFT—VALUE UNDER $60. Alcohol and tobacco are excluded.

➤ INFORMATION: **Revenue Canada** (✉ 2265 St. Laurent Blvd. S, Ottawa, Ontario K1G 4K3, ☎ 613/993–0534; 800/461–9999 in Canada).

IN NEW ZEALAND

Homeward-bound residents 17 or older may bring back $700 worth of souvenirs and gifts. Your duty-free allowance also includes 4.5 liters of wine or beer; one 1,125-ml bottle of spirits; and either 200 cigarettes, 250 grams of tobacco, 50 cigars, or a combination of the three up to 250 grams. Prohibited items include meat products, seeds, plants, and fruits.

➤ INFORMATION: **New Zealand Customs** (Custom House, ✉ 50 Anzac Ave., Box 29, Auckland, New Zealand, ☎ 09/359–6655, FAX 09/359–6732).

IN SWITZERLAND

Entering Switzerland, an overseas visitor 17 years or older may bring in 400 cigarettes or 100 cigars or 500 grams of tobacco; 2 liters of alcohol up to 15 proof; and a liter of alcohol over 15 proof. When entering from a European country, tobacco is restricted to 200 cigarettes or 50 cigars or 250 grams of tobacco. Medicine, such as insulin, is allowed for personal use only.

IN THE U.K.

If you are a U.K. resident and your journey was wholly within the European Union (EU), you won't have to pass through customs when you return to the United Kingdom. If you plan to bring back large quantities of alcohol or tobacco, check EU limits beforehand. From countries outside the EU, including Switzerland, you may bring home, duty-free, 200 cigarettes or 50 cigars; 1 liter of spirits or 2 liters of fortified or sparkling wine or liqueurs; 2 liters of still table wine; 60 ml of perfume; 250 ml of toilet water; plus £136 worth of other goods, including gifts and souvenirs. If returning from outside the EU, prohibited items include meat products, seeds, plants, and fruits.

➤ INFORMATION: **HM Customs and Excise** (✉ Dorset House, Stamford St., Bromley Kent BR1 1XX, ☎ 020/7202–4227).

IN THE U.S.

U.S. residents who have been out of the country for at least 48 hours (and who have not used the $400 allowance or any part of it in the past 30 days) may bring home $400 worth of foreign goods duty-free.

U.S. residents 21 and older may bring back 1 liter of alcohol duty-free. In addition, regardless of your age, you are allowed 200 cigarettes and 100 non-Cuban cigars. Antiques, which the U.S. Customs Service defines as objects more than 100 years old, enter duty-free, as do original works of art done entirely by hand, including paintings, drawings, and sculptures.

You may also send packages home duty-free: up to $200 worth of goods for personal use, with a limit of one parcel per addressee per day (and no alcohol or tobacco products or perfume worth more than $5); label the package PERSONAL USE and attach a list of its contents and their retail value. Do not label the package UNSOLICITED GIFT or your duty-free exemption will drop to $100. Mailed items do not affect your duty-free allowance on your return.

➤ INFORMATION: **U.S. Customs Service** (inquiries, ✉ 1300 Pennsylvania Ave. NW, Washington, DC 20229,

☎ 202/927–6724; complaints, ✉ Office of Regulations and Rulings, 1300 Pennsylvania Ave. NW, Washington, DC 20229; registration of equipment, ✉ Resource Management, 1300 Pennsylvania Ave. NW, Washington, DC 20229, ☎ 202/927–0540).

DINING

The restaurants we list are the cream of the crop in each price category; our focus is on regional cuisine. Properties indicated by an ✕🏠 are lodging establishments whose restaurant warrants a special trip (and will accommodate non-hotel guests). In regional chapters, price charts appear in the dining Pleasures and Pastimes section that follows each chapter introduction. In chapters devoted to a single city, price charts appear in the introductions to the dining section.

RESERVATIONS & DRESS

Reservations are always a good idea: we mention them only when they're essential or are not accepted. Book as far ahead as you can, and reconfirm as soon as you arrive. We mention dress only when men are required to wear a jacket or a jacket and tie.

DISABILITIES & ACCESSIBILITY

In Switzerland, most forms of public transportation offer special provisions, and accessible hotels are available in many areas of the country.

➤ LOCAL RESOURCES: **Mobility International Schweiz** (✉ Froburgstr. 4, CH-4600 Olten, ☎ 062/2068835, FAX 062/2068839) for information on special tours and travel. **Switzerland Tourism** (☞ Visitor Information, *below*) for a copy of "Swiss Hotel Guide for the Disabled," published by the Swiss Hotel Association. This detailed guide to Swiss hotels offering facilities for guests with disabilities distinguishes between properties appropriate for visitors in wheelchairs and those suitable for visitors with walking impairments.

DRIVING

Foreign visitors with either the Disabled Badge of their country or the International Wheelchair Badge mounted inside the windshield of their car are entitled to use parking spaces reserved for people with disabilities throughout the country. Motorists who cannot walk unaided can obtain a special permit for parking privileges, as well as the international badge mentioned above, from the local police authority.

LODGING

When discussing accessibility with an operator or reservations agent **ask hard questions.** Are there any stairs, inside *or* out? Are there grab bars next to the toilet *and* in the shower/tub? How wide is the doorway to the room? To the bathroom? For the most extensive facilities meeting the latest legal specifications **opt for newer accommodations.**

TRAIN TRAVEL

Throughout the Swiss Federal Railways, wheelchairs are often available; inform the stations ahead of time that you will need one. In addition, ramps or lifts and wheelchair-accessible toilets have been installed in more than 100 stations. All InterCity and long-distance express trains and more than two-thirds of the country's regional shuttle trains now have wheelchair compartments. A brochure describing services for disabled travelers is available (in French, German and Italian) from the Swiss Federal Railways (☞ Train Travel, *below*).

➤ COMPLAINTS: **Disability Rights Section** (✉ U.S. Department of Justice, Civil Rights Division, Box 66738, Washington, DC 20035-6738, ☎ 202/514–0301; 800/514–0301; 202/514–0301 TTY; 800/514–0301 TTY, FAX 202/307–1198) for general complaints. **Aviation Consumer Protection Division** (☞ Air Travel, *above*) for airline-related problems. **Civil Rights Office** (✉ U.S. Department of Transportation, Departmental Office of Civil Rights, S-30, 400 7th St. SW, Room 10215, Washington, DC 20590, ☎ 202/366–4648, FAX 202/366–9371) for problems with surface transportation.

TRAVEL AGENCIES

In the United States, although the Americans with Disabilities Act requires that travel firms serve the needs of all travelers, some agencies specialize in working with people with disabilities.

➤ TRAVELERS WITH MOBILITY PROBLEMS: **Access Adventures** (✉ 206 Chestnut Ridge Rd., Rochester, NY 14624, ☎ 716/889–9096), run by a former physical-rehabilitation counselor. **Accessible Vans of the Rockies, Activity and Travel Agency** (✉ 2040 W. Hamilton Pl., Sheridan, CO 80110, ☎ 303/806–5047 or 888/837–0065, FAX 303/781–2329). **Care-Vacations** (✉ 5-5110 50th Ave., Leduc, Alberta T9E 6V4, ☎ 780/986–6404 or 780/986–8332) has group tours and is especially helpful with cruise vacations. **Flying Wheels Travel** (✉ 143 W. Bridge St., Box 382, Owatonna, MN 55060, ☎ 507/451–5005 or 800/535–6790, FAX 507/451–1685). **Hinsdale Travel Service** (✉ 201 E. Ogden Ave., Suite 100, Hinsdale, IL 60521, ☎ 630/325–1335).

➤ TRAVELERS WITH DEVELOPMENTAL DISABILITIES: **Sprout** (✉ 893 Amsterdam Ave., New York, NY 10025, ☎ 212/222–9575 or 888/222–9575, FAX 212/222–9768).

DISCOUNTS & DEALS

Besides the various discount transportation passes (☞ Boat & Ferry Travel, *above and* Train Travel, *below*), there is a discount pass for Swiss museums. For a flat fee (30 SF for one month), the **Swiss Museum Passport** grants free entrance to over 240 museums throughout the country. You can buy the passports at the participating museums, many local tourist offices, and the main office.

Be a smart shopper and **compare all your options** before making decisions. A plane ticket bought with a promotional coupon from travel clubs, coupon books, and direct-mail offers may not be cheaper than the least expensive fare from a discount ticket agency. And always keep in mind that what you get is just as important as what you save.

➤ DISCOUNT MUSEUM PASS: **Swiss Museum Passport Office** (✉ Hornbachstr. 50, CH-8034 Zürich).

DISCOUNT RESERVATIONS

To save money **look into discount-reservations services** with toll-free numbers, which use their buying power to get a better price on hotels, airline tickets, even car rentals. When booking a room, always **call the hotel's local toll-free number** (if one is available) rather than the central reservations number—you'll often get a better price. Always ask about special packages or corporate rates.

When shopping for the best deal on hotels and car rentals **look for guaranteed exchange rates,** which protect you against a falling dollar. With your rate locked in, you won't pay more, even if the price goes up in the local currency.

➤ AIRLINE TICKETS: ☎ 800/FLY–4–LESS. ☎ 800/FLY–ASAP.

➤ HOTEL ROOMS: **Hotel Reservations Network** (☎ 800/964–6835). **International Marketing & Travel Concepts** (☎ 800/790–4682). **Steigenberger Reservation Service** (☎ 800/223–5652). **Travel Interlink** (☎ 800/888–5898).

PACKAGE DEALS

Don't confuse packages and guided tours. When you buy a package, you travel on your own, as if you had planned the trip yourself. Fly/drive packages, which combine airfare and car rental, are often a good deal. If you **buy a rail/drive pass** you may save on train tickets and car rentals. All Eurail- and Europass holders get a discount on Eurostar fares through the Channel Tunnel.

ELECTRICITY

To use your U.S.-purchased electric-powered equipment, **bring a converter and adapter.** The electrical current in Switzerland is 220 volts, 50 cycles alternating current (AC); wall outlets take Continental-type plugs, which have two round prongs.

If your appliances are dual-voltage you'll need only an adapter. Don't use 110-volt outlets, marked FOR SHAVERS ONLY, for high-wattage appliances such as blow-dryers. Most laptops operate equally well on 110 and 220 volts and so require only an adapter.

EMBASSIES

➤ AUSTRALIA: Consulate, ✉ chemin de Fins 2; ✉ Case Postale 172, CH-1211 Geneva, ☎ 022/7999100.

➤ CANADA: ✉ Kirchenfeldstr. 88, CH-3005 Bern, ☎ 031/3573200.

➤ UNITED KINGDOM: ✉ Thunstr. 50, CH-3015 Bern, ☎ 031/3597700.

➤ UNITED STATES: ✉ Jubiläumstr. 93, CH-3001 Bern, ☎ 031/3577011.

EMERGENCIES

Anglo-Phone (☎ 1575014), a 24-hour English-language hot line, gives information on what to do in an emergency, besides many other topics. Calls cost 2.13 SF per minute.

➤ CONTACTS: **Police** (☎ 117). **Ambulance** (☎ 144).

GAY & LESBIAN TRAVEL

For resources in Switzerland, a good starting point is **Dialogai** (✉ 11–13 rue de la Navigation, CH-1211 Geneva, ☎ 022/9064040, FAX 022/9064044), which has a library, tea room, bar and an English-speaking staff. You can pick up a copy of their guide, which lists gay-friendly contacts for Switzerland's French-speaking region and neighboring France (it's in French only).

➤ GAY- AND LESBIAN-FRIENDLY TRAVEL AGENCIES: **Different Roads Travel** (✉ 8383 Wilshire Blvd., Suite 902, Beverly Hills, CA 90211, ☎ 323/651–5557 or 800/429–8747, FAX 323/651–3678). **Kennedy Travel** (✉ 314 Jericho Turnpike, Floral Park, NY 11001, ☎ 516/352–4888 or 800/237–7433, FAX 516/354–8849). **Now Voyager** (✉ 4406 18th St., San Francisco, CA 94114, ☎ 415/626–1169 or 800/255–6951, FAX 415/626–8626). **Yellowbrick Road** (✉ 1500 W. Balmoral Ave., Chicago, IL 60640, ☎ 773/561–1800 or 800/642–2488, FAX 773/561–4497). **Skylink Travel and Tour** (✉ 1006 Mendocino Ave., Santa Rosa, CA 95401, ☎ 707/546–9888 or 800/225–5759, FAX 707/546–9891), serving lesbian travelers.

HEALTH

Your trip to Switzerland is likely to be one of the most disease-free of any in your life: It's a country that has well earned its reputation for impeccable standards of cleanliness. But even at the foot of an icy-pure 2,000-m (6,560-ft) glacier, you'll find the locals drinking bottled mineral water; you'll have to wrangle with the waiter if you want tap water with your meal. This is as much a result of the tradition of expecting beverages in a café to be paid for as it is a response to health questions. If you're traveling with a child under two years old, you may be advised by locals not to carry him or her on excursions above 2,000 m (6,560 ft); check with your pediatrician before leaving home. Adults should limit strenuous excursions on the first day at extra-high-altitude resorts, those at 1,600 m (5,248 ft) and above. Adults with heart problems may want to avoid all excursions above 2,000 m (6,560 ft).

MEDICAL PLANS

No one plans to get sick while traveling, but it happens, so **consider signing up with a medical-assistance company.** Members get doctor referrals, emergency evacuation or repatriation, hot lines for medical consultation, cash for emergencies, and other assistance.

➤ MEDICAL-ASSISTANCE COMPANIES: **International SOS Assistance** (✉ 8 Neshaminy Interplex, Suite 207, Trevose, PA 19053, ☎ 215/245–4707 or 800/523–6586, FAX 215/244–9617; ✉ 12 Chemin Riantbosson, 1217 Meyrin 1, Geneva, Switzerland, ☎ 4122/785–6464, FAX 4122/785–6424; ✉ 331 N. Bridge Rd., 17-00, Odeon Towers, Singapore 188720, ☎ 65/338–7800, FAX 65/338–7611).

HOLIDAYS

Jan. 1, Apr. 21–23 (Good Friday–Easter Sunday), May 1 (Labor Day), June 2 (Ascension), Aug. 1 (Swiss National Holiday), and Dec. 24–26.

INSURANCE

The most useful travel insurance plan is a comprehensive policy that includes coverage for trip cancellation and interruption, default, trip delay, and medical expenses (with a waiver for preexisting conditions).

Without insurance you will lose all or most of your money if you cancel your trip, regardless of the reason. Default insurance covers you if your tour operator, airline, or cruise line goes out of business. Trip-delay covers expenses that arise because of bad weather or mechanical delays. Study the fine print when comparing policies.

If you're traveling internationally, a key component of travel insurance is coverage for medical bills incurred if you get sick on the road. Such expenses are not generally covered by Medicare or private policies. U.K. residents can buy a travel-insurance policy valid for most vacations taken during the year in which it's purchased (but check pre-existing-condition coverage). British and Australian citizens need extra medical coverage when traveling overseas. Always **buy travel policies directly from the insurance company**; if you buy it from a cruise line, airline, or tour operator that goes out of business you probably will not be covered for the agency or operator's default, a major risk. Before you make any purchase **review your existing health and home-owner's policies** to find what they cover away from home.

➤ TRAVEL INSURERS: In the U.S. **Access America** (✉ 6600 W. Broad St., Richmond, VA 23230, ☎ 804/285–3300 or 800/284–8300), **Travel Guard International** (✉ 1145 Clark St., Stevens Point, WI 54481, ☎ 715/345–0505 or 800/826–1300). In Canada **Voyager Insurance** (✉ 44 Peel Center Dr., Brampton, Ontario L6T 4M8, ☎ 905/791–8700; 800/668–4342 in Canada).

➤ INSURANCE INFORMATION: In the U.K. the **Association of British Insurers** (✉ 51–55 Gresham St., London EC2V 7HQ, ☎ 020/7600–3333, FAX 020/796–8999). In Australia the **Insurance Council of Australia** (☎ 03/9614–1077, FAX 03/9614–7924).

LANGUAGE

Nearly 70% of the population of Switzerland speaks one dialect or another of German; Swiss German can be a far cry from high German, although standard German is generally understood. French is spoken in the southwest, around Lake Geneva, and in the cantons of Fribourg, Neuchâtel, Jura, Vaud, and most of the Valais. Italian is spoken in the Ticino. In the Upper and Lower Engadines, in the canton Graubünden, the last gasp of a Romance language called Romansh is still in daily use. There are several dialects of Romansh—five, in fact—so there's not much point in trying to pick up a few phrases. If you want to attempt communicating with the locals there, venture a little Italian. In the areas most frequented by English and American tourists—Zermatt, the Berner Oberland, Luzern—people in the tourist industry usually speak English. Elsewhere, you might not be as lucky. Ask before you plunge into your mother tongue—the person you're addressing may run to fetch the staff member who can converse with you on your own language terms. *See* the Swiss Vocabulary and Menu Guide at the back of the book for helpful words and phrases.

LANGUAGES FOR TRAVELERS

A phrase book and language-tape set can help get you started.

➤ PHRASE BOOKS & LANGUAGE-TAPE SETS: *Fodor's French for Travelers, Fodor's German for Travelers, Fodor's Italian for Travelers* (☎ 800/733–3000 in the U.S.; 800/668–4247 in Canada; $7 for phrasebook, $16.95 for audio set).

LODGING

Switzerland is as famous for its hotels as it is for its mountains, knives, and chocolates; its standards in hospitality are extremely high. Rooms are impeccably clean and well maintained, and they are furnished with comforts ranging from the simplest to the most deluxe. Prices are accordingly high: You will pay more for minimal comforts here than in any other European country. Americans accustomed to spacious motels with two double beds, a color TV, and a bath/shower combination may be disappointed in their first venture into the legendary Swiss hotel: Spaces are small, bathtubs cost extra, and single rooms may have single beds. What you're paying for is service, reliability, cleanliness, and a complex hierarchy of amenities you may not even know you need.

Where no address is provided in the hotel listings, none was necessary: In smaller towns and villages, a postal code is all you need. To find the hotel on arrival, watch for the official street signs pointing the way to every hotel that belongs to the local tourist association.

Some things to bear in mind when you check in: The standard double room in Switzerland has two prim beds built together with separate linens and, sometimes, sheets tucked firmly down the middle. If you prefer more sociable arrangements, ask for a "French bed," or *lit matrimoniale*—that will get you a single-mattress double. Some hotels may offer extra beds—for example, to expand a double room to a triple.

The lodgings we list are the cream of the crop in each price category. We always list the facilities that are available—but we don't specify whether they cost extra: When pricing accommodations, always ask what's included and what costs extra. In addition, assume that all rooms have private bath unless otherwise noted. Properties indicated by an ✕🏠 are lodging establishments whose restaurant warrants a special trip (and will accommodate non-hotel guests). In regional chapters, price charts appear in the lodging Pleasures and Pastimes section that follows each chapter introduction. In chapters devoted to a single city, price charts appear in the introductions to the dining section.

Assume that hotels operate on the European Plan (EP, with no meals) unless we specify that they use the Continental Plan (CP, with a Continental breakfast daily) or Breakfast Plan (BP, with a full breakfast daily). Particularly in ski resorts or in hotels where you'll be staying for three days

or more, you may be quoted a room price per person including *demipension* (half board). This means you've opted for breakfast included and to eat either lunch or dinner in the hotel, selecting from a limited, fixed menu. Unless you're holding out for gastronomic adventure, your best bet is to take half board. Most hotels will be flexible if you come in from the slopes craving a steaming pot of fondue, and they will subtract the day's pension supplement from your room price, charging you à la carte instead. A *garni* hotel is one without a restaurant on the premises.

APARTMENT & VILLA RENTALS

If you want a home base that's roomy enough for a family and comes with cooking facilities **consider a furnished rental.** These can save you money, especially if you're traveling with a group. Home-exchange directories sometimes list rentals as well as exchanges.

➤ INTERNATIONAL AGENTS: **At Home Abroad** (✉ 405 E. 56th St., Suite 6H, New York, NY 10022, ☎ 212/421–9165, FAX 212/752–1591). **Drawbridge to Europe** (✉ 5456 Adams Rd., Talent, OR 97540, ☎ 541/512–8927 or 888/268–1148, FAX 541/512–0978). **Europa-Let/Tropical Inn-Let** (✉ 92 N. Main St., Ashland, OR 97520, ☎ 541/482–5806 or 800/462–4486, FAX 541/482–0660). **Hometours International** (✉ Box 11503, Knoxville, TN 37939, ☎ 423/690–8484 or 800/367–4668). **Interhome** (✉ 1990 N.E. 163rd St., Suite 110, Miami Beach, FL 33162, ☎ 305/940–2299 or 800/882–6864, FAX 305/940–2911). **Rental Directories International** (✉ 2044 Rittenhouse Sq., Philadelphia, PA 19103, ☎ 215/985–4001, FAX 215/985–0323). **Rent-a-Home International** (✉ 7200 34th Ave. NW, Seattle, WA 98117, ☎ 206/789–9377, FAX 206/789–9379). **Vacation Home Rentals Worldwide** (✉ 235 Kensington Ave., Norwood, NJ 07648, ☎ 201/767–9393 or 800/633–3284, FAX 201/767–5510). **Villas and Apartments Abroad** (✉ 420 Madison Ave., Suite 1003, New York, NY 10017, ☎ 212/759–1025 or 800/433–3020, FAX 212/755–8316). **Villas**

SMART TRAVEL TIPS A TO Z

International (⊠ 950 Northgate Dr.,
Suite 206, San Rafael, CA 94903, ☎
415/499–9490 or 800/221–2260, FAX
415/499–9491). **Hideaways International** (⊠ 767 Islington St.,
Portsmouth, NH 03801, ☎ 603/430–
4433 or 800/843–4433, FAX 603/430–
4444; membership $99).

FARM STAYS

An unusual option for families seeking the local experience: Stay on a
farm with a Swiss family, complete
with children, animals, and the option
to work in the fields. Participating
farm families register with the
Schweizerischer Bauernverband
(Swiss Farmers Association), listing
the birth dates of their children,
rooms and facilities, and types of
animals your children can see. Prices
are often considerably lower than
those of hotels and vacation flats;
however, you should be reasonably
fluent in French or German, depending on the region of your stay. Further
information is available through
Switzerland Tourism (☞ Visitor
Information, *below*).

➤ ORGANIZATIONS: Contact the
Schweizerischer Bauernverband
(Swiss Farmers Association; ⊠ CH-
5200 Brugg, ☎ 056/4625111, FAX
056/4415348) or **Schweizer
Reisekasse** (Reka; ⊠ Neueng. 15,
CH-3001 Bern, ☎ 031/3296633, FAX
031/3296601) for listings.

HOME EXCHANGES

If you would like to exchange your
home for someone else's **join a home-
exchange organization,** which will
send you its updated listings of available exchanges for a year and will
include your own listing in at least
one of them. It's up to you to make
specific arrangements.

➤ EXCHANGE CLUBS: **HomeLink
International** (⊠ Box 650, Key West,
FL 33041, ☎ 305/294–7766 or 800/
638–3841, FAX 305/294–1448; $88
per year). **Intervac U.S.** (⊠ Box
590504, San Francisco, CA 94159,
☎ 800/756–4663, FAX 415/435–7440;
$83 per year).

HOSTELS

No matter what your age you can
**save on lodging costs by staying at
hostels.** In some 5,000 locations in
more than 70 countries around the
world, Hostelling International (HI),
the umbrella group for a number of
national youth-hostel associations,
offers single-sex, dorm-style beds and,
at many hostels, couples rooms and
family accommodations. Membership
in any HI national hostel association,
open to travelers of all ages, allows
you to stay in HI-affiliated hostels at
member rates (one-year membership
is about $25 for adults; hostels run
about $10–$25 per night). Members
also have priority if the hostel is full;
they're eligible for discounts around
the world, even on rail and bus travel
in some countries.

➤ ORGANIZATIONS: **Australian Youth
Hostel Association** (⊠ 10 Mallett St.,
Camperdown, NSW 2050, ☎ 02/
9565–1699, FAX 02/9565–1325).
**Hostelling International—American
Youth Hostels** (⊠ 733 15th St. NW,
Suite 840, Washington, DC 20005, ☎
202/783–6161, FAX 202/783–6171).
Hostelling International—Canada (⊠
400–205 Catherine St., Ottawa,
Ontario K2P 1C3, ☎ 613/237–7884,
FAX 613/237–7868). **Youth Hostel
Association of England and Wales** (⊠
Trevelyan House, 8 St. Stephen's Hill,
St. Albans, Hertfordshire AL1 2DY,
☎ 01727/855215 or 01727/845047,
FAX 01727/844126). **Youth Hostels
Association of New Zealand** (⊠ Box
436, Christchurch, New Zealand, ☎
03/379–9970, FAX 03/365–4476).
Membership in the U.S. $25, in
Canada C$26.75, in the U.K. £9.30,
in Australia $44, in New Zealand
$24.

HOTELS

When selecting a place to stay, an
important resource can be the Swiss
Hotel Association (SHA), a rigorous
and demanding organization that
maintains a specific rating system for
lodging standards. Eighty percent of
Swiss hotels belong to this group and
take their stars seriously. In contrast
to more casual European countries,
stars in Switzerland have precise
meaning: A five-star hotel is required

to have a specific staff-guest ratio, a daily change of bed linens, and extended-hour room service. A two-star hotel must have telephones, soap in the room, and fabric tablecloths in the restaurant. But the SHA standards cannot control the quality of decor and the grace of service. Thus you may find a four-star hotel that meets these technical requirements but has shabby appointments, leaky plumbing, or a rude concierge; a good, family-run two-star may make you feel like royalty.

Some rules of thumb: If you are looking for American-style, chain-motel-level comfort—a big bed, color TV, minibar, safe—you will probably be happiest in four-star, business-class hotels, many of which cater to Americans through travel agents and tour organizers; Best Western owns a number of four-star hotels in Switzerland. If you are looking for regional atmosphere, family ownership (and the pride and care for details that implies), and moderate prices, but don't care about a TV or minibar, look for three stars: Nearly all such rooms have showers and toilets. Two stars will get you tidy, minimal comfort with about a third of the rooms having baths. One-star properties are rare: They have no baths in rooms and no phone available in-house and generally fall below the demanding Swiss national standard. Several hotels in the SHA are specially rated *Landgasthof* or *relais de campagne,* meaning "country inn." These generally are rustic-style lodgings typical of the region, but they may range from spare to luxurious and are rarely set apart in deep country, as Americans might expect; some are in the midst of small market towns or resorts. The SHA distinguishes them as offering especially high-quality service, personal attention, and parking.

➤ TOLL-FREE NUMBERS: **Best Western** (☎ 800/528–1234). **Hilton** (☎ 800/445–8667). **Inter-Continental** (☎ 800/327–0200). **Marriott** (☎ 800/228–9290). **Le Meridien** (☎ 800/543–4300). **Radisson** (☎ 800/333–3333). **Ramada** (☎ 800/228–2828). **Renaissance Hotels & Resorts** (☎ 800/468–3571). **Sheraton** (☎ 800/325–3535). **Westin Hotels & Resorts** (☎ 800/228–3000).

INNS

Travelers on a budget can find help from the *Check-in E & G Hotels* guide (E & G stands for *einfach und gemütlich*: roughly, "simple and cozy"), available through Switzerland Tourism. These comfortable little hotels have banded together to dispel Switzerland's intimidating image as an elite, overpriced vacation spot and offer simple two-star standards in usually very atmospheric inns.

Other organizations can help you find unusual properties: The Relais & Châteaux group seeks out manor houses, historic buildings, and generally atmospheric luxury, with most of its properties falling into the $$$ or $$$$ range. A similar group, Romantik Hotels and Restaurants, combines architectural interest, historic atmosphere, and fine regional food. Relais du Silence hotels are usually isolated in a peaceful, natural setting, with first-class comforts.

MAIL & SHIPPING

POSTAL RATES

Mail rates are divided into first-class "A" (airmail) and second-class "B" (surface). Letters and postcards to the United States weighing up to 20 grams cost 1.80 SF first class, 1.10 SF second class; to the United Kingdom, 1.10 SF first class, .90 SF second class.

RECEIVING MAIL

If you're uncertain where you'll be staying, you can have your mail, marked "poste restante" or "postlagernd," sent to any post office in Switzerland. It needs the sender's name and address on the back, and you'll need proof of identity to collect it. You can also have your mail sent to American Express for a small fee; if you are a cardholder or have American Express traveler's checks, the service is free. Postal codes precede the names of cities and towns in Swiss addresses.

MONEY MATTERS

Despite increased competition across Europe, the recent decrease in the Swiss franc's value against other currencies, and the negligible inflation rate over the past several years, Switzerland remains one of the most expensive countries on the Continent for travelers, and you may find yourself shocked by the price of a light lunch or a generic hotel room. If you are traveling on a tight budget, avoid staying in well-known resorts and the most sophisticated cities; Geneva, Zürich, Zermatt, Gstaad, and St. Moritz are exceptionally expensive. If you are traveling by car, you have the luxury of seeking out small, family hotels in villages, where costs are relatively low. Unless you work hard at finding budget accommodations, you will average more than 150 SF a night for two—more if you stay in business-class hotels, with TV and direct-dial phone.

A cup of coffee or a beer costs about 3 SF in a simple restaurant; ordinary open wines, sold by the deciliter ("deci"), start at about 3 SF. All three beverages cost sometimes double that in resorts, city hotels, and fine restaurants. A plain, one-plate daily lunch special averages 14–18 SF. A city bus ride costs between 1.50 SF and 2.20 SF, a short cab ride 15 SF. Prices throughout this guide are given for adults. Substantially reduced fees are almost always available for children, students, and senior citizens. For information on taxes, *see* Taxes, *below.*

ATMS

You can withdraw money from ATMs in Switzerland as long as your card is properly programmed with your personal identification number (PIN). For use in Switzerland, your PIN number must be four digits long. Banks offer good, wholesale exchange rates.

➤ ATM LOCATIONS: **Cirrus** (☎ 800/424–7787). **Plus** (☎ 800/843–7587) for locations in the U.S. and Canada, or visit your local bank.

CREDIT CARDS

Credit cards can be used for cash advances at ATMs in Switzerland as long as they have been programmed with a four-digit personal identification number (PIN).

Throughout this guide, the following abbreviations are used: **AE**, American Express; **DC**, Diner's Club; **MC**, Master Card; and **V**, Visa.

➤ REPORTING LOST CARDS: **American Express** (☎ 800/327–2177 or call 336/393–1111 collect). **Diners Club** (☎ 800/234–6377 or call 702/797–5532 collect). **Master Card** (☎ 800/307–7309 or 0800/897092 toll-free). **Visa** (☎ 800/847–2911 or call 410/581–9994 collect).

CURRENCY

The unit of currency in Switzerland is the Swiss franc (SF), available in notes of 10, 20, 50, 100, 200, and 1,000. Francs are divided into centimes (in Suisse Romande) or rappen (in German Switzerland). There are coins for 5, 10, and 20 centimes. Larger coins are the ½-, 1-, 2-, and 5-franc pieces.

At press time (summer 1999), the Swiss franc stood at 1.44 to the U.S. dollar, 1.06 to the Canadian dollar, and 2.35 to the pound sterling.

CURRENCY EXCHANGE

For the most favorable rates, **change money through banks.** Although ATM transaction fees may be higher abroad than at home, ATM rates are excellent because they are based on wholesale rates offered only by major banks. You won't do as well at exchange booths in airports or rail and bus stations, in hotels, in restaurants, or in stores. To avoid lines at airport exchange booths **get a bit of local currency before you leave home.**

➤ EXCHANGE SERVICES: **International Currency Express** (☎ 888/842–0880 on East Coast; 888/278–6628 on West Coast). **Thomas Cook Currency Services** (☎ 800/287–7362 for telephone orders and retail locations).

TRAVELER'S CHECKS

Do you need traveler's checks? It depends on where you're headed. If you're going to rural areas and small towns, go with cash; traveler's checks are best used in cities. Lost or stolen checks can usually be replaced within 24 hours. To ensure a speedy refund, buy your own traveler's checks—don't let someone else pay for them: irregularities like this can cause delays. The person who bought the checks should make the call to request a refund.

Note that there is a limitation (300 SF) on the cashing of Eurocheques drawn on European banks.

OUTDOORS & SPORTS

BICYCLING

☞ Bike Travel, *above.*

BOATING

Holders of the Swiss Pass or Flexipass (☞ Train Travel, *below*) can go on boating excursions with Eurotrek's **Swiss Adventure program** (☎ 01/4620203, FAX 01/4631139).

CAMPING

Switzerland is ideal for campers, with approximately 450 sites throughout the country. All are classified with one to five stars according to amenities, location, and so on. The rates vary widely but average around 15 SF per night for a family of four, plus car or camper. For further details see the *Swiss Camping Guide,* published by the Swiss Camping Association, available at bookshops for 15 SF or from the **Camping and Caravaning Association** (☒ Box 24, CH-6004 Luzern, ☎ 041/2104822, FAX 041/2104822). Listings are also available from the **Touring Club of Switzerland** (☒ Ch. de Blandonnet 4, CH-1214 Vernier, ☎ 022/4172727, FAX 022/4172020) and from the **Swiss Campsite Association** (☒ CH-3800 Interlaken-Thunersee, ☎ 033/8233523, FAX 033/8232991).

To stay in most European campsites, you must have an **International Camping Carnet** verifying your status as a bona fide camper. This is available from any national camping association within Europe or from the **National Campers and Hikers Association** (☒ 4804 Transit Rd., Bldg. 2, Depew, NY 14043, ☎ 716/668–6242).

GOLF

There are 52 golf courses throughout Switzerland where you can rent clubs and play on a daily greens fee basis. For more information, contact the **Swiss Association of Golf** (☒ pl. Croix-Blanche 19, CH-1066 Epalinges-Lausanne, ☎ 021/7843531, FAX 021/7843536), which has a directory of all courses. It can also provide specific information, such as course fees and conditions.

HIKING

The Swiss Alps, naturally, are riddled with hiking trails; hiking is an especially popular pastime in the German-speaking areas of the country, such as the Berner Oberland. For suggested hiking itineraries, contact regional tourist offices; many bookstores also carry detailed topographical maps with marked trails. You can also contact the **Fédération Suisse de Tourisme Pédestre** (Im Hirsholm 49, CH-4125 Riehen, ☎ 061/6069340, FAX 061/6069345).

SKIING

A daily bulletin of ski conditions at 220 locations throughout Switzerland is available by calling 157/120120 (0.86 SF/min.); reports are in the local language. You can also check the Switzerland Tourism Web site (☞ Visitor Information, *below*). Applications to the **Swiss Alpine Club** should be addressed to the club at Sektion Zermatt, Mr. Edmond F. Krieger, Haus Dolomit, CH-3920 Zermatt (☎ FAX 027/9672610). Remember to include a passport-size photo. Excursions involve serious climbing; it's not necessary to be fluent in German. For a booklet of mountain-club huts, contact the Swiss Alpine Club (☒ Monbijoustr. 61, Postfach, CH-3000 Bern 23, ☎ 031/3701818 FAX 031/3701800). A hut directory, "Hütten der Schweizer Alpen," complete with color photos, can be ordered for 38 SF from **SAC-Buchauslieferung** (☒ Postfach 134, CH-7004 Chur, ☎ 081/2583335, FAX 081/2502666).

PACKING

Switzerland is essentially sportswear country. City dress is more formal. Men would be wise to pack a jacket

SMART TRAVEL TIPS A TO Z

and tie if dining in some of the great restaurants; otherwise, a tie and sweater is standard at night. Women wear skirts more frequently here than in America, especially women over 50, though anything fashionable goes. Except at the most chic hotels in international resorts, you won't need formal evening dress.

Even in July and August, the evening air grows chilly in the mountains, so **bring a warm sweater.** And **bring a hat or sunscreen,** as the atmosphere is thinner at high altitudes. Glaciers can be blinding in the sun, so **be sure to bring sunglasses, especially for high-altitude excursions.** Good walking shoes or hiking boots are a must, whether you're tackling medieval cobblestones or mountain trails.

To ensure comfort, **budget travelers should bring their own washcloth and soap,** not always standard equipment in one- and two-star-rated Swiss hotels. If you're planning on shopping and cooking, a tote bag will come in handy: Most groceries do not provide sacks, but sturdy, reusable plastic totes can be bought at checkout. Laundromats are rare, so laundry soap is useful for hand washing.

In your carry-on luggage **bring an extra pair of eyeglasses or contact lenses** and **enough of any medication you take** to last the entire trip. You may also want your doctor to write a spare prescription using the drug's generic name, since brand names may vary from country to country. In luggage to be checked, **never pack prescription drugs or valuables.** To avoid customs delays, carry medications in their original packaging. And don't forget to copy down and carry addresses of offices that handle refunds of lost traveler's checks.

CHECKING LUGGAGE

How many carry-on bags you can bring with you is up to the airline. Most allow two, but not always, so make sure that everything you carry aboard will fit under your seat, and get to the gate early. Note that if you have a seat at the back of the plane, you'll probably board first, while the overhead bins are still empty.

If you are flying internationally, note that baggage allowances may be determined not by piece but by weight—generally 88 pounds (40 kilograms) in first class, 66 pounds (30 kilograms) in business class, and 44 pounds (20 kilograms) in economy.

Airline liability for baggage is limited to $1,250 per person on flights within the United States. On international flights it amounts to $9.07 per pound or $20 per kilogram for checked baggage (roughly $640 per 70-pound bag) and $400 per passenger for unchecked baggage. You can buy additional coverage at check-in for about $10 per $1,000 of coverage, but it excludes a rather extensive list of items, shown on your airline ticket.

Before departure **itemize your bags' contents** and their worth, and label the bags with your name, address, and phone number. (If you use your home address, cover it so that potential thieves can't see it readily.) Inside each bag **pack a copy of your itinerary.** At check-in **make sure that each bag is correctly tagged** with the destination airport's three-letter code. If your bags arrive damaged or fail to arrive at all, file a written report with the airline before leaving the airport.

PASSPORTS & VISAS

When traveling internationally **carry a passport even if you don't need one** (it's always the best form of ID), and **make two photocopies of the data page** (one for someone at home and another for you, carried separately from your passport). If you lose your passport promptly call the nearest embassy or consulate and the local police.

ENTERING SWITZERLAND

All Australian, British, Canadian, New Zealand, and U.S. citizens need only a valid passport to enter Switzerland for stays of up to 90 days.

➤ U.K. CITIZENS: **U.S. Embassy Visa Information Line** (☎ 01891/200–290; calls cost 49p per minute, 39p per minute cheap rate) for U.S. visa information. **U.S. Embassy Visa Branch** (✉ 5 Upper Grosvenor Sq.,

London W1A 1AE) for U.S. visa information; send a self-addressed, stamped envelope. Write the **U.S. Consulate General** (✉ Queen's House, Queen St., Belfast BTI 6EO) if you live in Northern Ireland. Write the **Office of Australia Affairs** (✉ 59th fl., MLC Centre, 19-29 Martin Pl., Sydney NSW 2000) if you live in Australia. Write the **Office of New Zealand Affairs** (✉ 29 Fitzherbert Terr., Thorndon, Wellington) if you live in New Zealand.

PASSPORT OFFICES

The best time to apply for a passport or to renew is during the fall and winter. Before any trip, check your passport's expiration date, and, if necessary, renew it as soon as possible.

➤ AUSTRALIAN CITIZENS: **Australian Passport Office** (☎ 131–232).

➤ CANADIAN CITIZENS: **Passport Office** (☎ 819/994–3500 or 800/567–6868).

➤ NEW ZEALAND CITIZENS: **New Zealand Passport Office** (☎ 04/494–0700 for information on how to apply; 04/474–8000 or 0800/225–050 in New Zealand for information on applications already submitted).

➤ U.K. CITIZENS: **London Passport Office** (☎ 0990/210–410) for fees and documentation requirements and to request an emergency passport.

➤ U.S. CITIZENS: **National Passport Information Center** (☎ 900/225–5674; calls are 35¢ per minute for automated service, $1.05 per minute for operator service).

SENIOR-CITIZEN TRAVEL

Women over 62 and men over 65 qualify for special seasonal (and in some cases year-round) discounts at a variety of Swiss hotels. With married couples, at least one spouse must fulfill these conditions. Prices include overnight lodging in a single or double room, breakfast, service charges, and taxes. Arrangements can also be made for extended stays. Senior citizens are entitled to discounts on trains, buses, and boats, at all movie theaters in Switzerland, and, where posted, at museums and attractions.

To qualify for age-related discounts **mention your senior-citizen status up front** when booking hotel reservations (not when checking out) and before you're seated in restaurants (not when paying the bill). When renting a car ask about promotional car-rental discounts, which can be cheaper than senior-citizen rates.

➤ EDUCATIONAL PROGRAMS: **Elderhostel** (✉ 75 Federal St., 3rd fl., Boston, MA 02110, ☎ 877/426–8056, FAX 877/426–2166). **Interhostel** (✉ University of New Hampshire, 6 Garrison Ave., Durham, NH 03824, ☎ 603/862–1147 or 800/733–9753, FAX 603/862–1113). **Folkways Institute** (✉ 14600 Southeast Aldridge Rd., Portland, OR 97236-6518, ☎ 503/658–6600 or 800/225–4666, FAX 503/658–8672).

➤ LODGING: A special guide to hotels that offer senior discounts, *Season for Seniors*, is available from the Swiss Hotel Association (✉ Monbijoustr. 130, CH-3001 Bern, ☎ 031/3704111, FAX 031/3704444) or from **Switzerland Tourism** (☞ Visitor Information, *below*).

STUDENTS IN SWITZERLAND

Reduced student fees are often available for individual admission tickets, transportation, etc. An International Student Identification Card (ISIC), available through the Council on International Educational Exchange, is generally accepted. The Swiss Museum Passport (☞ Discounts & Deals, *above*) has a reduced student fee, and the Eurail Youth pass (☞ Train Travel, *below*) has a reduced fee for people between ages 12 and 25.

➤ STUDENT IDs & SERVICES: **Council on International Educational Exchange** (CIEE, ✉ 205 E. 42nd St., 14th fl., New York, NY 10017, ☎ 212/822–2600 or 888/268–6245, FAX 212/822–2699) for mail orders only, in the U.S. **Travel Cuts** (✉ 187 College St., Toronto, Ontario M5T 1P7, ☎ 416/979–2406 or 800/667–2887) in Canada.

TAXES

What you see is what you pay in Switzerland: Restaurant checks and hotel bills include all taxes.

VALUE-ADDED TAX (V.A.T.)

Switzerland's value-added tax is 7.5%; it can add a significant amount to already pricey bills. Culture vultures are one of the only groups not to be affected by the VAT, with theater and cinema tickets exempt.

However, on any one purchase of 550 francs or more from one store, refunds are available to nonresidents for clothes, watches, and souvenirs, but not for meals or hotel rooms. To **get a VAT refund,** pay by credit card; at the time of purchase, the store clerk should fill out and give you a red form and keep a record of your credit card number. When leaving Switzerland, you must hand-deliver the red form to a customs officer at the customs office at the airport, or if leaving by car or train, at the border. Customs will process the form and return it to the store, which will refund the tax by crediting your card. Europe Tax-Free Shopping is a V.A.T. refund service that makes getting your money back hassle-free. E.T.S. is Europe-wide and has 90,000 affiliated stores. In participating stores, **ask for the E.T.S. refund form** (called a Shopping Cheque). As is true for all customs forms, when leaving the European Union you get them stamped by the customs official. Then you take them to the E.T.S. counter and they will refund your money right there in cash, by check, or a refund to your credit card. All that convenience will cost you 20%—but then it's done.

➤ VAT REFUNDS: **Europe Tax-Free Shopping** (✉ 233 S. Wacker Dr., Suite 9700, Chicago, IL 60606-6502, ☎ 312/382–1101).

TELEPHONES

Cellular phones (*natels*) may be rented at either the Geneva (☎ 022/7178263) or Zürich (☎ 01/8165063) airports on a daily, weekly, or monthly basis. The rental desks are clearly indicated in each airport.

COUNTRY & AREA CODES

The country code for Switzerland is 41. When dialing a Swiss number from abroad, drop the initial 0 from the local area code. The country code is 1 for the U.S. and Canada, 61 for Australia, 64 for New Zealand, and 44 for the U.K.

DIRECTORY & OPERATOR INFORMATION

Dial 111 for information within Switzerland. All telephone operators speak English, and instructions are printed in English in all telephone booths. Precede the area-code number with 0 when dialing long-distance within Switzerland.

Anglo-Phone (☎ 1575014) is a 24-hour English-language information line giving details on hotels, restaurants, museums, nightlife, skiing, what to do in an emergency, and more. Calls cost 2.13 SF per minute.

INTERNATIONAL CALLS

You can dial most international numbers direct from Switzerland, adding 00 before the country code. If you want a number that cannot be reached directly, dial 1141 for a connection. Dial 1159 for international numbers and information. (Neighboring countries have their own information numbers: 1151 for Austria; 1152 for Germany; 1153 for France; and 1154 for Italy.) It's cheapest to use the booths in train stations and post offices: Calls made from your hotel cost a great deal more. Rates are lower between 3 PM and 7 PM and 8 AM and 10 AM (depending upon where you are calling), as well as on weekends and holidays. Normal rates for calls to the United States and to the United Kingdom cost about 0.75 SF a minute. If you're short on change and don't have a phone card, call from the phone cabins at the post office (although there is a 2 SF service charge): Tell the clerk what country you want to call, then step in and dial. The cost is clocked behind the desk, and you may pay with a credit card. There's no difference in price between phone cabins and public phone booths.

LONG-DISTANCE SERVICE

On January 1, 1998, the state monopoly on telecommunications ended. Rates are decreasing following the entrance of new companies into the market to compete with the state-owned Swisscom. There is direct dialing to everywhere in Switzerland. For local area codes, consult the pink pages and for international country and city codes, consult the green pages at the front of the telephone book.

AT&T, MCI, and Sprint access codes make calling long distance relatively convenient, but you may find the local access number blocked in many hotel rooms. First ask the hotel operator to connect you. If the hotel operator balks ask for an international operator, or dial the international operator yourself. One way to improve your odds of getting connected to your long-distance carrier is to travel with more than one company's calling card (a hotel may block Sprint, for example, but not MCI). If all else fails call from a pay phone.

➤ ACCESS CODES: **AT&T Direct** (☎ 800/435–0812). **MCI WorldPhone** (☎ 800/444–4141). **Sprint International Access** (☎ 800/877–4646 for other areas).

PUBLIC PHONES

To make a local call on a pay phone, pick up the receiver, put in a minimum of .60 SF, and dial the number. Digital readouts will tell you to add more as your time runs out. A useful alternative is the Swisscom phone card, available in 5 SF, 10 SF, or 20 SF units. You can buy them at the post office, train station, or kiosks, and you slip them into adapted public phones. The cost of the call will be counted against the card, with any remaining value still good for the next time you use it. If you drain the card and still need to talk, the readout will warn you: You can either pop in a new card or make up the difference with coins, although fewer and fewer phones still accept coins. Many phone booths now also accept Visa, MasterCard, and American Express cards but be sure to have a four-digit PIN code (☞ Credit Cards *in* Money, *above*).

TIME

Switzerland is six hours ahead of New York, nine hours ahead of Los Angeles, one hour ahead of London, and nine hours behind Sydney.

TIPPING

Despite all protests to the contrary and menus marked *service compris,* the Swiss *do* tip at restaurant meals, giving quantities anywhere from the change from the nearest franc to 10 SF for a world-class meal exquisitely served. Unlike American-style tipping, calculated by a percentage, usually between 10% and 20%, a tip is still a tip here: a nod of approval for a job well done. If, in a café, the waitress settles the bill at the table, fishing the change from her leather purse, give her the change on the spot—or calculate the total, including tip, and tell her the full sum before she counts it onto the tabletop. If you need to take more time to calculate, leave it on the table, though this isn't common practice in outdoor cafés. If you're paying for a meal with a credit card, try to tip with cash instead of filling in the tip slot on the slip: Not all managers are good about doling out the waiters' tips in cash. Tipping porters and doormen is easier: 2 SF per bag is adequate in good hotels, 1 SF per trip in humbler lodgings (unless you travel heavy). A fixed rate of 5 SF per bag applies to porter fees at the Geneva and Zürich airports.

TOURS & PACKAGES

On a prepackaged tour or independent vacation everything is prearranged so you'll spend less time planning—and often get it all at a good price.

BOOKING WITH AN AGENT

Travel agents are excellent resources. But it's a good idea to collect brochures from several agencies because some agents' suggestions may be influenced by relationships with tour and package firms that reward them for volume sales. If you have a special interest **find an agent with expertise in that area**; ASTA (☞ Travel Agencies, *below*) has a database of specialists worldwide.

Make sure your travel agent knows the accommodations and other services of the place they're recommending. Ask about the hotel's location, room size, beds, and whether it has a pool, room service, or programs for children, if you care about these. Has

SMART TRAVEL TIPS A TO Z

your agent been there in person or sent others whom you can contact?

Do some homework on your own, too: Local tourism boards can provide information about lesser-known and small-niche operators, some of which may sell only direct.

BUYER BEWARE

Each year consumers are stranded or lose their money when tour operators—even large ones with excellent reputations—go out of business. So **check out the operator.** Ask several travel agents about its reputation, and try to **book with a company that has a consumer-protection program.** (Look for information in the company's brochure.) In the United States, members of the National Tour Association and United States Tour Operators Association are required to set aside funds to cover your payments and travel arrangements in case the company defaults. It's also a good idea to choose a company that participates in the American Society of Travel Agent's Tour Operator Program (TOP); ASTA will act as mediator in any disputes between you and your tour operator.

Remember that the more your package or tour includes the better you can predict the ultimate cost of your vacation. Make sure you know exactly what is covered, and **beware of hidden costs.** Are taxes, tips, and transfers included? Entertainment and excursions? These can add up.

➤ TOUR-OPERATOR RECOMMENDATIONS: **American Society of Travel Agents** (☞ Travel Agencies, *below*). **National Tour Association** (NTA, ✉ 546 E. Main St., Lexington, KY 40508, ☎ 606/226–4444 or 800/682–8886). **United States Tour Operators Association** (USTOA, ✉ 342 Madison Ave., Suite 1522, New York, NY 10173, ☎ 212/599–6599 or 800/468–7862, FAX 212/599–6744).

TRAIN TRAVEL

The Swiss Federal Railways, or **CFF** (☎ 1572222, 1.19 SF/min.), has a very extensive network; trains and stations are clean, and, as you'd expect, service is extremely prompt. The cleanliness extends to the train station bathrooms—in most countries these are grim affairs, but in Switzerland's large city stations, look for "McClean" restrooms. They have nothing to do with the red-and-yellow hamburger chain; instead, they're immaculate, sleekly designed spaces with bathrooms, changing stations, showers, and a toiletries kiosk. Entrance is just under 2 SF.

Trains described as Inter-City or Express are the fastest, stopping only at principal towns. *Regionalzug/Train Régional* means a local train. If you're planning to use the trains extensively, get the official timetable ("Kursbuch" or "Horaire") for 16 SF; the portable, pocket version is called "Reka" and costs 12 SF.

Consider a first-class ticket only if the extra comfort is worth the price. The principal difference between first- and second-class is more space to yourself; the first-class cars are less crowded. Seat size is the same, upholstery fancier, and you usually will be delivered to track position closest to the station. **Make seat reservations** for trips during rush hours and in high season, especially on international trains.

If your itinerary requires changing trains, **bear in mind that the average connection time is six to eight minutes.**

CUTTING COSTS

To save money **look into rail passes.** But be aware that if you don't plan to cover many miles, you may come out ahead by buying individual tickets.

If Switzerland is your only destination in Europe, **there are numerous passes available** for visitors. The **Swiss Pass** is the best value, offering unlimited travel on Swiss Federal Railways, postal buses (☞ Bus Travel, *above*), lake steamers, and the local bus and tram services of 30 cities. It also gives reductions on many privately owned railways, cable cars, and funiculars. Available from Switzerland Tourism and from travel agents outside Switzerland, the card is valid for four days (216 SF second class; 324 SF first class); eight days (270 second class; 388 SF first class); 15 days (314 SF second class; 454 SF first class); or one month (430 SF second class;

626 SF first class). There is also a three-day **Flexipass** (216 SF second class; 324 SF first class), which offers the same unlimited travel options as a regular Swiss Pass for any three days within a 15-day period. The cost of a children's pass is half the cost of the adult pass. For information on the **Swiss Boat Pass,** *see* Boat Travel, *above;* for information on the Family Pass, *see* Children & Travel, *above*.

Within some popular tourist areas, **Regional Holiday Season Tickets,** usually issued for 15 days, give five days of free travel by train, postal buses, steamers, and mountain railways, with half fare for the rest of the validity of the card. Central Switzerland (Berner Oberland) offers a similar pass for seven days, with two days of free travel. Prices vary widely, depending upon the region and period of validity. Increasingly popular with tourists is a **Swiss Half-Fare Travel Card,** which allows half-fare travel for 30 days (90 SF) or one year (150 SF). Both passes are available from Switzerland Tourism (☞ Visitor Information, *below*) and local tourist boards, but to be on the safe side, inquire well in advance.

The **Swiss Card,** which can be purchased in the United States through Rail Europe and at train stations at the Zürich and Geneva airports and in Basel, is valid for 30 days and grants full round-trip travel from your arrival point to any destination in the country, plus a half-price reduction on any further excursions during your stay (144 SF second class; 175 SF first class). For more information about train travel in Switzerland, get the free "Swiss Travel System" or "Discover Switzerland" brochures from Switzerland Tourism (☞ Visitor Information, *below*).

Switzerland is one of 17 countries in which you can **use Eurailpasses,** which provide unlimited first-class rail travel, in all of the participating countries, for the duration of the pass. If you plan to rack up the miles, get a standard pass. These are available for 15 days ($554), 21 days ($718), one month ($890), two months ($1,260), and three months ($1,558). If your plans call for only limited train travel, **look into a Europass,** which costs less money than a EurailPass. Unlike with Eurailpasses, however, you get a limited number of travel days, in a limited number of countries, during a specified time period. For example, a two-month pass allows between 5 and 15 days of rail travel; costs range between $348 and $728. Keep in mind that the basic Europass is good only in France, Germany, Italy, Spain, and Switzerland, though you have the option of adding two "associate countries" (Austria, Hungary, the Netherlands, Belgium, Luxembourg, Greece, or Portugal).

In addition to standard Eurailpasses, **ask about special rail-pass plans.** Among these are the Eurail Youthpass (for those under age 26), the Eurail and Europass Saverpasses (which give a discount for two or more people traveling together), a Eurail Flexipass (which allows a certain number of travel days within a set period), the Euraildrive Pass and the Europass Drive (which combines travel by train and rental car). Whichever pass you choose, remember that you must **purchase your pass before you leave** for Europe.

Many travelers assume that rail passes guarantee them seats on the trains they wish to ride. Not so. You need to **book seats ahead even if you are using a rail pass**; seat reservations are required on some European trains, particularly high-speed trains, and are a good idea on trains that may be crowded—particularly in summer on popular routes. You will also need a reservation if you purchase sleeping accommodations.

FROM THE U.K.

With the Channel Tunnel completing a seamless route, you can leave London around noon on the Eurostar and (thanks to connections via Paris/Lyon on the superb French *train à grande vitesse,* TGV) have a late supper in Geneva.

The *Venice–Simplon–Orient Express* (✉ 20 Upper Ground, London SE1 9PD, ☎ 020/7928–6000) runs from London to Zürich. Information is also available from the tour company Abercrombie & Kent.

➤ TRAIN INFORMATION: **Rail Europe** (500 Mamaroneck Ave., Harrison, NY 10528, ☎ 914/682–5172 or 800/438–7245, ℻ 800/432–1329; 2087 Dundas E, Suite 106, Mississauga, Ontario L4X 1M2, ☎ 800/361–7245, ℻ 905/602–4198). **DER Travel Services** (✉ 9501 W. Devon Ave., Rosemont, IL 60018, ☎ 800/782–2424, ℻ 800/282–7474 for information or 800/860–9944 for brochures). **CIT Tours Corp.** (15 West 44th Street, 10th Floor, New York, NY 10036, ☎ 212/730–2400 or 800/248–7245 in the U.S., 800/387–0711 or 800/361–7799 in Canada). **Abercrombie & Kent** (✉ 1520 Kensington Rd., Oak Brook, IL 60521-2141, ☎ 630/954–2944 or 800/323–7308, ℻ 630/954–3324).

SCENIC ROUTES

Switzerland makes the most of its Alpine rail engineering, which cuts through the icy granite landscape above 2,000 m (6,560 ft), by offering **special trains** that run from one tourist destination to another, crossing over spectacular passes with panoramic cars. The *Glacier Express* connects the two glamourous resorts of Zermatt and Saint-Moritz, crawling over the Oberalp pass and serving lunch in a burnished-wood period dining car; the *William Tell Express* combines a rail crossing of the Saint Gotthard Pass with a cruise down the length of Lake Luzern. The *Golden Pass/Panoramic Express* climbs from the balmy waterfront of Montreux into the Alpine terrain around Interlaken and rolls on to Luzern via the Brünig Pass. The *Bernina Express* ascends from Chur to Saint-Moritz, then climbs over the magnificent Bernina Pass into Italy, where visitors can connect by postal bus to Lugano. The *Palm Express* route (summer only) combines all modes: You ride by bus from Saint-Moritz to Locarno in the Ticino, then take a train into Italy. From Domodossola you cross the Simplon Pass into Brig, and continue by rail to Zermatt or by bus to Saas-Fee. These sightseeing itineraries take from four to 11 hours travel time. For more information,

contact CFF (☞ *above*) or Railtour Suisse (✉ Chutzenstr. 24, CH-3000 17 Bern, ☎ 031/3780000, ℻ 031/3780222).

TRANSPORTATION AROUND SWITZERLAND

Switzerland offers perhaps the best transit network in Europe: Impeccable autoroutes studded with emergency phones; trams and buses snaking through city streets; steamers crisscrossing blue lakes; and, of course, the famous trains, whose wheels roll to a stop under the station clock just as the second hand sweeps 12.

It doesn't end there. Once on site, a web of tourist transportation gets you even closer to those spectacular views: Cogwheel trains grind up 45-degree slopes, lifts and gondolas sail silently to vantage points, tiny Alpine Metros bore through granite up to green tundra above 8,000 ft.

Traveling by car is the surest way to penetrate the Swiss landscape, but if you invest in a rail pass (☞ Train Travel, *above*), you will not feel cut off. Most Swiss trains intersect with private excursion networks and allow for comfortable sightseeing itineraries without huge layovers. And there's always a sturdy yellow postbus, following its appointed rounds with mountain-goat efficiency at minimal cost; connections to obscure villages and trails are free to holders of the Swiss Pass.

TRAVEL AGENCIES

A good travel agent puts your needs first. Look for an agency that has been in business at least five years, emphasizes customer service, and has someone on staff who specializes in your destination. In addition **make sure the agency belongs to a professional trade organization,** such as ASTA in the United States. If your travel agency is also acting as your tour operator *see* Buyer Beware *in* Tours & Packages, *above*.

➤ LOCAL AGENT REFERRALS: American **Society of Travel Agents** (ASTA, ☎ 800/965–2782 24-hr hot line, ℻ 703/684–8319). **Association of British Travel Agents** (✉ 55–57

Newman St., London W1P 4AH, ☎ 020/7637–2444, FAX 020/7637–0713). **Association of Canadian Travel Agents** (✉ 1729 Bank St., Suite 201, Ottawa, Ontario K1V 7Z5, ☎ 613/521–0474, FAX 613/521–0805). **Australian Federation of Travel Agents** (✉ Level 3, 309 Pitt St., Sydney 2000, ☎ 02/9264–3299, FAX 02/9264–1085). **Travel Agents' Association of New Zealand** (✉ Box 1888, Wellington 10033, ☎ 04/499–0104, FAX 04/499–0786).

VISITOR INFORMATION

For general information about Switzerland, contact the tourist offices before you go.

➤ TOURIST INFORMATION: Swiss National Tourist Office: **U.S.** (nationwide): (✉ 608 5th Ave., New York, NY 10020, ☎ 212/757–5944, FAX 212/262–6116). **El Segundo, CA:** (✉ 222 N. Sepulveda Blvd., Suite 1570, 90245, ☎ 310/335–5980, FAX 310/335–5982). **Chicago:** (✉ 150 N. Michigan Ave., Suite 2930, 60601, ☎ 312/630–5840, FAX 312/630–5848). **Canada:** (✉ 926 The East Mall, Etobicoke, Ontario M9B 6KI, ☎ 416/695–2090 or ☎ 514/333–9526, FAX 416/695–2774). **U.K.:** (✉ Swiss Centre, 1 New Coventry St., London W1V 8EE, ☎ 020/7734–1921, FAX 020/7437–4577).

➤ U.S. GOVERNMENT ADVISORIES: **U.S. Department of State** (✉ Overseas Citizens Services Office, Room 4811 N.S., 2201 C St. NW, Washington, DC 20520; ☎ 202/647–5225 for interactive hot line; 301/946–4400 for computer bulletin board; FAX 202/647–3000 for interactive hot line); enclose a self-addressed, stamped, business-size envelope.

WEB SITES

Do **check out the World Wide Web** when you're planning. You'll find everything from up-to-date weather forecasts to virtual tours of famous cities. Fodor's Web site, www.fodors.com, is a great place to start your on-line travels. For more information specifically on Switzerland, visit: **Switzerland Tourism** (www.switzerlandtourism.com or www.switzerlandvacation.ch), which

allows travelers to customize a vacation in Switzerland, and even to book it through an interactive travel planner; **Travel.Org** (www.travel.org/switz.html) for links and information on over a dozen cities, general travel tips, and more specialized topics like vegetarian restaurants; or **Swiss Federal Railways** (www.rail.ch), which broadcasts train schedules and time tables. The **Swissart Network** site (www.swissart.ch) has links to several museums, city art associations, and galleries; some information is in English. For information on outdoor activities, try **the Alps** (www.alpseurope.org/index.html), which highlights Alpine sports from ballooning to slalom courses. It covers France, Austria, and Italy as well as Switzerland. **Walking in Europe** (www.gorp.com/gorp/activity/europe/europe.html) has a special page on walking in the Alps.

WHEN TO GO

In July and August, Switzerland's best weather coincides with the heaviest crowds. June and September are still pleasant, and hotel prices can be slightly lower, especially in resorts. In May and June the mountains are at their loveliest, with Alpine flowers blooming and the peaks capped with snow; however, as ski season is over and high summer hasn't begun, this is often considered low season, and many resort hotels close down. Those that remain open reduce their prices considerably. Another low-season disadvantage: Some cable-car and cogwheel train operations take a break between the midwinter and midsummer rushes; some must wait for snow to clear before reopening. The most prestigious ski resorts charge top prices during the Christmas–New Year holidays but reduce them slightly in early January. February through Easter is prime time again. Many of the family-run, traditional hotels fill up a year ahead, and you'll have to settle for less appealing lodgings. Also, check with the resort for exact dates of high seasons: They vary slightly from region to region. Late autumn—from mid-October through early December—is the least appealing season for visiting the Alps,

SMART TRAVEL TIPS A TO Z

because there's usually little snow, no foliage, and a tendency toward dampness and fog. If you're sticking to the cities to shop and tour museums, you won't notice the doldrums that take over the resorts. The exception to the above rules of thumb: Ticino, the only portion of Switzerland south of the Alps, boasts a Mediterranean climate and declares high season from April through October. Many of its

hotels close down altogether from November through March.

CLIMATE

What follow are average daily maximum and minimum temperatures for major cities in Switzerland.

➤ FORECASTS: **Weather Channel Connection** (☎ 900/932–8437), 95¢ per minute from a Touch-Tone phone.

BERN

Jan.	36F	2C	May	65F	18C	Sept.	67F	19C
	25	– 4		47	8		50	10
Feb.	40F	4C	June	70F	21C	Oct.	56F	13C
	27	– 3		52	11		41	5
Mar.	49F	9C	July	74F	23C	Nov.	45F	7C
	34	1		56	13		34	1
Apr.	58F	14C	Aug.	72F	22C	Dec.	38F	36C
	40	48		56	13		29	– 2

GENEVA

Jan.	40F	4C	May	67F	19C	Sept.	70F	21C
	29	– 2		49	9		54	12
Feb.	43F	6C	June	74F	23C	Oct.	58F	14C
	31	– 1		56	13		45	7
Mar.	50F	10C	July	77F	25C	Nov.	47F	8C
	36	2		59	15		38	3
Apr.	59F	15C	Aug.	76F	24C	Dec.	40F	4C
	41	5		58	14		32	0

LUGANO

Jan.	43F	6C	May	70F	21C	Sept.	74F	23C
	29	– 2		50	10		56	13
Feb.	49F	9C	June	77F	25C	Oct.	61F	16C
	31	– 1		58	14		47	8
Mar.	56F	13C	July	81F	27C	Nov.	52F	11C
	38	3		61	16		38	3
Apr.	63F	17C	Aug.	81F	27C	Dec.	45F	7C
	45	7		59	15		32	0

ST. MORITZ

Jan.	29F	– 2C	May	50F	10C	Sept.	58F	14C
	11	–12		32	0		38	13
Feb.	34F	1C	June	59F	15C	Oct.	50F	10C
	13	–11		40	4		31	– 1
Mar.	38F	3C	July	63F	17C	Nov.	38F	3C
	18	– 8		41	5		22	– 6
Apr.	45F	7C	Aug.	61F	16C	Dec.	31F	– 1C
	25	– 4		41	5		14	10

ZÜRICH

Jan.	36F	2C	May	67F	19C	Sept.	68F	20C
	27	– 3		47	8		52	11
Feb.	41F	5C	June	74F	23C	Oct.	58F	14C
	29	– 2		54	12		43	6
Mar.	50F	10C	July	77F	25C	Nov.	45F	7C
	34	1		58	14		36	2
Apr.	59F	15C	Aug.	76F	24C	Dec.	38F	3C
	40	4		56	13		29	– 2

1 DESTINATION: SWITZERLAND

THE GOOD, THE BAD, AND THE TIDY

U P IN THE HOARY windswept heights and black fir forests of the Alps, an electric eye beams open a glistening all-glass door— and reveals the honey-gold glow of wood, the sheen of copper, the burnt-chocolate tones of ancient wooden rafters. Candles flicker; Sterno radiates blue-white flames under russet pots of bubbling fondue. The cheery *boomp-chick boomp-chick* of an accordion filters down from high-tech stereo speakers cleverly concealed behind oversize cowbells. Waitresses in starched black dirndls and waiters in bleached white ties scuttle briskly from kitchen to table, table to kitchen, while platters of gravy-laden veal, sizzling *Rösti* (hash brown potatoes), and rosy entrecôte simmer over steel trivets—preheated, electrically controlled—ready to be proudly, seamlessly served.

Coziness under strict control, anachronism versus state-of-the-art technology: strange bedfellows in a storybook land. Nowhere else in Europe can you find a combination as welcoming and as alien, as comfortable and as remote, as engaging and as disengaged as a glass cable car to the clouds. This is the paradox of the Swiss, whose primary national aesthetic pitches rustic Alpine homeyness against high-tech urban efficiency. Though they're proud, sober, self-contained, independent culturally and politically, disdainful of the shabby and the slipshod, painfully neat, rigorously prompt—the Swiss have a weakness for cuteness, and they indulge in incongruously coy diminutives: A German *Bierstube* becomes a *Stübli, Kuchen* (cake) becomes *Küchli, Wurst* becomes *Würstli, Pastete* (puff pastry) becomes *Pastetli,* and a *coupe* (glass) of champagne becomes a *Cüpli.*

It is lucky for tourists, this dichotomy of the folksy and the functional. It means your trains get you to your firelit lodge on time. It means the shower in your room runs as hot as a Turkish bath. It means the cable car that sweeps you to a mountaintop has been subjected to grueling inspections. It means the handwoven curtains are boiled and starched, and the high-thread-count bed linens are turned back with a chocolate at night. It means the scarlet geraniums that cascade from window boxes on every carved balcony are tended like prize orchids. It means the pipe smoke that builds up in the Stübli (cozy little pubs) at night is aired out daily, as sparkling clean, double-glazed windows are thrown open on every floor, every morning, to let sharp, cool mountain air course through hallways, bedrooms, and fresh-bleached baths.

Yet there is a stinginess that peeks around the apron of that rosy-cheeked efficiency. Liquor here is measured with scientific precision into glasses marked for one centiliter or two, and the local wines come in carafes reminiscent of laboratory beakers. Despite the fine linens and puffs of down that adorn each bed, double beds have separate mattresses with sheets tucked primly down the middle, sometimes so tightly you have to lift the mattress to loosen the barrier. And if you wash out your socks and hang them loosely on the shower rod in the morning, you may return at night and find them straightened, spaced, toes pointing the same direction, as orderly as little lead soldiers.

Nevertheless there is an earthiness about these people, as at ease with the soil as they are appalled by dirt. A banker in Zürich may rent a postage-stamp parcel of land in a crowded patchwork outside town, sowing tight rows of cabbages and strawberries, weeding bright borders of marigolds, and on Sunday he may visit his miniature estate, pull a chair out from the tidy toolshed, and simply sit and smoke, like Heidi's Alm-Uncle surveying his Alpine realm. An elderly woman may don knickers and loden hat and board a postbus to the mountains and climb steep, rocky trails at a brisk clip, cheeks glowing, eyes as icy bright as the glaciers above her. A family of farmers—grandparents, schoolgirls, married sons—unite for the hay cutting as if for Christmas dinner, standing shoulder to shoulder in the hip-high gold, swinging scythes from dawn to sunset.

There's a 21st-century counterpoint to this: the high-tech, jet-set glamour that splashes vivid colors across the slopes at St. Moritz, Gstaad, Zermatt, Verbier. Step out of a bulbous steel-and-glass cable car onto a concrete platform at 2,000 m (6,560 ft) and see Switzerland transformed, its workers' blue overalls and good wool suits exchanged for Day-Glo ski suits—mango, chartreuse, swimming-pool blue. Wholesome, healthy faces disappear behind mirrored goggles and war-paint sunblock, and gaudy skis and poles bristle militarily, like the pikes and halberds in the Battle of Sempach.

The contradictions mount: While fur-clad socialites raise jeweled fingers to bid at Sotheby's on Geneva's quai de Mont-Blanc, the women of Appenzell stand beside their husbands on the Landsgemeindeplatz and raise their hands to vote—a right not won until 1991. While digital screens tick off beef futures in Zürich, the crude harmony of cowbells echoes in velvet mountain pastures. While a Mercedes roars down an expressway expertly blasted through solid rock, a horse-drawn plow peels back thin topsoil in an Alpine garden plot, impossibly steep, improbably high.

And on August 1, the Swiss national holiday, while spectacular displays of fireworks explode in sizzling colors over the cities and towns, the mountain folk build the bonfires that glow quietly, splendidly, on every hillside of every Alp, uniting Swiss citizens as they celebrate their proud independence, their cultural wealth, and above all their diversity. It's that diversity and those quirky contradictions that make Switzerland a tourist capital—the folksy, fiercely efficient innkeeper to the world.

–Nancy Coons

NEW AND NOTEWORTHY

Skiers who annually converge on Graubünden resorts will have their path considerably smoothed; the **Vereina Tunnel,** stretching from Klosters to Susch/Lavin, is slated for completion in late fall 1999. The railway will load cars and whisk away twice an hour from each terminal—an especially big blessing when the Flüela Pass is closed by snow.

Luzern's world-renowned **Kultur- und Kongresszentrum,** the new home of the prestigious International Music Festival, plans to open a museum in its stunning complex by summer 2000.

Little visible damage remains from the series of severe avalanches in winter 1998–99. In some resorts and villages such as Wengen, however, buildings were demolished by snow slides.

Recent dips in the the Swiss franc's clout have eased the pain for American visitors, and tourism has begun to pick up steam.

WHAT'S WHERE

Zürich

Known as one of the leading financial centers of the world, Zürich at first sight may appear to be a modest, small-scale city, but the array of luxury shops along its Bahnhofstrasse and its renowned Opera reveal its cultural and material riches. Its Old Town, which straddles the River Limmat, has few high-rise buildings; Gothic guildhalls take the place of imperial palaces. In the distance, snow-clad peaks overlook the waters of the lake, dwarfing everything below.

Eastern Switzerland

Near Zürich, the cantons of Glarus, Schaffhausen, Thurgau, Saint-Gallen, and Appenzell, as well as the independent principality of Liechtenstein, are dominated by the Rhine River. With its obscure backcountry and thriving cities, the German-influenced region has everything from wood-shingle farmhouses to town houses adorned with oriel windows and frescoes. Still, the eastern cantons remain one of the most untouched regions of Switzerland.

Graubünden

Dominated by its trendy resorts—St. Moritz, Davos, Klosters, Arosa, Pontresina—Graubünden is nonetheless Switzerland's most culturally diverse and largest canton. German, Italian, and

Language Regions of Switzerland

GERMANY

FRANCE

Basel

Zürich

GERMAN

AUSTRIA

LIECHTENSTEIN

Bern

Fribourg

FRENCH

ROMANSH

St. Moritz

ITALIAN

Sierre

Bellinzona

Geneva

N

ITALY

| 0 | 60 miles |
| 0 | 90 km |

Romansh—the ancient dialect that is thought to date from 600 BC—are all spoken here, in a land where stalwart native farmers subsist alongside fur-clad tourists from abroad. This is also the site of Switzerland's only national park, probably the only place in the country where skiing is forbidden.

The Ticino

Italian in language, culture, and spirit, the Ticino is an irresistible combination of Mediterranean pleasures and Swiss efficiency. With its yacht-filled waterfront promenades of Locarno and Lugano and its constantly sunny climate, the Ticino is a canton set apart, a happy harbor for Switzerland's Italian-speaking minority.

Luzern and Central Switzerland

Endowed with a sophisticated transportation system that makes it one of the easiest regions to visit, central Switzerland is full of neat little towns, accessible mountains, and modest resorts. Centered around the Vierwaldstättersee, "the lake of the four forest cantons," the region is steeped in history: It is where the Oath of Eternal Alliance is said to have been renewed, and

it's also the birthplace of the legend of William Tell.

Basel

At the juncture of France and Germany, German-speaking Basel is a cultural capital with a sense of fun. Cultivated and yet down-home, it has more than 30 museums, Switzerland's oldest university, and some of the most diverse shopping in the country. All the same, beer and sausages are the snack of choice, and the annual Fasnacht (Carnival) is observed with a boisterousness that's unparalleled by other Swiss towns.

Fribourg, Neuchâtel, and the Jura

Unself-conscious and largely undiscovered, the cantons of Fribourg, Neuchâtel, and the Jura represent three very different worlds in western Switzerland. Fribourg, part German and part French, is full of medieval villages; Neuchâtel, French in language and culture, is beginning to shift its focus from watchmaking to tourism; and the isolated Jura Mountains, part German and part French, exist in a realm of their own.

Bern

Humble and down-to-earth, Bern is a city of broad medieval streets, farmers' markets, and friendly, slow-spoken people. It is also the federal capital of Switzerland and, more remarkably, a World Cultural Heritage city known for its sandstone arcades, fountains, flowers, and thick, sturdy towers.

Berner Oberland

The Bernese Alps concentrate the very best of rural Switzerland: panoramas of the Eiger, Mönch, and Jungfrau mountains; crystalline lakes, gorges, and waterfalls; and emerald slopes dotted with gingerbread chalets and cows with bells—not to mention world-class skiing. It's no secret, though: The Berner Oberland is among the most popular tourist destinations in Switzerland.

Valais

Alpine villages, famous peaks (the Matterhorn, most notably), world-class resorts (Zermatt, Saas-Fee, Crans, Verbier), and verdant vineyards are all reasons to visit the valley of the Rhone. This is the Switzerland of tumbledown huts, raclette eaters, and yodelers. Separated from the modern world by mountains, it feels like a land apart.

Vaud

Lausanne, Montreux, and the Alpes Vaudoises comprise one of Switzerland's most diverse regions. Centered around Lac Léman (also known as Lake Geneva), this French-speaking canton harbors some of the country's most famous cathedrals and castles, as well as Alpine villages, balmy lake resorts, and above all, its most verdant vineyards.

Geneva

As the headquarters of the United Nations, the World Health Organization, and the International Red Cross; an international mecca for writers and thinkers of every stripe; and a stronghold of luxurious stores and extravagant restaurants, Geneva is Switzerland's most cosmopolitan city. This is a city of wealth and influence, where the rustic chalets of hilltop villages seem worlds away.

PLEASURES AND PASTIMES

Dining

If you're looking for diverse dining experiences, you can't do much better than Switzerland, where French, Italian, or German cuisine may dominate, depending on which cantons you visit. In French areas (roughly Vaud, Geneva, Jura, Neuchâtel, and western parts of Fribourg and Valais) the cuisine is clearly Gallic, and wine stews, organ meats, and subtle sausages appear alongside standard *cuisine bourgeoise:* thick, rare beef entrecôte with a choice of rich sauces and *truite meunière* (trout dredged in flour and sizzled in butter). In the Ticino, the Italian canton, Italian cuisine appears virtually unscathed, particularly the Alpine-forest specialties of Piedmont and Lombardy (risotto, gnocchi, polenta, porcini mushrooms). The German cantons serve more pork than their neighbors and favor another standard dish that represents Switzerland though it vanishes in French-speaking or Italian-speaking areas: Rösti, a broad patty of hash-brown potatoes crisped in a skillet and often flavored with bacon, herbs, or cheese, is as prevalent in the German regions as fondue is in the French. Beyond the obvious cultural differences, Swiss cuisine is also influenced by the terrain: Mountain farmers have traditionally subsisted on such basic foods as raclette (cheese melted over boiled potatoes and garnished with pickled vegetables), while cities nurtured wealthy burghers and noblemen with the cream of the crops of outlying lands—milk-fed veal, fruits from low-lying orchards. Though fondue, Rösti, and veal are likely to be on any resort's menu these days, traces of these influences can still be found almost everywhere.

Hiking

When the snow melts and the mountain streams start to flow, Switzerland takes to the hills. That the Swiss Alps are the ultimate in hiking is no secret: On a sunny day in high season in the more popular vacation areas, footpaths can be almost as crowded as a line for World Series tickets. On narrow trails, hikers walk in single file, and the more aggressive pass on the left as if on the Autobahns of Germany. However, there is an almost infinite quantity of quiet, isolated routes to be explored; if you prefer to hike in peace, head for one of the less inhabited Alpine valleys—in the Valais or Graubünden there are several—and strike out on your own. Each of the regional tourist departments publishes suggested hiking itineraries, and major map publishers distribute excellent topographical maps of wilderness trails. In the German-speaking region especially, hiking is a deeply rooted tradition, and people of all ages and in all physical conditions head for well-beaten paths in jeans as often as knickers, woolen stockings, rucksacks, and hiking boots.

Regional Celebrations

Basel's extravagant pre-Lenten observance of Fasnacht (Carnival)—in which up to 20,000 costumed revelers fill the streets with the sounds of fifes and drums—is only one of the hundreds of festivals that the Swiss celebrate during the year. As if to prove that its spirit is vast despite its small size, almost every Swiss canton hosts its own popular celebration of one event or another. In Geneva, the Festival of the Escalade commemorates the heroic housewife who repelled the Savoyards by dumping hot soup on their heads. Lesser-known festivals range from the frivolous—in the Schlitteda Engiadinaisa, young unmarried men and women ride decorated sleighs through the villages of the Engadine—to the symbolic—in the Landsgemeinde, the citizens of Appenzell pay homage to their country's democratic tradition by conducting a vote by public show of hands.

Shopping

Swiss Army knives, Swiss watches, Swiss chocolate—what could be more . . . Swiss? Though you won't find many bargains in Switzerland anytime soon, you will find some uniquely Swiss treasures. Some of the best souvenirs of this pragmatic country are typically practical, such as watches, clocks, and Swiss Army knives. Others are more luxurious, such as sweet milk chocolate: Lindt, Nestlé, and Tobler are major manufacturers. Marvelous music boxes from the watchmaking country around Lake Neuchâtel are sold in specialty shops all over the country. Linens and good cottons—dish and tea towels, aprons, sheets—are another Swiss specialty, as are pottery and ceramics—most of them dark-glazed and hand-painted with simple designs. *Découpage* is the Swiss art of intricate sil-

houette paper-cutting. It's traditionally done with black paper, but it can also be found in color. Farm or *desalpage* (bringing cows down from mountain pastures) scenes are common motifs.

Skiing

Switzerland is Europe's winter playground, and its facilities are as technically advanced as its slopes are spectacular. As one recent skier put it, "There's just *more*"—more slopes; longer runs; more stunning, crisp scenery than you'll find in U.S. resorts. Any level of skier can find a resort to meet his or her needs, from a cozy family-oriented village with easy and moderate slopes to the world-class challenges at Crans-Montana, Verbier, Wengen, and Zermatt. Most of the resorts publish an area map showing their slopes and rating the trails for difficulty. Familiarize yourself with the resort's signs, including those warning of avalanche zones, before you set out. For an analysis of the best ski resorts, *see* Skiing Switzerland *in* Chapter 14.

Spectator Sports

If awards were given to countries with the most unusual sports competitions, Switzerland would win hands down. In the winter, the action centers around St. Moritz, where a frozen lake provides a novel setting for golf, polo, dogsled races, and horse races: In the Winter Golf Tournament, red balls on white "greens" are a festive sight; in the Racing Hounds Competition, a motley crew of canines races across 480 m (1,574 ft) of ice at an average speed of 90 kph (55 mph). Also in St. Moritz, the uniquely Swiss sport of *Skikjöring* involves skiers being pulled by galloping horses. Cows are the players in another, nonwinter event: In April, small towns throughout the Valais hold a *combat de reines,* or cow fight. Female cows head-butt each other (though some contestants have been known to just placidly chew their cud); the winner, *la reine* (the queen), is decorated and awarded with the best grazing ground. *Hornuss* is played in rural areas of the French-speaking cantons, particularly Fribourg and Vaud. Players wield wooden placards on sticks, tossing the placards into the air to stop a ball that is launched by a person wielding an extremely long, flexible implement that looks roughly like a golf club. Wrestling is a popular Swiss tradition: Men wear big baggy shorts of burlap and stand in sawdust rings; after the competition, costumed spectators sing and dance. Perhaps most unusual, stone-throwing competitions in Unspunnen (in the canton of Bern) take place every five years; 180-pound stones are used.

GREAT ITINERARIES

In a country as diverse as Switzerland, it makes sense to visit with a theme in mind. Below, we have outlined itineraries for culinary adventures and exploring historic castles. *Bon appétit* and happy exploring.

Swiss Gastronomy

This food-intensive itinerary offers aficionados an opportunity to travel from one great dining experience to another, sampling the very finest *haute gastronomie* at one stop, the most authentic regional classics—even the earthiest peasant cuisines—at another. Incidental pleasures—wandering in the Alps, for example, or strolling through medieval town centers in Switzerland's greatest cities—can be squeezed in between meals. Remember that reservations must be made well in advance. We'll start in Geneva, sampling its Lyon-influenced cuisine, then head east toward Lausanne and Crissier, where Philippe Rochat has succeeded the legendary (but retired) Fredy Girardet. Then it's northward to Basel, where his rival Jean-Claude Wicky at the restaurant Stucki competes for culinary stars. From Basel, it's an hour's journey to Küsnacht near Zürich, where the third of the Swiss triumvirate—Horst Petermann—reigns. After that, take a dip south to Luzern for regional cuisine. Now it's time for a little exercise: crossing the Alps into the Valais (the Rhône Valley), resting at Saas-Fee for a mountain-inn getaway, and following the Rhône back toward Geneva, stopping at Verbier, another mountain resort, for a gastronomic feast to tide you over for the journey home.

DURATION➤ Depending on your capacity for stellar meals—one or two per day—you can concentrate the highlights of this trip into nine marathon days or stretch it out over two weeks or more. If you're planning to pack it all into a few days, check opening days carefully—and always book ahead. Many restaurants in Geneva close weekends, and many elsewhere close Monday or Tuesday.

GETTING AROUND➤ Each of the stopovers is accessible by train, though some of the restaurants may require cabs or tram rides; a rental car will give you more flexibility for reaching country inns.

THE MAIN ROUTE➤ **1 night: Geneva.** Your first night, indulge in a hearty Lyonnaise bistro meal at Le Boeuf Rouge. For lunch the next day, head for the elite country-club atmosphere in the suburb of Cologny to rub shoulders with jet-set diners over bouillabaisse at Le Lion d'Or. Back in Geneva, have a relatively light Ticinese supper at La Favola. Incidental distractions to fill time between meals: world-class museums (especially the International Red Cross Museum), Old Town antiques shops, or the early Christian diggings under the cathedral.

1 night: Lausanne. Testing Phillipe Rochat's mettle at Restaurant de l'Hôtel de Ville in nearby Crissier may be the triumph of the trip—but reserve judgment for after Basel and Zürich. At night, head down to the waterfront at Ouchy and have a chic, light supper at the Café Beau-Rivage.

1 night: Basel. Two hours north, compare Jean-Claude Wicky with Rochat at lunch. Then, after visiting, say, the Münster and the history museum, relax in the downstairs bistro at the Teufelhof: The light specialties are prepared by Michael Baader, who is chef for the top-notch restaurant upstairs as well.

2 nights: Zürich. Have lunch at Petermann's Kunststuben, in the suburb of Küsnacht, where the gastronomy vies for the title "best in Switzerland." Then, after a thorough walking tour of Zürich's Old Town, you can settle in for an atmospheric, old-world evening at the Kronenhalle.

1 night: Luzern. For a total contrast and perhaps the most authentically *Swiss* meal of your tour, head for Galliker and a lunch of real farm food. Having absorbed the Lion Monument, crossed the Kapellbrücke, and toured the history museum, you can think about the evening meal:

A light, sophisticated river-fish meal at Rotes Gatter affords waterfront views.

1 night: Saas-Fee. From Luzern, allow for a full day's scenic mountain drive south over the Brünigpass, then on over the Grimselpass and down the Rhône Valley to Brig and the spectacular little resort of Saas-Fee. Once there, retreat to the isolated Waldhotel Fletschhorn for a sophisticated dinner and a bare minimum of one night to take in the mountain air.

1 night: Verbier. Following the Rhône back west toward Geneva, take one more Alpine side trip up to this famous ski resort to feast and sleep at Rosalp, the popular rustic-chic inn in the village center.

INFORMATION➤ *See* Chapters 2, 6, 7, and 11–13.

Castles and Cathedrals

Romantics, history buffs, and architecture fans will enjoy a circle tour that takes in some of the best of western Switzerland's medieval and Gothic landmarks. Start at Geneva, where the cathedral covers Christian history from Gallo-Roman times through Calvin. At Montreux, you'll visit the famous waterfront Castle of Chillon, where Lord Byron signed the pillar where his "Prisoner of Chillon" was manacled. In the green Fribourg countryside, the Gruyères Castle perches at the top of a tiny preserved village. The bilingual capital Fribourg is the last Catholic stronghold of western Switzerland, rooted in its single-tower cathedral. A jog down to the Berner Oberland and Thun takes you to the mighty Zähringen Castle along the waters of the Thunersee. Then head up to Bern, entirely fortified by the Zähringen dukes, with its spectacular Münster, and on to Basel, where its own Münster dominates the Old Town.

DURATION➤ Six days.

GETTING AROUND➤ All stops are easily accessible by expressway and connecting roads.

The complete itinerary works by rail, with most sites accessible on foot from the station; Gruyères has bus connections to the elevated castle and Old Town.

THE MAIN ROUTE➤ **1 night: Geneva.** The Cathédrale St-Pierre, begun during the 12th century, sinks roots into early Christianity: Immediately below its current structure, you'll find the *site archéologique,* where 3rd- and 5th-century ruins have been exposed.

1 night: Montreux. The Château de Chillon, partially surrounded by the waters of Lac Léman (Lake Geneva), may be the most completely and authentically furnished in Switzerland, with tapestries, carved fireplaces, ceramics, and painted wooden ceilings.

1 night: Gruyères. This craggy castle-village draws crowds to its ancient central street, souvenir shops, quaint inns, and frescoed castle, complete with dungeon and spectacular views.

1 night: Fribourg. The Last Judgment tympanum and Art Nouveau stained-glass windows of the Cathédrale St-Nicolas deserve attention—but leave time to explore the Old Town, with its multilevel fortifications constructed for the ubiquitous Zähringens.

1 night: Thun. If you're driving, cut across the rolling verdure of canton Fribourg toward Thun (by train, connect through Bern), where you'll see the Bernese Alps looming in all their splendor. Schloss Zähringen, which dates from 1191, features a knight's hall, tapestries, local ceramics, and an intimidating collection of weapons.

1 night: Bern. The Zähringens fortified this gooseneck in the River Aare; its 15th-century Münster features an unusually restored (full-color, painted) main portal.

1 night: Basel. In this historic, cosmopolitan city is a Münster with a lovely Romanesque portal and the tomb of the great humanist Erasmus.

INFORMATION➤ *See* Chapters 8–10, 12, and 13.

FODOR'S CHOICE

No two people will agree on what makes a perfect vacation, but it's fun and helpful to know what others think. We hope you'll have a chance to experience some of Fodor's Choices yourself while visiting Switzerland.

Flavors

⋆ The transfer is complete; the former Girardet, outside Lausanne, is now **Restaurant de l'Hôtel de Ville.** Philippe Rochat is no newcomer, though—having worked with Girardet for nearly 20 years, he maintains his mentor's standards. *$$$$*

⋆ You'll have to go off the beaten track to find one of the best chefs in Switzerland; the **Hôtel-Restaurant de la Gare** is in the village of Le Noirmont, practically on the French border. It's well worth the trek, as chef Georges Wenger adapts local Jura ingredients to sophisticated, seasonal cuisine. *$$$$*

⋆ The 20th-century art collection is as plentiful as the food at Zürich's **Kronenhalle,** where robust cooking in hearty portions draws a genial crowd. *$$$–$$$$*

⋆ Inside what was once the Heuberg mansion in Basel, the **Teufelhof** has an excellent restaurant, a chic Weinstube, and a trendy bar—there are even medieval ruins in the basement. The menus are always intriguing. *$$–$$$$*

⋆ At **Wirtschaft zum Frieden,** in Schaffhausen, you can opt for a daily plate lunch in an intimate stübli, a fancier meal in a tile-stove dining room, or selections from either menu in a private garden thick with wisteria. *$$–$$$*

⋆ In a 1677 inn at the hub of Chur, **Stern** carries on the age-old tradition of Graubündner culture, complete with local wine served in pewter pitchers and waitresses in folk costumes. *$–$$$*

⋆ Authentic Lyonnaise cuisine is the specialty at Geneva's **Boeuf Rouge,** where *boudin noir* (blood sausage) and *tarte Tatin* (caramelized apple tart) will make you think you've crossed the border. *$$*

⋆ Under a giant boar's head and century-old murals at **Bierhalle Kropf,** businesspeople, workers, and shoppers share crowded tables to feast on hearty Zürich cuisine. *$–$$*

⋆ Tucked in a tiny basement in an alleyway off Lugano's Old Town, **La Tinera** draws crowds of locals and tourists for its hearty meats, pastas, and local wine served in ceramic bowls. *$*

Comforts

⋆ Lausanne's **Beau Rivage-Palace** stands apart in neoclassic grandeur, with manicured waterfront grounds, and several first-class restaurants. *$$$$*

⋆ **Giardino,** in the small Ticinese village of Ascona, is decidedly decadent, from the pure linen sheets to the chauffeured Bentley. *$$$$*

⋆ In Geneva's Old Town, **Les Armures** is an archaeological treasure with original stonework, frescoes, and stenciled beams. *$$$$*

⋆ Overlooking green waterfront grounds on the Murtensee, the turn-of-the-century **Le Vieux Manoir au Lac** offers sumptuously decorated rooms. *$$$$*

⋆ A 600-year-old structure on the banks of the Limmat, **Zum Storchen** is one of Zürich's most atmospheric hotels. *$$$*

⋆ In Château-d'Oex, the 18th-century **Bon Acceuil** has low wood-beam ceilings, creaking floors, antiques, and fresh flowers inside and out. *$$*

⋆ A demure little inn on a residential hillside between Chillon and Montreux, **Masson** has offered peace and quiet to weary travelers since 1829. *$$*

⋆ With lead-glass windows, homespun linen, and pewter pitchers, the all-wood chalet **Ruedihus** in Kandersteg re-creates the atmosphere of the 1753 original. *$$*

⋆ Basel's **Krafft am Rhein** is a rare find in Swiss cities—it's an elegant little inn sitting directly on the right-bank waterfront, with mosaic floors, elaborate moldings, and a sinuous atrium stairwell. Try for a Rhine-side room. *$–$$*

Perfect Moments

⋆ When the sound of fife-and-drum music drifts from upstairs windows of guild houses in **Basel's Old Town,** you'll think the Middle Ages have dawned once again.

⋆ Feeding swans and ducks by the **Kapellbrücke** in Luzern is a favorite pastime of locals and tourists alike.

⋆ A herd of male red deer, antlers silhouetted, in the **Parc Nazional Svizzer** (Swiss National Park), is a memorable sight.

⋆ Drinking **steaming-fresh milk** in an Alpine barn, you'll understand why Heidi loved Switzerland.

Fireworks burst and mountain-farm bonfires smolder on the **Swiss National Holiday** (August 1).

For a festive, outdoorsy evening, rent a lap blanket for a summer night's outdoor performance of the **Tellspiel** at Interlaken.

Picturesque Villages and Towns

Clinging vertiginously to a hillside, its flower-filled balconies overlooking the sea, tiny **Gandria** retains the ambience of an ancient fishing village.

In the Lower Engadine, **Guarda** is a federally protected hamlet of architectural photo-ops, with cobblestone streets and flower boxes filled with red geraniums.

An eagle's-nest town set on a precarious 1,000-m (3,280-ft) slope in the Rhône Valley, **Isérables** is full of stone-shingled *mazots* (barns typical of the Valais) and narrow, winding streets.

Morcote, an old resort village below Lugano, has clay-color Lombard-style houses and arcades that look out on the waterfront.

In western Switzerland near Avenches, the ancient town of **Murten** (known in French as Morat) is a popular lake resort with a superbly preserved medieval center.

In the vineyard region of Vaud, the scenic **Corniche Road** joins cobblestone villages, such as St-Saphorin, and beckoning vineyards. The lake and mountain views—and the tastings of fruity, local wine—make this a memorable area.

On the Rhine River in eastern Switzerland, **Stein-am-Rhein** is a nearly perfectly preserved medieval village, replete with shingled, half-timber town houses boasting ornate oriels and flamboyant frescoes.

Views

The terrace café of the Disneyland-like **Château Gütsch** affords an idyllic view of Luzern and the Vierwaldstättersee.

In the **Emmental region** near Bern, the gentle hills begin to roll out village after beautiful village, dotted with many impressive examples of the classic Emmental farmstead.

From the summit station of Gornergrat, the snaggle-toothed **Matterhorn** steals the thunder from all surrounding peaks.

From the top of the 3,474-m (11,395-ft) **Jungfraujoch,** the Aletsch Glacier looks like a vast sea of ice.

With its mists, roaring water, jutting rocks, and bushy crags, the **Rheinfall,** from the Neuhausen side, appears truly Wagnerian.

Perched high above town, Bern's **Rose Garden** overlooks the entire Old Town.

The sunset from the south-facing hilltop resort of **Wengen** is a sublime way to end a day of skiing.

FESTIVALS AND SEASONAL EVENTS

Top seasonal events in Switzerland include Fasnacht (Carnival) celebrations in February and March, the Landsgemeinde open-air vote in Appenzell in April, the Montreux International Jazz Festival in July, the Menuhin Festival in Gstaad in August, Luzern's International Festival of Music from mid-August to mid-September, the Knabenschiessen (Boys' Shooting Contest) in Zürich in September, and the Escalade festival in Geneva in December. Events are named below as publicized by the host region, usually in the local language.

WINTER

➤ EARLY DEC.: **Geneva Escalade** commemorates the defeat of the Duke of Savoy, whose invading troops were repelled by a local woman dumping hot soup on their heads from atop the city walls.

➤ MID-JAN.: **Vogel Gryff Volksfest** is a colorful Basel tradition, with a costumed Griffin, a Lion, and a Wild Man of the Woods floating down the Rhine and dancing on the Mittlere Rheinbrücke.

➤ LATE JAN.: **Schlittedas Engiadinaisa** is a winter Engadine tradition in which young unmarried men and women ride decorated sleighs from village to village. **Château-d'Oex Hot Air Balloon Week** showcases the Vaud

resort's specialty.

➤ LATE JAN.–EARLY FEB.: St. Moritz's **Gourmet Festival** draws a host of top-tier chefs.

➤ EARLY FEB.: **Hom Strom** at Bad Scuol in the Lower Engadine observes the burning of Old Man Winter.

➤ LATE FEB.–EARLY MAR.: **Fasnacht** is observed throughout Switzerland, but nowhere more festively than in Basel, where it begins at 4 AM on the Monday after Ash Wednesday (March 13), with a drumroll and a costume parade. Luzern celebrates on the Thursday before Ash Wednesday, with a traditional **Fritschi** procession, distributing oranges to children. On the same day, Schwyz celebrates **Blätzli** with a mummers' procession of harlequins. Lugano celebrates Carnevale with a **Festa del Risotto**, with risotto and sausages served in the streets.

SPRING

➤ EARLY MAR.: **Good Friday** (April 21) processions take place in several southern villages, including Mendrisio in the Ticino, where the procession derives from a medieval Passion Play that is performed on Maundy Thursday as well.

➤ MID-MAR.: **Engadine Ski Marathon** covers the 42 km (26 mi) between Zuoz and Maloja.

➤ MAR.–MAY: **Primavera Concertistica** music festival takes place in Lugano.

➤ APR.: **Sechseläuten** in Zürich shows all its medieval guilds on parade and climaxes in the burning of the Böögg, a straw scarecrow representing winter.

➤ APR.: **Landsgemeinde** takes place in the town of Appenzell on the last Sunday of the month punctually at noon, with all citizens voting by public show of hands. Women voted for the first time in 1991.

➤ APR.: Small towns throughout the Valais hold a **Combat de Reines,** or cow fight, where female cows are pitted against each other in what amounts to a head-butting contest.

➤ APR.: Luzern's **Osterfestspiele** celebrates Easter with sacred music.

➤ APR.–MAY: The **International Jazz Festival—Bern** lasts five days in the federal capital.

➤ MID-APR.–MAY: The lovely lake town of Morges draws a crowd to its annual **Fête de la Tulipe** (Tulip Festival).

SUMMER

➤ MID-JUNE: **Grindelwald Country-Festival** brings American country-and-western groups to this mountain resort.

➤ LATE JUNE–MID-JULY: The **Zürich Festival** hosts dance, opera, theater, and more in several venues throughout the city.

➤ LATE JUNE–MID-SEPT.: **Wilhelm Tell** outdoor theater production, in Interlaken, has an epic-scale cast of locals.

➤ JULY: World-class artists perform at the **Montreux International Jazz Festival.**

➤ JULY–AUG.: **Engadiner Concert Weeks** bring outdoor classical music events to resorts throughout the region. **Festival International de l'Orgue Ancien** at Valère in Sion honors the 13th-century instrument within, the oldest functioning organ in the world.

➤ LATE JULY–AUG.: For more than two weeks the **Verbier Festival and Academy** hosts a classical music festival with an impressive guest roster.

➤ AUG. 1: **Swiss National Holiday** celebrates the confederation's birth in 1291 with fireworks and bonfires.

➤ EARLY AUG.: **Geneva Festival** celebrates with a techno parade and fireworks.

➤ AUG.: Locarno's **International Film Festival** unveils top new movies in the Piazza Grande.

➤ MID-AUG.: **Grächen Country Festival** imports American C&W music to the Alps. Vevey **International Festival of Film Comedy** honors comic classics on the outdoor screen.

➤ LATE AUG.: **International Folklore Festival** in

Fribourg celebrates its 25th anniversary.

➤ MID-AUG.–MID-SEPT.: The world-renowned **Internationale Musikfestwochen** in Luzern combines concerts, theater, and art exhibitions. In 2000 the theme will be "Metamorphoses." Davos **Young Artists in Concert** features tomorrow's classical music stars.

➤ AUG.–MID-SEPT.: **Yehudi Menuhin Festival** in Gstaad showcases world-class musicians. Lugano's **Blues to Bop Festival** brings authentic blues to the lakefront.

➤ LATE AUG.: Zürich's **Theaterspektakel** showcases avant-garde and mainstream playwrights as well as theater troupes from around the world.

➤ LATE AUG.–OCT.: **Vevey-Montreux Music Festival** invites important artists to these twin lake resorts.

➤ EARLY SEPT.: **Knabenschiessen** takes place in Zürich with a folk festival and fair.

➤ MID-SEPT.: **Bénichon,** a traditional autumn Fribourg feast, is held during the second week of September; it celebrates not only the return of the cows from the high pastures to the plains, but

also the season's final yield of hearty food.

➤ LATE SEPT.: The **Neuchâtel Wine Festival** is the biggest in the country.

➤ LATE SEPT.: **Etivaz Cheese Sharing** celebrates the division of spoils from the cheese cooperative with yodeling, wrestling, and other activities. **Fribourg Braderie** combines a citywide sidewalk sale, folk festival, and onion market.

➤ LATE SEPT.–EARLY OCT.: The small Vaud town of St-Cergue has an annual **Fête Desalpe,** a ritual for the cows coming down from the mountains. It lasts all of a Saturday morning, allowing hundreds of cows to parade the streets in amazing floral headgear. Another *desalpe* festival is held in October in Charmey, near Gruyères in Fribourg.

➤ OCT.: In Lugano, a traditional **Wine Harvest Festival** is held at the Piazza della Riforma and on the lakeside.

➤ LATE OCT.: **Olma Schweizer Messe für Land- und Milchwirtschaft** (agricultural and dairy fair) in Saint-Gallen gathers representatives of the farming industry from across Switzerland.

➤ LATE NOV.: Bern's **Zwiebelemärit** (Onion Market) celebrates the open market established for area farmers in gratitude for aid they gave Bern after the great fire of 1405.

2   ZÜRICH

Known as one of the leading financial
centers of the world, Zürich is a surprisingly
modest, small-scale city. Its Old Town, which
straddles the Limmat River, has just a handful
of high-rise buildings, and Gothic guildhalls
take the place of imperial palaces. In the
distance, snow-clad peaks overlook the
waters of the lake, a tantalizing promise of
the mountains beyond.

WHEN THE POUND STERLING sagged in the 1960s, the English coined the somewhat disparaging term "the gnomes of Zürich," which evoked images of sly little Swiss bankers rubbing their hands and manipulating world currencies behind closed doors. Yet the spirit that moves the Züricher doesn't come out of folkloric forests but rather from the pulpit of the Grossmünster, where the fiery Reformation leader Huldrych Zwingli preached sermons about idle hands and the devil's playthings. It's the Protestant work ethic that has made Zürich one of the world's leading financial centers and that keeps its workers on their toes. One Zwingli lesson stressed the transience of wealth, and Zürichers show native caution in enjoying their fabulous gains. Nor have they turned their backs on their humbler heritage: on a first visit, you might be surprised to see a graceful jumble of shuttered Gothic buildings instead of cold chrome-and-glass towers.

Updated by
Ian Plenderleith

Zürich is, in fact, a beautiful city, sitting astride the Limmat River where it emerges from the Zürichsee (Zürich Lake). Its charming Altstadt (Old Town), comprising a substantial part of the city center, is full of beautifully restored historic buildings and narrow, hilly alleys. In the distance, snowy mountains overlook the waters of the lake, and the shores are dominated by turn-of-the-century mansions. Only three high-rise buildings disturb the skyline, and even they are small by U.S. standards. There are not even any dominating castles to haunt the Züricher with memories of imperialism: in keeping with its solid bourgeois character, Zürich has always maintained a human scale.

The earliest known Zürichers lived around 4500 BC in small houses perched on stilts by the lakeside. The remains of 34 Stone Age and Bronze Age settlements are thought to be scattered around the lake. Underwater archaeologists have discovered a wealth of prehistoric artifacts dating back thousands of years, from Stone Age pottery and Bronze Age necklaces to charms made from boar fangs, bear teeth, and animal skulls; many relics are on display at the Schweizerisches Landesmuseum (Swiss National Museum) near the main train station.

In the 1st century BC, the Romans, attracted by Zürich's central location, built a customs house on a hill overlooking the Limmat River. In time, the customs house became a fortress, the remains of which can be seen on the Lindenhof, a square in the city center. The Romans were also accommodating enough to provide Zürich with its patron saints. Legend has it that the Roman governor beheaded the Christian brother and sister Felix and Regula on a small island in the river. The martyrs then picked up their heads, waded through the water, and walked up a hill before collapsing where the Grossmünster now stands.

When the Germanic Alemanni, ancestors of the present-day Zürichers, drove out the Romans in the 5th century, the region gradually diminished in importance until the Carolingians built an imperial palace on the Limmat four centuries later. Louis the German, grandson of Charlemagne, then founded an abbey here, appointing his daughter the first abbess; it was built on the site of what is now the Fraumünster, near the Bahnhofstrasse.

By the 12th century, Zürich had already shown a knack for commerce, with its diligent merchants making fortunes in silk, wool, linen, and leather. By 1336 this merchant class had become too powerful for an up-and-coming band of tradesmen and laborers who, allied with a charismatic aristocrat named Rudolf Brun, overthrew the merchants' town council and established Zürich's famous guilds. Those 13 original guilds never really lost their power until the French Revolution—and have yet to lose their prestige: every year, prominent Zürich businessmen dress up in medieval costumes for the guilds' traditional march through the streets, heading for the magnificent guildhalls that still dominate the Old Town.

If the guilds defined Zürich's commerce, it was the Reformation that defined its soul. From his pulpit in the Grossmünster, Zwingli galvanized the region, and he ingrained in Zürichers their devotion to thrift and hard work—so successfully that it ultimately led them into temptation: the temptations of global influence and tremendous wealth. The Zürich stock exchange, fourth largest in the world, after those of New York, London, and Tokyo, turned over 924 billion Swiss francs in domestic shares in 1998. However, Zürich is far from a cold-hearted business center. In 1916, the avant-garde Dadaist movement started here, when a group of artists and writers, including Tristan Tzara, Jean Arp, and Hugo Ball, rebelled against traditional artistic expression. Zürich also drew in Irish author James Joyce, who spent years re-creating his native Dublin in his *Ulysses* and *A Portrait of the Artist as a Young Man.* Now, the city's extraordinary museums and galleries and luxurious shops along the Bahnhofstrasse, Zürich's 5th Avenue, attest to its position as Switzerland's cultural—if not political—capital.

Pleasures and Pastimes

Dining

On German menus, the cuisine is called *nach Zürcher Art,* meaning cooked in the style of Zürich. What that means to Germans and to the rest of the world as well is meat, mushrooms, potatoes, butter, cream—and heartburn. Zürich's cuisine is one of the richest in the world, perfectly suited to the leaded-glass and burnished-oak guild houses. The signature dish, and one you'll encounter throughout both French and German Switzerland, is *geschnetzeltes Kalbfleisch,* or in French *émincé de veau:* bite-size slices of milky veal (and sometimes veal kidneys) sautéed in butter and swimming in a rich brown sauce thick with cream, white wine, shallots, and mushrooms. Its closest cousin is *geschnetzeltes Kalbsleber* (calves' liver), in similar form. Both are served at the table from broad copper chafing dishes with hot, fresh plates standing by to be filled when you've cleaned the first one. The inevitable accompaniment is *Rösti* (hash brown potatoes), in portions of equal scale—often the full 8-inch-diameter patty is a serving for one. You may also find *Spätzli,* or "little sparrows": flour-egg dough fingers, either pressed through a sieve or snipped, gnocchi style, and served in butter.

The flip side of Zürich's penchant for rich meats and heavy sauces is its sweet tooth: refined cafés draw crowds for afternoon pastries, and chocolate shops vie for the unofficial honor of making—and selling, by the thousands—the best chocolate truffles in town.

Guildhalls

In exploring the Old Town, you will want to enter at least one of the famous medieval union clubhouses scattered along the riverfront neighborhoods; the best way is to dine in one, as all but the Zunfthaus zur Meisen have been converted to public restaurants. Having polished off a traditionally meat-heavy meal, ask if you can have a peek into the other dining rooms—they are, for the most part, museum-perfect in their leaded-glass and Gothic-wood detail.

Museums

The wealth of Zürich bankers and industrialists gave rise to private art collections that are now part of the public art scene. Among the best is the Kunsthaus, with one of the world's best collections of Swiss art; the Museum Rietberg is famous for its East Asian collections. Many local museums host temporary design exhibitions, since Zürich was one of the centers of the graphic design industry early in the 20th century; the Museum für Gestaltung is devoted to all kinds of design.

Shopping

Many of Zürich's shopping finds lie hidden along the narrow streets between the Bahnhofstrasse and the Limmat River; these are peppered with designer boutiques. Quirky bookstores and antiques shops lurk in the sloping, cobblestone alleyways leading off Niedorfstrasse and Oberdorfstrasse. The fabled Bahnhofstrasse—famous because it's reputedly the most expensive street in the world—is dominated by large department stores and extravagantly priced jewelry.

EXPLORING ZÜRICH

From the northern tip of the Zürichsee, the Limmat River starts its brief journey to the Aare and, ultimately, to the Rhine—and it neatly bisects Zürich at the starting gate. The city is crisscrossed by lovely, low bridges. On the left bank are the Hauptbahnhof, the main train station, and Bahnhofplatz, a major urban crossroads and the beginning of the world-famous luxury shopping street, Bahnhofstrasse. The right bank constitutes the younger, livelier section of the Old Town known as Niederdorf. Most of the streets around the Rathausbrücke and the Grossmünster are pedestrian zones.

Scattered throughout the town are 13 medieval guildhalls, or *Zunfthäuser,* that once formed the backbone of Zürich's commercial society. Today most of these house atmospheric restaurants where high ceilings, leaded-glass windows, and coats of arms evoke the mood of the merchants at their trade. Often these restaurants are one floor above street level; in the days before flood control, the river would rise and inundate the ground floors.

Numbers in the text correspond to numbers in the margin and on the Zürich map.

Great Itineraries

IF YOU HAVE 1 DAY

Start in the small but luxuriously gentrified Old Town, taking time for window-shopping along the Bahnhofstrasse. Admire the Asian art and beautiful grounds at the Museum Rietberg; learn about Swiss history and culture at the Swiss National Museum; or stroll along the pretty Limmat River. Then cross over to the bustling Niederdorf to see the Grossmünster, the Rathaus, and—farther west, uphill—catch a temporary exhibition at the Kunsthaus.

IF YOU HAVE 3 DAYS

After exploring the city's churches and museums, consider opera or concert tickets. Or take a boat trip on the Zürichsee, followed by a trip to the outstanding Zürich Zoo. Consider a daylong side trip to well-preserved medieval Rapperswil, in the neighboring region of eastern Switzerland (☞ Chapter 3).

IF YOU HAVE 5 DAYS

For a taste of backcountry Switzerland, drive north through the scenic countryside up to Schaffhausen (☞ Chapter 3), passing the Rhine Falls and a slew of wood-shingle farmhouses. If art is more your interest, visit the Am Römerholz collection in the nearby art town of Winterthur (☞ Off the Beaten Path, *below*).

Bahnhofstrasse and the Old Town

Zürich's Old Town is home to several of Zürich's most important land-marks—the Lindenhof, St. Peters Kirche, the Fraumünster, and the Stadthaus—as well as its luxury shopping street, the world-famous Bahn-hofstrasse.

A Good Walk

Begin at the **Hauptbahnhof** ①, a massive 19th-century edifice now re-juvenated by a restoration. Directly behind the Hauptbahnhof is the **Schweizerisches Landesmuseum** ②, housed in an enormous 19th-cen-tury neo-Gothic mansion; behind that is a shady green park. Walk north-ward to the tip of the park, cross on the left-hand side of the bridge, turn south a bit along Sihlquai, and head up Ausstellungsstrasse to the **Museum für Gestaltung** ③, which holds an impressive collection of 20th-century graphic art. Back at the train station, look across Bahnhofplatz and you'll see traffic careening around a statue of **Alfred Escher,** the man who brought Zürich into the modern age.

Cross the square to the **Bahnhofstrasse,** Zürich's principal business and shopping boulevard. A quarter of the way up the street—about five blocks—veer left into the Rennweg and left again on Fortunagasse, an atmospheric medieval street well removed from the contemporary el-egance of the Bahnhofstrasse. Climb up to the **Lindenhof** ④, a quiet grass-less square with a view of the remains of the city's original Roman customs house and fortress. From here a maze of medieval alleys leads off to your right. Nestled among them, in one of the loveliest medieval squares in Switzerland, is **St. Peters Kirche** ⑤, whose tower has the largest clock face in Europe.

From St. Peters Kirche bear right on Schlüsselgasse and duck into a narrow alley, Thermengasse, which leads left; you'll walk directly over excavated ruins of **Roman baths**. At Weinplatz, turn right on Storchen-gasse, where some of the most elite boutiques are concentrated, and head toward the delicate spires of the **Fraumünster** ⑥. In the same square, you'll see two of Zürich's finest guildhalls, the **Zunfthaus zur Waag** ⑦ and **Zunfthaus zur Meisen** ⑧.

Wind left up Waaggasse past the Hotel Savoy to the **Paradeplatz** ⑨. Continue south on Bahnhofstrasse, which, as it nears the lake, opens onto a vista of boats, wide waters, and (on a clear day) distant peaks. At the Bürkliplatz, look to your right: those manicured parks are the front lawn of the **Hotel Baur au Lac**, the aristocrat of Swiss hotels. Be-yond, you'll see the modern structure of the **Kongresshaus** and the **Ton-halle,** where the Zürich Tonhalle Orchestra resides. Across General-Guisan-Quai is one of the local swans' favorite hangouts: the boat dock, which is the base for trips around the Zürichsee.

Here you can take General-Guisan-Quai west to Seestrasse to the **Mu-seum Rietberg** or turn left and cross the **Quaibrücke** (Quay Bridge) for one of the finest views in town, especially at night, when the flood-lighted spires are mirrored in the inky river, whose surface is disturbed only by drifting, sleeping swans.

TIMING

This side of Zürich's Old Town is surprisingly compact; half a day is enough time for a cursory visit. If you're planning on museum hop-ping, the Schweizerisches Landesmuseum and Museum Rietberg merit at least two hours apiece.

Sights to See

Alfred Escher. Leave it to Zürich to have a statue that honors not a saint, not a poet or artist, but rather the financial wizard who single-hand-

18

Zürich

0 ⸺ 200 yards

0 ⸺ 200 meters

KEY

AE American Express Office

i Tourist Information

⸺ Tram Line

edly dragged Zürich into the modern age back in the mid-19th century. Escher (1819–82) established the city as a major banking center, championed the development of the federal railways and the city's university, and pushed through the construction of the tunnel under the St. Gotthard Pass. ⊠ *In the middle of Bahnhofpl.*

Bahnhofstrasse. Zürich's principal boulevard offers luxury shopping and hulking department stores, while much shifting and hoarding of the world's wealth takes place discreetly behind the banks' upstairs windows. However, the long-standing story of the treasure trove below the Bahnhofstrasse was recently quashed—the subterranean vaults that once stored great piles of gold and silver now lie empty. In mid-1998 a local journalist was allowed access to the vaults; at the end of the dark labyrinths the scribe found nothing but empty rooms, the precious metals having been moved out to a site near the airport several years earlier. ⊠ *Runs north–south west of Limmat River.*

★ ❻ **Fraumünster** (Church of Our Lady). Of the church spires that are Zürich's signature, the Fraumünster's is the most delicate, a graceful sweep to a narrow spire. It was added to the Gothic structure in 1732; the remains of Louis the German's original 9th-century abbey are below. Its Romanesque choir is a perfect spot for meditation beneath the ochre, sapphire, and ruby glow of stained-glass windows by the Russian-born Marc Chagall, who loved Zürich. The Graubünden sculptor Alberto Giacometti's father, Giovanni Giacometti, executed the fine painted window in the north transept. ⊠ *Stadthausquai.* ☉ *May–Sept., Mon.–Sat. 9–6; Oct., Mon.–Sat. 10–5; Nov.–Feb., Mon.–Sat. 10–4; Mar.–Apr., Mon.–Sat. 10–5.*

OFF THE   **MUSEUM RIETBERG –** A prodigious gathering of art from India, China,
BEATEN PATH   Africa, Japan, and Southeast Asia is displayed in the neoclassical Villa
                 Wesendonck, once home to Richard Wagner (it was for the lady of the
                 house that he wrote his *Wesendonck Songs*). The rich collection
                 ranges from Cambodian Khmer sculptures and jade Chinese tomb art to Japanese Nô masks and Tibetan bronzes. From the city center, follow Seestrasse south about 1¾ km (1 mi) until you see signs for the museum; or take Tram 7 to the Rietberg Museum stop. ⊠ *Gablerstr. 15,* ☎ *01/2024528.* 🎟 *6 SF.* ☉ *Tues.–Sun. 10–5.*

❶ **Hauptbahnhof** (Main Railway Station). From the bustling main concourse of this immaculate 19th-century edifice you can watch crowds of people rushing to their famously on-time trains. Beneath lies a shopping mall, open daily (an exception to the closed-on-Sunday rule), with everything from grocery stores to clothing boutiques and bookshops. ⊠ *Between Museumstr. and Bahnhofpl.*

❹ **Lindenhof** (Linden Court). On this quiet square, overlooking the Old Town on both sides of the river, are the remains of the original Roman customs house and fortress and the imperial medieval residence. The fountain was erected in 1912, commemorating the day in 1292 when Zürich's women saved the city from the Hapsburgs. As the story goes, the town was on the brink of defeat as the imperial Hapsburg aggressors moved in. Determined to avoid this humiliation, the town's women donned armor and marched to the Lindenhof. On seeing them, the enemy thought they were faced with another army and promptly beat a strategic retreat. Today, the scene could hardly be less martial, as locals play boccie and chess under the trees. ⊠ *Bordered by Fortunag. to the west and intersected by Lindenhofstr.*

❸ **Museum für Gestaltung** (Design Museum). Innovative temporary exhibitions focus on topics such as architecture, poster art, graphic de-

sign, and photography. ⊠ *Ausstellungstr. 60,* ☎ *01/4462211.* ☜ *5 SF.*
☉ *Tues., Thurs., and Fri. 10–6, Wed. 10–9, weekends 11–6.*

❾ Paradeplatz (Parade Square). The hub of the Bahnhofstrasse and a tram
junction, this square is a great place to observe a microcosm of the local
upper crust—furrow-browed bankers striding to work while their fur-
trimmed wives struggle with half a dozen bags and the dilemma of where
to shop next. While you're at it, spoil your taste buds with incredible
chocolate from the Sprüngli café (☞ Shopping, *below*). ⊠ *Intersection of Bahnhofstr. and Poststr.*

★ ❺ St. Peters Kirche. Dating from the early 13th century, Zürich's oldest
parish church has the largest clock face in Europe. A church has been
on this site since the 9th century. The existing building has been considerably expanded over the years. The tower, for example, was extended in 1534, when the clock was added; the nave was rebuilt in 1705.
Keep an eye out for inexpensive or even free classical concerts. ⊠ *St.
Peterhofstatt,* ☎ *no phone.* ☉ *Weekdays 8–6, Sat. 8–4.*

★ ❷ Schweizerisches Landesmuseum (Swiss National Museum). Housed in
a gargantuan neo-Gothic building opened in 1889, the Swiss National
Museum owns an enormous collection of objects dating from the
Stone Age to modern times. There are costumes, furniture, early
watches, and a great deal of military history, including thousands of
toy soldiers reenacting battle scenes. In the hall of arms there's a splendid mural, painted by the late-19th-century Bernese artist Ferdinand
Hodler, *The Retreat of the Swiss Confederates at Marignano*—depicting a defeat in 1515 by the French that set Zürich back considerably after generations of prosperity. ⊠ *Museumstr. 2,* ☎ *01/2186511.*
☜ *Free.* ☉ *Tues.–Sun. 10:30–5.*

❽ Zunfthaus zur Meisen. This aristocratic baroque edifice, erected for the
city's wine merchants in the 18th century, houses the Swiss National
Museum's exquisite ceramics collection; the selection of 18th-century
porcelain is particularly strong and includes works by Zürich and
Nyon makers. Enter on the Fraumünster side. ⊠ *Münsterhof 20,* ☎
01/2212807. ☜ *Free.* ☉ *Tues.–Sun. 10:30–5.*

❼ Zunfthaus zur Waag. This circa-1637 guildhall was the meeting place
for linen weavers and hat makers. Today it houses a lovely restaurant
(☞ Dining, *below*). ⊠ *Münsterhof 8.*

Niederdorf

As soon as you step off the Quai Bridge on the right bank of the Limmat River, you'll notice a difference: The atmosphere is trendier and
more casual. The area is also the center of Zürich's nightlife—both upscale and down, with the city's opera house and its historic theater, as
well as plenty of bars and clubs.

As you explore the area along Münstergasse to Marktgasse, parallel
to the river, you'll notice a less Calvinistic bent. Each of the narrow
streets and alleys that shoot east off Marktgasse (which quickly becomes
Niederdorfstrasse) offers its own brand of entertainment. Marktgasse
eventually empties onto the Central tram intersection, opposite the main
train station; from there it's easy to catch a tram along the Bahnhofstrasse or the Limmatquai.

A Good Walk

Start at the Quai Bridge and head up Rämistrasse to Heimplatz, where
you'll find the **Schauspielhaus** ⑩. Across Heimplatz is the important
Kunsthaus ⑪ museum. Head back down Rämistrasse to Bellevueplatz—where you can catch a tram that will take you to the impres-

sive private **Stiftung Sammlung E. G. Bührle** collection—and follow Limmatquai downstream to the gaunt, imposing **Grossmünster** ⑫, with its distinctive stout twin towers.

Head back down the steps to the bank of the Limmat, where you'll find the 18th-century **Helmhaus** ⑬. Now an art museum, the Helmhaus is attached to the late-15th-century **Wasserkirche** ⑭, one of Switzerland's most delicate late-Gothic structures.

Along the Limmatquai, a series of guildhalls today houses popular and atmospheric restaurants, the 13th-century **Zunfthaus zum Rüden** ⑮, **Zunfthaus zur Zimmerleuten** ⑯, and the **Zunfthaus zur Saffran** ⑰ among them. Across the Limmatquai, the striking baroque **Rathaus** ⑱ seems to rise up from the river.

Head back across the Limmatquai and up into the Old Town streets, which meander past tiny houses, galleries, antiques shops, and neopunk boutiques. Follow Marktgasse to **Rindermarkt,** site of the historic home of the Swiss poet and novelist Gottfried Keller. The Rindermarkt joins the picturesque Neumarkt and Spiegelgasse streets at a tiny medieval square where you'll see a fine early Gothic tower, the **Grimmenturm.** There's another Gothic tower farther down Spiegelgasse at **Napfplatz,** used during the 14th century by Zürich bankers. Several artistic and political figures have called narrow Spiegelgasse home— Lenin lived at number 14 just before the Russian Revolution, and at number 12 the exiled young revolutionary German playwright Georg Büchner (1813–37) wrote *Woyzeck* before dying of typhoid. At the foot of the street a plaque marks the site of the Cabaret Voltaire, where the Dadaist movement took shape, conceived in Zürich by French exile Hans Arp, who in the 1920s proclaimed the new movement one that could "heal mankind from the madness of the age."

From Napfplatz, take Obere Zäune up to the broad medieval **Kirchgasse,** packed with antiques shops, galleries, and bookstores. From here you can either return to the Grossmünster or venture north to see the **Graphische Sammlung** ⑲, with its woodcuts, etchings, and engravings; or head to the **Zoologisches Museum** ⑳.

TIMING

A quick overview of the Niederdorf won't take more than a half day, but it's the kind of area where there is always something new to find, no matter how often you come back. Leave yourself extra time if you'd like to window-shop or invest a couple of hours in one of the galleries or museums, especially the Kunsthaus.

Sights to See

⑲ **Graphische Sammlung.** The impressive collection of the Federal Institute of Technology includes a vast library of woodcuts, etchings, and engravings by such European masters as Dürer, Rembrandt, Goya, and Picasso. Pieces from the permanent collection are often arranged in thematic exhibitions. Take Tram 6, 9, or 10 from the Bahnhofplatz or Central stops toward the ETH stop. ✉ *Rämistr. 101,* ☎ *01/6324046.* 📧 *Free.* ☉ *Mon., Tues., Thurs., and Fri. 10–5, Wed. 10–8.*

★ ⑫ **Grossmünster** (Great Church). Executed on the plump twin towers (circa 1781) of this impressive cathedral are classical caricatures of Gothic forms bordering on the comical. The core of the structure was built in the 12th century on the site of a Carolingian church dedicated to the memory of martyrs Felix and Regula, who allegedly carried their severed heads to the spot. Charlemagne is said to have founded the church after his horse stumbled over their burial site. On the side of the south tower an enormous stone Charlemagne sits enthroned; the original statue, carved in the late 15th century, is protected in the crypt. In keeping with what the 16th-century reformer Zwingli preached from the Grossmünster's pulpit, the interior is spare, even forbidding, with all luxurious ornamentation long since stripped away. The only artistic touches are modern: stained-glass windows by Giovanni Giacometti, and ornate bronze doors in the north and south portals, dating from the late 1940s. ⊠ *Zwinglipl.,* ☎ *01/2526144.* ⊙ *Late Mar.–Oct., daily 9–6; Nov.–mid-Mar., daily 10–5.*

⑬ **Helmhaus.** The open court of this museum once served as a linen market. Inside, there are changing exhibitions of contemporary art by Zürich-based artists, often of an experimental nature. In spring the museum hosts an exhibition of works from the city's annual competition for young artists. ⊠ *Limmatquai 31,* ☎ *01/2516177.* 🎟 *Free.* ⊙ *Tues., Wed., and Fri.–Sun. 10–6, Thurs. 10–8.*

Kirchgasse. Antiques, art, and book enthusiasts will delight in the shops on this street. No. 13 was Zwingli's last home before he was killed in battle (1531) while defending the Reformation.

★ ⑪ **Kunsthaus.** With a varied and high-quality permanent collection of paintings—medieval, Dutch and Italian baroque, and Impressionist—the Kunsthaus is possibly Zürich's best art museum. The collection of Swiss art includes some fascinating works, while others might be an acquired taste. Besides work by Ferdinand Hodler, with its mix of realism and stylization, there is a superb room full of Johann Heinrich Füssli paintings which hover between the darkly ethereal and the grotesque. Otherwise, Picasso, Klee, Degas, Matisse, Kandinsky, Chagall, and Munch are all satisfyingly represented. ⊠ *Heimpl. 1,* ☎ *01/2516765.* 🎟 *Varies with exhibition.* ⊙ *Tues.–Thurs. 10–9, Fri.–Sun. 10–5.*

OFF THE
BEATEN PATH

STIFTUNG SAMMLUNG E. G. BÜHRLE – One of Switzerland's best private art collections is owned by the E. G. Bührle Foundation. Though it's known especially for its Impressionist and post-Impressionist paintings and sculptures, the collection also includes religious sculpture as well as Spanish and Italian paintings from the 16th to 18th centuries. Take Tram 11 from Bellevueplatz, then Bus 77 from Hegibachplatz. ⊠ *Zollikerstr. 172,* ☎ *01/4220086.* 🎟 *9 SF.* ⊙ *Tues. and Fri. 2–5, Wed. 5–8.*

★ ⑱ **Rathaus** (Town Hall). Zürich's striking baroque town hall dates from 1694–98, and its interior remains as well preserved as its facade: There's a richly decorated stucco ceiling in the Banquet Hall and a fine ceramic stove in the government council room. ⊠ *Limmatquai 55,* ☎ *no phone.* ⊙ *Tues., Thurs., and Fri., 10–11:30.* 🎟 *Free.*

Rindermarkt (Cattle Market). Fans of Gottfried Keller, commonly considered Switzerland's national poet and novelist, will want to visit this street. The 19th-century writer's former home at No. 9 became famous thanks to his novel *Der Grüne Heinrich* (*Green Henry*). Opposite is the restaurant, **Zur Oepfelchammer** (☞ *Dining, below*), where Keller ate regularly. ⊠ *Street between Marktg. and Neumarkt.*

⑩ **Schauspielhaus.** During World War II this was the only German-language theater in Europe that wasn't muzzled by the Berlin regime, and it attracted some of the Continent's bravest and best artists. It's been presenting literary plays ever since it was built in 1884; today its productions aren't always so risky, but they are stunningly mounted and performed, in German of course. ⊠ *Rämistr. 34,* ☎ *01/2655858.*

⑭ **Wasserkirche** (Water Church). One of Switzerland's most delicate late-Gothic structures, this church displays stained glass by Giacometti. Both the church and the Helmhaus once stood on the island on which Felix

and Regula supposedly lost their heads. ⊠ *Limmatquai 31,* ☎ *no phone.*
⊙ *Wed. 9–11, 2–5.*

☾ ⑳ **Zoologisches Museum.** Engaging and high tech, the Zoological Museum allows you a close look in its accessible displays on Swiss insects, birds, and amphibians. You can examine butterflies and living water creatures through microscopes and listen to birdcalls as you compare avian markings. ⊠ *Karl Schmid-Str. 4,* ☎ *01/6343838.* 🎫 *Free.* ⊙ *Tues.– Fri. 9–5, weekends 10–4.*

⑮ **Zunfthaus zum Rüden.** Now housing one of Zürich's finest restaurants (☞ Dining, *below*), this 13th-century structure was the noblemen's guild-hall. Peek inside at the barrel-vaulted ceiling and 30-ft beams; or better yet, stay for a meal. ⊠ *Limmatquai 42.*

⑰ **Zunfthaus zur Saffran.** Portions of this guildhall for haberdashers date from as early as 1389. It is now a highly acclaimed restaurant, with beautiful old rooms and a facade facing the river. ⊠ *Limmatquai 54.*

⑯ **Zunfthaus zur Zimmerleuten.** Dating from 1708, this was the carpenters' guild. Its main restaurant draws business groups to a number of lovely dark-wood halls; its former storage cave houses a cozy restaurant, too (☞ Dining, *below*). ⊠ *Limmatquai 40.*

OFF THE
BEATEN PATH

WINTERTHUR – A wealth of fine art was donated to the textile town Winterthur by prosperous local merchants. One such denizen was Oskar Reinhart, whose splendid home now contains the huge **Am Römerholz** collection of paintings from five centuries, including works by Rembrandt, Manet, Renoir, and Cézanne. Winterthur is a half hour from Zürich by train, on the main rail route to Saint Gallen; fast trains depart daily from the main train station, about every half hour. By car, follow the autobahn signs for Winterthur–Saint Gallen. ⊠ *Stadthausstr. 6, Winterthur,* ☎ *052/2692741.* 🎫 *8 SF.* ⊙ *Tues.–Sun. 10–5*

ZÜRICH ZOO – This is one of Europe's outstanding zoos, with more than 1,500 animals and some 250 species, including Asian elephants, black rhinos, seals, and big cats. Set in a tree-filled park, it's just east of the city center and easily reached by Trams 5 and 6. ⊠ *Zürichbergstr. 221,* ☎ *01/2527100.* 🎫 *14 SF.* ⊙ *Nov.–Feb., daily 8–5; Mar.–Oct., daily 8–6.*

JAMES JOYCE'S GRAVE – Joyce, the inimitable Irish author, not only lived and wrote in Zürich, he died here as well. The city's most famous literary resident is buried in the Friedhof Fluntern (Fluntern Cemetery); atop his grave sits a contemplative statue of the writer, complete with cigar. A few steps away is the grave of another renowned author, Nobel Prize winner Elias Canetti. The cemetery is right next to the Tram 6 terminus. ⊙ *Mar.–Apr. and Sept.–Oct., daily 7–7; May–Aug., daily 7 AM–8 PM; Nov.–Feb., daily 8–5.*

DINING

The price categories listed below are slightly higher than those applied in other regional chapters, except in Geneva, which shares Zürich's inflated cost of living. There is a shortage of truly budget options, but keep in mind that daily prix-fixe menus are considerably cheaper, and even the glossiest places have business-lunch menus at noon—your best bet for sampling Zürich's highest cuisine at cut rates. For tight-budget travel, watch for posted *Tagesteller* listings: cheap menus of the day, with meat, potatoes, and possibly a hot vegetable, can still be found in the Niederdorf for under 20 SF.

CATEGORY	COST*
$$$$	over 90 SF
$$$	50 SF–90 SF
$$	30 SF–50 SF
$	under 30 SF

Prices are per person for a three-course meal (two-course meal in $ category), including sales tax and 15% service charge.

$$$$ ✕ **Baur au Lac Rive Gauche.** Though it has traded its self-important neo-Gothic decor for a light, Mediterranean look, businesspeople still flock to this traditional clubhouse-style institution. The cuisine is lighter and trendier now, with fresh seafood and salads, but the wine list still taps the Baur's impressive cave. ⊠ *Hotel Baur au Lac, Talstr. 1,* ☎ *01/2205060. Reservations essential. AE, DC, MC, V.*

$$$$ ✕ **La Rotonde.** Even when not illuminated by candlelight, the Dolder
★ Grand's haute-cuisine restaurant is one of Zürich's most grandiose spots. Housed in a great arc of a room, La Rotonde provides sweeping views over the terrace to the lake below. The atmosphere is formal, the staff attentive to a fault, the culinary style traditional French with a fashionably light touch—sweetbreads on a bed of gnocchi with asparagus and truffles, for instance. ⊠ *Kurhausstr. 65,* ☎ *01/2693870. AE, DC, MC, V. Jacket and tie.*

$$$$ ✕ **Petermann's Kunststuben.** Serious and chicly formal, this is one of
★ Switzerland's gastronomic meccas. Though it's south of city center, in Küssnacht on the lake's eastern shore, it's more than worth the investment of time, effort, and travel budget. Chef Horst Petermann never rests on his laurels: the ever-evolving menu may include lobster with artichoke and almond oil; grilled turbot with lemon sauce and capers; or Tuscan dove with pine nuts and herbs. ⊠ *Seestr. 160, Küssnacht,* ☎ *01/9100715. Reservations essential. AE, DC, MC, V. Closed Sun. and Mon., 2 wks in Feb. and 3 wks in late summer.*

$$$–$$$$ ✕ **Kronenhalle.** From Stravinsky, Brecht, and Joyce to Nureyev,
★ Deneuve, and Saint-Laurent, this beloved landmark has always drawn a stellar crowd. The atmosphere is genial, the cooking hearty, and the collection of 20th-century art astonishing. Every panel of gleaming wood wainscoting frames works by Picasso, Braque, Miró, or Matisse, collected by patroness-hostess Hulda Zumsteg, who owned the restaurant from 1921 until her death in 1985. Her son, Gustav, carries on the tradition, serving robust cooking in hefty portions: herring in double cream, tournedos with truffle sauce, duck *à l'orange* with red cabbage and Spätzli. There's no shame in ordering the sausage and Rösti just to take in the animated scene. ⊠ *Rämistr. 4,* ☎ *01/2516669. AE, DC, MC, V. Reservations essential.*

$$$ ✕ **Blaue Ente.** Part of a chic shopping gallery in a converted mill south
★ of the city center, this modern bar-restaurant draws well-dressed crowds from the advertising and arts scene. In a setting of whitewashed brick and glass, with jazz filtering through from the adjoining bar, guests sample *Zander* (pike-perch) roasted with bacon and sauerkraut, baked sea bass with basil cream sauce, or roast barbary duck with Spätzli. Take the No. 2 or 4 tram toward Wildbachstrasse. Reservations are advised. ⊠ *Seefeldstr. 223,* ☎ *01/4227706. AE, DC, MC, V.*

$$$ ✕ **Haus zum Rüden.** The most culinarily ambitious of Zürich's many Zunfthaus dining places, this fine restaurant is also the most architecturally spectacular, combining river views with a barrel-vaulted ceiling and 30-ft beams. Slick modern improvements—including a glassed-in elevator—manage to blend intelligently with the ancient decor. Innovations might include lobster lasagna in saffron sauce, veal in lime sauce, or beef fillet in port. It's especially impressive at night;

26

Dining ●

Adler's Swiss Chuchi, **7**
Baur au Lac
Rive Gauche, **24**
Bierhalle Kropf, **30**
Blaue Ente, **22**
Bodega Española, **17**
Haus zum Rüden, **11**
Hiltl Vegi, **35**
Hummer- und
Austernbar, **4**
Kronenhalle, **21**
La Rotonde, **14**
Mère Catherine, **13**
Odéon, **20**
Opus, **34**
Petermann's
Kunststuben, **23**
Reithalle, **37**
Rheinfelder
Bierhaus, **10**
Veltliner Keller, **31**
Zeughauskeller, **29**
Zunfthaus zur
Schmiden, **8**
Zunfthaus zur
Waag, **28**
Zunfthaus zur
Zimmerleuten/
Küferstube, **12**
Zur Oepfelchammer, **9**

Lodging ○

Adler, **7**
Baur au Lac, **24**
Central-Plaza, **1**
City, **36**
Dolder Grand, **14**
Florhof, **16**
Haus zum Kindli, **34**
Helmhaus, **19**
Leoneck, **3**
Limmathof, **5**
Neues Schloss, **25**
Rex, **2**
Rössli, **18**
St. Georges, **38**
Savoy Baur en
Ville, **27**
Splügenschloss, **26**
Wellenberg, **6**
Widder, **33**
Zum Storchen, **32**
Zürichberg, **15**

Zürich Dining and Lodging

KEY

AE American Express Office

i Tourist Information

Tram Line

0   200 yards
0   200 meters

ask for a window table. ⊠ *Limmatquai 42,* ☎ *01/2619566. AE, DC, MC, V.*

$$$ ✕ **Hummer- und Austernbar.** In a fin de siècle setting of polished wood, candles, and rich scarlet, you can have your fill of impeccably fresh lobster and oysters (*Hummer* means lobster; *Austern,* oysters), such as Brittany lobsters poached in champagne sauce. In August, the city's expatriate Swedes flock here for crayfish, a late-summer Nordic favorite. There's depth to the wine list, but champagne seems to be the beverage of choice. ⊠ *Hotel St. Gotthard, Bahnhofstr. 87,* ☎ *01/ 2118315. AE, DC, MC, V.*

$$$ ✕ **Veltliner Keller.** Though its rich, carved-wood decor borrows from Graubündner Alpine culture, this dining spot is no tourist-trap transplant: the house, built in 1325 and functioning as a restaurant since 1551, has always stored Italian-Swiss Valtellina wines, which were carried over the Alps and imported to Zürich. There is a definite emphasis on the heavy and the meaty, but the kitchen is flexible and reasonably deft with more modern favorites as well: grilled salmon, veal steak with Gorgonzola, and dessert mousses. ⊠ *Schlüsselg. 8,* ☎ *01/2254040. AE, DC, MC, V.*

$$ ✕ **Bodega Española.** The dark paneled interior of this Niederdorf spot is encircled with the coats of arms of old Spanish provinces and strung with garlands of onions and garlic. It specializes in big steaks, good seafood, omelets, and paella. Be sure to sample the excellent house Rioja (a Spanish-wine specialty shop adjoins, so the choice is extensive), and crown your meal with a Cuban cigar. ⊠ *Münsterg. 15,* ☎ *01/2512310. AE, DC, MC, V.*

$$ ✕ **Opus.** In this warm, bookish decor, you can enjoy a chic supper of Italian-inspired specialties: olive risotto with shrimp, duck breast with orange and balsamic vinegar sauce. The three-course lunch menu is a good value, especially the vegetarian version. On some winter weekends there's a hip salon or cabaret show between courses, with anything from the Singing Waiters to cigar-smoking evenings. ⊠ *Pfalzg. 1,* ☎ *01/2115917. AE, DC, MC, V.*

$$ ✕ **Zunfthaus zur Schmiden.** The sense of history and the decor alone— a magnificent mix of Gothic wood, leaded glass, and tile stoves—justify a visit to this popular landmark, the guild house of blacksmiths and barbers since 1412. All the Zürich meat classics are available in enormous portions (steaming double portions of geschnetzeltes, whole skillets of crisp Rösti), and there's a considerable selection of alternatives—fish among them. The guild's own house-label wine is fine. ⊠ *Marktg. 20,* ☎ *01/2515287. AE, DC, MC, V.*

$$ ✕ **Zunfthaus zur Waag.** Another, airier guildhall, its woodwork whitewashed, its leaded-glass windows looking out to the Fraumünster, this lovely dining spot offers generous portions of the local classics: richly sauced veal, butter-crisped salmon, and sizzling potatoes simmered in gleaming skillets and chafing dishes. ⊠ *Münsterhof 8,* ☎ *01/2110730. AE, DC, MC, V.*

$$ ✕ **Zunfthaus zur Zimmerleuten/Küferstube.** Although the pricier Zun-
★ fthaus upstairs is often overwhelmed with large banquets, at substreet level a cozy, candlelit haven called the *Küferstube* (Coopers' Pub) serves atmospheric meals in a dark-beamed, Old Zürich setting. Standard dishes have enough novelty to stand apart: goose soup with port, wild boar steak with red bilberry sauce, roast pork with smoked bacon, homemade cinnamon ice cream with wine-poached pear. ⊠ *Limmatquai 40,* ☎ *01/2520834. AE, DC, MC, V.*

$$ ✕ **Zur Oepfelchammer.** Dating from 1801, this was once the haunt of
★ Zürich's beloved writer Gottfried Keller. One section is a dark and heavily graffitied bar, with sagging timbers and slanting floors; there are also two welcoming little dining rooms with coffered ceilings and

plenty of carved oak and damask. Traditional meat dishes—calves' liver, geschnetzeltes Kalbfleisch, tripe in white wine sauce—come in generous portions; salads are fresh and seasonal. The place is always packed, and service can be slow, so stake out a table and plan to spend the evening. ⊠ *Rindermarkt 12,* ☎ *01/2512336. MC, V. Closed Sun., Mon.*

$–$$ ✕ Adler's Swiss Chuchi. A bit of an anomaly in a black-leather-and-
★ nose-ring neighborhood, this squeaky-clean, Swiss-kitsch restaurant has an airy, modern decor, with Alpine-rustic chairs, Big Boy–style plastic menus, and good home-cooked national specialties. Excellent lunch menus are rock-bottom cheap and served double quick; nights are reserved for fondue, reputedly the best in Zürich. ⊠ *Roseng. 10,* ☎ *01/2669696. AE, DC, MC, V.*

$–$$ ✕ Bierhalle Kropf. Under the mounted boar's head and restored cen-
★ tury-old murals depicting gallivanting cherubs, businesspeople, workers, and shoppers share crowded tables to feast on generous hot dishes and a great selection of sausages. The *Leberknödli* (liver dumplings) are tasty, the potato croquettes are filled with farmer's cheese and garnished with a generous fresh salad, and the *Apfelküchli* (fried apple slices) are tender and sweet. The bustle and clatter provide a lively, sociable experience and you'll more than likely get to know your neighbor. ⊠ *In Gassen 16,* ☎ *01/2211805. AE, DC, MC, V. Closed Sun.*

$–$$ ✕ Mère Catherine. This popular bistro with a Provençal veneer presents blackboard specials, with the chef turning out onion soup, duck liver terrine, seafood, and a few meat dishes—even American-raised *steak de cheval* (horse steak). The young, bohemian clientele also enjoys the restaurant's small, hipster-packed Philosoph bar next door. On warm evenings, opt for courtyard seating. ⊠ *Nägelihof 3,* ☎ *01/2622250. AE, MC, V.*

$–$$ ✕ Zeughauskeller. Built as an arsenal in 1487, this enormous stone-
★ and-beam hall offers hearty meat platters and a variety of beers and wines in comfortable, Germanic chaos. The waitstaff is harried and brisk, especially at lunchtime, when crowds are thick. Unlike the shabbier beer halls in Niederdorf, this is clean and bourgeois, reflecting its Paradeplatz location. They're not unaccustomed to tourists—menus are posted in English, Japanese, and at least 10 other languages—but locals consider this their home away from home. ⊠ *Bahnhofstr. 28, at Paradepl.,* ☎ *01/2112690. AE, DC, MC, V.*

$ ✕ Hiltl Vegi. Founded in 1898, when vegetarians were regarded as cranks and "grass eaters," this restaurant has more than proved its staying power. It was taken over in 1904 by Bavarian Ambrosius Hiltl, who married the cook; the current patron, Rolf Hiltl, is their great-grandson. In 1998 the restaurant celebrated its centennial with a cookbook revealing some, but not all, of the secrets contained in its flavorful lunchtime salad bar. At night there is an all-you-can-eat Indian buffet. ⊠ *Sihlstr. 28,* ☎ *01/2213870. AE, DC, MC, V.*

$ ✕ Odéon. This historic café-restaurant was once frequented by the pre-
★ revolutionary Lenin, who nursed a coffee and read the house's daily papers. Now the crowd is just as intense, and a tonic air of countercultural chic mixes with the cigarette smoke. You can nurse a coffee, too, or have a plate of pasta, a sandwich, or dessert; there's also a daily lunch menu for under 20 SF. The pharmacy next door used to be part of the café; an ongoing (but slow-motion) campaign aims to reintegrate the two. ⊠ *Limmatquai 2,* ☎ *01/2511650. AE, DC, MC, V.*

$ ✕ Reithalle. In a downtown theater complex behind the Bahnhofstrasse,
★ this old military riding stable now does its duty as a noisy and popular restaurant, with candles perched on the mangers and beams and heat ducts exposed. Young locals share long tables arranged mess-hall style to sample French and Italian specialties, many vegetarian, and an

excellent, international blackboard list of open wines. ⊠ *Gessnerallee 8,* ☏ *01/2120766. AE, MC, V.*

$ ✕ **Rheinfelder Bierhaus.** Dark and smoky, this solid old Niederdorf institution serves a rich *Rindspfeffer* (preserved beef stew) with homemade Spätzli; sausage standbys; and the pride of the Spanish/Romansch owners: an incongruous but freshly homemade paella, served on the last Tuesday of the month. ⊠ *Marktg. 19,* ☏ *01/2512991. No credit cards.*

LODGING

Spending the night in Zürich is as expensive as eating out, though the options are no more outlandishly priced than those in the prestigious ski resorts. Deluxe hotels—the five-star landmarks—average between 450 SF and 600 SF per night for a double, and you'll be lucky to get a shower and toilet in your room for less than 140 SF. Yet a full (if top-heavy) range of choices is available in the city center, so even if you're flying into Zürich-Kloten on your way to a mountain retreat, don't shy away from a stopover of a day or two. Luckily, almost all the hotels that cater to businesspeople during the week offer significantly cheaper weekend rates.

CATEGORY	COST*
$$$$	over 430 SF
$$$	300 SF–430 SF
$$	160 SF–300 SF
$	under 160 SF

Prices are for a standard double room, including breakfast, tax, and service charge.

$$$$ ▦ **Baur au Lac.** This highbrow patrician of Swiss hotels turns its broad
★   back to the commercial center while its front rooms overlook the lake, the canal, and the manicured lawns of its own private park. The signature classic room decor gleams with rich fabrics and such ultramodern comforts as triple-glazed windows and CD players. Lakeside corner junior suites (priced as deluxe doubles) are a relatively good value. In summer, meals (including breakfast) are served in the glassed-in pavilion along the canal; in winter, in the glowing Restaurant Français. ⊠ *Talstr. 1, CH-8022,* ☏ *01/2205020,* 🖷 *01/2205044. 107 rooms, 18 suites. 2 restaurants, bar, café, beauty salon, exercise room, dance club. AE, DC, MC, V.*

$$$$ ▦ **Dolder Grand.** Even if you're not staying here, you might wish to
★   indulge in afternoon English tea at this sprawling Victorian fantasy-manse sitting high over Zürich. Its opulence leaves you feeling like you're in a lavish period film—you half expect to see Jeremy Irons and Kate Winslet casting agonized glances at each other across the dining room. The exterior is a picturesque hodgepodge of turrets, cupolas, half-timbering, and mansards, while guest rooms, with Empire-cum-Euro-modern decor, are distinguished by their spaciousness and high ceilings. La Rotonde, the hotel's restaurant (☞ Dining, *above*), serves excellent traditional French haute cuisine. The funicular (free for guests) runs from the Römerhof. ⊠ *Kurhausstr. 65, CH-8032,* ☏ *01/2693000,* 🖷 *01/2693001. 149 rooms, 34 suites. Restaurant, bar, café, pool, beauty salon, 9-hole golf course, 5 tennis courts, ice-skating, parking (fee). AE, DC, MC, V.*

$$$$ ▦ **Savoy Baur en Ville.** The city's oldest hotel perennially improves itself, regularly sprucing up its rooms and amenities to maintain its conservative sleekness. The 35 rooms refurbished in 1998 with grey stone bathrooms, walk-in closets, and mixed-period furniture typify what the hotel calls its "past-modern" decor. It's directly on the Paradeplatz

at the hub of the banking, shopping, and sightseeing districts, and there are two fine restaurants—one French, one Italian—as well as a slick café-bar. ⊠ *Am Paradepl., Poststr. 12, CH-8022,* ☎ *01/2152525,* FAX *01/2152500. 112 rooms, 8 suites. 2 restaurants, bar. AE, DC, MC, V.*

$$$$ ⌑ **Widder.** Zürich's most captivating hotel was created when ten ad-
★ jacent medieval houses were gutted and combined—now steel fuses with ancient stone and time-worn wood. Behind every door is a fascinating mix of old and new; a guest room could mix restored 17th-century frescoes and stone floors with a leather bedspread and halogen bell jars. Each room has a private fax, and guests are provided with their own business cards upon check-in. Four suites have private roof terraces, while in the basement you can mosey into the wine cellar to sample and discuss the vintages. ⊠ *Rennweg 7, CH-8001,* ☎ *01/ 2242526,* FAX *01/2242424. 42 rooms, 7 suites. 2 restaurants, bar. AE, DC, MC, V.*

$$$ ⌑ **Central-Plaza.** Despite its landmark-quality exterior—it was built in 1883—this hotel aims to please a young crowd, with a fresh, if chain-style, decor: brass, bamboo, palms. The bars and theme restaurants all seem contrived to appeal to shopping-mall habitués: the King's Cave, for instance, has faux Gothic stone and "medieval" goblets. It's directly on the Central tram crossroads on the Niederdorf side, and the compact rooms are well protected against the sounds of the busy intersection below. ⊠ *Central 1, CH-8001,* ☎ *01/2515555,* FAX *01/2518535. 100 rooms. 2 restaurants, 2 bars. AE, DC, MC, V.*

$$$ ⌑ **Florhof.** This is an anti-urban-hotel, a gentle antidote to the bustle
★ of downtown commerce. In a dreamily quiet residential area by the Kunsthaus, this Romantik property pampers guests with its polished wood, blue-willow fabric, and wisteria-sheltered garden. The restaurant serves light, seasonal, fish-based menus, and meals on the terrace on a summer's night are positively rhapsodical. Two suites were added to the top story in April 1999. ⊠ *Florhofg. 4, CH-8001,* ☎ *01/ 2614470,* FAX *01/2614611. 33 rooms, 2 suites. Restaurant. AE, DC, MC, V.*

$$$ ⌑ **Neues Schloss.** Now managed by the Arabella-Sheraton chain, this small, intimate hotel in the business district, southeast of Paradeplatz, offers a warm welcome, good service, and dark, classic decor, the result of a complete refurbishment in early 1999. Its Le Jardin restaurant (closed Sundays) is popular with theater-goers for its pre-performance menu. ⊠ *Stockerstr. 17, CH-8022,* ☎ *01/2869400,* FAX *01/2869445. 58 rooms. Restaurant. AE, DC, MC, V.*

$$$ ⌑ **Splügenschloss.** Constructed at the turn of the century as luxury apart-ments, this Relais & Châteaux property maintains its ornate, historic decor. One room has been paneled completely in Graubünden-style pine; others are decorated in warm, pastel shades and many are fitted with antique wardrobes. The restaurant doubles as an exhibition space, with annual shows of artists such as Expressionist painter Gen Paul. The location—in a spare banking district—may be a little out of the way for sightseeing, but if you yearn for atmosphere, you'll find this worth the effort. ⊠ *Splügenstr. 2, CH-8002,* ☎ *01/2899999,* FAX *01/2899998. 50 rooms, 2 suites. Restaurant, bar. AE, DC, MC, V.*

$$$ ⌑ **Wellenberg.** This Niederdorf hotel makes a definite retro statement with its burled wood, black lacquer, Art Deco travel posters, and Hollywood photos. Guest rooms are relatively spacious, the central location is superb, and, if you're somehow feeling cut off from the outside world, you can bring your laptop and modem, get a password at reception, and plug into the Internet. ⊠ *Niederdorfstr. 10, CH-8001,* ☎ *01/2624300,* FAX *01/2513130. 45 rooms. Breakfast room, in-room data ports. AE, DC, MC, V.*

$$$ 🏨 **Zum Storchen.** The central location of this airy 600-year-old struc-
★   ture—tucked between the Fraumünster and St. Peters Kirche on the
     gull-studded bank of the Limmat River—is stunning, the hotel itself
     modern, impeccable, and intimately scaled. It has warmly appointed
     rooms with pretty toile de Jouy fabrics, some with French windows
     that open over the water. Both the lobby and the breakfast room have
     lovely river views; the former was renovated in 1998 in a soothing mus-
     tard yellow and now incorporates a "business corner" (a laptop com-
     puter, photocopier, fax, etc.). Deluxe corner rooms, with views toward
     both river and lake, are worth fighting for. ✉ *Weinpl. 2, CH-8001,* ☎
     01/2272727, FAX *01/2272700. 73 rooms. Restaurant, bar, café. AE, DC,
     MC, V.*

$$ 🏨 **Adler.** This once-shabby place, smack in the middle of Niederdorf,
     has metamorphosed into a smart, state-of-the-art hotel on a modest
     and affordable scale. From the gleaming lobby to the sleek, modular
     rooms, the ashwood-and-granite decor makes the most of tight spaces,
     and hand-painted murals of city landmarks remind you you're in
     Zürich. The restaurant off the lobby, Adler's Swiss Chuchi (☞ Din-
     ing, *above*), is known locally as a great place for fondue. ✉ *Roseng.
     10, CH-8001,* ☎ *01/2669696,* FAX *01/2669669. 52 rooms. Restaurant.
     AE, DC, MC, V.*

$$ 🏨 **City.** Close to the Bahnhofstrasse, the main train station, and the
     Löwenstrasse shopping district, this is a hotel in miniature, with small
     furnishings and baths and a high proportion of single rooms. An an-
     tique grandfather clock guards the lounge, and a model cow is stationed
     on the sun terrace (it was left over from a 1998 exhibition which dot-
     ted the entire city with bizarrely colored, life-sized model cattle). ✉
     Löwenstr. 34, CH-8021, ☎ *01/2171717,* FAX *01/2171818. 73 rooms.
     AE, DC, MC, V.*

$$ 🏨 **Haus zum Kindli.** This charming little bijou hotel could pass for a
     3-D Laura Ashley catalog, with every cushion and bibelot as artfully
     styled as a magazine ad. The result is welcoming, intimate, and a sight
     less contrived than many hotels' cookie-cutter decors. Even the Opus
     restaurant downstairs is filled with English bookcases and floral prints,
     and guests earn 10% off menu prices to vie with crowds of locals for
     a seat near the cabaret stage (☞ Dining, *above*). ✉ *Pfalzg. 1, CH-8001,*
     ☎ *01/2115917,* FAX *01/2116528. 21 rooms. AE, DC, MC, V.*

$$ 🏨 **Helmhaus.** In an assertively modernized 600-year-old building, this
     Old Town property softens its edges with bright florals, white furni-
     ture, and some lake views. It makes the most of its limited space, and
     service is crisply professional. Since it's near the Niederdorf, it's conve-
     nient for nightcrawling. ✉ *Schiffländepl. 30, CH-8001,* ☎ *01/2518810,*
     FAX *01/2510430. 25 rooms. Breakfast room. AE, DC, MC, V.*

$$ 🏨 **Rex.** Its parking-garage architecture brightened up with assertive
     colors and jazz posters, this foursquare property has some business-
     people's necessities (laptop jacks, desks big enough to spread your pa-
     pers on), without the depth of service offered by more expensive hotels.
     Its restaurant, the Blauer Apfel, draws a loyal, young-pro lunch clien-
     tele to its cool, blue-halogen-lighted tables. It's three stops from the Cen-
     tral tram station on the No. 15 line. ✉ *Weinbergstr. 92, CH-8006,* ☎
     01/3602525, FAX *01/3602552. 37 rooms. Restaurant. AE, DC, MC, V.*

$$ 🏨 **Rössli.** Ultra-small but friendly, this hotel is set in the heart of Ober-
★   dorf (the area around Oberdorfstrasse). The chic white-on-white decor
     mixes stone and wood textures with bold textiles and mosaic bathrooms,
     and extras include safes and bathrobes—unusual in this price range.
     Some singles are tiny, but all have double beds. ✉ *Rösslig. 7, CH-8001,*
     ☎ *01/2522121,* FAX *01/2522131. 16 rooms, 1 suite. Breakfast room,
     bar. AE, DC, MC, V.*

$$ 🏨 **Zürichberg.** This hotel is like the Dolder Grand's stepsister: both hotels share the same view from atop the prestigious hill that gave its name to both the neighborhood and the hotel. However, where the Dolder is flashy, the Zürichberg is down-to-earth—especially in its room rates. Its rooms are minimally but effectively furnished; all have parquet floors. In the Schneckenhaus (Snail House) annex, rooms radiate outward from a central, oval atrium. Run by the Zürich Women's Association, the hotel is alcohol-free. Tram 6 heads straight to the hotel from the Hauptbahnhof. ⊠ *Orellistr. 21, CH-8044,* ☎ *01/2683535,* FAX *01/2683545. 67 rooms. Restaurant, café. AE, DC, MC, V.*

$ 🏨 **Leoneck.** From the cowhide-covered front desk to the edelweiss-print curtains, this budget hotel wallows in its Swiss roots but balances this indulgence with no-nonsense conveniences: tile baths (albeit with cow-print shower curtains), murals, and built-in pine furniture. There isn't much space to stretch out, though, and the decor sometimes shows its wear. The adjoining restaurant, Crazy Cow, slings out its own Swiss kitsch (Rösti-burgers) in an over-the-top decor of milk cans, miniature Matterhorns, and the ubiquitous black-and-white bovine. ⊠ *Leonhardstr. 1, CH-8001,* ☎ *01/2542222,* FAX *01/2542200. 65 rooms. Restaurant. AE, DC, MC, V.*

$ 🏨 **Limmathof.** This spare but welcoming hotel inhabits a handsome, historic shell and is ideally placed on the Limmatquai, minutes from the Hauptbahnhof and steps from the Limmatquai and Central tram stops. All rooms have tile bathrooms and plump down comforters; TVs are available for an extra 22 SF. There's an old-fashioned wood-paneled Weinstube and a bright vegetarian restaurant that doubles as the breakfast room. ⊠ *Limmatquai 142, CH-8023,* ☎ *01/2614220,* FAX *01/2620217. 62 rooms. Restaurant, Weinstube. AE, DC, MC, V.*

$ 🏨 **St. Georges.** This simple former pension drenches its rooms in a milky, all-white look. Eleven rooms now offer full bathrooms; the rest, each under 100 square ft, share the shower and toilet down the hall. Take Tram 3 or 14 from the station to Stauffacher; it's another five minutes on foot. ⊠ *Weberstr. 11, CH-8004,* ☎ *01/2411144,* FAX *01/2411142. 40 rooms. Breakfast room. AE, MC, V.*

NIGHTLIFE AND THE ARTS

Nightlife

Of all the Swiss cities, Zürich has the liveliest nightlife. Niederdorf is Zürich's nightlife district, with cut-rate hotels, strip joints, and bars crowding along Marktgasse, which becomes Niederdorfstrasse. On Thursday and weekend nights, the streets flow with a rowdy crowd of club- and bar-hoppers. But the bars close early here, mostly between midnight and 2 AM: Zwingli hasn't lost his hold altogether.

Bars

Barrique (⊠ Marktg. 17, ☎ 01/2525941) is a vinotheque featuring a world-renowned wine list. The service may be surly at **Brasserie Federal** (⊠ Hauptbahnhof, ☎ 01/2171515), but you'll have the rare luxury of choosing from over 100 Swiss beers. **Champagnertreff,** in the Hotel Central (⊠ Central 1, ☎ 01/2515555), is a popular neo–Art Deco piano bar with several champagnes available by the glass. **Cranberry** (⊠ Metzgerg. 3, ☎ 01/2612772) stocks broad selections of rum and port; it also has a cigar room. The **James Joyce Pub** (⊠ Pelikanstr. 8, off Bahnhofstr., ☎ 01/2211828) is a beautifully tiled and panelled Irish pub where the wood is as dark as the Guinness. The **Jules Verne Panorama Bar** (⊠ Uraniastr. 9, ☎ 01/2111155) serves up cocktails with a wraparound view of downtown. The narrow bar at the **Kronenhalle**

(✉ Rämistr. 4, ☎ 01/2516669) draws mobs of well-heeled locals and internationals for its prize-winning cocktails. **Malatesta** (✉ Niederdorfstr. 15, ☎ 01/2514274) is a well-established bistro/hangout for locals 20–80. Serving a young, arty set until 4 AM, **Odéon** (☞ Dining, *above*) is a cultural landmark—Mata Hari danced here, though watch out for inflated prices after midnight.

Dancing

The medieval-theme **Adagio** (✉ Gotthardstr. 5, ☎ 01/2063666) books classic rock, jazz, and tango for well-dressed thirty-somethings. **Kaufleuten** (✉ Pelikanstr. 18, ☎ 01/2211505) is a landmark dance club that draws a well-dressed, upwardly mobile crowd. **Mascotte** (✉ Theaterstr. 10, ☎ 01/2524481), blasting funk and soul, is popular with all ages on weeknights and has a gay night on Sunday. **Oxa Dance Hall** (✉ Andreastr. 70, Oerlikon, ☎ 01/3116033) is a legendary techno club that draws thousands of casual young Swiss who dance all night (and to noon Sunday). Take Tram 14 from the Hauptbahnhof to the Oerlikon terminus. **Le Petit Prince** (✉ Bleicherweg 21, ☎ 01/2011739) attracts a chichi set; go ahead and request a tune, from disco to techno.

Jazz Clubs

Casa Bar (✉ Münsterg. 30, ☎ 01/2612002), long the sole bastion of jazz here, now has excellent competition. **Moods** (✉ Sihlamtstr. 5, ☎ 01/2018140), in an old train-station buffet, presents jazz groups four to five times a week. The popular **Widder Bar** (✉ Widderg. 6, ☎ 01/2242411), in the Widder Hotel (☞ Lodging, *above*), attracts local celebrities with its 800-count "library of spirits" and top-name acts.

The Arts

Despite its small population, Zürich is a big city when it comes to the arts; it supports a top-rank orchestra, an opera company, and a theater. Check *Zürich News,* published weekly in English and German, or "Züri-tipp," a German-language supplement to the Friday edition of the daily newspaper *Tages Anzeiger.* The city's annual **Züricher Festspiele**—a celebration of opera, ballet, concerts, theater, and art exhibitions—runs from late June through mid-July. You'll need to book well ahead for this—details are available from the tourist office or Info- und Ticketoffice (✉ Postfach 6036, CH-8023, ☎ 01/2154030). Tickets to opera, concert, and theater events can also be bought from the tourist office, while tickets for almost any event can be purchased in advance by telephone from **Fastbox**(☎ 0848/800800) or **Ticketline** (☎ 01/2256060). Depending on the event, **Musik Hug** (✉ Limmatquai 28–30, ☎ 01/2694100) makes reservations. Also try **Jecklin** (✉ Rämistr. 30, ☎ 01/2537676).

Film

Movies in Zürich are serious business, with films presented in the original language. Check newspapers and the ubiquitous posters and watch for the initials *E/d/f,* which means an English-language version with German (Deutsch) and French subtitles.

Music

The Zürich Tonhalle Orchestra, named for its concert hall, the **Tonhalle** (✉ Claridenstr. 7, ☎ 01/2063434), which was inaugurated by Brahms in 1895, enjoys international acclaim. There are also solo recitals and chamber programs here. Tickets sell out quickly, so book directly through the Tonhalle.

Opera

The permanent company at the **Opernhaus** (✉ Theaterpl., ☎ 01/2686666) is widely recognized and understandably difficult to drop in on if you haven't booked well ahead, but single seats can often be had at the last minute.

Theater

The venerable **Schauspielhaus** (☞ Exploring Zürich, *above*) has a long history of cutting-edge performances with a strong inventive streak; during World War II this was the only German-language theater in Europe that remained independent. Nowadays its main stage presents finely tuned productions (in German), while experimental works are given in the Keller (cellar). ⊠ *Rämistr. 34,* ☎ *01/2655858.*

During late August and early September, the **Theaterspektakel** takes place, with circus tents housing avant-garde theater and experimental performances on the lawns by the lake at Mythenquai.

OUTDOOR ACTIVITIES AND SPORTS

Bicycling

You don't get much for free in Switzerland, but one exception is Zürich's free bike rental program. For a refundable deposit of 20 SF and your passport you can borrow a bike. Over 300 bikes are available from six pick-up points; children's bicycles and child seats are available. The most central pick-up points are at platform 18 of the Hauptbahnhof, the Globus department store on the Bahnhofstrasse (☞ Shopping, *below*), and at Theaterplatz/Stadelhofen. The other pick-up points are the Enge railway station, the Altstetten railway station, and the marketplace in the Oerlikon suburb. Bikes are available from the train station year round; the other locations distribute bikes between early May and the end of October.

Golf

The nine-hole **Dolder Golf Club** (☎ 01/2615045) is near the Dolder Grand Hotel (☞ Lodging, *above*). **Golf & Country Club Zürich** (☎ 01/9180050), with 18 holes, is near the city center in Zumikon, a suburb of Zürich.

Running

The track closest to the center is at **Allmend Sportplatz** (⊠ Take Tram 13 to the last stop). The **Dolder Grand** Hotel (☞ Lodging, *above*) has a running path that winds through the forest; it's open to nonguests.

SHOPPING

Since Zürich voters opted for extended opening hours in 1998, many city-center stores are now open weekdays 9–8, Saturday 8–4. Many smaller shops, particularly in the Niederdorf area, open later in the morning or the early afternoon and are closed entirely on Monday.

Department Stores

ABM (⊠ Bellevuepl., ☎ 01/2614484) is cheap and cheerful. **Globus** (⊠ Bahnhofstr. and Löwenpl., ☎ 01/2266060) has a pricey but irresistible delicatessen in the basement, besides men's and women's designer clothes and housewares. **Jelmoli** (⊠ Bahnhofstr. and Seideng., ☎ 01/2204411) has topnotch merchandise and swarms of staffers. **Manor** (⊠ Bahnhofstr. 75, ☎ 01/2295111) is dependable and affordable.

Markets

At **Bürkliplatz** (⊠ Lake end of Bahnhofstrasse), there's a flea market open Saturday from 6 to 3:30 from May to October. There's a curio market on the **Rosenhof** (⊠ At intersection of Niederdorfstr. and

Marktg.) every Thursday 10–9 and Saturday 10–4 between April and
Christmas.

Shopping Streets

The store-lined **Bahnhofstrasse** concentrates much of Zürich's most
expensive (from elegant to gaudy) goods at the Paradeplatz end. There's
another pocket of good stores around **Löwenstrasse,** southwest of the
Hauptbahnhof. **Niederdorf** offers less expensive, younger fashions, as
well as antiques and antiquarian bookshops. The west bank's **Old
Town,** along Storchengasse near the Münsterhof, is a focal point for
high-end designer goods.

Specialty Items

Books

The antiquarian book shops in the upper streets of the Niederdorf area
are rich with discoveries—and most have selections of English books.
Buchhandlung Buchmann (✉ Kirchg. 40, ☎ 01/2512368) specializes
in art and art history. The **EOS Buchantiquariat Benz** (✉ Kirchg. 17
and 22, ☎ 01/2615750) is a superb general bookshop spread over two
storefronts. (Both shops sell second-hand books as well as antiquarian tomes.) Even more eclectic is **medieval art & vie** (✉ Spiegelg. 29,
☎ 01/2524720), selling books, music, and replicas of medieval artifacts, including reproduction medieval shoes, jewelry, and water bottles.

Chocolate

Sprüngli (✉ Paradepl., ☎ 01/2117616; ✉ Hauptbahnhof, ☎ 01/
2118483; ✉ Löwenpl., ☎ 01/2119612), the landmark chocolatier and
café for the wealthy Bahnhofstrasse habitués, concocts heavenly truffles and *Luxembourgli,* small, cream-filled cookies that require immediate
eating. Good, plain hot lunches and salads are also served. **Teuscher**
(✉ Storcheng. 9, ☎ 01/2115153; ✉ Jelmoli, Bahnhofstr. and Seideng., ☎ 01/2204387; ✉ Cafe Schober, Napfg. 4, ☎ 01/2518060) specializes in champagne truffles.

Collectibles

In the center of town, virtually every street has some kind of antique
or collectible shop. Especially intriguing are "modern antique" shops
which carry odds and ends from decades past. **Eselstein** (✉ Stadelhoferstr.
42, ☎ 01/2611056) stocks 1950s–70s items ranging from lamp shades
to standing ashtrays, plus odds and ends like Russian samovars. **Han-
nibal** (✉ St. Jakobstr. 39, ☎ 01/2426044) is a delightful lumber room
of postwar vases, chairs, pedal-operated trash bins, and rotary-dial telephones (remember them?).

Food

Inhale tempting smells from around the world at **H. Schwarzenbach**
(✉ Münsterg. 19, ☎ 01/2611315), an old-style, open-bin shop with
oak shelves lined with coffee, dried fruits, nuts, and grains. Or whet
your palate at **Scot & Scotch** (✉ Wohllebg. 7, ☎ 01/2119060) with any
one of 400 whiskeys from around the globe (nosing and tastings on
request).

Men's Clothes

The classic, elegant designs of **Giorgio Armani** (✉ Zinneng. 6, ☎ 01/
2212348) are found in the west bank's Old Town. **Trois Pommes** (✉
Storcheng. 6/7, ☎ 01/2110239) is the central boutique of a series of
designer shops scattered through the Storchengasse area; the racks are
heavily stacked with such high-profile international designers as Jil
Sander, Versace, Donna Karan, and Dolce & Gabbana.

Toys

AHA (⊠ Spiegelg. 14, ☎ 01/2131020) sells hypnotic, optical illusory gifts in styles and sizes to suit all ages. **Pastorini Spielzeug** (⊠ Weinpl. 3, ☎ 01/2287070) is a four-story mother lode of original and creative playthings, many hand-carved.

Women's Clothes

Beatrice Dreher Presents (⊠ In Gassen 14, ☎ 01/2111348) carries Chloë and Krizia. **En Soie** (⊠ Strehlg. 26, ☎ 01/2115902) carries gleaming, sometimes raw-textured silks, but although the fabrics are sophisticated, there's still an element of whimsy. You can snag some of last season's fashions at deep discounts at Trois Pommes' bargain-basement **Lagerverkauf** (⊠ Weinpl. 10, ☎ 01/2128318), where DKNY, Calvin Klein, and Dolce & Gabbana are jumbled on the racks. For the absolute latest, go to the main **Trois Pommes** (⊠ Storcheng. 6/7, ☎ 01/2110239) for Jil Sander, Alaïa, and Comme des Garçons.

ZÜRICH A TO Z

Arriving and Departing

By Car

The A2 expressway from Basel to Zürich leads directly into the city. A1 continues east to Saint Gallen. Approaching from the south and the St. Gotthard route, take **A14** from Luzern (Lucerne); after a brief break of highway (**E41**) it feeds into **A3** and approaches the city along the lake's western shore. You can take **A3** all the way up from Chur in Graubünden.

By Plane

AIRPORTS AND AIRLINES

Zürich-Kloten (⊠ 11 km/7 mi north of Zürich, ☎ 1571060) is Switzerland's most important airport and the 10th busiest in the world. It is served by some 60 airlines, including **American, United,** and, of course, **Swissair.** You can also catch domestic and European flights out of Kloten on **Crossair** (☎ 01/8164170), Switzerland's domestic airline.

BETWEEN THE AIRPORT AND THE CENTER

It's easy to take a **Swiss Federal Railways feeder train** directly from the airport to Zürich's **Hauptbahnhof** (main station; ☎ 1572222). Tickets cost 6.20 SF one way, and trains run every 10–15 minutes, arriving in 10 minutes. **Taxis** cost dearly in Zürich. A ride into the center costs 50 SF–60 SF and takes around 20 minutes. The **Airport Shuttle** (☎ 01/3001410) costs about 22 SF per person for a one-way trip and runs roughly every half hour to a series of downtown hotels.

By Train

There are straightforward connections and several express routes leading directly into Zürich from Basel, Geneva, Bern, and Lugano. All roads lead to the **Hauptbahnhof** (☎ 1572222) in the city center.

Getting Around

By Bus and Tram

VBZ-Züri-Linie, the tram service in Zürich, is swift and timely. It runs from 5:30 AM to midnight, every six minutes at peak hours, every 12 minutes at other times. All-day passes cost 7.20 SF and can be purchased from the same vending machines at the stops that post legible maps and sell one-ride tickets; you must buy your ticket before you board. Free route plans are available from VBZ offices, located at major crossroads (Paradepl., Bellevue, Central, Kluspl.). Stops are clearly signposted.

By Taxi

Taxis are very expensive, with an 8 SF minimum but no charge for additional passengers. An available taxi is indicated by an illuminated rooftop light.

Contacts and Resources

Embassies and Consulates

Contact the **United States** embassy in Bern (⊠ Jubiläumsstr. 93, ☎ 031/3577011). Contact the **Canadian** embassy in Bern (⊠ Kirchenfeldstr. 88, ☎ 031/3573200). There is a consulate for the **United Kingdom** (⊠ Minervastr. 117, ☎ 01/3833560) in Zürich.

Emergencies

Police (☎ 117). **Ambulance** (☎ 144). **Hospital** (⊠ Zürich Universitätsspital, Schmelzbergstr. 8, ☎ 01/2551111). **Doctors and dentists** can be referred in case of emergency by the English-speaking operators who man the *Notfalldienst* (Emergency Service) phones (☎ 01/2616100). **24-hour Pharmacy:** Bellevue Apotheke (⊠ Theaterstr. 14, ☎ 01/2525600).

English-Language Bookstores

Payot (⊠ Bahnhofstr. 9, ☎ 01/2115452) carries a good stock of English fiction despite the store's French focus. **Orell Füssli** (⊠ Füsslistr. 4, ☎ 01/2211060) also has English books and videos, and at press time had just taken over Stäheli, an English bookshop on the Bahnhofstrasse. Reopening was scheduled for autumn 1999, though probably under a new name.

Guided Tours

ORIENTATION

Three introductory **bus tours** are offered by the tourist office. **Cityrama's** daily tour covers the main city sights and then goes on to Rapperswil to see the rose gardens and castle. The trip lasts two hours, leaving at 11 AM; it costs 35 SF. The daily **Sights of Zürich** tour (32 SF) gives a good general idea of the city in two hours; it leaves at 10 AM, noon, and 2 PM, though there is no tour at 10 in winter. **In and Around Zürich** goes farther and includes an aerial cableway trip to Felsenegg. This is also a daily tour, starting at 9:30 AM (9 AM in winter); it takes 2½ hours and costs 39 SF for adults. All tours start from the Hauptbahnhof.

The tourist bureau also offers day trips by coach to Luzern, up the Rigi, Titlis, or Pilatus mountains, and the Jungfrau.

WALKING

Daily from May to October, the tourist office offers two-hour walking tours (18 SF) that start at the Hauptbahnhof. You can join a group with English-language commentary, but the times vary, so call ahead (☞ Visitor Information, *below*).

Travel Agencies

American Express (⊠ Uraniastr. 14, ☎ 01/2287777). **Kuoni Travel** (⊠ Bahnhofpl. 7, ☎ 01/2243333).

Visitor Information

Tourist service (⊠ Hauptbahnhof, CH-8023, ☎ 01/2154000). **Hotel reservations** (☎ 01/2154040, FAX 01/2154044).

3 EASTERN SWITZERLAND

Appenzell, Liechtenstein, Schaffhausen,
St. Gallen

Near Zürich, the cantons of Glarus,
Schaffhausen, Thurgau, St. Gallen, and
Appenzell, as well as Liechtenstein, are
dominated by the Rhine River. With its
secluded backcountry and thriving cities, the
German-influenced region has everything
from wood-shingle farmhouses to town
houses adorned with oriel windows and
frescoes. Still, the eastern cantons remain
one of the most untouched regions of
Switzerland.

Updated by
Katrin Gygax

DESPITE ITS PROXIMITY TO ZÜRICH, this Germanic region, bordered on the north by Germany and on the east by Austria, maintains a personality apart— a personality that often plays the wallflower when upstaged by more spectacular touristic regions. Lush with orchards and gardens, its north dominated by the romantic Rhine, with a generous share of mountains (including Mt. Säntis, at roughly 2,500 m/8,200 ft) and lovely hidden lakes, as well as the enormous Bodensee (Lake Constance), the region doesn't lack for variety—only tourists. Because the east draws fewer crowds, those who do venture in find a pleasant surprise: this is Switzerland sans kitsch, sans hard sell, where the people live out a natural, graceful combination of past and present. And although it's a prosperous region, with its famous textiles and fruit industry, its inns and restaurants cost noticeably less than those in regions nearby.

The region covers a broad sociological spectrum, from the thriving city of St. Gallen, with its magnificent baroque cathedral, to the obscure, Ozarklike backcountry of Appenzell, where women couldn't vote in cantonal elections until the federal court in Lausanne intervened on their behalf in 1990 (federal law had granted women the national vote in 1971). On the last Sunday in April in Appenzell City, you still can witness the *Landsgemeinde*, an open-air election counted by a show of hands.

Architecture along the Rhine resembles that of old Germany and Austria, with half-timbers and rippling, red-tile roofs. In cities like Schaffhausen, masterpieces of medieval frescoes decorate town houses, many of which have ornate first-floor bays called oriels. In the country, farmhouses are often covered with fine, feathery wooden shingles as narrow as Popsicle sticks and weathered to chinchilla gray. Appenzell has its own famous architecture: tidy narrow boxes painted cream, with repeated rows of windows and matching wood panels. The very countryside itself—conical green hills, fruit trees, belled cows, neat yellow cottages—resembles the naive art it inspires.

Pleasures and Pastimes

Dining

Your plate will feel the weight of German and Austrian influence in this most Teutonic of Swiss regions: portions are on a Wagnerian scale, and pork appears often. A side of *Spätzli* (little sparrows) or *Knöpfli* (little buttons) adds further heft: these are flour-egg dough fingers, either pressed through a sieve or snipped, gnocchi style, and served in butter. Another favorite side dish is *Hörnli* (little horns), crescent-shaped pasta with butter and cheese. You can also can order a full-meal portion of *Käseknöpfli* (cheese dumplings), which come smothered in a pungent cheese sauce.

All across Switzerland you'll find the St. Gallen bratwurst, called *Olmabratwurst* on its home turf (Olma is the name of an annual autumn agricultural exhibition here). In restaurants it's served with thick onion sauce and *Rösti* (hash brown potatoes), but in St. Gallen itself the locals eat it on the hoof, lining up at lunchtime at one of two or three outdoor stands, then holding the thick white-veal sausage in a napkin with one hand and a round, chewy chunk of whole-grain *Bürli* bread in the other.

In the quirky region of Appenzell, the famous Appenzeller cheese deserves its stardom, as among the fine hard cheeses of Switzerland it has the most complex, spicy flavor, with traces of nutmeg. Other Appenzeller treats include a variation of Graubünden's famous air-dried beef, here called *Mostbröckli* and steeped in sweet apple cider before drying. It is served in translucent slices, its moist, mildly sweet flavor countered with bits of pickled onion. *Bauernschublig* are dark dried-blood sausages. If you've got a sweet tooth, search out two regional specialties: Appenzeller *Biber* (honey cakes filled with almond and stamped with a design) and *Birnebrot* (thick dried-pear puree wrapped in glazed dough). *Chäsemagarone* is a rich, plain dish of large macaroni layered with butter, grated Appenzeller cheese, and butter-fried onions—it's often eaten with *Apfelmousse* (applesauce).

Eastern Switzerland is the country's orchard region, especially the Thurgau area. There are several fine fruit juices made here, as well as *Most* (sweet cider) and some good fruit schnapps. Among area wines, Berneck comes from the Rhine Valley, Hallau from near Schaffhausen, and crisp whites from Stein-am-Rhein.

CATEGORY	COST*
$$$$	over 70 SF
$$$	40 SF–70 SF
$$	20 SF–40 SF
$	under 20 SF

*Prices are per person for a three-course meal, including sales tax and 15% service charge

Hiking
Uncrowded hiking trails lead through all kinds of terrain, from rolling vineyards along the Rhine to isolated, rugged mountain wilderness above the Toggenburg Valley. This is a region of unspoiled nature, well-preserved villages, and breathtaking scenery.

Lodging
More and more hotels in this region are throwing away their Formica and commissioning hand-painted furniture to complement the beams they've so carefully exposed. However, bargain renovations tend toward the crisp, if anonymous, look of light, tongue-in-groove pine paneling and earth-tone, ceramic baths. The prices are somewhat lower on average here, with only slight variations from high to low season. Half board is rarely included. Hotel rates are generally calculated on a perperson basis; be sure to clarify the prices when reserving.

CATEGORY	COST*
$$$$	over 250 SF
$$$	180 SF–250 SF
$$	120 SF–180 SF
$	under 120 SF

*Prices are for a standard double room, including breakfast, tax, and service charge.

Exploring Eastern Switzerland

With their obscure backcountry and thriving cities, the cantons of Glarus, Schaffhausen, Thurgau, St. Gallen, and Appenzell are some of the most untouched in Switzerland. In the northern part of the region are the old Rhine city of Schaffhausen, the dramatic Rheinfall, and the preserved medieval town of Stein-am-Rhein. The Bodensee occupies the northeastern corner of Switzerland, just below Germany. Farther south are the textile center of St. Gallen, the quirky Appenzell region, and the resort area of the Toggenburg Valley. The tiny principality of Liechtenstein lies just across the eastern border, within easy driving distance.

Eastern Switzerland and Liechtenstein

Reichenau
ntersee
33
Gottlieben
13 **14** Konstanz
Arenenberg **15**
Kreuzlingen
perswil

31
GERMANY
Friedrichshafen

SWITZERLAND

Bodensee

Lindau

Weinfelden
16
Thur
14
Amriswil
Romanshorn

Arbon

Rorschach
Wil
7   A1   *Rorschacher-berg*
Abtwil   **16**
17   St.
St. Gallen   Margrethen   Lustenau
Gossau   Teufen
Stein   Altstätten
Herisau   **19**   Bühler
Bütschwil   Gais
8   *Rhein*
18
20   **Appenzell**
Urnäsch
Lienz   A13
16   *ALPSTEIN*
8   Schwägalp   **21** **Mt. Säntis**
AUSTRIA
Nesslau   Wildhaus   Haag
Unterwasser   **22**   Bendern
Alt   **Toggenburg**   6
St. Johann   **Valley**
CHURFIRSTEN   Buchs   **LIECHTENSTEIN**
Amden
Weesen   **23** **Vaduz**
27 **Walensee**   **24** **Triesenberg**
Näfels   A3   Plums   Steg
Flumserberg   **26**   3   **25** **Malbun**
Limth   A3
Sargans   A13
0   6 miles   Bad
0   9 km   N   Ragaz   TO   28
CHUR   Landquart

Numbers in the text correspond to numbers in the margin and on the Eastern Switzerland and Liechtenstein and Schaffhausen maps.

Great Itineraries

Although eastern Switzerland is topographically the country's lowest region, it's still fairly rugged. It will take only a short time to see the major sights, but they are spread throughout the region, so leave time each day to be in transit. Train travel here is more complicated than in neighboring areas, requiring more intercity changes, so plan your itinerary accordingly. If you want to get back into the Appenzell hills, though, you should rent a car. St. Gallen is a good excursion center for visiting the Bodensee, Appenzell, Mt. Säntis, and the principality of Liechtenstein; farther west, Schaffhausen offers easy access to the magnificent Rheinfall, medieval Stein-am-Rhein, and the Bodensee, as well.

IF YOU HAVE 1 OR 2 DAYS

If you are coming from Zürich, enter the region at its northernmost tip and start with the old Rhine city of ⛩ **Schaffhausen** ①–⑩, known for its medieval frescoes and baroque oriel windows. From there it's an easy excursion to the nearby **Neuhausen am Rheinfall** ⑪, the city known for its broad, dramatic series of falls. Just on the other side of Schaffhausen, spend an hour or two in tiny **Stein-am-Rhein** ⑫, a medieval gem situated on the river. Then dip south to ⛩ **St. Gallen** ⑰, a busy textile center with an active Old Town beside its grand, baroque cathedral. From St. Gallen you can explore the picture-pretty **Appenzell** ⑱.

IF YOU HAVE 3 OR 4 DAYS

With a little more time, you can spend your first two days in the northernmost areas, visiting ⛩ **Schaffhausen** ①–⑩, **Neuhausen am Rheinfall** ⑪, and **Stein-am-Rhein** ⑫; then make your way south, starting below Germany's Konstanz and following the southern coast of the Bodensee, a popular spot for local resorters. See the twin cities of **Kreuzlingen and Konstanz** ⑮ (the latter is in Germany) and ⛩ **Gottlieben** ⑭. Visit ⛩ **St. Gallen** ⑰ and ⛩ **Appenzell** ⑱, then trace the **Toggenburg Valley** ㉒, which runs in a great curve between Mt. Säntis and Wildhaus and draws Swiss tourists to its resorts and spas. Finally, head to the tiny principality of Liechtenstein to see the royal castle and explore its art and stamp museums and then go west to the isolated Walensee.

When to Tour Eastern Switzerland

Summers in eastern Switzerland provide the best weather and activities but also the greatest traffic, both on roads and in towns; spring and fall are good alternatives. Stein-am-Rhein receives enough coach tours to virtually paralyze the village with pedestrians during high season; if you go, arrive earlier in the day or come on a weekday when crowds are a bit thinner.

SCHAFFHAUSEN AND THE RHINE

Known to many Swiss as Rheinfallstadt (Rhine Falls City), Schaffhausen is the seat of the country's northernmost canton, which also shares its name. To gaze upon the grand, mist-sprayed Rheinfall, arguably the most famous waterfall in Europe, is to look straight into the romantic past of Switzerland. Goethe and Wordsworth were just two of the world's best-known wordsmiths to immortalize the Falls' powerful grandeur.

Schaffhausen

★ *48 km (29 mi) northeast of Zürich, 20 km (12 mi) east of Stein-am-Rhein.*

A city of about 35,000, Schaffhausen was, from the early Middle Ages on, an important depot for river cargoes, which—effectively stopped by the rapids and waterfall farther along—had to be unloaded there. The name *Schaffhausen* is probably derived from the skiff houses along the riverbank. The city has a small but beautiful *Altstadt* (Old Town), whose charm lies in its extraordinary preservation; examples of late Gothic, baroque, and rococo architecture line the streets. It doesn't feel like a museum, though; these buildings are very much in use, often as shops or restaurants, and lively crowds of shoppers and strollers throng the streets. Many streets (including Vorstadt, Fronwagplatz, Vordergasse, and Unterstadt) are pedestrians-only, and you can tell which ones are in this zone by the paving—the pedestrian streets are cobblestone.

A Good Walk

Upon entering the Old Town, it becomes obvious why Schaffhausen is also known as the Erkerstadt—the City of Oriel Windows. Begin your walk at the north end of the Old Town at the **Schwabentorturm** ①, where one of the two remaining defense towers houses one of the gates to the town. Continue along Vorstadt, glancing left and right at the oriel windows, many dating from the 17th century. If you cast your gaze up above the houses every now and then, you can see the other tower peek out above the rooftops. The brilliantly painted facade of **Zum Goldenen Ochsen** ② will be on your right—its oriel window is incredible. Vorstadt then leads into **Fronwagplatz** ③, with its clock tower and the Mohrenbrunnen and Metzgerbrunnen fountains at its north and south ends. Then veer right for a quick glance at the second tower, **Obertorturm**, and retrace your steps.

Continue east along the Vordergasse, where on your right you will first admire the **Haus zum Ritter** ④, probably the most famous fresco in Schaffhausen, followed by the **Schmiedstube** ⑤. Farther up the street to your left is the imposing St. Johannkirche. To the right of the church lies the **Haus zum Sittich**, a bright yellow structure with Renaissance oriel windows and relief sculpture. Take a left at the fork in the road up ahead to see the duplex **zur Wasserquelle** and **zur Zieglerburg** ⑥. Across from the duplex stands the Tellenbrunnen fountain.

Double back to the fork in the road and stroll down the tail end of Vordergasse. As you wait at the pedestrian crossing at Bachstrasse, the gray-and-white **Gerberstube** ⑦ welcomes you to this quieter part of town. Farther along the Unterstadt looking north is a group of odd houses with crooked and sharp angles. This is the entrance to the **Munot** ⑧. The meandering steps that lead to the tower are flanked by vineyards. Having enjoyed the view from the tower, double back to the pedestrian crossing at Bachstrasse. Cross the street and take the first left. You will come upon a cluster of large buildings that house the city library and the **Münster zu Allerheiligen** ⑨. Head west on Münsterplatz. This leads you straight to the entrances of the Münster and the **Museum zu Allerheiligen** ⑩. Now head up the hill to the government buildings on your left. The **Altes Zeughaus** (Old Armory), built by Johannes Jacob Meyer, is regarded as a good example of Swiss Renaissance architecture. From here, take any of the streets heading north to get back to the pedestrian zone.

TIMING

The entire walk takes about two hours, including the hike up to the Munot. You may want to linger at the Munot if there is clear weather, when the view is particularly good. A visit at the Museum zu Allerheiligen will add another hour. Keep in mind that the museum and cathedral are closed on Monday, and from noon to 2 on weekdays.

Sights to See

3 Fronwagplatz. This marketplace features the **Metzgerbrunnen,** a large, 16th-century fountain-statue of a prosperous burgher. The **clock tower** once held the market scales; its astronomical clock (1564) records not only the time but also eclipses, seasons, and the course of the moon through the zodiac. Across the square, a reproduction of the 1535 **Mohrenbrunnen** (Moor's Fountain) represents Kaspar of the Three Kings. The original fountain is stored in the Museum zu Allerheiligen (☞ *below*). Nowadays the square is lined with shops and cafés. It's a favorite place for young people to stroll, especially in the evening.

7 Gerberstube (Tanners' Guild House). The baroque building is known for its doorway framed by two lions. A two-handled tanner's knife used to stretch between the lions, but it unfortunately collapsed when nearby roadworks shook the neighborhood. Even without the knife, the doorway is still remarkable. A restaurant now occupies the building. ⊠ *Bachstr. 8.*

4 Haus zum Ritter (Knight's House). The city's finest mansion dates from 1492. Its fresco facade was commissioned by the resident knight, Hans von Waldkirch. Tobias Stimmer painted all three stories in classical themes, which are now displayed in the Museum zu Allerheiligen (☞ *below*); the contemporary replacement was made in the 1930s. ⊠ *Vorderg. 65.*

8 Munot. Built between 1564 and 1589 in full circle form based on an idea by Albrecht Dürer, the massive stone ramparts served as a fortress allowing the defense of the city from all sides. From its top are splendid Schaffhausen and Rhine Valley views. ⊠ *Munotstieg, Old Town.* 🎫 *Free.* ☉ *May–Sept., daily 8–8; Oct.–Apr., daily 9–5.*

9 Münster zu Allerheiligen (All Saints' Cathedral). This beautiful cathedral, along with its cloister and grounds, dominates the lower city. Founded in 1049, the original cathedral was dedicated in 1064, and the larger one that stands today was built in 1103. Its interior has been restored to Romanesque austerity with a modern aesthetic (hanging architect's lamps, Scandinavian-style pews). The **cloister,** begun in 1050, combines Romanesque and later Gothic elements. Memorial plates on the inside wall honor noblemen and civic leaders buried in the cloister's central garden. The enormous **Schiller Bell** in the courtyard beyond was cast in 1486 and hung in the cathedral tower until 1895. Its inscription, VIVOS—VOCO/MORTUOS—PLANGO/FULGURA—FRANGO ("I call the living, mourn the dead, stop the lightning"), supposedly inspired the German poet Friedrich von Schiller to write his "Lied von der Glocke" (*Song of the Bell*). You'll also pass through the aromatic **herb garden;** it's re-created so effectively in the medieval style that you may feel you've stepped into a tapestry. ⊠ *Klosterpl. 1,* ☎ *052/6254377.* 🎫 *Free.* ☉ *Tues.–Fri. 10–noon and 2–5, weekends 10–5.*

10 Museum zu Allerheiligen (All Saints' Museum). This museum, on the cathedral grounds, houses an extensive collection of ancient and medieval historical artifacts, as well as displays on Schaffhausen industry. Temporary exhibitions on various themes reach international caliber. Museum literature is available only in French or German.

Schaffhausen

Fronwagplatz, **3**
Gerberstube, **7**
Haus zum Ritter, **4**
Munot, **8**
Münster zu
Allerheiligen, **9**
Museum zu
Allerheiligen, **10**

Schmiedstube, **5**
Schwabentorturm, **1**
Zum Goldenen
Ochsen, **2**
Zur Wasserquelle/
Zur Zieglerburg, **6**

⊠ *Klosterpl. 1,* ☎ *052/6330777.* 🎦 *Free.* ☉ *Tues.–Sat. 10–noon and 2–5, weekends 10–5 (May–Oct. only).*

❺ **Schmiedstube** (Smiths' Guild House). With its spectacular Renaissance portico and oriel dating from 1653, this building is an embodiment of Schaffhausen's state of suspended animation. Framed over the door are the symbols of the tongs and hammer for the smiths and that of a snake for doctors, who depended on smiths for their tools and thus belonged to the guild. ⊠ *Vorderg. 61.*

❶ **Schwabentorturm** (Swabian Gate Tower). Once a part of the city wall, the tower dates from 1370. Inside the arch on the keystone is a relief from 1933 with a wise caution for anyone crossing the street: LAPPI TUE D'AUGE UF ("Open your eyes, you idiot!"). The tower's counterpart, the **Obertorturm**, lies just off the Fronwagplatz (☞ *above*).

❷ **Zum Goldenen Ochsen** (At the Golden Ox). This late-Gothic building had a Renaissance-style portico and oriel window added to it in 1608. Flanking the windows are three floors of exterior frescoes depicting historic and mythological figures, most from the Trojan War. ⊠ *Vorstadt 17.*

❻ **Zur Wasserquelle** and **Zur Zieglerburg.** The rococo duplex dates from 1738; since they're private residences, you can see them only from the outside. Across the street are the **Tellenbrunnen,** a fountain-statue of William Tell copied from the 1522 original, and, farther up Vordergasse, the **St. Johannkirche,** whose Gothic exterior dates from 1248. ⊠ *Pfarrhofg. 2.*

Dining and Lodging

$$–$$$ ✕ **Theater Restaurant Schaffhausen.** As the name suggests, this bistro and restaurant is connected to Schaffhausen's city theater. The downstairs bistro is decorated with theater paraphernalia; a cozy alcove in the rear has a door leading directly backstage for actors who want a quick snack between scenes. The elegant upstairs restaurant has a view of the Herrenacker square. Choose from a cross section of European cuisine: Swiss sausage salad; Norwegian smoked salmon; Italian ravioli stuffed with ricotta and spinach; and the quintessentially Parisian *entrecôte "Café de Paris".* ⊠ *Herrenacker 23,* ☎ *052/6250558. MC, V. Closed Sun.–Mon.*

$$–$$$ ✕ **Wirtschaft zum Frieden.** You can choose from a variety of delight-
★ ful settings in this unpretentious, traditional restaurant. There's an intimate (read: tiny) Stübli full of waxed and weathered wood; a graceful tile-stove dining room with antiques; and a small private garden thick with wisteria and luxuriant trees. You can have a cheap, generous *Tagesteller* (daily special) in the Stübli, an ambitious meal upstairs, or choices from both menus in the garden, where the locals crowd to drink on a summer evening with carafes of local wine. The menu includes home-smoked salmon, homemade Knöpfli, a *Friedentopf* ("peace stew") of fillets of pork, veal, and beef, lamb noisettes, and veal kidneys, and poached plums for dessert. ⊠ *Herrenacker 11,* ☎ *052/ 6254715. AE, DC, MC, V. Closed Sun.*

$ ✕ **Restaurant Falken.** This busy restaurant caters to crowds with a palate for simple, local fare—Rösti, *Geschnetzeltes* (small pieces of veal in cream sauce), and breaded fish. The *Tagesteller* (daily special) is an especially good deal at lunchtime. Though plain, the wooden facade and interior create Gemütlichkeit without the clichés. It is an excellent choice for families; it even houses its own small bowling alley! ⊠ *Vorstadt 5,* ☎ *052/6253221. AE, DC, MC, V.*

$$$$ ✕⊞ **Rheinhotel Fischerzunft.** This modern Relais & Châteaux prop-
★   erty is a bit out of place in such a medieval city. Of its 10 rooms—some
in fussy florals, others in sleek jewel-tone solids—seven have river
views, but everyone shares the lovely Rhine view at breakfast. The restaurant's mixed nautical and Asian decor reflects the chef's Franco-Chi-
nese leanings: he trained in Hong Kong and has created a brilliant, eclectic
cuisine with such dishes as crayfish wrapped in Thai noodles, deep fried
and served with lentil sprouts. ⊠ *Rheinquai 8, CH-8200,* ☎ *052/
6253281,* ℻ *052/6243285. 6 rooms, 4 suites. Restaurant. AE, DC,
MC, V.*

$$$ ⊞ **Kronenhof.** This fine, quiet city hotel in the heart of Schaffhausen's
★   Old Town has a traditional, shutter- and flower-trimmed facade. A top-
to-bottom renovation will continue through summer 2000. Rooms are
being redone six at a time, so their styles will vary, but the final look
is crisp, with birchwood furniture and abstract prints. Renovated
rooms also tend to be larger, as some older ones are being combined.
The restaurant plans to retain its excellent, refined versions of local
dishes, including trout, herring, and rich soups. ⊠ *Kirchhofpl. 7, CH-
8200,* ☎ *052/6256631,* ℻ *052/6244589. 38 rooms, 2 suites. Restau-
rant, bar. AE, DC, MC, V.*

$$-$$$ ⊞ **Park-Villa.** Despite the no-nonsense elevator tacked onto the exte-
rior, this Belle Epoque–style mansion, built by a local industrialist, has
been transformed into a small hotel with surprisingly little disruption
to its grand but familial style. Many of the original furnishings—in-
laid pieces, chandeliers, Persian rugs—remain. The upper floors are mod-
ern but retain their eccentric shapes, and some have Rhine or fortress
views. The fine old garden room is luxurious and a steal (the toilet is
down the hall); all the other rooms have full baths. The hotel sits slightly
apart, and uphill, from the Old Town. ⊠ *Parkstr. 18, CH-8200,* ☎
052/6252737, ℻ *052/6241253. 21 rooms, 4 suites. Restaurant, bar,
tennis court. AE, DC, MC, V.*

$$ ⊞ **Promenade.** This solid, simple, Edwardian hotel, on the same residential hill as the Park-Villa (☞ *above*), offers spare, Formica-and-
beige rooms, a garden restaurant, and modest fitness equipment.
There's a pretty park walk to the viaduct and the Old Town. ⊠ *Fäsen-
staubstr. 43, CH-8200,* ☎ *052/6248004,* ℻ *052/6241349. 37 rooms.
Restaurant, exercise room. AE, DC, MC, V.*

$ ⊞ **Löwen.** At the edge of suburban Herblingen, where the bedroom
community seems to melt back into its origins as a half-timber country town, this quintessential old guest house still draws the locals to
its pub and serves regional standards in its restaurant. Rooms, however, are all modern, with ceramic tile and modern pine paneling. ⊠
Im Höfli 2, CH-8207 Herblingen, ☎ *052/6432208. 7 rooms. Restaurant, pub. No credit cards.*

Outdoor Activities and Sports
Bicycles—a popular mode of transportation—can be rented at the
train station in Schaffhausen (☎ 051/2234500).

Neuhausen am Rheinfall

★ ⑪ *3 km (1¾ mi) south of Schaffhausen.*

Adjacent to Neuhausen, on the north bank of the Rhine, a series of
magnificent waterfalls powers the city's industry (arms, railroad cars,
aluminum). The **Rheinfall** is 150 m (492 ft) wide, drops some 25 m
(82 ft) in a series of three dramatic leaps, and is split at the center by
a bushy crag straight out of a 19th-century landscape painting. The
effect—mists, roaring water, jutting rocks—is positively Wagnerian;
Goethe saw in the falls the "ocean's source." There is a footpath,

Rheinuferstrasse, that leads from Schaffhausen's Old Town along the river to the falls (a 25- to 35-minute walk). It's marked with the standard, yellow hiking trail signs. From Neuhausen there's a good view toward the Schloss Laufen.

Stein-am-Rhein

★ ⑫   *20 km (13 mi) east of Schaffhausen.*

Stein-am-Rhein, a nearly perfectly preserved medieval village and one of Switzerland's most picturesque towns, lies at the point where the Rhine leaves the Bodensee. Crossing the bridge over the river, you see the village spread along the waterfront, its foundations and docks rising directly out of the water. Here, restaurants, hotels, and souvenir stands occupy 16th- and 17th-century buildings, and the Rhine appears to be a narrow mountain stream—nothing like the sprawling industrial trade route it becomes farther downstream.

The **Rathausplatz** and main street are flanked by tight rows of shingled, half-timber town houses, each rivaling the next for the ornateness of its oriels, the flamboyance of its frescoes. The elaborate decor usually illustrates the name of the house: *Sonne* (Sun), *Ochsen* (Ox), *Weisser Adler* (White Eagle), and so on. Most of the artwork dates from the 16th century. The **Rathaus** (Town Hall) itself was built between 1539 and 1542, with the half-timber upper floors added in 1745; look for its fantastical dragon waterspouts, typical of the region.

The Benedictine **Kloster St. Georgen** (Monastery of St. George), a curious half-timber structure built in 1005, houses a small museum of woodwork and local paintings and also shelters a cloister. ⊠ *Edge of Old Town, just upstream from the last bridge over the Rhine before the Bodensee. Museum:* ⊙ *Weekdays 9–noon and 2–5, Sat. noon–4.*

Directly above the town atop vineyards and woods stands the 13th-century hilltop castle of **Hohenklingen,** which now houses a restaurant and offers broad views of the Rhine Valley and the lake beyond. ⊠ *Above Schaffhausen.*

Dining and Lodging

$$–$$$$ ✕ **Sonne.** Upstairs, you'll find a formal dining room (ceiling beams,
★   damask, and Biedermeier) where chef Philippe Combe's inventive, contemporary cuisine—Rhine fish, crisp duck with cabbage—commands top prices. Downstairs in the Weinstube, he offers a daily plate and simple light lunches, dished up in a spare, chic, gentrified pub: more beams, stone, stucco, parquet—and exposed pipes painted maroon. The Weinstube benefits from the kitchen upstairs; it offers homemade pastas, simple but sophisticated stews, and selections from the fine wine list. ⊠ *Rathauspl.,* ☎ *052/7412128. AE, DC, MC, V. Closed Tues.– Wed.*

$$ ✕ **Der Rote Ochse.** The beautiful frescoed facade invites its admirers into this warm little *Weinstübli* (wine parlor), where dark antiques surround a *Kachelofen* (tile stove) and candles glow on the tables. The simple menu is thick with hearty cuisine—a variety of sausages such as *Bauernschübli* (farmer's sausage), local cheeses, but also delicious homemade pastas. When they say the food is regional, they mean it: all ingredients are obtained from the village and surrounding areas. ⊠ *Rathauspl. 129,* ☎ *052/7412328. No credit cards. Closed Mon.*

$$$$ ⊡ **Chlosterhof.** Its brick-and-angled-glass exterior seems utterly misplaced in this medieval setting, but this hotel worked hard to face as many rooms as possible toward the Rhine. Inside, the look is modern, suburban, and business-class despite token vaulting in the lobby and scattered antiques; indeed, the focus is on entertaining conference

groups and their spouses. The rooms have sleek, dark-pine cabinetry and some four-poster beds, but the creamy pastels and carpets say up-scale international chain. Suites claim the best Rhine views. ⊠ *Oehninger-str. 201, CH-8260,* ☎ *052/7424242,* FAX *052/7411337. 44 rooms, 27 suites. 4 restaurants, bar, in-room VCRs, indoor pool, sauna, exercise room, dance club. AE, DC, MC, V.*

$$ ★ 🏨 **Rheinfels.** Even some of the bathrooms have ceiling beams in this fine old waterfront landmark, which was built between 1508 and 1517. The public spaces have creaking pine-plank floors and suits of armor on display, and every room—modernized in beige and rose tones, with all-tile bath—has a Rhine view. The hotel's suite is in essence an apartment; it has its own separate entrance, a one-car garage, and a boat jetty. The restaurant specializes in top-quality fresh-water fish at reasonable prices. Both the hotel and the restaurant are closed on Wednesday. ⊠ *Rhig. 8, CH-8260,* ☎ *052/7412144,* FAX *052/ 7412522. 16 rooms, 1 suite. Restaurant. MC, V.*

$–$$ ★ 🏨 **Adler.** With one of the most elaborately frescoed 15th-century fa-cades on the Rathausplatz, this hotel has a split personality: its inte-rior is airy, slick, and immaculate, with gray industrial carpet, white stucco, and blond wood throughout. The cabinetry is built-in, the baths are tile, and the windows are double glazed. A young, local fam-ily runs the hotel; other families will fit right in. The cheerful restau-rant serves good regional cooking, along with some French cuisine. ⊠ *Rathauspl. 15, CH-8260,* ☎ *052/7426161,* FAX *052/7414440. 25 rooms. Restaurant. AE, DC, MC, V.*

$ ★ 🏨 **Bleiche.** This private farmhouse lodging, on a hill high over the Rhine Valley about a mile from the village center, offers a chance to sleep under deep shingled eaves and wake to the sound of cowbells. The rooms are rock-bottom simple (linoleum, a mix of dormitory and collectible furniture), with showers down the hall, but the setting is surpassingly beautiful. A friendly German-speaking woman runs it. ⊠ *Bleicherhof, CH-8260,* ☎ *052/7412257. 5 rooms. No credit cards.*

$ 🏨 **Zur Rheingerbe.** Right on the busy waterfront promenade, this small inn has wood-panel ceilings and big furniture reminiscent of Sears (sculptured carpet, spindle beds). Some rooms overlook the Rhine. The first-floor restaurant has a full-length bay window along the riverfront. The hotel and restaurant are closed on Wednesday. ⊠ *Schifflände 5, CH-8260,* ☎ *052/7412991,* FAX *052/7412166. 7 rooms. Restaurant. AE, DC, MC, V.*

En Route Fourteen kilometers (9 miles) east of Stein-am-Rhein, the town of **Steckborn** has some fine old houses, including the Baronenhaus and the Gerichtshaus; it's also home to **Turmhof Steckborn**, a half-timber waterfront castle built in 1342 and now housing a small local museum containing artifacts from prehistoric times through the Roman and Ale-mannic settlements. ☎ *052/7611378.* ☉ *May–Oct., Wed., Thurs., and Sat. 3–5.*

Arenenberg

⑬ *20 km (12 mi) east of Stein-am-Rhein, 40 km (25 mi) east of Schaffhausen.*

Just east of Stein-am-Rhein, the Rhine opens up into the Untersee, the lower branch of the Bodensee. In its center lies the German island of Reichenau. Charles the Fat, great-grandson of Charlemagne, was buried here.

The villages on either side of the Untersee are dominated by castles. On the Swiss side, behind the village of Mannenbach (nearly opposite

Reichenau), the **castle at Arenenberg** was once home to the future Napoléon III and serves today as a museum with furnishings and artwork from the Second Empire. ⊠ *Behind Mannenbach,* ☎ *071/ 6641866.* 🖾 *5 SF.* ☉ *Tues.–Sun. 10–5.*

Gottlieben

⑭ *5 km (3 mi) east of Arenenberg, 45 km (28 mi) east of Schaffhausen.*

The village of Gottlieben has a Dominican monastery-castle, where the Protestant reformers Jan Hus and Jerome of Prague were imprisoned in the 15th century by order of Emperor Sigismund and Pope John XXII. Pope John was himself confined in the same castle a few years later. Today, though the castle can be viewed only from the outside, Gottlieben offers a romantic, half-timber waterfront promenade—and two fine old hotels—before you reach the urban complex of Kreuzlingen and Germany's Konstanz.

Lodging

$$$ 🏨 **Drachenburg und Waaghaus.** On the misty banks of the Rhine be-
★ tween the Bodensee and the Zellersee rises this half-timber apparition of onion domes, shutters, and gilt gargoyles. The original house, the early 18th-century Drachenburg, lies across a walk from the second building, the Waaghaus. A third house was added for overflow guests. The Drachenburg has gleaming old staircases, four-poster beds, brocade, chaise lounges, and crystal sconces throughout the labyrinth of rooms and parlors; rooms in the other buildings follow this elegant lead. The scale is grand but cozy, and Rhine-view rooms are furnished like honeymoon suites. Three restaurants vary in ambience, the most sophisticated being the one in the original house. ⊠ *AmSchlosspark, CH-8274,* ☎ *071/6667474,* 📠 *071/6691709. 58 rooms, 2 suites. 3 restaurants, bar. AE, DC, MC, V.*

$$ 🏨 **Krone.** Immediately downstream from the Drachenburg und Waaghaus (☞ *above*), this member of the Romantik chain is smaller, cheaper, and a tad more generic than its flamboyant neighbor, though it dates from the same era. Standard doubles are done in mild, classic beiges; the suites are quite baroque and have lake views. Breakfast is served in a beam-and-herringbone-ceiling hall overlooking the Rhine. The glowing dark-wood restaurant offers nouvelle-influenced seafood as well as lake fish. ⊠ *Seestr., CH-8274,* ☎ *071/6692323,* 📠 *071/ 6668069. 22 rooms, 3 suites. Restaurant. AE, DC, MC, V.*

FROM THE BODENSEE TO ST. GALLEN

Along the shores of the Bodensee, orchards stripe rolling hills which slowly rise to meet the foothills of the Alps around St. Gallen. Two thousand years ago this region lay on the northeastern border of the Roman Empire, Arbon (Arbor Felix) being the first stop on the trade route for goods coming into the Empire from points east. Today the region is mostly rural, with clusters of farmhouses dotting the grassy slopes. In summer the lake teems with vacationers, but otherwise it's a distinctly tranquil area.

Bodensee

Known in English as Lake Constance, the Bodensee is about 65 km (40 mi) long and 15 km (9 mi) wide, making it second in size in Switzerland only to Lac Léman (Lake Geneva). The strong German flavor of the towns on its Swiss edge is seasoned with a resort-village mellowness; sometimes palm trees fringe the waterfront. This isn't the Mediterranean, though; as the lake is not protected by mountains, it is turbulent in stormy weather and even on fine days is exposed to the wind. Compared with Switzerland's usual crystalline lakes, the Bodensee is gloomy and brooding; nonetheless, it draws European vacationers in summer for swimming, windsurfing, and fishing. Many Swiss have built tidy homes along the lakefront.

Outdoor Activities and Sports

HIKING

As a summer resort destination, the area around the Bodensee is usually thronged with hikers. For timed hiking itineraries, topographical maps, and suggestions on the areas best suited to your style of wandering, consult the **Tourismusverband Ostschweiz** (Tourist Association of Eastern Switzerland; ☞ Visitor Information *in* Eastern Switzerland A to Z, *below*).

SWIMMING

People do swim in the Bodensee; there are several **public beaches**, usually more grass than sand. Most have changing rooms and concession stands. **Arbon** (☎ 071/4461333) has a gravel beach—getting into the water can be a little rough on tender feet. **Kreuzlingen** (☎ 071/6881858) has some sand at the water's edge, though you'll be spreading your towel on the grass. **Romanshorn** (☎ 071/4631147) has a similar setup. **Rorschach** (☎ 071/8411684) has a pocket-size beach.

Kreuzlingen and Konstanz

⑮ *7 km (4 mi) east of Gottlieben, 46 km (28 mi) east of Schaffhausen.*

The big German city of Konstanz, with its Swiss twin of Kreuzlingen, dominates the straits that open into the Bodensee. Though Kreuzlingen itself offers little of interest to travelers, Konstanz has a lovely, concentrated *Altstadt* (Old Town) area. It's easily accessible from the Swiss side, though your passport may be checked even if you pass on foot. Konstanz belonged to Switzerland until 1805; today the two border towns share the dominant German influence.

En Route   About halfway between Kreuzlingen and Rorschach (follow Highway 13 east along the Bodensee), you'll come to the small town of **Romanshorn.** An industrial town and an important ferry port for Friedrichshafen in Germany, this is also a surprisingly enjoyable resort with fine views of the Swiss and Austrian mountains.

Between Romanshorn and Rorschach on Highway 13, **Arbon** (known to the Romans as Arbor Felix) lies on a little promontory jutting out into the Bodensee, surrounded by lovely meadows and orchards. It was a Celtic town before the Romans came in 60 BC and built military fortifications. Evidence of the Romans can be found in an interesting collection of relics in the late-Gothic St. Martinskirche.

Rorschach

⑯ *41 km (25 mi) southeast of Kreuzlingen, 80 km (49 mi) southeast of Schaffhausen.*

The lake resort of Rorschach, a port on the Bodensee, lies on a protected bay at the foot of the Rorschacherberg, an 883-m (2,896-ft) mountain covered with orchards, pine forests, and meadows. For generations, Rorschach has carried on a thriving grain trade with Germany, as the imposing baroque **Kornhaus** (Granary), built in 1746, attests. There's a public beach here, too (☞ Bodensee, *above*).

Outdoor Activities and Sports

SAILING

There are several sailing schools in Goldach, a small town 5 km (3 mi)
west of Rorschach, including **Segelschule Rorschach** (☎ 071/8448989).

St. Gallen

❶⑰ *14 km (9 mi) southwest of Rorschach, 94 km (59 mi) southeast of
Schaffhausen.*

Switzerland's largest eastern city, St. Gallen is a bustling city with students dominating its streets during the school year. The narrow streets
of the *Altstadt* (Old Town) are flanked by a wonderful variety of boutiques and antiques shops. The city has been known for centuries as
both an intellectual center and the source of some of the world's finest
textiles. St. Gallus, an Irish missionary, came to the region in 612 to
live in a hermit's cell in the Steinach Valley. In 720 an abbey was
founded on the site where he died. Soon a major cultural focus in medieval Europe, the abbey built a library of awesome proportions.

★ The abbey was largely destroyed in the Reformation and was closed
down in 1805, but its magnificent rococo **Stiftsbibliothek** (Abbey Library), built in 1758–67, still holds a collection of more than 100,000
books and manuscripts. The library hall itself is one of Switzerland's
treasures. Visitors enter behind the cathedral. Large gray carpet slippers are worn to protect the magnificently inlaid wooden flooring. The
hall is a gorgeous explosion of gilt, frescoes, and undulating balconies,
but the most striking aspect by far is the burnished woodwork, all luminous walnut and cherry. Its contents, including illuminated manuscripts
that are more than 1,200 years old and incunabula, comprise one of
the world's oldest and finest scholarly collections. Also on display, incongruously, is an Egyptian mummy dating back to 700 BC. ⊠ *Klosterhof 6c*, ☎ *071/2273416.* ☜ *5 SF.* ☉ *Apr.–Oct., Mon.–Sat. 9–noon and
1:30–5, Sun. 10–noon and 1:30–4; Nov.–Mar., Mon.–Sat. 9–noon and
1:30–4. Closed first 3 weeks in Nov.*

★ The **Kathedrale** (Cathedral) is impressive in its own right. Begun in 1755
and completed in 1766, it is the antithesis of the library, though the
nave and rotunda are the work of the same architect, Peter Thumb:
the scale is outsize and the decor light, bright, and open despite spectacular excesses of wedding-cake trim. ⊠ *Klosterhof,* ☎ *071/2273415.*
☉ *Weekdays 9–6:30, Sat. 9–5, Sun. noon–7.*

The grounds of the abbey and the cathedral border the **Old Town,** which
demonstrates a healthy symbiosis between scrupulously preserved Renaissance and baroque architecture and a thriving modern shopping
scene. The best examples of oriel windows, half-timbering, and frescoes can be seen along Gallusstrasse, Schmiedgasse, Marktgasse, and
Spisergasse, all pedestrian streets. For a good picnic spot, head to the
Mühleggbahn, a self-service funicular that runs up the hillside to a lovely
view of St. Gallen and the Bodensee. Once up top, take two immediate right turns to the wooden stairs leading to a paved path with park
benches. ⊠ *Off the Abbey end of the Old Town,* ☎ *071/2439595.* ☜
1.50 SF. ☉ *Daily 6 AM–11:30 PM.*

St. Gallen's history as a textile capital dates from the Middle Ages, when
convent workers wove linen toile of such exceptional quality that it
was exported throughout Europe. The industry expanded into cotton
and embroidery and today dominates the top of the market. To enjoy
some marvelously ornate old embroidery, visit the **Textilmuseum** (Textile Museum). Its lighting is dim to protect the delicate fabrics and its
captions are all in German, but the work speaks for itself. ⊠ *Vadianstr.*

2, ☏ 071/2221744. ⊠ 5 SF. ☉ Nov.–Mar., weekdays 10–noon and 2–5; Apr.–Oct., Mon.–Sat. 10–noon and 2–5.

Dining and Lodging

$$$$ ✕ **Am Gallusplatz.** This is St. Gallen's grandest restaurant in terms of both the cuisine and decor. The menu is based on market-fresh seasonal ingredients and may include saffron perch with new potatoes, or spinach crêpes with fresh coriander. There's also an enormous wine list. The dining room impresses with its cross-vaulted ceilings and heavy chandeliers. ⊠ Gallusstr. 24, ☏ 071/2233330. AE, MC, V. Closed Mon.

$$–$$$ ✕ **Zum Goldenen Schäfli.** Of the first-floor (second-floor to Americans) restaurants that are St. Gallen's trademark, this is the most popular, and its slanting floors groan under crowds of locals and tourists. The low ceiling and walls are all aged wood. The menu offers hearty regional standards with a special twist: sweetbreads in mushroom sauce, tripe in Calvados sauce, lake fish with almonds. ⊠ Metzgerg. 5, ☏ 071/2233737. AE, DC, MC, V. Closed Sun. No lunch Sat.

$$ ✕ **Schlössli.** Tidy, bright, and modern despite its setting in a historic
★ building, this first-floor landmark has a less woody atmosphere than its peers, the Bäumli and the Schäfli, but better cooking. The Käsespätzli are homemade and the salads fresh and good, especially the main-course salad with duck liver. The café draws casual families and locals playing a favorite card game, Jass, at lunch; businesspeople choose the only slightly more formal dining room that adjoins it. ⊠ Am Spisertor, Zeughausg. 17, ☏ 071/2221256. AE, DC, MC, V. Closed Sun. No lunch Sat.

$–$$ ✕ **Weinstube zum Bäumli.** All dark, glossy wood and lead glass, this 500-year-old first-floor (second floor to Americans) beauty serves classic local fare (veal, bratwurst, Rösti) to tourists, businesspeople, and workers, who share tables comfortably in the midst of the noisy bustle. ⊠ Schmiedg. 18, ☏ 071/2221174. MC, V. Closed Sun.–Mon.

$$$$ ⊞ **Einstein.** Tucked back into a slope at the edge of the Old Town, this former embroidery factory is now a sleek, upscale business-class hotel, with Hilton-like interiors (polished cabinetry, lacquered rattan, subdued florals), a uniformed staff, and a five-star attitude. The generous breakfast buffet, laid out in the skylighted top-floor loft that serves as the à la carte restaurant by night, is not included in the room price. ⊠ Berneggstr. 2, CH-9001, ☏ 071/2200033, FAX 071/2275577. 65 rooms, 3 suites. Restaurant, bar. AE, DC, MC, V.

$$$ ⊞ **Gallo.** Now a relatively cheap business hotel, this graceful former apartment house is set beside a busy road but has double-glazed windows to shut out the roar. The location is not particularly convenient to the Old Town (Bus 3, named Heiligkreuz, stops at nearby Olma or carries you into the center), but interiors are fresh and attractive, with big tile baths and bright-color lacquer; two lovely attic doubles have beams and dormer windows. There is a great Italian restaurant on the ground floor. ⊠ St. Jakobstr. 62, CH-9000, ☏ 071/2452727, FAX 071/2454593. 24 rooms. Restaurant. AE, DC, MC, V.

$$$ ⊞ **Im Portner & Pförtnerhof.** The original old Im Portner Hotel, in the
★ Old Town, is comfortable but undistinguished with its gold carpet, Naugahyde, and mix-and-match rooms. But across the street, the annexed Pförtnerhof stands apart: the big, bay-window, half-timber house has been restored and stylishly updated. The rooms combine antiquity (leaded glass, painted woodwork, stone niches) with high tech (halogen and lithos). ⊠ Bankg. 12, CH-9000, ☏ 071/2229744, FAX 071/2229856. 17 rooms. Restaurant, café. AE, DC, MC, V.

$$ ⊞ **Elite.** In the modern deco style of the 1950s, this Old Town spot has a functional air and a friendly staff. Half the rooms have baths; the others have sinks and cost less. The back rooms are quieter. ⊠ Metz-

gerg. 9/11, CH-9004, ☎ 071/2221236, ℻ 071/2222177. 26 rooms, 13 with bath. Breakfast room. AE, DC, MC, V.

$–$$ ▣ **Vadian.** A narrow town house tucked behind half-timber landmarks in the Old Town, this is a discreet and tidy little place with an alcohol-free policy. Most of its tiny rooms have been updated with beige stucco, knotty pine, and new tile baths. Rooms without bath cost less. ✉ *Gallusstr. 36, CH-9000, ☎ 071/2236080, ℻ 071/2224748. 13 rooms, 6 with bath. Breakfast room. AE, DC, MC, V.*

Outdoor Activities and Sports

🐾 **Säntispark.** Just outside St. Gallen lies this year-round, family-friendly sports and spa extravaganza. There is something to please (and exhaust) everyone—racquet sports, bowling, minigolf, billiards. Children can dive into the wave pool at the water park and enjoy the rides and playgrounds. For relaxing, there's a solarium, sauna, and massage center. Equipment can be rented; most activities cost under 20 SF. ✉ *From the main train station in St. Gallen, 15 mins by Bus 7 (Abtwil), or by car along Hwy. N–1, exit Winkeln. ☎ 071/3131555. ▦ Pay per activity. ☉ Daily 9 AM–11 PM.*

Shopping

ANTIQUE PRINTS

An outstanding assortment of antique prints of Swiss landscapes and costumes is sold at a broad range of prices at **Graphica Antiqua** (✉ Oberer Graben 46, near the Einstein Hotel, ☎ 071/2235016). The pictures are cataloged alphabetically by canton for easy browsing.

TEXTILES AND EMBROIDERY

For a region world-renowned for its textiles and embroidery, it's surprisingly difficult to find the real thing at a single store. There are a few excellent exceptions, including **Rocco Textil** (✉ Spiserg. 41, ☎ 071/2222407), which has a small but wonderful selection of St. Gallen embroidery, linens, and lace; they're an especially good source for custom work. **Saphir** (✉ Bleichestr. 9, ☎ 071/2236263) carries a high-quality collection of embroidered handkerchiefs, bed and table linens, and bolts of embroidered fabric and lace—all from the St. Gallen region. **Sturzenegger** (✉ St. Leonhardstr. 12, ☎ 071/2224576), the better-known embroidery firm, established in 1883, sells its own line of linens and lingerie, designed and manufactured in the factory a block away.

Appenzell

⑱ *20 km (12 mi) south of St. Gallen, 98 km (60 mi) southeast of Schaffhausen.*

Isolated from St. Gallen by a ridge of green hills, Appenzell is one of Switzerland's most eccentric regions. Fellow Swiss think of its people as hillbillies, citing their quirky sense of humor and old-fashioned costumes. The city of St. Gallen melts away into undulating hills spotted with doe-skin cows, a steep-pastured, isolated verdure reminiscent of West Virginia or the Ozarks. Prim, symmetrical cottages inevitably show rows of windows facing the valley. Named Appenzell after the Latin *abbatis cella* (abbey cell), the region served as a sort of colony to the St. Gallen abbey, and its tradition of fine embroidery dates from those early days. The perfect chance to see this embroidery is during a local festival, such as the Alpfahrten, when cows are herded down the mountains. Women wear tulle coifs and dresses with intricate embroidery and lace, often with an edelweiss motif; men wear embroidered red vests and suspenders decorated with edelweiss or cow figures. These traditional costumes are taken very seriously; they can cost thousands of francs, but in this case, pride supersedes economy. A small highway (No. 3) leads into the hills through Teufen; the quaint Appenzell–Teufen–Gais rail line also serves the region.

The town of Appenzell blends some of the best and worst of the region, offering tourists a concentrated and somewhat self-conscious sampling of the culture. Its streets lined with bright-painted homes, bakeries full of *Birnebrot* (pear bread) and souvenir *Biber* (almond and honey cakes), and shops full of embroidery (which, on close examination, often turns out to have been made in China), Appenzell seems to watch the tourists warily and get on with its life while profiting from the attention. Its **Landsgemeindeplatz** in the town center is the site of the famous open-air elections (until 1991, for men only), which take place the last Sunday in April. Embroidery has become big business here, but it's rare to find handmade examples of the local art; though women still do fine work at home, it's generally reserved for gifts or heirlooms. Instead, large factories have sprung up in Appenzell country, and famous fine-cotton handkerchiefs sold in specialty shops around the world are made by machine here at the Dörig, Alba, and Lehner plants.

The **Museum Appenzell** showcases handicrafts and local traditions, regional history, and an international embroidery collection—it's a good general overview of the area's history and culture. The building itself dates from 1560 and was residential until 1985, when the museum collection was moved here from the Rathaus (town hall) next door. An English-language guide is available. ⊠ *Hauptg. 4,* ☎ *071/7889631.* 🎫 *5 SF.* ☉ *Apr.–Oct., daily 10–noon and 2–5; Nov.–Mar., Tues.–Sun. 2–4.*

Dining and Lodging

$$ ✕ **Traube.** The understated, traditional interior lacks personality, but in the summer months it opens up onto a terrace overlooking a lovely landscaped garden hidden from major streets. The menu is heavy on pork and potatoes, but the selection is wide enough to please most palates. Fondue and Appenzeller *Chäshörnli* (cheese and macaroni) round off the the mostly heavy offerings. The daily special is usually under 20 SF. ⊠ *Marktg. 7,* ☎ *071/7871407. MC, V. Closed Mon.*

$$$ ✕🏠 **Appenzell.** This comfortable lodging has all the gabled
★ Gemütlichkeit of its neighbors, with rows of shuttered windows and a view over the Landsgemeindeplatz. Homey rooms, warmed with polished wood, owe their airiness to the traditional multiple windows. The fine woodwork and antiques in the breakfast room are remnants of the previous house on the property. The restaurant offers fresh interpretations of regional fare, such as the *Hauptgass* (an Appenzeller cheese gratin with pork, prosciutto, and tomato), plus a selection of health and vegetarian dishes, which are rare in these parts. You certainly won't have to squint at your menu; the room is so brightly lit it has an almost clinical atmosphere. ⊠ *Landsgemeindepl., CH-9050,* ☎ *071/7874211,* 🅵🅰🆇 *071/7874284. 16 rooms. Restaurant, breakfast room, café, patisserie, no-smoking rooms. AE, DC, MC, V.*

$–$$ ✕🏠 **Hof.** One of Appenzell's most popular restaurants serves hearty
★ regional meats and cheese specialties, such as *Käseschnitte* (cheese toast) and Käsespätzli, to locals and tourists who crowd elbow to elbow along shared tables and raise their voices to be heard over the clatter from the service bar. The all-modern, rustic-wood decor and ladder-back chairs, the knotty pine, and the display of sports trophies add to the local atmosphere. Upstairs, groups can rent up to 58 beds in cheap summer-camp dormitory lodgings and play skittles after dinner. ⊠ *Engelg. 4, CH-9050,* ☎ *071/7872210,* 🅵🅰🆇 *071/7875883. 10 rooms. AE, DC, MC, V.*

$$$ 🏨 **Löwen.** Wising up to the tourists' quest for "typical" local decor, the owners of this renovated 1780 guest house furnished several rooms in authentic Appenzeller styles, with embroidered linens and built-in woodwork (canopy beds, armoires) painted with bright designs and naive local scenes—some actually reflecting the view from the window. Standard rooms in dormitory-style oak also are available for a slightly lower price. ⊠ *Hauptg. 25, CH-9050,* ☎ *071/7872187,* ℻ *071/7872579. 17 rooms, 9 suites. Restaurant, bar, sauna. AE, DC, MC, V.*

$$$ 🏨 **Säntis.** A member of the Romantik hotel group, this prestigious hotel has a somewhat new and formal ambience, though the earliest wing has been a hotel-restaurant since 1835. Old-style touches—inlaid wood furnishings, painted beams—mix comfortably with the jewel-tone rooms and gleaming walnut cabinetry; some rooms have four-poster or canopy beds. The main first-floor restaurant serves slightly Frenchified regional specialties in either of two wood-lined dining rooms, one Biedermeier, the other a folksy Appenzeller style. A cherry-wood Stübli at street level attracts locals. Guests can borrow bikes for free. ⊠ *Landsgemeindepl., CH-9050,* ☎ *071/7881111,* ℻ *071/7881110. 31 rooms, 6 suites. Restaurant, bar, sauna. AE, DC, MC, V.*

$ 🏨 **Freudenberg.** This is a cookie-cutter modern chalet, but its vantage point on a velvety green hillside overlooking town is the most scenic and tranquil you'll find here. Built in 1969, it still has dormlike rooms and sculptured carpet in harvest gold, but some rooms have balconies, and the broad, shaded terrace café—festive in the evening with strings of yellow lights—lets you take in the picture-pretty views. ⊠ *Behind the train station, CH-9050,* ☎ ℻ *071/7871240. 7 rooms. Restaurant, café. AE.*

Shopping

CHEESES

Picnickers can sample the different grades of Appenzeller cheese and its unsung mountain rivals at **Mösler** (⊠ Hauptg., ☎ 071/7871317). **Sutter** (⊠ Marktstr. 8, ☎ 071/7871227) also has a good selection of local cheeses.

EMBROIDERY

True, locally made hand embroidery is rare in Appenzell. Many handkerchiefs that beautifully reproduce the blindingly close work that locals no longer pursue have been hand-stitched in Portugal. Though an odd souvenir, they capture the spirit of Appenzell handwork better than much of the pretty, though broad, machine work available in the stores. **Margreiter** (⊠ Hauptg. 29, ☎ 071/7873313) carries a large stock of machine-made handkerchiefs from the local Dörig, Alba, and Lehner factories, many decorated with edelweiss or other Alpine flowers. **Trachtenstube** (⊠ Hauptg. 23, ☎ 071/7871606) offers high-quality local handiwork—lace, embroidery, and crafts.

LIQUEURS

Butchers, bakers, and liquor shops up and down the streets offer souvenir bottles of **Appenzeller Bitter** (Alpenbitter), a very sweet aperitif made in town. A well-balanced **eau-de-vie** called Appenzeller Kräuter, made of blended herbs, is another specialty.

Stein

🔟 *13 km (8 mi) northwest of Appenzell, 94 km (58 mi) southeast of Schaffhausen.*

The quiet village of Stein (not to be confused with Stein-am-Rhein) consists of little more than sturdy old farmhouses and red-roofed homes with the obligatory geraniums in window boxes. At the **Schaukäserei** (showcase dairy), modern cheese-making methods are demonstrated. Note that cheese is made 9–2 only. ☎ 071/3685070. ☒ *Free.* ☉ *Mar.– Oct., daily 8–7; Nov.–Feb., daily 9–6.*

The **Appenzeller Volkskunde Museum** (Folklore Museum) displays Appenzell arts and crafts, local costumes, and hand-painted furniture. ☎ 071/3685056. ☒ *7 SF.* ☉ *Nov.–Mar., Sun. 10–5; Apr.–Oct., Tues.– Sat. 10–noon and 1:30–5, Sun. 10–6.*

Urnäsch

⑳ *10 km (6 mi) west of Appenzell, 110 km (68 mi) southeast of Schaffhausen.*

If you're interested in a traditional festival, you'll want to head to this modest, countryside town on December 21 or January 13. New Year's and "Old New Year's" (according to the Julian calendar) are celebrated with an early-morning parade of *Chläuse*, men done up in amazingly complicated masks, huge headpieces, and costumes made of bark, moss, and branches. Some of the *Chläuse* wear enormous cowbells around their necks as well. It's a good idea to reserve a table for lunch at one of the local restaurants so you don't get left out in the cold— the parade draws crowds of spectators. Contact the Urnäsch tourist office (☞ Visitor Information *in* Eastern Switzerland A to Z, *below*) for more information.

The **Museum für Appenzeller Brauchtum** (Museum of Appenzeller Tradition) displays costumes, cowbells, a cheese wagon, and examples of farmhouse living quarters. ☎ 071/3642322. ☒ *4 SF.* ☉ *May–Oct., daily 1:30–5; Apr., Wed. and weekends 1:30–5 and by appointment; Nov.– Mar., by appointment only.*

Mt. Säntis

㉑ *11 km (7 mi) south of Urnäsch, 121 km (75 mi) southeast of Schaffhausen.*

A pleasurable high-altitude excursion out of Appenzell takes you west to Urnäsch, then south to the hamlet of Schwägalp, where a cable car carries you up to the peak of Mt. Säntis, at 2,502 m (8,209 ft) the highest in the region, with beautiful views of the Bodensee as well as of the Graubünden and Bernese Alps. The very shape of the summit—an arc of jutting rock that swings up to the jagged peak housing the station— is spectacular. ☎ 071/3656565. ☒ *27 SF round-trip.* ☉ *July–Aug., daily 7:30–7; May, June, and Sept., daily 7:30–6:30; Oct.–Apr., 8:30–5; departures every 30 mins. Closed for 3 wks in Jan.*

Toggenburg Valley

㉒ *Entrance 11 km (7 mi) south of Mt. Säntis, 132 km (82 mi) southeast of Schaffhausen.*

A scenic, pre-Alpine resort area popular with locals but relatively unexplored by outsiders, this is an ideal place for skiers and hikers who hate crowds. In the rugged Upper Toggenburg, weather-boarded dwellings surround the neighboring resorts of Wildhaus (birthplace of religious reformer Huldrych Zwingli), Unterwasser, and Alt-St. Johann—all of which draw Swiss families for winter skiing and summer hiking excursions into the Churfirsten and Alpstein mountains. As they lie within shouting distance of each other, the ski facilities can be shared, and the jagged teeth of the mountains behind provide a dramatic backdrop.

If you're interested in the Reformation, you may want to make a pilgrimage to Wildhaus's **Zwinglihaus,** the farmhouse where Huldrych Zwingli was born in 1484. His father was president of the village's political commune, and the house was used as a meeting place for its council. A small museum within displays some restored furniture from his time, though not from his family, and an impressive collection of period Bibles. The fire-and-brimstone preacher celebrated his first mass in the town's Protestant church and went on to lead the Protestant Reformation in Zürich. ✉ *Schönenboden, Wildhaus/Lisighaus,* ☎ 071/9992178. ☞ *Free.* ☉ *June–mid-Nov. and Jan.–mid-Apr. Tues.–Sun. 2–4.*

Skiing

Equally popular with locals, the triplet ski resorts of Wildhaus, Unterwasser, and Alt-St. Johann combine forces to draw visitors into the Churfirsten "paradise" in the Toggenburg Valley. Here you'll find altitudes and drops to suit even jaded skiers, the most challenging starting on the 2,076-m-high (6,809-ft-high) Gamserrugg and winding down 1,000 m (3,280 ft) to Wildhaus itself; a medium-difficult rival winds from Chäserrugg (2,262 m/7,419 ft) all the way down to Unterwasser. A one-day pass for all three resorts costs 43 SF; a five-day pass costs 170 SF; a seven-day pass costs 212 SF. There are ski schools in all three resorts. For more information and reservations, call ☎ 071/9999911, ℻ 071/9992929.

Alt-St. Johann, at 900 m (2,952 ft), has one chairlift and two T-bars. **Unterwasser,** at 910 m (2,985 ft), has one funicular railway, one cable car, four T-bars, 50 km (31 mi) of downhill runs, 45 km (28 mi) of cross-country trails, and 27 km (17 mi) of ski-hiking trails. At 1,098 m (3,601 ft), **Wildhaus** offers skiers four chairlifts, five T-bars, 50 km (31 mi) of downhill runs, 45 km (28 mi) of cross-country trails, and 27 km (17 mi) of ski-hiking trails.

Outdoor Activities and Sports

RACQUET SPORTS
Wildhaus (☎ 071/9991211) has two outdoor courts. **Unterwasser** has three outdoor tennis courts and a tennis-squash center (☎ 071/9993030).

LIECHTENSTEIN AND THE WALENSEE

When you cross the border from Switzerland into the principality of Liechtenstein, you will be surrounded by license plates marked FL: This stands for Fürstentum Liechtenstein (Principality of Liechtenstein). You are leaving the world's oldest democracy and entering a monarchy that is the last remnant of the Holy Roman Empire—all 157 square km (61 square mi) of it. If you blink, you may miss it entirely.

This postage-stamp principality was begun at the end of the 17th century, when a wealthy Austrian prince, Johann Adam von Liechtenstein, bought out two bankrupt counts in the Rhine Valley and united their lands. In 1719 he obtained an imperial deed from Emperor Karl VI, creating the principality of Liechtenstein. The noble family poured generations of wealth into the new country, improving its standard of living, and in 1862 an heir, Prince Johann the Good, helped Liechtenstein introduce its first constitution as a "democratic monarchy" in which the people and the prince share power equally.

Today the principality's 32,000 citizens enjoy one of the world's highest per-capita incomes and pay virtually no taxes. Its prosperous (though discreet) industries range from jam making to the molding of false teeth. Ironically, prosperity has built the lower reaches of Liechtenstein into a modern, comfortable, bourgeois community, full of big, new cream-color bungalows that hardly seem picturesque to tourists seeking traces of the Holy Roman Empire.

Vaduz (Liechtenstein)

㉓ *15 km (9 mi) southeast of the Toggenburg Valley, 159 km (98 mi) southeast of Schaffhausen.*

Arriving in downtown Vaduz (there are exits from the A–13 expressway from both the north and the south), a visitor could make the mistake of thinking Liechtenstein's only attraction is its miniature scale. Liechtenstein's small **Briefmarkenmuseum** (Stamp Museum) demonstrates the principality's history as a maker of beautifully designed, limited-edition postage stamps. Have your passport stamped for 2 SF at the **Fremdenverkehrszentrale** (tourist office) (☞ Visitor Information *in* Eastern Switzerland A to Z, *below*) in the same building. ✉ *Städtle 37,* ☎ *075/2366105.* 🎟 *Free.* ☺ *Apr.–Oct., daily 10–noon and 1:30–5:30; Nov.–Mar., daily 10–noon and 1:30–5.*

The **Liechtensteinische Staatliche Kunstsammlung** (Liechtenstein State Museum of Art) displays an ever-changing fraction of the country's extraordinary art collection, including graphic art, paintings (with works by Rembrandt and Rubens), and pieces from the world-famous art collection of the prince, which concentrates on Greek and Roman mythological art. ✉ *Städtle 37,* ☎ *075/2322341.* 🎟 *5 SF.* ☺ *Apr.–Oct., daily 10–noon and 1:30–5:30; Nov.–Mar., daily 10–noon and 1:30–5.*

The **Ski Museum Vaduz** is a small shrine to Switzerland's (and the Alps') preferred pastime. Here you'll find numerous variations on the theme, including skis, sleds, ski fashion, and literature. ✉ *Bangarten 10,* ☎ *075/2321502.* 🎟 *5 SF.* ☺ *Weekdays 2–6.*

At the top of a well-marked hill road (you can climb the forest footpath behind the Engel hotel) stands **Vaduz Castle.** Here, His Highness, Johannes Adam Pius, reigning prince of Liechtenstein, duke of Troppau and Jaegerndorf, reigns in a gratifyingly romantic fortress-home with striped medieval shutters, massive ramparts, and a broad perspective over the Rhine Valley. Originally built in the 12th century, the castle was burned down by troops of the Swiss Confederation in the Swabian Wars of 1499 and partly rebuilt during the following centuries, until a complete overhaul that started in 1905 gave it its present form. It is not open to the public, as Hans-Adam enjoys his privacy. He is the son of the late, beloved Franz Josef II, who died in November 1989 after a more than 50-year reign. Franz Josef's birthday, August 15, is still celebrated as the Liechtenstein national holiday; Hans-Adam—the last living heir to the Holy Roman Empire—has been known to join the crowds below to watch the fireworks while wearing jeans.

Dining and Lodging

$ ✕ **Wirthschaft zum Löwen.** Though there's plenty of French, Swiss, and
★ Austrian influence, Liechtenstein has a cuisine of its own, and this is the place to try it. In a wood-shingle landmark farmhouse on the Austrian border, the friendly Biedermann family serves tender homemade *Schwartenmagen* (the pressed-pork mold unfortunately known as headcheese in English), pungent *Sauerkäse* (sour cheese), and Käseknöpfli, plus lovely meats and the local crusty, chewy bread. Be sure to try the region's wines. ✉ *FL-9488 Schellenberg,* ☎ *075/ 3731162. No credit cards.*

$$$–$$$$ ✕🏨 **Real.** Here you'll find rich, old-style Austrian-French cuisine in
★ this Relais & Châteaux establishment, prepared these days by Martin Real, son of the unpretentious former chef, Felix Real—who, in his re-

tirement, presides over the 20,000-bottle cellar. There's an abundance of game in season, richly sauced seafood, and soufflés. The extraordinary wine list includes some rare (and excellent) local samplings, some from the family vineyard. Downstairs, the more casual Stübli atmosphere is just right for *Geschnetzeltes mit Rösti* (veal bits in cream sauce with hash-brown potatoes); upstairs, the guest rooms are small but airily decorated. ⌧ *Städtle 21, FL-9490,* ☎ *075/2322222, FAX 075/ 2320891. 11 rooms, 2 suites. Restaurant. AE, DC, MC, V.*

$$ ✕🖾 **Engel.** This elegant, centrally located hotel-restaurant has a comfortable local ambience despite the tour-bus crowds. The restaurant downstairs dishes up home cooking, and there's a *Biergarten* (beer garden) where Liechtensteiners meet. Upstairs, the more formal restaurant serves Chinese cuisine. The guest rooms are in fresh colors, with tile bathrooms. ⌧ *Städtle 13, FL-9490,* ☎ *075/2361717, FAX 075/ 2331159. 20 rooms. Restaurant, pub. AE, DC, MC, V.*

$$$$ 🖾 **Park-Hotel Sonnenhof.** A garden oasis—and a Relais & Châteaux property—commanding a superb view over the valley and mountains beyond, this hillside retreat offers understated luxury minutes from downtown Vaduz. Rooms are being renovated one by one; older rooms are decorated in homey pastels, the newer ones in gold and bright colors. Public areas are full of antiques, rugs, woodwork, and familial touches. The excellent French restaurant is exclusively for guests. ⌧ *Mareestr. 29, FL-9490,* ☎ *075/2321192, FAX 075/2320053. 17 rooms, 12 suites. Restaurant, indoor pool, sauna. AE, DC, MC, V.*

Outdoor Activities and Sports

BICYCLES AND MOTORCYCLES

In Vaduz, bikes and small motorcycles can be rented from **Hans Melliger** (☎ 075/2321606).

TENNIS

Vaduz (☎ 075/2327720) has public covered courts on Schaanerstrasse. Covered courts are also accessible in nearby **Schaan** (☎ 075/2332343). Rental equipment is available.

Shopping

POTTERY

Though shops on the main street of Vaduz carry samples of the local dark-glaze pottery painted with folksy flowers and figures, the central source is **Schaedler Keramik** (⌧ Nendeln, 8 km/5 mi north of Vaduz on the main highway, ☎ 075/3731414). Simpler household pottery is available for sale as well as the traditional and often ornate hand-painted pieces. Pottery-making is demonstrated daily; it's open weekdays 8– noon and 1:30–6.

STAMPS

Liechtenstein is sometimes called the unofficial, per capita world champion of stamp collecting. To buy some of its famous stamps, whether to send a postcard to a philatelist friend or to invest in limited-issue commemorative sheets, you must line up with the tour-bus crowds at the popular **post office** (⌧ Städtle).

Triesenberg

㉔   *3 km (2 mi) southeast of Vaduz, 162 km (100 mi) southeast of Schaffhausen.*

This cluster of pretty chalets clings to the mountainside, with panoramic views over the Rhine Valley. Triesenberg was settled in the 13th century by immigrants from the Valais in southwestern Switzerland. The **Walser Heimatmuseum** (Valais Heritage Museum) traces the culture of these immigrants. Furnishings and tools from farmers and craftsmen are displayed, and an entertaining 20-minute slide show (in English) illustrates their Alpine roots. ⊠ *Dorfenzentrum,* ☎ *075/2621926.* ▦ *2 SF.* ☉ *Sept.–May, Tues.–Fri. 1:30–5:30, Sat. 1:30–5; June–Aug., Tues.–Fri. 1:30–5:30, Sat. 1:30–5; Sun. 2–5.*

Malbun

㉕ *5 km (3 mi) southeast of Triesenberg, 167 km (103 mi) southeast of Schaffhausen.*

In winter, this 1,600-m-high (5,250-ft-high) mountain resort near the Austria border draws crowds of local families who come for the varied slopes, many of which are well suited to beginners. England's Prince Charles and Princess Anne learned to ski here while visiting the Liechtenstein royal family in Vaduz. In summer, Malbun becomes a quiet, unpretentious resort with reasonable prices.

Skiing

Malbun is a sunny, natural bowl with low, easy slopes and a couple of difficult runs; you can ride a chairlift to the top of the Sareiserjoch and experience the novelty of skiing from the Austrian border back into Liechtenstein. Facilities are concentrated at the center, including hotels and cafés overlooking the slopes. The resort also has a ski school (☎ 075/2639770). One-day lift tickets cost 35 SF; six-day passes cost 140 SF.

Lodging

$ 🏠 **Alpenhotel.** This 85-year-old chalet, well above the mists of the Rhine, has been remodeled and has added a modern wing. The old rooms are small, with creaky pine trim; the higher-priced new rooms are modern stucco. The Vögeli family's welcoming smiles and good food have made it a Liechtenstein institution. ⊠ *FL-9490,* ☎ *075/2631181,* 𝐅𝐀𝐗 *075/2639646. 21 rooms. Restaurant, café, indoor pool. AE, DC, MC, V.*

Outdoor Activities and Sports

Liechtenstein has a 162-km (100-mi) network of Alpine hiking trails, and another 243 km (150 mi) of valley hiking. **Malbun** and **Steg** are ideal starting points for mountain hikes. You can get trail maps at the tourist office or at magazine kiosks.

Flumserberg

㉖ *25 km (15 mi) west of Malbun, 122 km (75 mi) southeast of Schaffhausen.*

On the windswept, timberless slopes overlooking the Walensee and the Churfirsten Mountains, this resort is the site of one of the world's longest cableways. Over a distance of about 3 km (1¾ mi), a procession of little four-seater cabins reaches up to the rocky summit at **Leist,** 2,056 m (6,743 ft) up.

Skiing

Flumserberg, spanning 1,200 m–2,222 m (3,936 ft–7,288 ft), has five cable cars, 10 chairlifts, four T-bars, 60 km (40 mi) of downhill runs, 21 km (13 mi) of cross-country trails, and 20 km (12 mi) of mountain trails. The runs are suitable for beginner to intermediate skiers. You can also endeavor to skate, skibob, night ski, or snowboard in the newly constructed Funpark. A ski school (☎ 081/7333939) provides help for the less proficient. The German-only *Schneebericht* (☎ 081/7201510) gives current information on snow conditions. One-day lift tickets cost 46 SF; six-day passes, 194 SF.

Walensee

 5 km (3 mi) northwest of Flumserberg, 127 km (78 mi) southeast of Schaffhausen.

Between Liechtenstein and Zürich, the spectacular, mirrorlike lake called the Walensee is a deep emerald gash that stretches 16 km (10 mi) through the mountains, reflecting the jagged Churfirsten peaks. At the western end of the lake, **Weesen** is a quiet, shady resort noted for its mild climate and lovely lakeside walkway. Six kilometers (4 miles) north of Weesen on a winding mountain road lies **Amden,** perched 950 m (3,116 ft) above the Walensee in the relatively undiscovered region south of the Churfirsten Mountains. With its balance of up-to-date resources and traditional atmosphere, it is rarely penetrated by foreigners.

Skiing

Despite its small size, **Amden** is a major winter sports center, offering modest skiing in a ruggedly beautiful setting. Easy and medium slopes with unspectacular drops and quick, short-lift runs provide good weekend getaways for crowds of local Swiss families. The highest trails start at 1,700 m (5,576 ft); there are a chairlift, three T-bars, one children's lift, 25 km (16 mi) of downhill runs, and 8 km (5 mi) of cross-country trails—also a ski school (☎ 055/6111127), skating on a natural ice rink, and walking paths. One-day lift tickets cost 29 SF; six-day passes cost 110 SF.

Outdoor Activities and Sports

For sports enthusiasts, **Amden** also has a public skating rink (☎ 055/6111413), the heated indoor pool **Hallenbad Amden** (☎ 055/6111588), and an outdoor tennis court (☎ 055/6111413).

OFF THE
BEATEN PATH

RAPPERSWIL – Between the Walensee and Zürich, this small town on Zürichsee (Lake Zürich) offers pleasant views and summertime waterfront strolls. Three rose gardens in the town center, including one for people with disabilities, account for Rapperswil's claim as the "Swiss City of Roses." A forbidding 13th-century **castle** looks like part of a gothic novel, with a trio of grave towers. Inside is the small **Polenmuseum** (☎ 055/2101862; ⊠ 4 SF) highlighting the history of Polish immigrants to Switzerland. It's open on weekends from 1 to 5 between November and March, and daily from 1 to 5 between April and October. The castle's walkway faces a small deer park and affords a view of Zürich; from the terrace you'll see the Glarus Alps. At the **Knie's Kinderzoo** (Children's Zoo), there are dolphin shows, 70 types of animals from around the world, elephant and pony rides, and plenty of creatures to feed and pet. (Elephant rides are not given on rainy days.) Follow signs; it's near the train station. ⊠ About 36 km (22 mi) northwest of Weesen and 40 km (24 mi) southeast of Zürich. Children's Zoo: ☎ 055/2206767. ⊠ 7 SF. ☺ Mid-Mar.–Oct., daily 9–6.

EASTERN SWITZERLAND A TO Z

Arriving and Departing

By Car

The A–1 expressway from Zürich heads for St. Gallen through Winterthur. To reach Schaffhausen from Zürich, take A–1 to Winterthur, then head north on the cantonal highway E–41/15. You also can leave Zürich by way of the A–4 expressway past Kloten Airport, crossing through Germany briefly and entering Schaffhausen through Neuhausen am Rheinfall. From the south, the **A–13** expressway, shared with Austria, leads you from Chur along Liechtenstein to the east end of the Bodensee; from there, you take A–1 into St. Gallen.

By Plane

Zürich-Kloten Airport (☎ 1571060), the most important in Switzerland, lies in Zürich, about 48 km (30 mi) south of Schaffhausen, about 75 km (46 mi) west of St. Gallen, and 130 km (81 mi) northwest of Liechtenstein.

By Train

A connection by train from the Zürich Hauptbahnhof into the **SBB Bahnhof Schaffhausen** (☎ 051/2234500) takes about 40 minutes; into **SBB Bahnhof Saint Gallen** (☎ 040/671040) or Sargans, about an hour. Connections from the south (Graubünden) are more complicated, as both Austria and the Alps intervene.

Getting Around

By Boat

Swiss Federal Railways provides regular year-round service on the Bodensee through **Schweizer Bodensee Schifffahrt Gesellschaft** (Swiss Bodensee Cruiseline Co., ☎ 071/4633435), though fewer boats run in winter. (You'll travel free if you have a Swiss Pass.) There is also **Verkehrsverein Untersee am Rhein** (☎ 052/7612604), with a cruise-ship route on the Walensee and a Rhine cruise between Schaffhausen and Kreuzlingen-Konstanz. The Swiss Boat Pass allows half-fare travel (☞ Boat Travel *in* Smart Travel Tips A to Z).

The **Untersee und Rhein** ship company (✉ Freierpl. 7, CH-8202 Schaffhausen, ☎ 052/6254282, or contact the Schweizerische Bodenseeschiffahrtsgesellschaft AG at Romanshorn ☎ 071/4633435) offers a winning combination of a boat ride on the Rhine with romantic views of storybook castles, citadels, and monasteries. Boats run regularly up- and downstream, docking at Schaffhausen, Stein-am-Rhein, Gottlieben, Konstanz, and Kreuzlingen. Prices vary according to the distance traveled. A one-way trip from Schaffhausen to Kreuzlingen takes about 4½ hours.

By Bus

The famous yellow **postbuses** provide much of the public transport in areas not served by trains, particularly smaller towns and, of course, Liechtenstein, which has no rail service. The bus schedules are usually posted outside the town post office, but you can also obtain information from any train station.

By Cable Car

Although there are a few scattered across the region, the most popular and spectacular cable-car rides are up Mt. Säntis from Schwägalp and to the Ebenalp via Appenzell-Wasserauen.

By Car

Driving in eastern Switzerland allows you to see the best of this region, with its highway along the Bodensee and pretty back roads in Appenzell. Neither St. Gallen nor Schaffhausen is a big enough city to warrant all-out panic, although you'll find it easiest to head directly for the center and abandon the car for the duration of your visit. Try to get into a parking lot, as finding a spot on the street can be difficult. In Schaffhausen, there's a big lot by the Stadttheater on Herrenacker. In St. Gallen, the Old Town is surrounded by underground parking lots. You'll find entrances on Burggraben, Oberergraben, and, most conveniently, on St. Georgenstrasse, right by the abbey.

By Train

Rail connections are somewhat complicated in this area, especially if you want to visit more of Appenzell than its major towns. Schaffhausen and St. Gallen are the main hubs from which regional trains head into the countryside and along the Bodensee. The only railroads into the country are the narrow-gauge line between St. Gallen and the town of Appenzell, which passes Teufen and Gais, and the Gossau–Appenzell–Wasserauen line. To see more of the territory, you may return to St. Gallen on this same line by way of Herisau.

Although there is no regional rail pass available for eastern Switzerland, the general Swiss Pass (☞ Train Travel *in* Smart Travel Tips A to Z) includes St. Gallen and Schaffhausen city transit as well as overall rail privileges. You cannot enter Liechtenstein by rail; the international express train that passes between Switzerland and Austria doesn't bother to stop. From the train stations at Buchs or Sargans, you can catch a postbus (☞ By Bus, *above*) into Vaduz.

Contacts and Resources

Emergencies

Police (☎ 117). **Ambulance** (☎ 144). **Doctor, dentist, late-night pharmacies** (☎ 111). **Medical assistance** in St. Gallen (☎ 071/2261111).

Guided Tours

WALKING

The **Schaffhausen tourist office** (☞ Visitor Information, *below*) gives guided walking tours with English commentary of the Old Town, the monastery, and the Munot.

Visitor Information

The tourist office for all of eastern Switzerland is based in St. Gallen: **Tourismusverband Ostschweiz** (Tourist Association of Eastern Switzerland; ✉ Bahnhofpl. 1a, CH-9001, ☎ 071/2273737, FAX 071/2273767).

There are small regional visitor information offices throughout eastern Switzerland. **Appenzellerland** (✉ Hauptg. 4, CH-9050 Appenzell, ☎ 071/7889641; ✉ CH-9063 Stein, ☎ 071/3685050). **Schaffhausen** (✉ Fronwagturm 4, CH-8201, ☎ 052/6255141). **Liechtenstein** (✉ Städtle 37, FL-9490 Vaduz, ☎ 075/2321443). **Thurgau** (✉ Gemeindehaus, CH-8580 Amriswil, ☎ 071/4118181) services the Bodensee. **Urnäsch** (✉ Dorf 91, CH-9107, ☎ 071/3641777).

4 GRAUBÜNDEN

Arosa, Davos, St. Moritz

Dominated by its trendy resorts—St. Moritz,
Davos, Klosters, Arosa, Pontresina—
Graubünden is nonetheless Switzerland's
most culturally diverse and largest canton.
German, Italian, and Romansh—the ancient
dialect that is thought to date from 600
BC—are all spoken here, in a land where
stalwart native farmers subsist alongside the
fur-clad jet set.

THOUGH THE NAMES OF ITS RESORTS—St. Moritz, Davos, Klosters, Arosa, Pontresina—register almost automatic recognition, the region wrapped around them remains surprisingly unsung, untouched by the fur-clad poseurs who make stage sets out of its sports centers, aloof to the glamour trends—quirky, resilient, and decidedly apart. Nowhere in Switzerland will you find sharper contrasts than those between the bronze seven-day citizens who jet into St. Moritz and the stalwart native farmers who nurse archaic dialects and gather their crops by hand as their Roman-Etruscan forefathers did.

Updated by
Kara
Misenheimer

Graubünden is the largest canton in Switzerland, covering more than one-sixth of the entire country. As it straddles the continental divide, its rains pour off north into the Rhine and Inn rivers and south into the Italian River Po. The land is thus riddled with bluff-lined valleys, and its southern half basks in crystalline light: except for the Italian-speaking Ticino, it receives the most sunshine in the country. Its 150 valleys are flanked by dense blue-black wilderness and white peaks, among them Piz Buin (3,313 m/10,867 ft) in the north and Piz Bernina (4,050 m/13,284 ft) in the south.

Of all the Swiss cantons, Graubünden is the most culturally diverse. To the north it borders Austria and Liechtenstein, and in the east and south it abuts Italy. Dialects of both German and Italian are widely spoken. But the obscure and ancient language called Romansh (literally, "Roman") is spoken by almost 20% of the population, harking back to the 1st century BC, when the area was a Roman province called Rhaetia Prima. Some say the tongue predates the Romans and trace its roots back as far as 600 BC, when an Etruscan prince named Rhaetus invaded the region.

Though anyone versed in a Latin language can follow Romansh's simpler signs (*camara da vacanza* is vacation apartment; *il büro da pulizia* the police office), it is no easy matter to pick it up by ear. Nor do the Graubündners smooth the way: Rhaetian Romansh is fragmented into five subdialects beyond its codified form, so that people living in any of the isolated valleys of the region might call the same cup a *cuppina,* a *scadiola,* a *scariola,* a *cuppegn,* a *tazza,* or a *cupina.* The name *Graubünden*—Les Grisons (French), I Grigioni (Italian), and Il Grischun (Romansh)—means "gray confederation," referring to the 14th-century rebellion against Hapsburg rule. With these dialects and their derivatives cutting one valley culture neatly off from another, it's no wonder the back roads of the region seem as removed from the modern mainstream as the once-a-century world of Brigadoon.

Pleasures and Pastimes

Dining

In this relatively exotic region of Switzerland, with its myriad dialects and potent blend of Latin and German blood, the cuisine is as novel and unexpected as its culture. Though you hear of little but the ubiquitous *Bündnerfleisch* (air-dried beef pressed into rectangular loaves and shaved into chewy, translucent slices), you will find a much broader range of delights. Italian influence is strong here, but—unlike the Ticinese to the southwest, who borrow from Italy wholesale—the Graubündners have evolved their own versions and incorporate Germanic styles as well. Takeoffs on gnocchi (potato-based pasta) and *Spätzli* (tiny flour dumplings) coexist here, with relatives of *Rösti* (hash brown potatoes) and polenta asserting their own local flavor.

Originating in isolated rural areas, the cuisines of Graubünden are earthy and direct, with sausages, potatoes, cheese, and cabbage as staples and onions, garlic, bacon, and dried fruits providing the hearty flavors. You may feel you've stepped back to the Middle Ages when you sit down to *pizzoccheri neri* (little buckwheat dumplings swimming in garlic) or to *maluns* (grated potatoes stirred in pools of butter until they form crisp balls) served with tart applesauce. *Capuns* or *krutkapuna* are bundles of Swiss chard smothered in butter and cheese and flavored with dried meat, and *hexenpolenta* is a harmless dish of cornmeal mush sweetened with raisins and apples.

In many kitchens, these down-to-earth treats are making a comeback in either traditional or more modern interpretations. On tourist menus, though, you're sure to see token regional specialities—robust *Gerstensuppe* (barley soup), *Engadiner Nusstorte* (a chewy walnut-and-honey cake found in every bake shop), and the inevitable (but wonderful) variety of cold local meats offered as a *Bündnerplatte*.

Watch for the annual winter Gourmet Festival in St. Moritz, when world-renowned chefs serve their specialties in host restaurants and hotels. The Grand Gourmet Finale is a gargantuan feast prepared by 30 chefs on the frozen St. Moritz Lake. For reservations call the St. Moritz tourist office (☞ Visitor Information *in* Graubünden A to Z, *below*).

CATEGORY	COST*
$$$$	over 80 SF
$$$	50 SF–80 SF
$$	20 SF–50 SF
$	under 20 SF

*Prices are per person for a three-course meal (two-course meal in $ category), including sales tax and 15% service charge

Farmhouse Vacations

An unusual alternative to the typical resort experience can be found on more than 70 high- and low-altitude Bündner farms providing apartments or rooms for rent. Most have pastures full of cows and other domestic animals, sell farm products, and offer voluntary participation in daily chores. The booklet "Farm Holidays," available from Graubünden Holidays (☞ Visitor Information *in* Graubünden A to Z, *below*), includes a list of participating families with descriptions of the various scenarios and available activities. Knowing some German is practically a prerequisite, as the host families usually don't speak English.

Lodging

Of all the regions in Switzerland—each trading on its homeyness, its quaintness, its own take on a storybook setting—Graubünden delivers the most, as its hoteliers invest fortunes in preserving Alpine coziness inside and out. Unlike other parts of Switzerland, where hotels radiate warmth and history from their shuttered facades but have interiors as stark as hospital rooms, Graubünden hotels are often softened from within with wood. The source is *Arvenholz*, the prized Alpine pine (*Pinus cembra*), thick with knots and rich in natural color—a color that deepens from buff to burnished toffee over the decades. You'll see this lovely wood in original installations, lovingly preserved, or in new but well-crafted beds, armoires, end tables, and even ceilings. Whether plain or elaborately carved, the effect is welcoming and unmistakably Swiss.

Prices in this popular region are comparatively high—even if you leave exorbitant St. Moritz out of the curve—and they stay that way most of the year. Winter prices are highest, summer's close behind. Take note: hotels publish tariffs in various ways; double-check to see whether you're paying per person or per room, as well as whether you have *demipension* (half-board).

CATEGORY	COST*
$$$$	over 300 SF
$$$	200 SF–300 SF
$$	120 SF–200 SF
$	under 120 SF

Prices are for a standard double room, including breakfast, sales tax, and 15% service charge.

Skiing and Snow Sports

With Davos as the site of the first ski lift in history, St. Moritz as the world's ritziest resort, and a host of other justifiably famous winter wonderlands within its confines, Graubünden easily earns its reputation as the ultimate winter destination. You'll find downhill skiing at all levels, as well as cross-country and off-piste skiing, snowboarding, carving, and a multitude of other winter activities—from curling, skating, and tobogganing to more unusual spectator sports, such as dogsled racing, kite skiing, and ski *joering*, in which participants are pulled on skis by a horse. If it's played summers on green surfaces, it's done here winters on white turf: Silvaplana and other resorts have snow golf, and St. Moritz hosts polo and horse racing on its frozen lake. Convenience is a growing trend at some resorts: the New Technology Centers (☎ 081/9367900) in the Flims/Laax area will equip you with a ski suit, skiing or snowboarding equipment, and a day ski pass, all for a flat fee of about 100 SF.

Trains

The bright red narrow-gauge trains of the Rhätische Bahn were designed with sightseeing in mind. Along with the legendary, panoramic *Glacier Express* from St. Moritz to Zermatt, which takes you up and over the barren backbone of Switzerland near Andermatt, trains throughout the region traverse spectacular glacial terrain, crossing bridges built unbelievably high over mountain gorges, cutting through mountainsides by way of viaducts. Even as the most desolate landscapes pass by, signs of civilization are never far behind: the lofty little villages, serviced by tiny train stations, show once again the Swiss affinity for access and for making the impossible seem routine.

Wines

Graubünden has its own distinctive wines: red pinot noir, white Riesling Silvaner, and pinot gris from the Bündnerherrschaft, the sunny region around Maienfeld, Jenins, and Malans. The unique Veltliner, a hearty red Nebbiolo is actually grown over the border in Valtellina, which was ceded to Italy in 1815 (and was before then known as the Veltlin). The wine has always been brought into Graubünden, where it is aged and bottled as a product that is, at least in spirit, Swiss.

Exploring Graubünden

The region is fairly neatly bisected, by a spine of 2,987-m (9,800-ft) peaks, into two very different sections connected only by the Julier Pass, the Albula Pass, and the Flüela Pass. In the northwest, the region's capital, Chur, is flanked by ancient villages and a few lesser-known ski resorts. Farther east is the wild and craggy Prättigau region, which includes the resorts of Klosters and Davos as well as the Flüela Pass. The other half of the canton is comprised of the famous Engadine region, home to mountain-ringed lakes and sophisticated resorts: Sils-Maria, Pontresina, and St. Moritz—as well as the magnificent Parc Naziunal Svizzer.

Numbers in the text correspond to numbers in the margin and on the Graubünden map.

Great Itineraries

IF YOU HAVE 1 OR 2 DAYS

If you've yet to indulge in some of the world's most varied and exclusive sports, shopping, and nightlife activities—at high altitude and with over-the-top attitude—concentrate on ⊞ **St. Moritz** ⑬. If you're in search of Alpine splendor at a lower-key resort, head to ⊞ **Pontresina** ⑫, with its stately hotels and sweeping views, or to ⊞ **Sils** ⑭, in its inspiring setting of mountain-mirroring lakes.

IF YOU HAVE 3 OR 4 DAYS

Start at the region's capital ⊞ **Chur** ②, then continue to ⊞ **Klosters** ④, where the British royal family vacations. Alternatively, head from Chur to ⊞ **Arosa** ③—set apart by an isolated feel and old-village character.

IF YOU HAVE 5 OR MORE DAYS

From the bases in the three-day itinerary, above, visit the Upper and Lower Engadine valleys. Here, the **Parc Naziunal Svizzer** ⑨ (open June to October only) is a magnificent, federally protected preserve of virtually virgin wilderness. For a day or two of pampering, visit the resort town of ⊞ **Scuol.** If you're traveling by car, detour to visit the pretty village of **Guarda** ⑦ for an afternoon. Heading toward the Upper Engadine you can turn off at Samedan for ⊞ **Pontresina** ⑫ or continue on to **St. Moritz** ⑬ or **Sils** ⑭. Climb the Julier Pass heading north to **Tiefencastel** ⑮ (if you're going that way, you could also leave the region via the San Bernardino Pass towards Lugano).

When to Tour Graubünden

Though the tourism industry breathlessly awaits winter, when Graubünden's resorts fill to capacity, summer is popular as well. Thanks to a score of warm-weather sports such as hiking, cycling, golfing, windsurfing, and even hot-air ballooning, the area is now pleasurably active year round. Avoid November, early December, and May, when most resorts close for preparations and annual renovations. From late September to late October, the weather is typically temperate, with clear skies and the gleaming yellow colors of its golden fall.

HEIDI COUNTRY, CHUR, AND AROSA

Outcropped hills, forlorn-looking castle ruins, and craggy peaks sloping down to sheltered vineyards highlight area's topography—and history—as you enter the canton from Sargans or Vaduz. Though it's the gateway to Graubünden, this region has a catchier claim to fame: It was here that the legendary Heidi enjoyed the fresh air and rustic pleasures of the Alps.

Maienfeld

❶ *17 km (11 mi) north of Chur.*

Above this graceful little village full of fountains, vineyards, and old stucco houses, the Zürich author Johanna Spyri set *Heidi,* the much-loved children's story of an orphan growing up with her grandfather on an isolated Alpine farm. Taken away to accompany the invalid Clara in murky Frankfurt, she languishes until returning to her mountain home. Spyri spent time in Maienfeld and hiked the mountains behind, but it's questionable whether actual people inspired her tale. Nonetheless you can hike from the Heidihof Hotel along the Heidiwanderweg (Heidi hiking path), across steep open meadows and up thick forest switch-

Graubünden

HESAPLANA

AUSTRIA

SWITZERLAND

Madrisahorn

Küblis Saas

U VALLEY   Landquart   Mezzaselva   Albeina

Gotschnagrat

ein   Parsenn
Weissfluhjoch   4 Klosters

Strela   Wolfgang

chatzalp   5 Davos   Jakobshorn
Frauenkirch   Rinerhorn   28   Weisshorn   L. Lavin   Guarda 7

Glaris   Flüelapass   27   Ardez   Tarasp   Vulpera
Susasca   Susch   6   Piz d'Arpiglias

Schwarzhorn   Grialetsch   Piz   Piz
Glacier   Vadret   Nuna

Piz   Zernez
Vadret   8

A L B U L A   Inn   Parc Naziunal Svizzer   9
(Swiss National Park)   28

S-chanf   Zuoz   27

O B E R - E N G A D I N E   Lago del
Gallo

Albulapass

Albula Tunnel   Bever

Samedan   10   Muottas
Muragl   ITALY

Corviglia   Celerina   11   Punt Muragl   Piz
Languard   KEY

Piz   13   ——————— Rail Lines
air   St. Moritz   12   Pontresina   •••••• Cable Car/
Funicular

3   Champferer   Piz   Flaz   Bernina   – – – Regional
See   Rosatsch   Pass   Boundary Lines

Silvaplana   Silvaplaner   🎿 Ski Resorts
See   Diavolezza

Sils   14   Piz   Piz
Corvatsch   Morteratsch   N

ilser   Val Roseg   29
See   Piz   Piz   Piz
Bernina   Tschierva   0   10 miles

Maloja Pass   Piz   0   15 km
Roseg   Piz
Palü

SILVRETTA   GRUPPE

Piz Buin

Scuol

Ftan

Vereina Tunnel

Champferer

Rosatsch

Piz Nuna

backs to what have now been designated **Peter the Goatherd's Hut** and
the **Alm-Uncle's Hut**—and take in awesome Rhine Valley views from
flowered meadows that would have suited Heidi beautifully. The enthusiasm for the story will even result in an entire **Heididorf** (Heidi Village). The Heidi House opened in summer 1999; it's an 1880s homestead
outfitted to the hilt with Heidi-appropriate furnishings. Other sections
of the village will be under construction through 2001. ☎ *081/3023626.*
🖃 *5 SF.* ☉ *Mar.–Nov. 10–5.*

When you've had enough of the high meadows, back in town you can
visit wine merchants or have a meal in the Knight's Hall of **Schloss Bran-
dis,** a Toggenburger castle-tower with its earlier portions dating from
the 10th century. ☎ *081/3022423. Closed Mon.–Tues.*

Chur

❷ *17 km (11 mi) south of Maienfeld.*

Now the region's capital and a small city of 33,000 with a bustling
downtown and a busy rail crossroads, Chur is actually the oldest con-
tinuously settled site in Switzerland; there are traces of habitation
from as far back as 3000 BC–2500 BC. The Romans founded Curia Rae-
torium on the rocky terrace south of the river; from here, they protected the Alpine routes that led to the Bodensee. By AD 284 it served
as the capital of the flourishing Roman colony Rhaetia Prima. Its heyday, however, evident throughout the Old Town even now, was during the Middle Ages, when it was ruled by bishops and bishop-princes.
Narrow streets, cobblestone alleys, hidden courtyards, and ancient shuttered buildings abound; the city's symbolic citadel is the massive 12th-
century Kathedrale St. Maria Himmelfahrt.

The **Rathaus** (Town Hall), a landmark of the Old Town, was built as
two structures in 1464 and connected in 1540. Its striking deep roof,
topped with a lantern tower, follows the odd form of the joined buildings—one end is narrower than the other. (The steep roof is hard to
see from street. Go to the opposite side for a better look.) Inside, the
Grosser Ratsaal (Large Council Chamber) has a timber ceiling dating
from 1493 and an 18th-century ceramic stove. The **Bürgerratskammer**
(Citizens' Council Chamber) has Renaissance wall panels and another
ceramic stove, this one from 1632. Embedded in the wall beside the
door opening onto Reichsgasse there's a rod of iron about a foot
long—the standard measure of a foot or shoe before the metric system
was introduced. Although the hall is generally closed to the public (it's
still used by the city), you can contact the tourist office (☞ Graubünden A to Z, *below*) to arrange a visit. ⊠ *Old Town, Untertor.*

Though its unremarkable facade doesn't attract much notice, the early
18th-century **Altes Gebäude** (literally, Old Building) mansion was built
for a Chur statesman who was one of the most important leaders in
Graubünden at the time. This is also the site where Jürg Jenatsch, a
17th-century Graubünden dictator, was assassinated. ⊠ *Poststr. 14,
Old Town.*

The slender, spired **Kirche St. Martin** (St. Martin's Church) was built
in 1491 in the late-Gothic style after a fire destroyed the 8th-century
original. Since 1526, it has been a Protestant church. On your right as
you enter are three stained-glass windows created in 1919 by Augusto
Giocometti, the father of the Graubünden sculptor Alberto Giacometti.
The steeple dates from 1917; with permission from the sacristan, you
can climb to the top to see the bells. ⊠ *Evangel. Kirchgemeinde,
Kirchg. 12,* ☎ *081/2522292.*

The **Rätisches Museum** (Rhaetic Museum) is housed in the 1675 mansion of the von Buol family. Its collection includes not only furnishings and goods from the period, but also archaeological finds from the region, both Roman and prehistoric. It's a thorough, evocative overview of the canton's development. ⊠ *Hofstr. 1,* ☎ *081/2572889.* 🎫 *5 SF.* ⊙ *Tues.–Sun. 10–noon and 2–5.*

The **Oberer Spaniöl,** another luxurious mansion from the 1640s, stands across from the Rhaetic Museum (☞ *above*). There's a beautiful coat of arms signifying the owner's alliance with a Chur burgomaster. ⊠ *Kirchg. 16. Closed to the public.*

The stone archway under the **Hof-Torturm** (Court Gate Tower) leads into the residence of the strong bishop-princes of Chur, once hosts to Holy Roman emperors who passed through on their way between Italy and Germany—sometimes with whole armies in tow. The bishops were repaid for their hospitality by imperial donations to the people. The thick fortifications of the residence demonstrate the disputed powers of the bishops; by the 15th century, irate inhabitants who rebelled again and again were rebuffed and punished with excommunication. By 1526 the Reformation broke the domination of the Church—although the city remains a Catholic bishopric today. The Hofkellerei restaurant is now at the site. ⊠ *Hof 1.*

The centerpiece of Chur is the **Kathedrale St. Maria Himmelfahrt** (Cathedral of the Assumption), built between 1151 and 1272 in a mix of styles that spanned the century and drew on influences from across Europe. The capitals of the columns are worked in a distinctly Romanesque style, carved with fantastical, evil beasts; at their bases are clustered less threatening animals, many recognizable from the region—including sheep and the humble mountain marmot. In the choir, a magnificent three-side altar, elaborately carved in gilded wood, dates from the 15th century. The structure built on this site in prehistoric times was supplanted by a Roman castle, a bishop's house in 451, and a Carolingian cathedral during the 8th century. The marble panels under the altars of St. Laurentius and St. Fidelis have been preserved from this earliest church. ⊠ *Hof.* ☎ *081/2529250.* ⊙ *Daily 8–7.*

Obere Gasse, once the main street through Chur and a major route between Germany and Italy, is now lined with small shops, cafés, and an open-air theater that draws local crowds. At the end stands the 16th-century **Obertor** (Upper Gate), guarding the bridge across the Plessur River. ⊠ *Old Town, between the Obertor and Arcaspl.*

At the **Kutschensammlung** (Coach Museum), a collection of turn-of-the-century carriages and sleighs, buffed to a picture-book high sheen, harkens back to the era of romance. One 1880 sleigh has a fur blanket and jingle bells straight out of Hans Christian Andersen's *The Ice Queen.* ⊠ *Hotel Stern, Reichg. 11,* ☎ *081/2523555.* 🎫 *Free.* ⊙ *Daily by appointment.*

Dining and Lodging

$–$$ ✕ **Controversa.** With a sleek, modern look to match its forward-looking menu—at last, a salad bar with everything from lamb's lettuce to beets—this lively, young restaurant offers a dose of nontradition in a very traditional town. In addition to salads, options range from superb carpaccio to such daring pasta dishes as tagliatelle with sliced chicken, mango, and hot curry sauce. Patrons frequent the bar into the wee hours. ⊠ *Steinbruchstr. 2,* ☎ *081/2529944. AE, DC, MC, V.*

$–$$$ ✕🏨 **Stern.** This is a rare find: a historic inn in the hub of a city with ★ a restaurant that serves authentic regional cooking—moderately priced. Built in 1677, this Romantik hotel has modern, wood-warmed rooms, a fireplace lounge, and a lovely restaurant wrapped in seasoned Arvenholz. Unusual dishes range from *Kalbsleber dolce brusco* (breaded liver in sweet red wine sauce with raisin polenta and dried fruit compote) to air-dried beef with dried apples and pears; all are served with anise bread and local wine by waitresses in folk costume. ⊠ *Reichg. 11, CH-7000,* ☎ *081/2523555,* 𝔽𝔸𝕏 *081/2521915. 58 rooms. Restaurant, Stübli. AE, DC, MC, V.*

$ ✕⌂ **Zunfthaus zur Rebleuten.** This atmospheric wooden house in the middle of Old Town was the meeting place of wine producers back in 1483. Wine and regional specialties—particularly lamb dishes and the mean cheese fondue—are the draw. There are a dozen affordable, no-frills rooms. The restaurant's closed on Sunday and Monday. ⊠ *Pfisterpl. 1, CH-7000,* ☎ *081/2571357,* 𝔽𝔸𝕏 *081/2571358. 12 rooms. AE, DC, MC, V.*

$$–$$$ ⌂ **ABC Terminus.** This business hotel is just yards from the train station. Despite its sterile appearance—the exterior a corporate metal-and-glass box—the amenities and rooms are state-of-the-art. Be sure to request a room that does not face the tracks. ⊠ *Bahnhofpl., CH-7000,* ☎ *081/2526033,* 𝔽𝔸𝕏 *081/2525524. 31 rooms. Sauna. AE, DC, MC, V.*

Nightlife
The futuristic **Giger Bar** (⊠ Comercialstr. 23, ☎ 081/2537506) is as close as you'll come to the flight deck of the *Starship Enterprise.* The strange space was created by 1980 visual effects Oscar winner H. R. Giger, a Chur native who designed the sets for the film *Alien.*

Outdoor Activities and Sports
Chur has an indoor **swimming pool** (⊠ Sportanlagen Obere Au, ☎ 081/2544288) for the aquatically inclined.

Arosa
★ ❸ *29 km (18 mi) east of Chur.*

Although idyllic, high-altitude Arosa is one of the best-known and most popular of Graubünden's winter and summer sports centers, its modest size, isolation, and natural beauty set it apart. There is none of the rush of Davos or the pretension of St. Moritz: this is a friendly, family-oriented spot staffed by upbeat, down-to-earth people. There are a few grand hotels with social ambitions, but their guests seem to keep a lid on it: Even the most well-heeled rarely dress for dinner.

The village lies at the end of a spectacular, winding 30-km (19-mi) road that cuts through a steep-walled valley and climbs through tiny steepled towns on grades of more than 12%. The town is concentrated into two sections: at the end of the valley (Inner-Arosa) and around the lake and train station (Ausser-Arosa). The road empties into a sheltered, sunny mountain basin at the end of the Schanfigg, the valley source of the Plessur, a basin surrounded by white peaks and centered on two broad, accessible lakes. Cars should be left in the lakeside lots when possible, as a convenient free bus shuttles through the town, and traffic is forbidden between midnight and 6 AM.

Although the town has a slick, busy commercial center, it's strung along a narrow shelf with broad southern views, and within moments you can melt into the wilderness here on good mountain trails—they're even impeccably groomed for winter wandering. There are four skating rinks—one indoors—and the skiing at all levels of difficulty is among the best in Switzerland. The altitude ensures good snow, and pistes lead directly down into the village.

From Arosa, you can take a cable car up to the Weisshorn (2,653 m/8,700 ft) for views over resorts, lakes, and a sweep of peaks. Gondola cars take you from Arosa to Hörnli (2,513 m/8,701 ft) for similar views from a different perspective.

Skiing

Open to ski tourism since 1877, Arosa is remote and humble in comparison to the worldly resorts of Gstaad and St. Moritz. Closely screened in by mountains, the 5,900-ft-high resort is family oriented, with runs suitable for every level of skier. Arosa's 16 lifts have an hourly capacity of 21,000 people and cover 70 km (43 mi) of trails. Its facilities don't match those of Davos, the not-too-distant neighbor that an unbreachable rock barrier renders light years away, but they are sufficient for the guests that the resort welcomes in high season, mostly at the end of December, February, and Easter. With the exception of one heavily trafficked strategic run, Arosa does not have snowmaking; nevertheless, it has often been possible to ski throughout an entire season despite poor snowfall. A one-day lift ticket costs 49 SF; a six-day pass costs 228 SF.

Beginners and children can enjoy the sunny and gentle slopes of **Pratschli.** Maniacs who want a battering will find on **Weisshorn** (2,654 m/8,700 ft) the black piste of their dreams. Most of the runs, however, are intermediate—even those of the **Hörnli** (2,460 m/8,200 ft), served by a cable car. These slopes are so broad and clear that moonlight and torchlight skiing is organized regularly, generally following fondue or raclette and wine in a restaurant high on the mountain—to the tunes of a *Ländlerkapelle,* a musical ensemble typical of German Switzerland. More than 150 instructors are staffed out of Arosa's official **Swiss Ski School** (☎ 081/3771150).

Dining and Lodging

$$$$ ✕ **Zum Wohl! Sein.** Eighteen hundred different wines await in the cellar of this restaurant, and chef Beat Caduff can recommend and retrieve a bottle in mere minutes. He's also a mastermind of modern Swiss-European cuisine with a traditional twist—somewhat fanatical in finding the freshest ingredients and insisting on serving seven-course meals only. His specialties include *Wildessenz,* a precious quantity of steaming bouillon obtained by simmering pounds of vegetables, choice meats, and plenty of red wine for hours. Reserve a week in advance and prepare to stay several hours—it's an eating event. ⊠ *Hohe Promenade, in Hotel Anita,* ☎ *081/3771109. Reservations essential. AE, DC, MC, V. Closed Mon. No lunch.*

$$ ✕ **Grischuna.** Although most of the best food can be found in hotels in this accommodating resort, the Grischuna merits a stop for its comfortable ambience and regional decor—wood, ceramics, farm tools, game trophies. Its simple menu includes local cold meat and cheese dishes, as well as trout and horse steak. ⊠ *Poststr.,* ☎ *081/3771701. No credit cards.*

$$ ✕🏠 **Arve Central.** Although it's set back slightly from the main street, this hotel lives up to its name, with neither the elevation nor the isolation of its competitors. Yet it's solid and slickly done, with pristine stucco and knotty pine, and good views on the south side. (The back rooms have neither balcony nor view.) The restaurant, all richly detailed knotty pine, offers some of the best food in town: the changing menu updates French classics, with a focus on fish and game prepared with herbs. ⊠ *Off Poststr., CH-7050,* ☎ *081/3770252,* 𝖥𝖠𝖷 *081/3774271. 48 rooms. 2 restaurants, bar, hot tub, sauna. AE, DC, MC, V.*

$$ ✕🏠 **Hold.** This busy, happy, family place—full of books and toys and
★ hikers—is just across the road from the luxurious Kulm and sits literally at the foot of the slopes. The rooms are simple and bright, with

blond wood; the back rooms are larger, with big tile baths. The restaurant serves skiers'-appetite standards—fried fish, entrecôtes, and fondues. Keen supporters of folk culture, the owners host Alphorn and yodeling weeks on the premises during Arosa's summer music festival. Even beginners can enroll. ⊠ *Poststr., CH-7050 Inner-Arosa,* ☎ *081/3771408,* 🖷 *081/3774927. 18 rooms. Restaurant, café. AE, DC, MC, V.*

$$$$ 🏨 **Kulm.** For a luxury hotel with roots in 1882, this hotel's look is re-
★ freshingly young and sporty, with various decor influences that mingle to an almost confusing degree. You wonder: is this Vail? Santa Fe? Mykonos? Oslo? There are miles of curving stucco and glass, heavy beams and high-tech fixtures, chintz and primitive prints. The wraparound windows take in acres of green hills or snowy slopes. Indeed, the hotel's position is its biggest draw, as it stands on the farthest edge of town at the base of the slopes: You can ski home at the end of the day. ⊠ *Poststr., CH-7050 Inner-Arosa,* ☎ *081/3778888,* 🖷 *081/3778889. 137 rooms. 3 restaurants, 2 cafés, tennis court, bowling, health club, dance club, baby-sitting. AE, DC, MC, V.*

$$$$ 🏨 **Waldhotel National.** First a health retreat, then a military hospital, this member of the Relais du Silence group became a hotel in 1965 and is consistently upgraded and refined. Northern rooms look over the forest and southern ones have the spectacular Arosa view; all are done in shades of rose and blue, with those in the Arven wing glowing with golden Swiss pine. Above the town and set in its own expansive, wooded park, it offers a peaceful retreat. The Kachelofastübli is a local favorite and an alternative to the formal dining room. Rates are demipension only. ⊠ *Prätschlistr., CH-7050 Ausser-Arosa,* ☎ *081/ 3771351,* 🖷 *081/3773210. 94 rooms. Restaurant, bar, indoor pool, massage, sauna. AE, DC, MC, V. Closed mid-Sept.–early Dec. and late Apr.–mid-June.*

$$ 🏨 **Alpina.** This hotel just above the main street, with views over the Untersee and the mountains, strikes an appealing balance between old and new. Built in 1908, it also has a more modern wing added in 1983, which has rustic furnishings, farm implements, and kitchen-equipped apartment units. The rooms in the higher, original building combine dark wood with newer Euro-style furnishings and superior views. The common rooms are comfortable, the dining areas bright and spacious, and the friendly management eager to please. ⊠ *Off Poststr., CH-7050,* ☎ *081/3771658,* 🖷 *081/3773752. 35 rooms. Restaurant, bar, café, Stübli, sauna. AE, DC, MC, V. Closed mid-Oct.–mid-Dec. and mid-Apr.–mid-June.*

$$ 🏨 **Panorama Raetia.** Among the bank of hotels on the shelf over the main street, the Raetia has the broadest sweep of view from both its original wing, which dates from the 1890s, and its new wing, built during the 1950s. As if they knew they couldn't top the beauty of its Bündnerstübli, with its original Arvenholz aged to burnished gold, its owners have left the newer portions untouched; try to look at the '70s-style avocado-and-shocking-orange decor in a retro light. ⊠ *Poststr., CH-7050 Ausser-Arosa,* ☎ *081/3770241,* 🖷 *081/3772279. 40 rooms. Restaurant, Stübli. AE, DC, MC, V.*

$–$$ 🏨 **Sonnenhalde.** The automatic Arvenholz door that welcomes you to
★ this chaletlike *garni* (without a restaurant) hotel is your first sign of its happy marriage of charm and modern comfort. There are no tired furnishings here—rooms are bright and large, with wall-to-wall wood and tasteful, minimalist decor. Admire the hand-detailed wooden armoires as you head down the hall to the steam bath, or come back from the ski lifts just behind the house. With rooms that easily accommodate extra beds (for an additional fee), this good-value gem surpasses the standards within its class and some of the those in the category above.

✉ *Sonnenbergstr. and Poststr., CH-7050 Inner-Arosa,* ☎ *081/3771531,* FAX *081/3774455. 23 rooms. Sauna, steam room. No credit cards.*

Nightlife and the Arts

To find out what's happening in Arosa, check the *Wochenbulletin,* published (partially in English) every two weeks.

BARS

The Casino's **Espresso Bar** (☎ 081/3773940) is a trendy *Treffpunkt* (meeting point). There's a popular piano bar at **Hotel Carmenna** (☎ 081/3771766).

CASINOS

Arosa's **Kursaal** (Casino; ✉ Poststr., ☎ 081/3775051) has a roulette wheel with the usual 5 SF gambling limit—but the casino's 75 slot machines, set up after their ban was withdrawn in 1994, are its prized novelty.

DANCING

For dancing and discos, **Gada** (☎ 081/3771766) has a Wild West theme and live music. The **Kitchen Club** (✉ Hotel Eden, ☎ 081/3787106) is a disco inside an original 1907 kitchen, where a young crowd dances among old pots and pans while the DJ perches above antique aluminum refrigerators. The après-ski crowd here is decidedly city chic—you should change out of your ski bibs first. **Nuts** (☎ 081/3773940) is open until 3 AM. The tiny **Tschuetta Dancing-Bar** (☎ 081/3771949) manages to squeeze a live band in front of a '70s-style, rainbow-color backdrop.

MUSIC

There are **organ concerts** in Arosa's mountain chapel from Christmas through mid-April, Tuesday at 5.

Outdoor Activities and Sports

CROSS-COUNTRY AND SNOWSHOEING

Langlaufschule Geeser (☎ 081/3775152) gives lessons and leads excursions. If you opt for snowshoeing, the rental equipment is included with your excursion fee.

HIKING

The tourist office offers an unusual hiking package—it will not only book your hotel ahead of time, but it will also deliver your luggage to your destination so you're free of heavy bags on your trip (☞ Hiking *in Davos, below;* Guided Tours *in Graubünden A to Z, below*).

HORSEBACK RIDING

Call **L. Messner** (☎ 081/3774196), which leads guided horseback tours. It also has horse-drawn carriage rides in summer and sleigh rides in winter.

PARAGLIDING

Contact **Flying School Arosa** (☎ 079/4361788).

SKATING

Arosa has no fewer than four skating rinks: the indoor **Eissporthalle** (☎ 081/3771745), **Offene Kunsteisbahn Obersee** (☎ 081/3771745), **Natureisbahn Hof Maran** (☎ 081/3770185), and **Natureisbahn Inner-Arosa** (☎ 081/3772930); the last three are outdoors.

SWIMMING

There's a free bathing **beach** on the Untersee.

TENNIS

There are three public courts at the **Hof Maran** (☎ 081/3770185).

PRÄTTIGAU

The name means "meadow valley," and it's just that—a lush landscape of alternating orchards, pastures, and pine-covered mountains. Here are the renowned ski resorts of Davos and Klosters, which attract skiers from all over the world. The predominant language is German, though most towns still have Romansh names that date from ancient times.

Klosters

❹ *26 km (19 mi) southeast of Landquart.*

Once a group of hamlets, Klosters has become a small but chic resort town, framed between striking peaks. There's an aesthetic scattering of weathered-wood and white-stucco chalets and a clock-tower church, the only remnant of the medieval monastery that gave the town its name. Klosters is famed for its skiing—British royal family members are faithful visitors—and makes the most of its access to the slopes of the Parsenn, which afford some of the finest skiing anywhere.

The starting point for the best of the Klosters-Parsenn runs is the **Weissfluhjoch,** reached by a cable-car ride from town to the Gotschnagrat, a short ski run, and then a second cable car. The run back to Klosters, almost 10 km (6 mi), drops around 1,495 m (4,900 ft). The variety of runs from the Weissfluhjoch and the Gotschnagrat is almost unlimited, but the best-known are those that lead north all the way to Küblis or south to **Wolfgang.** The **Madrisa** slopes, reached by the Albeina gondolas, are popular with both skiers and sunbathers.

A brief outing to the folk museum **Nutli-Hüschi** will illustrate how far this resort has evolved from its mountain roots: a pretty wood-and-stone chalet, built in 1565, has been restored and fitted with the spare furnishings of its day, including kitchen tools and a children's bed that lengthens as the child grows. ⊠ *Monbielerstr. at Talstr.,* ☎ *081/4102020.* ☜ *3 SF.* ☉ *Jan.–mid-Apr. and end of June–mid Oct., Wed. and Fri. 4–6.*

Skiing

Along with its twin resort Davos (☞ *below*), Klosters is known for its vast range of trails and facilities, with their hundreds of kilometers of downhill runs divided nearly equally among easy, moderate, and difficult pistes. More rural than Davos, Klosters is favored by the British royal family for its access to 315 km (196 mi) of maintained runs and 55 lifts in a half-dozen ski areas. **Küblis,** a red (moderately difficult) run leads toward the town of Landquart, and you can return to Klosters or Davos on a short train ride, free with your ski pass. **Wolfgang** is a very difficult descent that takes you over near Davos's lake. The sunny **Madrisa** slopes, on the other hand, are quite easy; you'll see lots of parents teaching their children to ski. There's a snowboard park here as well. For instruction, contact Kloster's branch of the **Swiss Ski School** (☎ 081/4102028). Lift tickets to the combined Davos/Klosters areas cost 52 SF for one day, 223 SF for six days.

Dining and Lodging

$$$ ✕ **Alte Post.** In this warm, woody, local favorite, pleasantly cluttered with ceramics and game trophies, choose from a straightforward menu thick with game and salmon. There are token French classics and a few Swiss standards, but the old-style dishes are a forte: rabbit in thyme, *tête de veau* (veal head) vinaigrette, beef with marsala and risotto, and lots of trout and lamb. If you like salmon, go for the *Lachsmenu* (prix-fixe salmon menu), with salmon in every dish but the sorbet. The restaurant is slightly apart from the town center but worth the trip.

⊠ *Doggilochstr. 136, Klosters-Aeuja,* ☎ *081/4221716. DC, MC, V. Closed Mon. and Tues. and mid-Apr.–early June.*

$$ ✕ **Höhwald.** This is a friendly, touristy restaurant up the hill from Klosters in Monbiel, with a large, open terrace that takes in valley and mountain views. There are hearty soups, cheese specialties (such as *Chäsgatschäder,* bread soaked in milk with grated cheese, all fried like a big pancake), Bündner meats, and a local mix of Italian and country cooking, stressing game. The fruit tarts are fresh and homemade. ⊠ *Monbiel,* ☎ *081/4223045. AE, MC, V. Closed early Apr.–late May.*

$$ ✕ **Wynegg.** The English—including a few crowned heads—come here
★ to drink pints après-ski, eat enormous platters of local cold meats, and enjoy the cozy, slightly kitschy surroundings, with all the checkered tablecloths and cuckoo clocks. ⊠ *Landstr. 205,* ☎ *081/4221340. AE, MC, V. Closed mid-Apr.–mid-Dec.*

$$$ ✕⌂ **Walserhof.** Of the high-end hotels in Klosters, this is the most so-
★ phisticated, having struck a smart balance between old and new. It was built in 1981 with the weathered materials from an old farmhouse. Its restaurant and café are paneled with ancient carved wood; stone, stucco, and quarry tile are used elsewhere. The only drawback is its location, on the main road through town; the best views take in either the street or fairly well-developed fields behind. The superb restaurant pairs international and regional dishes; local specialties could include trout in cider, cabbage dumplings with wild mushrooms, game terrines, or lamb stew with polenta. ⊠ *Landstr. 141, CH-7250,* ☎ *081/4102929,* 𝗙𝗔𝗫 *081/4102939. 10 rooms, 3 suites. Restaurant, Stübli. AE, DC, MC, V. Closed mid-Apr.–mid-June.*

$$$-$$$$ ⌂ **Chesa Grischuna.** Although it's directly in the town center at the crossroads, this creaky 1890 mountain farmhouse qualifies as a country inn—as well as one of the most popular places to stay. Every room is full of old carved wood, and some have balconies to take in the sun. There are antiques and regional knickknacks throughout, and plenty of public spaces, as this is a sociable place: whether you bowl in the vaulted cave, play cards, or dance to the piano music at happy hour, you'll be surrounded by Klosters regulars. Prices are high for the limited facilities (no elevator, a couple of rooms without bath), but you pay for the coveted social mix. ⊠ *Bahnhofstr. 12, CH-7250,* ☎ *081/ 4222222,* 𝗙𝗔𝗫 *081/4222225. 25 rooms, 23 with bath. Restaurant, bar, bowling. AE, MC, V. Closed late May–early July.*

$$-$$$ ⌂ **Albeina.** This large and luxurious chalet-style resort complex lies in the lower valley of Klosters-Dorf, with easy access to skiing—but it provides its own activities regardless of season or weather. Rooms are tastefully decorated, with duvets and floral detail. The popular Dörfyi Bar draws regulars, sometimes royals. ⊠ *CH-7252 Iltisweg,* ☎ *081/ 4232100,* 𝗙𝗔𝗫 *081/4232121. 80 rooms. Restaurant, bar, indoor pool, 2 tennis courts, boccie, Ping-Pong, playground. AE, DC, MC, V. Closed mid-Apr.–mid-June.*

$$ ⌂ **Rätia.** Set in Klosters-Dorf, in the broad, quiet valley west of the
★ center, this Relais du Silence hotel lives up to the group's name. It's a classic vacation lodge, with logs in the fireplace, a beam-timber dining hall, and balconies facing up toward the slopes. In summer, you can have tea on the broad porch under hanging geraniums; in winter, a schnapps by the fire after skiing to the doorstep from the Gotschnagrat. As a farmhouse, it started taking in guests and expanded to a neighboring home; in the 1970s a new wing was added. Most rooms have natural-tone decor with wood accents; some have tile baths. ⊠ *CH-7252 Gäuggeliweg,* ☎ *081/4224747,* 𝗙𝗔𝗫 *081/4224749. 24 rooms, 20 with bath. Restaurant, bar. AE, DC, MC, V. Closed mid-Apr.–mid-June.*

$$ 🏠 **Silvapina.** This delightful hotel, which enjoys the same valley posi-
★ tion as the Rätia (☞ *above*), places emphasis on family, as the own-
ers have three children of their own and the father was born under the
very roof he now repairs. The weathered-wood Victorian-style chalet
was built in 1931, with a new wing added in 1960. Rooms in the new
wing are spare white with pine touches; older rooms have lovely, bur-
nished wood everywhere. The sitting rooms and dining area are fresh
and tidy. There's even a private tennis court. ✉ *Silvapena-Weg 6, CH-
7252,* ☎ *081/4221468,* FAX *081/4224078. 15 rooms. Restaurant, Stübli,
sauna, tennis court. AE, MC, V. Closed late Apr.–mid-May.*

Nightlife

Revelers dance at **Casa Antica** (☎ 081/4221621), a 300-year-old con-
verted barn, late into the night. It's closed from mid-April to mid-July.
Chesa Bar (☞ Chesa Grischuna, *above*) is a popular after-dinner spot,
with piano music and several intimate bar areas. It's closed from mid-
April to mid-December.

Outdoor Activities and Sports

PARAGLIDING

Grischa Flying School (☎ 081/4222070) will sign you up for introductory
sessions or passenger flights.

SKATING

Kloster's **Sportszentrum** (Doggilochstr. 11, ☎ 081/4102131) offers rinks
for skating, hockey, and curling in season.

SWIMMING

The local municipal heated outdoor **swimming pool** (Doggilochstr., ☎
081/4221524) is open in summer; it's also got a restaurant and table
tennis.

TENNIS

There are seven sand courts (five of which are floodlighted) to reserve
at the **Sportszentrum** (☞ *above*).

TREKKING

Snowshoe treks are led by **Trek Out** (☎ 081/4223800). Information is
also available from the Klosters branch of the **Swiss Ski School** (☞ Ski-
ing, *above*).

Davos

❺ *11 km (7 mi) south of Klosters.*

With a reputation nearly as far-flung as those of St. Moritz and Gstaad,
Davos is one of Switzerland's most esteemed winter resorts—famed
for its ice sports as well as its skiing. At 1,560 m (5,117 ft), this high-
est "city" in Europe is good for cold-weather sports even in the sog-
giest of winters.

Davos lies at the end of the Davos Valley, which runs parallel to the
Upper Engadine though they're separated by the vast Albula chain, at
some points more than 3,000 m (9,840 ft) high. On the opposite side
of the valley stands the Strela chain, dominated by the **Weissfluh.** The
open, sunbathed slopes of the **Strela** range provide magnificent skiing.
The Parsenn funicular railway runs from Davos up to Weissfluhgipfel,
2,844 m (9,328 ft) high, and the upper end of the **Parsenn** run. From
there you can ski down over vast, open snowfields to the town, a drop
of around 1,000 m (3,280 ft). Or, striking off to the northeast, you
come to Davos's neighboring resort: Klosters (☞ *above*). On the op-
posite side of the valley is the Jakobshorn, flanked by the Disma and
Sertig valleys; you have direct access to the well-equipped **Brämabüel-**

Jakobshorn ski area, reached by cable car and lift from Davos-Platz. In addition, there are more than 75 km (47 mi) of prepared cross-country ski trails.

Take note: this is a capital for action-oriented sports enthusiasts and not necessarily for anyone seeking a peaceful, rustic mountain retreat. Davos-Dorf and its twin, Davos-Platz, are strung along the valley in one noisier-than-average urban strip, with traffic, timed parking, department stores, and trendy bars. But except for a few token historic structures, most of Davos consists of awkward concrete-balcony hotels and apartment buildings. In town, the bracing mountain air that drew Davos's first visitors, tuberculosis sufferers taking medical cures, can be offset by the exhaust of city traffic. Yet this Alpine metropolis is surrounded by dramatic mountain passes, green hillsides, and farms punctuated by weathered sheds and outbuildings. And no matter how densely populated and fast-paced the twin towns become, the slopes are still spectacular and the regulars return.

Among the town's few architectural highlights, the late-Gothic **Kirche St. Johann** (Church of St. John the Baptist) stands out by virtue of its windows by Augusto Giacometti. Nearby is the 17th-century **Rathaus** (Town Hall). ⊠ *Rathausstutz 2, Davos-Platz.*

The **Kirchner Museum** houses the world's largest collection of works by Ernst Ludwig Kirchner, the German Expressionist artist who came to Davos in 1917 to cure his failing health and stayed to paint. ⊠ *Promenade 82, Davos-Platz,* ☎ *081/4132202,* ⊡ *7 SF.* ☉ *Tues.–Sun. 2–6.*

Skiing

More urbane than its connecting cousin resort Klosters, Davos (1,560 m/5,116 ft) extends more than 35 km (22 mi) along a relatively sheltered valley floor, the Prättigau, which opens onto a fantastic panorama at higher elevations. Spanning from Laret (1507 m/4,942 ft) to Monstein (1,626 m/5,333 ft), the commune of Davos is Switzerland's second largest and can accommodate some 24,000 visitors on 315 km (196 mi) of runs.

At the southeast end of Davos, the easy west-facing pistes bask in afternoon sun. On the other side of the valley, the steep slopes of the **Parsenn** challenge hordes of experts. Locals and others in the know often prefer to ski on the other side of the valley at **Rinerhorn,** where the slopes, less crowded but nearly as interesting, lead to the hamlet of **Glaris,** 7 km (4½ mi) from the center of Davos. A must for the skilled skier: the descent from **Weissfluhgipfel** (2,844 m/9,330 ft) to **Küblis** (814 m/2,670 ft)—a magnificent 15-km-long (9-mi-long) piste with a vertical drop of 2,000 m (6,560 ft). Lift tickets to the combined Davos/Klosters areas cost up to 52 SF for one day (depending on which areas you choose to ski in), 223 SF for six days. Lessons are given by a branch of the Swiss Ski School (Schneesportschule Davos, ☎ 081/4167171).

Dining and Lodging

$$$$ ✕▥ **Davoserhof.** With lovely Jakobshorn views from its south side;
★ fresh, pretty rooms in taupe, paisley, and pine; and all-white tile baths, this is one of the most welcoming hotels in town—without taking into account its restaurants, which are two of the region's finest. During the World Economic Forum conference that takes place here every February, you'll be hard-pressed to find a table either in the intimate old Davosstübli, with its burnished Arvenholz and ceramic stove, or in the elegant, piney Jenatschstübe. In spring and summer, everyone eats on the broad terrace overlooking the green hills and mountains. Chef Kurt Jaussi, something of a wunderkind, creates such innovative dishes as

salt-encrusted turbot (for two). ⊠ *Berglistutz 2, CH-7270,* ☎ *081/ 4156666,* FAX *081/4156667. 22 rooms. 2 restaurants, bar, dance club. AE, DC, MC, V. Closed mid-Apr.–mid-July.*

$–$$$$ ✕ 🖬 **Hubli's Landhaus.** Though on the busy mountain highway between
★ Davos and Klosters, this country inn is quiet as well as comfortable and attractive with its somewhat modernized rustic decor (scarlet, stucco, dark pine, and wrought iron). But the strong point by far is the food: chef Felix Hubli prepares sophisticated fare (turbot with wild mushrooms and ginger, squab with leeks and truffles) and serves it in two lovely dining rooms: one for visitors, one for demipension guests, who—considering the à la carte prices—are getting a terrific deal. ⊠ *Kantonstr., CH-7265 Davos-Laret,* ☎ *081/4162121,* FAX *081/4163342. 20 rooms, 19 with bath. Restaurant. AE, V. Closed mid-Apr.–early June.*

$$$$ 🖬 **Golfhotel Waldhuus.** Right at the edge of the Davos golf course, with the leisurely *pock-pock* of a tennis game echoing next door, this Relais du Silence property re-creates a suburban country club on the outskirts of an Alpine city. Solid, sunny, and serene, with plenty of pine and stucco to soften its prefab feel, it offers late sun on the terrace, a fireplace in the lobby, and the soothing tunes of a pianist in its bar. The rooms are decorated in country-casual miniature prints and pink linens; public spaces are in pink, lace, and dried flowers. The restaurant serves standards with nouvelle twists such as pike quenelles with squid-ink pasta. ⊠ *Mattastr. 58, CH-7270,* ☎ *081/4168131,* FAX *081/4163939. 47 rooms. Restaurant, bar, indoor pool, sauna, driving range, 2 tennis courts, exercise room. AE, DC, MC, V. Closed early Apr.–late June.*

$$$$ 🖬 **Steigenberger Belvedere.** With its neoclassical stone fireplace and wedding-cake white plaster details, this is a grand hotel in the full sense of the word: it sweeps the length of a hillside with south-facing balconies, and its interiors are lavished with period detail. Rooms range from Arvenholz-rustic to period greens and pastels; many have been outfitted with hardwood floors. It's worth it to pay for superior-class rooms, as rooms with north and end views (and decors) are distinctly inferior. ⊠ *Promenade 89, CH-7270,* ☎ *081/4156000,* FAX *081/ 4156001. 141 rooms. 2 restaurants, bar, café, indoor pool, sauna. AE, DC, MC, V. Closed early Apr.–late May.*

$$$ 🖬 **Ochsen.** Over the past few years, this modest hotel, run by an ambitious young team, has had its rooms redone in pastels and pine. Though it's centrally located, a few upper rooms rise high enough to take in Jakobshorn views. The welcoming dining-breakfast room is wall-to-wall Arvenholz (with Graubünder specialties to match), and the *Stübe* (tavern) is a down-to-earth, local watering hole. ⊠ *Talstr. 10, CH-7270,* ☎ *081/4135222,* FAX *081/4137671. 47 rooms. Restaurant, bar, Stübli. AE, DC, MC, V. Closed early Apr.–early May.*

Nightlife and the Arts

BARS AND CASINO

After 3 AM, hipsters gather for live music and snacks at **EX Bar** (⊠ Promenade 63, ☎ 081/4135645), hopping until 6 AM. **Hotel Europe** (Promenade 63, ☎ 081/4135921) has two popular bars, the chic **Tonic Piano Bar,** serving until 3 AM, and the homey **Cabanna Bar.** In addition, there's a **casino** in the hotel with more than 100 slot machines.

DANCING

At 10:30 PM the Cabanna Bar becomes the **Cabanna Club** (☎ 081/ 4135921), whose techno decor and loud music lure a rowdy crowd. **Pöstli** (⊠ Promenade 42, ☎ 081/4137676) is a winter-only institution with live bands ranging from rock to folk and pop. The **Rotliechtli** (⊠ Davoserhof Hotel; ☞ *above*) has a bar and a dance floor.

Outdoor Activities and Sports

GOLF

Golf Club Arosa (☎ 081/3774242) has a nine-hole course. **Golf Club Vulpera** (☎ 081/8649688) also has nine holes. There's an 18-hole golf course at **Golfplatz Davos** (☎ 081/4165634).

HIKING

Threaded with more than 450 km (280 mi) of marked walks and mountain trails, Davos offers an unusual hiking package. The itinerary, which runs up to seven days, includes walking from Davos to Arosa, and then on to Lenzerheide, with overnights along the way; for more information, contact the tourist office (☞ Visitor Information *in* Graubünden A to Z, *below*).

PARAGLIDING

Delta- und Gleitschirmschule Davos (☎ 081/4136043) gives lessons and offers tandem flights during Davos's summer and winter seasons.

SAILING AND WINDSURFING

Sailing and windsurfing are popular on the Davos lake. To rent boats or take a lesson with a sailing school, call **Segelschule Davosersee** (☎ 081/4161577) or **Hans Heierling** (☎ 081/4165918).

SKATING

Davos has long been reputed as an important ice-sports center, with its enormous **Sportzentrum Eisbahn** (⊠ Talstr. 41, ☎ 081/4153600) speed-skating rink. The Eisstadion maintains one indoor and two outdoor rinks; you might also look into the skating tournament schedule if you'd like to watch a competition.

SPORTS CENTERS

The **Sports & High Altitude Center Davos** (☎ 081/4153600) offers field and ice-sports facilities for amateurs and Olympians alike.

SWIMMING

Davos has an indoor-outdoor swimming **pool** complex (Hallenbad Davos, ⊠ Promenade 90, ☎ 081/4136463). You can also swim from the **Strandbad** (open beach; ☎ 081/4161505) in the Davos lake.

RACQUET SPORTS

Tennis and Squash Center Davos (⊠ Clavadelerstr., ☎ 081/4133131) has four indoor and five outdoor tennis courts, plus two squash and four badminton courts.

En Route The main road from Davos leads into the Engadine by way of the spectacular **Flüelapass** (Flüela Pass). For 16 km (13 mi) you climb southeast over mild grades and modest switchbacks. Dense larch forests give way to pine, then to fir, and finally, above the timberline, to a rocky, desolate waste of boulders and jutting cliffs. Ahead, on the left, are the rocky slopes of the **Weisshorn** (3,086 m/10,119 ft), with the **Schwarzhorn** (3,147 m/10,319 ft) to the right. Toward the summit, even in August, you may drive through snow. You'll pass between two small lakes: the Schottensee and the Schwarzsee. At the summit (2,383 m/7,816 ft), 14 km (9 mi) from Davos, is the **Flüela Hospiz** (☎ 081/4161747), a picturesque wooden chalet with a windmill, where you can get refreshments and a night's lodging at reasonable rates.

The descent from the Flüela Pass into the Romansh region of the Lower Engadine takes you through a narrow valley and across the River Susasca, in sight of the 3,229-m (10,600-ft) Piz Vadret, to the base of the great **Grialetsch**—a spectacular mass of jagged ice and snow. The road winds, following the increasingly torrential river and its deep, rocky gash, down to Susch, where the Susasca flows into the River Inn, or in Romansh, En.

Take note: with the opening of the Vereinalinie and its train service from Klosters to Sagliains (☞ Getting Around by Car *in* Graubünden A to Z, *below*) in November 1999, the Flüela Pass will no longer be cleared for road traffic in winter.

LOWER ENGADINE

Like Dorothy landing in Oz, you may find your sudden arrival in this, the most picturesque and novel of Graubünden's many valleys, something of a shock. You'll hear of people talk of *Schellenursli* (a legendary munchkin of a little boy with a bell), and there's even a sort of Scarecrow—for *Hom Strom* in February the children of Scuol make a figure out of hay to burn the winter away. Festivals and folklore abound, as do dense, fairy-tale forests and quaint village settings. "Allegra!" is the proper greeting on the street, reflecting the Romansh language and Latinate culture that have developed without obstruction here. The Roman roots of the region are also demonstrated in the houses—typically squat stucco bungalows with deep Etruscan-arch doors, thick Mediterranean walls, and sunken windows. Watch for such functional features as built-in wooden benches at front entrances and for the ever-present decorative sgraffiti—the signature of the Engadine. An underlayer of dark gray stucco is whitewashed; then designs, images, and sometimes sayings are scraped into the paint to reveal the undercolor. The Lower Engadine—more enclosed than its upper counterpart—shares the region's dry, crisp "champagne" climate.

Susch

⑥ *27 km (17 mi) east of Davos.*

Susch guards the entrance to the Lower Engadine, guarded itself by the magnificent Piz d'Arpiglias (3,289 m/9,930 ft). Here the River Susasca tumbles into the Inn, and the small town seems to cling to the banks of the roaring, white-water torrent as it heads on its way to the Danube. Though Susch was partially burned in 1925, its houses remain stubbornly traditional in style, and the streets are lined with sgraffitied structures, their windows spilling geraniums, their heavy wooden doors often half ajar to display interiors quirkily furnished with crockery, copper, antiques, and stuffed game.

The two towers of **Kirche St. Jon** (Church of St. John) stand high over the river, one Romanesque, the other—like the body of the church—dating from 1515. During a restoration in 1742, the late-Gothic style of the windows was changed, but in 1933, on the evidence of recently discovered fragments, they were restored to their original form.

Guarda

★ ⑦ *7 km (4 mi) east of Susch.*

Between Susch and the resort towns of Scuol, Vulpera, and Tarasp, a scenic valley passes through several gorges and then emerges into flowered plains and a pleasant chain of hamlets: Lavin, Guarda, Ardez, and Ftan. Each offers a new show of fine sgraffitied homes, but Guarda deserves a leisurely exploration among its steep, patterned-cobble streets. The federal government protects the architecture, and row upon row of the vivid dark-on-white etchings, contrasting sharply with the bright red geraniums lined up on the windowsills, draws pedestrians from one photogenic stop to another. As its name implies,

Guarda ("watch") sits high on a hillside looking out over the valley and the 3,001-m (9,840-ft) peaks to the south.

Lodging

$$$$ ⛆ **Meisser.** This brightly colored lodge lives up to its picturesque setting, with sgraffiti and flower boxes outside, antiques and Arvenholz inside. There are a grand Victorian dining hall with pine wainscoting and parquet and a more casual porch restaurant with spectacular valley views. Some rooms are simple and modern, though you can have a splendid carved-pine room if you pay a little bit more. An adjacent, renovated 17th-century farmhouse has six suites. ⊠ *CH-7545,* ☎ *081/8622132,* ☎ *081/8622480. 21 rooms, 6 suites. Restaurant, playground. AE, DC, MC, V.*

Scuol, Vulpera, and Tarasp

13 km (8 mi) east of Guarda.

Sometimes grouped under the name Bad Scuol-Tarasp-Vulpera, these three towns effectively form a vacation and health resort complex whose waters from some 20 mineral springs have historically been used for liver cures. Beautifully located in the open valley of the Inn, with wooded hillsides backed by mountains—the Silvretta on one side and the Engadiner Dolomites on the other—all three towns have been popular summer resorts, frequented mostly by Swiss and Germans. Today they fill up in winter as well, thanks to the network of gondolas and ski lifts on the unobstructed south-facing slopes of Motta Naluns—and the reputation of its snowboard school, the oldest in Europe.

Scuol, the most urban of the three, has a busy downtown and a small but exemplary *Altstadt* (Old Town) with five functional fountains from which you can taste-test normal tap water against that from a local spring source. For the inside-and-out spa experience, head to the **Bogn Engiadina Scuol,** where the calming blue interior, fantastical aquatic murals, and shifting reflections from backlit pools start relaxing you before your toes even touch the water. Six indoor or outdoor basins range in temperature from 64 to 98.6 degrees; there are also saunas, solariums, and steam rooms. A special Roman-Irish ritual treatment (54 SF; reservations required) alternates between moist and dry heat, massage, and mineral baths. If you prefer to drink the water, at least four mineral-fortified varieties are available. ⊠ *Town center,* ☎ *081/8612000.* ☎ *23 SF.* ☺ *Daily 10–10.*

The other two towns lie on the other side of the river. Vulpera is draped along the valley floor, with large hotels and an old cure house, the Trinkhalle, with its mineral spring. Tarasp stands apart, little more than a cluster of houses scattered over green hillsides.

From Scuol and Vulpera, a bus goes up to the historic **Schloss Tarasp** (Tarasp Castle). It's an impressive castle, a rambling fantasy perched 153 m (500 ft) above the valley floor. The main tower and chapel date from the 11th century, when the castle was the stronghold of the knights of Tarasp. Long a source of discord between the powerful bishop of Chur and the count of Tyrol, it was the seat of the Austrian governors until the early 19th century, when Graubünden joined the Swiss Confederation. Today it's owned by a foundation in association with the Hesse family. You must join a tour to see the interior. The schedule varies quite a bit; call ahead for tour days and times. Catch the bus that runs from the Scuol post office or train station to the Tarasp post office roughly once an hour. From the Tarasp post office, it's about a 10 minute walk. The bus ride itself takes 15 minutes. You could also walk the entire route (about 1½ hours) by taking the yellow-marked path from Scuol over the Punt'Ota bridge. ☎ *081/8649368.* ☉ *Late Dec.–mid-Oct.*

Skiing and Snowboarding

The region's ski area centers around 15 gondolas and lifts going up **Motta Naluns** (near Scuol), at elevations between 1,250 and 2,800 m (4,100 and 9,184 ft). The 80 km (50 mi) of trails include the 12-km (7½-mi)*Traumpiste* (Dream Run), a good run of medium difficulty, with a few tough areas. It's kept open the entire season for descents to the valley. Lift tickets cost 43 SF for one day, 189 SF for six days.

Snowboarding is extremely popular on these broad, sunny slopes. For a primer, try **The School** (☎ 081/8648220) or **Schweizer Schneesportschule Scuol** (☎ 081/8641723). If you're stiff at the end of the day, you could treat yourself to a trip to the Scuol spa (☞ *above*).

Dining and Lodging

$$$ ✕🏨 **Chastè.** Many Swiss hoteliers are proud to claim even a second
★ generation of family ownership; this hidden treasure has spent 500 years under the Pazeller family's care. It started as a farm, then supplied provisions to builders for the Tarasp Castle, which looms on the hill above. It eventually drew overnight guests—and today it's an impeccable, welcoming inn with every comfort. The Pazellers have preserved the bulging, sgraffitied stucco exterior, and behind the magnificently carved wood door, extraordinary effort has been made to match and modernize. Each room varies a bit: a canopy bed here, an antique trunk there, and honey-colored Arvenholz everywhere. Rudolf Pazeller himself is the chef and offers a small but sophisticated menu; his fish dishes, such as the fish terrine, are outstanding. ✉ *CH-7553 Tarasp,* ☎ *081/8641775,* 🖷 *081/8649970. 20 rooms. Restaurant, bar, Stübli, sauna, steam room. No credit cards.*

$$$ 🏨 **Guardaval.** This member of the Romantik chain, built in 1693, preserves its original wing, with its stucco vaulting and heavy beams, but has altered the rest to keep rooms up-to-date. The dining/breakfast room shows off mountain views through two stories of windows, and the public areas are dripping with atmosphere (carved and painted antique furniture, ibex antlers). Rooms have spare decor in white and pine. Because the building is protected by historic preservation laws, a few rooms in the older portion still don't have full baths—but their arched ceilings and ancient wood compensate. ✉ *Doess, CH-7550 Scuol,* ☎ *081/8641321,* 🖷 *081/8649767. 45 rooms. Restaurant, bar, café, sauna, steam room. AE, DC, MC, V.*

$$–$$$ 🏨 **Villa Maria.** This simple hillside retreat above the Trinkhalle has an elite, genteel air, with flowers on the antique furniture and Oriental rugs on the quarry tile. The rooms are homey but fresh, and some have balconies overlooking the forested valley. A little restaurant downstairs has a fireplace and other rustic touches and serves good *cuisine du marché* (menus based on fresh market produce); the chef grows his vegetables out back. ✉ *CH-7552 Vulpera,* ☎ *081/8641138,* 🖷 *081/8649161. 15 rooms. Restaurant, bar, café. No credit cards.*

$$ 🏨 **Engiadina.** This typical Engadine house, with sgraffiti, oriels, vault-
★ ing, and beams, was built during the 16th century in the lower, older section of Scuol. Newer guest rooms are done in beige tones touched with bright reds or blues, while four older units surround you with Arvenholz. Spacious, loftlike apartments can be rented in a second house. The immaculate *ustaria* (simple restaurant) and *Arvenstube* (separate dining room) have a welcoming, country feel, with light wood, blue linens, and cushions in every corner. ✉ *Old Town, near Plaz Foun-*

tain, CH-7550 Scuol, ☎ *081/8641421,* 📠 *081/8641245. 11 rooms, 4 apartments. Restaurant, breakfast room. No credit cards.*

$ 🏨 **Traube.** This fresh, friendly inn reflects the personal touch: the rooms are all wood, the baths are all tile, and the public areas—in parquet and pine, with antiques and a ceramic stove—are pristine. Locals are drawn to the warmth of the pub and the candlelit restaurant, which serves hearty risottos, gratins, and homemade Nusstorte. Although it's in town, there are a garden and a sun terrace with mountain views. ✉ *Stradun, CH-7550 Scuol,* ☎ *081/8641207,* 📠 *081/8648408. 19 rooms. Restaurant, Stübli, sauna. AE, DC, MC, V.*

Outdoor Activities and Sports

ICE SPORTS
Open-air ice rinks for hockey and skating are available in Scuol at **Sportanlage Trü** (☎ 081/8612000). **Eishalle Gurlaina** (☎ 081/8640272) in Scuol has indoor facilities for skating, hockey, and curling.

PARAGLIDING
For paragliding and flyovers (beginners to advanced gliders), call **Hang Loose** (☎ 075/2300705).

RAFTING AND CANOEING
Swissraft (✉ Scuol, ☎ 081/9115250) organizes daily rafting expeditions of varying difficulties on the River Inn from early June to mid-September. **Eurotreck** (✉ Scuol, ☎ 081/4620203) runs canoeing excursions for experienced canoers from early June to mid-September.

TENNIS
Reserve sand courts in Scuol through **Tennis Club Scuol-Tarasp-Vulpera** (☎ 081/8640643); the courts are available from mid-May to mid-October. **Robinsons Club Schweizerhof** (☎ 081/8611700) in Vulpera has two indoor courts and two outdoor sand courts. You can also rent equipment.

Zernez

8 *6 km (4 mi) south of Susch.*

This friendly little crossroads is the last town before the higher valley of the Inn. Here, hordes of serious hikers sporting loden hats, knickers, warm kneesocks, and sturdy boots come to stock up on picnic goods, day packs, and topographical maps before setting off for the Swiss National Park (☞ *below*); it's also a good overnight spot for park visits. (Keep in mind that many places are closed in November and May.)

Dining and Lodging

$–$$ 🏨 **Bär-Post.** After a first life as a post stop in the late 1800s, this has been a family-run hotel since 1905. The common and guest rooms take a cue from the pale yellow, blue-trimmed exterior—they pass on lumberjack plaid (prevalent in this hiker's mecca) in favor of Arvenholz and pastels. All rooms have baths with either tub or shower. The high-ceiling, parquet-floor dining room doubles as a breakfast space. ✉ *CH-7530,* ☎ *081/8515500,* 📠 *081/8515599. 46 rooms. Restaurant, sauna, solarium, pool (summer only). AE, DC, V.*

$ 🏨 **Bettini.** Clean, bright, and local to the bone—this solid old road-
★ house is one of the town's best hotels. Game trophies hang on the knotty pine walls, rustic antiques stand in the hallways, and lovely valley views open from the dining hall, which serves dependable (if predictable) meals. A few back rooms have balconies with the same valley views; two rooms without bathrooms are a real bargain. ✉ *CH-7530,* ☎ *081/8561135,* 📠 *081/8561510. 25 rooms. Restaurant, café. AE, DC, MC, V.*

$ ⊡ **Piz Terza.** This *garni* hotel (one without a restaurant) is completely
★   modern behind its traditional facade; its rooms have slick, plain, built-
in cabinetry and a utilitarian look. Yet the back rooms have balconies
that survey the valley, and each has its own blooming geranium—an
indication of the management's friendly approach to bargain hotel service. The public pool is across the street; the Swiss National Park
house just a block away. ⊠ *CH-7530,* ☎ *081/8561414,* ⨳ *081/
8561415. 20 rooms. No credit cards.*

Parc Naziunal Svizzer

★ ❾   *Entrance 12 km (7 mi) east of Zernez, 18 km (11 mi) southeast of Susch.*

The Swiss National Park is a magnificent federal preserve of virtually
virgin wilderness. Although its 169 square km (105 square mi) cover
only 1% or 2% of the territory of a U.S. or Canadian national park,
it has none of the developments that typically hint of "accessibility"
and "attraction": no campgrounds, no picnic sites, no residents. It also
has few employees: just a handful of staffers run the visitor center, and
the rangers live outside the park. This is genuine wilderness, every leaf
protected from all but nature itself. Dead wood is left to rot, insects
to multiply, and only carefully screened scholars are allowed to perform preapproved experiments. As a result, the park contains large herds
of ibex with long, curving horns; delicate, short-horned chamois; huge
red deer and tiny roe deer; and vast colonies of marmots. They are wild
animals, however, and are not likely to line up for Twinkies by the road:
without binoculars (for rent at the visitor center), you're unlikely to
get a good look.

This is no satisfaction-guaranteed African safari. You may feel more
privileged at the sight of a group of ibex on a distant hill or great herds
of male red deer, their antlers silhouetted above a snowy ridge, than
when snapping close-up pictures of a dozen Yellowstone bison. But if
the big game makes no appearance, rein in your expectations and try
to follow the park's advice: "Appreciate a butterfly or an ant as much
as a herd of chamois."

Other signs, flyers, and brochures reiterate the park's philosophy of
restriction and conservation, adopting an almost scolding tone in five
languages: "Wastepaper and other residues disfigure natural beauty.
Take them with you! Don't pick a single flower! Leave your dog at
home!" The list of prohibitions includes hunting, fishing, camping, pick-
ing berries, taking plants (with or without the roots), grazing cattle,
carrying guns, skiing, making commercial movies, even making loud
noises. Nonetheless, the wildlife gives a wide berth to paths where, on
fine summer days, foot traffic becomes so thick that hikers have to walk
in single file and ask permission to pass.

The trails and settings themselves are magnificent. From small parking lots off the park's only highway (visitors are encouraged to take
postbuses into their starting point), a series of wild, rough, and often
steep trails takes off into the coniferous forests. From Parking 7, the
Il Fuorn–Stabelchod–Val dal Botsch trail marks botanical and natural
phenomena with multilingual signs (some in English) and leads to a
spectacular barren ridge at 2,340 m (7,672 ft); the round-trip takes about
three hours.

Another three-hour route, from picturesque S-chanf (pronounced sss-
chonpf) to Trupchun, takes the Höheweg, or high road, into a deep
glacial valley where ibex and chamois often gather; the return, by a
riverside trail, passes a handy log snack bar—just across the park border and thus permitted. Visitors are restricted to the trails except at

designated resting places, where broad circles are marked for hikers to collapse in and have lunch. The visitor center provides detailed maps and suggested routes, including time estimates; it also has an introductory film, displays on wildlife and geology, and scientific hiking guides. ⊠ *Nationalpark–Haus, CH-7530, Zernez, leaving the village toward Ofenpass,* ☎ *081/8561378.* ▣ *4 SF.* ☉ *June–Oct., Mon. and Wed.– Sun. 8:30–6, Tues. 8:30–10 PM.*

Dining and Lodging

$$
★ ✕▦ **Il Fuorn.** This mountain inn was built in 1894 in the middle of what is now the Swiss National Park, and it is the only commercial property that remains there. It makes an ideal base for hikers tackling more than one route, and it's easily accessible from the park's only highway. There are big pine beams inside, a pretty wooden Stübli, and a choice of either old-style rooms without bath (though there are sinks in the rooms) or pine-and-stucco rooms with bath in the new wing, added in 1980. The plain, meaty Swiss cooking is augmented by a generous salad bar. ⊠ *CH-7530,* ☎ *081/8561226,* ℻ *081/8561801. 32 rooms, 12 with bath. Restaurant, café, Stübli. AE, DC, MC, V.*

Outdoor Activities and Sports

HIKING

The **Swiss National Park** (☎ 081/8561378) charts out a series of spectacular all-day or half-day ventures, for large groups only, into the wilderness preserves, some of them covering steep and rough trails.

En Route   Drive south along the River Inn from the Swiss National Park toward its source, past S-chanf and Zuoz, the first towns of the Upper Engadine and both full of Engadine-style houses. The drive is lovely, a mild but steady climb past snowcapped peaks and the roaring river. You may notice an increase in the number of Jaguars and Mercedeses and the occasional Rolls as you approach St. Moritz.

UPPER ENGADINE

Stretching from St. Moritz to Zernez and with a gate to the vast Parc Naziunal Svizzer (Swiss National Park) at S-chanf, this is one of the country's highest regions—1,800 m (5,904 ft)—and one of its most dazzling. From mountain peaks, such as Piz Bernina and Piz Corvatsch, you can swoosh down world-class slopes or simply take in the dizzying view. **Engadine Concert Weeks** (☎ 081/8426573), Switzerland's international chamber-music festival, involves some 20 world-class concerts between mid-July and late August held in Sils, Silvaplana, St. Moritz, Pontresina, Celerina, Samedan, La Punt, Zuoz, and S-chanf.

Samedan

🔟   *27 km (17 mi) south of Zernez, 33 km (20 mi) southeast of Susch.*

This small, cozy (if less prestigious) resort near St. Moritz has an impressive 18-hole golf course (the highest in Europe), is nearest to the Upper Engadine's airport, and offers magnificent views of the awe-inspiring Bernina chain to the south: **Piz Bernina** (4,057 m/13,300 ft), **Piz Palü** and **Piz Roseg** (3,932 m/12,900 ft), **Piz Morteratsch** (3,752 m/12,300 ft), **Piz Tschierva** (3,569 m/11,700 ft), **Piz Corvatsch** (3,447 m/11,300 ft), and **Piz Rosatsch** (3,111 m/10,200 ft). An intricate network of funiculars, cableways, and lifts carries the surrounding resorts' visitors up to overlooks, cafés, hiking trails, and ski pistes that offer an infinite combination of views of these peaks.

Celerina

⑪ *2 km (1 mi) south of Samedan, 3 km (1¾ mi) northeast of St. Moritz.*

Though in the shadow of St. Moritz, Celerina (Schlarigna in Romansh) still sits in the sunny spotlight as a first-rate ski resort in its own right, with easy access to the facilities of its glamorous neighbor. An attractive cluster of Engadine houses characterizes its oldest neighborhood. Its most striking landmark is the 15th-century church of **San Gian** (St. John), which has a richly painted wooden ceiling. ☉ *Mid-Dec.–mid-Apr., Mon. and Wed. 2–4, Fri. 10:30–noon.*

En Route   Between Celerina and Pontresina, in the direction of the Bernina Pass, you'll find **Punt Muragl,** the base of the funicular up to the summit of **Muottas Muragl.** A 15-minute ride takes you to an altitude of 2,456 m (8,055 ft), 702 m (2,300 ft) above the valley floor. From the top you get an eagle's-eye view of St. Moritz, the nearby watershed of **Piz Lunghin,** and the chain of lakes that stretches almost 16 km (10 mi) toward Maloja. In winter you can panorama-sled back down on a rather adventuresome, curvy 4.2-km (2.6-mi) course through open fields and forests; it's BYO sled, or you can rent one at the top.

Pontresina

⑫ *4 km (2 mi) south of Celerina, 6 km (4 mi) east of St. Moritz.*

Lying on a south-facing elevated shelf along the Bernina Valley, Pontresina is an exceptionally picturesque resort. From here you can see clear across to the Roseg Valley, once filled with the Roseg Glacier. The glacier has retreated now to the base of Piz Roseg itself. To the left and southeast, the Flaz River winds through the mountain-framed valley from its source, the Morteratsch Glacier, which oozes down from Piz Bernina. The altitude of Pontresina (1,830 m/6,000 ft) ensures wintry weather, and its access to skiing on the slopes of Diavolezza (2,974 m/9,751 ft) is convenient (☞ Skiing *in* St. Moritz, *below*). It is also a superb base for hiking and biking, either to the glaciers or into the heights around them, for fine overviews—and for mountaineering as well. There are concerts presented here summer mornings in the shaggy-pine Tais Woods, and you can take a horse-drawn carriage up the Val Roseg anytime. Though the main streets are built up with restaurants, shops, and services, the dazzling resort still has the feel of a balanced vacation retreat. In the off seasons, generally between Easter and mid-June and mid-October through Christmas, many hotels are closed.

Dining and Lodging

$$–$$$ ✕ **Berghotel Muottas Muragl.** Many say this high-altitude dining ex-
★   perience is not to be missed. Turn off the road to the funicular station—the restaurant's another 8,055 ft up. If you've arrived before sunset and reserved a window table, you'll see the entire chain of shimmering Upper Engadine lakes. A local wine makes a good toast; then sample regional specialties such as pizzoccheri neri or capuns. By the time you're sipping espresso, the sun will be slipping into the perfect V formed by the Maloja Pass. The funicular fare up from the valley is around 15 SF round trip. ⊠ *Off the highway by Punt Muragl, between Samedan and Pontresina,* ☎ *081/8428232. AE, DC, MC, V.*

$ ✕ **Café Puntschellas.** Either way you look here you can't go wrong:
★   you'll face either the Roseg Valley or the spread of fresh-made pastries. The menu can satisfy all kinds of cravings, from bowls of breakfast muesli to hearty dinner Spätzli and risottos served in ceramic crocks. Locals know to ask for the beignet-like *quarkinis* with vanilla sauce—as well as a seat on the terrace. ⊠ *Via Mulin,* ☎ *081/8388030. MC, V.*

$$$$ ✕⊡ **Kronenhof.** Started on this scenic site as a coach stop for post horses
★ running Veltliner wine over the Bernina Pass and developed in three
graceful wings, this grandest of luxury structures was completed in 1898,
and very little has been changed. If the views from the lobby bay don't
dazzle you, the baroque splendor of the decor will, as the ceilings—
already thick with elaborate moldings—are gilded and frescoed to the
maximum with pink cherubs and blushing nymphs. The rooms are tastefully done, with unassuming pastels and Biedermeier furniture. The lawn
that sprawls out toward the Roseg Valley is a social center in summer
and winter, with tennis courts doubling as an ice rink and a pavilion
for taking in winter sun. The Kronenstübli, all barrel-vaulted Arvenholz, serves international cuisine du marché—such as lobster with ginger butter—and the wine may be drawn from the still-functioning
Veltlinerkeller (wine cellar) below. ✉ *Via Maistra, CH-7504,* ☎ *081/*
8420111, ⅣX *081/8426066. 93 rooms. 2 restaurants, bar, café, indoor*
pool, outdoor pool, beauty salon, massage, 2 tennis courts, boccie, bowl-
ing, ice-skating. AE, DC, MC, V.

$ ✕⊡ **Roseggletscher.** Hike up the ruggedly beautiful Roseg Valley or
★ take a horse-drawn carriage to this isolated, modern though traditionally
styled hotel. The restaurant, where you can either be served or visit
the cafeteria line, offers simple regional favorites except in fall, when
the owner brings in game from the surrounding countryside; his trophies adorn the walls. This is a very popular lunch spot for hikers, bikers, and cross-country skiers, who reward themselves with a selection
from the massive dessert buffet. The rooms are spartan but fresh; besides the usual doubles and singles, there are some larger rooms that
can accommodate half a dozen people or more, making it a good spot
for hiking parties. ✉ *Via Maistra, CH-7504,* ☎ *081/8426445,* ⅣX *081/*
8426886. 13 rooms, 3 dorm rooms. 2 restaurants, cafeteria. No credit
cards.

$$$$ ⊡ **Walther.** If the elaborate Kronenhof is Dionysus, the Walther is Apollo,
★ strictly classical with its discreet pastels and sleek, unfussy wood.
Though built in 1907, the look is contemporary, save for a few ornate
moldings. The rooms have built-in pine cabinetry; those with south-
facing balconies are most in demand. The state-of-the-art pool is in a
glass-and-pine pavilion that opens onto a wooded garden. The clientele is younger than at the Kronenhof. ✉ *Via Maistra, CH-7504,* ☎
081/8426471, ⅣX *081/8427922. 62 rooms, 9 suites. Restaurant, bar,*
indoor pool, hot tub, massage, sauna, steam room, health club. AE,
DC, MC, V.

$$$ ⊡ **Saratz.** At a time when grand hotels have been going downhill, if
★ not out of business, this 19th-century grande dame has reopened its
doors. It's a success story involving four brothers and a family legacy:
now a modern lobby and a 60-room wing, done in porous, toast-color
tufa in the spirit of the hotel's original stone portals, extend the prop-
erty lengthwise. The interiors, with their warm schemes of yellow-green
and orange-red, make for an effective bridge between new and old; guests
can choose a room with gilt-mirror grandeur (in the Chesa Nuova sec-
tion) or one with stricter '90s lines (Ela Tuff). For another shot of el-
egance, dine in the period, à la carte restaurant. The hotel easily
accommodates travelers with children, demonstrating their commit-
ment with everything from family-friendly, suite-style rooms and a kinder-
garten to special cereals on a kid-size breakfast bar. The views on the
Roseg Valley from the lobby terrace, or from anywhere within the hotel's
extensive park, are inspiring. Rates are aggressively low for the cate-
gory, but you're charged an extra fee for rooms on the east and south
sides. ✉ *Via Maistra, CH-7504,* ☎ *081/8394000,* ⅣX *081/8394040.*
92 rooms. Restaurant, bar, indoor pool, outdoor pool, hot tub, mas-
sage, sauna, steam room. AE, DC, MC, V.

$$$ 🏨 **Schweizerhof.** This 1907 landmark modernized its lobbies and common rooms with sleek lines and yellow and gray leather. Guest rooms are more traditional, with Arvenholz accents; corner bay rooms have panoramic, southwestern views. The restaurant specializes in classic Swiss and vegetarian dishes, with regional Bündnerherrschaft and Veltliner wines. The public pool is across the street. ✉ *Via Maistra, CH-7504,* ☎ *081/8420131,* 📠 *081/8427988. 70 rooms. Restaurant, bar, café, hot tub, sauna. AE, DC, MC, V.*

$$–$$$ 🏨 **Bernina.** This comfortable hotel goes the straightforward route with modern, spring-tone prints, pine furniture, and tile baths. Splendid views can be taken in from balconies and luxury corner doubles or from the restaurant and the Stübli's big sun terrace overlooking the mountains—perhaps providing inspiration to the regular crowds of skiers and hikers. ✉ *Via Maistra, CH-7504,* ☎ *081/8426221,* 📠 *081/8427032. 47 rooms. Restaurant, café, Stübli, sauna, steam room. AE, DC, MC, V.*

Nightlife and the Arts

BARS AND LOUNGES

Popular nightspots include **Piano-Bar** (✉ Sporthotel, ☎ 081/8426331), a cozy, blond-wood bar; the trendy **Pöstli-Keller** (✉ Hotel Post, ☎ 081/8426318), geared toward a younger crowd; and **Cento Bar** (✉ Hotel Müller, ☎ 081/8426341), a local hangout with rustic furnishings. **Bar "Pitschna Szena"** (✉ Hotel Saratz, ☎ 081/8394000) makes unique use of the leftover sign from the old Hotel Saratz.

DANCING

Sarazena (✉ Via Maistra, ☎ 081/8426353), in an old Engadine house, starts the night as a moodlit restaurant; at 11 this makes way for a dance floor and a disco beat, which goes until 3 AM.

MUSIC

The **Kurorchester Pontresina** plays chamber concerts daily between mid-June and mid-September at 11 AM in the Taiswald (Tais Forest) free of charge.

Outdoor Activities and Sports

BICYCLING

Conventional and mountain bikes can be rented at **Fähndrich-Sport** (☎ 081/8427155), **Flück Sport** (☎ 081/8426262), and **Michel Massé** (☎ 081/8426824).

CARRIAGE AND SLEIGH RIDES

Horse-drawn carriages or, in winter, sleigh rides can be booked through **L. Costa** (☎ 081/8426057), **M. Keiser** (☎ 081/8426620), or **P. Thom** (☎ 081/8426543).

FISHING

Trout fishing in the Lej Nair and Lej Pitschen Mountain lakes is free for Pontresina guests in season from mid-June to mid-September. For license information, contact the tourist office (☞ Visitor Information *in* Graubünden A to Z, *below*).

FLYOVERS AND HELICOPTER TRIPS

Scenic flights via glider or helicopter can be arranged through **Heli Bernina** (☎ 081/8524677). The **Samedan Airport** (☎ 081/8525433) also organizes flight excursions.

HIKING

Pontresina provides a network of paths of varying difficulty and guided excursions to the Swiss National Park, including sunrise walks, mushroom hunting in season (usually August–September), and glacier hiking. Call the tourist office (☞ Visitor Information *in* Graubünden A to Z, *below*) for info. If you are staying in Pontresina overnight, the tours are free of charge; day visitors pay a small fee.

MOUNTAINEERING AND CLIMBING

Bergsteigerschule Pontresina (Pontresina Mountain Climbing School; ⊠ Via Maistra, CH-7504, ☎ 081/8388333) is the biggest school in Switzerland and offers rock and ice instruction for beginners and advanced climbers, plus private guided tours. Along with the tourist office and the ski school, it's in the Rondo Congress, Cultural and Information Center.

RAFTING

For white-water rafting excursions on the Flaz River call **Michel Massé** (☎ 081/8426824).

SKATING

There's a large natural ice-skating rink in winter by the public indoor swimming pool, **Pontresina Hallenbad** (⊠ Gemeindeverwaltung, ☎ 081/8427341 or 081/8428257 for both). Ten curling rinks with instructors and ice hockey are available at **Sportpavilion Roseg** (⊠ Via Maistra, ☎ 081/8426346 or 081/8426349) from December through March.

SWIMMING

In addition to an indoor pool, **Pontresina Hallenbad** (☞ *above*) offers a sauna, a solarium, and a sunbathing terrace.

TENNIS

Thirteen public tennis courts are available in Pontresina at different hotels; inquire at the hotels or at the tourist office. There are two public artificial grass/artificial sand tennis courts and two sand courts at the **Sportpavilion Roseg** (☞ *above*).

St. Moritz

★ ⑬   *5 km (3 mi) west of Pontresina, 85 km (53 mi) southeast of Chur.*

Who put the *ritz* in St. Moritz? The approach to this celebrated city may surprise newcomers who, having heard the almost magical name dropped in the same breath as Paris and Rome, expect either a supremely cosmopolitan Old World capital or a resort whose spectacular natural setting puts other resorts to shame. It is neither. What makes St. Moritz's reputation is the people who go there and who have been going there, generation by generation, since 1864, when hotelier Johannes Badrutt dared a group of English resorters—already summer regulars—to brave the Alpine winter as his guests. They loved it, delighted in the novelty of snowy mountain beauty—until then considered something to be avoided—and told their friends. By the turn of the century, St. Moritz, Switzerland, and snow were all the rage.

Not that St. Moritz had been a stranger to tourism before that. Since 1500 BC, when Druidic Celts first passed through, people have made the pilgrimage here to take healing waters from its mineral springs. The Romans had a settlement here, and later a church was founded on the site, dedicated to Mauritius, an early Christian martyr. The first historical reference to the town dates from 1139; and in 1537 Paracelsus, the great Renaissance physician and alchemist, described the health-giving properties of the St. Moritz springs. It is said that in the late 17th century the duke of Parma led a retinue of 25 followers over the mountain passes to taste the waters.

In fact, 70% of the latter-day pilgrims who visit St. Moritz come from abroad, still the cosmopolitan mix of socialites, blue bloods, and celebs that made the resort's name. St. Moritz catches social fire around the winter holidays—some New Year's Eve events have guest lists closed a year in advance—but the glitter fades by spring. Very ordinary people fill the streets come summer—the same hikers you might meet in any resort—and hotel prices plummet.

Then visitors see St. Moritz for what it really is: a busy, built-up old resort city sprawled across a hillside above an aquamarine lake, the St. Moritz See, surrounded by forested hills and by graceful, though not the region's most dramatic, peaks. Piz Rosatsch, with its glacier, dominates the view, with Piz Languard (3,263 m/10,699 ft) on the east and Piz Güglia (2,285 m/7,492 ft) on the west. St. Moritz-Dorf is the most like a downtown, with busy traffic and competitive parking in the shopping district. St. Moritz-Bad, the original spa-resort at the base of the lake, now bristles with brutish modern housing worthy of a Costa Moritza. The town shows its best face from a distance, especially at dusk: from the *See* promenade—the popular walk around the lake—modern edges soften and the lake reflects the darkening mountains, warm hotel lights, and the grace that first made St. Moritz a star.

Even a hundred years of hype have not exaggerated its attractions as a winter sports center. The place that twice hosted the Olympic games (1928 and 1948)—and trademarked the shining sun as its logo—is still a sports marketing mecca, with excellent facilities for ice-skating, bob-sledding, ski jumping, riding, and even winter golf, polo, and horse racing. But it does not have a corner on fine skiing: it shares a broad complex of trails and facilities with Sils, Silvaplana, Celerina, and Pontresina; only the slopes of Corviglia, Marguns, and Piz Nair are directly accessible from town.

One of the few reminders that the now-contemporary St. Moritz was once an Engadine village is the **Engadine Museum,** a reproduction of the traditional, sgraffitied home. Tools, furniture, and pottery, all displayed in rooms restored in different styles, explain the local way of life. ⊠ *Via dal Bagn 39,* ☎ *081/8334333.* ⊡ *5 SF.* ☺ *June–Oct., weekdays 9:30–noon and 2–5, Sun. 10–noon; Dec.–Apr., weekdays 10–noon and 2–5, Sun. 10–noon.*

Skiing

As a resort of superlatives—it's the oldest (its thermal springs were known 3,000 years ago), the most snobbish, and the most chichi—St. Moritz obviously could not be content with only one ski area. It has three: one on each side of the valley, **Corviglia** and **Corvatsch,** and another in reserve, 20 minutes away by car—**Diavolezza-Lagalp. Piz Corviglia, Piz Nair,** and **Grisch,** on the northwestern slopes of St. Moritz, are ideal terrain for family skiing and snowboarding, with 80 km (50 mi) of generally easy runs, wide and well groomed, restaurants here and there, and lift service more than sufficient except for several days in high season. **Corviglia**—site of the principal ski competitions of the Winter Olympics in 1928 and 1948—offers, in spite of its exceptionally sunny location, ideal conditions for intermediate skiers. The elevation (1,647 m/5,400 ft) and the snowmaking machines here and at **Marguns** defy even calamitous snow seasons. **Diavolezza** and **Lagalp** have extensive facilities, and from February on you can ski the awe-inspiring glacier descent from Diavolezza to **Morteratsch.** Skiing is also snow-secure on the **Corvatsch,** with its panoramas on Piz Bernina and Piz Palü from its own perch at 3,451 m (11,319 ft) above Surlej. The long tobogganing **Cresta Run** (☎ 081/8334609 or 081/8333117) rips riders headfirst at speeds of up to 85 mph down an icy track from St. Moritz to Celerina. It's generally a spectator attraction, although a crash course (pardon the pun) may be available. It runs from mid-December to late

February. St. Moritz also has a branch of the official **Swiss Ski School** (☎ 081/8338090). Lift tickets cost 54 SF for one day, 258 SF for six.

Dining and Lodging

$$$$ ✕ **Jöhri's Talvò.** Roland Jöhri's cuisine continues to garner compliments. His restaurant, in a 350-year-old Engadine house, is near enough to St. Moritz to be convenient but far enough away from town to provide a peaceful setting. Both the cooking and decor reflect Jöhri's philosophy: to marry the best of Graubünden tradition with classic French elegance, from the delicate linens softening weathered woodwork to the light sauces that curb the heartiness of local capuns, pizzoccheri, and maluns. A popular fish menu combines lobster, shellfish, and other fresh catches; the desserts are elaborate works of art. ⊠ *Champfèr, about 100 m/330 ft from the postbus stop,* ☎ *081/8334455. AE, DC, MC, V. Reservations essential. Closed mid-Apr.–mid-June and mid-Oct.–mid-Dec.*

$$$ ✕ **Chesa Veglia.** This 17th-century *Bauernhof* (farmhouse) retains its raw beams and native carvings within a theme restaurant so self-consciously restored you may think you're in an American mall—an effect enhanced by the restaurant's fragmentation into three theme rooms (an upscale grill, a Stübli, and a pizzeria). Despite the rustic setting, the main menu aspires to international cuisine; you can order *côte de boeuf à la moelle et aux truffes* (beef with marrow and truffles), carpaccio, and terrine *de lièvre* (hare pâté) at prices that are St. Moritz–high. There are good fruit tarts at teatime, when the atmosphere is at its most convincing; later, you'll find dinner and dancing with live entertainment and piano music in the grill. ⊠ *Via Veglia 2,* ☎ *081/8372800. AE, DC, MC, V.*

$$ ✕ **Engiadina.** With its plain linoleum and pine, this could pass for a St. Moritz diner, though its raison d'être is fondue—with champagne fondue its house specialty. Other favorites are cheap *steak-frîtes* (steak with french fries), escargots, and side orders of Spätzli. It's a popular oddity in this ritzy resort. ⊠ *Off Schulhauspl.,* ☎ *081/8333265. AE, DC, MC, V. Closed Nov.*

$$ ✕🏠 **Meierei.** On a winding, private forest road partway around the
★ lake, this *Landgasthof* (country inn) is a rural mirage, an incongruity in the city but spiritually allied to the mountains and lake. It started in the 17th century as a farm where the bishop stopped over when traveling; later, it became a dairy restaurant and—about 150 years ago—a hotel. Today it's sought out for its restaurant, which serves light meals and such modern combinations as pumpkin gnocchi with lobster. Its sun terrace is also a popular meeting spot for day hikers and walkers. (If you're not a guest, you'll have to walk in, as only guests may drive in.) The rustic themes of the dining areas are loosely translated into guest-room decor, with most rooms combining brown tones and wood with green-tone carpet. Some have newer, all-tile baths. ⊠ *Off the eastern shore of St. Moritz Lake, CH-7500,* ☎ *081/8333242,* 📠 *081/8338838. 10 rooms. Restaurant, café. No credit cards. Closed May and Nov.*

$–$$ ✕🏠 **Veltlinerkeller.** This bright, genial restaurant has nothing swanky
★ about it—just lots of wood, ancient moldings in the form of grapes, a few outsize game trophies, and a welcoming wood fire where the meat is roasted while you watch. The owner mans the grill, and his touch with Italian-Romansh cooking is light and straightforward. In addition to grilled meats and whole trout, there are good and varied homemade pastas served family style from crockery bowls. The nine double rooms upstairs are finished in slick quarry tile and stucco, with cotton floral prints and all-tile baths. ⊠ *Via dal Bagn, St. Moritz-Bad,*

CH-7500, ☎ 081/8334009, ℻ 081/8333741. *9 rooms. Restaurant, bar, Stübli. No credit cards.*

$$$$ ⊞ **Badrutt's Palace.** With its pseudo-Gothic stone and mismatched sprawl of architectural excess, the Palace is pure Hollywood, all glitz and conspicuous consumption. Winter is its prime time: flagrant and showy, with Rolls-Royces and Lear jets discharging guests willing to pay more per night than for a transatlantic flight, it is crammed with beautiful people and wealthy wannabes who made token appearances on the slopes before checking in at the hairdresser. This place definitely has its standards—jacket and tie for public rooms, for example. Nowhere in Switzerland will you find more facilities—the hotel even has its own ski school and a private cinema. The restaurant is as vast as a mess hall, beswagged and chandeliered; the Grill-Room is a celadon jewel box and enjoys a culinary reputation beyond the guest list. Rooms are surprisingly discreet and rather like a lot of other hotel rooms at a third the price—but it's not the drapes you're paying for. ⊠ *Via Serlas 27, CH-7500,* ☎ *081/8371000,* ℻ *081/8372999. 180 rooms, 40 suites. 3 restaurants, bar, indoor pool, outdoor pool, hot tubs, massage, sauna, 4 tennis courts, health club, squash, ice-skating, cinema, dance club, nightclub, nursery. AE, DC, MC, V. Closed late Aug.–mid-Dec. and early Apr.–early July.*

$$$$ ⊞ **Carlton.** If you want luxury without blatant glitz, consider this un-
★   sung hotel, which stands slightly above the city center in a supersunny location with fine views. Built in 1913, it's now bright and modern, without a scrap of Arvenholz, its white-marble lobby more like a performing-arts center than a Belle Epoque hotel. Blue runners lead upstairs to the plush bar/sitting room and regal dining rooms. Guest rooms have every modern amenity; some lean toward contemporary lines, others evoke eras gone by with crystal chandeliers and fine carpets. The baths are state-of-the-art Euro style, and the beautiful glassed-in pool has views over the lake and a sun terrace. ⊠ *Via J. Badrutt 11, CH-7500,* ☎ *081/8331141,* ℻ *081/8332012. 99 rooms, 6 suites. Restaurant, bar, indoor pool, beauty salon, massage, sauna, health club, nursery. AE, DC, MC, V. Closed mid-Sept.–mid-Dec. and early Apr.–mid-June.*

$$$$ ⊞ **Kulm.** This luxury hotel can claim its share of St. Moritz superlatives: it was the first hotel here (1856) *and* the first house to have electricity in all of Switzerland (1878). Modern comfort has come a long way since: for instance, the Panorama Healthclub, with a saltwater grotto and fitness gym. Elsewhere, the hotel's discreetly done in slightly old-fashioned good taste—cream, gold, scarlet. The facilities are top quality, the breakfast room is pure Wedgwood, and the à la carte restaurant—Rôtisserie de Chevaliers—is a romantic vaulted space, serving (predictably enough) old-style haute cuisine. ⊠ *Via Maistra, CH-7500,* ☎ *081/8321151,* ℻ *081/8332738. 200 rooms. Restaurant, bar, indoor pool, massage, sauna, 3 tennis courts, health club. AE, DC, MC, V. Closed mid-Sept.–early Dec. and early Apr.–late June.*

$$$$ ⊞ **Schweizerhof.** This big-city hotel in the center of town was built in 1896 and is still grand. Public areas are heavy with carved wood and moldings, and the Victorian splendor is almost oppressive. A lighter touch is the painted ceiling of the guests' dining room, with its glittering birch forest. Guest rooms leave romantic fantasy behind—they're slick postmodern with burled-wood cabinets and contemporary color schemes. There's a popular piano bar and a lively Stübli that draws a young après-ski crowd. The Acla restaurant, at street level, serves casual Italian and Austrian meals. ⊠ *Via dal Bagn 54, CH-7500,* ☎ *081/8370707,* ℻ *081/8370700. 72 rooms, 8 suites. 2 restaurants, 4 bars, sauna, health club, nursery. AE, DC, MC, V.*

$$$$ 🏨 **Steffani.** Although it was built in 1869, the Steffani is now a standard city business-class hotel; as it's owned by Best Western, it's tailored to match American tastes. Despite its age, it now has a heavy, modern look, with some stylized local details but more stress on function and dependability than history. The facilities are ample, the staff is welcoming and its Lapin Bleu restaurant is frequently sought out by non-guests. It's open throughout the off-season—in fact it hasn't been closed one day since 1930. ⊠ *Via Somplaz 1, CH-7500,* ☎ *081/8332101,* 𝔽𝔸𝕏 *081/8334097. 75 rooms, 5 suites. 3 restaurants, 3 bars, indoor pool, hot tub, massage, sauna, bowling, dance club. AE, DC, MC, V.*

$$$–$$$$ 🏨 **Crystal Hotel.** If the spacious lobby of this modern hotel has a touch of familiarity, it may be because an American interior decorator lent a hand—there's a long, low-slung feel to it. Rooms are done in wood and patterned red fabrics, with luxurious bath products and Arvenholz in the baths. Though there's little hope for a truly broad view—it's flanked by buildings and a parking garage—the facilities are ample, the fitness center is equipped to get all of St. Moritz in shape, and its location is convenience itself—it's steps from the valley station for connections to Corviglia. If you're sore after a tough day on the slopes, try the sauna's Turkish bath. ⊠ *Via Traunter Plazzas 1, CH-7500,* ☎ *081/8362626,* 𝔽𝔸𝕏 *081/8362627. 80 rooms. Restaurant, bar, massage, sauna, health club. AE, DC, MC, V. Closed early Oct.–mid-Dec. and early Apr.–late May.*

$$$ 🏨 **Waldhaus am See.** This is another world, a good hotel perched on ★ a peninsula overlooking the lake and mountains with a merely peripheral view of St. Moritz's urban turmoil (well filtered through double glass) across the highway. With a big, sunny balcony, dining rooms with views, and a clientele ranging from family clans to seniors, it's a vacation lodge geared to leisurely one- to two-week stays. The reasonably priced restaurant stocks more than 1,500 wines, and owner-entrepreneur Claudio Bernasconi has introduced Switzerland's most extensive whiskey bar (as well as his handpicked selection of ties for sale). Rooms are plain, with pine trim and some dated plumbing, though many modern baths have been added in recent years. Sunny corner doubles have tiny bays over the lake. ⊠ *About 200 m/650 ft from the train station on the eastern side of the lake, CH-7500,* ☎ *081/8337676,* 𝔽𝔸𝕏 *081/8338877. 50 rooms. Restaurant, sauna, exercise room. DC, MC, V.*

$$–$$$ 🏨 **Eden.** Just up from the center of town, on a hilltop, this small hotel *garni* has been in the same family since it opened in the 1890s. Such personal touches as the buffed original Arvenholz in some guest rooms and an antique swan sleigh that serves as part of the breakfast buffet reflect a genteel air and the owner's singular style. Most rooms have modern lines with wood accents; be prepared for some bright tiles in the bathrooms. ⊠ *Off Via Maistra, CH-7500,* ☎ *081/8336161,* 𝔽𝔸𝕏 *081/8339191. 35 rooms. Breakfast room. No credit cards. Closed mid-Oct.–mid-Dec. and late Apr.–mid-June.*

$$–$$$ 🏨 **Landguard.** This delightful little hotel stands between the Eden and ★ the Kulm (☞ *above*), sharing their lovely mountain views. Such restored regional details as sgraffiti, carved ceilings, and fine darkened pine in some rooms preserve the best from its earlier days. The big corner rooms deserve the top price they command; back rooms look over town. All-tile baths add modern sparkle. ⊠ *Off Via Maistra, CH-7500,* ☎ *081/8333137,* 𝔽𝔸𝕏 *081/8334546. 22 rooms. Breakfast room. AE, DC, MC, V. Closed mid-Oct.–early Dec. and mid-Apr.–mid-June.*

Nightlife and the Arts

To find out what's happening in the arts world, check *St. Moritz Aktuell* or the booklet "Engadin," which offers weekly events information for the Upper Engadine resorts in local languages plus English.

BARS AND LOUNGES

Bobby's Pub (⊠ Gallaria Badrutt, at Via dal Bagn 52, ☎ 081/8334767) has an English atmosphere. A casual crowd congregates at the **Cava-Bar** in the Steffani (☎ 081/8322101; ☞ Dining and Lodging, *above*). The **Muli Bar,** in the Hotel Schweizerhof's (☞ Dining and Lodging, *above*) former library, offers country music après-ski. The Schweizerhof's **Piano Bar** has a champion bartender who serves exotic cocktails to upscale crowds in a tiny Jugendstil lounge. The hotel's pine **Stübli,** open all year, draws casual young people après-ski with a live guitarist and snacks, including raclette in winter. The **Renaissance Bar** in Badrutt's Palace (☞ Dining and Lodging, *above*), with American-style bar stools and tables, has an open fireplace; the awe-inspiring lobby lounge, also in the hotel, has a pianist evenings.

CASINOS

The casino in **St. Moritz** (⊠ Via Veglia 15/Via Maistra 28, ☎ 081/8321080) supplements its roulette with 75 slot machines. It's open until 3 AM.

CLUBS

The **Grand-Bar Nightclub** in Badrutt's Palace (☞ Dining and Lodging, *above*) has dancing to live music. **La Volière** (⊠ Suvretta House, ☎ 081/8321132) is a very formal nightclub, requiring evening dress.

DANCING

Absolut (⊠ Via Maistra 10, ☎ 081/8336398) draws movers and shakers. The **King's Club** of Badrutt's Palace (☞ Dining and Lodging, *above*), with its urban-decay decor—graffiti, neon, dated Keith Haring look—attracts the jet set at holiday time; prepare for a massive cover charge. **Vivai** is a popular disco club in the Steffani (☞ Dining and Lodging, *above*).

MUSIC

The **St. Moritz Kurorchester,** a 13-piece summer chamber group, plays free concerts summer mornings at 10:30 between late June and mid-September in the Heilbadzentrum concert hall (⊠ off via Mezdi, St. Moritz-Bad) or in the park just in front of the hall if the weather is fine.

Outdoor Activities and Sports

BICYCLING

You can rent both conventional and mountain bikes at the **Corviglia Tennis Center** (☎ 081/8331500). Bicycles can also be rented at the **Rhaetian Railway station,** though their use is restricted to bike trails. Mountain bikes also are available, but they are rarely permitted on pedestrian trails.

BOBSLEDDING

With enough advance notice (a few days to a week), bob-taxi rides can be booked down the world's last remaining natural ice course of its kind, the **Olympic Bob Run** (☎ 081/8334110 or 081/8300200) from St. Moritz to Celerina. You ride behind an experienced driver. You can also call ahead for start times to watch training sessions and races. The bob run is generally open from Christmas through February.

GOLF

St. Moritz and Samedan share Switzerland's oldest 18-hole golf course, **Engadine Golf Samedan** (☎ 081/8525226), along the River En.

For **hang gliding** or paragliding call ☎ 081/8332416. In winter, tandem **Delta glider flights** (☎ 079/3532159) are offered with certified pilots—you take off on skis from the Corviglia and land on the frozen lake more than 2,000 ft below.

SAILING AND WINDSURFING

Arnoud Missiaen (☎ 081/8289229) heads a windsurfing school. The **Segelschule St. Moritz** (☎ 081/8334056) gives sailing lessons.

SKATING

Ludains (☎ 081/8335030), an artificial outdoor skating rink in St. Moritz-Bad, is open from July to April.

SWIMMING

You can swim in **Lake Nair,** near St. Moritz. For indoor swimming, try the **Hallenschwimmbad** (☎ 081/8336025), a municipal pool and sauna in St. Moritz-Bad; it has coed and single-sex hours.

TENNIS

Corviglia Tennis Center (☎ 081/8331500) in St. Moritz-Bad has four outdoor and four indoor tennis courts, with staff instructors. The local tourist office (☞ Visitor Information *in* Graubünden A to Z, *below*) can tell you about other available courts.

Sils, Sils-Baselgia, and Sils-Maria

⑭ *13 km (8 mi) southwest of St. Moritz.*

The Lower Engadine Valley broadens into green meadows punctuated by a series of crystalline lakes: the little Champferer See, just past St. Moritz; the larger Silvaplaner See, headed by the small hillside resort of Silvaplana, and the long sprawl of the Silser See, accessible from the land bar that separates the two bodies of water. On this green lowland 13 km (8 mi) from St. Moritz stands the resort complex of Sils (Segl in Romansh), connecting Sils-Baselgia and, farther back against the mountains, Sils-Maria. From Sils the highway heads over the Maloja Pass (1,816 m/5,953 ft) and crosses into Italy.

Although the flat setting and expanding new housing make Sils-Maria look like an American suburban country club, Sils-Maria is a resort with old-Engadine flavor and inspiring views. Friedrich Nietzsche called it "the land of silver colors" and wrote *Also Sprach Zarathustra* (*Thus Spoke Zarathustra*) in his house here, which is now **Stiftung Nietzsche Haus.** The collection inside displays transcriptions of the writer's manuscripts (in German) right next to originals in his own fascinatingly scrawly script. An array of photos and mementos gives homage not only to Nietzsche, but to a host of other literati who put their thoughts on paper while staying with Nietzsche or while vacationing in town—from Thomas Mann to Anne Frank. ⊠ *Next to Hotel Edelweiss,* ☎ *081/8265369.* 🎫 *6 SF.* 🕙 *Mid-Dec.–Apr. and June–Nov., Tues.–Sun. 3–6.*

Dining and Lodging

$ ✕🗊 **Chesa Marchetta/Pensiun Andreola.** You won't find a more pleas-
★ ant and complete regional experience than in this tiny twin pension and restaurant run by two sophisticated sisters; not only do they decorate with taste, but they also serve authentic local dishes. The sgraffitied pension is furnished in pine and chic cotton prints, while the neighboring restaurant is an Arvenholz gem, perfectly preserved since 1671. The menu is limited to one main dish a night—homemade pasta with lamb, perhaps, or polenta with veal—with permanent options of *plain in pigna* (potato gratin with homemade sausage) or fondue chi-

noise; but there are always cold local meats and Engadiner Nusstorte. Meals are served evenings only, snacks from 3:30 on. ⊠ *Sils-Maria, CH-7514,* ☎ *081/8265232,* 🖷 *081/8266260. 10 rooms, 6 without bath. Restaurant, Stübli. No credit cards.*

$$$$ 🏨 **Waldhaus.** Hermann Hesse, Thomas Mann, C. G. Jung, Marc Cha-
★   gall, Albert Einstein, and Richard Strauss all found solace in this hill-
top forest retreat, high above the meadow that separates Lake Sils and Lake Silvaplana and offers spectacular views in all directions. You can have tea on the terrace, surrounded by tall evergreen woods, or play tennis on the courts just below; either way, you'll be accompanied by the hotel's resident string trio, which adds to the sense of Wagnerian idyll. Even the indoor pool, built of pine and rock, takes in forest views. The building itself is steeped in tradition and creaky grandeur, with its heavy marble pillars, burnished parquet, and Asian runners. The rooms range from spare (chenille and parquet) to splendid (bay windows with fine panoramas), but the public areas are consistently gracious, especially the formal dining room, where in winter the white-draped tables and iciclelike light fixtures mirror the snow-blanketed landscape outside. ⊠ *CH-7514,* ☎ *081/8385100,* 🖷 *081/8385198. 140 rooms. Restaurant, bar, Stübli, indoor pool, beauty salon, massage, steam room, miniature golf, 4 tennis courts. MC, V.*

$$ 🏨 **Chesa Randolina.** This hotel in Sils-Baselgia laps up sun from its position set back from the Sils lake. The architecture is low-slung but pure Engadine, with stucco vaulting, beams, and pine in nearly every room; the best have long balconies facing south. There's a broad, spacious lounge with a stone fireplace and a cozy restaurant (hotel guests only) with a sgraffitied ceiling. ⊠ *CH-7515,* ☎ *081/8265151,* 🖷 *081/8265600. 37 rooms. Restaurant, bar. No credit cards.*

$$ 🏨 **Privata.** Tucked into a green corner at the edge of the village, this
★   tidy, fresh, Engadine-style inn is full of personal touches: antiques, paintings done by past guests, and trophies from the owner's former days as a ski champion. The parlors have fireplaces and inlaid stone floors, and there's a lovely garden in back. Decorated in white and pine, most rooms have good views, though the hotel behind spoils a few. Some upper rooms have tiny balconies with chairs. The restaurant is open only to inn guests and the fresh-baked *Zopf* (braided bread) at Sunday breakfast is a good reason to get up early. ⊠ *Sils-Maria, CH-7514,* ☎ *081/ 8265247,* 🖷 *081/8266183. 25 rooms. Restaurant. No credit cards.*

Nightlife and the Arts

Small **chamber ensembles** perform from late June through September at 4 or 4:30 on the Konzerztplatz in Sils-Maria; in bad weather, they move to the schoolhouse.

Outdoor Activities and Sports

DOGSLEDDING

Turn yourself over to **Sämy Stöckli** (☎ 079/4404166) and his mushing crew; 12 snow-hungry huskies will pull you across extraordinary frozen-lake landscapes near Sils.

PARAGLIDING

In Sils-Baselgia, contact instructor **Andrea Kuhn** (☎ 081/8265400).

BOATING, SAILING AND WINDSURFING

Rowboats can be rented from **Schifffährtgesellschaft Silsersee** (☎ 081/ 8265343) in Sils-Maria. **Surf-Schule Malojawind** (☎ 081/8265877) in Sils-Maria offers sailing and windsurfing instruction. Silvaplana's **Surf- und Segelschule** (☎ 081/82655786) also provides lessons. On any lake excursion, watch out for the "Maloja Wind," which blows in daily in summer at 11 AM like a punctual Swiss train.

SPORTS CENTERS

Sils's **Muot Marias** (☎ 081/8385050) is a well-equipped sports center with a cafeteria. Silvaplana has the **Sportcèntrum Mulets** (☎ 081/8289362), with two sand tennis courts, a soccer field, an ice rink, a playground, and a training room.

TENNIS

Sils has four public courts, booked through the **Waldhaus Hotel** (☎ 081/8266666) or the tourist office (☞ Visitor Information *in* Graubünden A to Z, *below*).

JULIER ROUTE TO SAN BERNARDINO PASS

The Julier Pass is one of the three great Alpine passes known to have been used by the Romans (the Grand St. Bernard and the Splügen are the other two)—though even in those days, the Julier was favored because of its immunity to avalanches. The present road, built between 1820 and 1826, is dominated by three mountains, Piz Julier, Piz Albana, and Piz Polaschin, and near the top it is marked by two pillars, about 1½ m (5 ft) high, which are said to be the remains of a Roman temple. The terrain here is barren, windswept, and rocky—the perfect place to imagine an open stage for marching legions.

About 16 km (10 mi) beyond the summit of the Julier Pass is the village of **Bivio**: once a Roman settlement named Stabulum Bivio, it is called Bivio in Italian and Swiss German, and Beiva in Romansh—and residents speak all three.

Tiefencastel

⓯ *44 km (27 mi) northwest of Sils, 29 km (18 mi) south of Chur.*

Where the Julia flows into the Albula, you'll find this valley town, buried deep in the mountain forests and accessible only by steep, winding roads; it was entirely destroyed by fire in 1890. Above the rebuilt town, the tall white church of **St. Ambrosius** still stands out against the background of fir trees that cover the encroaching hills.

En Route   From Tiefencastel, the road forks: you can drive north on Route 3 toward Chur (☞ *above*) through Lenzerheide (1,525 m/5,000 ft), a year-round resort known for moderate slopes for beginning skiers and a good 18-hole golf course, or cut west to Thusis. The Thusis route is particularly spectacular via the Rhaetian Railway (☞ Getting Around by Train *in* Graubünden A to Z, *below*), as it passes through 16 tunnels, one of them more than 5 km (3 mi) long, and across 27 bridges and viaducts. The most celebrated of these is the **Solis Viaduct,** the center arch of which is 42 m (137 ft) across and 89 m (293 ft) high.

Thusis, surrounded by high mountains and thick forest, has a late-Gothic church (1506) and the ruins of the old Schloss Hohenrhaetien, perched on rocky heights to guard the entrance to the ancient road Via Mala.

Leading south from Thusis, the **Via Mala** writhes south along the bottom of a deep ravine crisscrossed by bridges. It has been replaced by the new highway, but you can still see the old Via Mala by leaving the highway about 5 km (3 mi) after Thusis and following the traffic signs marked VIA MALA toward the San Bernardino Pass. On foot, you can descend 321 steps into the gorge to see the bridges that, in various epochs, have been strung across the treacherous water.

At Zillis, famous for the painted wooden ceiling in its St. Martinskirche (St. Martin's Church), the Via Mala ends, and A13 leads south and west toward the **Splügenpass** (the southbound entrance into Italy). Just west of the Splügenpass is the **San Bernardino Pass** (Little St. Bernard Pass). There is an easy express tunnel through the pass these days, 8 km (5 mi) long, but the tortuous climb up the old highway rewards drivers (and postbus passengers) with astonishing perspectives: as you begin to ascend, the Rheinwald Valley opens below, and you see the first currents of the Hinter, or Lower, Rhine; beyond looms its source, the glacier of the **Zapporthorn** (3,154 m/10,340 ft). This pass is closed in winter, and may also receive snowfall at other times of year.

GRAUBÜNDEN A TO Z

Arriving and Departing

By Bus
You can take the Swiss **postbus** system's *Palm Express* (☎ 081/8376764) from Ascona or Lugano in the Ticino over the Maloja Pass and into St. Moritz.

By Car
As Graubünden is dense with mountains and thin on major highways, drivers usually enter either by way of the San Bernardino Pass from Ticino or from the north past Liechtenstein, both on **A13**, the region's only expressway; it traces the Rhine to its main source.

By Plane
Oberengadine Regional Airport (✉ Samedan, 5 km/3 mi from St. Moritz, ☎ 081/8525433) is served mainly by charter flights from Air Engiadina, Crossair, and Classic Air. At 1,707 m (5,600 ft), it's the highest airport in Europe.

By Train
The only main **Swiss Federal Railway** (SBB) trains to enter Graubünden come into Chur at the Rhätische Bahn (☎ 081/2539121). From there, the fine local **Rhaetian Railway** (RhB) takes over, with its broad network of narrow-gauge track. For general information on SBB and RhB, call the Rhätische Bahn.

To make the most of the Rhaetian Railway systems, you can take famous scenic train routes in or out of the region. The **Bernina Express** runs from Chur to St. Moritz via the Albula route and on to Italy past the spectacular Bernina peaks. The glamorous **Glacier Express** connects St. Moritz with Zermatt via the Oberalp Pass, crossing 291 bridges and spectacular Alpine terrain on its 7½-hour route. The train pulls a burnished-wood period dining car; you can reserve a table through the **Schweizerische Speisewagen Gesellschaft** (✉ CH-7000 Chur, ☎ 081/2521425). Seat reservations for these trains are mandatory; contact the appropriate tourist offices (☞ Visitor Information, *below*) or the railway itself.

Getting Around

By Bus
Postbuses are a dramatic way to lumber up Alpine switchbacks over the region's great passes—that is if you're not inclined to motion sickness. You can also use them to make circle tours with some careful study of the schedule. Information is available at all post offices.

By Car

The A13 expressway cuts a swift north–south route through Graubünden. If you want to get back into the deep farmlands, you'll definitely need a car. Fine valley highways connect the rest of the area, though to move from one resort to another you may have to crawl over a mountain pass. If you're traveling in winter, make sure to check on the status of the passes; weather is obviously a major player. The San Bernardino, Oberalp, Albula, and Flüela passes are normally closed, but the Bernina and Julier are usually open to car traffic. The **Vereinalinie,** opened in November 1999 by the Rhätische Bahn to cover the stretch from Klosters to Susch/Lavin, makes a safe alternative to the sometimes treacherous drive over the Flüela pass. Cars are loaded on rails and zipped through the 11.5-mi **Vereina Tunnel** into the Lower Engadine; the cost ranges from 27 to 40 SF per car.

By Train

The **Rhaetian Railway** (☞ Arriving and Departing, *above*) consists of 375 km (243 mi) of track and 117 tunnels and offers unusually thorough coverage of the terrain. Without resorting to cogwheel supports, some of the trains climb stiff mountain grades of up to 7%. Holders of the Swiss Pass (☞ Train Travel *in* Smart Travel Tips A to Z) travel free on all RhB lines.

Contacts and Resources

Emergencies

Police: Upper Engadine (☎ 081/8641414); Arosa (☎ 081/3771938); Klosters (☎ 081/4221236); St. Moritz (☎ 081/8333017). **Ambulance:** Klosters (☎ 081/4221713); St. Moritz (☎ 081/8518888). **Hospital**: Upper Engadine/Samedan (☎ 081/8518888); Davos (☎ 081/4148888). **Doctors: Upper Engadine referral** (☎ 081/8525657). Available doctors, dentists, and emergency pharmacies are listed in local newspapers under "Notfalldienst" (**emergency service**) and in the city or resort's tourist periodical.

Guided Tours

HIKING

Arosa, Davos, and Lenzerheide-Valbella offer an unusual **hiking package:** they'll book your hotel and deliver your bags ahead. You can walk from Davos to Arosa one day and from Arosa to Lenzerheide the next. A seven-day program lets you spend more time in each resort. Contact local tourist offices (☞ Visitor Information, *below*).

WALKING

The **Arosa** tourist office (☞ Visitor Information, *below*) offers guided tours and nature walks every morning and afternoon from June through October; you can visit a cheese maker, a regional museum, and a 15th-century chapel. The **Pontresina** tourist office (☞ Visitor Information, *below*) offers guided walking tours of its Old Town, full of typical Engadine houses, from mid-June to mid-October. It also offers guided botanical excursions, sunrise viewings, glacier tours, and hiking trips to the Swiss National Park, plus mushroom-picking outings in season (usually August–September). If you are staying in Pontresina, the tours are free; day visitors pay a small fee.

Visitor Information

Graubünden Holidays (✉ Alexanderstr. 24, CH-7001 Chur, ☎ 081/3026100, FAX 081/3021414) is the tourist-information headquarters for the canton. The local **Chur** city tourist office (✉ Grabenstr. 5, CH-7002 Chur, ☎ 081/2521818) offers leaflets for self-paced walks around the Old Town, as well as guided tours departing from the Town Hall. One

helpful thing to keep in mind: the Bündner Herrschaft/Maienfeld
tourist office (☞ *below*) stays open seven days a week. (Most tourist
offices are closed on Sunday or all weekend.)

Arosa (✉ Kurverein, Poststr., CH-7050, ☎ 081/3787020). **Bündner
Herrschaft/Maienfeld** (✉ Autobahn Raststätte Heidiland, CH-7304,
☎ 081/3026100). **Davos** (✉ Promenade 67, CH-7270, ☎ 081/
4152121). **Klosters** (✉ Kur & Verkehrsverein, Alte Bahnhofstr. 6,
CH-7250, ☎ 081/4102020). **Pontresina** (✉ Rondo Center, CH-7504,
☎ 081/8388300). **St. Moritz** (✉ Kur & Verkehrsverein, Via Maistra
12, CH-7500, ☎ 081/8373333). **Scuol** (☎ 081/8612222). **Sils** (✉
CH-7514 Sils-Maria, ☎ 081/8385050). **Zernez** (✉ Verkehrsverein, CH-
7530, ☎ 081/8561300).

5 THE TICINO

Locarno, Lugano

Italian in language, culture, and spirit, the Ticino is an irresistible combination of Mediterranean pleasures and Swiss efficiency. With its yacht-filled waterfront promenades of Locarno and Lugano and its sunny climate, the Ticino is a canton set apart, a happy harbor for Switzerland's Italian-speaking minority.

Updated by
Susan Tuttle-
Laube

NEWCOMERS TO THE OLD WORLD, a little weak on their geography, might hear the names Lugano, Ascona, Locarno, Bellinzona and assume—quite naturally—they're in Italy. Color photographs of the region might not set them straight: nearly every publicity shot shows palm trees and mimosas, red roofs and loggias, azure waters and indigo skies. Surely this is the Italian Mediterranean or the coast of the Adriatic. But behind the waving date palms are telltale signs: fresh paint, manicured gardens, punctual trains. There's no mistake about it: it's a little bit of Italy, but the canton Ticino is decidedly Swiss.

For the German Swiss, it's a little bit of paradise. They can cross over the Saint Gotthard or San Bernardino passes and emerge in balmy sunshine, eat gnocchi and polenta in shaded *grotti* (rustic outdoor restaurants), drink merlot from ceramic bowls, taste *gelato* (ice cream) while gazing at the waters of Lago di Maggiore (Lake Maggiore)—and still know their lodging will be strictly controlled by the Swiss Hotel Association. They don't even have to change money. The combination is irresistible, and so in spring, summer, and fall they pour over the Alps to revel in low-risk Latin delights.

And the Ticinese welcome them like rich, distant cousins, to be served and coddled and—perhaps just a bit—despised. For the Italian-speaking natives of the Ticino—a lonely 8% of the Swiss population—are a minority in their own land, dominated politically by the German-speaking Swiss, set apart by their culture as well as by their language. Their blood and their politics are as Mediterranean as their climate: in a battle over obligatory seat belts, the Ticinese consistently voted to reject the federal intrusion. They were voted down by their Germanic neighbors—a 70% majority—and they protested. It was brought to vote again, and again they were defeated. Nowadays the Ticinese defy the federal law—and their policemen, Ticinese themselves, of course, turn a blind and supportive eye.

Their Italian leanings make perfect sense: an enormous mountain chain cuts them off from the north, pushing them inexorably toward their lingual roots. Most of the territory of the Ticino belonged to the pre-Italian city-states of Milan and Como until 1512, when the Swiss Confederation took it over by force. It remained a Swiss conquest—oppressed under the then-tyrannical rule of Uri, Schwyz, and Unterwalden, the very cantons now revered for forming the honorable Confederation of Switzerland—until 1798, when from the confusion of Napoléon's campaigns it emerged a free canton, and in 1803 it joined the confederation for good.

It remains a canton apart nonetheless, graceful, open, laissez-faire. Here you'll instantly notice differences in manner and body language among Ticinese engaged in conversation; you'll also notice fewer English-speaking Swiss. The climate, too, is different: there's an extraordinary amount of sunshine here—more than in central Switzerland and even in sunny Italy immediately across the border, where Milan and Turin often are haunted by a grim overcast of gray. Mountain-sports meccas aside, this is the most glamorous of Swiss regions: the waterfront promenades of Lugano, Locarno, and Ascona, lined with pollards, rhododendrons, and bobbing yachts, blend a rich social mix of jet-set resorters. A few miles' drive brings the canton's impoverished past into view— the foothill and mountain villages are still scattered with low-roof stone peasants' cabins, but nowadays those cabins often prove to have been gentrified as chic vacation homes.

Although they're prosperous, with Lugano standing third in banking, after Zürich and Geneva, the Ticinese hold on to their past, a mountain-peasant culture that draws them to hike, hunt, and celebrate with great pots of risotto stirred over open outdoor fires. It's that contrast—contemporary glamour, earthy past—that grants travelers a visit that's as balanced, satisfying, and as unique as a good merlot.

Pleasures and Pastimes

Dining

Of all the Swiss regions, this can be the most pleasurable to eat in, as the stylish and simple cuisine of Italy has been adopted virtually intact. Because the Ticinese were once a poor mountain people, their everyday cooking shares the earthy delights of another once-poor mountain people, the Piedmontese, whose steaming polenta and rib-sticking gnocchi break bread with game and meaty porcini mushrooms. *Manzo brasato* (savory braised beef with vegetables) and osso buco are standards, as are polenta *con carne in umido* (with meat stew), *busecca* (vegetable soup with tripe), and any number of variations on risotto. If you look and ask, you might be lucky enough to find *trota in carpione* (trout marinated in red wine and vinegar and served as a cold hors d'oeuvre). Game offerings usually include *coniglio* (rabbit), *lepre* (hare), and *capretto* (roast kid).

As in the rest of Switzerland, local cold meats come in a broad variety, from myriad salamis to prosciutto *crudo*, the pearly pink, cured, raw ham made famous in Parma. Any food product made locally is called *nostrano*, and the prosciutto crudo nostrano is worth asking for, as you won't find a match for its forthright, gamey flavor back home. Eat it with bread and sweet butter to balance the salt.

Most cooks import Italian cheeses—Parmigiano-Reggiano, sharp pecorino—though there are good, hard, white mountain varieties (Piora, Gesero) in most shops. Tiny *formaggini*—little molds of ultra-fresh goat cheese—taste best with coarsely ground black pepper and olive oil. Or try the *zincarlin*, a fresh cheese mixed with parsley, garlic, and pepper.

The best place to sample these down-to-earth delicacies is in a grotto, one of the scores of traditional country restaurants scattered across the region. Some of them are set deep in the mountains and forests, little more than a few rows of picnic tables and a string of festive lights. Some serve only cold meats, but a few offer a daily hot dish or two. To experience an authentic grotto, avoid the ones with *ristorante* in their names; the categories of eating establishments are carefully regulated, so these will always be pricier—and not the real thing. The local wine is merlot; a warm, generous, ruby wine counted as one of the top Swiss reds. The wine is poured into an individual *boccalino*, a traditional ceramic pitcher, or a small ceramic bowl, to be drunk from like a cup. Instead of beer to quench locals' thirsts, a mix of *gazosa* (lemon-lime soda) and *vino nostrano* (the house red wine) is de rigueur. If you want a real Italian-style espresso, one-finger deep and frothing with golden foam, ask for *un liscio*. Otherwise they'll serve it with cream, Swiss style—and might even charge you extra. If you want a shot of grappa (grape brandy) thrown in, ask for it *corretto*—literally, "correct." Or finish off your meal with a shot of *Nocino*, a traditional walnut liqueur also known as *Ratafiá* (from *rata fiat,* meaning "it's done"). Walnuts picked before San Giovanni's day (June 25) are soaked in grappa and mixed with a secret combination of herbs and spices. Most Nocino is produced privately from closely guarded recipes—no two taste alike.

CATEGORY	COST*
$$$$	over 80 SF
$$$	50 SF–80 SF
$$	20 SF–50 SF
$	under 20 SF

Prices are per person for a three-course meal (two-course meal in $ category), including sales tax and 15% service charge

Lodging

The hotel industry of this Mediterranean region of Switzerland capitalizes on its natural assets, with lakeside views of Lago di Lugano and Lake Maggiore, and swimming pools and terraces that pay homage to the omnipresent sun. As the Ticino is at its best in spring and fall, and packed with sunseekers in summer, many hotels close down for the winter. Tourist offices often publish lists of those remaining open, so if you're planning to come in low season—and even in January the lake resorts can be balmy—check carefully. Keep in mind that most hotels are not air-conditioned, in spite of hot spells in July and August. Places which might catch a breeze off the lake, like lakefront or hillside lodging, are more comfortable in high summer. Although these are vacation resorts, they do not depend on the *demipension* (half-board) system as much as their mountain counterparts, but arrangements can be made.

CATEGORY	COST*
$$$$	over 300 SF
$$$	180 SF–300 SF
$$	120 SF–180 SF
$	under 120 SF

Prices are for a standard double room, including breakfast, tax, and service charge.

Mountain Valleys

Valle di Blenio, Valle Maggia, Valle Verzasca, Valle Leventina, and other mountain valleys just a short distance from the major cities, are rugged reminders of the region's modest history. Stone peasant homes, called *rustici*, dot the valleys, some cut so deeply into the land that the sun never quite reaches bottom. Driving these valleys can be disorienting, for time seems to have stopped; you'll encounter whole villages perched on craggy mountainsides in apparent defiance of gravity.

Waterfront Promenades

Switzerland's sunniest waterfronts—with boating, swimming, charming cafés, fine dining, and shops of all sorts—are in the Ticino. Palm-lined promenades in Lugano, Locarno, and Ascona offer tremendous views overlooking rugged Italian Alps.

Exploring the Ticino

The canton is divided into two geographic regions by the small mountain range (554 m/1,817 ft) called Monte Ceneri, which rises up south of the valley below Bellinzona. Extending northeast and northwest of Monte Ceneri in the windswept Sopraceneri region are several mountainous valleys, including Valle di Blenio, Valle Maggia, Valle Verzasca, and Valle Leventina. Included in this region north of, or literally, "above" Monte Ceneri are Locarno and Ascona, which share a peninsula bulging into Lake Maggiore. The more developed southern region, Sottoceneri ("below Ceneri"), is home to business and resort towns, notably Lugano.

Numbers in the text correspond to numbers in the margin and on the Ticino and Lugano maps.

Great Itineraries

Lugano and Locarno alone provide an overview of the region, but completing the picture requires forays to the less touristy waterfront village of Ascona, the mountain stronghold of Bellinzona, and the rural, rugged mountain valleys beyond.

IF YOU HAVE 1 OR 2 DAYS

Concentrate on ⊡ **Lugano** ⑦–⑲, exploring the waterfront shops, venturing east to the Villa Favorita, and riding a funicular up Monte Brè. On the second day, take in the sights of the serene hillside city ⊡ **Locarno** ③ and the former fishing village of **Ascona** ⑥, both on the shore of Lake Maggiore.

IF YOU HAVE 3 OR 4 DAYS

In addition to all of the above, explore the medieval fortifications of **Bellinzona** ①, the canton's capital, and tiny **Campione** ㉑, an Italian enclave on Swiss territory. Also take a drive through the wilds of the Ticino, into any of the numerous rugged valleys, and discover the tiny, ancient villages perched on the mountainsides. A perfect sample would be a drive through **Valle di Blenio** ②, where peasant life has carried on virtually unchanged for centuries.

When to Tour the Ticino

Lush and Mediterranean, the Ticino is gorgeous in springtime; the season starts as early as mid-March here, making the region a popular late-winter escape. In summertime, lakeside activity surges, and the weather can at times be hot. Warm summer nights are incredibly romantic, particularly on the Lago di Lugano. Crowds fill the promenades at Lugano and Locarno throughout the summer, but neither waterfront becomes unpleasantly jammed—although the road from Bellinzona to Locarno and Lugano is usually packed.

SOPRACENERI

The mountainous valleys of Valle di Blenio, Valle Maggia, Valle Verzasca, and Valle Leventina reach like the fingers of a hand south from the Alps into the basin of Lake Maggiore and Monte Ceneri in the Sopraceneri. At the tips are the sun-kissed resorts of Locarno and Ascona, both on Italy's Lake Maggiore. Here the true spirit of the canton is still evident in the numerous, small valley communities, some with less than 100 inhabitants—but nonetheless, each politically autonomous. The Sopraceneri reveals a slightly slower-paced, homier side of the Ticino, leaving the flashier offerings to Lugano in the south.

Bellinzona

★ ❶   *128 km (79 mi) south of Luzern, 150 km (93 mi) south of Saint-Moritz.*

All roads lead to Bellinzona, the fortified valley city that guards the important European crossroads of the Saint Gotthard and San Bernardino routes. Its importance through the ages makes itself evident: massive fortified castles—no fewer than three—rise over its ancient center. They were built by the noble Sfórza and Visconti families, the dukes of Milan who ruled northern Italy and environs for centuries and held this crucial juncture until 1422, when the Swiss Confederates began a violent century of battling for its control. Bellinzona passed to the Swiss Confederation in 1503. Ironically, the names of the castles built in part to keep the Swiss at bay were then changed to Schwyz, Uri, and Unterwalden—the three core cantons of the Swiss Confederation. Eventually the names were changed again and the

113

KEY

Rail Line
Cable Car/ Funicular
Regional Boundary Lines
Ski Resorts

N

0   8 miles
0   12 km

ITALY

S33
Cuzzago

S. Maria Maggiore

S337

CENTOVALLI

Gordevio

Cardada
Tegna
Intragna
Camedo
Ronco
Brissago
Valmara

Corippo
Cimetta
L. di Vogorno

Gordola
Gordola

Locarno
Ascona

3
6

Maggia
Lago Maggiore

13

Germignana

S34

Verbania

Laveno-Mombello

Citiglio

S394

Ghirla

Ponte Tresa

S233

Lago Maggiore

Gorduno

Sementina

Monte Ceneri

A2

Quartino

A13

Bellinzona
Pludo
Giubiasco

1

Agno

Lugano
7 — 19

Monte San Salvatore

Melide

Morcote
22

Riva San Vitale

23

Paradiso di Lugano

Monte Brè

Gandria
20

Campione
21

Lago di Lugano

Lago di Lugano

Monte Generoso

Mendrisio
2

A2

ITALY

Porlezza

Lugano

S340

Argegno

Lago di Como

ITALY

fortresses are known today as Castelgrande, Castello di Montebello, and Castello di Sasso Corbaro.

The three castles have been exceptionally well restored and each merits a visit, but the city itself should not be overlooked: it is a classic Lombard town, with graceful architecture, red cobblestones, and an easy, authentically Italian ambience. It is relatively free of tourists and thus most revealing of the Ticino way of life.

Pick up a map in the tourist office in the **Palazzo Civico** (⊠ Via Camminata, ☎ 091/8252131), a splendid Renaissance structure heavily rebuilt in the 1920s. Its courtyard is framed by two stacked rows of delicate vaulted arcades, with airy loggias at the top. The **Old Town,** with its heavy-column arcades, wrought-iron balconies, and shuttered facades, exhibits the direct influence of medieval Lombardy. It's a small area, distinguished by its red cobblestones.

The **Castelgrande** was begun in the 6th century, though the current structure dates from the 1200s. The massive exterior is dominated by two heavy, unmatched towers and the remaining portion of a crenellated wall that once stretched all the way to the river. Renovations and modern additions have created an elaborate new complex of restaurants (☞ Dining, *below*) and museums, including art and archaeology exhibitions. The 14th-century ceiling murals, created to embellish the wooden ceiling of a local villa (now demolished), offer a peek at privately commissioned decorative art. ⊠ *Monte San Michele,* ☎ *091/ 8258145.* ⛶ *4 SF; 8 SF combination ticket for Castelgrande, Castello di Montebello, and Castello di Sasso Corbaro.* ☉ *Feb.–Dec., Tues.– Sun. 10–6.*

The imposing late-Renaissance facade of the **Chiesa Collegiata di San Pietro e San Stefano** (Church of St. Peter and St. Stephen), begun in the 16th century, stands across from the Castelgrande. Its interior is lavishly frescoed in the baroque style by late-18th-century Ticino artists. ⊠ *Piazza Collegiata,* ☎ *091/8252605.*

The most striking of Bellinzona's three castles is the **Castello di Montebello.** Its oldest, center portion dates from the 13th century; there are also a palace and courtyard from the 15th century, with spectacular walkways around the top of the encircling walls. The center structure houses an attractive, modern **Museo Civico** (Municipal Museum), with exhibits on local history and architecture, including an impressive collection of Gothic and Renaissance stone capitals. ⊠ *Salita ai Castelli,* ☎ *091/8251342.* ⛶ *4 SF, 8 SF combination ticket for Castelgrande, Castello di Montebello, and Castello di Sasso Corbaro.* ☉ *Feb.– Dec., Tues.–Sun. 10–6.*

The lofty **Castello di Sasso Corbaro** is a typical Sforza structure, designed by a Florentine military engineer and built in 1479 for the duke of Milan, who insisted the work be completed in six months. In the dungeon, there's a branch of the **Museo dell'Arte e delle Tradizioni Popolari del Ticino** (Museum of Traditional Ticino Arts and Crafts), displaying coins, stamps, historic photographs of Bellinzona, and a fine exhibit of Ticino folk costumes. Ambitious walkers can reach it in about 45 minutes by going uphill from the Castello di Montebello along a switchback road through woods; if you are driving, follow signs. ☎ *091/8255906.* ⛶ *4 SF, 8 SF combination ticket for Castelgrande, Castello di Montebello, and Castello di Sasso Corbaro.* ☉ *Feb.–Dec., Tues.–Sun. 10–6.*

Chiesa San Biagio (Church of St. Biagio), one of Bellinzona's two Italianate churches, is a spare medieval treasure guarded on the exterior by an outsize fresco of a soldierly Christ. The 12th-century, late-Romanesque structure suggests a transition into Gothic style. Natural alternating redbrick and gray stone complement fragments of exquisitely colored 14th-century frescoes. ⊠ *Via San Biagio 13, Bellinzona-Ravecchia,* ☎ *091/8252505.*

Built at the end of the 15th century, **Chiesa Santa Maria delle Grazie** (Church of the Holy Virgin) displays a split transept in the Franciscan style, with a dividing wall spectacularly frescoed by an unknown 15th-century Lombard artist. The central image is a crucifixion scene; the surrounding panels depict the life of Christ. ⊠ *Via Convento 5,* ☎ *091/78252663.*

The city's art gallery, **Villa dei Cedri,** sporadically dips into its coffers—made up of a donated private collection—and hangs worthwhile exhibits. Behind the garden and grounds, the city maintains a tiny vineyard used to produce its very own merlot, available for sale inside. ⊠ *Piazza San Biagio 9,* ☎ *091/8218520.* 🖭 *8 SF.* ☉ *Mid-Nov.–Mar., Tues.–Sun. 10–noon and 2–5; Apr.–mid-Nov., Tues.–Sat. 10–noon and 2–6, Sun. 10–6.*

Dining and Lodging

$$–$$$
★
╳ **Castelgrande.** Now that the oldest of the city's castles has been renovated, its chic, modern restaurant merits a visit. Don't expect a quick cafeteria lunch served to shorts-clad tourists: this is a serious experience, with a daringly cool, post-Memphis decor and sophisticated efforts from the Italian chef, such as goose liver with blueberries or pigeon and pearl onions in sweet-and-sour sauce. The wine list flaunts more than 70 Ticino merlots. The terrace has a lighter atmosphere; it's a great spot to soak up views and sunshine. ⊠ *Monte San Michele,* ☎ *091/8262353. AE, DC, MC, V. Closed Mon.*

$$
╳ **Osteria Sasso Corbaro.** From the heights of the ancient Castello Sasso Corbaro, this atmospheric restaurant serves meals inside a beautifully restored hall or outside, at stone tables, in the shady, walled-in courtyard. The cooking is simple and regional, with cold and grilled meats, trout, and seasonal vegetables. Good local wines toast a holiday air, as the restaurant opens only in high season. ⊠ *Castello Sasso Corbaro,* ☎ *091/8255532. AE, DC, MC, V. Closed Mon. and Nov.–Apr.*

$–$$
╳ **Montebello.** At this spot on a hill above the center in the adjoining suburb of Daro, you can relax under a grape arbor at linen-covered tables and enjoy an authentic meal in true Italian style: easygoing and elegantly simple. From a standing menu and a list of daily specials, sample carpaccio, homemade pasta, and frothy zabaglione. ⊠ *Via alla Chiesa 3, Bellinzona-Daro,* ☎ *091/8258395. AE, DC, MC, V. Closed Sun.*

$
╳🏠 **Grotto Paudese.** Immaculate, friendly, and family-run, this grotto-cum-bed-and-breakfast perches high above the town in the tiny hamlet of Paudo. Its handful of rooms are tastefully simple if small; they squeeze in the occasional antique chest of drawers. There's also an unsurpassed view of the twinkling valley and the Alps beyond. The adjoining grotto is warmly traditional, turning out a robust daily meal (homemade pasta, polenta, and the like). The inn is roughly a 15-minute drive from Bellinzona. Going east into the Val Morobbia, follow signs for Piannezo and then for Paudo. ⊠ *CH-6582 Paudo,* ☎ FAX *091/8571468. 4 rooms. Restaurant, bar. MC, V.*

En Route To see the deep countryside of the Ticino—beyond its resorts and cities—follow the A–2 expressway north from Bellinzona toward Saint Gotthard; after 17 km (11 mi), exit at **Biasca,** a miniature Bellinzona itself, as it guards two major access roads from the north.

Valle di Blenio

❷ *17 km (11 mi) north of Bellinzona, 80 km (49 mi) north of Lugano.*

North of Biasca toward Olivone is the Valle di Blenio, a characteristic Ticinese valley cutting deeper and higher into wild, rocky country. Its villages mingle tidy suburban cottages with the architectural signature of Ticino life: ancient stone houses, some little more thans huts, with ramshackle roofs of odd-size slabs. This is the *rustico* once inhabited by mountain peasants starving under the harsh rule of the Swiss-German confederates. Today the heirs of both those ancient lines happily profit from a new twist: the Ticinese now rent their *rustici* to wealthy tourists—most of them Swiss-German—seeking to escape the pressures of urban prosperity. In these villages—Largario, Ponto Valentino, Prugiasco—you'll see the real, rural Ticino.

Locarno

❸ *21 km (13 mi) west of Bellinzona, 39 km (24 mi) northwest of Lugano.*

Superbly placed on the sheltered curve of the northernmost tip of Lake Maggiore and surrounded on all sides by mountains, Locarno is Switzerland's sunniest town. Subtropical flora flourishes here, with date palms and fig trees, bougainvillea, rhododendron, even aloe vera burgeoning on the waterfront. Its fauna is no less colorful: every spring, summer, and fall the arcaded streets and cafés teem with exotic characters in fur coats and T-shirts, lamé, leather—and sunglasses. You don't show your face in Locarno without a stylish set of shades.

In August, Locarno makes worldwide news with its film festival, showcasing the latest cinema on an outdoor screen in the Piazza Grande; it is also host to international artists in concert. Its facilities haven't just drawn culture hounds: here, in 1925, Briand, Stresemann, Mussolini, and Chamberlain initiated the Locarno Pact, securing the peace—albeit temporarily—in Europe.

Locarno's raison d'être is its waterfront, which has a graceful promenade curving around the east flank of the bay and a beach and public pool complex along the west. Its clear lake is often still as glass, reflecting the Ticinese Alps across to the south. Locarno's Lombard-style arcades and historic landmarks continually draw visitors inland as well. There are a few pedestrian streets in the heart of the Old Town.

★ The **Piazza Grande** is the heart of the Old Town and its social center, too: from under the crowded arcades shoppers spill onto open ground to lounge in cafés and watch each other drink, smoke, and pose. **Chiesa Nuova** (New Church; ⊠ Via Cittadella) is an exuberantly decorated baroque church (1630) with an enormous statue of St. Christopher on the facade. Down the street from the New Church, the **Casa dei Canonici** (House of the Canons; ⊠ Via Cittadella) dates from the same period; note the lovely interior courtyard (it's now a private house).

The 17th-century **Chiesa di Sant'Antonio** (Church of St. Anthony) lies at the end of **Via Sant'Antonio**, a fine, narrow street lined with splendid old houses in both medieval and flamboyant baroque styles. Immediately to the right of the Church of St. Anthony stands the **Casa Rusca,** an 18th-century residence that now serves as the city art gallery. Its permanent collections include the work of Jean Arp, and temporary exhibits highlight both Swiss and international artists. ⊠ *Via Sant'Antonio,* ☎ *091/7563185.* ☜ *5 SF.* ☉ *Tues.–Fri. 10–6.*

The heavy, frescoed **Chiesa di San Francesco** (Church of St. Francis) and its convent date from the mid-15th century; legend has it that it was founded by St. Anthony of Padua. The emblems on its Renaissance facade show Locarno's social distinctions of the era: the eagle represents the aristocrats; a lamb, the country folk; and the ox (unkind, surely), the citizens. In its sanctuary, concerts are performed every spring and fall; contact the tourist office (☞ Visitor Information *in* The Ticino A to Z, *below*) for more information. ⊠ *Via S. Francesco.*

Built in 1300 as a stronghold of the dukes of Milan, **Castello Visconteo** was soon virtually destroyed by the invading Swiss Confederates. Today it contains a **Museo Civico e Archeologico** (Municipal and Archaeological Museum), with Roman relics, including a major glass collection, and Romanesque sculpture. ⊠ *Piazza Castello 2,* ☎ *091/ 7563180.* ☜ *5 SF.* ☾ *Apr.–Oct., Tues.–Sun. 10–5.*

★ You can get to the **Santuario Madonna del Sasso** (Sanctuary of the Madonna of the Rock) via a five-minute funicular ride to a high plateau (the funicular is close to the train station). The sprawling church complex is where, in 1480, Brother Bartolomeo da Ivrea saw a vision of the Virgin Mary; the sanctuary was begun seven years later and gradually enlarged to include a convent, a museum, and side galleries. Within the sanctuary, you'll find Bramantino's *The Flight into Egypt* (1520) and *Christ Carried to the Sepulcher,* a dramatic, Caravaggiesque procession scene painted in 1870 by Antonio Ciseri, from nearby Ascona. You'll also see naive-art votive gifts to the Madonna from peasants who've survived everything from family tragedies to fender benders. ⊠ *Via Santuario 2, Orselina,* ☎ *091/7436265.* ☾ *Sanctuary: daily 6:30 AM–8 PM; church: daily 6:30 AM–7 PM; museum: weekdays 2–4:30, Sun. 10–noon and 2–5.*

Dining and Lodging

$$$$ ✕ **Centenario.** Set back from the waterfront east of the urban tangle,
★ this gracious *ristorante* serves innovative Franco-Italian cuisine that is unashamedly nouvelle and absolutely top quality, from its moderately priced business lunch to the all-out *menu de dégustation* (sampling menu). Specialties include risotto in merlot with crayfish tails, rack of roe deer, and tangy lemon soufflé. You can have an aperitif on the lakefront terrace before sitting down to a meal surrounded by quarry tile, Persian rugs, and gleaming silver. ⊠ *Lungolago 13, Locarno-Muralto,* ☎ *091/ 7438222. AE, DC, MC, V. Closed Sun. and Mon.*

$–$$ ✕ **Casa del Popolo.** While the politics might lean left at this popular restaurant, the Italian favorites are done just right. Try the amazingly delicate *Picatta alla Milanese* (veal cutlets pounded thin, coated in egg, and sautéed), the spicy *Penne all'arrabbiata* (pasta with red pepper and tomato sauce), or any of the 20 types of pizza. Red-checked tablecloths and occasional appearances by the local *politico* round it all out. ⊠ *Piazza Corporazione,* ☎ *091/7511208. No credit cards.*

$$$–$$$$ ✕▥ **Reber au Lac.** This richly landscaped oasis at the end of the waterfront row holds a roomy, comfortable hotel dating from 1886 and still in the Reber family. The interiors exude patrician calm with pleasing touches like antique Venetian glass lamps, lacy duvet covers, and the occasional bit of gilt or wrought iron. Awning-shaded balconies overlook the lake or pool, and interiors are done in tasteful pastels— no two rooms are alike. The Grill Room has a good reputation among locals for its Franco-Italian cuisine and creative fish menus served in a Spanish setting. ⊠ *Viale Verbano 55, CH-6600 Locarno-Muralto,* ☎ *091/7358700,* ℻ *091/7358701. 60 rooms, 8 suites. 2 restaurants, 2 bars, no-smoking rooms, pool, sauna, tennis court, beach, business services. AE, DC, MC, V. Closed mid-Nov.–Feb.*

$$$ ✕▥ **Belvedere.** Well above the city, this wonderfully situated hotel has
★ gone all out, with interiors in postmodern beech, lacquer, and marble. All rooms face south; the suites in the wing on the hill offer particu-

larly breathtaking views. The elegant dining hall, with its frescoes, elaborately trimmed vaults, and a massive stone fireplace, is all that remains of the original building, a private home built in 1680. L'Affresco, the formal restaurant, serves upscale Italian specialties; look for the turbot in a potato crust and the homemade pastas. You can reach the Belvedere by funicular from the train station or on foot in a five-minute uphill walk; Mr. Taylor, the energetic, Welsh proprietor, is a gracious host. ⊠ *Via ai Monti della Trinità 44, CH-6601,* ☎ *091/ 7510363,* FAX *091/7515239. 52 rooms, 12 suites. 3 restaurants, bar, no-smoking rooms, pool, hot tub, sauna, health club, bicycles, playground, business services. AE, DC, MC, V.*

\$\$–\$\$\$ ✕⊞ **Dell'Angelo.** At the end of the Piazza Grande and the long row of Lombardy arcades, this downtown hotel fits right in: it was based on a 1674 structure, with ground-floor arches and iron-trim balconies. The interior isn't entirely in keeping, however—an incongruous, silver-mirrored elevator zips you up to spare, walnut-grain Formica and beige stucco rooms. A lively pizzeria at street level serves pizzas cooked in a wood-burning oven and grilled meats; you can choose from the same menu in the restaurant upstairs, where you'll eat amid chintz and damask under the faded remains of frescoed vaulting. ⊠ *Piazza Grande, CH-6601,* ☎ *091/7518175,* FAX *091/7518256. 55 rooms. Restaurant, pizzeria. AE, DC, MC, V.*

\$\$–\$\$\$ ✕⊞ **Hotel Navegna.** It may not look like much from outside, but this is a true diamond in the rough, right on the lake farther up shore from the promenade. The rooms are simply furnished, but the kitchen is the real magnet. The inventive Ticinese cooking earns raves for gregarious owner Enrico Ravelli. Navegna is close to rail tracks (luckily there are no night trains) so you may wish to request a lake view. ⊠ *Via alla Riva 2, CH-6648 Locarno-Munusio,* ☎ *091/7432222,* FAX *091/7433150. 22 rooms. 2 restaurants, bicycles. MC, V. Closed Dec.–Feb.*

\$–\$\$\$ ✕⊞ **Cittadella.** This popular dining spot in the Old Town offers inexpensive regional food—pizzas, pastas, simply prepared fish—in its casual downstairs trattoria and fine fish dishes in the more formal restaurant upstairs. The preparation is light, the flavors subtle with oils and herbs. Upstairs are a handful of newly done (1999), pleasing rooms, some up under the rafters, all with classic stone tile floors in cream and red. They may be simple, but they're a great bargain. ⊠ *Via Cittadella 18, CH-6600,* ☎ *091/7515885,* FAX *091/7517759. 11 rooms. Restaurant. AE, DC, MC, V.*

Nightlife and the Arts

BARS

Amalur Music Bar (⊠ Via Torretta 7, ☎ 091/7516414) is open year-round; it keeps going until 3 or 4 AM. The piano bar/jazz club **La Bussola** (⊠ Lungolago, Locarno-Muralto, ☎ 091/7436095) is a favorite among locals; it's closed on Tuesday. **Palm'Arte** (⊠ Hotel La Palma au Lac, Viale Verbano 29, Locarno-Muralto, ☎ 091/7353636) is a good piano bar; it's closed Tuesday during the high season and from December to February.

CASINO

The **Kursaal** (Casino; ⊠ Via Largo Zorzi 1, Piazza Grande, ☎ 091/ 7511535) has 195 slot machines and *boule* (a type of roulette), with a federally imposed 5 SF limit. It's open every day from noon to 2 AM, until 4 AM on Friday and Saturday nights.

FILM

The **Locarno International Film Festival,** gaining ground from Cannes on the prestige front because of the caliber of the films it premieres, takes place every August in the Piazza Grande. The 2000 festival will run August 2–12. For information, contact: Festival Internazionale del Film Locarno (✉ Via B. Luini 3/a, CH-6601 Locarno, ☎ 091/7562121).

MUSIC

The **I Feel Good Funk Festival,** a new, annual, open-air event staged in the Piazza Grande, hosts local and international funk artists. It's slated to run in late June 2000. The **Back Home Again–American Music Festival Locarno** is scheduled for June 9–11, 2000. The musical menu has a little of everything, from Cajun and country to bluegrass and blues.

OFF THE
BEATEN PATH

CIMETTA – A winter sports center with views of Monte Rosa, the Swiss Alps, and the Italian Apennines, Cimetta (1,672 m/5,482 ft) can be reached only by chairlift; first you must catch a cable car (near the train station) to Cardada, then a chairlift to the resort. But don't be put off; the ride is part of the fun: as the lake falls away below, you sail over flowery meadows and wooded hills. Cimetta is also a hiker's paradise. Renovations are currently being made on both the cable car and chairlift, with reopening planned for spring 2000. For information, call the chairlift company at ☎ 091/7566115 or 091/7566117.

Valle Verzasca

❹ *12 km (7 mi) north of Locarno, 25 km (15½ mi) north of Lugano.*

A short drive along the A–13 highway through the wild and rugged mountain gorge of the Valle Verzasca leads to **Corippo,** where a painterly composition of stone houses and a 17th-century church are all protected as architectural landmarks.

About 12 km (7 mi) north of Corippo, in the town of **Lavertezzo,** you'll find a graceful double-arch stone bridge, the **Ponte dei Salti,** dating from 1700. The mountain village of Sonogno lies at the end of the 26-km (16-mi) valley.

Valle Maggia

❺ *4 km (2 mi) northwest of Locarno, 30 km (19 mi) northwest of Lugano.*

A drive through this rugged, agricultural valley that stretches northwest from Locarno will give you a sense of the tough living conditions endured for centuries by Ticinese peasants, who today mine granite. The valley is cut so far into the earth that sunlight in winter never seems to reach bottom—a stark contrast to sunny Locarno only a short distance south. Until the 1920s, many Valle Maggia natives immigrated to the United States; some returned, bringing with them several English phrases that still pepper the local Ticinese dialect. As you pass through Gordevio, Maggia, Someo, and Cevio—the valley's main village—you'll feel as if you're in a time capsule: there's little commercialization, and the mostly 17th-century houses call to mind a movie set. Bignasco, just beyond Cevio, is the last village before the valley splits in two continuing north.

OFF THE
BEATEN PATH

MOGNO – Beyond Bignasco to the east lies the Val Lavizzara. At Peccia the road splits again, with Val Sambuco to the east. Nearly at the end of this valley, in tiny Mogno, stands a beautiful, modernist chapel built in 1994 by world-renowned Ticinese architect Mario Botta, who designed the San Francisco Museum of Modern Art. For information, contact Associazione Ricostruzione Chiesa di Mogno, CH-6696 Fusio (open Apr.– Oct.).

Ascona

❻ *3 km (1¾ mi) west of Locarno.*

Though it's only a few minutes from Locarno, tiny Ascona has a life of its own. Little more than a fishing village until the turn of the century, the town was adopted by a high-minded group of northerners who arrived to develop a utopian, vegetarian artists' colony on **Monte Verità,** the hillside park behind the waterfront center. Influenced by Eastern and Western religions as well as the new realms of psychology, its ideals attracted thousands of sojourners, including dancer Isadora Duncan and psychologist C. G. Jung. You can visit the group of Monte Verità buildings, including the unusual, flat-roof, wooden **Casa Anatta,** and view papers and relics of the group's works. ⊠ *Monte Verità, between waterfront and town center,* ☎ *091/7910327 or 091/7910181 for the Monte Verità Foundation.* 🖼 *6 SF.* ⏰ *Apr.–June, Sept., and Oct., Tues.–Sun. 2:30–6; July and Aug., Tues.–Sun. 3–7.*

Monte Verità's influence spread and its reputation grew throughout the world. Today the still-small village of 5,000 attracts artists, art restorers, and traditional bookbinders to its ancient, narrow streets. On ★ the waterfront, however, it's a sun-and-fun scene, with the **Piazza Motta** (isolated from traffic as a pedestrian zone) crowded with sidewalk cafés and the promenade on the water's edge swarming with boats. Behind Piazza Motta, a charming labyrinth of lanes leads uphill past artisan galleries (not all showing gallery-quality work) to **Via Borgo,** lined with contemporary shops and galleries.

OFF THE BEATEN PATH

BRISSAGO ISLANDS – From Ascona, an easy excursion by car or bus leads to Brissago, a flowery lakefront resort at the lowest elevation in Switzerland. The main attraction, however, lies offshore: the Brissago Islands, two floral gems floating in Lake Maggiore, have been federally preserved as botanical gardens, with more than 1,000 species of subtropical plants. Plaques identify the flora in Italian, German, and French; an English guide to the plants is for sale at the gate (5 SF). You may have lunch or drinks at the island's restaurant, in a beautifully restored 1929 villa that now doubles as a seminar center and offers lodging to groups. Individuals must leave with the last boat back to the mainland—usually around 6—so check schedules carefully when you plan your excursion. You can buy tickets at the entrance or with the boat ticket; group and Swiss Boat Pass (☞ Boat Travel *in* Smart Travel Tips A to Z) discounts apply. ⊠ *Boats depart regularly from Brissago, Porto Ronco, Ascona, and Locarno,* ☎ *091/7914361.* 🖼 *Boat: 11 SF round-trip from Ascona; island: 6 SF.*

Dining and Lodging

$$$–$$$$ ✕ **Ascolago.** There's a potent Italian influence in this hotel restaurant's menu; seasonal specialties might include stuffed quail with goose liver and champagne sauerkraut or freshly caught lake perch with herbs. Besides the bright, open dining room there's a spacious terrace overlooking the lake. It's popular—reservations are essential if you want to snag a table for dinner. ⊠ *Hotel Ascolago,* ☎ *091/7912055. V. Closed mid-Nov.–mid-Dec. and Mon. Oct.–May.*

$$ ✕ **Ristorante Stazione.** Going west from Locarno into the picturesque Centovalli you'll come to the tiny town of Intragna—and near its train station you will find this little gem. Agnese Broggini has spent almost 30 years offering a bright, cheerful place to stop and have a special meal of risotto, chicken, or other Ticino specialties. Sixty varieties of merlot are offered. ⊠ *Intragna,* ☎ *091/7961212. AE, DC, MC, V. Closed Dec.–Feb.*

$$$$ ✕▦ **Giardino.** Glamorous, atmospheric, cosmopolitan—this hotel
★ feels like the kissing cousin of a Mediterranean villa. Portuguese ceramics, Florentine floor tiles, Veronese marble, ceramic room-number
plaques in della Robbia style, and even a Swiss-baroque, carved-wood
conference chamber from Zürich's Bierhalle Kropf have been imported. The luxury of this Relais & Châteaux property borders on deca-
dence: the sheets are pure linen, ground-floor rooms have small, private
gardens, and there's a landscaped pool, not to mention a chauffeured
Bentley, an antique-bus shuttle service, and pink bicycles for guest use.
The charming manager, Hans Leu, keeps things grounded—he'll even
pick you up at the train station on his pink Harley, if you like. The
restaurants are excellent: Aphrodite, with modern Italian and vegetarian
cuisine, rates among the best in Switzerland. The Osteria runs close
behind with its regional Italian specialties. Varied weekly programs include a sunrise mountaintop breakfast, lunch on the hotel's boat, simple hikes and bike-and-picnic excursions. On Sundays there's Teatro
Giardino: dinner theater including ballet one week, singing waiters, jazz,
or opera the next. Prepare to be spoiled. ⊠ *Via Segnale 10, CH-6612,*
☎ *091/7910101, FAX 091/7921094. 54 rooms, 18 suites, 5 apartments.*
3 restaurants, bar, pool, beauty salon, hot tub, steam room, bicycles,
baby-sitting. AE, DC, MC, V. Closed mid-Nov.–mid-Mar.

$$$–$$$$ ▦ **Casa Berno.** This Relais du Silence hotel manages absolute isola-
tion; it's on a forest road tucked into a hillside far above the town and
lake. Its self-containment (there's even a magazine-and-tobacco shop
in the lobby and a shuttle bus to town) and the aura of dated gentil-
ity, projected by the avocado brocade and Picasso prints in cream
frames, appeal to relaxed vacationers who want to laze by the big pool
overlooking the lake, have drinks and lunch on the broad roof terrace,
and get away from it all—completely. Multi-level terraces catch the best
views—from the Brissago Islands to Bellinzona. Room decor ranges
from polished, dark wood to white wood with red or blue accents. Re-
quest a room on one of the top floors for the most sweeping views.
Demipension is standard, but menus can be modified. ⊠ *CH-6612,*
☎ *091/7913232, FAX 091/7921114. 65 rooms. 2 restaurants, bar, café,*
pool, massage, beauty salon, sauna, health club, mountain bikes. AE,
DC, MC, V. Closed Nov.–mid-Mar.

$$$–$$$$ ▦ **Castello Seeschloss.** Dating from 1250, though completely rebuilt
★ within, this Romantik property is a romantic enough hotel as is—not
even taking into account its garden setting and position across from
the waterfront. Its interior is rich with frescoes, beams, vaults, and heavy
masonry, recently lightened with a contemporary touch. Each room is
different: a wrought iron bed in the back tower, a blue wooden canopy
bed in room 203, or the lavishly redone front tower room with a loft.
Most impressive are the lakeside rooms, which have original 16th- to
18th-century frescoes. There are a private courtyard for summer-night
dining and an isolated pool. Honeymooners, take note: deluxe rooms
in the towers start at prices not much higher than standard doubles.
⊠ *Piazza Motta, CH-6612,* ☎ *091/7910161, FAX 091/7911804. 45*
rooms. 2 restaurants, bar, no-smoking rooms, pool. AE, DC, MC, V.
Closed mid-Nov.–mid-Mar.

$$–$$$ ▦ **Piazza.** This tidy, modest member of the familial Minotel chain, in
the middle of the Piazza Motta, looks first and foremost like a café,
and you have to wend your way through crowded tables to get to the
reception area. The throngs are enjoying at ground level what you'll
see better from your room: the pollards, park benches, and blue ex-
panse of the waterfront. The rooms can be tiny, but they're well
equipped. ⊠ *Lungolago G. Motta 29, CH-6612,* ☎ *091/7911181, FAX*
091/7912757. 37 rooms. Restaurant, café. AE, DC, MC, V. Closed Nov.–
mid-Mar.

$–$$$ 🏠 **Tamaro.** The shuttered windows of this 18th-century patrician house look out on the waterfront; inside, you can lounge in sitting rooms richly furnished with antiques, books, and even a grand piano. The rooms range from lavish corner doubles with lake views and repro antiques to tiny, bathless quarters overlooking the courtyard that are an excellent value. There's a private sun terrace high over the street with fine lake views. ⊠ *Piazza G. Motta 35, CH-6612,* ☎ *091/7910282,* 🟥 *091/7912928. 51 rooms, 37 with bath. 3 restaurants, café, pool, bicycles, meeting room. AE, DC, V. Closed mid-Nov.–mid-Mar.*

Nightlife and the Arts

The ideals that brought Isadora Duncan here still bring culture to Ascona: Every year it hosts Ascona New Orleans Jazz and the Settimane Musicali di Ascona series of world-class classical music concerts (☞ Music, *below*). The lakefront piazza serves as an open-air stage for almost daily summer entertainment, with mime, theater, and live pop bands. Locarno's August film festival is only a cab ride away across the peninsula.

BARS AND DANCING

Young disco enthusiasts flock to **Happyville** (⊠ Fontanelle 3, ☎ 091/7914922). The **Lago Bar** (⊠ Via Moscia 2, ☎ 091/7911065) discotheque also draws a young crowd, and it has a piano bar upstairs. More sedate dancers go to **Piper Bar** (⊠ Via Aerodromo 3, ☎ 091/7911374) for live music. **La Tana** (⊠ Via Locarno 110, ☎ 091/7911381) has an orchestra and striptease acts. Note that most bars and clubs are open only during the tourist season (Easter–late October), but La Tana is open year-round.

MUSIC

Ascona New Orleans Jazz (☎ 091/7910090) seeks out performers a cut above standard Dixieland and swing groups and brings an amazing international selection of them to its open-air bandstands; in 2000 the festival will run from late June to early July. The **Settimane Musicali** (Musical Weeks; ☎ 091/7910093) bring in full orchestras, chamber groups, and top-ranking soloists to Ascona and Locarno; in 2000 they will run from late August to late October.

THEATER

The **Teatro di Locarno** (⊠ Palazzo Kursaal, via Largo Zorzi 1, ☎ 091/7566151) hosts international theatrical companies from October through May. For tickets, contact the the tourist office (☞ Visitor Information *in* The Ticino A to Z, *below*).

SOTTOCENERI

Although Monte Ceneri is no Everest, it marks the borderline between the vast differences of the Sopraceneri and its southern cousin "below" the Ceneri. The Sottoceneri is the Ticino with attitude, where culture and natural beauty join forces with business and cash. The resort town of Lugano is an international glamour magnet, but even there the incredible scenery and native Ticinese warmth haven't been completely upstaged.

Lugano

45 km (28 mi) southeast of Ascona, 39 km (24 mi) southeast of Locarno.

Strung around a sparkling bay like Venetian glass beads, with dark, conical mountains rising primordially out of its waters and icy peaks framing the scene, Lugano earns its nickname as the Rio of the Old

World. Of the three world-class waterfront resorts, Lugano tops Ascona and Locarno for architectural style, sophistication, and natural beauty. This is not to say that it has avoided the pitfalls of a successful modern resort: There's thick traffic right up to the waterfront, much of it manic Italian style, and it has more than its share of concrete waterfront high-rise hotels with balconies skewed to produce "a room with a view" regardless of aesthetic cost. Yet the sacred *passeggiata*—the afternoon stroll to see and be seen that winds down every Italian day—asserts the city's true personality as a graceful, sophisticated resort—not Swiss, not Italian . . . just Lugano.

A Good Walk

Begin at the **Piazza della Riforma** ⑦, which is dominated by the **Palazzo Civico** ⑧, or town hall. Look up to the gable above the clock to see the city's coat of arms. (The building also houses the tourist office.) On the western side of the square, where the Piazza connects to the Via Nassa, is Lugano's oldest monument, the **Pretorio** (1425). Also on this side, the Piazza della Riforma bleeds into the **Piazza Rezzonico**, which contains a large fountain by Otto Maraini (1895).

Heading out of the Piazza della Riforma on the north side, onto the Via Luvini, you enter the **Old Town**, where narrow streets are lined with chic Italian clothing shops and small markets offering pungent local cheeses and porcini mushrooms. Soon you come to the **Piazza Dante**; turn left down Via Pessina, which will lead you into the **Piazza Cioccara** on your right. Here is where the funicular from the train station terminates.

From the Piazza Cioccara, walk up the shop-lined staircase street of Via Cattedrale. On your left is the **Cattedrale di San Lorenzo** ⑨. Take a moment to enjoy the view from the church square. Continue up to the right of the church on Via Paolo Ragazonni to the Hotel Federale; there you can leave the Via Paolo Ragazonni and take the foot path through the gardens under the train station. Go up the steps to reach the station. At the southern end of the train station square, follow the Via Maraini to visit **Parco del Tassino** ⑩—the park entrance is just past the bridge over the tracks.

Retrace your steps back to the station and either walk or take the funicular back down to Piazza Cioccara. Turn right onto the Via Pessina and follow it into the lively **Piazza Maraini**. Here you can start a leisurely stroll down the **Via Nassa**, which runs between the Piazza della Riforma and the Piazza Luini. It's characterized by a long row of porticos, many housing chic designer clothing shops. Nestled among the medieval and modern buildings on the right, between Piazza San Carlo and Piazza Battaglini, is the 17th-century, baroque church **San Carlo Borromeo**. The street ends at the **Chiesa di Santa Maria degli Angioli** ⑪, facing the lake at the Piazza Luini.

Across the road, spreading south along the lakefront promenade, is the **Giardino Belvedere** ⑫. At the west end of the gardens, an incongruous **bust of George Washington** stands on the lake promenade in its own little gazebo. "Georgio" Washington never visited Lugano; this image was erected in 1859 by a grateful Swiss engineer who had made his fortune in America. At this far end of the gardens, directly across the Riva Antonio Caccia, is the **Museo d'Arte Moderna** ⑬.

Head back northeast along the waterfront promenade and at the Imbarcadero Centrale (central boat wharf), take the underpass to cross the road, coming back up at the Piazza della Riforma. Leave the piazza at the northeast side through a portico onto the Via Canova. After crossing over the Via della Posta/Via Albrizzi, you'll come to the **Museo**

Cantonale d'Arte ⑮. Continue straight ahead to the 17th-century San Rocco church, with its neo-baroque facade. Just past the church on your left you'll find a small pedestrian entranceway into the **Quartiere Maghetti**—a town within a town. It's a tangle of streets full of porticoes, little squares, shops, and offices, a modern take on old forms, created in the early 1980s by the architects Camazind, Brocchi, and Sennhauser. Exit the Quartiere Maghetti back onto Via Canova and continue east, crossing Via Stauffacher. On your left is the open Piazza dell'Independenza. Cross over the wide Corso Elvezia to enter the **Parco Civico** ⑯. Inside the grounds, in addition to the 60,000 square meters (nearly 15 acres) of greenery, you'll find the **Museo Civico di Belle Arti** ⑰ and **Museo Cantonale di Storia Naturale** ⑱. From here, you can opt to spend the afternoon at the **Lido** ⑲, the city's public beach and pool, just east of the park across the River Cassarate. Or you can head back to town along the waterfront promenade, known as **Il Lungolago** ⑭, and take in the stunning mountain views: straight ahead, the rocky top of Monte Generoso (1,702 m/5,579 ft), and flanking the bay at right and left, respectively, Monte San Salvatore and Monte Brè.

TIMING

It is best to walk through the city in the morning, before it gets too hot. A quick overview, without much time in the museums or parks, would take a couple of hours. Or make a day of it, taking in the main sights in the morning, stopping for lunch, and then spending the afternoon in the museums or on the Lido. Remember that the museums are closed on Monday.

Sights to See

⑨ **Cattedrale di San Lorenzo** (Cathedral of St. Lawrence). Behind this church's early Renaissance facade is a richly frescoed baroque interior with a baptismal font dating back to 1430. The church has premedieval origins: it became a collegiate church in 1078. Eight hundred years later it became a cathedral. ✉ *Via Cattedrale.*

★ ⑪ **Chiesa di Santa Maria degli Angioli** (Church of St. Mary of the Angels). The simple facade doesn't prepare you for the riches within. Begun in the late 15th century, the church contains a magnificent fresco of the *Passion and Crucifixion,* as well as *The Last Supper* and *Madonna with the Infant Jesus,* all by Bernardino Luini (1475–1532). ✉ *Piazza Luini.*

⑫ **Giardino Belvedere** (Belvedere Gardens). This lakefront sculpture garden frames a dozen modern sculptures with palms, camellias, oleanders, and magnolias. At the far west end there's a public swimming area. ✉ *On the lake side of Quai Riva Antonio Caccia near the Piazza Luini.* 🎫 *Free.* ⏰ *Daily, 24 hours.*

⑲ **Lido.** The city's public beach has two swimming pools and a restaurant. To reach it you'll have to cross the Cassarate River, heading east from the Parco Civico; follow the riverbank left to the main street, Viale Castagnola, and then turn right. The main swimming-area entrance is just ahead on the right. Everyone from families to scenesters comes here to cool off. ☎ *091/9714041.* 🎫 *7 SF; changing cabins 3 SF.* ⏰ *May, June, and Sept., daily 9:30–6; July and Aug., daily 9–7.*

★ ⑭ **Il Lungolago** (waterfront promenade). This 2-km (1-mi) lakefront path lined with pollarded lime trees, funereal cypresses, and palm trees stretches from the lido all the way to the Paradiso neighborhood and is the place to see and be seen, while taking in the views, of course. At night luminous fountains turn the lake near the Parco Civico into a special attraction.

⑬ **Museo d'Arte Moderna** (Museum of Modern Art). In addition to interesting temporary exhibitions, such as shows of Soutine or Modigliani, this museum displays an enormous permanent collection of works by international artists such as Henri Rousseau, Monet, Pissarro, and Futurist artist Umberto Boccioni. Ticinese artists are represented as well. Museum literature is available in English. ⊠ *Villa Malpensata, Riva Antonio Caccia 5,* ☎ *091/9944370.* 🎫 *10 SF.* ☉ *Tues.–Sun. 9–7.*

⑮ **Museo Cantonale d'Arte** (Cantonal Art Museum). A group of three palaces dating from the 15th to the 19th centuries was used for this museum. Its permanent and temporary exhibits span paintings, sculpture, and photography, including some important avant garde works. The permanent collection holds works by Klee, Turner, Degas, Renoir, and Hodler as well as contemporary Ticinese artists. Descriptive material is available in English. ⊠ *Via Canova 10,* ☎ *091/9104780.* 🎫 *Permanent collection: 7 SF; temporary exhibits: 10 SF.* ☉ *Wed.–Sun. 10–5, Tues. 2–5.*

⑱ **Museo Cantonale di Storia Naturale** (Cantonal Museum of Natural History). A museum since 1854, it contains exhibits on fossils, animals, and plants (there's a large section on mushrooms), mostly those typical of the region. ⊠ *Viale Cattaneo 4, in the Parco Civico,* ☎ *091/ 9115380.* 🎫 *Free.* ☉ *Tues.–Sat. 9–noon and 2–5.*

⑰ **Museo Civico di Belle Arti** (Muncipal Art Museum). Reopened in 1998 after extensive renovations, the museum, located in the Villa Ciani, contains hundreds of works by Swiss and European artists from the 15th to the 20th century. English-language museum literature is available. ⊠ *Villa Ciani, in the Parco Civico,* ☎ *091/9236163.* 🎫 *5 SF.* ☉ *Tues.–Sun. 9–7.*

⑧ **Palazzo Civico** (Town Hall). This neoclassical Lombard structure dates from 1844. Inside there is a large inner yard surrounded by a four-sided arcade, with a wide vestibule on the piazza side. It houses the town council and tourist office. ⊠ *Piazza della Riforma.*

⑯ **Parco Civico** (City Park). A green oasis in the city center, the park has cacti, exotic shrubs, and more than 1,000 varieties of roses, as well as an aviary, a tiny deer zoo, and a fine view of the bay from its peninsula. ⊠ *Area south of Viale Carlo Cattaneo, east of Piazza Castello.* 🎫 *Free.* ☉ *Daily, 24 hours.*

☚ ⑩ **Parco del Tassino** (Tassino Park). Situated on a plateau just behind and south of the train station, this park offers lovely bay views from among its rose gardens. A small deer park and playground make it very child-friendly. ⊠ *Take Bus 2 east to San Domenico stop in Castagnola, or use the funicular from Old Town to the train station.* 🎫 *Free.*

★ ⑦ **Piazza della Riforma** (Reformation Square). In the early 19th century, several buildings were removed in order to enlarge the square—giving more room to the 20th century café tables. Commonly referred to as simply "la Piazza", it's the social and cultural heart of the city and the site of markets and open-air music performances. ⊠ *Just north of the Imbarcadero Centrale (main boat wharf).*

OFF THE
BEATEN PATH

VILLA FAVORITA – This splendid 16th-century mansion in Castagnola houses a portion of the extraordinary private art collection of the Baron von Thyssen-Bornemisza. Although, after a scandalous international divorce battle, portions of the collection were transferred to Spain, a significant display of 19th- and 20th-century paintings and watercolors from Europe and America remains. Artists represented include Giorgio de Chirico, Frederick Church, Lucien Freud, Edward Hopper, Jackson

Lugano

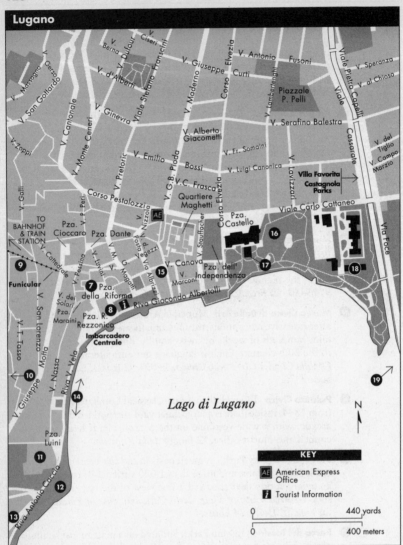

Lago di Lugano

KEY

AE American Express Office

i Tourist Information

0 ——— 440 yards

0 ——— 400 meters

Cattedrale di
San Lorenzo, **9**

Chiesa di Santa Maria
degli Angioli **11**

Giardino
Belvedere, **12**

Lido, **19**

Il Lungolago, **14**

Museo d'Arte
Moderna, **13**

Museo Cantonale
d'Arte, **15**

Museo Cantonale di
Storia Naturale, **18**

Museo Civico di Belle
Arti, **17**

Palazzo Civico, **8**

Parco Civico, **16**

Parco del Tassino, **10**

Piazza della
Riforma, **7**

Pollock, and Andrew Wyeth. The villa gardens are also worth a stroll; they're planted with native and exotic flora. Take Bus 1 in the direction of Castagnola or take the 40-minute walk from town, heading east along the lake on Viale Castagnola, which turns into Via Riviera past the Castagnola wharf. You may want to call ahead, as opening hours and entrance fees can change during special exhibitions. ⌧ *Strada Castagnola, Via Rivera 14,* ☏ *091/9721741.* ⌧ *12 SF; 5 SF for park only.* ☺ *Easter–Oct., Fri.–Sun. 10–6.*

CASTAGNOLA PARKS – For an idyllic daytime excursion, combine a trip to the Villa Favorita (☞ *above*) with one or both of the parks adjacent to it. The **Parco degli Ulivi** (Olive Park) spreads over the lower slopes of Monte Brè and offers a romantic landscape of silvery olive trees mixed with cypress, laurel, and wild rosemary; you enter it from the Gandria Footpath (Sentiero di Gandria). **Parco San Michele** (St. Michael Park), also on Monte Brè, has a public chapel and a broad terrace that overlooks the city, the lake, and, beyond, the Alps. From Cassarate, walk up the steps by the lower terminus of the Monte Brè funicular.

MONTE SAN SALVATORE, MONTE BRÈ, MONTE GENEROSO – The serious view hound may want to reach the top of one of the three peaks which define the landscape around Lugano. **Monte Brè** has a funicular which takes you up from the east end of Lugano in Cassarate, although it's also possible to drive, cycle, or hike to the crest. At the top are several well-marked hiking trails, and there is an "art trail" in the mountaintop village of Brè—a path studded with pieces of sculpture (a guided tour can be booked at the funicular station). **Monte San Salvatore** can be reached via the funicular in Paradiso. At the top are a huge relief model of the entire Sottoceneri region, marked "nature itinerary" paths pointing out flower and tree specimens, and other marked hikes down and around the area. For yet more spectacular views, take a boat from Lugano across to Capolago where you can take the 40-minute cogwheel train up **Monte Generoso**. At the top are a restaurant, café, and lots of marked hiking trails. *Monte San Salvatore:* ☏ *091/9852828.* ⌧ *18 SF round trip.* ☺ *Mid-Mar.–mid-Nov. 8:30–7. Monte Brè:* ☏ *091/9713171.* ⌧ *19 SF round trip.* ☺ *Feb.–Dec. 9:10–noon and 12:45–6:30. Monte Generoso:* ☏ *091/6481105.* ⌧ *46 SF round trip.* ☺ *Dec.–Oct. Trains up at 10, 11, noon, 2, and 3:30; trains down at 1:45, 4:15, and 5:15.*

SWISSMINIATUR – You'll feel like Gulliver walking in Lilliput at this novel but slightly kitschy open-air park filled with detailed models of the architectural highlights of Switzerland built on a scale of 1:25. There's a tiny Chillon, the Cathedral of Lausanne, the Parliament buildings of Bern, a recent reproduction of the Lausanne Olympic Museum, and exquisitely detailed reproductions of Swiss trains, boats, and cable-car systems—all fully functional. Carefully landscaped on the waterfront, the park has a playground for kids who lose interest while Dad is still watching the trains. If you're driving, take the highway going south (direction Mendrisio–Chiasso) and exit at Melide; the train from Lugano to Melide stops right in front of the park. ⌧ *Melide, below Lugano,* ☏ *091/6401060.* ⌧ *11 SF.* ☺ *Mid-Mar.–Oct., daily 9–6.*

Dining and Lodging

$$$$
★ ✕ **Al Portone.** Silver and lace dress up the stucco and stone here, but the ambience is strictly easy. Chef Roberto Galizzi pursues *nuova cucina* (contemporary cuisine, Italian style) with ambition and flair, and he rarely resorts to gimmickry while putting local spins on Italian classics. You might choose roast veal kidneys with balsamic vinegar, lobster salad, seafood carpaccio, or simple creamed potatoes with priceless

white truffle. Or you could *lascia fare a Roberto* (leave it to Robert)— as he calls his menu *de dégustation*. ⊠ *Viale Cassarate 3, Lugano/Cassarate,* ☎ *091/9235511. AE, DC, MC, V. Closed Sun. and Mon.*

$$$ ✕ **Galleria.** Though the decor aspires to formal hauteur, with its contemporary appointments and very modern art, family warmth permeates the restaurant, making it a comfortable source of good traditional Italian cooking: pasta, veal favorites, and good, plain grilled fish, as well as a fine little list of local and Italian wines. ⊠ *Via Cantonale 4, Lugano/Manno,* ☎ *091/6108761. AE, DC, MC, V. Closed Sun., 2nd and 3rd wks. of Aug.*

$$$ ✕ **Locanda del Boschetto.** The grill is the first thing you see in this no-
★ nonsense, low-key ristorante, a specialist in pure and simple seafood *alla griglia* (grilled). The decor is a study in linen and rustic wood, and the service is helpful and down to earth. ⊠ *Via Boschetto 8,* ☎ *091/ 9942493. AE, DC, MC, V. Closed Mon., 1st and 2nd wks. of Nov.*

$$$ ✕ **Santabbondio.** Ancient stone and terra-cotta blend with pristine pas-
★ tels in this upgraded grotto, where subtle, imaginative, new Franco-Italian cuisine *du marché* (menus based on fresh market produce) is served in intimate, formal little dining rooms and on a shady terrace. Watch for lobster risotto, scallops in orange-basil sauce, or eggplant ravioli to confirm what locals assert: chef Martin Dalsass is the canton's best. There's a good selection of open wines. You'll need a cab to get here, but it's worth the trip. ⊠ *Via Fomelino 10, Lugano/Sorengo,* ☎ *091/9932388. AE, DC, MC, V. Closed Mon., 1st wk. of Jan., last wk. of Feb. No lunch Sat., no dinner Sun.*

$–$$ ✕ **Al Lago.** A short drive into the countryside north of Lugano, you'll
★ find this soothing, sunny, lakeside spot in the wooded wetland of a nature preserve on Origlio lake. Calabrian chef Francesco Ferraro recreates a Mediterranean cuisine; the extensive antipasto buffet is delightful, but don't overlook the fresh fish and pasta dishes from various regions in Italy. ⊠ *Origlio,* ☎ *091/9451333. AE, DC, MC, V. Closed Tues., Jan. and 1st two wks. of Nov.*

$–$$ ✕ **Da Raffaelle.** Having a meal in this family-run Italian restaurant feels like being let in on a neighborhood secret. Start with a pasta, like their marvelous, homemade *orecchiette* (ear-shaped pasta) with seasonal vegetables, then try something from the grill, like *gamberoni all griglia* (grilled shrimp). The staff does not speak English, but their warmth needs no translation. The restaurant is just outside the city in a residential neighborhood, but easily reached by car or bus (take Bus 8 or 9 from the train station to the last stop, Viganello). ⊠ *Contrada dei Patrizi 8/Via Pazzalino, Viganello,* ☎ *091/9716614. AE, MC, V. Closed Sun., last wk. of July and 1st two wks. of Aug. No lunch Sat.*

$ ✕ **Grotto Figini.** Absolutely authentic, this grotto pulls in a rowdy local crowd for a *boccalino* of good merlot and a satisfying, rib-sticking meal of polenta and grilled meats. Don't expect English or other tourists, and don't take the stares when you first walk in too personally. It's in a short stretch of woods on a hill in Gentilino, above Lugano-Paradiso. After your meal you can stroll down the shady road to see old *grotti* hidden in the overgrown hillside. ⊠ *Via ai Grotti, Gentilino,* ☎ *091/9946497. V. Closed Mon., mid-Dec.–Feb.*

$ ✕ **La Tinera.** Tucked down an alley off Via Pessina in the Old Town,
★ this cozy basement taverna squeezes loyal locals and tourists onto wooden benches for authentic regional specialties, hearty meats, and pastas. Regional wine is served in traditional ceramic bowls. ⊠ *Via dei Gorini 2,* ☎ *091/9235219. AE, DC, MC, V. Closed Sun., Aug.*

$$$$ ✕▥ **Ticino.** In this 500-year-old palazzo (protected as a historical mon-
★ ument) in the heart of the Old Town, shuttered windows look out from every room onto a glassed-in garden. The vaulted halls are lined with art and antiques, and the rooms are unpretentious yet elegant, with

pleasing details like embroidered towels and special mattresses. The formal restaurant, full of dark-wood wainscoting and leather banquettes, blends Ticinese with French cuisine; it's famous for its rack of lamb with herbs and fresh seafood. The hotel is a Romantik property, and it's only steps away from the funicular to the train station. There's a two-night minimum stay. ⊠ *Piazza Cioccara 1, CH-6901,* ☎ *091/ 9227772,* FAX *091/9236278. 18 rooms, 2 suites. Restaurant, bar, no-smoking rooms, library. AE, DC, MC, V. Closed Jan.*

$$$$ ✕🖫 **Villa Principe Leopoldo and Residence.** This extravagantly furnished
★   garden mansion, on a hillside high over the lake (Collina d'Oro, or Golden Hill), offers Old World service and splendor to match. It was built in 1868 on behalf of Prince Leopold of Hohenzollern. There's a stunningly arranged pool-and-terrace complex encircled by a double staircase—a slightly baroque touch of Bel Air. The rooms are grace-fully lush in muted tones and marble. Fabulous creations from chef Dario Ranza, like lobster risotto or sea bass baked in a salt crust, make din-ing here a notable experience. ⊠ *Via Montalbano 5, CH-6900,* ☎ *091/ 9858855,* FAX *091/9858825. 70 rooms, 4 suites. 3 restaurants, bar, no-smoking rooms, pool, hot tub, massage, sauna, indoor golf, tennis court, health club, business services, meeting rooms. AE, DC, MC, V.*

$$$$ 🖫 **Splendide Royale.** This landmark was first converted from a villa
★   to a hotel in 1887, and much of the Victorian luster of its public spaces—with their marble, pillars, terrazzo, and antiques—has been respectfully preserved. Since a wing was added in the '80s, you can choose between sleek rooms decorated in beech, beige, and gold or more florid period rooms in the original wing. All rooms are air-conditioned and have heated floors in the bathrooms; they offer lake or garden views from their balconies or terraces. There's also an attractive S-shape in-door pool. ⊠ *Riva A. Caccia 7, CH-6900,* ☎ *091/9857711,* FAX *091/ 9857722. 96 rooms, 8 suites. Restaurant, piano bar, indoor pool, mas-sage, sauna, business services, meeting rooms. AE, DC, MC, V.*

$$$–$$$$ 🖫 **Du Lac.** This comfortable, bright hotel offers more lakefront lux-ury than do some glossier hotels down the same beach. Owned by one family since it was founded in 1920, Du Lac was completely rebuilt in 1962 and renovated over the past few years. Huge, impressive, needle-work tapestry art reproductions, handmade by the owner's father, cover the walls of the open lobby and restaurant. The rooms are all spacious and face the lake; those on the sixth floor are the quietest. The hotel has a private swimming area on the lake. ⊠ *Riva Paradiso 3, CH-6902 Lugano/Paradiso,* ☎ *091/9941921,* FAX *091/9941122. 52 rooms, 1 suite. Restaurant, bar, no-smoking rooms, pool, whirlpool bath, massage, sauna, exercise room, beach, waterskiing, meeting room. AE, DC, MC, V. Closed Jan.–mid-Mar.*

$$$ 🖫 **Alba.** This solid little hotel, isolated on its own landscaped grounds
★   and lavish inside to the extreme, is ideal for lovers with a sense of camp or honeymooners looking for romantic privacy. Mirrors, gilt, plush, and crystal adorn the public areas; in the guest rooms, the beds are all ruffles and swags in deep rose and velvet, and cut-glass chandelier lamps stand on the night-tables. The garden is studded with palms—a lovely place for a drink. ⊠ *Via delle Scuole 11, CH-6902 Lugano-Paradiso,* ☎ *091/9943731,* FAX *091/9944523. 25 rooms, 1 suite. Restaurant, bar, pool. AE, DC, MC, V.*

$$$ 🖫 **International au Lac.** Just a stone's throw from the lake and next to the Church of St. Mary of the Angels, this big, old-fashioned, friendly hotel offers many lake-view rooms. The interiors are floridly decorated, with many paintings and antiques, and heavy plush furniture. The large garden and pool in the back make you forget you're downtown. Side rooms are quieter, and only the top floor is air-conditioned. ⊠ *Via Nassa*

68, CH-6901, ☎ 091/9227541, FAX 091/9227544. *80 rooms. Restaurant, pool, garden. AE, DC, MC, V. Closed Nov.–Easter.*

$$$ ☐ **Park-Hotel Nizza.** Tucked into the dense tropical foliage of the
★   lower slopes of Monte San Salvatore and well above the lake, this former villa is an attractive combination of luxurious parlors and modern comforts. Most rooms are small, with a hodgepodge mix of old and new furnishings, but all are quiet and comfortable; lake panoramic views don't cost extra. The hotel has its own farm and vineyards on the hill behind—the source of organic produce for the restaurant. They even make their own wine, with some very original labels designed by the owner. Summer meals are served in the garden, and there's a weekly special farmer's breakfast and evening cocktail party. ⊠ *Via Guidino 14, CH-6902 Lugano-Paradiso,* ☎ *091/9941771,* FAX *091/ 9941773. 29 rooms. 2 restaurants, bar, no-smoking rooms, pool, whirlpool bath, children's playground, free parking. AE, MC, V. Closed mid-Dec.–mid-Mar.*

$$ ☐ **San Carlo.** Ideally located on the main shopping street, a block from the waterfront, and only 150 yards from the funicular, this friendly hotel is clean, small, and quiet; it's one of the better deals in town. The breakfast room is small, so breakfast in bed is encouraged. ⊠ *Via Nassa 28, CH-6900,* ☎ *091/9227107,* FAX *091/9228022. 22 rooms. Breakfast room. AE, DC, MC, V.*

$–$$ ☐ **Flora.** In this 100-year-old, family-run lodging, the rooms are spare and the decor just recently emerging from the 60's, but most bathrooms are new and the restaurant has been spruced up. Some rooms have balconies, and there's a sheltered garden terrace. ⊠ *Via Geretta 16, CH-6902,* ☎ *091/9941671,* FAX *091/9942738. 40 rooms. Restaurant, bar, outdoor pool, TV room. AE, DC, MC, V. Closed Nov.–Mar.*

$ ☐ **Dishma.** The welcoming owners of this hotel, the Abgottspons, make it a bargain worth seeking out. The rooms are clean and bright and the flowers on the balconies have won the owners awards. The public rooms are a riot of colors, souvenirs, and knickknacks; there's a mynah bird to talk to near the elevator. The restaurant is non-smoking (rare in these parts) and they even have a coin-operated washer and drier for guests. ⊠ *Vicolo Geretta 6, CH-6902 Lugano-Paradiso,* ☎ *091/9942131,* FAX *091/9941503. 35 rooms. Restaurant, bar, TV room, coin laundry. AE, MC, V. Closed Dec.–Feb.*

$ ☐ **Zurigo.** Ideally central and handy to parks, shopping, and the waterfront promenade, this spartan hotel offers quiet comfort. Its rates are affordable even in high season and all the rooms have been freshly done over (late 1998–1999). Those on the Via Pioda side are quieter. ⊠ *Corso Pestalozzi 13, CH-6900,* ☎ *091/9234343,* FAX *091/9239268. 28 rooms. Breakfast room. AE, DC, MC, V. Closed Nov.–mid-Mar.*

Nightlife and the Arts

BARS

Caffè Caruso (⊠ Piazza Riforma 4, ☎ 091/9211979) is a popular, Italian-style café and bar. The piano player strikes up a tune nightly, sometimes with a singer, at **Principe Leopoldo** (⊠ Via Montalbano 5, ☎ 091/ 9858855). There's also nightly piano music at the **Splendide Royale** (⊠ Riva Antonio Caccia 7, ☎ 091/9857711).

CASINO

The **Kursaal** (⊠ Via Stauffacher 1, ☎ 091/9233281) has a restaurant, disco, bar, slot machines, movie theater, and gaming room.

DANCING

La Canva (⊠ Riva Paradiso 18, ☎ 091/9941218) is popular among locals. **Capo San Martino** (⊠ Via Cantonale, Pazzallo, ☎ 091/9945570) is in nearby Paradiso; it combines a disco with a pizzeria. **Titanic**

(✉ Via Cantonale, Pambio-Noranco, off A–2 exit for Lugano-Sud, ☎ 091/9856010) is the Ticino's biggest disco, with three dance floors.

MUSIC

There is a free **Blues to Bop Festival** in the Piazza della Riforma scheduled for the first weekend in September 2000. The **Estival Jazz** (second weekend in July 2000) offers free outdoor concerts in the Piazza della Riforma. From April to June, the city hosts its **Primavera Concertistica di Lugano,** with top-level orchestras and conductors.

Shopping

You'll find all the glossy-magazine designers in the beautiful shops along the car-free **Via Nassa** in the Old Town. Cute novelty shops and antiques stores line the staircase street of **Via Cattedrale.** If it's Italian designer clothing bargains you're after, you could explore the factory outlet store called **Fox Town** (✉ Via Angelo Maspoli, Mendrisio, ☎ 091/6462111) in nearby Mendrisio—it's open every day, including Sunday.

Gandria

⑳ *7 km (4 mi) east of Lugano.*

Although today its narrow waterfront streets are crowded with tourists, the tiny historic village of Gandria merits a visit, either by boat from Lugano (☞ Getting Around by Boat *in* The Ticino A to Z, *below*) or by car, as parking is available just above the town. It clings vertiginously to the steep hillside; a labyrinth of stairways and passageways and flower-filled balconies hang directly over open water. Souvenir and crafts shops now fill its backstreet nooks, but the ambience of an ancient fishing village remains.

OFF THE BEATEN PATH

CANTINE DI GANDRIA – Across Lake Lugano from Gandria—almost in Italy—this tiny village has a small **Museo Doganale** (Customs Museum; ☎ 091/9104811 or 9239843), casually known as the "Smugglers' Museum." Here you'll learn the romantic history of clandestine trade through displays of ingenious containers, weapons, and contraband. You can catch a boat from the jetty. ☎ *091/9715223 or 091/9234610 for boat schedule information.* ✉ *Free.* ☉ *Apr.–Oct., daily 1:30–5:30.*

Campione

㉑ *18 km (11 mi) south of Gandria, 12 km (7 mi) south of Lugano.*

In the heart of Swiss Italy lies Campione. Here, in this southernmost of regions, the police cars have Swiss license plates but the policemen inside are Italian; the inhabitants pay their taxes to Italy but do it in Swiss francs. Its narrow streets are saturated with history and the surrounding landscape is a series of stunning views of Lake Lugano and Monte San Salvatore.

In the 8th century, the lord of Campione gave the tiny scrap of land, less than a square kilometer (½ square mi) in area, to the monastery of St. Ambrosius of Milan. Despite all the wars that passed it by, Campione remained Italian until the end of the 18th century, when it was incorporated into the Cisalpine Republic. When Italy unified in 1861, Campione became part of the new Kingdom of Italy—and remained so. There are no frontiers between Campione and Switzerland, and it benefits from the comforts of Swiss currency, customs laws, and postal and telephone services. Despite its miniature scale, it has exercised disproportionate influence on the art world: in the Middle Ages, a school of stonemasons, sculptors, and architects from Campione and the surrounding region worked on the cathedrals of Milan, Verona, Cremona, Trento, and Modena—even Hagia Sophia in Istanbul.

Nightlife and the Arts

Today, Campione is a magnet for gamblers, as its large, glittering **Casino** (✉ Piazza Milano 1, ☎ 091/6401111) offers visitors to conservative Switzerland a chance to play for higher stakes than the usual 5 SF: following Italian law, the sky's the limit here. The casino has a restaurant, dancing, and a show; this is jacket-and-tie territory.

Riva San Vitale

㉓ *9 km (5½ mi) south of Campione, 13 km (8 mi) south of Lugano.*

At the south end of Lake Lugano sits Riva San Vitale, which rivals Campione for its odd history: in 1798 its people objected to new boundaries and declared themselves an independent republic. Their glory lasted 14 days before a small cantonal army marched in and convinced them to rejoin Switzerland. A 5th-century **Battistero** (Baptistery) remains, still containing its original stone immersion font.

Four kilometers (2 miles) south of Riva San Vitale is little **Mendrisio,** cradle of the Ticinese wine industry. It's known for its medieval processions, which take place on the Thursday and Friday before Easter.

Morcote

★ **㉒** *6 km (4 mi) northwest of Riva San Vitale, 10 km (6 mi) south of Lugano.*

At the southernmost tip of the glorious Ceresio Peninsula waterfront is the atmospheric, old resort-village of Morcote, its clay-color, Lombard-style houses and arcades looking directly over the waterfront. A steep and picturesque climb leads up to the **Chiesa di Madonna del Sasso** (Church of the Madonna of the Rock), with its well-preserved 16th-century frescoes; its elevated setting affords wonderful views.

THE TICINO A TO Z

Arriving and Departing

By Bus

The **Palm Express** scenic postbus and train route carries visitors from St. Moritz to Lugano or Ascona via the Maloja Pass and Italy. It takes about four hours and can be arranged at any train station or tourist office (☞ Visitor Information, *below*). You can also contact **Railtour Suisse** (✉ ☎ 031/3780000).

By Car

There are two major gateways into the Ticino: the **St. Gotthard Pass** in the northwest and the **San Bernardino Pass** to the northeast. From the Saint Gotthard Pass, the swift **A–2** expressway leads down the Valle Leventina to Bellinzona, where it joins with **A–13**, which cuts south from the San Bernardino. A–2 directs the mingled traffic flow southward past Lugano to Chiasso and the Italian border, where the expressway heads directly to Como and Milan. Alternately there's the **St. Gotthard tunnel**—17 km (11 mi) of dense air and darkness speeding you through the Alps rather than over them. If traffic is light, it can cut an hour off your travel time, but if the passes are closed and it's holiday migration time, tunnel traffic can be nasty.

By Plane

The nearest international airport is in Italy. **Malpensa** (✉ About 50 km/31 mi northwest of Milan), which was enlarged and reopened in fall 1998, is now one of the biggest hubs in southern Europe. Some flights from the international **Linate** (⊠ Less than 10 km/6 mi east of Milan) will be transferred to Malpensa. For air-traffic **information** for both airports and information on connections with Milan, call 0039/ 2/74852200. You can continue into the Ticino via rail, car, or taxi. Crossair (☎ 084/8852000 for central reservations), Switzerland's domestic airline, connects directly into the domestic **Aeroporto Lugano-Agno** (⊠ 7 km/4½ mi west of Lugano, Agno, ☎ 091/6051226 or 091/ 6101212) from **Zürich's** Kloten Airport (☎ 1571060) and from **Geneva's** Cointrin (☎ 1571500), as well as from other European destinations. There's a shuttle bus connecting Agno airport with Lugano, which operates on request (☎ 079/2214243). Call upon arrival.

By Train

The Saint Gotthard route connects south from Zürich, cuts through the pass tunnel, and heads into Bellinzona and Lugano. Side connections lead into Locarno from Brig, crossing the Simplon Pass and cutting through Italy. Swiss Pass (☞ Train Travel *in* Smart Travel Tips A to Z) travelers do not have to pay Italian rail fares to cross from Brig to Locarno via Domodossola. Trains connect out of Zürich's airport and take about three hours; from Geneva, catch the Milan express, changing at Domodossola, Locarno, and Bellinzona. Trains do not go directly into Ascona but stop at Locarno: you must connect by taxi or local bus. For train information from Lugano, call 1572222 (1.19 SF/min).

Getting Around

By Boat

Lake Lugano and northern Lake Maggiore are plied by graceful steamers that carry passengers from one waterfront resort to another, offering excellent views of the mountains. Steamer travel on Lake Lugano is included in the Lugano Regional Passes (☞ By Train, *below*) and the Swiss Pass (☞ Train Travel *in* Smart Travel Tips A to Z); tickets can be purchased near the docks before departure. On Lake Lugano, the **Navigation Company of Lake Lugano** (⊠ Casella Postale 56, CH-6900 Lugano, ☎ 091/9715223 or 091/9234610) offers cruise-boat excursions around the bay to Gandria and toward the Villa Favorita.

Boats owned by **Navigazione Lago Maggiore-Bacino Svizzero** (⊠ Lungolago Motta, CH-6600 Locarno, ☎ 091/7511865) cruise Lake Maggiore. Discounts are given for Swiss and Swiss Boat passes (☞ Train Travel *and* Boat Travel *in* Smart Travel Tips A to Z) and the Locarno Regional Pass (☞ By Train, *below*).

By Bus

There is a convenient postbus sightseeing system here that tourists can use—easily—to get around the region, even into the backcountry. La Posta (post and telegraph office) publishes illustrated booklets with suggested itineraries and prices; you can get them through the **Autopostale Ticino-Moesano** (⊠ Via S. Balestra, CH-6905 Lugano, ☎ 091/8078520/ 28) or through local tourist and post offices. Postbus excursion prices are reduced with the Locarno or Lugano Regional Pass (☞ By Train, *below*) and are free with the Swiss Pass (☞ Train Travel *in* Smart Travel Tips A to Z).

By Car

A car is a real asset here if you intend to see the mountain valleys— and a hindrance in the congested, urban lakeside resorts. Lugano is particularly difficult to drive through, and traffic between Bellinzona and Locarno can move at a crawl during high season. There's a handful of basic main roads between towns, but secondary roads peter out. Wherever you are in the Ticino, the Italian (read: fast and risky) driving style dominates.

By Train

Secondary rail connections here are minimal and can make all but the most mainstream rail sightseeing a complicated venture; most excursions will require some postbus connections. Nevertheless, there are **Regional Passes:** Lugano's offers seven days' unlimited travel on most rail and steamer lines, with 50% reductions on various other excursions and modes of transit (92 SF); or three days' travel within seven consecutive days (70 SF). In Locarno/Ascona, the seven-day Regional Pass offers unlimited travel on local rail and steamer trips and 50% reductions on chairlift and funicular rides (76 SF, available through tourist offices). Compare the Locarno and Lugano passes carefully before choosing; many of their discounted facilities overlap. As the Swiss Pass doesn't cover all the transport facilities of the Lake Lugano region, Regional Passes are offered to its holders at a discount.

Contacts and Resources

Emergencies

Police: (☎ 117). **Medical assistance/ambulance:** (☎ 144). Lugano civic **hospital** (☎ 091/8056111). Lugano **dental clinic** (☎ 091/9350180).

Guided Tours

ORIENTATION

The *Wilhelm Tell Express* carries you by paddle steamer and rail from Luzern over the Saint Gotthard Pass and into Locarno and Lugano with a guide and running commentary in English. Contact Lake Lucerne Navigation Centre SGV (⊠ Werftestrasse 5, P.O. Box 4265, CH-6005 Luzern, ☎ 041/3676767) or inquire at rail stations. The *Bernina Express,* Europe's highest Alp-crossing railway, takes you from Chur to St. Moritz in the *Glacier Express;* then you cross the Alps over the Bernina Pass into Italy (in summer it's even possible in an open-air train car) and continue into Lugano. Several variations are possible. Both offer discounts for Swiss Pass and Swiss Boat Pass holders (☞ Train Travel *and* Boat Travel *in* Smart Travel Tips A to Z). Inquire at any railway station for information and reservations.

Guided walks are available in all regions covering cultural, historical, architectural, and natural interests. Wonderfully detailed English-language brochures with maps are available from local tourist offices for both guided and self-guided tours.

Visitor Information

The principal tourist authority for the Ticino is **Ticino Turismo** (⊠ Villa Turrita, Via Lugano 12, CP 1441, CH-6501 Bellinzona, ☎ 091/8257056, FAX 091/8253614).

Local offices: Ascona (⊠ Casa Serodine, Box 449, CH-6612, ☎ 091/7910090). **Bellinzona** (⊠ Palazzo Civico, Box 1419, CH-6500, ☎ 091/8252131). **Biasca** (⊠ CH-6710, ☎ 091/8623327). **Blenio** (⊠ CH-6716 Acquarossa, ☎ 091/8711765). **Brissago Islands** (⊠ CH-6614 Brissago, ☎ 091/7931170). **Locarno** (⊠ Via Largo Zorzi, CH-6601, ☎ 091/7510333). **Lugano** (⊠ Palazzo Civico, CH-6901, ☎ 091/9133232). **Mendrisiotto e Basso Ceresio** (⊠ Via Angelo Maspoli 25, CH-6850 Mendrisio, ☎ 091/6465761).

6 LUZERN AND CENTRAL SWITZERLAND

Luzern, Engelberg, Weggis, Schwyz, Zug

Endowed with a sophisticated transportation system that makes it one of the easiest regions to visit, central Switzerland is full of neat little towns, accessible mountains, and modest resorts. Centered around the Vierwaldstättersee, the Lake of the Four Forest Cantons, the region is steeped in history: it is where the Oath of Eternal Alliance is said to have been renewed, and it's also the birthplace of the legend of William Tell.

AS YOU CRUISE DOWN THE LEISURELY sprawl of the Vierwaldstättersee (Lake Luzern), mist rising off the gray waves, mountains—great loaflike masses of forest and stone—looming above the clouds, it's easy to understand how Wagner could have composed his *Siegfried Idyll* in his mansion beside this lake. This is inspiring terrain, romantic and evocative. When the waters roil up, you can hear the whistling chromatics and cymbal clashes of Gioacchino Rossini's thunderstorm from his 1829 opera, *Guillaume Tell*. It was on this lake, after all, that William Tell—the beloved, if legendary, Swiss national hero—supposedly leapt from the tyrant Gessler's boat to freedom. And it was in a meadow nearby that three furtive rebels and their cohorts swore an oath by firelight and planted the seed of the Swiss Confederation.

Updated by
Katrin Gygax

The Rütli Meadow, a national landmark on the western shore of Lake Luzern, is the very spot where the Confederates of Schwyz, Unterwald, and Uri are said to have met on the night of November 7, 1307, to renew the 1291 Oath of Eternal Alliance—Switzerland's equivalent of the U.S. Declaration of Independence. With this oath, the world's oldest still-extant democracy was formed, as the proud charter territories swore their commitment to self-rule in the face of the oppressive Hapsburgs and the Holy Roman Empire. Every August 1, the Swiss national holiday, citizens gather in the meadow in remembrance of the oath, and the sky glows with the light of hundreds of mountaintop bonfires.

William Tell played an important role in that early rebellion, and his story, especially as told by German poet and playwright Friedrich von Schiller in his play *Wilhelm Tell* (1805), continues to stir those with a weakness for civil resistance. Though there are no valid records to prove his existence, and versions of the legend conflict with historical fact, no one denies the reality of his times, when central Switzerland—then a feudal dependent of Austria but by its own independent will not yet absorbed into the Holy Roman Empire—suffered brutal pressures and indignities under its local rulers. The mythical Gessler was one of those rulers, and his legendary edict—that the proud Swiss should bow before his hat suspended from a pole in the village square at Altdorf—symbolizes much crueler oppressions of the time. Schiller's Tell was a hero through and through: brisk, decisive, a highly skilled helmsman as well as marksman, and not one for diplomatic negotiations—he refused to kneel. Tell's famous punishment: to shoot an apple off his young son's head before a crowd of fellow townsmen; if he refused, both would be killed. Tell quietly tucked an arrow in his shirt bosom, loaded another into his crossbow, and shot the apple clean through. When Gessler asked what the second arrow was for, Tell replied that if the first arrow had struck his child, the second arrow would have been for Gessler and would not have missed.

For this impolitic remark, Tell was sentenced to prison. While deporting him across Lake Luzern, the Austrians (including the ruthless Gessler) were caught in a violent storm (remember your Rossini) and turned to Tell, the only man on board who knew the waters, to take the helm. Unmanacled, he steered the boat to a rocky ridge, leapt free, and pushed the boat back into the storm. Later he lay in wait in the woods near Küssnacht and, as Gessler threatened to ride down a woman begging mercy for her imprisoned husband, shot him in the heart. This act of justified violence inspired the people to overthrow their oppressors and swear the Oath of Eternal Alliance around a roaring bonfire, laying the groundwork for the Swiss Confederation.

Pretty romantic stuff. Yet for all its potential for drama, central Switzerland and the area surrounding Lake Luzern are tame enough turf: neat little towns, accessible mountains, smooth roads, resorts virtually glamour-free—and modest, graceful Luzern (Lucerne) astride the River Reuss much as it has been since the Middle Ages.

An eminently civilized region, Zentralschweiz (Central Switzerland) lacks the rustic unruliness of the Valais, the spectacular extremes of the Berner Oberland, the eccentricity of Graubünden. Nor does it have the sophistication and snob appeal of jet-set resorts or the cosmopolitan mix of Geneva, Basel, and Zürich. Instead, the area radiates tradition. Villages range neatly around their medieval centers; houses are tidy, pastel, picture-book cottages, deep-roofed and symmetrical, each rank of windows underscored with flowers. Luzern, the capital, hosts arts festivals and great shopping but little native industry. Serene and steady as the Reuss that laps at the piers of its ancient wooden bridges, it's an approachable city in an accessible region.

Central Switzerland's popularity with tourists has spawned an infrastructure of hotels, restaurants, museums, excursions, and transportation that makes it one of the easiest places in Switzerland to visit, either by car or by rail—and one of the most rewarding. As Wagner exclaimed, perhaps carried away a bit by his own waterfront idyll: "I do not know of a more beautiful spot in this world!"

Pleasures and Pastimes

Dining

Rooted in the German territory of Switzerland and the surrounding farmlands, central Switzerland's cuisine is down-home and hearty, though its specialties offer some variety from the veal-and-*Rösti* (hash brown potatoes) found everywhere else. In the heights, there are Alpine cheese specialties (*Aelpler Magrone*—pasta, butter, cheese, and fried onions); in the orchard country around Zug, there are such cherry specialties as *Zuger Kirschtorte,* a rich yellow cake soaked with cherry schnapps. Pears from the local orchards are dried, then spiced and poached in sweetened red *Dole* (wine). Luzern takes pride in its *Kügelipaschtetli,* puff-pastry nests filled with tiny veal meatballs, chicken, or sweetbreads; mushrooms; cream sauce; and occasionally raisins.

But here the real *cuisine du marché,* based on fresh market ingredients, focuses on lake fish. Lake Luzern and its neighboring Zugersee (Lake Zug) produce an abundance of *Egli* (perch), *Hecht* (pike), *Forellen* (trout), and *Felchen* (whitefish); Zug produces its own exclusive *Röteln,* a red-bellied relative of the trout. Restaurants—especially along waterfronts—trade heavily in these freshwater products, whether they come from the region or not. Ask, and you may get an honest answer: the sources vary, but the tradition and style of preparation remain local. In Zug, whole fish may be baked with sage, bay leaves, shallots, cloves, and plenty of white wine and butter; a Luzern tradition has them sautéed and sauced with tomatoes, mushrooms, and capers.

CATEGORY	COST*
$$$$	over 70 SF
$$$	40 SF–70 SF
$$	20 SF–40 SF
$	under 20 SF

*Prices are per person for a three-course meal (two-course meal in $ category), including sales tax and 15% service charge.

Hiking

Since Switzerland's 1991 septicentennial, celebrating the 700-year anniversary of its confederation, central Switzerland has marked and developed a historic foot trail, the Swiss Path, which covers 35 km (21½ mi) of lakefront lore along the southernmost branch of Lake Luzern. You'll trace the mythical steps of William Tell and the genuine steps of medieval forerunners, climb through steep forests and isolated villages, and visit the holiday resort of Brunnen. Complete information and maps can be requested through Central Switzerland Tourism (☞ Visitor Information *in* Luzern and Central Switzerland A to Z, *below*). The videocassette "Hiking the Swiss Path" is available through branches of Switzerland Tourism.

Lodging

Luzern provides a convenient home base for excursions all over the region, though villages are peppered with small, shuttered guest houses, and you may easily find an overnight spot as you drive through the countryside. As the terrain and climate vary radically between balmy lakefronts and icy heights, check carefully for high and low seasons before booking ahead. Such water-sport resorts as Weggis and Vitznau cut back service considerably in winter, just when Engelberg comes alive. Luzern, unlike most Swiss urban areas, has high and low seasons, and prices drop by as much as 25% in the winter, approximately November through March. Rates are usually calculated on a per-person basis, so it is wise to confirm the rates, particularly if you're traveling as anything other than a couple.

CATEGORY	COST*
$$$$	over 350 SF
$$$	250 SF–350 SF
$$	120 SF–250 SF
$	under 120 SF

Prices are for a standard double room, including breakfast, tax, and service charge.

Shopping

Although Luzern no longer produces embroidery or lace, you can find a wide variety of Swiss handiwork of the highest quality, crafts, and watches in all price categories. High-end watch dealers Gübelin and Bucherer offer inexpensive souvenirs to lure shoppers into their luxurious showrooms; smaller shops carry Tissot, Rado, Corum, and others—but prices are controlled by the manufacturers. Watch for closeouts on out-of-date models.

Exploring Luzern and Central Switzerland

Though called the Lake of the Four Forest Cantons, Lake Luzern and its environs take in not only the four cantons that abut the lake—Luzern, Uri, Schwyz, and Unterwalden—but the canton of Zug as well. Unterwalden itself is divided politically into two half-cantons: Obwalden (upper) and Nidwalden (lower). It was the canton of Schwyz that gave Switzerland its name.

The narrow, twisting lake flows from Flüelen, where the Reuss opens into the Urnersee, its southernmost leg. This is the wildest end of the lake, where much of the Tell story was set. The north end of the lake is flanked by the region's highest points, Mt. Pilatus (2,121 m/6,953 ft) and Mt. Rigi (1,798 m/5,894 ft). Luzern lies in a deep bay at the lake's northwest extreme and at the point where the rivers Reuss and Emme part ways. Zug stands apart, on the northern shore of its own Lake Zug, which is divided from Lake Luzern by the mass of Mt. Rigi.

Numbers in the text correspond to numbers in the margin and on the Central Switzerland and Luzern (Lucerne) maps.

Great Itineraries

When visiting this multiterrain area, you must change modes of transit frequently to see it all; part of the region's interest is the variety of boat trips, train rides, and drives you'll take to reach the sights. On any given day, you may walk through the lovely Old Town of Luzern, ascend Mt. Pilatus by cable car and descend by cogwheel train, take a lake steamer, or drive through the Rütli Meadow.

IF YOU HAVE 1 OR 2 DAYS

Take in the Old Town sights of ⊡ **Luzern** ①–⑮, then consider a half-day boat trip on the Vierwaldstättersee, which gives you the opportunity to see the sights of the region from the lake itself. **Mt. Pilatus** ⑯ offers central Switzerland's best mountaintop panoramas. Allow yourself a half day to ascend the mountain.

IF YOU HAVE 3 OR MORE DAYS

In addition to all of the above, take a trip to **Einsiedeln** ㉗, with its 9th-century Benedictine monastery. A combined train and cable-car trip from ⊡ **Weggis** ⑳ will take you to the summit of **Mt. Rigi**, where you can see as far as the Black Forest and Mt. Säntis and even spend the night in the hotel at the top. If you're traveling by car, you can follow the course of a lake steamer from Luzern, driving to the Saint Gotthard Pass along the lakefront highway (A2).

When to Tour Luzern and Central Switzerland

If you don't mind negotiating heavy traffic, particularly in Luzern, summer is the ideal season for boat excursions and great views from the tops of Mt. Pilatus and Mt. Rigi. In fall, when the crowds thin, you'll find crisp weather around the mountains and the lake. This isn't a big ski area, so wintertime tends to be quiet, even in Luzern.

LUZERN

57 km (36 mi) southwest of Zürich.

Luzern city is a convenient home base for excursions all over central Switzerland. The countryside here is tame, and the vast Vierwaldstättersee (Lake Luzern) offers a prime opportunity for a lake steamer cruise.

Where the River Reuss flows out of Lake Luzern, Luzern's Old Town straddles the narrowed waters. The greater concentration of life bustles along the river's right bank. The city's signature sights include the Kapellbrücke, a covered wooden bridge, and the moving Löwendenkmal (☞ *below*). There are a couple of passes available for discounts for museums and sights in the city. One is a museum pass that costs 25 SF and grants free entry to all museums for one month. If you are staying in a hotel, you may also want to pick up a special visitor's card; once stamped by the hotel, it entitles you to discounts at most museums and other tourist-oriented businesses as well. Both are available at the tourist office (☞ Visitor Information *in* Luzern and Central Switzerland A to Z, *below*).

Old Town and Beyond

A Good Walk

Start at the new **Kultur- und Kongresszentrum** ① by the train station, which gives you a beautiful view of all the places you'll see in Luzern. Walk down Bahnhofstrasse to the modern bridge, the **Rathaus-Steg**, and head north to the **Altes Rathaus** ②, across the bridge. (This late-

Tschamut

Bürglen

Alidorf **24**

17

Erstfeld

Flüelen **23**

Reuss

Amsteg

2

2

Urnersee

Wassen

Göschenen

Obere Alppass

Andermatt **26**

2

Göscheneralp See

TO ST GOTTHARD PASS

Sustenhorn

Dammastock

Titlis

Engelberg **18**

Trübsee

11

Gadmen

Aa

Grafenort

Innertkirchen

Guttannen

9

Sarnen

Kaiserstuhl

Meiringen

Lungern See

4

Sarner See

Brienzwiler

A8

4

Bränzer Rothorn

TO INTERLAKEN

N

KEY

———	Rail Lines
⋯⋯⋯	Cable Car/ Funicular
	Tunnels
– – –	Regional Boundary Lines
– – –	Ferry
⛷	Ski Resorts

4 miles

0 km

Luzern (Lucerne)

14

13

12

Löwen-platz

Löwen-str.

Weystrasse

Denkmalstr.

Zürichstrasse

Fluhmattstrasse

Bergstrasse

Kapuzinerweg

Abendweg

Landschaustrasse

Dreilindenstr.

Dreilindenstr.

Hitzlisbergstr.

Adligenswilerstr.

11

Zinggentorstr.

Haldenstrasse

Museggstrasse

Hertensteinstr.

St. Leodegar-Str.

Haldenstrasse

Kursaal (Casino)

Carl Spittelerquai

AE

Schweizerhofquai

Nationalquai

Schwanen-Platz

Vierwaldstättersee

N

Furrengasse

Rathausquai

10

Kapell-brücke

Seebrücke

Bahnhofstrasse

Theaterstr.

Pilatusstrasse

Frankenstrasse

Zentralstrasse

Inseliquai

Bahnhof-platz

Bahnhof

Europa-platz

1

KEY	
——	Rail Lines
••••	Funicular
▦▦▦	Tramway
AE	American Express Office

0   200 yards

0   200 meters

Renaissance style building is on **Rathausquai,** the city's main avenue.) Just to the right of the Rathaus is the **Am Rhyn-Haus** ③, now a Picasso museum. Turn left and climb the stairs past the ornately frescoed Zunfthaus zur Pfistern (☞ Pfistern *in* Dining and Lodging, *below*), a guildhall dating from the late 15th and early 16th centuries, to the **Kornmarkt,** where the grinding din of the grain market was once heard. Cut left to the **Weinmarkt** ④. Leave the square from its west end, turn right on Kramgasse, and head west across the Mühlenplatz to the **Spreuerbrücke** ⑤, an unlikely exhibition space for dark paintings of the medieval plague epidemic. Crossing the bridge to the left bank, you'll find a pair of museums, the **Natur-Museum** ⑥ and the **Historisches Museum** ⑦. From the end of the Spreuerbrücke, cut back upriver along Pfistergasse, veer left on Bahnhofstrasse, and turn right into Münzgasse to the **Franziskanerkirche** ⑧. Return to Bahnhofstrasse and head to the **Jesuitenkirche** ⑨. Continuing east past the Rathaus-Steg Bridge, you'll see the **Kapellbrücke** ⑩, the oldest of its kind in Europe.

After crossing the Kapellbrücke, break away from Old Town through thick pedestrian and bus traffic at Schwanenplatz to Schweizerhofquai. Double back and take the first right, St. Leodegarstrasse, to the **Hofkirche** ⑪; go back down the church steps, turn right, and continue on to Löwenstrasse. Turn right and walk up to Löwenplatz and the **Bourbaki-Panorama** ⑫ (closed for renovations until winter 2000), which dominates the square like a remnant from a Victorian world's fair. Beyond the plaza, up Denkmalstrasse, is the **Löwendenkmal** ⑬, called by Mark Twain "the most mournful and moving piece of stone in the world." Immediately adjoining the small park that shades the lion lies the **Gletschergarten** ⑭. Return down Denkmalstrasse and, at Löwenplatz, turn right on Museggstrasse, which cuts through an original city gate and runs parallel to the watchtowers and crenellated walls of Luzern, constructed around 1400. The fifth tower is **Zytturm** ⑮.

TIMING

The Old Town is easy to navigate and ideal for walking. You can take in the sights on this route in about three hours; to this add another hour each to see the Natur-Museum and Historisches Museum, and time to linger awhile at the Kapellbrücke and the Löwendenkmal. Note that both the Natur-Museum and the Historisches Museum are closed Monday; the Gletschergarten is closed Monday from mid-November through February.

Sights to See

❷ **Altes Rathaus** (Old Town Hall). In 1606, the Luzern town council held its first meeting in this late-Renaissance style building, built between 1599 and 1606. It still meets here today. ⊠ *Rathausquai, facing the end of Rathaus-Steg.*

❸ **Am Rhyn-Haus** (Am Rhyn House). Also known as the Picasso Museum, this spot contrasts a beautiful, 17th-century building with its modern holdings. The collection consists mainly of works from the last 20 years of Picasso's life, including his "Déjeuner sur l'Herbe" and giant iron sculptures, along with more than 100 photos of the artist. ⊠ *Furreng. 21,* ☎ *041/4101773.* ☜ *6 SF.* ☉ *Apr.–Oct., daily 10–6; Nov.–Mar., daily 11–1 and 2–4.*

⑫ **Bourbaki-Panorama.** This enormous conical wooden structure was created between 1876 and 1878 as a genuine, step-right-up tourist attraction and is, in its undiluted period form, as interesting for its novel nature as for its content. At the top of wide entry stairs, the conical roof covers a sweeping, wraparound epic painting of the French Army of the East retreating into Switzerland at Verrières—a famous episode in the

Franco-Prussian War. It was painted by Édouard Castres of Geneva, who was aided by many uncredited artists, including Ferdinand Hodler. As you walk around the circle, the imagery seems to pop into three dimensions; in fact, with the help of a few strategically placed models, it does. There's a recorded commentary in English. The Bourbaki-Panorama is closed for renovations until February 2000. ☒ *Löwenpl.*, ☎ *041/4109942.* 🎫 *3 SF.* ☉ *Call for hours after reopening.*

⑧ Franziskanerkirche (Franciscan Church). After more than 700 years, this church, despite persistent modernization, retains its 17th-century choir stalls and carved wooden pulpit. The barefoot Franciscans once held a prominent social and cultural position in Luzern, which took a firm Counter-Reformation stance and remains more than 70% Roman Catholic today. ☒ *Franziskanerpl., just off Münzg.*

⑭ Gletschergarten (Glacier Garden). The bedrock of this 19th-century tourist attraction was excavated between 1872 and 1875 and has been dramatically pocked and polished by Ice Age glaciers. A private museum on the site displays impressive relief maps of Switzerland. ☒ *Denkmalstr. 4,* ☎ *041/4104340.* 🎫 *7 SF.* ☉ *May–mid-Oct., daily 8–6; Mar., Apr., and mid-Oct.–mid-Nov., daily 9–5; mid-Nov.–Feb., Tues.–Sat. 10:30–4:30, Sun. 10–5.*

⑦ Historisches Museum (Historical Museum). Housed in the late-Gothic armory dating from 1567, this stylish institution exhibits city sculptures, Swiss arms, and flags. Reconstructed rooms depict rural and urban life; it's also got the original Gothic fountain from the Weinmarkt (☞ *below*). ☒ *Pfisterg. 24,* ☎ *041/2285424.* 🎫 *4 SF.* ☉ *Tues.–Fri. 10–noon and 2–5, weekends 10–5.*

⑪ Hofkirche. This sanctuary of St. Leodegar was first part of a monastery founded in 750. Its Gothic structure was mostly destroyed by fire in 1633 and rebuilt in late-Renaissance style, so only the towers of its predecessor were preserved. The carved pulpit and choir stalls date from the 17th century, and the 80-rank organ (1650) is one of Switzerland's finest. It's still used for the church's concerts, which are held several times each month. Outside, Italianate loggias shelter a cemetery for patrician families of Old Luzern. ☒ *St. Leodegarstr. 6,* ☎ *041/4105241. Closed Fri. 10–noon, 2:30–5.*

OFF THE BEATEN PATH

VERKEHRSHAUS – Easily reached by steamer, car, or Bus 2, the Swiss Transport Museum is almost a world's fair in itself, with a complex of buildings and exhibitions both indoors and out, including dioramas, live demonstrations, and a "Swissorama" (360-degree screen) film about Switzerland. Every mode of transit is discussed, from stagecoaches and bicycles to jumbo jets and space capsules. The museum also has Switzerland's first IMAX theater. If you're driving, head east on Haldenstrasse at the waterfront and make a right on Lidostrasse (it's also signposted). ☒ *Lidostr. 5,* ☎ *041/3704444.* 🎫 *16 SF.* ☉ *Mar.–Oct., daily 9–6; Nov.–Feb., daily 10–5.*

★ ⑨ Jesuitenkirche (Jesuit Church). Constructed in 1666–77, this baroque church with a symmetrical entrance is flanked by two onion-dome towers, added in 1893. Go inside: its vast interior, restored to mint condition, is a rococo explosion of gilt, marble, and epic frescoes. Nearby is the Renaissance **Regierungsgebäude** (Government Building), seat of the cantonal government. ☒ *Bahnhofstr., just west of Rathaus-Steg,* ☎ *041/2100756.* ☉ *Daily 6 AM–6:15 PM.*

★ ⑩ Kapellbrücke (Chapel Bridge). The oldest wooden bridge in Europe snakes diagonally across the Reuss. When built in the early 14th century, it served as the division between the lake and the river. Its shingle roof and grand, stone water tower are to Luzern what the Matterhorn is to Zermatt, but considerably more vulnerable, as a 1993 fire proved. Almost 80% of this fragile monument was destroyed, including many of the 17th-century paintings inside; restorations are still underway. However, a walk through this dark, creaky landmark will take you past polychrome copies of the 112 gable panels, painted by Heinrich Wägmann during the 17th century and depicting Luzern and Swiss history, stories of St. Leodegar and St. Mauritius, Luzern's patron saints, and coats of arms of local patrician families. ⊠ *Between Seebrücke and Rathaus-Steg, connecting Rathausquai and Bahnhofstr.*

★ ❶ **Kultur- und Kongresszentrum** (Culture and Congress Center). Architect Jean Nouvel's stunning glass and steel building manages to both jolt and fuse with its ancient milieu. The lakeside center's roof is a cantilevered, oversized, flat plane; shallow water channels thread inside, and immense glass plates mirror the surrounding views. The main magnet is the concert hall, opened in 1998. Although the lobbies are rich in blue, red, and stained wood, the hall itself is refreshingly pale, with acoustics so perfect you can hear the proverbial pin drop. Among the annual music events is the renowned International Music Festival (☞ Nightlife and the Arts, *below*). A museum with both permanent and rotating exhibits was slated to open in summer 2000. ⊠ *Europapl.,* ☎ 041/2207070.

★ ⓭ **Löwendenkmal** (Lion Monument). The Swiss officers and 760 guards officers who died defending Louis XVI of France at the Tuileries in Paris in 1792 are commemorated here. Designed by Danish sculptor Berthel Thorwaldsen and carved out of a sheer sandstone face by Lucas Ahorn of Konstanz, this 19th-century wonder is a simple, stirring image of a dying lion. The Latin inscription translates: "To the bravery and fidelity of the Swiss." ⊠ *Denkmalstr.*

☝ ❻ **Natur-Museum** (Natural History Museum). Unusually modern display techniques bring nature lessons to life: The museum focuses on local natural history, with model panoramas of early Luzern settlers and live animals for children to meet. ⊠ *Kasernenpl. 6,* ☎ 041/2285411. ☞ 5 SF. ☉ *Tues.–Sat. 10–noon and 2–5, Sun. 10–5.*

❺ **Spreuerbrücke.** This narrow, weathered, all-wood covered bridge dates from 1408. Its interior gables hold a series of eerie, well-preserved 17th-century paintings by Kaspar Meglinger of the *Dance of Death.* Medieval in style and inspiration, they chronicle the plague that devastated all of Europe in the 14th century. ⊠ *Between Geissmattbrücke and Reussbrücke, connecting Zeughaus Reuss-Steg and Mühlenpl.*

❹ **Weinmarkt** (Wine Market). What is now the loveliest of Luzern's several fountain squares drew visitors from all across Europe in the 15th to 17th centuries with its passion plays. Its Gothic central fountain depicts St. Mauritius (patron saint of warriors), and its surrounding buildings are flamboyantly frescoed in 16th-century style. ⊠ *Square just west of Kornmarkt, north of Metzgerainli.*

⓯ **Zytturm.** The clock in this fifth watchtower, was made in Basel in 1385 and still keeps time. ⊠ *North of and parallel to Museggstr.*

Dining and Lodging

$$$ ✕ **Old Swiss House.** Conceived as self-consciously as its name implies—no doubt to satisfy the romantic expectations of the flood of English tourists heading for the Lion Monument—this popular establishment pleases crowds with its beautifully contrived collection of 17th-cen-

tury antiques, its leaded glass, and an old-world style now pleasantly burnished by more than 130 years of service. The standing menu includes specialties from around the country: cheese croquettes, veal and Rösti, lake fish, and Swiss chocolate mousse. ⊠ *Löwenpl. 4, ☎ 041/ 4106171. AE, DC, MC, V. Closed Mon. and Feb.*

$$$ ✕ **Rotes Gatter.** This chic restaurant in the Des Balances hotel (☞ *below*)
★ has a combination as desirable as it is rare: soigné decor, shimmering river views, and a sophisticated menu with fish dishes such as curry cream scallops or the house specialty, meat and fish fondue. There's a more casual, less expensive bistro area as well. ⊠ *Weinmarkt, ☎ 041/ 4103010. AE, DC, MC, V.*

$$ ✕ **Galliker.** Step past the ancient facade into a room roaring with local
★ action, where Luzerners drink, smoke, and wish each other *Guten Appetit*. Brisk, motherly waitresses serve up the dishes *Mutti* used to make: fresh *Kutteln* (tripe) in rich white wine sauce with cumin seeds; real *Kalbskopf* (chopped fresh veal head) served with heaps of green onions and warm vinaigrette; and authentic Luzerner Kügelipaschtetli. Desserts may include dried pears steeped in pinot noir. Occasional experiments in a more modern mode—such as ginger ice cream—prove that Peter Galliker's kitchen is no museum. ⊠ *Schützenstr. 1, ☎ 041/ 2401002. AE, DC, MC, V. Closed Sun., Mon., and 3 wks in Aug.*

$$ ✕ **Rebstock/Hofstube.** At the opposite end of the culinary spectrum from Galliker (☞ *above*), this up-to-date kitchen offers modern, international fare, including rabbit and lamb, as well as East Asian and vegetarian specialties. But you're still in Switzerland: the chewy breads, baked up the street, are so beautiful that they're displayed as objets d'art. The lively bentwood brasserie hums with locals lunching by the bar, while the more formal old-style restaurant glows with wood and brass under a low-beamed parquetry ceiling. ⊠ *St. Leodegarpl. 3, ☎ 041/4103581. AE, DC, MC, V.*

$ ✕ **Pfistern.** One of the architectural focal points of the Old Town waterfront, this floridly decorated old guild house—the guild's origins can be traced back to 1341—offers a good selection of moderate meals in addition to higher-price standards. Lake fish and *pastetli* (meat pies with puff pastry) are worthy local options. Inside, it's woody and publike, if slightly down-at-the-heels, but in summer the small first-floor balcony may provide the best seat in town. ⊠ *Kornmarkt 4, ☎ 041/ 4103650. AE, DC, MC, V.*

$$$$ ✕▥ **Palace Hotel.** This waterfront hotel drinks in the broadest possi-
★ ble lake views. Built in 1906, it's been brilliantly refurbished so that its classical look has a touch of postmodernism. Rooms are large enough for a game of badminton, and picture windows afford sweeping views of Lake Luzern and Mt. Pilatus. The hotel's elegance seeps into its restaurant, Mignon, as well. The contemporary cuisine—rosemary beef tenderloin in olive oil and black pepper jus, for example—is faultlessly prepared and formally presented. Reservations are essential. ⊠ *Haldenstr. 10, CH-6002, ☎ 041/4100404, ℻ 041/4101504. 178 rooms, 45 suites. Restaurant, bar, massage, 2 saunas, steam room, health club, parking (fee). AE, DC, MC, V.*

$$$ ✕▥ **Wilden Mann.** The city's best-known hotel offers its guests a gra-
★ cious and authentic experience of Old Luzern, with stone, beams, brass, hand-painted tiles, and burnished wood everywhere. (Even the street is atmospheric—across the way is a 16th-century pharmacy.) Standard rooms have a prim 19th-century look. The hotel's reputation extends to its restaurants; the Burgerstube, which began in 1517 as a rest stop for Saint Gotthard travelers, is cozy with its dark beams and family crests, while vaulting and candlelight give the Liedertafel restaurant a more formal atmosphere. On either side, young chef Andreas Stübi strikes a fine balance between old-style local cooking and savvy French

cuisine: smoked salmon tartare wrapped in Rösti with dill sauce; duck breast with dandelion honey and balsamic vinegar. ⊠ *Bahnhofstr. 30, CH-6003,* ☎ *041/2101666,* ℻ *041/2101629. 35 rooms, 8 suites. 2 restaurants. AE, DC, MC, V.*

$$$$ 🏨 **Château Gütsch.** This "castle," built in 1888, is not exactly authentic, but honeymooners, gullible romantics, and other neophytes seeking out storybook Europe enjoy the Disneyland-like experience: the turrets and towers worthy of a mad Ludwig of Bavaria; the cellars, crypts, and corridors lined with a hodgepodge of relics; not to mention the magnificent hilltop site above Luzern. Fantasy-style rooms are decked out for romance, some with four-poster canopy beds, all with grand baths. The restaurant is known for its dramatic views of Luzern, and there are wine tastings in the atmospheric cellar. You can get a funicular up to the hotel (2 SF); catch it where Pfistergasse meets Baselstrasse. ⊠ *Kanonenstr., CH-6002,* ☎ *041/2494100,* ℻ *041/2494191. 28 rooms, 3 suites. 2 restaurants, pool, free parking. AE, DC, MC, V.*

$$$$ 🏨 **National Hotel.** In this monumental landmark, founded in 1870 and once home base to Cesar Ritz, the inner sanctums have been restored to florid splendor, down to the last cupola, crown molding, and Corinthian column. The hotel's mansarded facade stretches the length of two city blocks, dominating the lakeside promenade. Rooms are French provincial with brass beds, the domed bar is decked with mahogany and aglitter with crystal, and the marble-columned breakfast hall may be the most splendid in Switzerland—even without the lake view. ⊠ *Haldenstr. 4, CH-6003,* ☎ *41/4190909,* ℻ *041/4190910. 78 rooms, 10 suites. 4 restaurants, breakfast room, café, piano bar, indoor pool, sauna, health club, parking (fee). AE, DC, MC, V.*

$$$$ 🏨 **Schweizerhof.** Built in 1844 and expanded in the 1860s, this imposing structure has hosted Napoléon III, Leo Tolstoy, and Mark Twain—and Richard Wagner lived here while his lakefront home at Tribschen was being completed. Rooms have a sweeping view of the lake and mountains. At press time, the hotel planned to be closed through December 1999 for renovation. ⊠ *Schweizerhofquai 3, CH-6002,* ☎ *041/4100410,* ℻ *041/4102971. 116 rooms. Restaurant, café, bar, free parking. AE, DC, MC, V.*

$$$ 🏨 **Des Balances.** This riverfront property, built in the 19th century on
★ the site of an ancient guildhall, gleams with style. State-of-the-art tile baths, up-to-date pastel decor, and one of the best sites in Luzern (in the heart of the Old Town) make this the slickest in its price class. Rear rooms look toward the Weinmarkt. The restaurant Rotes Gatter (☞ *above*) is so good that you may want to eat every meal in the hotel. ⊠ *Weinmarkt, CH-6000,* ☎ *041/4103010,* ℻ *041/4106451. 50 rooms, 7 suites. Restaurant. AE, DC, MC, V.*

$$$ 🏨 **Hofgarten.** This gracious 12th-century house off the end of the Schweizerhofquai reflects the creative mind of owner Claudia Moser. The rooms are an eclectic mix of colors and themes. One contains a 5-ft-tall antique stove (still operable) while another is called the Ship Room and resembles the interior of a clipper ship. The Hofgarten also offers Luzern's only all-vegetarian restaurant, whose dishes could satisfy even a meat lover. ⊠ *Stadthofstr. 14, CH-6006,* ☎ *041/4108888,* ℻ *041/4108333. 18 rooms. Restaurant, parking (fee). AE, DC, MC, V.*

$$$ 🏨 **Montana.** This 1910 palace glows with beeswaxed beauty, its luxurious original woodwork, parquet, and terrazzo in superb condition. The public rooms flank the ground floor's south side and on a clear day offer a magnificent view of the lake and the Alps. The guest rooms echo Art Deco, with bold patterns and funky furniture. Those in back overlook a hillside, while the front doubles (slightly costlier) have balconies overlooking the city and lake. The building is perched on a slope above town, accessible by funicular from the lakeshore Haldenstrasse

or by car. TV is available by request only. ⊠ *Adligenswilerstr. 22, CH-6002,* ☎ *041/4106565,* FAX *041/4106676. 55 rooms, 10 suites. Restaurant, bar, free parking. AE, DC, MC, V.*

$$ ⛨ **Des Alpes.** This historic hotel, with a terrific riverfront location in the bustling heart of the Old Town, has an interior resembling a laminate-and-vinyl chain motel. The rooms, however, are generously proportioned, tidy, and even sleek; front doubles, several with balconies, overlook the water and promenade. Cheaper back rooms face the Old Town; those on higher floors have rooftop views and plenty of light. ⊠ *Rathausquai 5, CH-6003,* ☎ *041/4105825,* FAX *041/4107451. 45 rooms. Restaurant, café. AE, DC, MC, V.*

$$ ⛨ **Diana.** This is a city hotel, on the south bank and off the main shopping street, but it's reached through a quiet park. Newly decorated rooms may have built-in fixtures in sleek beech or warm knotty pine; some have French windows that open onto balconies. In the oldest rooms, a bleak Formica look, a holdover from the '60s, prevails. Jugendstil touches remain in the corridors, and the public areas are modern but worn. ⊠ *Sempacherstr. 16, CH-6003,* ☎ *041/2102623,* FAX *041/2100205. 38 rooms. Breakfast room. AE, DC, MC, V.*

$$ ⛨ **Krone.** Spotless and modern, this hotel softens its edges with pastel linens and walls; in one of the interior walls you may find a stone prayer shrine retained from the original structure. The rooms facing the Weinmarkt have high ceilings and tall windows that let in floods of sunshine. Rooms to the back have no direct sunlight but are still bright and a little larger. The restaurant downstairs has a sinful dessert menu (try the crepes!) and sprawls out onto the Weinmarkt in the summer; it has a no-alcohol policy. ⊠ *Weinmarkt 12, CH-6004,* ☎ *041/4194400,* FAX *041/4194490. 25 rooms. Restaurant, deli, outdoor café. AE, DC, MC, V.*

$–$$ ⛨ **Goldener Stern.** This plain and pleasant former wine cellar has restored its fine 17th-century exterior to present a scrubbed face to the world. Pristine linens soften the modern rooms; windows, some looking over the Franciscan Church, are double-glazed. The Stübli is popular with locals. ⊠ *Burgerstr. 35, CH-6003,* ☎ *041/2275060,* FAX *041/2275061. 18 rooms. Restaurant. AE, MC, V.*

$ ⛨ **Schlüssel.** This spare, no-nonsense lodging on the Franziskanerplatz attracts young bargain hunters; several of its rooms overlook the square's Franciscan church and fountain (be prepared for morning church bells). It's a pleasant combination of tidy new touches (quarry tile, white paint) and antiquity: you can have breakfast or a simple hot meal in a low, cross-vaulted "crypt" and admire the fine old beams in the lobby. ⊠ *Franziskanerpl. 12, CH-6003,* ☎ *041/2101061,* FAX *041/2101021. 11 rooms. Breakfast room. AE, MC, V.*

$ ⛨ **Tourist.** Despite its friendly, collegiate atmosphere, this cheery dorm-
★ like spot is anything but a backpackers' flophouse. It has a terrific setting on the Reuss around the corner from the Old Town. Its spare modern architecture is brightened with fresh, trendy colors and framed prints, and rooms that don't have the river view face Mt. Pilatus instead. The staff is young and helpful, and the coed four-bed dorms (sex-segregated in high season) draw sociable travelers with their rock-bottom prices. There are also seven private-bath doubles. Shared baths are well maintained. ⊠ *St. Karli Quai 12, CH-6003,* ☎ *041/4102474,* FAX *041/4108414. 35 dormitory rooms. Coin laundry. AE, DC, MC, V.*

Nightlife and the Arts

For information on goings-on around town, get a copy of the *Luzern City Guide,* published by the city seasonally; it's available at the tourist office (☞ Visitor Information *in* Luzern and Central Switzerland A to Z, *below*). It's bilingual (German/English).

Nightlife

BARS AND LOUNGES

Château Gütsch (✉ Kanonenstr., ☎ 041/2494141) draws a sedate dinner-and-dancing crowd. **Mr. Pickwick** (✉ Rathausquai 6, ☎ 041/4105927) serves up pints English style. The **National Hotel** (☞ Dining and Lodging, *above*) mixes drinks in both its glossy American-style bar and its imposing lobby lounge. The **Palace Hotel** (☞ Dining and Lodging, *above*), like the National, has two American-style bars.

CASINOS

The most sophisticated nightlife in Luzern is found in the **Casino** (✉ Haldenstr. 6, ☎ 041/4185656), a turn-of-the-century building on the northern shore by the grand hotels. You can play *boule* (a type of roulette) in the Gambling Room (5 SF limit, federally imposed), dance in its club **Vegas,** watch the cabaret in the **Red Rose,** or have a Swiss meal in **Le Chalet** while watching a folklore display.

The Arts

FILM

Movie theaters, concentrated on the south bank along Pilatusstrasse and Bahnhofstrasse, usually present films in their original language.

FOLKLORE

The ***Night Boat*** (☎ 041/3194978), which sails from the Landungsbrücke every evening from May through September, offers meals, drinks, and a folklore show during a pleasant lake cruise. Performances at the **Stadtkeller** (✉ Sternenpl. 3, ☎ 041/4104733) come with Valais-cheese specialties, yodelers, dirndled dancers, and more.

MUSIC

Luzern, the cultural hub of central Switzerland, annually hosts the **International Music Festival** for three weeks in August. The 1998 festival inaugurated the festival's new lakeside home, the Kultur- und Kongresszentrum (✉ Europapl.). Outstanding performers come from all over the world; guests scheduled for 1999 included soprano Cecilia Bartoli, conductor Zubin Mehta, and the Berlin Philharmonic Orchestra. For further information on the festival, contact **International Musikfestwochen** (✉ Hirschmanttstr. 13, CH-6002, ☎ 041/2264400, FAX 041/2264460). The **Allgemeine Musikgesellschaft Luzern** (AML), the local orchestra in residence, offers a season of concerts from October through June at the Kunsthaus (✉ Moosstr. 15, ☎ 041/2105050).

THEATER

The **Luzerner Theater** (✉ Theaterstr. 2, ☎ 041/2106618), directly on the waterfront on the Bahnhof side of town, is home to Luzern's principal theater group, which stages plays in German and operas, usually in the original language.

Outdoor Activities and Sports

Bicycling

The standard Swiss practice of renting bicycles from the **train station** (☎ 051/2273261) comes in handy here, as the lake-level terrain offers smooth riding.

Boating

Pedal-, motor-, and sailboats are available in Luzern through **Bucher & Co.** (☎ 041/4102055). **SNG Luzern** (✉ Alpenquai 11, ☎ 041/3680808), open daily 11–6, offers 60-minute boat tours for 13 SF. **Werft**

Herzog AG (☎ 041/4104333) specializes in exclusive yacht excursions for as many as 12 passengers.

Golf

Golfplatz Dietschiberg (✉ Just above Luzern, near the city center, ☎ 041/4209787) has an 18-hole course open to visitors.

Swimming

At the **Lido** (✉ Lidostr., ☎ 041/3703806), past the casino and near the Verkehrshaus, you can swim in Lake Luzern. The Lido was reopened after renovations in summer 1999.

Tennis

Tennisclub Carlton Tivoli (✉ Haldenstr., ☎ 041/3703137) has four outdoor courts available. However, no rental equipment is available.

Windsurfing

Contact **Kempf Sport AG** (✉ Bahnhofstr. 24, ☎ 041/2101057).

Shopping

The best shopping in the region is concentrated in Luzern, which, although it no longer produces embroidery or lace, still offers a wide variety of Swiss handiwork as well as the luxury goods appropriate to its high profile. During the summer, most shops remain open in the evening until 9 and open on Sunday morning after 11. On Thursday night year-round, shops stay open until 9.

Department Stores

The main department store in town is **Globus** (✉ Pilatusstr. 4, ☎ 041/2270707); it's a good place to hunt for souvenirs. **Migros** (✉ Hertensteinstr. 44, ☎ 041/4106363; ✉ Letzihof mall, Hirschengraben 41, ☎ 041/2405571) specializes in groceries and also has inexpensive stationery and office supplies.

Embroidery

For fine handcrafted lace and embroidery, visit **Neff** (✉ Löwenstr. 10, ☎ 041/4101965), if not to buy, just to browse. The main producer of Swiss embroidery is **Sturzenegger** (✉ Schwanenpl. 7, ☎ 041/4101958) of Saint Gallen, which sells its own machine-made lace and embroidered goods as well as Hanro and Calida underwear. The store also stocks a conservative line of women's dresses and blouses.

Handicrafts and Gifts

Aux Arts du Feu (✉ Schweizerhofquai 2, ☎ 041/4101401) offers high-end china and crystal. **Ordning & Reda** (✉ Hertensteinstr. 3, ☎ 041/4109506) is an upscale Swedish stationer featuring precision writing instruments and brightly colored, handmade, recycled-paper products. **Schmid-Linder** (✉ Denkmalstr. 9, ☎ 041/4104346) carries an extensive line of Swiss embroidery and linen as well as cuckoo clocks, cowbells, and a large stock of wood carvings from Brienz, in the Berner Oberland.

Markets

A **flea market** takes place every Saturday from 8 to 4 at Untere Burgerstrasse. For locally made crafts, there's a **Handwerksmarkt** on the Weinmarkt on the first Saturday of every month.

Watches

Competition is fierce, and the two enormous patriarchs of the watch business advertise heavily and offer inexpensive souvenirs to lure shoppers into their luxurious showrooms. **Bucherer** (✉ Schwanenpl., ☎ 041/3697700) represents Piaget and Rolex. **Gübelin** (✉ Schweizerhofquai 1, ☎ 041/4105142) is the exclusive source for Audemars Piguet, Patek Philippe, and its own house brand.

Women's Clothing

The czarina of women's fashion in Luzern is **Christina De Boer,** who runs a group of designer boutiques: De Boer (⊠ Weggisg. 29, ☎ 041/ 4102022), De Boer Rive Gauche (⊠ Pilatusstr. 14, ☎ 041/2108916), De Boer's Esprit (⊠ Kornmarkt, ☎ 041/4102776), and Christina De Boer (⊠ Weggisg. 29, Werchlaube, ☎ 041/4106239). **McStore/Maglia Poletti** (⊠ Furreng. 7, ☎ 041/4102115) stocks such hip Euro designers as Apropos, Annex, Pink Flamingo (all Swiss designers), and Paul Smith, as well as Poletti's own line of knits in wool, silk, and cotton.

LUZERN ENVIRONS

Mt. Pilatus

⑯ *10 km (6 mi) southwest of Luzern.*

This 2,121-m (6,953-ft) mountain was named either from the Latin *pileatus* (wearing a cap), to refer to its frequent cloud covering, or, more colorfully, for the ghost of Pontius Pilate, who supposedly haunts the summit: his body, it was said, was brought here by the devil. For centuries it was forbidden to climb the mountain and enrage the ghost, who was said to unleash deadly storms. Unlike Queen Victoria, who rode to the summit by mule in 1868, you can now reach it by cable car for a hefty 78 SF in summer, 43 SF in winter.

Take a bus from the train station in Luzern to the suburb of Kriens, where you catch a tiny, four-seat cable car that flies silently up to Fräkmüntegg (1,403 m/4,600 ft); then change to the 40-seat cable car that sails through open air up the rock cliff to the summit station (1,696 m/5,560 ft). From here a 10-minute walk takes you to the **Esel,** at the center of Pilatus's multiple peaks, where views unfold over the Alps and the sprawling, crooked Lake Luzern.

A pleasant variation for the return trip to Luzern from Mt. Pilatus involves riding a steep cogwheel train, often down gradients inclined nearly 48%, through four tunnels that pierce sheer rock, to Alpnachstad. From there, take the train or the ferry, which leaves from the jetty across from the train station, back to Luzern. To go on to Engelberg get off the Luzern-bound train at Hergiswil, where you can cross the track and climb aboard the small, private Stans-Engelberg train that heads up the Engelbergertal (Engelberg Valley). If you are coming straight from Luzern, trains run every hour to Engelberg.

Stans

⑰ *10 km (6 mi) east of Mt. Pilatus, 10 km (6 mi) south of Luzern.*

In the heart of lush valley terrain and mossy meadows, Stans is an old village whose appealing Old Town center is dotted with the deep-roof houses typical of central Switzerland. This was the home of the beloved Heinrich Pestalozzi, the father of modern education. When the French army invaded the village in 1798, slaughtering nearly 2,000 citizens, it was Pestalozzi who gathered the orphaned children into a school, where he applied his progressive theories in the budding science of psychology to the practice of education. Instead of rote memorization and harsh discipline, Pestalozzi's teaching methods emphasized concrete examples (using plant specimens to teach botany, for example) and moral as well as intellectual development—quite a liberal education. He also championed the idea of children's individuality.

The bell tower of Stans's **Pfarrkirche St. Peter und St. Paul** (Church of Saints Peter and Paul) is in Italian Romanesque style (with increasing numbers of arched windows as the tower rises), though the incongruous steeple was added in the 16th century; the church as it stands dates from the Renaissance period. ⊠ *Knirig. 1,* ☎ *041/6109261.*

On the town square stands a 19th-century **monument to Arnold von Winkelried,** a native of Stans who martyred himself to lead the Swiss Confederates to victory over the Austrians at the battle of Sempach in 1386. The Austrians, armed with long spears, formed a Roman square so that the Swiss, wielding axes and halberds, couldn't get in close enough to do any damage. Shouting, "Forward, confederates, I will open a path!" von Winkelried threw himself on the spears, clasping as many of them as he could to his breast—creating an opening for his comrades. ⊠ *Knirig., in front of Church of Saints Peter and Paul.*

Another native son, from the neighboring village of Flüeli, is Niklaus von Flüe, who saved the Confederation again, nearly 100 years after von Winkelried, with his wise council at the Diet of Stans in 1481. He was canonized in 1947.

En Route A two-part journey on a nostalgic 1893 funicular and an ultramodern cable car takes you to the **Stanserhorn** (1,891 m/6,200 ft), from whose peak you can see the lakes; the Titlis, at 3,050 m (10,000 ft) the highest point in central Switzerland; and even the Jungfrau.

Engelberg

⑱ *12 km (8 mi) south of Stans, 27 km (17 mi) south of Luzern.*

At the top of the village of Obermatt, Engelberg (1,000 m/3,280 ft) is a popular resort for skiers from nearby Zürich, but its slopes are limited in comparison to those of Saint-Moritz, Wengen, and Zermatt. Engelberg clusters at the foot of its Benedictine **Kloster** (monastery) founded in 1120; inside there's one of the largest organs in the country. Until the French invaded in 1798, massacring thousands, this monastery ruled the valley. ⊠ *Signposted,* ☎ *041/6371143.* ⊙ *Mon.–Sat. 10–4.*

OFF THE BEATEN PATH **TITLIS –** This is perhaps the most impressive of the many rocky peaks that surround the Obermatt's long, wide bowl. Thanks to a sophisticated transportation system that benefits skiers, hikers, climbers, and tourists alike, it's possible to ride a small cable car up to the tiny mountain lake (and famous ski area) called **Trübsee** (1,801 m/5,904 ft). From there, change to a larger cable car, which rotates to give 360-degree panoramas, and ascend to Stand and ultimately to the summit station on the Titlis. There's an ice grotto (serving drinks from a solid-ice bar) and a panorama restaurant: views take in the Jura Mountains, the Graubünden and Bernese Alps, and what, from this perspective, seems like the puny Pilatus. 🎫 *75 SF round-trip.*

Skiing

At the base of the 3,021-m-high (9,906-ft-high) **Titlis,** Engelberg has two funicular railways, seven cable cars, 13 lifts, 45 km (28 mi) of downhill runs, 34 km (21 mi) of cross-country trails, 3½ km (2 mi) of toboggan runs, and ice-skating. About half the runs are intermediate level, and there are plenty of easy slopes as well; advanced skiers will have relatively slim pickings. A **ski school** (☎ 041/6373040) and **snowboard school** (☎ 041/6374050) are in the **Tourist Center** (☞ Visitor Information *in* Luzern and Central Switzerland A to Z, *below).*

Dining and Lodging

$$–$$$ × **Bierlialp.** The pizzas at this trattoria are incredible: delicious 18-inch, ★ stone-oven-baked extravaganzas—and that's a single serving! The modern decor is softened by warm candlelight and an even warmer

welcome. For a more elaborate entree, try *Tagliatelle Nere* (black noodles, fish, and shrimp with a pepper-cream sauce) or the truffle ravioli. ⊠ *Dorfstr. 21,* ☎ *041/6371717. AE, MC, V.*

$$ ✕⊞ **Hess.** Though it was gutted and rebuilt back in 1984, this old mountain lodge retains the character you expect from a hotel run by the family that founded it in 1884. The pine-and-chintz rooms are fresher than those decorated in dark wood; corner doubles are bright, with fine views. Southern mountain views look over the road. The public areas are rustic but grand, with parquet floors, game trophies, and a huge fireplace in the main lounge. The restaurant, Tudor-Stübli, is known for satisfying dishes such as veal with porcini risotto; Mr. Hess does some of the cooking himself. ⊠ *Dorfstr. 50, CH-6390,* ☎ *041/6371366,* 𝔽𝔸𝕏 *041/6373538. 40 rooms, 4 suites. Restaurant, piano bar, sauna, exercise room, dance club. AE, DC, MC, V. Closed May and Nov.*

$ ✕⊞ **Alpenclub.** This is a very Swiss find: a cozy, old-fashioned chalet,
★ every square inch pine-paneled and dark-timbered, with down-quilted beds, a glowing fondue Stübli, and a quiet sun terrace looking out on snowy peaks. It's lively, casual, and, above all, cheap. It draws mobs of young skiers to its disco-bar and pizzeria, and families to its firelit restaurant (all serve à la carte only). Though it stands slightly beyond the urbanized center, it's not for quiet retreats, at least in ski season. ⊠ *Dorfstr. 5, CH-6390,* ☎ *041/6371243,* 𝔽𝔸𝕏 *041/6370337. 8 rooms. Restaurant, bar, pizzeria, Stübli. AE, DC, MC, V. Closed May–June.*

$$$ ⊞ **Edelweiss.** Walk a few minutes uphill from the center of town to
★ find this 1903 hotel. It's perfect if you're looking for organized activities: skiing, snowman-building, or sleigh-rides in winter; biking, river-rafting, or wellness courses in summer. Rooms are outfitted with modern, Scandinavian-style wood furniture, some with beautiful old bathroom fixtures. A fixed, four-course dinner is served nightly, although special needs (vegetarian, low sodium) can be accommodated. Children have a supervised playroom. ⊠ *Terracestr., CH-6390,* ☎ *041/6370737,* 𝔽𝔸𝕏 *041/6373900. 50 rooms. Restaurant, bar, sauna, free parking. AE, DC, MC, V.*

$$$ ⊞ **Treff Regina Titlis.** In a resort haunted by fading grand hotels from a bygone Victorian boom, this central high-rise, a little bit of Dallas in the Alps, strikes a jarring note. Built in 1983 on the ashes of its predecessor, it has fresh, solid rooms with warm wood accents, balconies with views, and generous facilities. If you're looking for quiet, reserve a room at the back of the hotel, away from the street. ⊠ *Dorfstr. 33, CH-6390,* ☎ *041/6372828,* 𝔽𝔸𝕏 *041/6372392. 96 rooms, 28 suites. 2 restaurants, bar, café, indoor pool, sauna, exercise room, parking (fee). AE, DC, MC, V.*

$$ ⊞ **Europe.** Built in 1908, this Jugendstil beauty offers modern amenities in a bright, elegant setting. Some of the rooms are simple to the point of being bland, but others have small chandeliers and beautifully detailed, mirrored wardrobes. Step onto the wrought-iron balconies and gaze up at the Titlis or down at the neighboring park; if you score one of the rooms over the front entrance, you'll have especially incredible views. The restaurant, for hotel guests only, serves contemporary cuisine and traditional Swiss favorites. The hotel also houses a hotel management school, so you might find yourself being practiced on every now and then. ⊠ *Dorfstr. 40, CH-6390,* ☎ *041/6370094,* 𝔽𝔸𝕏 *041/ 6372255. 59 rooms, 7 suites. Restaurant, bar. AE, DC, MC, V.*

$$ ⊞ **Schweizerhof.** Though the exterior suggests a once-grande dame, this lovely old fin de siècle structure has been attentively remodeled inside to combine fresh, light, new knotty-pine looks with plush Edwardian comforts. Guest rooms are modern and airy. The south-side views are fine, especially from rooms with balconies. Bay-window corner doubles are worth asking for. Four family suites with separate bed- and living rooms make this a perfect option for families and small groups. ✉ *Dorfstr. 42, CH-6390,* ☎ *041/6371105,* 𝔽𝔸𝕏 *041/ 6374147. 30 rooms, 10 suites. Restaurant, sauna, steam room, exercise room. AE, DC, MC, V.*

Outdoor Activities and Sports

MOUNTAIN BIKING

Mountain biking is very popular here; there's a well-traveled path from the Jochpass to the Trübsee. Free biking maps are available at the tourist office. You can rent bikes from **Amstutz** (✉ Dorfstr. 39, ☎ 041/6371268). Also try **Bike 'n' Roll Rock'n Ice** (✉ Titlizentru, Dorfstr. 31, ☎ 041/6374691). Another source is **Gisin Sport** (✉ Klosterg. 8, ☎ 041/6374939).

TENNIS

The **Sportcenter Erlen** (✉ Engelbergstr. 11, ☎ 041/6373494) has two indoor courts and six outdoor courts; they also rent equipment.

VIERWALDSTÄTTERSEE TO SAINT GOTTHARD AND EINSIEDELN

From Luzern, you can take a lake steamer all the way down to the Urnersee (the southern leg of Lake Luzern); or you can drive the same route along the lakefront highway, continuing on to the historic pilgrimage town of Einsiedeln. Either trip will involve switching to train or cable car if you want to climb to Rigi Kulm, the summit of Mt. Rigi.

If you choose to go by boat, depart at any convenient time (schedules are available at the ticket and tourist offices; *see* Visitor Information *in* Luzern and Central Switzerland A to Z, *below*) from the main docks by the train station (or, by car, past the casino along the waterfront drive); the boat will be marked for Flüelen. First-class seats are on top; each level has a restaurant-café. The exterior seats are only slightly sheltered; if you want to sit inside, you may feel obligated to order a drink. Take advantage of the boat's many stops—you can get on and off at will.

Bürgenstock

⑲ *20 km (13 mi) southeast of Luzern.*

Most Flüelen-bound boats go to the base of the Bürgenstock, where visitors can take a funicular to the isolated resort at the top of a ridge. Though the plateau isn't terribly high—only 458 m/1,500 ft—it rises dramatically above the water and offers striking views over the lake region; that's why a small colony of luxury hotels has mushroomed here, most of them owned by the Frey family. Bürgenstock also can be approached by car, up a narrow, steep road, from Stansstad, on the road between Luzern and Stans.

Weggis

★ **⑳** *25 km (15 mi) northeast and across the lake from Bürgenstock, 20 km (12 mi) northeast of Luzern.*

Weggis is a summer resort town known for its mild, almost subtropical climate. There's a pretty waterfront park and promenade; and as it's far from the auto route and accessible only by the secondary road, you get a pleasant sense of isolation. The famed **Mt. Rigi** (1,800 m/5,900 ft) is just a cable-car ride away from Weggis: follow signs for the Rigibahn, a station high above the resort (a 15-minute walk). From here you can ride a large cable car to **Rigi-Kaltbad**, a small resort on a spectacular plateau; walk across to the electric rack-and-pinion railway station and ride the steep tracks of the Vitznau–Rigi line to the summit of the mountain. Take an elevator to the Hotel **Rigi-Kulm** (☞ *below*) to enjoy the views indoors or walk to the crest (45 minutes) to see as far as the Black Forest in one direction and Mt. Säntis in the other. Or consider climbing to the top, staying in the hotel, and getting up early to see the sun rise over the Alps—a view that astounded both Victor Hugo and Mark Twain. With Lake Lucern on one side and Lake Zug on the other, Mt. Rigi can seem like an island.

You have the option of returning to Luzern from Weggis by taking a different railway down, from Rigi to Arth-Goldau; the two lines were built by competing companies in the 1870s in a race to reach the top and capture the lion's share of the tourist business. The line rising out of the lakefront resort of Vitznau won, but the Arth-Goldau line gets plenty of business, as its base terminal lies on the mainstream Saint Gotthard route. The round-trip fare from Vitznau or Arth-Goldau to Rigi-Kulm is 56 SF.

Skiing

Mt. Rigi, at 1,798 m (5,900 ft), has two funicular railways, three cable cars, seven lifts, 30 km (19 mi) of downhill runs, 14 km (9 mi) of cross-country trails, 14 km (9 mi) of ski-hiking trails, and curling.

Dining and Lodging

$$$ ✕ **Renggli's.** This restaurant is ideally located on the waterfront, with its own private dock and a terrace overlooking the lake. The eclectic cuisine ranges from refined vegetarian dishes to more exotic fare, such as poached guinea fowl with a mango-curry sauce. Standards are jazzed up, too: steamed white fish with apple cider–herb sauce, for instance. ✉ *Seestr. 21,* ☎ *041/3900370. AE, DC, MC, V.*

$$$ ☷ **Albana.** From this lush Art Nouveau hotel, you can drink in fabulous lake and mountain views. The public areas are its best feature; they're grand from top to bottom. Three magnificent rooms have 15-foot ceilings, one painted with cherubs and clouds and trimmed in gold leaf. A pair of 100-year-old Venetian chandeliers glistens; under the original period furniture shine buffed parquet floors. The dusty-pink and white rooms, however, are outfitted with modern furniture; white-tile bathrooms have tubs with room to stretch out. Eight rooms have the original parquet floors—these are the ones to ask for. The restaurant's menu is imaginative—for instance, "herb cappuccino" (soup) and lamb enveloped in Rösti with a white bean ragout. The hotel is a short walk uphill from the boat landing. ✉ *Luzernerstr. 26, CH-6353,* ☎ *041/3902141,* ☏ *041/3902959. 57 rooms. Restaurant, bar, sauna, steam room. AE, DC, MC, V.*

$$–$$$ ☷ **Beau-Rivage.** Built in 1908 but much modernized, this attractive
   ★   business-class resort concentrates its comforts on a small but luxurious waterfront site, with a restaurant above the manicured lawn, a small swimming pool with mountain views, and lounge chairs at the lake's edge. Its rooms glow with rosy wood, brass, and pastel fabrics. It's at the center of town, near the boat landing. ✉ *Gotthardstr. 6, CH-6353,* ☎ *041/3901422,* ☏ *041/3901981. 40 rooms. Restaurant, bar, outdoor pool. AE, DC, MC, V. Closed Nov.–Mar.*

$$ ☷ **Rigi-Kulm.** If you find the novelty of mountaintop stopovers appealing, this high-altitude hotel is for you; built in 1950 and rather generic, it still has the air of a rugged but genteel lodge. Southern rooms have rustic decor and great views. (Be warned, however: mountainside transportation makes this an awkward home base for excursions, and if it's raining during your stay, the views disappear.) A short walk from the summit, at 1,800 m (5,900 ft), it is accessible by cable car from Weg-

gis to Rigi-Kaltbad, then by cogwheel rail; or by cogwheel from Vitznau or Arth-Goldau. Or you can climb up from Weggis, allowing either three hours or, as Mark Twain required, three days, depending on your penchant for resting. If you'd like to follow an old romantic tradition, get up at the crack of dawn to see the sun rise over the Alps. ✉ *CH-6410,* ☎ *041/ 8550303,* ℻ *041/8550041. 40 rooms. Restaurant, café. AE, DC, MC, V.*

Outdoor Activities and Sports

The tourist office at Weggis (☞ Visitor Information *in* Luzern and Central Switzerland A to Z, *below*) rents **bicycles.** Weggis maintains several public **tennis** courts; call the tourist office for information. Windsurfing lessons and rentals in Weggis are available through the **Hotel Hertenstein** (☎ 041/3901444).

Vitznau

㉑ *4 km (2½ mi) southeast of Weggis, 26 km (16 mi) east of Luzern.*

For a quintessentially scenic, quiet spot, stop over in Vitznau, a tiny waterfront resort that competes with Weggis in balmy weather, although its main claim to fame is the palatial Park Hotel, built in 1902.

Lodging

$$$$ 🏨 **Park Hotel.** This isolated but lavish retreat dominates the tiny lake-
★ front village of Vitznau. Constructed in 1902 and enlarged in 1985, it's a vaulted and beamed Edwardian dream in impeccable modern form. Even the corridors are grand, with massive oak triple doors and Persian runners stretching over quarry tile. Rooms have timeless pastels, and lakefront rooms command dreamy Alpine views. The back rooms overlook the slopes of the Rigi, dotted with grazing cows. With the hotel's restaurants and all the activities available, you could easily find yourself not wanting to budge. ✉ *Kantonstr., CH-6354,* ☎ *041/ 3970101,* ℻ *041/3970110. 74 rooms, 30 suites. 2 restaurants, café, indoor pool, outdoor pool, miniature golf, 2 tennis courts, beach, dock, waterskiing, playground. AE, DC, MC, V. Closed Nov.–Mar.*

$$ 🏨 **Rigi.** Less than half the price of the grandiose Park (☞ *above*), this solid lodging has modernized interiors and a welcoming Stübli atmosphere in its public areas. Corner rooms have balconies with a lake view; four rooms have small kitchenettes. The hotel is just one block from the boat landing and close to the Rigibahn (which means there's some traffic noise during the day). Both the restaurant and the less formal Stübli serve good, simple fish dishes, and there's a pleasant garden terrace. ✉ *Hauptstr., CH-6354,* ☎ *041/3972121,* ℻ *041/3971825. 36 rooms. Restaurant, Stübli. AE, DC, MC, V.*

$ 🏨 **Schiff.** Commanding much the same view as the Park (though the
★ Park itself clouds some of its lakefront beauty), this plain old roadhouse perches on the hill across the street and offers cheap, no-bath rooms in '50s summer-cottage styles. The vine-trellised terrace restaurant, wide open to the water and mountain skyline, serves inexpensive lake-fish dishes. It's down-to-earth and decidedly friendly. ✉ *Kantonstr., CH-6354,* ☎ *041/3971357,* ℻ *041/3972498. 6 rooms. Restaurant. AE, DC, MC, V. Closed Oct.–Nov.*

Outdoor Activities and Sports

BIKING

Rent bikes through the **Hotel Vierwaldstättersee** (✉ Hauptstr., ☎ 041/3972222).

TENNIS

The **Park hotel** (✉ Hertensteinstr. 34, ☎ 041/3901313) in Weggis, four km away, rents court time to nonguests for 35 SF an hour. Rental equipment is available. The **Seehotel Vitznauerhof** (⊠ Seestr., ☎ 041/3997777) has a court and equipment to rent.

WATER SPORTS

Motorboats and paddleboats are for rent through **Anker Travel** (⊠ Zihlstr. ☎ 041/3971707). You can swim in the bay, which is naturally warmer than Luzern's Lido.

En Route   From Vitznau, a boat tour will take you across Lake Luzern to **Beck-**
★   **enried,** from which a cable car leads up to **Klewenalp** (1,601 m/5,250 ft), a small winter-sports and summer resort overlooking the lake. The area is excellent for hiking, with breathtaking panoramic views of the lake and mountains on clear days. You can get a hiking trail map from newsstands or local tourist offices (☞ Visitor Information *in* Luzern and Central Switzerland A to Z, *below*). If you're driving, you could also follow the north shore to **Gersau,** a tiny lake resort that from 1332 to 1798 was an independent republic—the world's smallest. From Gersau the boat snakes around the sharp peninsula of the Seelisberg; the 1980 completion of a 9¼-km (6-mi) tunnel across the peninsula, south of the lake, opened the way for even swifter north–south travel between Luzern and points north and the Saint Gotthard route and points south.

At the south end of Lake Luzern, past the Seelisberg peninsula, the narrow, majestic **Urnersee** is the wildest and most beautiful leg of the lake. Along its shores lie some of the most historic—or, at least, romantic—landmarks in the region. The **Schillerstein,** on the right as you cruise past the peninsula, is a natural rock obelisk extending nearly 26 m (85 ft) up out of the lake; it bears the simple dedication: TO THE AUTHOR OF *WILHELM TELL*, FRIEDRICH VON SCHILLER. 1859.

Rütli Meadow

★ ㉒   *15 km (10 mi) northwest of Altdorf on Urnersee, 35 km (22 mi) south-east of Luzern.*

Perhaps the most historically significant site in central Switzerland, the Rütli Meadow, just above the Rütli dock, is where the confederates of Schwyz, Unterwald, and Uri are said to have met in 1307 to renew the 1291 Oath of Eternal Alliance. The **Tellsplatte,** on the east side of the lake, at the foot of the Axen Mountain, is the rocky ledge onto which Tell, the legendary rebellious archer, leapt to escape from Gessler's boat, pushing the boat back into the stormy waves as he jumped. There is a small chapel here, built around 1500 and restored in 1881; it contains four frescoes of the Tell legend, painted at the time of restoration.

Another monumental event took place here centuries later: amid threats of a 1940 German invasion, General Guisan, Swiss army commander-in-chief, summoned hundreds of officers to the meadow to reaffirm their commitment to the Swiss Confederation in a secret, stirring ceremony.

Altdorf

㉓   *20 km (12 mi) south of Rütli Meadow, 35 km (22 mi) southeast of Luzern.*

Schiller's play *Wilhelm Tell* sums up the tale for the Swiss, who perform his play religiously in venues all over the country—including the town of Altdorf, just up the road from the Rütli Meadow. Leave the steamer at Flüelen, the farthest point of the boat ride around the lake, and connect by postbus to Altdorf, the capital of the canton Uri and, by popular if not scholarly consensus, the setting for Tell's famous apple-shooting scene. There is a much-reproduced **Tell monument** in the village center, showing a proud father with crossbow on one shoulder,

Finally, a travel companion that doesn't snore on the plane or eat all your peanuts.

When traveling, your MCI WorldCom Card is the best way to keep in touch. Our operators speak your language, so they'll be able to connect you back home—no matter where your travels take you. Plus, your MCI WorldCom Card is easy to use, and even earns you frequent flyer miles every time you use it. When you add in our great rates, you get something even more valuable: peace-of-mind. So go ahead. Travel the world. MCI WorldCom just brought it a whole lot closer.

You can even sign up today at www.mci.com/worldphone or ask your operator to make a collect call to 1-410-314-2938.

EASY TO CALL WORLDWIDE

1 Just dial the WorldPhone access number of the country you're calling from.
2 Dial or give the operator your MCI WorldCom Card number.
3 Dial or give the number you're calling.

France ♦	0-800-99-0019
Germany	0800-888-8000
Ireland	1-800-55-1001
Italy ♦	172-1022
Spain	900-99-0014
Sweden ♦	020-795-922
Switzerland ♦	0800-89-0222
United Kingdom To call using BT To call using CWC	0800-89-0222 0500-89-0222

For your complete WorldPhone calling guide, dial the WorldPhone access number for the country you're in and ask the operator for Customer Service. In the U.S. call 1-800-431-5402.

♦ Public phones may require deposit of coin or phone card for dial tone.

EARN FREQUENT FLYER MILES

AmericanAirlines
AAdvantage

Continental Airlines
OnePass

△ Delta Air Lines
SkyMiles

✈ MILEAGE PLUS.
United Airlines

U·S AIRWAYS
DIVIDEND MILES

MCI WorldCom, its logo and the names of the products referred to herein are proprietary marks of MCI WorldCom, Inc. All airline names and logos are proprietary marks of the respective airlines. All airline program rules and conditions apply.

The first thing you need overseas is the one thing you forget to pack.

FOREIGN CURRENCY DELIVERED OVERNIGHT

Chase Currency To Go® delivers foreign currency to your home by the next business day*

It's easy–before you travel, call 1-888-CHASE84 for delivery of any of 75 currencies

Delivery is free with orders of $500 or more

Competitive rates– without exchange fees

You don't have to be a Chase customer–you can pay by Visa® or MasterCard®

 CHASE

THE RIGHT RELATIONSHIP IS EVERYTHING.®

1•888•CHASE84
www.chase.com

*Orders must be placed before 5 PM ET. $10 delivery fee for orders under $500.
©1999 The Chase Manhattan Corporation. All rights reserved. The Chase Manhattan Bank. Member FDIC.

the other hand grasping his son's hand; it was sculpted by Richard Kissling in 1895.

Outdoor Activities and Sports

BIKING

You can rent bikes at the train station (☎ 041/8701008) in Altdorf. Mountain bikes and motorbikes can be rented and serviced in Altdorf through **Mototreff** (✉ Flüelerstr. 20, ☎ 041/8709737).

WATER SPORTS

You can rent pedal boats and motorboats in Flüelen at **Herr F. Kaufmann** (✉ Seestr. 1, Flüelen, ☎ 041/8701575).

Bürglen

㉔ *3 km (1¾ mi) southeast of Altdorf, 40 km (25 mi) southeast of Luzern.*

Tell was supposedly from the tiny town of Bürglen, just up the road from Altdorf. The **Tell Museum** devoted to him displays documents and art on the legend. ✉ *Postpl.,* ☎ *041/8704155.* 💠 *4 SF.* ☉ *May–Oct., daily 10–11:30 and 2–5; July and Aug., daily 10–5.*

Andermatt

㉕ *25 km (15 mi) south of Bürglen (exit the A2 expressway at Göschenen), 67 km (41 mi) southeast of Luzern.*

Andermatt serves as a crossroads for traffic arriving from the Furka Pass, the Oberalp Pass, and the Saint Gotthard Pass. It's a relaxing little backwater (no tracts of condos here), with lovely valley hiking and, thanks to its level terrain, fine cross-country skiing. It's much more of a local spot than a sunglasses-and-celebrities resort. From the top of **Gemsstock,** approached by cable car from the town, it is said you can see 600 Alpine peaks.

Skiing

A high, sheltered plateau at the crossroads of three passes—the Gotthard, the Furka, and the Oberalp—**Andermatt** (1,449 m/4,750 ft) is easily accessible from all directions. It has five cable cars, 10 lifts, 55 km (34 mi) of downhill runs, and 20 km (12 mi) of cross-country trails and a snowboard fun park. The ski runs are especially suited for intermediate to advanced skiers. The German-language **snow hot line** (☎ 041/8870181) reports on the latest conditions.

Outdoor Activities and Sports

MOUNTAIN BIKING

Mountain biking is popular here; to rent bikes, call **Christen Sport** (✉ Gotthardstr. 55, CH-6490, ☎ 041/8871251), which stocks summer-sports and snow equipment.

OFF THE BEATEN PATH

SAINT GOTTHARD PASS – This ancient passage started as a narrow path in the 13th century; a railway was not completed until 1882, and the new tunnel was finished in 1980. In these bleak and icy heights, the watershed of both the Rhine and the Rhône, you may spot eerie, partially concealed military facilities dug deep into the rock and see soldiers drilling in the snow: it's the Swiss army, refining its Alpine defense skills. The pass closes in winter but in summer it's a great mountain-biking destination. Take the old road that's closed to traffic; it's known as Alte Gotthardstrasse and runs alongside the main road. There's a hotel at the top; you can gaze at the breathtaking views and have a simple meal at its terrace restaurant.

Schwyz

 30 km (20 mi) north of Andermatt (via Hwy. 8 or the A2 expressway—exit just past Altdorf), 44 km (27 mi) east of Luzern.

This historic town is the capital of the canton Schwyz, root of the name Switzerland, and source of the nation's flag. Switzerland's most precious archives are stored here as well. Traces of an independent settlement at Schwyz have been found from as far back as the Bronze Age (2500 BC–800 BC), but it was its inhabitants' aid in the 1291 Oath of Allegiance that put Schwyz on the map. You can see the beautifully scripted and sealed original document as well as battle flags and paintings of the period in Schwyz's **Bundesbriefmuseum** (Federal Charters Museum). ✉ *Bahnhofstr. 20,* ☎ *041/8192064.* 🎟 *Free.* 🕐 *Daily 9:30–11:30 and 2–5.*

Schwyz has several notable baroque churches and a large number of fine old patrician homes dating from the 17th and 18th centuries, not least being the **Ital-Redinghaus** with its magnificent interior, antique stoves, and fine stained glass. A visit to this grand house includes a peek inside the neighboring **Bethlehemhaus,** the oldest wooden house in Switzerland, dating from 1287. ✉ *Rickenbachstr. 24,* ☎ *041/8114505.* 🎟 *2 SF.* 🕐 *May–Oct., Tues.–Fri. 2–5, weekends 10–noon and 2–5.*

Curiously, many of Schwyz's splendid houses owe their origin to the battlefield. The men of Schwyz had a reputation as fine soldiers and were in demand in other countries as mercenaries during the 16th and 17th centuries. They built many of the houses you can see today with their military pay. Schwyz's most famous landmark is the **Rathaus** (Town Hall); its richly frescoed exterior (1891) depicts the Battle of Morgarten, where the Austrian army was defeated by the Swiss. The building is still used as the town hall. ✉ *Hauptpl. 1.*

Einsiedeln

 27 km (18 mi) northeast of Schwyz, 69 km (43 mi) northeast of Luzern.

A minor summer and winter resort, Einsiedeln has been a pilgrimage site since AD 946. It is also the home of the **Black Madonna,** still on display in the **Benedictine monastery** after more than a thousand years. The monastery was founded in Charlemagne's time, when Meinrad, a Hohenzollern count and monk, chose the remote site to pursue his devotions in solitude. The abbess of Zürich gave him an image of the Virgin Mary, for which he built a little chapel, and Meinrad lived in peace, fed—the story goes—by two ravens who brought him supplies. When he was murdered by brigands seeking treasure, the ravens followed the thieves to Zürich and shrieked over their heads until they were arrested. A monastery was built over Meinrad's grave. When it was completed, the bishop of Konstanz was invited to consecrate it, but as he began the ceremony, a voice was heard crying out in the chapel three times, "Brother, desist: God himself has consecrated this building." A papal bull acknowledged the miracle and promised a special indulgence to pilgrims.

Through the ages the monastery of Einsiedeln has been destroyed many times by fire, but the Black Madonna has always been saved. When Napoléon's armies plundered the church, hoping to carry off the sacred image, it had already been taken to the Tirol in Austria for safekeeping. Today the Black Madonna is housed in a black-marble chapel just inside the west entrance to the church. When seen from a distance, its color appears to be a rich bronze, not black, and there is something quaint and gentle about the figure despite its jeweled splendor. The present abbey structure was built by Caspar Moosbrugger in 1735 and decorated by the famous brothers Egid Quirid and Cosmos Damian Asam; it is one of the finest late-baroque churches of its kind, the impressive simplicity and grace of the exterior contrasting vividly with the exuberance of its ornate interior. In front of the church, a grand square surrounds a golden statue of the Virgin Mary with a large gilt crown. Around the base, water trickles from 14 spouts, and pilgrims, to be sure of good luck, traditionally drink from each one in turn.

Einsiedeln is just off the A3 autobahn that connects Zürich with eastern Switzerland. You can take this autobahn to return to Luzern, but a more interesting route is via Alosen and Unterägeri by the Ägerisee, to Zug (☞ *below*), famous for its Old Town.

The Arts

Einsiedeln remains a center for religious pomp and ceremony and celebrates a **Festival of the Miraculous Dedication** every September 14. Every five years some 700 citizens, coached by the monks, perform *Das Grosse Welttheater* (*the Great World Drama*) before the abbey church. A religious drama on life and the problems of humankind, it was first performed before the Court of Spain in 1685. The next performance of this historic pageant takes place in summer 2003.

Zug

㉘ *27 km (17 mi) north of Einsiedeln, 28 km (18 mi) northeast of Luzern (via A14 and A4).*

On arriving at the train station in Zug, you may be surprised to find that it is bustling, modern, and full of multinational corporations. Its contemporary life unfurls around the remnants of ancient ramparts, and its lakefront neighborhood seems frozen in another century. From the train station area on Alpenstrasse you can head straight for the waterfront of the **Zugersee** (Lake Zug). This landscaped promenade and park has fine views of the Pilatus, Rigi, and the Bernese Alps—including the Eiger, the Mönch, and the Jungfrau.

Zug's Old Town is dominated by the **Rathaus** (Town Hall), which was completed in the early 16th century. Inside, there are exhibits of gold and silver work as well as embroideries, wood carvings, stained glass, and the flag Peter Kolin held until he perished in the battle of Arbedo (1422), when 3,000 Swiss tried valiantly to hold off 24,000 Milanese soldiers. Unfortunately, you'll see these fine furnishings only if you dine in the **Rathauskeller** (☞ Dining and Lodging, *below*), one of the best— but most expensive—restaurants in central Switzerland. ⊠ *Oberaltstadt 1. Closed to the public.*

By passing through a gate under the Zytturm (Clock Tower), you'll come upon the waterfront **Kolinplatz,** dedicated to the prominent local Kolin family, and dominated by a fountain topped by a statue of Wolfgang Kolin. South of the Kolinplatz, up a small hill, is the **Kirche St. Oswald** (Church of St. Oswald), built in the 15th and 16th centuries; its delicate spires rise high above the town.

The Burg, a former Hapsburg residence, has a half-timber exterior so heavily restored it looks like a Disney set for *Snow White*. It now houses the **Burg-Museum,** focusing on archaeology, art, and history from Zug. ⊠ *Kirchenstr. 11,* ☎ *041/7283297.* ☞ *5 SF, free Sun.* ☉ *Tues.–Fri. 2– 5, weekends 10–noon and 2–5.*

NEED A
BREAK?
While waiting for your return train, stop at the patisserie-café **Meier** (✉ Alpenstr. 14, ☎ 041/7111049) for coffee and a slice of the famous Zug Kirschtorte—though called cherry cake, the only cherry you'll find is the heavily alcoholic essence that soaks the delicate yellow cake and butter cream. (The café shares its space with the tourist office.)

The most atmospheric streets of Zug are the **Oberaltstadt** and the Unteraltstadt, tight lanes closed in on each side by narrow, shuttered 16th-century town houses now in the beginning throes of gentrification: the storefronts are full of arts and crafts, ceramics, and jewelry.

Dining and Lodging

$$$$ ✕ **Rathauskeller.** Upstairs in this historic landmark you are surrounded by a museumlike collection of medieval regional treasures but are served nothing but cutting-edge cuisine. The emphasis is on good fish (scallops marinated in olive oil and lemon juice), meats (tender rabbit fillet with wild mushroom risotto), and a minimum of visual fuss. Downstairs, in the traditional, dark little Stübli you can order simpler, cheaper dishes from the same kitchen. ✉ *Oberaltstadt 1,* ☎ *041/7110058. AE, V. Closed Sun. and Mon.*

$-$$ ✕ **Aklin.** This 500-year-old Altstadt landmark offers *Grossmutters Küche* (Grandmother's cooking)—*Kalbskopf* (chopped veal head), *Siedfleisch* (boiled beef), and lake fish—on candlelit wooden tables by a ceramic-tile stove in the upstairs restaurant or in the atmospheric, casual bistro downstairs. ✉ *Kolinpl. 10,* ☎ *041/7111866. AE, DC, MC, V. Closed Sun.*

$$-$$$ ⌂ **Ochsen.** Although the notch-gabled facade has been preserved at this 16th-century landmark on the imposing Kolinplatz in Zug's Old Town, the interior is strictly upscale-chain. Hints of architectural detail have been sanded away, and the buffed wood of the restaurant looks more Scandi-sleek teak now than Swiss; it's hard to believe that Goethe was once a guest here. The rooms are high-tech chic; the best are at the far back (above a tiny courtyard) and—of course—looking over the Kolinplatz fountain toward the lake. The restaurant deserves its good reputation for fine local dishes: meats, Rösti, and its specialty, lake fish. ✉ *Kolinpl. 11, CH-6301,* ☎ *041/7293232,* FAX *041/7293222. 46 rooms. Restaurant. AE, DC, MC, V.*

Outdoor Activities and Sports

At 436 m (1,430 ft), Zug has 9 km (6 mi) of **cross-country ski** trails, 17 km (11 mi) of **ski-hiking** trails, and **curling.** You can rent bicycles from the train station (☎ 041/7113988).

LUZERN AND CENTRAL SWITZERLAND A TO Z

Arriving and Departing

By Car

It's easy to reach Luzern from Zürich by road, approaching from national expressway **A3** south, connecting to **A4** via the secondary **E41** in the direction of Zug, and continuing on A4, which turns into the **A14,** to the city. A convenient all-expressway connection between the two cities won't be open for over a decade. Approaching from the southern, Saint Gotthard Pass route (**A2**) or after cutting through the Furka Pass by rail ferry, you descend below Andermatt to Altdorf, where a tunnel sweeps you through to the shores of the lake. If you're heading for resorts on the north shore, leave the expressway at Flüelen and follow the scenic secondary route. From Basel in the northwest, it's a clean sweep by the A2 to Luzern.

By Plane

The nearest international airport is **Zürich-Kloten** (⊠ Approximately 54 km/33 mi northeast of Luzern, ☎ 1571060). **Swissair** (☎ 800/221–4750 in the U.S.; 0171/434–7300 in the U.K.) flies in most often from the United States and the United Kingdom.

By Train

Luzern functions as a rail crossroads, with express trains connecting hourly from Zürich, a 49-minute trip, and every two hours from Geneva, a 3½- to 4-hour trip changing at Bern. Trains enter from the south via the Saint Gotthard Pass from the Ticino and via the Furka Pass from the Valais. For rail information, call the **Bahnhof** (train station; ⊠ Bahnhofpl., ☎ 1572222).

The **Wilhelm Tell Express,** a cooperative effort of Swiss Federal Railways and lake steamers, operates daily from May through October; a boat ride takes you from Luzern to Flüelen, then a train zips to Lugano. The journey, without stopovers, takes six hours. For information, contact the Luzern tourist office (☞ Visitor Information, *below*).

Getting Around

By Boat

It would be a shame to see this historic region only from the shore; some of its most impressive landscapes are framed along the waterfront, as seen from the decks of one of the cruise ships that ply the lake. Rides on these are included in a **Swiss Pass** (☞ Train Travel *in* the Gold Guide) or a **Swiss Boat Pass** (☞ Boat Travel *in* the Gold Guide). Individual tickets can be purchased at Luzern's departure **docks** (⊠ Near the train station, ☎ 041/3676767); the fee is based on the length of your ride. Any combination of transportation can be arranged, such as a leisurely cruise from Luzern to Flüelen at the lake's southernmost point, lasting about 3½ hours and costing 64 SF; the return train trip, via the Arth–Goldau line, takes little more than an hour. The **Tell Pass** (☞ By Train, *below*) gives you free boat rides.

By Bus

The postbus network carries travelers faithfully, if slowly, to the farthest corners of the region. It also climbs the Saint Gotthard and the Furka passes (remember, these are closed in winter). For schedules and prices, check at the post office nearest your home base or pick up a copy of the *Vierwaldstättersee Fahrplan,* a booklet (50 rappen) that covers cruise ships and private railways as well as postbuses, available at the local tourist office (☞ Visitor Information, *below*). If you're staying in a Luzern hotel, you will be eligible for the special **Guest-Ticket,** offering unlimited rides for two days for a minimal fee of 8 SF. The **Tell Pass** (☞ By Train, *below*) includes postbus discounts.

By Car

Although Mt. Rigi and Mt. Pilatus are not accessible by car, nearly everything else in this region is. The descent from Andermatt past the Devil's Bridge, which once carried medieval pilgrims from the Saint Gotthard and drew thrill seekers during the 19th century, now exemplifies awe-inspiring Swiss mountain engineering: from Göschenen, at 1,106 m (3,627 ft), to the waterfront, it's a four-lane expressway.

By Train

Swiss National Railways is enhanced here by a few private lines (to Engelberg, Pilatus, the Rigi Kulm) that make it possible to get to most sights. If you don't have a Swiss Pass, there's a central Switzerland regional discount pass, called the **Tell Pass.** The 15-day pass grants you five days of unlimited free travel on main routes, 10 days at half fare. The seven-day pass gives you two days free, five at half fare. (Besides the CFF lines, most private rail lines will also accept the pass.) The ticket can be bought at rail or boat ticket offices, on a cruise boat, from travel agencies, or from the tourist office (☞ Visitor Information, *below*). The 15-day pass costs 175 SF second class, 196 SF first class; the seven-day pass costs 128 SF second class, 139 SF first class. Plan your itinerary carefully to take full advantage of all discount rates, and before you buy a regional pass, add up your excursions à la carte. Remember that many routes always charge half price. All boat trips and the private excursions to Rigi and Pilatus are free to holders of regional passes—but getting to the starting point may cost you half price. If you plan to cover a lot of ground, however, you may save considerably. Choose your free days in advance: you must confirm them *all* with the first inspector who checks your pass.

Contacts and Resources

Emergencies
Police (☎ 117). **Medical, dental, and pharmacy referral** (☎ 111). **Auto breakdown**: Touring Club of Switzerland (☎ 140); Swiss Automobile Club (☎ 041/2100155).

Guided Tours
The **Luzern tourist office** (☞ Visitor Information, *below*) offers a guided walking tour of Luzern with English commentary. It takes about two hours and cost 15 SF, including a drink. **Schiffahrtsgesellschaft des Vierwaldstättersees** (✉ Werftestr. 5, CH-6002 Luzern, ☎ 041/3676767) offers historic and Alpine theme cruises with English commentary.

Visitor Information
The principal tourist office for the whole of central Switzerland, including the lake region, is **Zentralschweiz Tourismus** (Central Switzerland Tourism; ✉ Alpenstr. 1, CH-6002 Luzern, ☎ 041/4184080, FAX 041/4107260). The main tourist office for the city of **Luzern** (✉ Frankenstr. 1, ☎ 041/4107171) is near the Bahnhof. There's also an accommodations service.

Local offices: **Altdorf** (✉ Rathauspl., CH-6460, ☎ 041/8720450). **Andermatt** (✉ Offizieles Verkehrsbüro, Gotthardstr. 2, CH-6490, ☎ 041/8871454). **Einsiedeln** (✉ Hauptstr. 85, ☎ 055/4184488). **Engelberg** (✉ Klosterstr., CH-6390, ☎ 041/6373737). **Schwyz** (✉ Bahnhofstr. 32, CH-6440, ☎ 041/8101991). **Stans** (✉ Engelbergstr. 34, CH-6370, ☎ 041/6108833). **Vitznau** (✉ Seestr., CH-6354, ☎ 041/3980035). **Weggis** (✉ Seestr. 5, CH-6353, ☎ 041/3901155). **Zug** (✉ Alpenstr. 16, CH-6300, ☎ 041/7110078).

7 BASEL

At the juncture of France and Germany,
German-speaking Basel is a cultural capital
with a sense of fun. Cultivated and yet
down-home, it has more than 30 museums,
Switzerland's oldest university, and some of
the most diverse shopping in the country. All
the same, beer and sausages are the snack
of choice, and the annual Carnival is
observed with a boisterousness that's
unparalleled in other Swiss towns.

Updated by
Kara
Misenheimer

THOUGH IT LACKS THE GILT AND GLITTER of Zürich and the Latin grace of Geneva, in many ways quiet, genteel Basel (Bâle in French) is the most sophisticated of Swiss cities. At the frontier between two of Europe's most assertive personalities, France and Germany, and tapped directly into the artery of the Rhein (Rhine), it has flourished on the lifeblood of two cultures and grown surprisingly urbane, cosmopolitan, worldly wise. It is also delightfully eccentric, its imagination fed by centuries of intellectual input: Basel has been host to Switzerland's oldest university (1460) and patron to some of the country's—and the world's—finest minds. A northern center of humanist thought and art, it nurtured the painters Konrad Witz and Hans Holbein the Younger as well as the great Dutch scholar Erasmus. And it was Basel's visionary lord mayor Johann Rudolf Wettstein who, at the end of the Thirty Years' War, negotiated Switzerland's groundbreaking—and lasting—neutrality.

Every day, 27,500 French and German commuters cross into Basel. Banking activity here is surpassed only by that of Zürich and Geneva, and every month representatives of the world's leading central banks meet behind closed doors in the city center at the Bank for International Settlements, the world's central bank clearinghouse. Enormous international pharmaceutical firms—Novartis and Roche—crowd the riverbanks. Yet Basel's population hovers around a modest 200,000; its urban center lies gracefully along the Rhine, no building so tall as to block another's view of the cathedral's twin spires. Two blocks from the heart of the thriving shopping district you can walk 17th-century residential streets cloaked in perfect, otherworldly silence.

The disproportionate number of museums per capita is a reflection of Basel's priorities: the city has more than 30, including the world-class Kunstmuseum (Museum of Fine Arts), the Jean Tinguely Museum, and the Beyeler Foundation. As high culture breeds good taste, Basel has some of the most varied, even quirky, shopping in Switzerland; antiquarian book stores, calligraphers, and artisans do business next to sophisticated designer shops and famous jewelers. But you can still get a beer and a sausage here: Baslers almost exclusively speak German or their own local version of *Schwyzerdütsch,* called *Baseldütsch.* On Freiestrasse, the main shopping street, dense crowds of shoppers stand outside a local butcher's, holding bare *Wienerli* (hot dogs) and dipping the pink tips into thick golden mustard. They also indulge in *Kaffe und Kuchen*—the late-afternoon coffee break Germans live for—but Baslers do it differently. Instead of the large slices of creamy cake, they select tiny sweet gems—two or three to a saucer, but petite nonetheless—and may opt for a delicate Chinese tea.

The Celts were the first to settle here, some 2,000 years ago, on the site of the Münster (cathedral). During the 1st century BC the Romans established a town at Augst, then called Colonia Augusta Raurica; the ruins and the theater can be visited today, 10 minutes by car outside town. By the 3rd century, the Romans had taken the present cathedral site in Basel proper, naming the town Basilia (royal stronghold). Germanic invaders banished them in 401, and it was not until the Holy Roman Emperor Henry II took Basel under his wing in the 11th century that stability returned. His image and that of his wife, Kunegunde, adorn the cathedral and the Rathaus (Town Hall). Henry built the original cathedral—on the site of a church destroyed by a raiding band of Hungarian horsemen in 916—and established Basel as one of the centers of his court. In 1006 the bishop of Basel was made ruler of the town, and throughout the Middle Ages these prince-bishops gained and exerted enormous temporal and spiritual powers. Though the prince-bishops are no more, Basel still uses one of their symbols in its coat of arms—a striking black staff.

Yet Basel is first and foremost a Renaissance city in the literal sense of the word: a city of intellectual and artistic rebirth, its flourishing river commerce bringing with it a flow of ideas. In 1431 the Council of Basel, an ecumenical conference on church reform, was convened here, bringing in—over a period of 17 years—the great sacred and secular princes of the age. One of them, who later became Pope Pius II, granted permission for the founding of the university and established Basel as the cultural capital it remains today.

Art and academia over the ages haven't made Basel stuffy, however. The Baslers' Lenten celebration of Fasnacht (related to Mardi Gras, or Carnival) turns the city on its ear. The streets are filled with grotesquely costumed revelers bearing huge homemade lanterns scrawled with comments and caricatures relating to local current events. Although the festivities last only three days, you'll see masks, drums, and fifes displayed and sold everywhere all year long, and hear strains of fife-and-drum marches wafting from the guild houses' upper windows; they're rehearsing for Fasnacht. Like confetti lodged between the cobblestones, there always seems to be a hint of Fasnacht, age-old and unpredictable, even in Basel's most sedate and cultivated corners.

Pleasures and Pastimes

Dining
When the Alemanni hordes sent the Romans packing, they brought their Germanic cuisine as well, and for the most part the German style stuck. When Baslers eat home-style, it's inevitably sausage, schnitzel, *Spätzli* (tiny flour dumplings), and beer. The city is full of comfortable haunts lined with carved wood and thick with the mingled odors of cooking meat and cigar smoke.

Yet the proximity of the Rhine has given Basel a taste for river fish, too, and if Basel could claim a regional specialty, it would be salmon. Salmon became so commonplace in Basel's golden age that some cooks refused to prepare it more than twice a week. Basel's better restaurants often feature the meaty pink fish (though it's likely imported, as the Rhine has suffered from pollution), served in a white-wine marinade with fried onions on top—*nach Basler-Art* (Basel style). Try it with a bottle of the fruity local Riesling-Sylvaner.

Fasnacht
Dating back to the Middle Ages, Switzerland's best-known Carnival is a must-see if Basel is on your early-spring travel itinerary. Beginning at 4 AM the morning after Ash Wednesday, the Morgenstraich opens the event with a blast of fifes and drums loud enough to wake the living, the dead, and the hard-of-hearing too. As it happens, no one's sleeping at all: they're waiting for the start of colorful masked processions that traverse the Old Town until dawn and continue for several days. Nearby Liestal stages its own spectacular and more primitive ceremony the night before, when burning stacks of wood are paraded through the town and heaped together. Crackling torches are carried on participants' backs, while increasingly larger blazing logpiles are pulled behind on wagons. The flames flare splendidly against the town's medieval *Tor* (gate) as each passing group rushes through.

Museums
With a renowned gallerist's hand-picked paintings (the Fondation Beyeler), an homage to unique mechanized art (the Tinguely Museum),

and the world's oldest public art collection (the Kunstmuseum), Basel
easily earns high rank in the art world. But the city goes even further
with additional museums of astounding variety—from collections featuring design and caricature to paper, printing, and pharmaceutical history. The larger museums, such as the Historisches Museum, publish
guides in English. Also, the tourist office has a museum guidebook (in
English) that describes the highlights of Basel's collections.

EXPLORING BASEL

The Rhine divides the city of Basel into two distinct sections: the whole
of the Old Town lies in Grossbasel (Greater Basel), the commercial,
cultural, and intellectual center. The opposite bank, to the northeast,
is Kleinbasel (Little Basel), a Swiss enclave on the "German" side of
the Rhine that is the industrial quarter of the city. Unless you are visiting on business and meeting at the convention center east of the
river, your time on the right bank will probably be limited to a waterfront stroll and possibly a good night's sleep, as some hotels are here.

*Numbers in the text correspond to numbers in the margin and on the
Basel map.*

Great Itineraries

IF YOU HAVE 1 OR 2 DAYS

Begin with a stroll through Basel's Old Town, making sure to see the
Münster and the sweeping views from the church's Rhine terrace, the
Pfalz. Art enthusiasts could decide to circle from here directly to the
Kunstmuseum, while shoppers may want to head down one of the winding alleyways into the Freiestrasse or the Marktplatz. A leisurely, late-
afternoon walk across the Mittlere Rheinbrücke and upstream along
the sunny Kleinbasel riverside promenade (Oberer Rheinweg) is a
good way to see the town in its best light.

On the following day, take in some of the city's smaller museums, perhaps in the picturesque St. Alban quarter. From here, take a ferry boat
across the river and head east to the Tinguely Museum. Or, organize
your day around a trip to Riehen; the Fondation Beyeler's stunningly
well-rounded (and beautifully presented) collection of 20th-century art
can be reached in a mere 20 minutes by tram.

IF YOU HAVE 3 TO 5 DAYS

Given the luxury of several days, you can explore even more of Basel's
museums. In season, make sure to take a boat trip to the Roman ruins
of Augusta Raurica, east of Basel. You could also take a driving tour
of the small villages scattered south of Basel: Balsthal, Holderbank,
Oberer Hauenstein, Langenbruck, and Liestal.

Old Town

Standing in the middle of the Marktplatz or even watching river traffic from the Mittlere Rheinbrücke, it's easy to envision the Basel of centuries ago. On a bend of the Rhine, Basel's Old Town is full of majestic
Gothic spires and side streets that have remained largely unchanged
since the 1600s. Still, much of the delicately preserved architecture of
the Old Town incorporates impressive, state-of-the-art museums and
miles of shop-lined pedestrian zones.

A Good Walk

Six bridges link the two halves of the city; the most historic and picturesque is the **Mittlere Rheinbrücke** ①. Start at its Grossbasel end, near
the tourist office. On the corner of what is now a chain restaurant (Churrasco) at Schifflände, you can see a facsimile of the infamous

Lällekönig ②, a 15th-century gargoyle once mechanized to stick out his tongue and roll his eyes at his rivals across the river.

Walking across the bridge, you'll see Basel's peculiar, gondolalike ferry boats, attached to a high wire and angling silently from shore to shore, powered only by the swift current of the river (you can ride one for 1.20 SF). Across the Rhine, pause at the seated **statue of Helvetia,** one of Basel's many tongue-in-cheek sculptures.

Back across the Mittlere Rheinbrücke in Grossbasel, turn left up a steep alley called the **Rheinsprung,** banked with 15th- and 16th-century houses. Turn right at Archivgässlein, and you'll come to the **Martinskirche** ③, the oldest parish church in town, dating from 1288.

Continue along Martinsgasse, on your left, to the elegant neighboring courtyards of the **Blaues und Weisses Haus** ④, meeting place of kings. Just beyond, turn left and head toward the fountain adorned by a mythical green basilisk into the Augustinergasse. At No. 2 is the entrance to the **Naturhistorisches Museum** ⑤ and the **Schweizerisches Museum der Kulturen** ⑥. Under one roof, you will find one of the world's foremost natural history and prehistory collections.

Augustinergasse leads into the Münsterplatz, dominated by the striking red-sandstone 12th-century **Münster** ⑦, burial place of Erasmus and Queen Anna of Hapsburg. Walk around to the church's river side to a terrace called the **Pfalz,** which affords wide views of the river, the Old Town, and, on a clear day, the Black Forest.

From the Münsterplatz, head down Rittergasse, past its elegant villas and courtyards, to the first busy cross street. Ahead of you is St. Alban-Vorstadt, which leads to the **St. Alban-Tor** ⑧, one of the original 13th-century medieval city gates. St. Alban-Tal leads from St. Alban-Vorstadt down to St. Alban-Rheinweg on the Rhine to the **Basler Papiermühle/Schweizer Papiermuseum und Museum für Schrift und Druck** ⑨ and **Museum für Gegenwartskunst** ⑩.

Leaving the museums by way of the St. Alban-Rheinweg along the riverside, ascend the Wettstein Bridge stairs and head left onto St. Alban-Graben. Here is the imposing **Kunstmuseum** ⑪, home of one of Europe's oldest public collections. Continue down St. Alban-Graben to the next cross street and veer right on Steinenberg, which goes by the **Kunsthalle** ⑫.

Just beyond the gallery, the whimsical Tinguely-Brunnen or **Fasnacht-Brunnen** puts on a show on the Theaterplatz. (A Richard Serra sculpture, normally covered in graffiti, also punctuates the square.) Rather than head down Steinenberg, you can turn left on Elisabethenstrasse and see the **Haus zum Kirschgarten** ⑬, which houses the collections of the Basel Historical Museum. Or go along Steinentorstrasse to the **Zoologischer Garten** ⑭ directly west of the SBB train station.

At the end of Steinenberg lies the bustling Barfüsserplatz. Here the **Puppenhaus Museum** ⑮ displays toys from the 18th and 19th centuries while the **Historisches Museum** ⑯ exhibits annals and objects out of Basel's proud past in the mid-14th-century Franciscan **Barfüsserkirche,** or Church of the Discalced Friars.

Behind the tram concourse on Barfüsserplatz, follow the pedestrian zone to Leonhardsberg, which leads left up the stairs to the late-Gothic **Leonhardskirche** ⑰. Continue along the church walk into Heuberg street, the spine of one of the loveliest sections of old Basel. A network of small streets threads through the quarter, lined with graceful old houses from many periods: Gothic, Renaissance, baroque, Biedermeier. Heuberg

170

26

PEDESTRIAN ZONE

Rebgasse

Riehenstrasse

Wettsteinallee

Wettsteinallee

TO DEUTSCHE BUNDESBAHN (BADISCHER BAHNHOF)

Schwarzwaldstr.

Riehentorstr.

am Rheinweg

Wettsteinstrasse

Wettsteinplatz

Grenzacherstrasse

25

Solitude Park

Theodorsgraben-Anlage

Schaffhauser-Rheinweg

Wettstein-brücke

Rhein

7

St. Alban-Rheinweg

St. Alban-Rheinweg

10

9

St. Alban-Tal

Weidengasse

Ritterg.

St. Alban-Graben

St. Alban-Vorstadt

11

8

Zürcherstrasse

Dufourstrasse

Malzgasse

St. Alban-Anlage

Gellertstrasse

Aeschengraben

Lange Gasse

Hardstrasse

St. Alban-Ring

Gartenstrasse

St. Jakobs-Str.

Schule

Engelgasse

Peter Merian-Str.

Rosenfeld Park

Münchensteinerstrasse

Kant. Handelsschule

St. Alban

Sissacherstr.

N2

Nauenstr.

St.-Jakobs-Str.

Hochstrasse

Tellstrasse

Münchensteinerstr.

Güterbahnhof Wolf

feeds into Spalenvorstadt, which will take you ahead two blocks to the **Holbeinbrunnen,** styled from a drawing by Hans Holbein.

The Spalenvorstadt stretches ahead to the impressive 14th-century **Spalentor** ⑱, another of Basel's medieval city gates. Spalengraben curves north from here past the buildings of the Universität, one of the six oldest universities in German-speaking Europe. Nearby Petersplatz is the site of the 13th-century **Peterskirche** ⑲ and the lively Saturday *Flohmarkt* (flea market).

Petersgasse, behind the Peterskirche, presents an exemplary row of houses, some only a single window wide. Several small streets scale downhill from here, among them the Totengässlein, which leads past the **Pharmazie-Historisches Museum** ⑳. The steep stairs wind on in the direction of the **Marktplatz** ㉑, the historic and modern heart of Basel, with its towering **Rathaus** ㉒.

Leading off the south end of the Marktplatz, main shopping streets Freiestrasse and Gerbergasse are lined with international shops and department stores. The north end heads toward **Fischmarkt** ㉓. Marktgasse leads past the historic **Drei Könige Hotel** ㉔. If you're feeling energetic, walk to the **Tinguely Museum** ㉕ by crossing over the Mittlere Rheinbrücke and heading east toward Solitude Park on Kleinbasel's sunny waterfront promenade Oberer Rheinweg. Or take a tram (No. 6 from Barfüsserplatz, Marktplatz, or Schifflände; No. 2 from Bankverein or Munstermesse in the direction of Riehen-Grenze) to the **Fondation Beyeler** ㉖, with its modern art collection and green park.

TIMING

Moving at a rapid clip you can see the major sights, as well as a cross section of the cultural and artistic collections, in three to five hours. A more leisurely itinerary, including strolling, Old Town shopping along the Spalenburg, and museums on the Kleinbasel side, will while away the better part of at least one day, if not two. Keep in mind that many museums are closed Monday.

Sights to See

🖐 ❾ **Basler Papiermühle/Schweizer Papiermuseum und Museum für Schrift und Druck** (Basel Paper Mill/Swiss Museum of Paper, Writing, and Printing). Though its name sounds esoteric, this museum, in a beautifully restored, medieval waterfront mill house, is surprisingly accessible. A functioning waterwheel and demonstrations of papermaking, typesetting, and bookbinding show how the site still practices the ancient craft. You can watch the 12-step papermaking process, beginning with the pulpy raw material simmering in the "Visitors' Vat." Kids can try out quills and ink or spell their names in pieces of type for printing. Most descriptions have an English translation, but some special exhibits are in German only. ⊠ *St. Alban-Tal 35/37*, ☎ *061/2729652.* 🎫 *9 SF.* ☉ *Tues.– Sun. 2–5.*

❹ **Blaues und Weisses Haus** (Blue House and White House). Built between 1762 and 1768 for two of the city's most successful silk merchants, these were the residences of the brothers Lukas and Jakob Sarasin. In 1777 the emperor Joseph II of Austria was a guest in the Blue House and subsequent visitors, including Czar Alexander of Russia, Emperor Francis of Austria, and King Friedrich Wilhelm III of Prussia, who met for dinner here in 1814, take this historical site's guest book over the top. The restored, twin-like houses are both white with blue trim, but they're distinguished by their gates: one is intricate iron (Blue House) and the other stately wood. ⊠ *Martinsg.*

㉔ **Drei Könige Hotel** (Three Kings Hotel). The statues on the facade depict three wise men who visited here nearly a millennium ago, in 1032 to be precise. Rodolphe II, king of Burgundy; Holy Roman emperor Konrad II; and the latter's son, the future Heinrich III, held a meeting here that joined Burgundy to the Holy Roman Empire. The young general Napoléon Bonaparte stayed here in 1797 (the suite has been named for him and redecorated in opulent Empire style), followed by other stellar guests: the kings of Italy, Princess Victoria, Charles Dickens, and Picasso (who once spent the night on the balcony admiring the view). In 1887 the great Hungarian-born Jewish writer Theodor Herzl stayed here during the first Zionist Congress, which laid the groundwork for the founding of the state of Israel. ⊠ *Blumenrain 8.*

Fasnacht-Brunnen (Carnival Fountain). Created by the internationally famous Swiss artist Jean Tinguely, known for his work in mechanized media, this witty, animated construction was commissioned by the city in 1977 to carry on Basel's tradition of fountain sculpture. Its nine busy metal figures, in Tinguely's trademark whimsical style, churn, lash, and spray with unending energy. ⊠ *Theaterpl.*

㉓ **Fischmarkt** (Fish Market). Fishmongers once kept the catch fresh for the market on this square, whose fountain basin served as a sort of communal cooler. The fountain itself dates from 1390 and upholds figures of the Virgin Mary, St. Peter, and John the Baptist. ⊠ *Marktg., northwest of Marktpl.*

★ ㉖ **Fondation Beyeler** (Beyeler Foundation). In the Basel suburb of Riehen, art dealers Ernst and Hedy Beyeler established a permanent public home for their astonishingly well-rounded collection of 20th-century art. Architect Renzo Piano's building uses simple, introverted lines to direct attention to the 175 paintings and objects. Rightly so, as the collection's catalog reads like a who's who of modern artists—Cézanne, Matisse, Lichtenstein, Rauschenberg.

In this limpid setting of natural light and openness, Giacometti's wiry sculptures stretch toward the ceiling while Monet's water lilies seem to spill from the canvas into an outdoor reflecting pool. Indigenous carved figures from New Guinea and Nigeria stare into faces on canvases by Klee and Dubuffet. And a stellar selection of Picassos is juxtaposed with views on blue skies and neighboring fields.

The harmony of the collection notwithstanding, personal preference is a perceivable theme, and there is a strong sensation of being invited into an intimate space. With local enthusiasm generating capacity crowds on weekends, however, you may feel as though you've brought half of Basel with you. The tram trip from Schifflände takes about 20 minutes. Although there isn't much museum literature in English, an English-language tour is offered. ⊠ *Baselstr. 77, CH-4125 Riehen,* ☎ *061/6459700.* ☞ *8 SF.* ☉ *Thurs.–Tues. 11–5, Wed. 11–8.*

⑬ **Haus zum Kirschgarten** (Kirschgarten House). This 18th-century home was built as a palace for a young silk-ribbon manufacturer. Nowadays it contains the 18th- and 19th-century collections of the city's Historical Museum, displayed as furnishings in its period rooms. ⊠ *Elisabethenstr. 27,* ☎ *061/2711333.* ☞ *5 SF, 1st Sun. of month free.* ☉ *Tues.–Sun. 10–5.*

★ ⑯ **Historisches Museum** (Historical Museum). Housed within the **Barfüsserkirche** (Church of the Discalced Friars), which was founded by the barefoot Franciscans in 1250 and rebuilt during the mid-14th century, the museum has an extensive collection of tapestries, wooden sculptures, coins, armor, and other vestiges of Basel's past. An underground gallery displays fully reconstructed **medieval and Renaissance guild rooms,** complete with stained glass, ceramic stoves, and richly carved wood. Downstairs, in the back of the church, the **Münster Treasury** contains priceless reliquaries in gold. Despite its status as one of the finest examples of Franciscan architecture north of the Alps, the church was deconsecrated in the 19th century and turned into a warehouse until it was rescued in 1894 and converted to the present-day museum. Most museum descriptions are in German only. ⊠ *Barfüsserpl., Steinenberg 4,* ☎ *061/2710505.* ▣ *5 SF, 1st Sun. of month free.* ☉ *Wed.–Mon. 10–5.*

Holbeinbrunnen (Holbein Fountain). Created by an unknown 16th-century stonemason, this whimsical fountain is a bundle of copies. It depicts a group of dancing farmers, copied from a drawing by Hans Holbein; above stands a bagpiper, copied from a Dürer engraving. The fountain itself is a copy, the original having been moved to the Historical Museum. ⊠ *Spalenvorstadt, 2 blocks up the tram tracks toward Spalentor.*

★ ⑫ **Kunsthalle** (Basel Art Gallery). Managed through Basel's community of artists, the Basler Kunstverein, this museum has hosted precedent-setting exhibits of contemporary art since 1872. In addition to showing several modern masters early in their careers (Klee and Picasso), the gallery was the first in Europe to display works by American abstract expressionists. Recent exhibits have featured Christopher Wool and Maurizio Cattelan. An on-site theater shows video installations, performances, and local and foreign films. ⊠ *Steinenberg 7,* ☎ *061/2069900.* ▣ *9 SF.* ☉ *Tues.–Sun. 11–5, Wed. 11–8:30.*

★ ⑪ **Kunstmuseum** (Museum of Fine Arts). In a city known for its museums, the Kunstmuseum is Basel's heirloom jewel. It was built in 1932–36 to house one of the oldest public collections of art in Europe, owned by the city since 1661; the imposing facade gives way to an inner courtyard studded with statues. Inside is the world's largest assemblage of paintings by Hans Holbein the Younger, an exceptional group of works by Konrad Witz, and, in fact, such a thorough gathering of the works of their contemporaries that the development of painting in the Upper Rhine is strikingly illuminated. Other Swiss artists are well represented: from the 18th-century Alpine landscapes of Caspar Wolf through Klimt-like Ferdinand Hodler. The museum's other forte is its international 20th-century collection, from Georges Braque to Jasper Johns. Most museum materials are in German only, but English descriptions are sometimes provided for special exhibits. ⊠ *St. Alban-Graben 16,* ☎ *061/2066262.* ▣ *7 SF includes admission to Museum für Gegenwartskunst; 1st Sun. of month free.* ☉ *Tues.–Sun. 10–5.*

★ ❷ **Lällekönig.** When a famous gate tower on the Grossbasel side was destroyed, with it went the notorious Lällekönig, a 15th-century gargoyle of a king once mechanized by clockwork to stick out his tongue and roll his eyes at the "lesser" citizens across the river. Kleinbasel residents take symbolic revenge even today, though. Every year during the Vogel Gryff festival, a birdlike figure dances to the midpoint of the bridge, gives the Lällekönig a flash of his backside, and takes the party back to Kleinbasel. You can see a facsimile of the Lällekönig on the corner of what is now a chain restaurant (Churrasco) at Schifflände 1. The mechanized original still ticks away and sticks out his tongue in the nether regions of the Historical Museum. ⊠ *Schifflände.*

⑰ **Leonhardskirche** (St. Leonard's Church). Like virtually all of Basel's churches, this one was destroyed in the 1356 quake and rebuilt in the Gothic style, although its Romanesque crypt remains. Its High Gothic wooden pulpit is distinctive. Free organ concerts are held on Friday evening. ⊠ *Heuberg.* ⊙ *Daily 10–5.*

㉑ **Marktplatz.** Fruits, flowers, and vegetables are sold every morning from open stands in this central square, Basel's historic and modern heart. In fall and winter passersby purchase bags of hot roasted chestnuts, the savory smoke of which fills the square. ⊠ *Tram crossroads at the foot of Rathaus, south of Marktg.* ⊙ *Market: Tues., Thurs., and weekends 6–1:30; Mon., Wed., and Fri. 6 AM–6:30 PM.*

❸ **Martinskirche** (St. Martin's Church). The acoustics inside make this church popular for concerts, although it's rarely used for services. The lower portions of the tower date from 1288, making it the oldest parish church in town; the greater part was rebuilt after the earthquake of 1356. The fountain outside, with the statue of a warrior dressed for battle, dates from the 16th century. ⊠ *Martinsg.*

★ ❶ **Mittlere Rheinbrücke** (Middle Rhine Bridge). This is Basel's most historic and best-known bridge. First built around 1225, the bridge made possible the development of an autonomous Kleinbasel and the consequent rivalry that grew between the two half-towns. The wooden bridge was replaced in stone at the turn of the 20th century, its 1478 chapel reconstructed at the center of the new bridge. ⊠ *Schifflände.*

★ ❼ **Münster** (Cathedral). On the site of a 9th-century Carolingian church and replacing a cathedral consecrated by Henry II in 1019, Basel's current cathedral was built during the 12th century in an impressive transitional style, late Romanesque and pre-Gothic. The Münsterplatz square itself is one of the most satisfying architectural ensembles in Europe, its fine town houses set well back from the cathedral, the center filled with pollarded trees.

Since much of the building was destroyed in the 1356 earthquake, the Romanesque and pre-Gothic influences diminished with the rebuilding of the church in Gothic style. But the facade of the north transept, called the **Galluspforte** (St. Gall's Door), survives from the original structure and stands as one of the oldest carved portals in German-speaking Europe—and one of the loveliest. Slender, fine-tooled columns and rich, high-relief, and freestanding sculptures frame the door. Each of the Evangelists is represented by his symbol: the angel for Matthew, an ox for Luke, a bulbous-chested eagle for John, a slim-limbed lion for Mark. Above, around the window, a wheel of fortune flings little men off to their destiny.

Inside on the left, following a series of tombs of medieval noblemen whose effigies recline with their feet resting on their loyal dogs, stands the strikingly simple **tomb of Erasmus.** Below the choir, you can see the delicately rendered death portraits on the double **tomb of Queen Anna of Hapsburg** and her young son Charles, from around 1285. The vaulted **crypt** was part of the original structure and still bears fragments of murals from 1202. ⊠ *Münsterpl.* ⊙ *Easter–mid-Oct., weekdays 10–6, Sat. 10–noon and 2–5, Sun. 1–5; mid-Oct.–Easter, Mon.–Sat. 10–noon and 2–4, Sun. 2–4.*

NEED A BREAK?
It's hard to beat the plaza tables of **Café zum Issak** (⊠ Münsterpl. 16, ☏ 061/2617711) for scenic value; you look straight up at the cathedral's towers. The house favorite, *gaggocino,* is an elaborate, semisweet hot chocolate with alpine peaks of white froth. They're closed Monday; no credit cards accepted.

---

❿ **Museum für Gegenwartskunst** (Museum of Contemporary Art). Carrying Basel's art collections up to the present, this museum focuses on works from the 1970s on. The fittingly modern building looks as though it has shouldered its way in between the street's half-timber houses. Inside are selections by artists such as Frank Stella, Bruce Naumann, and photographer Cindy Sherman. The language of the exhibition materials typically corresponds to the nationality of the artists. ⊠ *St. Alban-Rheinweg 60,* ☎ *061/2728183.* ☞ *7 SF includes admission to Kunstmuseum; 1st Sun. of month free.* ☉ *Tues.–Sun. 11–5.*

☝ ❺ **Naturhistorisches Museum** (Natural History Museum). Under the same monumental roof as the Schweizerisches Museum der Kulturen (☞ *below*), this museum outlines the history of the earth and its current and one-time inhabitants, from mammoths to insects. There is also a focus on local fossil finds and indigenous minerals from the Alps and Jura regions. Most descriptive materials are in German only. ⊠ *Augustinerg. 2,* ☎ *061/2665500.* ☞ *6 SF includes admission to Schweizerisches Museum der Kulturen; free Sun.* ☉ *Tues.–Sun. 10–5.*

⑲ **Peterskirche** (St. Peter's Church). Living evidence of the late-Gothic heyday of Basel, the 13th-century St. Peter's Church sits across from **Petersplatz,** a lovely park next to the **Universität** (University). In the rose-lighted chapel are some interesting 15th-century frescoes. ⊠ *Just across Peters-Graben from Peterspl.*

⑳ **Pharmazie-Historisches Museum** (Museum of Pharmaceutical History). Although pharmaceuticals as the topic of an entire museum may seem like too much of a necessary thing, this collection showcases Basel's roots in the industry that dominates the banks of the Rhine today. There are recreated old-fashioned pharmacy counters, all kinds of beakers and flacons, plus a bizarre array of old remedies that now seem like candidates for a witches' brew. The museum is housed in Zum Vorderen Sessel, a home once frequented by Erasmus. You can request an English-language information sheet. ⊠ *Totengässlein 3,* ☎ *061/ 2617940.* ☞ *Free.* ☉ *Weekdays 9–noon and 2–5.*

☝ ⑮ **Puppenhaus Museum** (Doll House Museum). Bordering on the Barfüsserplatz, this museum, opened in 1998, has several floors stuffed with 18th- and 19th-century toys and classic miniature toy furnishings. The main stars here are stuffed themselves; more than 2,000 teddy bears are exhibited in perhaps the world's most complete collection representing major manufacturers. The museum's collections are organized not by toy type but by themes—don't be surprised to see a teddy bear driving a model Formula 1 racecar. ⊠ *Steinenvorstadt 1,* ☎ *061/ 2259595.* ☞ *7 SF.* ☉ *Daily 11–5.*

★ ㉒ **Rathaus** (Town Hall). This late-Gothic edifice, built to honor the city's entry into the Swiss Confederation in 1501, towers over the Marktplatz. Only the middle portion actually dates from the 16th century; pseudo-Gothic work was added in 1900. A massive clock with figures of the Madonna, the emperor Henry II, and his wife, Kunegunde, adorns the center of the facade, and all around is a series of colorful frescoes, painted in 1608. Step into the courtyard, where the frescoes continue. ⊠ *Marktpl.*

NEED A
BREAK?

Choose a few jewel-like pastries and order loose-leaf-brewed tea in the carved-wood, clubby upstairs tearoom of the **Café Schiesser** (⊠ Marktpl. 19, ☎ 061/2616077), steeping since 1870.

Rheinsprung. Fifteenth- and 16th-century houses and a handful of ink makers' shops line this steep little alley in Grossbasel. Number 11 housed Basel's university when it was first founded, in 1460. ⊠ *Grossbasel, parallel to and south of Rhine, between Eiseng. and Stapfelbg.*

⑧ St. Alban-Tor. This original medieval city gate is set amid a lovely garden near remnants of the town's ramparts. Parts of the gate date from the 13th century. ⊠ *St. Alban-Berg.*

⑥ Schweizerisches Museum der Kulturen (Swiss Museum of World Cultures). After walking in from the cobblestone street, you'll suddenly find yourself at a woven-palm "culthouse" from Papua, New Guinea. This is one of the world's foremost ethnographic collections, with 32,000 non-European pieces from the far corners of the globe. The extensive ground-floor exhibits on Oceania and Melanesia include standing pole figures, dance staffs, and bristling headdresses. The museum shares its space with the Natural History Museum (☞ *above*). Key elements of the collection have English-language information sheets. ⊠ *Augustinerg. 2,* ☎ *061/2665500.* ☑ *6 SF includes admission to Natural History Museum; free Sun.* ☉ *Tues.–Sun. 10–5.*

⑱ Spalentor. Like the St. Alban-Tor (☞ *above*), the Spalentor served as one of Basel's medieval city gates, beginning in the 14th century. More imposing than graceful, it has a toothy wooden portcullis; also note Basel's coat of arms atop the gate. ⊠ *Spalenvorstadt.*

Statue of Helvetia. What would the woman pictured on most Swiss coins do if freed from the confines of currency? With spear and shield set aside (and suitcase already packed!) this humanistic interpretation shows her seemingly contemplating the possibilities from a perch not far from the border of her homeland and the wide world beyond. ⊠ *Kleinbasel, right bank of Rhine, near Mittlere Rheinbrücke.*

★ **㉕ Tinguely Museum.** Ticinese architect Mario Botta, creator of the San Francisco Museum of Modern Art, designed this museum dedicated to the life and work of Switzerland's well-known 20th-century master of mechanized art, Jean Tinguely. Much of the collection is the gift of his widow, artist Niki de Saint Phalle. Born in Fribourg, Tinguely is best known for his whimsical *métamécaniques* (mechanical sculptures), which transform normally inhuman machinery into ironic and often macabre statements: *Le Ballet des Pauvres,* from 1961, suspends a hinged leg with a moth-eaten sock, a horse tail and fox pelt, a cafeteria tray, and a blood-soaked nightgown, all of which dangle and dance on command. The Barca, a wing projecting over the Rhine, has a splendid river view of Basel. Many of the museum's "sculptures" play on timers, typically every five to 15 minutes, and it pays to wait and see them in action. Schedules are listed on each work's nameplate, and information sheets are available in English. ⊠ *Grenzacherstr. 210,* ☎ *061/6819320.* ☑ *5 SF.* ☉ *Wed.–Sun. 11–7.*

☙ **⑭ Zoologischer Garten** (Zoological Garden). Famed for its armored rhinoceroses (it has had great luck breeding them) as well as its pygmy hippopotamuses, gorillas, and Javanese monkeys, this is no ordinary zoo. It's very child-friendly and the enormous restaurant-pavilion in the center of the zoo serves kid-size meals. Buy a booklet with a map to find your way, or you may end up wandering in circles. ⊠ *Binningerstr. 40,* ☎ *061/2953535.* ☑ *10 SF.* ☉ *May–Aug., daily 8–6:30; Mar.–Apr. and Sept.–Oct., daily 8–6; Nov.–Feb., daily 8–5:30.*

OFF THE
BEATEN PATH

LANGENBRUCK AND ENVIRONS – In the German-speaking countryside south of Basel, known as the Baselbiet, is a handful of stately little villages with sturdy old guest houses and a range—from medieval to Roman—of historic sites to explore. Take the winding forest road (A12) west of the freeway between Liestal and Oensingen, watching for Balsthal, Holderbank, Oberer Hauenstein, and Langenbruck; the industrial stretch just south of Liestal is less attractive. Landgasthof Bären (☎ 062/

3901414) in Langenbruck offers superb regional cooking, inexpensive prix-fixe menus, and locally brewed beer.

VITRA DESIGN MUSEUM – Ten kilometers (six miles) across the border in the German town of Weil am Rhein, this museum is a startling white geometric jumble designed by American architect Frank Gehry as part of an avant-garde building complex associated with the Vitra furniture manufacturer. The Gehry section generally hosts traveling architectural exhibits. The permanent collection, including the soaring Wall of Chairs (just what it sounds like), is displayed in the nearby Vitra Fire Station, accessible only on the guided tour. To get here by car, take A5/E35 north from Basel toward Karlsruhe; turn right just after German customs onto Route 532, parallel to the parking lot, and turn left after exiting at Weil am Rhein. The museum is 1½ km (about 1 mi) ahead on the right. Or from the Deutscher Bahnhof in Basel, take Bus 5 (toward Kandern) to the Vitra stop. Bring your passport and call ahead to arrange for an English-speaking tour guide. ✉ *Charles-Eames-Str. 1, Weil am Rhein, Germany,* ☎ *49/7621/7023200.* 🎫 *DM 10.* ☉ *Tues.–Fri. 2–6, weekends 11–5. Guided tours Wed.–Fri. at 2.*

Colonia Augusta Raurica (Augst)

Founded in 44–43 BC, Augst is the oldest Roman establishment on the Rhine. The site is reachable by car from Basel in 10 minutes, or from mid-May to mid-October, via a leisurely boat trip up the river. To view the restoration areas scattered around the almost suburban neighborhood, be prepared to do some walking.

A Good Tour

A scenic 1½-hour boat ride will take you to Kaiseraugst, known for its thermal spas. From there, walk uphill, following the signs to the ruins of **Augusta Raurica,** a 2,000-year-old Roman settlement that's been almost entirely rebuilt. Stop in for a map and a peek at the excavated ancient treasures in the **Römermuseum,** which is itself a reconstructed Roman house. Boats (Basler Personenschiffahrts-Gesellschaft, ✉ Depart from the Schifflände, behind the Drei Könige Hotel, ☎ 061/6399500) to Augst leave up to three times a day in high season. For a round-trip fare of about 32 SF, you'll cruise slowly up the Rhine, passing the Old Town and the cathedral.

TIMING

Augst merits at least a half day, slightly more if you go by boat. Drinks and cold snacks are available on all cruises, hot meals on some. The last boat returning to Basel each day leaves Augst around 5 PM.

Sights to See

★ **Augusta Raurica.** The remains of this 2,000-year-old Roman settlement have been extensively rebuilt (one suspects the Swiss might have done the same with Rome's Colosseum if they had they gotten their hands on it), with substantial portions of the ancient town walls and gates, streets, water pipes, and heating systems all in evidence. The 2nd-century theater has been restored for modern use, and open-air plays and concerts are staged in summer; contact the Römermuseum for details.

Römermuseum (Roman Museum). Roman daily life is vividly depicted in this rebuilt, ochre-hued home. Everything—from the thermal baths to the ancient board games in the sitting room—has been completely recreated. The museum also exhibits a treasure trove of Roman-era coins and silver unearthed in 1962. The objects, dating mostly from the 4th century, are believed to have been buried by the Romans in 350 to protect them from the ravages of the Alemanni, the German tribes who drove the Romans out of Switzerland. Another exhibit, running through 2001, demonstrates how a typical day, even 2,000 years ago, revolved around religion, money, and pleasures of the palate. Trilingual (English/French/German) brochures are available. ⊠ *Giebenacherstr. 17, Augst,* ☏ *061/8162222.* ☐ *5 SF.* ⊙ *Mar.–Oct., Mon. 1–5, Tues.–Sat. 10–5, Sun. 10–6; Nov.–Feb., Tues.–Sat. 10–noon and 1:30–4, Sun. 10–noon and 1:30–5, Mon. 1–4.*

DINING

Of course, Basel can't help but show the sophistication of generations of cosmopolitan influence, and it has a surprising number of innovative French and international restaurants—some of them world-class (and priced accordingly). In fact, dining in Basel is a pricey venture, whether your sausage is stuffed with lobster and truffles or merely pork scraps. To keep expenses down, stick to beer-hall fare or watch posted menus for lunch specials.

CATEGORY	COST*
$$$$	over 70 SF
$$$	40 SF–70 SF
$$	20 SF–40 SF
$	under 20 SF

Prices are per person for a three-course meal (two-course meal in $ category), excluding drinks, tax, and 15% service charge.

$$$$ ✕ **Stucki.** Chef Jean-Claude Wicky continues in the vein of the late master chef Hans Stucki at what is still one of Basel's best spots. Classics
★ include pigeon in truffle coulis (liquid puree of cooked vegetables), duck à l'orange, and grilled lobster in tarragon sabayon. The service at this restaurant, in the leafy residential neighborhood of Bruderholz, is formal and the seating competitive: reserve as far ahead as possible. ⊠ *Bruderholzallee 42,* ☏ *061/3618222. Reservations essential. AE, DC, MC, V. Closed Sun.–Mon.*

$$$ ✕ **Chez Donati.** The new millennium will mean a new regime for this old-school Italian restaurant once frequented by Warhol and Tinguely. Having catered to well-heeled Baslers for many generations, the Donati family will pass on the silver serving spoon to a yet-unknown successor. One can only hope that traditions such as the decadent dessert trollies and the thin-pounded *vitello* (veal) and truffles will continue. ⊠ *St. Johanns-Vorstadt 48,* ☏ *061/3220919. AE, DC, MC, V. Closed Mon.–Tues. and mid-July to mid-Aug.*

$$$ ✕ **St. Alban-Eck.** This café, a five-minute walk behind the Kunstmuseum, shows a glimpse of Basel's French blood. In a half-timber historic home, it's a real *petit coin sympa* (friendly little corner), with plank wainscoting in natural wood, framed historic prints, and net curtains. The cuisine gracefully mixes German and French favorites: grilled entrecôte, sole, salmon, and *foie de veau à la Riehen* (liver with onions, apple, and smoked bacon). ⊠ *St. Alban-Vorstadt 60,* ☏ *061/2710320. AE, DC, MC, V. Closed Sun. No lunch Sat.*

$$$ ✕ **Schlüsselzunft.** This historic guildhall holds an elegant little restaurant with a ceramic stove and rustic appointments, as well as an inexpensive, open-atrium courtyard café called the Schlüsselhöfli. The restaurant, which draws business-lunch crowds, serves well-bred French food and cuisine *Bâloise,* meaning liver with onions and the local salmon dish; the café serves shoppers cheap international plates. ⊠ *Freiestr. 25,* ☏ *061/2612046. Reservations essential in restaurant. AE, DC, MC. Closed Sun.*

180

Dining
Brauerei Fischerstube, **11**
Café Papiermühle, **20**
Café Pfalz, **12**
Chez Donati, **1**
Löwenzorn, **4**
St. Alban-Eck, **18**
Schlüsselzunft, **8**
Stucki, **17**
Teufelhof, **7**
Zum Goldenen
Sternen, **19**
Zum Schnabel, **6**

Lodging
Bad Schauenburg, **21**
Basel, **5**
Central, **16**
Drei Könige, **2**
Euler, **14**
Krafft am Rhein, **10**
Merian am Rhein, **9**
Rochat, **3**
Schweizerhof, **15**
Steinenschanze, **13**
Teufelhof, **7**

PEDESTRIAN
ZONE

Rebgasse

Riehenstrasse

Riehentorstr.

Wettsteinallee

Wettsteinallee

TO DEUTSCHE
BUNDESBAHN
(BADISCHER BAHNHOF)

Schwarzwaldstr.

11

Rheinweg

Wettsteinstrasse

Wettsteinplatz

Grenzacherstr.

Solitude
Park

Theodorsgraben-
Anlage

Schaffhauser-Rheinweg

Wettstein-
brücke

Rhein

St. Alban-Rheinweg

St. Alban-Rheinweg

Ritterg.

St. Alban-
Graben

19

20

St. Alban-Tal

Weidengasse

St. Alban-Vorstadt

18

Zürcherstrasse

Dufourstrasse

Malzgasse

St. Alban-Anlage

Gellertstrasse

Aeschengraben

Lange Gasse

Hardstrasse

Alban-Ring

Gartenstrasse

St. Jakobs-Str.

Schule

Engelgasse

Peter Merian-Str.

Rosenfeld
Park

Münchensteinerstrasse

Kant.
Handelsschule

St. Alban

Sissacherstr.

21

Lindenhofstr.

N2

Nauenstr.

Hochstr.

Bruderholzstr.

Tellstrasse

Münchensteinerstr.

St. Jakobs-Str.

17

Güterbahnhof
Wolf

$$–$$$$ ✕ **Teufelhof.** Owners Monica and Dominique Thommy have trans-
★   formed a grand old Heuberg mansion into a top gastronomic restau-
rant, a chic Weinstube, a trendy bar, two theaters, and guest rooms (☞
Lodging, *below*); there are even medieval ruins in the basement. The
formal restaurant Bel Étage's decor is almost minimalist, showcasing
a few artworks and a star-pattern parquet floor. Michael Baader's
masterly guidance might result in such inventions as grouper in oys-
ter sauce with *spaghettini* and glazed celery or beef in Stilton and bal-
samic vinegar with polenta soufflé. Wines by the glass come in
astonishing variety, and you can buy by the bottle in the house wine
shop. The casual, high-tech, and warm-wood Weinstube serves a crowd
of low-key, upscale bohemians. The café-bar is tiny and usually crowded
with new-wave artists. ⊠ *Leonhardsgraben 47/Heuberg 30,* ☎ *061/
2611010. AE, MC, V. Restaurant closed Sun.–Mon. No lunch Sat.*

$$ ✕ **Zum Goldenen Sternen.** Dating from 1506, this *Gasthof* claims to
be the oldest restaurant in Switzerland, though the building has been
moved from town center to its current Rhine-side site. The impeccable restoration retains the antique beams, stenciled ceilings, and un-
varnished planks, yet without seeming contrived. Though it could
easily play a secondary role, the food almost lives up to the setting: it's
classic French, only slightly updated. Game and seafood are specialties. ⊠ *St. Alban-Rheinweg 70,* ☎ *061/2721666. AE, DC, MC, V.*

$–$$ ✕ **Café Papiermühle.** With the splashing of the paper mill's waterwheel
★   in the background, this is a comfortable local spot for lunch or a coffee break (they're open only until 6 PM). The hand-scrawled chalkboard
and printed menus are not translated but most often include two multicourse meals in the 15- to 20-SF range, brunch favorites (vegetable
quiche, *Birchermüsli,* granola mixed with yogurt and fruit), salads, soups,
and pasta dishes. Handsignals, however, are all you'll need to point
out one of the homemade cakes. ⊠ *St. Alban-Tal 35,* ☎ *061/2724848.
No credit cards. Closed Mon.*

$ ✕ **Brauerei Fischerstube.** If you're serious about local color, venture a
★   few steps beyond the tourist pale and try a home brew here. The Fischerstube brews its own lagers and ales in the deep, frothing copper
·   tanks behind the bar. The house label is Ueli Bier, named for a jester-
like Fasnacht clown; the timid can taste it at the upscale Teufelhof (☞
Lodging, *below*). Pretzels hang on wooden racks on the sanded wooden
tables, and the menu includes such local dishes as *Fleischkäse* (sausage
loaf) with eggs and *frites* (french fries), rump steak, and just plain *Würstli*
(sausage) from the grill. There's a beer garden in back. ⊠ *Rheing. 45,*
☎ *061/6926635. Reservations not accepted. AE, DC, MC, V.*

$ ✕ **Café Pfalz.** This bookish little self-service café, down a narrow
street below the cathedral, dishes out veggie plates, muesli, sausage,
and quiche in a trim beech-wood-and-black contemporary setting. A
salad bar, juicer, and one hot daily special add to the options. ⊠ *Münsterberg 11,* ☎ *061/2726511. No credit cards.*

$ ✕ **Löwenzorn.** This is a classic, comfortable gathering place for plain
Germanic food. Though the menu is a hodgepodge of fondues, fish,
and Italian dishes as well as standard local fare, regulars come here
for beer, a full plate, and some laughs with the friendly staff. With stained-
glass lamps resembling Fasnacht lanterns, woodwork, ceramic stoves,
and a roof garden, it's a nice mix of bistro and beer hall. ⊠ *Gemsberg
2,* ☎ *061/2614213. AE, DC, MC, V. Closed Sun.*

$ ✕ **Zum Schnabel.** This dark-green and aged-wood *Wirtshaus* (inn)
has a clubby, unpretentious feel, with multiple variations on Basel-brewed
beer. Sausage, pork, steak and, of course, *Rösti* (hash brown potatoes)
reign. If you're in the mood for linens, candles, and a more serious meal,
climb up to the lovely, wood-lined dining area. ⊠ *Trillengässlein 2,* ☎
061/2614909. MC, V. Closed Sun.

LODGING

With its industry, its banking, and its conference center, this is a business city first. As a result, hotel prices tend to be steep, bargains in short supply, and comforts—TV, minibar, phone—more important than atmosphere in the all-out competition for expense-account travelers. When there's a conference in town, every bed for miles can be filled; book well ahead. Hotel reservations can be made through the **Basel Hotel Reservation Service** at the City Information office and at the tourist office (☞ Visitor Information *in* Basel A to Z, *below*).

CATEGORY	COST*
$$$$	over 300 SF
$$$	200 SF–300 SF
$$	140 SF–200 SF
$	under 140 SF

Prices are for a standard double room, including breakfast, tax, and service charge.

$$$$ 🏨 **Drei Könige.** An integral part of Basel history even before the first ★ bridges drew the distant banks of the Rhine together, this riverside hotel began in the 11th century as a small inn; it later became a coach stop, and today it's a landmark of the modern city. Expanded to its present form in 1835, it was bought by the family du Boisrouvray in 1976; corridors are lined with a fascinating variety of their portraits. The furnishings have regained their 19th-century grandeur, with ravishing colors of cream, gilt, and powder blue; ornate woodwork, paintings, and tapestries nudge the opulence factor even higher. All rooms have big, tile baths with recessed lighting and modern fixtures; balconied rooms and rooms with river views cost more. The formal French restaurant serves haute cuisine on the broad, awning-shaded Rhine terrace, which is heated well into fall. There's also a more casual brasserie. ⊠ *Blumenrain 8, CH-4001,* ☎ *061/2615252,* 🏦 *061/2612153. 80 rooms, 7 suites, bar. AE, DC, MC, V.*

$$$$ 🏨 **Euler.** An archetypal little Old World luxury hotel, this landmark ★ draws a loyal business clientele, which mingles with local and international bankers over a *Cüpli* (glass of champagne) in the famous leather-and-red-velvet bar. Duvets billow like baking bread out of the bed frames in some of the cushier rooms and suites; standard rooms are furnished in a classic but spare style, with reproduction antique furnishings. All have triple-glazed windows to cut out tram-traffic noise. ⊠ *Centralbahnpl. 14, CH-4051,* ☎ *061/2724500,* 🏦 *061/2715000. 55 rooms, 9 suites. Restaurant, bar. AE, DC, MC, V.*

$$$ 🏨 **Basel.** This all-modern hotel built in 1975 has become part of the Old Town neighborhood, its bars and restaurants filling with locals after work. The wood-walled rooms are accented with contemporary leather furniture and chrome; polished marble adds luster to the baths. There are two no-smoking floors. The clientele is almost exclusively businesspeople, but there's plenty of room on weekends. ⊠ *Münzg. 12, CH-4051,* ☎ *061/2646800,* 🏦 *061/2646811. 68 rooms, 4 suites. 2 restaurants, café. AE, DC, MC, V.*

$$$ 🏨 **Merian am Rhein.** Built in 1972 to blend with the neighboring land-★ mark Café Spitz, this has a modern, airy look, with touches of gray wood, russet leather, le Corbusier chairs, and live plants. Café Spitz has been a meeting place since the early 13th century, but you wouldn't guess it to look at it; now it's done in light wood, linens, and halogen, with fish dominating the wall decor and the menu. ⊠ *Rheing. 2, CH-4005,* ☎ *061/6810000,* 🏦 *061/6811101. 65 rooms. Restaurant, café, in-room VCRs. AE, DC, MC, V.*

$$$ ▩ **Schweizerhof.** This bastion of the station area, once a luxury hotel, now bestows on business travelers the proud personal service once lavished on such musical stars as Toscanini. Built in 1864 and in the same family since 1896, it is filled with antiques and faience, though its marble floors and wing chairs mingle with faded updates from the '50s and '60s. The most recently modernized rooms mix Biedermeier with beech and pine, though the big front bays are done in rose plush and rosewood. Staff cuts have cost this landmark its official fifth star, if not its five-star style. ✉ *Centralbahnpl. 1, CH-4002,* ☎ *061/2712833,* FAX *061/2712919. 75 rooms. Restaurant, bar. AE, DC, MC, V.*

$$$ ▩ **Teufelhof.** In addition to its bars, theaters, medieval ruins, and
★   restaurants (☞ Dining, *above*), this Basel bastion of style and gourmandise has a small guest house whose eight rooms are works of art in their own right: each is decorated by a different artist and redesigned by another artist every other year. By contrast, the serenely simple 25 rooms of the adjoining Galerie Hotel function collectively as a canvas for one particular artist; these are also redecorated by another artist annually. There's a food and wine shop in the archaeological cellar, and there's even a pair of small theaters that put on various performances (cabaret, satire) from mid-September to early May. In-room TVs are available upon request. ✉ *Leonhardsgraben 47/Heuberg 30, CH-4051,* ☎ *061/2611010,* FAX *061/2611004. 33 rooms. 2 restaurants, bar, café, 2 theaters. AE, MC, V.*

$$ ▩ **Bad Schauenburg.** Ten kilometers (6 miles) southeast of Basel, this charming country inn has suites done in Biedermeier-period antiques and a restaurant serving *cuisine de marché.* Take the main road to Liestal, then follow the signs after the turnoff in Frenkendorf. ✉ *Schauenburgerstr., CH-4410 Liestal,* ☎ *061/9062727,* FAX *061/9062700. 31 rooms, 3 suites. Restaurant. AE, DC, MC, V.*

$$ ▩ **Central.** If you hadn't just picked up your key from the reception
★   desk of a five-star hotel, you might have reservations about your reservation in an economical *garni* down an alleyway near the train station. But this hotel is under the same management as the nearby Euler (☞ *above*), and the larger hotel's care and professionalism carry over. Rooms can be on the small side but are tasteful and cheerful, with hardwood floors and dashes of strong color—tangerine bedspreads, bouquet-patterned drapes, and poppy-red baths. Check in at the Euler's main entrance on Centralbahnhofplatz. ✉ *Kücheng. 7, CH-4051,* ☎ *061/2724200,* FAX *061/2715000. 23 rooms. Bar. AE, DC, MC, V.*

$$ ▩ **Rochat.** Built in 1898 across from the university, this modest but roomy property offers plain, if mildly institutional, comforts in its main brownstone building or in an adjacent annex. Some rooms have large new bathrooms with either a shower or a tub. The three rooms without a private bath cost less. The restaurant is alcohol-free. ✉ *Petersgraben 23, CH-4051,* ☎ *061/2618140,* FAX *061/2616492. 50 rooms, 47 with bath. Restaurant, café. AE, DC, MC, V.*

$–$$ ▩ **Krafft am Rhein.** A rare find in Swiss cities, this is an elegant little
★   mansion of an inn directly on the right-bank waterfront, with mosaic floors, elaborate moldings, chandeliers, and a sinuous atrium stairwell. The accommodating management more than makes up for any wear and tear. Some higher-price Rhine-side rooms have polished wood floors, Biedermeier beds, and Oriental runners; others still have '50s mix-and-match. Those without bath fall into the $ category. There's a traditional dining room with Rhine views for breakfast and dinner, but the downstairs Zem Schnooggeloch (Mosquito's Den) is where everyone gathers for German-style food. The waterfront terrace café is justifiably popular. ✉ *Rheing. 12, CH-4058,* ☎ *061/6909130,* FAX *061/ 6909131. 52 rooms, 45 with bath. Restaurant. AE, DC, MC, V.*

$ Steinenschanze. Despite its awkward, isolated position above the
★   busy highway and behind the nightlife district, this bargain hotel is clean,
welcoming, and bright, with good-size rooms, blue-and-white-tile
baths, and tasteful Scandinavian furniture. The harsh parking garage
lines have been softened by recessed lighting and a scattering of plants,
posters, and knickknacks. Back rooms are quiet; there's a garden behind and a breakfast buffet with fresh cheeses (included in the rate).
⊠ *Steinengraben 69, CH-4051,* ☎ *061/2725353,* F̄AX *061/2724573.
55 rooms. Breakfast room. AE, DC, MC, V.*

NIGHTLIFE AND THE ARTS

For a complete listing of events in Basel, pick up a copy of *Basel Live,*
a booklet published every two weeks. It is written partially in English.
Basel, another listings publication, comes out every three months and
is fully bilingual (German/English). Both are available at the tourist office and usually at hotel desks. If you'd like to play it by ear, the
Steinenvorstadt is crowded with cinemas, bars, and young people,
while on the Kleinbasel side, there are more late-night bars along the
Oberer Rheinweg.

Nightlife

Bars and Lounges

Brauner Mutz (⊠ Barfüsserpl., ☎ 061/2613369) is a big, landmark beer
hall with long wooden tables and a beer in every hand. **Campari Bar**
(⊠ Steinenberg 7, ☎ 061/2728383), behind the Basel Art Gallery and
the Tinguely fountain, draws a young, artsy crowd with pop-art paraphernalia and loud pop music. The **Euler Bar** (⊠ Centralbahnpl. 14,
☎ 061/2724500), inside the Hotel Euler, draws a conservative business crowd after work. **Zum Sperber** (⊠ Münzg. 12, ☎ 061/2612433),
behind the Hotel Basel, fills tables and bar stools with well-heeled workers at happy hour; there's live music some evenings.

Dancing and Nightclubs

Atlantis (⊠ Klosterberg 13, ☎ 061/2721780) hosts a regular roster of
live blues, rock, and alternative bands in a loftlike setting. **Casper's** (⊠
Blumenrain 10, ☎ 061/2613050) is an upscale discotheque with a cover
charge. **Hazy-Club** (⊠ Heuwaage, ☎ 061/2619982) has a top orchestra and show. At **Le Plaza Club** (⊠ Am Messepl., ☎ 061/6923206) the
DJ spins pop hits. **Singerhaus** (⊠ Marktpl., ☎ 061/2616466) is a traditional nightclub with a good show; the bar opens at 7, and dancing
starts at 9.

The Arts

Film

Movies in Basel are usually shown in the original language with sub-
titles. Newspaper listings can be deciphered, but most houses are along
Steinenvorstadt in the Old Town, and times are prominently posted.
Prices vary depending on how close to the screen you choose to sit.

Music

Stadtcasino (⊠ Steinenberg 14, ☎ 061/2726657, F̄AX 061/2725822),
along with its restaurants and piano bar, hosts the Basel Symphony Orchestra, the Basel Chamber Orchestra, and visiting performers. Tickets are sold at the theater box office one hour before performance.
Advance bookings can be made at **Musikhaus au Concert** (⊠ Aeschenvorstadt 24, ☎ 061/2721176). The **Musik-Akademie der Stadt Basel**
(⊠ Leonhardsgraben 4–6) is an important academy with top-quality
international performers. Book as for the Stadtcasino (☞ *above*).

Theater
Basel Stadttheater (⊠ Theaterstr. 7, ☎ 061/2951133), hosts opera, operetta, and dance, as well as drama (usually in German). Book in advance weekdays 10–1 and 3:30–6:45, Saturday 10–6:45. The box office opens one hour before the performance. The **Komödie** (⊠ Steinenvorstadt 63) performs light German-language theater in an intimate atmosphere. Book through the Stadttheater (☞ *above*) or at the box office one hour before the curtain.

OUTDOOR ACTIVITIES AND SPORTS

Golf
Golf and Country Club Basel (⊠ Hagenthal-le-Bas in France, ☎ 33/03/89685091) is one of the most beautiful golf courses in Europe, with attractive views of the Jura, Black Forest, and Vosges mountains. It is open to visitors; bring your passport.

Squash
Sportcenter Paradies (⊠ Bettenstr. 73, ☎ 061/4859580) has good squash facilities (try to make a reservation if you're going during the week); there are eight courts, and you can rent equipment there.

Tennis
Sporthalle St. Jakob (⊠ Schänzli, ☎ 061/3117209) has two indoor and three outdoor courts to reserve, but no rental equipment.

SHOPPING

Though first impressions here may suggest yet another modern pedestrian shopping district, it's worth a closer look. There are still a lot of lone-wolf, quirky shops that contain extraordinary treasures.

Department Stores
Whether you're in need of socks, toothpaste, or chocolate on the cheap, department store chains **Manor** (⊠ Greifeng. 22, ☎ 061/6959511) and **EPA** (⊠ Gerberg. 4, ☎ 061/2699250) have items to get by on, plus groceries in the basement. **Globus** (⊠ Marktpl. 2, ☎ 061/2615500) is a nicer version, with gourmet edibles and sleeker clothes. In what can often be a somewhat barren area, **Migros** (⊠ Centralbahnpl., ☎ 061/2799745), open at its SBB train station location until 10 PM, is a good place to buy provisions.

Shopping Streets
The major, central shopping district stretches along **Freiestrasse** and **Gerbergasse**, though lower-price shops along **Steinenvorstadt** cater to a younger crowd. Streets radiating left, uphill from the Gerbergasse area, feature more one-of-a-kind boutiques. Most antiquarian bookshops concentrate their business on **Klosterberg** through Elisabethenstrasse to Aeschengraben.

Specialty Stores

Antique Books
Among many fine competitors, **Erasmushaus/Haus der Bücher** (⊠ Bäumleing. 18, ☎ 061/2723088) has one of the largest collections of fine old and used books, mostly in German but including some multilingual art publications.

Calligraphic Paraphernalia

Abraxas (✉ Rheinsprung 6, ☎ 061/2616070) is a great source for fine writing tools and paraphernalia, from thick papers and delicate fountain pens to luxurious sealing waxes and reproductions of antique silver seals. **Scriptorium am Rhysprung** (✉ Rheinsprung 2, ☎ 061/2613900) mixes its own ink and carries calligraphy pens.

Coins

Münzen und Medaillen AG (✉ Malzg. 25, ☎ 061/2727544) is a good place to find coins and medals dating from antiquity to the mid-19th century.

Crafts and Gifts

Though primarily specializing in home furnishings, **Atelier Baumgartner** (✉ Spalenberg 8, ☎ 061/2610843) also stocks Swiss and European handicrafts, including much-loved figurines, music boxes, and nutcrackers from the Erzgebirge region of Germany. **Heimatwerk** (✉ Schneiderg. 2, ☎ 061/2619178) sells Swiss crafts from traditional ceramics to linen dish towels and children's wooden toys. Basel-made specialties include embroidered silk ribbons. Highly specialized handiwork comes from **Johann Wanner** (✉ Spalenberg 14, ☎ 061/2614826), who commissions hand-blown, hand-painted, hand-embroidered, and hand-molded ornaments; tin Victorian miniatures; Advent cards; tartan ribbons; cards; and candles—all solely for Christmas. **zem Baselstab** (✉ Schnabelg. 8, ☎ 061/2611016) has Fasnacht figurines and other Basel paraphernalia.

Food Specialties

The famous **Läckerli-Huus** (✉ Gerberg. 57, ☎ 061/2612322) sells a variety of sweets but highlights the local specialty—*Leckerli,* a chewy spiced cookie of almond, honey, dried fruit, and kirsch. A large selection of gift canisters and a shipping service make getting gifts home a cinch. **Bachmann** (✉ Gerberg. 51, ☎ 061/2613583; ✉ Blumenrain 1, ☎ 061/2614152; and ✉ Centralbahnpl. 7, ☎ 061/2712627) also carries the primly packaged, lovely little sweets that set Basel apart. **Glausi's** (✉ Spalenberg 12, ☎ 061/2618008) ages its own cheeses, which are sold alongside myriad fresh Swiss specialties. **Schiesser** (✉ Marktpl., ☎ 061/2616077), a convivial tearoom opened in 1870, sells carefully crafted (and costly) confections in its downstairs shop.

Linens

Caraco (✉ Gerberg. 77, Falknerstr. entrance, ☎ 061/2613577) sells handmade Swiss lace and embroidered goods as well as imports. **Langenthal** (✉ Gerberg. 26, ☎ 061/2610900) offers mostly Swiss products: tea towels, tablecloths, and folk-style aprons. **Sturzenegger** (✉ Freiestr. 62, ☎ 061/2616867) specializes in household linens made in Saint Gallen, the Swiss textile capital.

Lingerie

Beldona (✉ Freiestr. 103, ☎ 061/2731170) stocks Swiss cotton lingerie. **Fogal** sells its famous Swiss hosiery at two locations (✉ Freiestr. 44, ☎ 061/2617461; ✉ Freiestr. 4, ☎ 061/2611220); both branches set out trays of clearance goods. **Sturzenegger** (☞ Linens, *above*) also carries an extensive line of Hanro and Calida underwear.

Men's Clothes

K. Aeschbacher (✉ Schnabelg. 4, ☎ 061/2615058) carries unique Swiss silk ties, scarves, robes, and pajamas. For the smoking-jacket set, **Renz** (✉ Freiestr. 2a, ☎ 061/2612991) has a small but impeccable selection of fine Swiss-cotton pajamas, Hanro underwear, and classic Scottish cashmeres.

Shoes

Kropart (⊠ Schneiderg. 16, ☎ 061/2615133) specializes in trendy, comfort-oriented styles. **Müki** (⊠ Münsterberg 14, ☎ 061/2712436) focuses on functional yet stylish European-made kids' shoes—from patent leather loafers to fun-colored fleece house slippers. **Rive Gauche** (⊠ Schneiderg. 1, ☎ 061/2611080) carries high-end designer shoes—the place to get a Prada fix.

Toys

Bercher & Sternlicht (⊠ Spalenberg 45, ☎ 061/2612550) has miniature trains and accessories. **Spielegge** (⊠ Rümelinspl. 7, ☎ 061/2614488) places an emphasis on wood, with chisel-carved puppets and whimsical Decor puzzles watercolored with fairy-tale scenes. Slightly less folksy than Heimatwerk (☞ Crafts and Gifts, *above*), **Spielhuus** (⊠ Eiseng. 8, ☎ 061/2649898) is a good source for board games and reasonably priced children's toys, as well as Fasnacht costumes.

Women's Clothes

Trois Pommes (⊠ Freiestr. 74, ☎ 061/2729255) dominates the high end, with Jil Sander, Versace, Armani, and Valentino. **S.T.O.C.K. Fashion** (⊠ Eiseng. 6, ☎ 061/2620007) sounds the siren call of a bargain; you'll find mostly cut-rate French and Italian styles.

BASEL A TO Z

Arriving and Departing

By Car

The German autobahn **A5** enters Basel from the north and leads directly to the Rhine and the city center. From France, the auto route **A35** (E9) peters out at the frontier, and secondary urban roads lead to the center. The A2 autobahn leads off to the rest of Switzerland. As the most interesting and scenic portions of Basel are riddled with pedestrians-only streets, it is advisable to park your car for the duration of your visit.

By Plane

EuroAirport (⊠ Just across the border in France, ☎ 061/3253111) is shared by Basel, Mulhouse, and Freiburg in Germany. Direct flights link Basel to most major European cities. The nearest intercontinental airport is **Kloten** outside **Zürich** (⊠ Approximately 80 km/50 mi southeast of Basel, ☎ 1571060). There are connecting flights from Zürich into Basel's airport on **Crossair** (☎ 061/3253636 for reservations or 084/8852000 within Switzerland), Switzerland's domestic airline.

BETWEEN THE AIRPORT AND THE CITY CENTER

By Bus. Regular bus service runs between the airport and the train station in the city center. The trip takes about 15 minutes and costs 2.60 SF per person; call 061/3252511 for schedules and information.

By Taxi. One-way fare from the airport to the Basel center is approximately 35 SF; it takes about 15 minutes in light traffic and up to 30 minutes at rush hours (around noon, 2 PM, and between 5 PM and 7 PM). There are normally cabs at the taxi stand, but if you do need to call one from the airport (in France), you must dial two prefixes: 19 to get out of the country, then 4161, then the number; the cost is negligible. Taxi companies: **Mini Cab** (☎ 061/2711111); **33er Taxi** (☎ 061/6333333); **Taxi-Zentrale** (☎ 061/2712222).

By Train

There are two main rail stations in Basel. The **SBB** (Schweizerische Bundesbahnen; ⊠ Centralbahnstr., ☎ 061/1572222) connects to Swiss destinations as well as to France and its trains. The **DB** (Deutsche Bundesbahn, locally known as the Badischer Bahnhof; ✉ North of the Rhine in Kleinbasel, Schwarzwalderstr. and Riehenstr., ☎ 061/6901111) connects to Germany and to the SBB. Arriving in Basel from France, you get off on the French side of the border; carry your bags through a small customs station, where your passport will be checked; then either continue into the open track area to find your connection or exit left into the city center. Arriving from Germany at the DB station, you walk through a customs and passport check as well.

Getting Around

The best way to see Basel by far is on foot or by tram, as the landmarks, museums, and even the zoo radiate from the Old Town center on the Rhine, and the network of rails covers the territory thoroughly. Taxis are costly, less efficient, and less available than the ubiquitous tram. Parking in the city center is competitive, and in some areas nonexistent. If you've driven in by car, you'll save time and hassle by heading straight for an all-day garage such as the Parkhaus Elisabethen on Heuwaage near the SBB train station. Rates run from 10 to 20 SF per day.

By Tram and Bus

Most trams run every six minutes all day, every 12 minutes in the evening. Tickets must be bought at the automatic machines at every stop (most give change). Stops are marked with green-and-white signs; generally the trams run from 5:30 or 6 in the morning until midnight or shortly thereafter. As long as you travel within the central Zone 10, which includes even the airport, you pay 2.80 SF per ticket. If you are making a short trip—four stops or fewer—you pay 1.80 SF. *Mehrfahrtenkarten* (multijourney cards) allow you 12 trips for the price of 10 and can be purchased from the ticket office at Barfüsserplatz. *Tageskarten* (day cards) allow unlimited travel all day within the central zone and cost 7.20 SF. You can buy day cards at most hotels as well as through the above sources. Holders of the Swiss Pass (☞ Train Travel *in* the Gold Guide) travel free on all Basel public transport systems.

Contacts and Resources

Emergencies
Police (☎ 117). **Hospital** (✉ Kantonsspital, Petersgraben 2, ☎ 061/2652525). **Medical emergencies and late-night pharmacy** referral (☎ 061/2611515).

English-Language Bookstores
Bider & Tanner (✉ Aeschenvorstadt 2 (at Bankverein), ☎ 061/2069999) has a good range of fiction and nonfiction, plus travel-focused and intercultural publications. **Jäggi** (✉ Freiestr. 32, ☎ 061/2615200) shelves plenty of best-sellers.

Guided Tours
Basel Tourismus (☞ Visitor Information, *below*) organizes daily tours of the city by bus, departing at 10 AM from the Euler hotel by the SBB. The tours last about 1¾ hours and cost 20 SF. They also lead two-hour walking tours Sunday and Monday in summer for 10 SF. Commentary is in English. **Basler Personenschiffahrt** (✉ Departing from Schifflände by Mittlere Brücke, ☎ 061/6399500) offers boat trips on the Rhine to Augst for 32 SF round-trip.

Travel Agencies
American Express (✉ Steinenvorstadt 33, ☎ 061/2813380).

Visitor Information

Basel Tourismus (Basel Tourism; ⊠ Schifflände 5, ☎ 061/2686868, FAX 061/2686870) is on the Rhine just left of the Mittlere Brücke, at the Schifflände tram stop. The Basel Tourism branch at the **SBB center** (⊠ Bahnhof, ☎ 061/1572222) will help you with hotel reservations. **City Information** (⊠ Bahnhof, SBB, ☎ 061/2713684) also provides hotel and museum information.

8 FRIBOURG, NEUCHÂTEL, AND THE JURA

Unpretentious and largely undiscovered, the regions of Fribourg, Neuchâtel, and Jura represent three very different worlds. Fribourg, two-thirds French and one-third German, is full of medieval villages and rolling farmland; Neuchâtel, French in language and culture, sparkles from the shores of its glittering lakes to the precision time pieces of its watchmaking industry; and the Jura is a realm of sunny, high plateaux and deeply cleft valleys, horses and hidden streams.

Updated by
Susan Rose

SHOULDERED BY THE MORE PROMINENT CANTONS of Bern and Vaud, the cantons of Fribourg, Neuchâtel, and Jura are easily overlooked by hurried visitors. If they do stop, it is usually for a quick dip into Fribourg and Gruyères. That leaves the rest of this largely untouched area to the Swiss, who enjoy its relatively unspoiled nature and relaxed approach to life: a hiker stops to enjoy the view while sipping a crisp Fendant wine; a family shares homemade sausage and crusty bread at a riverside picnic.

While the strict cantonal borders are a messy reflection of historic power struggles, the regional boundaries are unmistakable, even to an outsider. Fribourg starts in the pre-Alpine foothills above Charmey and rolls down across green hills, tidy farms, and ancient towns until it reaches the silty shores of the Murten, Neuchâtel, and Biel lakes. The region of Neuchâtel begins in these silt-rich fields (which grow everything from lettuce to tobacco), sweeps across the lake to the chateaux- and vineyard-lined western shore of Lake Neuchâtel and rises up to the craggy valleys of the Jura Mountains. The Jura is a deceptive region: its smoky, forested slopes, sheltering the "arc" of the Jurassian watch-making industry, suddenly flatten out onto open, sunny plateaux, gentle pastures, and low-roofed farm houses. Each of the cantons meanders along a porous line where French meets German; it's not unusual in certain towns to walk into a *boulangerie* selling dark *Vollkornbrot* (wholegrain bread) or to find a family named Neuenschwand that hasn't spoken German for generations. If you're looking for an untouristy experience, this is an excellent place for exploring.

Pleasures and Pastimes

Bicycling

Each region has miles of bicycle routes to choose from, and route maps can be picked up in most tourist offices. Swiss Federal Railways (CFF/SBB) offers reasonably priced rentals, including mountain bikes and children's bikes, at many train stations throughout the three cantons. Bicycles must be reserved at least one day in advance; in summer you should call at least three days in advance. Call the local tourist office or train station for details. In addition, tourist offices in Fribourg run a unique program called "Bike Broye." They've charted twenty different biking itineraries (a vineyard or abbey tour, for example) which can be paired with an overnight package. Contact local tourist boards for more information. To reserve an overnight package, contact the Avenches Tourist Office (☞ Visitor Information *in* Fribourg, Neuchâtel, and the Jura A to Z, *below*) at least three weeks in advance. (If you plan to do the tour in July, book at least two months in advance.)

Cheese

The name *Fribourg* immediately brings to mind *fondue fribourgeoise,* as the canton combines its two greatest cheeses—Gruyère and Vacherin—for a creamy *moitié-moitié* (half-and-half) blend. The Vacherin can be melted alone for an even creamier fondue; potatoes can be dipped instead of bread. From the Jura comes the Vacherin Mont d'Or—wood-ringed cheese so creamy you can spoon it out—or the Tête de Moine, the "monks head" cheese which is stuck on a metal post and shaved off in nutty-flavored ruffles.

You can find many places to view cheese being made; but those familiar cows that relieve the saturation of green in the Fribourg countryside yield more than cheese: we owe them an additional debt of gratitude for producing *crème-double*, a Gruyères specialty that rivals Devonshire cream. A rich, extra-thick, high-fat cream that—without whipping—almost supports a standing spoon, it is served in tiny carved-wood *baquets* (vats), to be spooned over a bowl of berries or a giant meringue, another regional specialty. When it's not pasteurized, you'll get a whiff of green meadows and new-mown hay.

Dining
In these three regions you'll reap the benefits of a great palette of tastes. Each region enjoys robust, seasonal food: perch from the lakes, trout from the streams, game and mushrooms from the forested highlands, plenty of savory, spicy sausage, and of course, the dairy products of Fribourg and Gruyères. These flavors are well paired with a fruity Fendant or crackling Vully wine.

The traditional autumn Fribourg feast, called Bénichon (Kilbi in Swiss German), embodies the region's love of fundamental food. Like the American Thanksgiving, it is a harvest feast that fetes not only the return of the cattle from the high pastures to the plains, but the season's final yield: chimney-smoked ham, served hot with *moutarde de Bénichon* (sweet mustard); mutton stew with plump raisins and potato puree; and tart *poires-à-Botzi* (pears poached and lightly caramelized). The main feast takes place during the second week of September, but restaurants across the region serve versions of Bénichon all fall.

In the lake towns, menus are thick with *perche* (perch), *sandre* (a large cousin of the perch), *bondelle* (a pearly fleshed trout found exclusively in Lake Neuchâtel), or *silure* (catfish).

Mushrooms are another strong suit, from the delicate *Schwämli* to the delicacy of the Jura, the *bolets*—fat, fleshy mushrooms with a meaty texture and taste. These are particularly wonderful when served with local rabbit or venison, and a glass of red Neuchâtel pinot noir.

CATEGORY	COST*
$$$$	over 70 SF
$$$	40 SF–70 SF
$$	20 SF–40 SF
$	under 20 SF

*Prices are per person for a three-course meal (two-course meal in $ category), including tax and 15% service charge.

Hiking and Walking
Fribourg is ideal hiking and walking country for every level of difficulty, with its rugged pre-Alps and flat lake lands. Hiking in the Jura offers open terrain and thick forest. All trails are well marked by yellow signs, and hiking maps are available at local tourist offices. If city wandering is more your style, the city of Neuchâtel has one of the country's largest pedestrian zones, the first Swiss city to designate such a zone. The winding streets of Fribourg are a tougher workout.

Lodging
As relatively untouristed cantons, Fribourg, Neuchâtel, and Jura have a less developed hotel infrastructure, which means fewer lodging choices but also more authentically homey hotels. Fribourg is by far the best-equipped, though there's only a handful of choices in the city itself. In Neuchâtel, most lodgings are along the lake; as you venture inland, there are fewer available. In the Jura, not all towns have hotels; you may prefer to make excursions from Neuchâtel or contact the tourist offices for recommendations.

CATEGORY	COST*
$$$$	over 250 SF
$$$	180 SF–250 SF
$$	120 SF–180 SF
$	under 120 SF

*Prices are for a standard double room, including breakfast, tax, and service charge.

Snowshoeing

This newly updated winter sport, involving lightweight plastic *raquettes de neige* that allow snow hikers to leave the trail, was revived in the Jura resort of St-Cergue a few years ago. You'll find hook-sole snowshoes in many Swiss sports shops and good company on the relatively gentle Jura Mountain slopes.

Exploring Fribourg, Neuchâtel, and the Jura

These three regions are roughly organized like a hand. At the wrist are the Alpine foothills of Fribourg; these curve gently down to the palm of flatter Neuchâtel, with the long ellipse of Lake Neuchâtel. The Jura's rugged fingers form valleys in the Jura Mountains and finally rest on the plateaux. The formal cantonal borders defy the Swiss penchant for neatness since they're based on medieval land-holdings. For instance, the present-day cantonal borders of Fribourg still surround odd bits belonging to other cantons, such as the town of Avenches, which technically belongs to Vaud.

Numbers in the text correspond to numbers in the margin and on the Fribourg, Neuchâtel, and the Jura map.

Great Itineraries

Though the major sights themselves require only a little time, they are grouped together in distant regions. You can explore much of this area by train with great ease, but renting a car will save you some time and allow you to go at your own pace (though many places are connected by two-lane roads often used by tractors).

IF YOU HAVE 1 OR 2 DAYS

Plan your itinerary according to your starting point. If you're coming from the east (Bern, Basel, or Zürich), start with the old town and lakefront promenade of ⌧ **Neuchâtel** ⑩; go on to the lakeside town of medieval **Murten** ⑨, then continue to ⌧ **Fribourg** ①. Make a side trip to **Gruyères** ③ on your way to Lausanne or Geneva. If you're coming from the south (Geneva or Lausanne), reverse the order.

IF YOU HAVE 3 OR MORE DAYS

More time allows you to leisurely crawl over ancient ramparts, wander through a medieval town, and visit a 17th-century château. Visit ⌧ **Fribourg** ①, then cut south to the castle at **Gruyères** ③; from there, circle northwest through the ancient towns of **Bulle** ④, **Romont** ⑤, **Payerne** ⑥, **Avenches** ⑧, and **Murten** ⑨. From Murten, go on to ⌧ **Neuchâtel** ⑩, then head south along the *route du vignoble* (vineyard route) to the château town of **Grandson** ⑪ and the spa town of **Yverdon-les-Bains** ⑫. Or you can go northwest from Neuchâtel through watchmaking country to **La Chaux-de-Fonds** ⑬; then go on to enjoy the natural beauty of the Jura, perhaps stopping at **Saignelégier** ⑭ to go horseback riding or cross-country skiing.

When to Tour Fribourg, Neuchâtel, and the Jura

Throughout the year you'll encounter lighter tourist traffic here than in any other region. Summer is a lovely time in the Jura, when forest glades become ripe with the smells of the woods. Fribourg is also pleasant in summer, but crowds tend to pick up, especially in Gruyères. Spring and fall are beautiful times to visit anywhere in this region.

FRIBOURG

With its landscape of green, rolling hills against the craggy peaks of the pre-Alps, Fribourg is one of Switzerland's most rural cantons; its famous Fribourgeois cows—the Holsteins (black and white, the colors of the cantonal coat of arms)—provide the canton with its main income, although light industry is replacing the cows. Fondue was invented here; Gruyère cheese and Switzerland's famous double-cream both originated here.

Fribourg

★ ❶ *34 km (21 mi) southwest of Bern.*

Between the rich pasturelands of the Swiss plateau and the Alpine foothills, the Sarine River twists in an S-curve, its sandstone cliffs joined by webs of arching bridges. Situated in one of the curves of the river is the old (nearly a thousand years behind it) city of Fribourg. The city grew in overlapping layers; it's an astonishing place of hills and cobblestones, medieval passageways and worn wooden stairs, red-orange rooftops and sudden views. Only on foot can you discover its secret, medieval charm.

Fribourg is a stronghold of Catholicism; it remained staunchly Catholic even during the Reformation. The evidence is everywhere, from the numerous chapels and religious orders to the brown-robed novitiates walking the sidewalks. Fribourg University, founded in 1889, remains the only Catholic university in Switzerland. It is also the only bilingual institution of its kind and reflects the region's peculiar linguistic agility. Two-thirds of the people of Canton Fribourg are native French speakers, one-third are native German speakers, and many switch easily between the two. In the *Basse-Ville* neighborhood, old-timers still speak a unique mixture of the two languages called *Boltz*. The city is officially bilingual, although French predominates.

At its very core, and a good place to start a walk, is the **Basse-Ville** (Lower City), tucked into a crook of the river, where you'll find the 11th through 16th century homes of the original village. The Bernese would come here for the lucrative Sunday business, since the extremely Catholic Fribourgeois were not allowed to work. It's now a lively café and cellar-theater scene. The oldest bridge in this city of bridges is the **Pont de Berne** (Bern Bridge), so called because it was then the only access to the territory of Bern. It's made entirely of wood. All Fribourg's bridges were once like this but were modernized; in the 19th century, engineers even built a series of spectacular suspension bridges strung high across the valley. Those bridges have been replaced by the solid, concrete arches you see today.

As the town expanded from the Basse-Ville, it crossed the river over the **Pont du Milieu** (Middle Bridge) to a narrow but nevertheless inhabitable bank, the **Planche-Inférieure**, a row of tightly packed houses. As the town prospered, it spread to the more stately 16th- and 17th-century **Planche-Supérieure,** a large, sloping, open triangular *place* (square) that was once the busy livestock market; it is now lined with several upscale restaurants and cafés. From here you can make a small detour to the **Chapelle de Lorette** (Loreto Chapel), once a favored pilgrimage site, at the far end of the square.

Fribourg, Neuchâtel, and the Jura

KEY

Rail Lines

Regional
Boundary Lines

Ski Resort

0 ___ 8 miles
0 ___ 12 km

N

SWITZERLAND

TO BASEL

Delémont

Les Rangiers

St-Ursanne

Porrentruy

Glovelier

Montfaucon

Saignelégier

Le Noirmont

Les Bois

La Chaux-de-Fonds

Le Locle

La Brévine

FRANCE

Doubs

JURA

FRANCHES-MONTAGNES

Tavannes

Moutier

Grenchen

Büren

Soncebox

Mt. Soleil

St-Imier

Chasseral

Vue des Alpes

NEUCHÂTEL

Colombier

La Sauge

Neuchâtel

St. Blaise

La Neuveville

Bieler See

Nidau

Biel/Bienne

Aarberg

Aare

Wohlensee

Aare

SOLOTHURN

BERN

Birs

Zihlkanal

Aare Kanal

When the **Pont St-Jean** was built in the 17th century, making the northern bank of the river readily accessible, the merchant houses and walled cloisters of the **Neuve-Ville** (New Town) popped up. From the steep, cobbled rue Grand-Fontaine, you can spy narrow passageways and hidden courtyards; or you can take the *funiculare* up and walk down the Route des Alpes to the **Hôtel de Ville,** or *Rathaus* (Town Hall). This is the seat of the cantonal parliament; it was built on the foundations of the château of Berthold IV of Zähringen, who founded the town of Fribourg in 1157. The symmetrical stairways were added in the 17th century, as were the clockworks in the 16th-century clock tower. The Place de Tilleul (Linden Square) has its own dramatic history (☞ Murten, *below*); nowadays it buzzes with a busy local market every Saturday morning. ✉ *Pl. de Tilleul.*

From the Place de Tilleul, the shop-lined rue de Lausanne and rue des Alpes climb upwards; their tightly spaced, 18th century buildings hide terraced gardens of surprising size. The 19th- and 20th-century section of the city begins at the top of rue de Lausanne. Here a McDonalds hides behind an 18th century facade and part of the ancient, stone city wall can be seen in the grocery section of the Placette department store. Nearby are the main buildings of the university.

NEED A
BREAK?

Belonging to the old, local Perriard family and sometimes still called that by townspeople, the **Confiserie Bürgisser** (✉ 61 rue de Lausanne, ☎ 026/3223489) has the best chocolate for miles around. Stop for a *ristrette* (espresso) or a *renversée* (coffee with milk) and a slice of rich, black truffle torte or caramelly nut torte. It's closed Monday.

A block away from the Hôtel de Ville is the **Cathédral St-Nicolas** (St. Nicholas Cathedral), which rears up from the gray, 18th century buildings in striking Gothic unity. Its massive tower was built in the 15th century, three centuries after the body of the cathedral was begun in 1283. It draws the Catholic powers of not only Fribourg but also Geneva and Lausanne, whose cathedrals now serve the Protestant faith. Above the main portal, a beautifully restored tympanum of the Last Judgment shows the blessed being gently herded left toward Peter, who holds the key to the heavenly gates; those not so fortunate head right, led by pig-face demons, into the jaws and cauldrons of hell. Inside the enormous structure you can see its famous 18th-century organ, built by Fribourger Aloys Mooser, as well as the rare 1657 organ built by Sebald Manderscheidt (completely restored in 1998). The exceptional stained-glass windows, dating from 1895 through 1936, are beautifully executed in a pre-Raphaelite and Art Nouveau style reminiscent of America's Louis Comfort Tiffany. In the **Chapelle du St-Sépulcre** (Chapel of the Holy Sepulcher) a group of 13 polished-wood figures dating from 1433 movingly portrays the entombment of Christ. If you can handle the stairs, climb up the tower. ✉ *3 rue des Chanoines,* ☎ *026/3223945.* ▨ *Free.* ☉ *Mon.–Sat. 7:30–7, Sun. 9–7.*

From the cathedral, slip through the rue des Épouses (street of the married) to the Grand Rue, lined with 18th century patrician homes. At the end of this street is the Sarine-spanning **Pont de Zaehringen** (Bridge of Zähringen), with views over the Pont de Berne, the Pont de Gottéron, and the wooden remains of the ancient towers that once guarded the entrance to the city. You're now in the area where Duke Berthold IV first established his residence and "founded" the city in 1157—so claims the Hotel Duc Berthold (☞ Dining and Lodging *below*).

The 13th-century **Église des Cordeliers** (Church of the Franciscan Friars), north of the Cathédrale St-Nicolas, is attached to a Franciscan friary; the lightness of its white walls and the rose, gray, and alabaster-colored ceiling contrast with the Gothic darkness of the cathedral. A 16th-century polyptych by the anonymous Nelkenmeister, or Maîtres à l'Oeillet (who signed their works only with red and white carnations) hangs over the high altar. A carved wood triptych, believed to be Alsatian, and a 15th-century retable by the Fribourg artist Hans Fries depicting the temptation of St. Anthony adorn the side walls. At the entrance to the *Kreuzgang/Cloître* (cloister) leading to the friary is a 13th-century, five-paneled fresco depicting the birth of the Virgin Mary. ⊠ *6 rue de Morat,* ☎ *026/3471160.* 🎫 *Free.* 🕐 *Mon.–Sat. 9–6, Sun. noon–6.*

Near the Church of the Franciscan Friars, on rue de Morat, are a couple of fascinating museums. The **Musée d'Art et d'Histoire de Fribourg** (Fribourg Museum of Art and History) occupies a Renaissance mansion and, incongruously, an old slaughterhouse connected to it by an underground passage. The graceful gray-stone Ratzé mansion, built in 1581–84, displays a concentration of local art from the 11th to 18th centuries as well as a strong collection on Fribourg archaeology. The museum's most striking aspect, however, is the 19th-century slaughterhouse, a stark stone structure modernized with steel and glass blocks to display a provocative mix of sacred sculptures (many from the cathedral) and the black whimsy of Jean Tinguely. The sun-washed attic gallery displays 19th- and 20th-century paintings from Delacroix and Courbet to Ferdinand Hodler. Cool your heels in the museum sculpture garden next to one of Niki de Saint Phalle's voluptuous figures. ⊠ *12 rue de Morat,* ☎ *026/3055140.* 🎫 *Permanent collection free; temporary expositions 5 SF–10 SF.* 🕐 *Tues.–Sun. 10–5, additional hrs Thurs. 8 PM–10 PM.*

Espace Jean Tinguely–Niki de Saint Phalle was once the city's tram terminal. The kinetic, metallic sculptures of Jean Tinguely (1925–91), a native Fribourgeois and an "ethnologist of the modern age," are paired with the oversized, joyously colorful works of his then wife, Niki de Saint Phalle. ⊠ *2 rue de Morat,* ☎ *026/3055140.* 🎫 *5 SF.* 🕐 *Wed.–Sun. 10–5, additional hrs Thurs. 8 PM–10 PM.*

Skiing

Winter sports in the *Alpes fribourgeoises* are popular; there are a variety of areas and possibilities for alpine and cross-country skiing, snowboarding, and luge (sledding). A bilingual (French/German) report on ski conditions for this entire area is available by calling ☎ 1573821.

Schwarzsee, (Lac Noir in French), a popular family resort in the Fribourg alps, lies at the end of a valley only 26 km (16 mi) southeast of Fribourg, nestled below several 2,000-m (6,560-ft) peaks; its lifts go up to 1,750 m (5,740 ft) for medium runs with spectacular views. At 1,050 m (3,449 ft), the mountain has three ski areas with 10 lifts, 25 km (15 mi) of downhill runs, and 10 km (6 mi) of cross-country trails. Parking can be difficult on weekends, but the post bus runs here from Fribourg. For the ski report in German, call ☎ 026/4121660.

Dining and Lodging

$$–$$$ ✕ **L'Aigle Noir.** The views of the Alps and the Old Town make this a worthwhile stop—especially if you can get a seat on the flagstone terrace in good weather. It mixes old and new; the building is a 17th-century nobleman's house on a narrow, cobbled backstreet, but the furnishings are modern, both in the restaurant and in the casual café. The food is a step above *cuisine bourgeoise*—beef with béarnaise sauce comes with delicate waffle chips instead of *frites* (french fries), and there are touches of ginger and mint. ⊠ *10 rue des Alpes,* ☎ *026/3224977. AE, DC, MC, V. Closed Sun.–Mon.*

$–$$ ✕ **Café du Midi.** This 17th-century, low-ceilinged, wood-paneled restau-
★ rant—the air thick with the smell of melting cheese—serves the best
fondue in Fribourg. You can stick to the traditional *moitié-moitié* or
try something different like the garlicky, herb-scented *fondue marseil-
laise.* Reservations recommended on weekends. ⊠ *25 rue Romont,* ☎
026/3223133. No credit cards.

$$$$ ✕▦ **Auberge de Zaehringen.** The oldest private house in Fribourg, now
★ a lovely auberge, has been owned by only three families during its 700
years. The restaurant offers elegant dishes such as a juniper-perfumed
rack of lamb with sweetbreads—and a view little changed for nearly
eight centuries. A gleaming suit of armor greets you in the warmly lighted
brasserie, with its great 17th-century wooden beams overhead. Choose
from specialties such as wild mushrooms cooked on a bed of crisp cabbage and served on puff pastry with a delicate thyme and rosemary
sauce, or a saffron fish soup. The two guest rooms are vast and luxurious, furnished with antiques, lush fabrics, and marble baths. Free cab
service to the hotel is offered from the train station if you telephone
in advance. Reservations are essential at the restaurant on weekends.
⊠ *13 rue de Zaehringen, CH-1700,* ☎ *026/3224236,* ℻ *026/3226908.
2 rooms. 2 restaurants, bar. DC, MC, V. Closed Mon. No dinner Sun.*

$$$ ✕▦ **Au Sauvage.** Once a gathering spot for Lower Town locals, this
renovated 17th-century auberge guards its spark of friendliness. Each
room has architectural details that remind you of its past. Thick me-
dieval walls might hide a TV or a collection of silver; white-tiled bath-
rooms include old-fashioned walnut vanities. The dining room, part
of which is under the original vaulted ceiling, is small but not cramped.
The sophisticated menu could include beef filet with Gorgonzola or
fish in a delicate ginger-lime sauce; for dessert, try plums lightly baked
with cream and served with cinnamon ice cream. The restaurant is
closed on Sunday and Monday. ⊠ *12 Planche-Supérieure, CH-1700,* ☎
026/3473060, ℻ *026/3473061. 17 rooms. Restaurant, bar. AE, DC,
MC, V.*

$$$$ ▦ **Golden Tulip.** This modern, multi-storied box within walking dis-
tance of the train station sits next to a park studded with a spouting
Tinguely fountain. The blue, gold, and walnut decor runs throughout
the hotel, except for the sedate green of the club-style bar. All rooms
have modem hook-ups. ⊠ *14 Grand Places, CH-1700,* ☎ *026/3519191,*
℻ *026/3519192. 130 rooms. Restaurant, bar, non-smoking floors, free
parking. AE, DC, MC, V.*

$$$ ▦ **Hotel Duc Berthold.** Berthold IV himself is said to have lived in this
ancient building in the 12th century. The smallish rooms have a com-
fortable, old-fashioned air with their delicate florals, creamy linens, and
reproduction antique furniture. Triple-glazed windows keep out the din
from the heavily trafficked Zähringen Bridge. ⊠ *5 rue des Bouchers,
CH-1700,* ☎ *026/3508100,* ℻ *026/3508181. 37 rooms. 2 restaurants,
bar, coffee shop. AE, DC, MC, V.*

$$ ▦ **Elite.** It's spare, slightly overpriced, and a bit dark, but it's conve-
niently located between the train station and the pedestrian zone of
the rue Romont. ⊠ *7 rue du Criblet, CH-1700,* ☎ *026/3223836,* ℻
026/3224036. 36 rooms. Restaurant, bar/café, sauna. AE, DC, MC, V.

Nightlife

An 18th-century inn, seemingly in the middle of nowhere, has been turned
into **Planet Edelweiss,** a lively *restaurant de nuit* and disco. The crowd
is wonderfully diverse; don't be surprised to spot a hefty farmer next
to a Bernese banker. Cordon bleu cooking is served under strings of
colored lights amidst papier mâché farm animals. It stays open until

2 AM Sunday to Tuesday, 3 AM on Wednesday and Thursday, and 4 AM on Friday and Saturday. It's about a five-minute drive northeast of town; a taxi from the train station would cost about 20 SF. ✉ *Mariahilf, Düdingen,* ☎ *026/4920505. AE, MC, V.*

Broc

❷ *33 km (20 mi) south of Fribourg.*

This otherwise unassuming town has a tantalizing draw for chocoholics. The **Nestlé** *chocolaterie* (chocolate factory), founded by Alexandre Cailler in 1889 and bought by Nestlé in 1929, offers a 40-minute tour with a video showing how the mundane and the exotic team up to make something irresistible the world over. Following the tour—fairly enough—is a chocolate tasting. Chocolate-brown road signs along the road from Gruyères (☞ *below*) indicate the way. ✉ *CH-1636,* ☎ *026/ 9215151.* ☜ *Free.* ☉ *May–Oct., weekdays 9–11 and 1:30–4. Reservations essential.*

Gruyères

★ ❸ *5 km (3 mi) south of Broc, 35 km (21 mi) south of Fribourg.*

The castle village of Gruyères rises above the plain on a rocky crag, its single, cobbled main street lined with medieval houses in perfect condition. With its traditional crest bearing a crane (*grue* in French), Gruyères is a perfect specimen of a medieval stronghold: It was once the capital of the idyllic Alpine estates of the Burgundian counts of Gruyères. The town is entirely car-free, so if you're driving, you'll need to park in one of three lots outside town and walk in (a short distance); arrive early to beat the crowds.

There were 19 counts holding political power over the region between 1080 and 1554; the last was Michael I of Gruyères, a lover of luxury and a big spender who expanded the estates and then fled his creditors, leaving vast holdings to Fribourg and Bern. In 1848 a wealthy Geneva family bought the old **château.** As patrons of the arts, they hosted the artist Corot; some of his panels grace the castle's drawing room. In a tour of the castle, you can also see the 13th-century dungeon and the living quarters, decorated in 16th- and 17th-century styles with tapestries, frescoes, and grand fireplaces. ✉ *CH-1663,* ☎ *026/9212102.* ☜ *5 SF.* ☉ *June–Sept., daily 9–6; Mar.–May and Oct., daily 9–noon and 1–5; Nov.–Feb., daily 9–noon and 1–4:30.*

Gruyères is known for its blue-and-white, or dark red-and-white pottery decorated with the *grue,* carved wooden spoons, creamy, nutty cheeses (Vacherin and Gruyère, spelled without the town's *s*), and the 48%-butterfat crème-double, which is dipped from a wooden *barque* and served with a bowl of berries or crumbly, sweet meringues. Before going up the hill to Gruyères, you can visit the demonstration **fromagerie** (cheese dairy), where the famous cheese is produced with fully modernized equipment. ☎ *026/9211410.* ☜ *Free.* ☉ *Daily 8–7; demonstrations at 10 and 2.*

For a more historical look at cheese-making, visit the Magnin family **fromagerie d'alpage** in nearby Moléson-sur-Gruyères. Here you can see first-hand how the true Gruyère cheese, called *Gruyère d'alpage,* gets its delicate, complex flavor. The family still makes cheese over an open fire in their low-roofed chalet. An exhibit explains the development of cheese-making since the 17th century; a 40-minute video in English describes the process. If all this gets your appetite going, there is also a small restaurant serving raclette and fondue. ✉ *Signposted.*

☎ 026/9211044. 📷 3 SF. ☉ Daily 9:30–7; demonstrations mid-May–mid-Oct., daily at 9 and 2.

OFF THE BEATEN PATH

CHARMEY, CRÉSUZ, LA VALSAINTE – If you're traveling by car from Gruyères, take the old Fribourg road (before you enter Bulle) and head north through Broc; soon after Broc the road splits and the right-hand branch heads into a valley toward Charmey/Jaun. Once you've passed Crésuz, but before reaching Charmey, cut left and take the narrow, winding road into La Valsainte. Peaceful and green, with few villages, the valley runs its way upward along a stream, past the austere and impressive Chartreux Monastery (founded by followers of St. Bruno at the end of the 13th century).

Skiing

Gruyères/Moléson, at 1,100 m (3,609 ft), offers skiing up to 2,002 m (6,568 ft), with wraparound views of the pre-Alps and on to Lake Geneva. It has three cable cars, four lifts, 20 km (12 mi) of downhill ski runs, and 8 km (5 mi) of cross-country trails. **Charmey,** a family resort at 900 m (2,953 ft), lies in a bowl surrounded by forested peaks; its one ski area stretches between Vounetz, at 1,627 m (5,337 ft), and the village itself. Slopes are of medium difficulty at best. The resort's charms lie more in its bucolic isolation (the *fête de la désalpe*, the procession of the cows coming down from the mountains, is celebrated every October). Charmey has eight lifts, including a gondola; 20 km (12 mi) of downhill runs; and 25 km (16 mi) of cross-country trails.

Dining and Lodging

$$$$ ✕ **Pinte des Mossettes.** In this spot that's truly away from it all, in-
★   credibly fresh preparations come with a dash of sophistication. From the terrace of this tiny restaurant, under a spreading chestnut, you can count the low, spreading roofs of the chalets dotting the steep hillsides. Owner-chef Judith Baumann, who won acclaim in 1998 as Switzerland's female chef of the year, prepares a monthly menu based on local ingredients and often homegrown produce. The menu translates into high-flown poetics: "a crown of Bresse poultry" or veal with rosemary essence. ⊠ *Road between Gruyères and La Valsainte, Cerniat,* ☎ FAX *026/9272097. AE, DC, MC, V. Closed Nov.–mid-Mar.*

$$ ✕ **Auberge de la Halle à Pied Cheval.** The unfussy interior of this medieval house, with its massive raftered ceiling, cool plaster walls edged with burgundy, and smooth stone floor, welcomes you like a 16th-century burgher's home. Choose a terrace according to its view: people-watching (front) or the town ramparts and the mountains (back). Then savor traditional Gruyères dishes, such as fondue with potatoes, macaroni with onions, and crème-double with raspberries. Another plus: the restaurant is less touristy than others on the main street. ⊠ *CH-1663,* ☎ *026/9212178. AE, DC, MC, V.*

$$ ✕🏨 **Le Vieux Chalet.** This self-conscious, carefully reconstructed "chalet," built in 1959, has tried to be as authentic as possible; the setting, the fabulous view from the large terrace, and the filling, traditional food make it worth the stop. Try the cheese dishes, such as Rösti with Vacherin, local ham, and berries with Gruyère crème-double. For an overnight, there are six bedrooms, all done in knotty pine. The restaurant is closed Tuesday. ⊠ *Road from Gruyères to Charmey, in direction of Jaun Pass, CH-1653 Crésuz,* ☎ *026/9271286. 6 rooms. Restaurant, café. AE, MC, V. Closed Dec.–mid-Feb.*

$$–$$$ 🏨 **Hostellerie des Chevaliers.** You need never mingle with the busloads
★   except in passing the upper parking lot, as this idyllic, atmospheric hotel stands aloof, well off the main tourist drag. It even has the same views as the castle, and back rooms overlook the broad valley. The decor is

a warm regional mix of antiques, handsome woodwork, and ceramic stoves—sometimes a little eccentric, as in the baths, which have been outfitted with teal or pumpkin tiles, and rooms, festooned with rich jewel tones and lavish prints. ⊠ CH-1663, ☎ 026/9211933, FAX 026/9212552. 32 rooms. Restaurant. AE, DC, MC, V. Closed Dec.–Feb.

$$ ⊞ **Fleur de Lys.** From its vaulted, stenciled reception area to its pine-
★ and-beam restaurant, this is a welcoming little hotel (originated in the 17th century) with pretty wood-paneled rooms and a wonderful rear terrace and garden that look over the mountains and castle. ⊠ CH-1663, ☎ 026/9212108, FAX 026/9213605. 10 rooms. Restaurant, café, bar. AE, DC, MC, V. Closed mid-Jan.–mid-Feb.

$ ⊞ **De Ville.** Directly on the picturesque main street, with back rooms overlooking the valley, this old family inn has been modernized with quarry tile, stucco, and pine. Five rooms are doubles with a shower instead of a full bath; there are also a triple and a pair of quads, all with full bath. ⊠ CH-1663, ☎ 026/9212424, FAX 026/9213628. 8 rooms. Restaurant. AE, DC, MC, V. Closed Jan.

Bulle

❹ 5 km (3 mi) northwest of Gruyères (toward the A12 expressway), 31 km (19 mi) southwest of Fribourg.

A small town of fewer than 10,000 people, Bulle condenses the attractions of a larger town: a castle (not open to the public), three-storied patrician houses lining the cobblestone main street, and a scenic backdrop so perfect that you might think it's been painted. You can learn about Gruyères traditions at the **Musée Gruérien,** with its displays of folk costumes, handicrafts, and farm tools—it even has a full reproduction of a flagstone farmhouse kitchen and dining room. ⊠ pl. du Cabalet, ☎ 026/9127260. ☞ 4 SF. ☉ Tues.–Sat. 10–noon and 2–5, Sun. 2–5.

Romont

❺ 15 km (9 mi) northwest of Bulle, 49 km (30 mi) southwest of Fribourg.

The best way to approach this 13th-century town of two broad streets is to leave the highway and drive up to its castle terrace. The fortress's 13th-century ramparts surround the town, forming a belvedere from which you can see the Alps—from Mont Blanc to the Berner Oberland—as well as other notable buildings: the 12th-century **Cistercian convent,** the 17th-century **Capuchin monastery,** and the lovely 13th-century *Collégiale,* one of the purest examples of a Gothic church in Switzerland, with period windows, sculptures, choir stalls, a screen, and an altarpiece. Inside the castle, the **Musée du Vitrail** (Stained Glass Museum) shimmers with crisscrossing shafts of colored light from the glass panels, both ancient and contemporary. A slide presentation traces the development of the craft, while a workshop area demonstrates current techniques. ⊠ Château, ☎ 026/6521095. ☞ 6 SF. ☉ Apr.–Oct., Tues.–Sun. 10–1 and 2–7; Nov.–Mar., weekends 10–noon and 2–6.

Payerne

❻ 15 km (9 mi) north of Romont, 18 km (11 mi) southwest of Fribourg.

The market town of Payerne has a magnificent 11th-century **église abbatiale** (abbey church), one of the finest examples of Romanesque art in Switzerland. Recent efforts have restored it to its functioning austere abbey, with a grand barrel-vaulted sanctuary and primitive capital carvings on the pillars. The meandering streets below the church are filled with pastel-painted, 18th-century buildings, now shops and

restaurants. ☎ 026/6626704. ⊠ 3 SF. ⊙ May–Oct., Mon.–Sat. 9–noon
and 2–6; Nov.–Apr., Tues.–Sat. 9–noon and 2–6.

Estavayer-le-Lac

❼ *7 km (4 mi) northwest of Payerne, 51 km (32 mi) southwest of Neuchâtel.*

On the shore of Lake Neuchâtel, this modest but charming lake town
has retained much of its medieval architecture, from the arcades of the
town center to the gracious, multitowered medieval **Château de
Chenaux,** which now houses city government offices. The humorous
and quirky **Musée de Grenouilles** (Frog Museum) displays 108 embalmed
frogs posed like people in scenes of daily life from the 19th century up
through the mid-1900s. Other exhibits include an authentic 17th-cen-
tury kitchen, various military and household artifacts dredged from
Lake Neuchâtel, and more than 200 Swiss railroad lanterns, some up
to 100 years old. ⊠ rue des Musées, CH-1470, ☎ 026/6632448. ⊠
3 SF. ⊙ Mar.–June and Sept.–Oct., Tues.–Sun. 9–11 and 2–5; July–Aug.,
daily 9–11 and 2–5; Nov.–Feb., weekends 2–5.

Avenches

★ **❽** *5 km (3 mi) northeast of Estavayer-le-Lac, 13 km (8 mi) northeast of
Fribourg.*

Avenches (technically in Canton Vaud) is the old capital of the Helve-
tians, which, as Aventicum, grew into an important city that reached
its peak in the 2nd century AD. In its prime, the Roman stronghold was
surrounded by some 6 km (4 mi) of 2-m-high (6-ft-high) stone walls.
The Alemanni destroyed it in the 3rd century. The town's **castle** was
built at the end of the 13th century by the Bishops of Lausanne and
has belonged to the town since 1804. Aside from its Renaissance-style
facade and portal, you'll find a tiny museum dedicated to Swiss avia-
tors (open on weekends from 2–4) and a small art gallery (open
Wednesday through Sunday, 2–6). Closed Dec.–Mar.

You can still see the remains of a Roman forum, a bathhouse, and an
amphitheater—today the **Musée et Théâtre Romains** (Roman Museum
and Theater)—where bloodthirsty spectators once watched the games.
Now opera-lovers gather here for an annual July evening spectacle; contact the tourist office well in advance for tickets. The collection of Roman
antiquities at the museum is noteworthy, including an excellent copy
of a gold bust of Marcus Aurelius, unearthed at Avenches in the 1920s,
the original of which is in Lausanne. ☎ 026/6751730. ⊠ 2 SF. ⊙ Apr.–
Sept., Tues.–Sun. 10–noon and 1–5; Oct.–Mar., Tues.–Sun. 2–5.

Murten

★ **❾** *6 km (4 mi) northeast of Avenches, 17 km (11 mi) north of Fribourg.*

The ancient town of Murten, known in French as Morat, is a popular
resort on Lac de Morat (Murten Lake), with a boat-lined waterfront,
windsurfer rentals, grassy picnic areas, and a promenade. It was here,
on June 22, 1476, that the Swiss Confederates—already a fearsomely
efficient military machine—attacked with surprising ferocity and won
a significant victory over the Burgundians, who were threatening Fribourg under the leadership of Duke Charles the Bold. Begun as a siege
12 days earlier, the battle cost the Swiss 410 men, the Burgundians
12,000. The defeat at Murten prevented the establishment of a large
Lothringian kingdom and left Switzerland's autonomy unchallenged
for decades. Legend has it that a Swiss runner, carrying a linden branch,

ran from Murten to Fribourg to carry the news of victory. He expired by the town hall, and a linden tree grew from the branch he carried. Today, to commemorate his dramatic sacrifice, some 15,000 runners participate annually on the first Sunday in October in a 17-km (11-mi) race up the steep hill from Murten to Fribourg. As for the linden tree, it flourished in Fribourg for some 500 years, until 1983, when it was ingloriously felled by a car and replaced with a steel sculpture.

Bilingual Murten/Morat has a superbly preserved medieval center. Leave your car in the parking area before the 13th century gates and stroll the fountain-studded cobblestone streets; you can even climb up the worn wooden steps of the town ramparts. The **Musée Historique** (Historical Museum) is in the town's old mill, complete with two water-powered mill wheels; on view are prehistoric finds, military items, and trophies from the Burgundian Wars. ⊠ *Historic center,* ☎ *026/6703100.* ☜ *4 SF.* ☉ *Oct.–Dec. and Mar.–Apr., Tues.–Sun. 2–5; May–Sept., Tues.–Sun. 10–noon and 2–5; Jan.–Feb., weekends 2–5.*

Dining and Lodging

$$$$ ✕▥ **Le Vieux Manoir au Lac.** Just one kilometer (½ mile) south of Murten
★ on Lake Murten, this stately mansion is a graceful mix of half-timbering and turrets, with a deep Fribourg roofline. Sprawling comfortably across a manicured park near the lakefront, it exudes a manorial grace you won't find elsewhere in Switzerland, even in other Relais & Châteaux properties. The decor is an eclectic mix of parquet and Persian rugs, wing chairs, Biedermeier, and country prints; rooms are a rich blend of chintz, gingham, and toile de Jouy. The restaurant offers a choice of seasonal sampling menus, each with a French/Continental bent; options might include roast lamb with mustard sauce or a lasagna of asparagus with truffle butter. A winter garden allows you to dine in a room bathed with light, just yards from the shore of the lake. ⊠ *rue de Lausanne, CH-3280 Meyriez,* ☎ *026/6786161,* ℻ *026/6786162. 30 rooms. Restaurant. AE, DC, MC, V. Closed mid-Dec.–mid-Feb.*

$$$ ✕▥ **Schiff.** This low, white-fronted building below the town nabbed an ideal setting; its sheltered terrace gives directly onto a shady park and the waterfront promenade. Inside, homey touches such as Persian rugs, antiques, and shining gilt add character. The restaurant, Lord Nelson, wraps around the garden and serves ambitious French cuisine on the terrace or in a room with a nautical theme, both with lake views. Specialties may include risotto with porcini mushrooms and pigeon breast or classic local trout, perch, or pike, sold by weight. (The restaurant is closed on Wednesday and Thursday.) The Schiff is a "velo-hotel;" bicycles are welcome, and they can help you rent one in town. ⊠ *Ryf 53, CH-3280,* ☎ *026/6702701,* ℻ *026/6703531. 15 rooms. Restaurant, bar, café. AE, DC, MC, V.*

$$–$$$ ✕▥ **Weisses Kreuz.** Though it shares great lake views with other ho-
★ tels in town, this lodging has more to offer: the devotion—even obsession—of its owners (it has been in one family since 1921). There are two buildings, and though you might be tempted by lakeside panoramas, consider the wing with Old Town views across the street; it's furnished in extraordinary style with complete antique bedroom sets—Biedermeier, Art Nouveau, Louis XVI, Empire. Simpler rooms, in Scandinavian pine or high-tech style, cost less. The lovely formal dining room is known for its broad array of fish specialties: whitefish with chanterelles and cucumbers, timbale of three lake fish, pike braised in dill. ⊠ *Rathausg. 31, CH-3280,* ☎ *026/6702641,* ℻ *026/6702866. 27 rooms. Restaurant, café. AE, DC, MC, V. Closed mid-Dec.–mid-Feb.*

$$ ▥ **Krone.** Not all of Murten is "bourgeois chic." The quirky Krone has its own following and what it lacks in tidiness it makes up in character (including the owner, a self-styled cowboy). Rooms are small, clean, and patched, with a mix of furniture veering toward shabby, but the views from the back rooms are great. The standard-Swiss restaurant is locally known as a good, casual place to eat. ⊠ *5 Rathausg., CH-3280,* ☎ *026/6705252,* FAX *026/6703610. 33 rooms. Restaurant, bar, 2 cafés. AE, DC, MC, V.*

LAC NEUCHÂTEL

The region of Neuchâtel belonged to Prussia from 1707 to 1857, with a brief interruption caused by Napoléon and a period of double loyalty to Prussia and the Swiss Confederation between 1815 and 1857. Yet its French culture remains untouched by Germanic language, diet, or culture. Some boast that the inhabitants speak "the best French in Switzerland," which is partly why so many summer language courses are taught here.

Neuchâtel

★ ⑩ *28 km (17 mi) north of Murten, 48 km (30 mi) northwest of Fribourg.*

The city of Neuchâtel, at the foot of the Jura mountains, flanked by vineyards and facing southeast, enjoys remarkable views across Lac Neuchâtel and the whole crowded range of the middle Alps, from the majestic mass of Mont Blanc to the Bernese Oberland. (Lac Neuchâtel, at 38 km/24 mi long and 8 km/5 mi wide, is the largest in the country.) A prosperous city, Neuchâtel has a reputation for precision work, beginning with watchmaking in the early 18th century. It possesses an air of almost tangible dignity; in the lower part of town, bordering the placid lake, broad avenues are lined with imposing yellow-sandstone buildings which inspired author Alexandre Dumas to call it "a city with the appearance of an immense *joujou* dressed in butter". The overall effect is of unruffled but compact grandeur—the castle and cathedral look gracefully down on the city's bustling Old Town and market place thronged with lively, urban street life.

The extent of French influence in Neuchâtel is revealed in its monuments and architecture, most notably at the **Église Collégiale** (Collegiate Church), a handsome Romanesque and Burgundian Gothic structure dating from the 12th century, with a colorful tile roof. (For anyone not wanting to climb steep streets, the church and prison tower may be reached from the Promenade Noire off the Place des Halles by an inconspicuous elevator—*Ascenseur publique.*) The church contains a strikingly realistic and well-preserved grouping of life-size painted figures called *le cénotaphe,* or monument to the counts of Neuchâtel; dating from the 14th and 15th centuries, this is considered one of Europe's finest examples of medieval art. It was restored between 1997 and 1999. Grouped around the church are the ramparts and cloisters of the 12th-century **château,** which today houses the cantonal government. A tour of the château (available in English) is the only way to see the cantonal high courtroom, a fascinating display of every family crest that ever married into the governing dynasty of Neuchâtel. ⊠ *12 rue de la Collegiale,* ☎ *032/8896000.* 🎫 *Free.* ◷ *Daily 8–6.*

The **Tour des Prisons** (Prison Tower), which adjoins the Collegiate Church, affords panoramic views from its turret. On your way up, stop in one of the original wooden prison cells; on the landings you can see models of the city as it evolved from the 15th through the 18th centuries. ⊠ *rue Jeanne de Hochberg,* ☎ *032/8896000.* 🎫 *50 centimes.* ◷ *Daily 8–6.*

The **architecture of the Old Town** demonstrates a full range of French styles, far beyond the Gothic. Along rue des Moulins are two perfect specimens of the Louis XIII period, and—at its opposite end—a fine

Louis XIV house anchors the Place des Halles (market square), also notable for its turreted 16th-century **Maison des Halles**. The **Hôtel de Ville** (⊠ Rue de l'Hôtel de Ville), opened in 1790 east of the Old Town, is by Pierre-Adrien Paris, Louis XVI's architect. There are several fine patrician houses, such as the magnificent **Hôtel DuPeyrou** (⊠ 1 av. DuPeyrou, east of Old Town), home of the friend, protector, and publisher of Jean-Jacques Rousseau, who studied botany in the nearby Val-de-Travers. Most of the Old Town is a pedestrian zone, though public buses do run through it.

★ For connoisseurs not only of art but of art museums, the **Musée d'Art et d'Histoire** (Museum of Art and History) merits a pilgrimage. Thanks to a remarkably unprovincial curator, it displays a deep collection of paintings gathered under broad themes—nature, civilization—and mounted in a radical, evocative way. Fifteenth-century allegories, early Impressionism, and contemporary abstractions pack the walls from floor to ceiling: interacting, conflicting, demanding comparison. You may climb a platform (itself plastered with paintings) to view the higher works. This aggressive series of displays is framed by the architectural decorations of Neuchâtel resident Clement Heaton, whose murals and stained glass make the building itself a work of art.

This novel museum also has the honor of hosting three of this watch-making capital's most exceptional guests: the **automates Jaquet-Droz**, three astounding little androids, created between 1768 and 1774, that once toured the courts of Europe like young mechanical Mozarts. Pierre Jaquet-Droz and his son Henri-Louis created them, and they are moving manifestations of the stellar degree to which watchmaking had evolved by the 18th century. One automaton is called **Le Dessinateur** (the Draughtsman). A dandy in satin knee pants, he draws graphite images of a dog, the god Eros in a chariot pulled by a butterfly, and a profile of Louis XV. **La Musicienne** (the Musician) is a soulful young woman who plays the organ, moving and breathing subtly with the music, and actually striking the keys that produce the organ notes, also authentic. **L'Écrivain** (the Writer) dips a real feather in real ink and writes 40 different letters, capital and lowercase; like a primitive computer, he can be programmed to write any message simply by changing a steel disk. The automates are viewable only on the first Sunday of the month, at 2, 3, or 4, or by appointment, but an audio-visual show and a close-up view of them is enough to re-create the thrill. ⊠ *quai Léopold-Robert*, ☎ *032/ 7177925.* ▣ *7 SF; free Thurs.* ☉ *Tues.–Sun. 10–5, Thurs. 10–9.*

Ⓒ The **Papiliorama** and **Nocturama** literally crawl with life; two separate domes contain two completely different tropical biospheres. The **Papiliorama** pulses with humid tropical plants, lily ponds, more than a thousand living butterflies, dwarf caimans (*crocodilians*), tortoises, birds, fish, and gigantic tropical insects—the latter, fortunately, in cages. The **Nocturama** is filled with bats, opossums, raccoons, skunks, and other nocturnal creatures. Just 5 km (3 mi) from Neuchâtel, you can get there by car or train. ⊠ *Marin,* ☎ *032/7534344.* ▣ *Both domes: 11 SF.* ☉ *Apr.–Sept., daily 9–6; Oct.–Mar., daily 10–5.*

Dining and Lodging

$–$$ ✕ **Du Banneret.** This popular restaurant, built of yellow Neuchâtel sandstone in late-Renaissance style, is across from a colorful fountain. Lying at the foot of the rue du Château, the brasserie is a cozy gathering place, where the chef often emerges to greet his guests. The brasserie has a low, beamed ceiling with huge stones framing the windows facing the fountain; the dishes are mostly regional fare, such as homemade pasta with fresh wild mushrooms or lake trout. In the upstairs dining room, the food takes a strong Italian twist. ⊠ *1 rue Fleury,* ☎ *032/7252861. AE, DC, MC, V. Closed Sun.*

$ ✕ **Le Cardinal Brasserie.** At one of the most authentic cafés in the Old Town, stop and have a perfect café crème or light meal along with the Neuchâteloise. A molded ceiling, etched windows, and blue and green decorative tile from 1905 give it a turn-of-the-century feel. Daily specials might include a plate of smoked salmon, trout, or leg of rabbit. ⊠ *9 rue du Seyon,* ☎ *032/7251286. No credit cards.*

$$$ ✕▦ **Auberge de l'Aubier.** Just a 10-minute drive west from Neuchâtel, this small auberge on the lake is akin to an eco-retreat. There are solar panels on the barn, rainwater is used in the washing machines, and you can be sure the kitchen's ingredients are fresh—the auberge runs its own organic farm. Each guest room has an individual theme, and on a clear day you can make out Mont Blanc. Vegetarian food takes an imaginative twist, such as the *gallets de cèreal* (whole-grain patties) served with an herb-flavored, sour-cream-like sauce. It's a good idea to make a reservation in advance. ⊠ *CH-2205 Montézillon,* ☎ *032/7303010,* ℻ *032/7303016. 15 rooms. Restaurant, shop, meeting rooms. AE, MC, V. No smoking.*

$ ✕▦ **Du Marché.** Opening directly onto the Place des Halles, this is a delightful place for a hearty plat du jour or a carafe of local wine. Inside, pass through the lively bar-café to the steamy, old-wood brasserie for a bowl of tripe in Neuchâtel wine or salt pork with lentils. Upstairs, a pretty little dining room serves more sophisticated fare. Plain, functional rooms with tidy tile bathrooms down the hall are an excellent value. ⊠ *4 Pl. des Halles, CH-2000,* ☎ *032/7245800,* ℻ *032/7214742. 10 rooms. Restaurant, café. AE, DC, MC, V.*

$$$$ ▦ **Beau-Rivage.** This thoroughly elegant, restored 19th century hotel
★ sits gracefully on the lakeshore; on clear days there's a splendid view of the Alps. Its warmly lighted, high-ceiling, wild cherry wood interior exudes a feeling of stately calm. Each of the spacious rooms has a modem hookup with fax availability; bathrobes hang in the white tiled bathrooms. (Two-thirds of the rooms have lake views.) The sophisticated dining room, done in pale green, has a magnificent view, not to mention a fine selection of after-dinner cigars and brandies. ⊠ *1 esplanade du Mont Blanc, CH-2001,* ☎ *032/7231515,* ℻ *032/ 7231616. 65 rooms. Restaurant, bar. AE, DC, MC, V.*

$$-$$$$ ▦ **La Maison du Prussien.** Ten minutes from the bustle of Neuchâtel in the gorge of Vauseyon, this 16th-century restored mill, part of the Romantik chain, nestles alongside a roaring woodland stream. The polished beams, stone walls, terra-cotta floors, and lush views from every window make it softly romantic. Every room or suite has a name and a unique decor; three have fireplaces. Take the tunnels under Neuchâtel toward La Chaux-de-Fonds, exit toward Pontarlier-Vauseyon, and then watch for the hotel's signs. ⊠ *Au Gor du Vauseyon, CH-2006,* ☎ *032/7305454,* ℻ *032/7302143. 6 rooms, 4 suites. Restaurant, brasserie, café. AE, DC, MC, V.*

$$ ▦ **Alpes et Lac.** This modest hotel across from the train station overlooks the tile rooftops, the sparkling lake, and the white-capped Alps. The building's renovation preserved the ancient parquet floors and stone steps; along the pale yellow corridors, fresh flowers hide in niches. The gold-and-red checked bedspreads in the medium-sized rooms echo the colors found throughout this sunny hotel. A lovely park surrounds the terrace. ⊠ *2 pl. de la Gare, CH-2002,* ☎ *032/7231919,* ℻ *032/ 7231920. 30 rooms. 2 restaurants. AE, DC, MC, V.*

Outdoor Activities and Sports

BIKING

Neuchâtel has about 400 km (248 mi) of marked mountain-bike trails. You can rent mountain bikes at **Alizé** (⊠ pl. du 12-Septembre, ☎ 032/ 7244090) or through the train station. Free trail maps are available at the tourist office (☞ Visitor Information *in* Fribourg, Neuchâtel, and the Jura A to Z, *below*).

There's an 18-hole golf course at **Voëns sur St-Blaise** (☎ 032/7535550).

There are **public beaches** at nearly every village and resort around Lake Neuchâtel and Lake Murten, plus a **municipal complex** (✉ Nid du Crô Rte des Falaises 30, ☎ 032/7214848) with outdoor and indoor pools, open daily, in Neuchâtel.

Nightlife

For night owls, Neuchâtel has an ever-changing selection of *restaurants de nuit* and *bars musicaux*, establishments that pulse with disco music till the wee hours of the morning and sometimes serve food (along the lines of *steak-frites*) to keep you going. The best-known for food, if you don't mind loud music and smoke, is the techno-metallic **Garbo Café** (✉ 5–7 rue des Chavannes, ☎ 032/7243181). **Casa d'Italia** offers a more varied menu without the disco (✉ 1 rue de Prebarreau, off the rue de l'Ecluse, ☎ 032/7250858). **La Rotonde** (✉ 14 Faubourg du Lac, ☎ 032/7244848) squeezes in four different discos under one roof but does not serve food. **Seven** (✉ 3 av. de la Gare, ☎ 032/7100705) is for fans of European techno. **Le Shakespeare** (✉ 7 rue des Terreaux, ☎ 032/7258588), a bar/pub, remains the most conservative.

En Route   Just a few miles west of Neuchâtel lie some of Switzerland's best **vineyards,** their grapes producing chiefly white and rosé wines that are light and slightly sparkling. The wines are bottled before the second fermentation, so they have a rather high carbonic-acid content. The tourist office has a map of the *route du vignoble* (Vineyard Road). Three of the larger vintners are **Cave Jungo et Fellerman** in Cressier (☎ 032/7571162), **Caves de Cortaillod** in Cortaillod (☎ 032/8412064), and **Château Boudry** in Tour de Pierre (☎ 032/8421098). If you'd like to arrange a tasting, your best bet would be to call and set up an appointment. Neuchâtel's biggest annual festival is the winemakers' three-day celebration of the grape harvest, the *fête des vendanges*. It's celebrated the last weekend of September with parades and fanfare throughout the city.

Grandson

⓫ *29 km (18 mi) southwest of Neuchâtel.*

This lakeside village in Canton Vaud has a long history. It is said that in 1066 a member of the Grandson family accompanied William of Normandy (better known as the Conqueror) to England, where he founded the English barony of Grandison. Otto I of Grandson took part in the Crusades. When the Burgundian Wars broke out in the late 15th century, the **Château de Grandson** (Grandson Castle), built in the 11th century and much rebuilt during the 13th and 15th centuries, was in the hands of Charles the Bold of Burgundy. In 1475 the Swiss won it by siege, but early the next year their garrison was surprised by Charles, and 418 of their men were captured and hung from the apple trees in the castle orchard. A few days later the Swiss returned to Grandson and, after crushing the Burgundians, retaliated by stringing their prisoners from the same apple trees. After being used for three centuries as a residence by the Bernese bailiffs, the castle was bought in 1875 by the de Blonay family, which restored it to its current impressive state, with high, massive walls and five cone turrets. Inside, you can see a reproduction of a Burgundian war tent, *oubliettes* (dungeon pits for prisoners held *in perpetua*), torture chambers, and a model of the Battle of Grandson, complete with 20-minute slide show. Cassette-guided tours of the town are available at the castle reception desk. ☎ 024/4452926. ✉ 8 SF. ☉ Apr.–Oct., daily 9–6; Nov.–Jan., Sat. 1–5 and Sun. 9–5 or by request; Feb.–Mar., Mon.–Sat. 8:30–11:30 and 1:30–5, Sun. 9–5.

Yverdon-les-Bains

⑫ 6 km (4 mi) southwest of Grandson, 36 km (22 mi) southwest of Neuchâtel.

This pastel-colored lakefront town at the southernmost tip of Lake Neuchâtel has been appreciated for its thermal waters and sandy, willow-lined shoreline since the Romans first invaded and set up thermal baths here. In the 18th century its fame spread across Europe; today the **Thermal Center** (✉ ave. des Bains 22; ☎ 024/4230232) is completely up-to-date, offering medicinal as well as recreational pools.

On a point of land jutting into the lake sits the turreted, mid-13th-century **Château de Yverdon-les-Bains.** Most of the castle is now a museum, with exhibits on locally found prehistoric and Roman artifacts, Egyptian art, natural history, and of course, local history. The 12th-century trade boats on the lower floor suggest the lake's importance at one time. A special room is dedicated to the famous Swiss educator Johann Heinrich Pestalozzi (1746–1827), who spent 20 years here. His influential ideas on education led to school reforms at home and in Germany and England. ☎ 024/4259310. ✉ 6 SF. ☉ June–Sept., daily 10–noon and 2–5; Oct.–May, Tues.–Sun. 2–5.

In front of Yverdon's Hôtel de Ville (Town Hall)—notable for its Louis XV facade—stands a bronze monument of Pestalozzi, grouped with two children. The charming, bustling town center is closed to traffic. Along the waterfront you'll find parks, promenades, a shady campground, and a 5 km (3 mi) stretch of little beaches.

THE JURA

Straddling the French frontier from Geneva to Basel is a range of low-riding mountains (few peaks exceed 1,500 m) that fall steeply down to the mysterious river Doubs to the north and to the lakes to the south. The secret of this region, known as the Jura, is the sunny plateau atop the mountains, especially in the Montagnes Neuchâteloise and the Franches-Montagnes in the Jura canton. These lush pastures and gentle woods have excellent hiking, biking, horseback-riding, and cross-country skiing opportunities—perfectly organized yet unspoiled. (La Brévine, between Le Locle and Les Verrières, is known as the Swiss Siberia.) Administratively, the Jura region is shared by four cantons: Jura, Vaud, Neuchâtel, and Basel. Culturally, it is unified by language (French, except for Basel), economy, and spirit. Watchmaking concentrates around Le Locle and La Chaux-de-Fonds, while horse breeding and tourism flourish in the Franches-Montagnes.

En Route   From Neuchâtel into the Jura Mountains, the A20 highway climbs 13 km (8 mi) from Neuchâtel to the **Vue des Alpes,** a parking area on a high ridge that affords, as the name implies, spectacular views of the Alps, including Mont Blanc.

La Chaux-de-Fonds

⑬ 22 km (14 mi) north of Neuchâtel.

During the early 18th century, watchmaking was introduced in La-Chaux-de-Fonds (called Tschaux by locals) as a cottage industry to create income for an area otherwise completely dependent on farming. Over the years, the town became the watchmaking capital of Switzerland. Destroyed by fire at the end of the 18th century, the city was rebuilt on a grid plan around the central, broad, tree-lined avenue Léopold-Robert. It is a city of incongruities: pastel-painted townhouses and stone villas, working-class cafés and cultural institutions. It is a city that rewards effort.

Famed architect Charles-Édouard Jeanneret, otherwise known as Le Corbusier, was born here. His birthplace can be seen, although not toured, along with the École d'Art, where he taught, and several villas he worked on between 1906 and 1917. Only one of his buildings is open to the public: the **Villa turque,** north of the main avenue. It has a glowing, terracotta brick facade, rounded wings, and curved edges. The tourist office has a brochure outlining a walk that passes by his buildings. ⊠ *147 rue du Doubs,* ☎ *032/9123131.* ⊡ *Free.* ⊙ *Sat. 11–4 or by appointment.*

The **Musée des Beaux-Arts** (Museum of Fine Arts), a striking neoclassical structure, was designed by Le Corbusier's teacher L'Éplattenier; it contains a furniture set, an oil painting (*Seated Woman*), and a tapestry (*Les Musiciens*) by Le Corbusier. There are also works by such other Swiss artists as Léopold Robert and Ferdinand Hodler. ⊠ *33 rue des Musées,* ☎ *032/9130444.* ⊡ *6 SF, Sun. free 10–noon.* ⊙ *Tues.–Sun. 10–noon and 2–5.*

★ The **Musée International d'Horlogerie** (International Timepiece Museum) displays a fascinating collection of clocks and watches that traces the development of timekeeping and the expansion of watchmaking as an art form. You can see audiovisual presentations on the history and science of the craft, observe current repairs on pieces from the collection in an open work area, and browse the gift shop, which sells replicas as well as the latest timepieces by stellar local watchmaking firms (Corum, Girard-Perregaux, Ebel, and so on). ⊠ *29 rue des Musées,* ☎ *032/9676861.* ⊡ *8 SF.* ⊙ *Oct.–May, Tues.–Sun. 10–noon and 2–5; June–Sept., Tues.–Sun. 10–5.*

Lodging

$$ ⊞ **Fleur-de-Lys.** This friendly spot has a standard interior with a few extra perks: fresh fruit and snacks along with the usual amenities (minibar, TV, safe). Though the hotel sits on the main thoroughfare, the rooms—done in muted colors—are quiet. The restaurant is popular with locals. ⊠ *13 av. Léopold-Robert, CH-2300,* ☎ *032/9133731,* FAX *032/9135851. 28 rooms. Restaurant, bar, meeting room. AE, DC, MC, V.*

$ ⊞ **Du Cheval Blanc.** Behind the spring-green front of this warm, hospitable, 18th-century *routier* are clean, comfortable rooms with dormer windows. It's within easy walking distance of the museum and train station. ⊠ *16 rue Hôtel-de-Ville, CH-2300,* ☎ *032/9684098,* FAX *032/ 9684055. 13 rooms. Restaurant. V.*

Skiing

La Chaux-de-Fonds is very close to cross-country ski areas and some modest downhill runs as well. The **Tête-de-Ran,** beyond Vue des Alpes, tops 1,400 m (4,592 ft) and allows skiers to take in panoramic views toward the Bernese Alps. Together, **Vue des Alpes, Tête-de-Ran, La Corbatière,** and **Le Locle** count 31 lifts, 27 km (16 mi) of downhill runs, and 400 km (nearly 250 mi) of cross-country trails. Call ☎ 157/ 160130 for a bilingual (French/German) bulletin on ski conditions.

En Route **LE NOIRMONT –** Twenty minutes by car or train from La Chaux-de-
★ Fonds on the way to Saignelégier is one of Switzerland's top gourmet restaurants, Hôtel-Restaurant de la Gare. Chef Georges Wenger creates

an atmosphere of rural gentility. He mixes French and Jurassiènne influences and has made himself an expert on updating the Jura's regional specialties, with dishes such as roasted quail with wild garlic and new carrots with pistachios, grilled tuna with grapefruit and laurel, and an assortment of local cheeses. The three rooms and two mansard suites, all tastefully decorated and equipped with extravagant bathrooms, overlook the hiking and skiing trails in the valley beyond. ⊠ *2 rue de la Gare, CH-2340,* ☎ *032/9531110,* FAX *032/951059. 5 rooms. Restaurant. AE, MC, V. Closed Mon. and Tues.*

Saignelégier

⑭ *26 km (16 mi) northwest of La Chaux-de-Fonds, 36 km (22 mi) southwest of Delémont.*

A small, fairly modern town set in rolling pastures, Saignelégier is known mostly for its lush surroundings, horseback riding, and cross-country skiing. The *Marché-Concors National de Chevaux* (National Horse Fair), held since 1897, takes place on the second Sunday in August and draws crowds from throughout Switzerland and France, as does the *fête des Montgolfières* (Hot-Air Balloon Festival) the second weekend of October. It's also a good place for bicycling (rentals available at the train station).

Lodging

$ 🏨 **Du Soleil.** For the bohemian at heart, the Soleil is a great gathering place. Local artwork hangs in the café—a warm spot with massive wood ceiling beams and worn kitchen tables. Live music, often jazz, wafts from the indoor baby grand or the tree-shaded garden. Rooms are spartan but clean; all have writing desks. It's just across from the town's equestrian center. ⊠ *CH-2350,* ☎ *032/9511688,* FAX *032/9512295. 7 rooms, 1 dormitory. Restaurant, café, terrace. MC, V.*

Outdoor Activities and Sports

BICYCLING

As soon as the snow melts, cyclists hit the cross-country tails. The Chemin de Fer du Jura (Jura Railway) offers special "Rent-a-Bike" packages; call the local train station or the central office in Saignelégier (☎ 032/9511822). Call at least three days in advance.

HORSEBACK RIDING

This is terrific horseback-riding country. Many individual farms offer weekend riding packages geared for families; contact the tourist office for information (☞ Visitor Information *in* Fribourg, Neuchâtel, and the Jura A to Z, *below*). You can also rent horses at the **Manège de Saignelégier** (☎ 032/951755).

SPORTS CENTER

The modern **Centre de Loisirs** (☎ 032/9512474) has an impressive array of facilities: a covered 25-m swimming pool, indoor ice rink, gymnasium, weight room, even conference rooms and a restaurant. There are cross-country ski tracks nearby. A map in front of the sports center displays a network of nearby trails for biking or hiking; trails are clearly indicated with yellow markers.

St-Ursanne

⑮ *22 km (14 mi) west of Delémont, 27 km (17 mi) from Saignelégier.*

This lovely, quiet medieval town in a valley carved by the River Doubs is best known to outdoors enthusiasts—fishermen, bicyclists, canoeists, and kayakers. The 12th-century church, **la Collégiale,** is a mixture of Romanesque and early Gothic architecture; the large cloisters are Gothic. The old stone bridge over the River Doubs, with its statue of

St. John of Nepomuk, the patron saint of bridges, best catches the romantic spirit of St-Ursanne. Local restaurants often serve perch and trout from the Doubs.

Porrentruy

⑯ *13.5 km (8 mi) northwest of St-Ursanne, 28 km (mi) from Delémont.*

A small detour toward the French border brings you to the center of the Ajoie region and to this city that has an excellently preserved medieval town center. It is worth the journey just to view the impressive **Château de Porrentruy** towering over the Old Town, now used by cantonal offices. This was once the seat of the prince-bishops of Basel; the 13th-century Tour Réfouse (refuge tower) next to the castle provides a beautiful view and is always open to the public. The Porte de France, a remnant of the walls of the city, and the old stone houses alongside it dramatically reflect a medieval character.

Delémont

⑰ *81 km (50 mi) northeast of Neuchâtel.*

Nestled in a wide, picturesque valley, this is the administrative seat of the Jura canton; though it's on the French-German language divide, the official language is French. From the 11th century until the 18th century, Delémont was annexed by the bishop-princes of Basel, who often used it as a summer residence. The town center is still atmospheric, with its cobblestones and innumerable 17th-century fountains. A mile northeast of town is the pilgrimage church **Chapelle du Vorbourg,** perched on a wooded outcropping. The door is usually open; masses are held Sunday and holidays at 9:30 AM.

En Route Between La Chaux-de-Fonds and Delémont (just 11 km/6½ mi south of Delémont), the medieval town of **Moutier** produces the creamy, piquant Vacherin Mont d'Or, or the smooth textured Tête de Moine (monk's head) cheese eaten in finely shaved ruffles, the only reminder of the town's once-renowned monastery of Bellelay.

FRIBOURG, NEUCHÂTEL, AND THE JURA A TO Z

Arriving and Departing

By Car

An important and scenic trans-Swiss artery, the A12 expressway, cuts from Bern to Lausanne, passing directly above Fribourg; a parallel northwestern route approaches from Basel by expressway (**A1**) to Solothurn, then changes to a secondary highway and follows the northwestern shore of Lake Neuchâtel, with brief sections of expressway at Neuchâtel itself and from Yverdon on down to Lac Léman. A slow but scenic route along A18 cuts from Basel through the Jura by way of Delémont.

By Plane

Geneva's **Cointrin** Airport (✉ 138 km/86 mi southwest of Fribourg, ☎ 022/7177111) is the second-busiest international airport in Switzerland. Frequent flights from the United States and the United Kingdom arrive on **Swissair** and other international carriers via Cointrin. Bern's small airport, **Belp** (✉ 34 km/21 mi northeast of Fribourg, ☎ 031/9613411), services **Crossair** (☎ 084/8852000), and **Air Engiadina** (☎ 084/8848528 for reservations).

By Train
The main train route between Basel, Zürich, and Geneva passes through the **Fribourg station** (⊠ ave. de la Gare, ☎ 157/2222, 1.19 SF/min) between Bern and Lausanne. Trains generally arrive twice an hour.

Getting Around

By Boat
There are boat trips on the lakes of Neuchâtel, Murten (Morat), and Biel (Bienne), as well as on the Aare River and the Broye Canal, a natural wildlife sanctuary. Schedules vary seasonally, but in summer are frequent and include evening trips. Contact **Compagnie de la Navigation** (☎ 032/7534012) for more information.

By Bus
Postbus connections, except in the principal urban areas, can be few and far between; plan excursions carefully using the bus schedules available at the train station.

By Car
The charms of this varied region can be seen best by car, and there are scenic secondary highways throughout. Keep in mind that some towns, like Gruyères, are car-free or have pedestrians-only centers; in these cases, parking lots are easy to find.

By Train
Secondary connections are thin, but they allow visits to most towns. To visit Gruyères, you must take a bus out of Broc.

Contacts and Resources

Emergencies
Police: (☎ 117). Fribourg (☎ 117 or 026/3051818). Neuchâtel (☎ 117 or 032/7222222). **Ambulance or medical emergency:** (☎ 026/4225500). Fribourg and Neuchâtel (☎ 117). **Medical and dental referrals:** Fribourg (☎ 026/3223343). Neuchâtel (☎ 032/7222222).

Guided Tours
Guided walks of Neuchâtel with English commentary are available for groups of up to 30 persons. They last about two hours and cost 75 SF. Contact the tourist office (☞ *below*) for information.

Visitor Information
The regional office for canton Fribourg is based in **Fribourg** (⊠ 1107 rue de la Glâne, CH-1700, ☎ 026/4025644, FAX 026/4023119). The regional office for canton Neuchâtel (as well as its city tourist office) is based in **Neuchâtel** (⊠ Hôtel des Postes, CH-2000, ☎ 032/8896890, FAX 032/8896291). The Jura's regional office is found in **Saignelégier** (⊠ 1 rue de la Gruere, CH-2350, ☎ 032/9521952, FAX 032/9521955).

Local tourist offices: **Avenches** (⊠ 3 pl. de l'Église, CH-1580, ☎ 026/6751159). **Estavayer-le-Lac** (⊠ pl. du Midi, CH-1470, ☎ 026/6631237). **Fribourg** (⊠ 1 av. de la Gare, CH-1700, ☎ 026/3213175, FAX 026/3223527). **Gruyères** (⊠ CH-1663, ☎ 026/9211030). **La Chaux-de-Fonds** (⊠ 1 Espacité, CH-2302, ☎ 032/9196895). **Murten** (⊠ 6 Franz-Kirchg., CH-3280, ☎ 026/6705112). **Porrentruy** (⊠ 5 Grand Rue, CH-2900, ☎ 032/4665959). **St-Ursanne** (⊠ CH-2882, ☎ 032/4613716). **Yverdon-les-Bains** (⊠ 1 pl. Pestalozzi, CH-1400, ☎ 024/4236290).

9 BERN

With an Excursion to the Emmental

Humble and down-to-earth, Bern is a city of broad medieval streets, farmers' markets, and friendly, slow-spoken people. It is also the federal capital of Switzerland and, more remarkably, a World Cultural Heritage city known for its sandstone arcades, fountains, and thick, sturdy towers. A short drive outside the city will take you to the farm-sprinkled lowlands of the Emmental region.

Updated by
Susan Tuttle-
Laube

THOUGH BERN IS THE SWISS CAPITAL, you won't find much cosmopolitan nonsense here: the *cuisine du marché*, based on the freshest ingredients available in the local market, features fatback and sauerkraut; the annual fair fetes the humble onion; and the president of the Swiss Confederation often takes the tram to work. It's fitting, too, that a former Swiss patent-office clerk, Albert Einstein, began developing his theory of relativity in Bern. Warm, friendly, down-to-earth, the Bernese are notoriously slow-spoken; ask a question and then pull up a chair while they formulate a judicious response. Their mascot is a common bear; they keep some as pets in the center of town. Walking down broad medieval streets past squares crowded with farmers' markets and cafés full of shirt-sleeve politicos, you might forget that Bern is the geographic and political hub of a sophisticated, modern, and prosperous nation.

Although Bern is full of patrician houses and palatial hotels, there is no official presidential residence: The seven members of the coalition government, each of whom serves a year as president, have to find their own places to live when in Bern.

Bern wasn't always so self-effacing. It earned its pivotal position through a history of power and influence that dates from the 12th century, when Berchtold V, duke of Zähringen and one of the countless rulers within the Holy Roman Empire, established a fortress on this gooseneck in the River Aare. A descendent of the German Alemanni tribes, whose penetration into Switzerland can roughly be measured by the areas where Swiss German is spoken today, he chose Bern not only for its impregnable location—it's a steep promontory of rock girded on three sides by the river—but also for its proximity to the great kingdom of Burgundy, which spread across France and much of present-day French-speaking Switzerland.

By the 14th century, Bern had grown into a strong urban republic. When the last Zähringens died, the people of Bern defeated their would-be replacements and, shedding the Holy Roman Empire, became the eighth canton to join the rapidly growing Swiss Confederation. It was an unlikely union: aristocratic, urban Bern allied with the strongly democratic farming communities of central Switzerland. But it provided the Bernese with enough security against the Hapsburg Holy Roman Empire to continue westward expansion.

Despite a devastating fire that laid waste to the city in 1405, by the late 15th century the Bernese had become a power of European stature—a stature enhanced exponentially by three decisive victories over the duke of Burgundy in 1476 and 1477. Aided by the other cantons and prompted by Louis XI, king of France and bitter enemy of the Burgundians, the Bernese crushed Charles the Bold and drove him out of his Swiss lands. Not only did the Bernese expand their territories all the way west to Geneva, but they also acquired immense wealth—great treasures of gold, silver, and precious textiles—and assumed the leading role in Switzerland and Swiss affairs.

Bern stayed on top. Through the 17th and 18th centuries, the city's considerable prosperity was built not so much on commerce as on the export of troops and military know-how. The city and her territories functioned essentially as a patrician state, ruled by an aristocracy that saw its raison d'être in politics, foreign policy, the acquisition of new lands, and the forging of alliances. At the same time, her landed gentry continued to grow fat on the fruits of the city's rich agricultural lands. Napoléon seized the lands briefly from 1798 until his defeat in

1815, but by the 1830s the Bernese were back in charge, and when the Swiss Confederation took its contemporary, democratic form in 1848, Bern was a natural choice for its capital.

Yet today it's not the massive Bundeshaus (Houses of Parliament) that dominates the city but instead its perfectly preserved arcades, fountains, and thick, stalwart towers—all remnants of its heyday as a medieval power. They're the reason UNESCO granted Bern World Cultural Heritage status, along with the Egyptian pyramids, Rome, Florence, and the Taj Mahal.

Pleasures and Pastimes

Arcades

Like a giant cloister, Bern is crisscrossed by *Lauben* (arcades) that shelter stores of every kind and quality. Stout 15th-century pillars support the low vaulted roofs, which extend to the edge of the pavement below. At the base of many arcades, nearly horizontal cellar doors lead down into interesting underground eateries and businesses. Combined with Bern's sturdy towers and narrow cobbled streets, the arcades distinguish the city as one of the country's best-preserved medieval towns.

Flowers

Geranium-filled window boxes are as common a sight in Bern as ruins are in Rome. In 1897 Bern formed a preservation society to encourage citizens to decorate their houses with flowers. In 1902 this society began to decorate the public fountains and then, a few years later, the windows of buildings in the Old Town. In 1984 Bern won the title of Europe's most floral city, and the geranium is the city's official flower. The hillside Rosengarten (Rose Garden), flourishing with some 160 varieties, and the city's flower market have added to Bern's renown as a blossoming city.

Fountains

Throughout Bern, scores of brilliantly colored and skillfully carved fountains—their bases surrounded by flowers—provide relief from the structural severity of the medieval houses that form their backdrop. Like the stelae of Athens, these fountains remind the Bernese of their virtuous forbears: witness the Anna Seilerbrunnen, an ode to temperance and moderation, and the Gerechtigkeitsbrunnen, with a personification of Justice standing over several severed heads. Most are the work of Hans Gieng, who created them between 1539 and 1546.

Markets

In the Middle Ages, Bern was a great marketing center, and markets today—with stands hawking everything from geraniums to meats—are still an integral part of daily life. The lone surviving market from medieval Bern is the Zwibelemärit (Onion Market), which takes place on the fourth Monday in November. Draped from scores of stalls are long strips of onions woven into the shapes of dolls, animals, and even alarm clocks. The Onion Market dates from the 1405 fire: in gratitude for assistance given by Fribourg, Bern granted farmers the right to sell their onions in the city's market square.

Museums

As the nation's capital, Bern offers a satisfying concentration of museums, including the stellar Kunstmuseum, full of fine art, and its massive Historisches Museum, displaying war trophies and church treasures. All uniquely Swiss are the original Museum für Kommunikation; the Schweizerisches Alpines Museum, exploring the Alps and their conquest; and the Schweizerisches Schützenmuseum, about the innately Swiss love of sharpshooting.

EXPLORING BERN

Because Bern stands on a high, narrow peninsula formed by a goose-neck in the Aare, its streets seem to follow the river's flow, running in long parallels to its oldest, easternmost point; from afar, its uniform red-tile roofs seem to ooze like glowing lava down the length of the promontory. The Old Town was founded on the farthest tip and grew westward; its towers mark those stages of growth like rings on a tree.

Numbers in the text correspond to numbers in the margin and on the Bern map.

Great Itineraries

IF YOU HAVE 1 OR 2 DAYS

You can visit Bern's Old Town in a single day; but two days will allow you a more leisurely pace, with plenty of time for museums and shopping. Starting at the main train station, the Hauptbahnhof, you can move eastward through the towers, fountains, and arcades of the Old Town to the site of Bern's founding at Nydeggkirche. Across the Aare are more museums, the Rosengarten, and the embassy row of Thunstrasse. Back on the north side of the river, the Münster and the Bundeshaus are not to be missed.

IF YOU HAVE 3 TO 5 DAYS

If you're making an extended stay in Bern, spend the first few days as above, exploring the town. To help round out the city's history, visit the Historisches Museum, or try the Naturhistorisches Museum, which is considered one Europe's best natural history museums. Then escape for a half- or full-day drive through the Emmental to experience a landscape that has been left virtually untouched since the 19th century (☞ Excursion to the Emmental, *below*). If you're anxious to get an even closer look at the mountains, head into the Berner Oberland, one hour away. You can visit the Jungfrau region by train, taking the Interlaken–Grindelwald–Klein Scheidegg–Jungfraujoch route (and, weather permitting, Wengen) in a single long day (☞ Chapter 10).

Old Town

Now a pedestrian zone, the old city center west of the river retains a distinctly medieval appeal—thanks to the 1405 fire that destroyed its predominantly wooden structures. The city was rebuilt in sandstone, with arcades stretching on for some 6 km (4 mi).

As medieval as it may look, this old city is decidedly modern, with countless shops concentrated between the Hauptbahnhof (main train station) and the Zytgloggeturm (Clock Tower)—especially on Spitalgasse and Marktgasse. Beyond, along Kramgasse and Gerechtigkeitsgasse and, parallel to them on the north, Postgasse, there are quirkier, bohemian spots and excellent antiques stores. You may hear the Bernese calling the area east of the clock tower the *Altstadt* (Old Town), as its 800 years of commerce give it seniority over the mere 15th-century upstarts to the west.

A Good Walk

Start on the busy Bahnhofplatz in front of the grand old Schweizerhof Hotel, facing the Hauptbahnhof. To your left is the **Heiliggeistkirche** ①. If you turn right down the Bollwerk, away from the church, and veer right down Genfergasse, you'll reach the **Kunstmuseum** ② on the right at Hodlerstrasse. If you turn left and go back up Bollwerk just past the church, you'll come to the beginning of Spitalgasse on your left. Head down this wide street and walk *outside* the arcades (keeping an eye out for trams) to see some of the city's stunning architecture; if you walk inside the sheltered walkways, you'll be seduced by modern shops and cafés.

Head for the **Pfeiferbrunnen,** or Bagpiper Fountain. At the edge of the Bärenplatz stands the **Käfigturm** ③, once a medieval city gate. Continue down Marktgasse past the **Anna Seilerbrunnen,** an allegory on moderation, and the **Schützenbrunnen,** or Marksman Fountain, a tribute to a troop commander from 1543.

Just beyond and spreading to your left lie the Kornhausplatz and the imposing 18th-century **Kornhaus** ④, now a popular restaurant (☞ Dining, *below*). In the Kornhausplatz, the ogre depicted in the **Kindlifresserbrunnen** is worth a second look: he's munching on a meal of small children.

Dominating town center, the mighty **Zytgloggeturm** ⑤ entertains with its hourly mechanical puppet performance. Continue down Kramgasse, a lovely old street with many guild houses, some fine 18th-century residences, more arcades, and, of course, more fountains: first the **Zähringerbrunnen,** or Zähringen Fountain, a monument to Bern's founder Berchtold V, then the powerful depiction of Samson on the **Simsonbrunnen.** Between the fountains on your right at No. 49 is the **Einsteinhaus** ⑥, once Albert Einstein's apartment and workplace.

Turn left at the next opening (Kreuzgasse) and make a brief diversion to the Rathausplatz and, at its north end, the **Rathaus** ⑦ itself. Across from it stands the **Vennerbrunnen,** or Ensign Fountain, with the figure of a Bernese standard-bearer.

Return as you came and turn left on the main thoroughfare, now called Gerechtigkeitsgasse. You'll pass the **Gerechtigkeitsbrunnen,** or Justice Fountain. Beyond are some lovely 18th-century houses. At No. 7 is the Gasthaus zum Goldenen Adler (☞ Lodging, *below*). Built between 1764 and 1766, it has a particularly captivating coat of arms by locksmith Samuel Rüetschi.

A left turn at the bottom of Gerechtigkeitsgasse will take you steeply down Nydegg Stalden through one of the oldest parts of the city; the **Nydeggkirche** ⑧ is on your right. The sudden quiet of this ancient neighborhood is magical. Down the hill stands the **Läuferbrunnen,** the image of a city herald. Take the Untertorbrücke, or Lower Gate Bridge, across the Aare.

From here, it's a short, steep climb to the east end of the high Nydeggbrücke. If you're feeling energetic, it's well worth crossing the road and either climbing a small path to the left, turning right at the top; or turning right and then left to walk up the broader Alter Aargauerstalden, where you'll turn left. Either will bring you to the **Rosengarten** ⑨, its roses in spectacular bloom from June to October.

Head back down to the Nydeggbrücke but don't cross it yet: on your left, facing the Old Town, you'll find the famous **Bärengraben** ⑩, home to the city's mascots.

Cross the bridge and turn left up Junkerngasse, notable for its fine old houses. Number 59 is the elegant 15th-century **Béatrice von Wattenwyl House,** where the Swiss government gives receptions. In contrast, No. 51 has a gorgeous, unrestored, painted facade which stands out in its dilapidated grandeur. At the top of Junkerngasse, you come to the pride of the city: the magnificent Gothic **Münster** ⑪. On leaving the cathedral, head left to the terrace on its south side. Many of the square's chestnut trees are from the original 18th-century planting. Look east, in the direction you just came from, for a view of the impressive south-side facades of the patrician houses and their gardens leading down to the **Matte** neighborhood.

Cross the Münsterplatz, passing by the **Mosesbrunnen.** Follow Münstergasse, taking a moment to check out No. 62 (the Mayhaus)—the huge, enclosed, 1895 balcony connecting two 16th-century houses is held up by a muscled figure whose facial expression is worth a double take. At the street's end turn left into Casinoplatz, where you'll find the so-called **Casino** (actually a restaurant and concert locale). At this point, by crossing the river on the panoramic Kirchenfeldbrücke to Helvetiaplatz, you can visit six major museums that are conveniently grouped together. Just across the bridge, immediately on your left, you'll see the contemporary **Kunsthalle** ⑫. On your right is the **Schweizerisches Alpines Museum** ⑬, for armchair climbers and real ones, too. Across the square behind the massive fountain of Mother Helvetica is the **Historisches Museum** ⑭, where armor and arms, tapestries, and church treasures illustrate Bern's 15th-century victory over Burgundy.

Leaving the history museum, turn left and follow Bernastrasse a half block down. Adjoining the museum at the back is the **Schweizerisches Schützenmuseum** ⑮. Continue down Bernastrasse to the **Naturhistorisches Museum** ⑯. On leaving the museum, head left and then turn left onto Hallylerstrasse, then left again onto Helvetiastrasse, where you'll find the **Museum für Kommunikation** ⑰, tracing the evolution of the Swiss mail system. When you are done with the museums, you can nip down the Thunstrasse for a look at the impressive buildings that make up Embassy Row.

Head back over the Kirchenfeldbrücke, toward Casinoplatz, but turn left into the little alley just after crossing the bridge and stroll along the terrace behind the **Bundeshaus** ⑱. This spot affords another fine view across the river and, in good weather, to the distant Alps; at the bridge end of the parapet is a diagram to help you pick out the principal peaks. You can walk around the Bundeshaus into the Bundesplatz and then into the traffic-free (and bear-free) Bärenplatz. On Tuesday and Saturday mornings, a lively market spills into surrounding streets.

TIMING

You can tour the Old Town in a single day, leaving extra time for the Bärengraben, Münster, and Rosengarten (in clear weather). If you'll be in Bern longer, leave an afternoon for at least one of the many museums, or indulge your whims in the arcade shops. Crowds can be considerable on weekends, so plan accordingly. Arrive at the Zytgloggeturm five minutes before the hour at the very latest: the mechanical figures spring into action at precisely four minutes to, and it's best to leave time to claim a spot on the street.

Sights to See

★ � ❿ **Bärengraben** (Bear Pits). Since the late 1400s, the Bear Pits have been digs for the city's mascots: fat brown bears that clown and beg for carrots, which vendors provide for tourists and loyal townsfolk. According to legend, Berchtold V announced that he would name the new city for the first animal he killed. It was a bear, of course; in those days the woods were full of them. The German plural for bears is *Bären,* and you'll see their images everywhere in Bern: on flags, the city coat of arms, buildings, statues, chocolates, and umbrellas, and—of course— as stuffed toys. Note that, in spite of its name, you won't find the real critters at Bärenplatz, but rather at the east end of the peninsula just across the river. ⊠ *South side of Nydeggbrücke.*

⑱ **Bundeshaus** (Houses of Parliament). This hulking, domed building is the beating heart of the Swiss Confederation and meeting place of the Swiss National Council. Free guided tours (in English) include entry to the parliamentary chambers, where there's a spectacular mural of

Bern

KEY
Rail Lines
AE American Express Office

300 yards
300 meters

Bärengraben, 10
Bundeshaus, 18
Einsteinhaus, 6
Heiliggeistkirche, 1
Historisches
Museum, 14
Käfigturm, 3
Kornhaus, 4

Kunsthalle, 12
Kunstmuseum, 2
Münster, 11
Museum für
Kommunikation, 17
Naturhistorisches
Museum, 16
Nydeggkirche, 8

Rathaus, 7
Rosengarten, 9
Schweizerisches
Alpines Museum, 13
Schweizerisches
Schützenmuseum, 15
Zytgloggeturm, 5

Lake Luzern, considered the cradle of the Confederation. ⊠ *Bunde-spl.*, ☎ *031/3228522.* ◷ *Tours Mon.–Sat. at 9, 10, 11, 2, 3, and 4; Sun. at 9, 10, 11, 2, and 3. Can vary according to Parliament sessions.*

❻ Einsteinhaus (Einstein's House). For a bit of recent history, you can visit the apartment and workplace of Albert Einstein. It was during his stay here that, at the age of 26, he published his *Special Theory of Relativity.* ⊠ *Kramg. 49,* ☎ *031/3120091.* 🎫 *3 SF.* ◷ *Tues.–Fri. 10–5 and Sat. 10–4. Closed Dec.–Jan.*

❶ Heiliggeistkirche (Church of the Holy Ghost). Completed in 1729, the sanctuary adds a bit of baroque flamboyance to the otherwise medieval Old Town. The ornateness also contrasts with the neighborhood—not exactly Bern's nicest. ⊠ *Spitalg. 44, across from Hauptbahnhof.*

★ ⓮ Historisches Museum (Historical Museum). Much of this enormous, enlightening collection is booty from victories over Burgundy, including magnificent tapestries "acquired" in 1476–77, when the Bernese pushed Charles the Bold back into France. There are armor and arms, lavish church treasures (including 15th- and 16th-century stained-glass windows), and the original Last Judgment sculptures from the cathedral's portal. Don't miss the novel three-way portrait of Calvin, Zwingli, and Luther. Among the important exhibitions about the outside world is an exceptional Islamic collection. ⊠ *Helvetiapl. 5,* ☎ *031/3507711.* 🎫 *5 SF.* ◷ *Tues.–Sun. 10–5.*

❸ Käfigturm (Prison Tower). A city entrance from the 13th and 14th centuries (later restored in the 18th century), when the limits of Bern extended only this far west, the Käfigturm served as a prison until 1897. ⊠ *Marktg. 67.*

❹ Kornhaus (Granary). The imposing 18th-century Kornhaus has a magnificent cellar, now a popular Bernese restaurant (☞ Dining, *below*), which once held wine brought to town by farmers as a tribute to the patrician city government. The upper stories, extensively renovated in 1998, now house the Forum für Media und Gestaltung (Forum for Media and Design), which hosts exhibitions and events devoted to design, architecture, contemporary media, video, photography, and applied art. ⊠ *Kornhauspl. 18.* ☎ *031/3129110.* 🎫 *Varies with exhibition/event.* ◷ *Tues.–Fri. 10–7, weekends 10–5.*

⓬ Kunsthalle (Art Gallery). Not to be confused with the traditional Kunstmuseum, this ground-breaking contemporary art venue has no permanent collection, but displays temporary exhibits of living artists, usually before you've heard of them. Built in 1918 in heroic classical style to boost local artists—Kirchner, Klee, Hodler—it grew to attract the young Kandinsky, Miró, Sol LeWitt, Richard Long, Cy Twombly—and a parade of newcomers of strong potential. ⊠ *Helvetiapl. 1,* ☎ *031/3510031.* 🎫 *6 SF.* ◷ *Tues. 10–9, Wed.–Sun. 10–5.*

★ ❷ Kunstmuseum (Art Museum). Just down the hill and three blocks from the Hauptbahnhof, this important museum displays the third-largest art collection in Switzerland—and the largest gathering of works by Paul Klee in the world, with more than 2,000 examples of this native son's skills. From another Bern native, the symbolist Ferdinand Hodler, there are striking allegories (some enormous), landscapes, and portraits; works by Swiss artists Stauffer, Anker, and Böcklin are also shown. But the Kunstmuseum's concentration is not entirely Swiss, with masterworks ranging from Fra Angelico to Cézanne, Rouault, and Picasso. It also has a cafeteria and a cinema. ⊠ *Hodlerstr. 8–12,* ☎ *031/3110944.* 🎫 *6 SF.* ◷ *Tues. 10–9, Wed.–Sun. 10–5.*

Matte. In the narrow row houses below the patrician residences of Junkerngasse, laborers once lived along the banks of the Aare. In those days, as today, the neighborhood was called *Matte,* and was the most sociable, raucous part of town. In the same tradition that produced Cockney rhyming slang, there developed a bizarre dialect—*Matten-englisch*—that can still be heard today, though it has grown so rare that its proponents have formed a club to keep it alive. Spotted with Yiddish and Gypsy terms, the dialect derives its name from *Matten* (lowland or meadow) and *Englisch* (unintelligible). Even if you don't hear the local tongue, Matte is a lovely old neighborhood to wander, with tiny shops tucked here and there. From the cathedral terrace, take the 183 steps or ride the funky little outdoor elevator (1 SF) down to the river. There's a flea market here on Mühleplatz every third Saturday from May through October. ⊠ *Off Gerberg. and below Junkerng.*

★ ⑪ **Münster** (Cathedral). Started in 1421 by master mason Matthäus Ensinger, Bern's famous cathedral was planned on lines so spacious that half the population could worship in it at one time. The smaller church on the site was kept intact and functioning during construction. Only later was it demolished and removed piece by piece through the main portal of the new cathedral, whose construction went on for centuries. Even the Reformation, the impact of which converted it from a Catholic to a Protestant church, did not halt the work. Daniel Heinz directed construction for 25 years (from 1573 to 1598), completing the nave and the tower. The finishing touch, the tip of the 100-m (328-ft) steeple (the highest in Switzerland), was added only in 1893. Today you can ascend it by a dizzying 254-step spiral staircase to enjoy a panorama of red roofs, the Aare, and if the weather is clear, the Bernese Alps.

The cathedral has two outstanding features, one outside and one in. Outside is the **main portal,** with a magnificent representation of the Last Judgment (1490) composed of 234 carved figures—heaven is on the left, hell on the right. This work was completed immediately before the Reformation, but it escaped destruction by the iconoclasts who emptied the niches of the side portals. The main portal was recently restored and painted in vivid—some may say jarring—colors. Green demons with gaping red maws and ivory-skin angels with gilt hair appear with Technicolor intensity.

Inside the church, while the elaborately carved pews and choir stalls are worth attention, note the **stained glass,** especially the 15th-century windows of the choir, dealing as much with local heraldry as with Christian iconography. ⊠ *Münsterpl. 1,* ☎ *031/3110572.* ☉ *Easter Sun.–Oct. 31, Tues.–Sat. 10–5 and Sun. 11:30–5; Nov.–Easter Sun. Tues.–Fri. 10–noon and 2–4, Sat. 10–noon and 2–5, Sun. 11:30–2.*

⑰ **Museum für Kommunikation** (Communications Museum). Housed in a modern building behind the Historical Museum, this high-concept, interactive museum (formerly known as the Schweizerisches PTT Museum) has detailed documents, art, and artifacts of early technology relating to the history of the mails in Switzerland. There's a magnificent stamp and postmark collection, one of the largest and most valuable in the world, exhibited in sleek sliding-glass trays. ⊠ *Helvetiastr. 16,* ☎ *031/3575555.* ☞ *5 SF.* ☉ *Tues.–Sun. 10–5.*

★ ☾ ⑯ **Naturhistorisches Museum** (Museum of Natural History). Considered one of Europe's finest museums of natural history, this beloved institution has a huge display area with a slick, skylit four-story wing. It has enormous, evocative wildlife dioramas, as well as row upon row of Victorian oak-and-beveled-glass cases mounting varied species of mammals like so many butterflies. Its quirkiest trophy: the stuffed body of Barry, a St. Bernard that saved more than 40 people in the Alps in the last century. There's also a splendid collection of Alpine minerals. ✉ *Bernastr. 15,* ☎ *031/3507111.* 🖾 *5 SF.* ☉ *Mon. 2–5, Tues., Thurs.–Fri. 9–5, Wed. 9–8, weekends 10–5.*

OFF THE
BEATEN PATH

TIERPARK DÄHLHÖLZLI – Here is a zoo with a difference: parts of it are in a natural woodland park along the Aare river and can be visited anytime day or night. The habitats back onto public walkways; come by at the right moment, and you'll get a peek at the animals behind the trees. The proper zoo part has some exotic species and a vivarium full of reptiles and fish. The majority of the zoo's creatures are European: wolves, chamois, lynx, seals, and—of course—bears. The zoo is an easy trip south on Bus 18. ✉ *Tierparkweg. 1,* ☎ *031/3571515. Habitats:* 🖾 *Free.* ☉ *Daily 24 hrs. Zoo, Vivarium, Petting Zoo:* 🖾 *7 SF.* ☉ *Apr.–Sept., daily 8–6:30; Oct.–Mar., daily 9–5.*

❽ Nydeggkirche (Nydegg Church). Built in 1341–46, the Nydegg Church stands on the ruins of Berchtold V's first fortress (destroyed about 1260–70), the site of Bern's founding. You can see parts of the original foundation below the chancel; there's also a wooden pulpit from 1566. ✉ *Nydegg.,* ☎ *031/3116102.* ☉ *Mon.–Sat. 10–noon and 2–5:30; Sun. 10–noon.*

❼ Rathaus (Town Hall). Bern's stately Town Hall is the seat of the cantonal government. Along with the city's arcades, it was built after the great fire of 1405 and still retains its simple Gothic lines. It's not open to the public. ✉ *Rathauspl. 2.*

★ **❾ Rosengarten** (Rose Garden). In this splendidly arranged and well maintained garden, some 160 varieties of roses bloom from June to October. One of Bern's most popular gathering places, this is a great vantage point from which to admire the Jungfrau, Eiger, and Mönch—on clear days only. ✉ *Alter Aargauerstalden.* 🖾 *Free.* ☉ *Daily sunrise–sunset.*

⓭ Schweizerisches Alpines Museum (Swiss Alpine Museum). This arcane but eye-opening museum of the Alps has topographical maps and reliefs and displays illustrating the history of mountain climbing, alongside epic art and fine old photos. There's an enormous model of the Berner Oberland (indispensable for getting your bearings if you're headed for that region) under a magnificent Hodler mural of the tragic conquest of the Matterhorn. ✉ *Helvetiapl. 4,* ☎ *031/3510434.* 🖾 *5 SF.* ☉ *Late Feb.–mid-Oct., Mon. 2–5, Tues.–Sun. 10–5; mid-Oct.–late Feb., Mon. 2–5, Tues.–Sun. 10–noon and 2–5.*

⓯ Schweizerisches Schützenmuseum (Swiss Rifle Museum). Run by the Swiss Marksmen's Association, the institution pays homage to this very Swiss art. With a large collection of guns in every imaginable form, the museum traces the evolution of firearms from 1817; with trophies, it celebrates centuries of straight shooting, as Swiss sharpshooters have always measured themselves against the apple-splitting accuracy of archer William Tell. ✉ *Bernastr. 5,* ☎ *031/3510127.* 🖾 *Free.* ☉ *Tues.–Sat. 2–4, Sun. 10–noon and 2–4.*

★ **❺ Zytgloggeturm** (Clock Tower). Bern's oldest building, the mighty Clock Tower, was built in 1191 as the western gate to the then-smaller city. Today it dominates the town center with its high copper spire and a massive astronomical clock and calendar, built on its east side in 1530. As an added attraction, a delightful group of mechanical figures performs every hour. To see the puppet show, it's best to take up a position at the corner of Kramgasse and Hotelgasse at least five minutes before the hour: you won't be the only one there.

At four minutes to the hour, heralded by a jester nodding his head and ringing two small bells, the puppet show begins. From a small arch on the left appear a couple of musically inclined bears—a drummer and a piper—leading a procession made up of a horseman with a sword, a bear wearing a crown, and lesser bears, each carrying a gun, a sword, or a spear. When the procession ends, a cockerel on the left crows and flaps his wings, a knight in golden armor above hammers out the hour, and Father Time, on a throne in the middle, beats time with a scepter in one hand and an hourglass in the other. ⊠ *Kramg.*

DINING

Although Bern strikes a diplomatic balance in heading French-Swiss and German-Swiss politics, its Teutonic nature conquers Gaul when it comes to cuisine. Dining in Bern is usually a down-to-earth affair, with Italian home cooking running a close popular second to the local standard fare: German-style meat and potatoes. The most widespread specialty is the famous *Bernerplatte*, a meaty version of Alsatian *choucroûte*—great slabs of salt pork, beef tongue, smoky bacon, pork ribs, and mild pink pork sausages cooked down in broth and heaped on a broad platter over juniper-scented sauerkraut, green beans, and boiled potatoes. When a waitress eases this wide load onto the table before you, you may glance around to see who's sharing: one serving can seem enough for four. Another meaty classic is the Berner version of *Ratsherrtopf*, traditionally enjoyed by the town councillors: veal shank cooked in white wine, butter, and sage.

CATEGORY	COST*
$$$$	over 80 SF
$$$	50 SF–80 SF
$$	20 SF–50 SF
$	under 20 SF

Prices are per person for a three-course meal (two-course meal in $ category), including sales tax and 15% service charge

$$$$ ✕ **Bellevue-Grill.** When Parliament is in session, this haute-cuisine
★ landmark in the Bellevue Palace (☞ Lodging, *below*) is transformed from a local gourmet mecca to a political clubhouse where movers and shakers confer over unusual dishes such as roast breast of duck in a sauce with a hint of coffee or beef fillet with truffle noodles. The ambience is one of pure luxury. ⊠ *Kocherg. 3–5,* ☎ *031/3204545. Reservations essential. Jacket and tie. AE, DC, MC, V.*

$$$$ ✕ **Schultheissenstube.** The intimate, rustic dining room, with a club-
★ like bar and an adjoining, even more rustic, all-wood *Stübli* (tavern-café), looks less like a gastronomic haven than a country pub. Yet the cooking is sophisticated, international, and imaginative—consider lightly smoked lamb on a bed of saffron lentils, quail breast and duck liver on choucroûte, oyster and champagne risotto—and the wine list, encyclopedic. ⊠ *Hotel Schweizerhof (☞ Lodging, below), Bahnhofpl. 11,* ☎ *031/3268080. Reservations essential. Jacket and tie in dining room. AE, DC, MC, V. Closed Sun. and July.*

$$$ ✕ **Jack's Brasserie.** Sometimes referred to by locals as the Stadt Restaurant (City Restaurant), this dining room at street level, with high ceilings, wainscoting, and roomy banquettes is airy, bustling, urbane, and cosmopolitan. Enjoy a drink here by day at bare-top tables or settle in at mealtime for smartly served Swiss standards, French bistro classics, or a great Sunday brunch. ⊠ *Hotel Schweizerhof (☞ Lodging, below), Bahnhofpl. 11,* ☎ *031/3268080. AE, DC, MC, V.*

$$$ ✕ **Verdi.** Named for the Italian opera composer, this restaurant is nothing if not theatrical. There are framed pieces of opera memorabilia, carved wood ceilings, chandeliers, velvet drapes, and occasionally even opera singers to entertain guests between courses. Amazingly,

it isn't the least bit kitschy. Chef Giovanni D'Ambrogio even cooks specialties from Verdi's hometown region of Emilia-Romagna. Try his spaghetti Scarpara, with an excellent, garlicky tomato sauce, or the sliced steak on a bed of arugula with Parmesan. Reservations are essential if you want to even get near this popular spot on weekends. ⊠ *Gerechtigkeitsg. 5,* ☎ *031/3126368. AE, DC, MC, V.*

$$$ ✗ **Zimmermania.** This deceptively simple bistro has been in business
★ for more than 150 years and is a local favorite for authentic, French bourgeois cooking. The owner visits Paris regularly to update his exceptional seasonal menu. Try their cheese soufflé or veal kidneys in mustard sauce or any of their ocean fish specialties. For a special vintage, ask for the separate French wine list. ⊠ *Brunng. 19,* ☎ *031/3111542. AE, MC, V. Closed Sun.–Mon.*

$$–$$$ ✗ **Kornhauskeller.** Extensive renovations in 1998 have carefully and reverently lifted this historic spot from beer hall to high society. The vaulted ceilings and frescoes in the old city wine cellar below the Granary are nothing short of spectacular. They're now enhanced by the chic marriage of culture and history; besides the dining room there's a whiskey lounge and humidor. The menu covers all bases, from local fare to French, Italian, and even Asian dishes; the wine list is extensive. An offshoot at street level, the Kornhaus Café, makes a good stop for a light lunch, supper, or cocktail. A reservation is a good idea. ⊠ *Kornhauspl. 18,* ☎ *031/3277272. AE, DC, MC, V.*

$$–$$$ ✗ **Zum Zähringer.** For a quiet meal out of range of the city's bustle, head down to the river to this restaurant in the Matte neighborhood. The emphasis here is on fresh and local ingredients. The staff will even tell you the name of the farmer who provides the pork. The menu changes according to the season and the whims of the chef—you might find delicate pumpkin ravioli, a meaty veal shank with a subtle wine sauce, or an original vegetarian dish. One constant: the daily fish special is always a hit. ⊠ *Badg. 1,* ☎ *031/3113270. MC, V. Closed Sun.*

$$ ✗ **Brasserie zum Bärengraben.** Directly across from the Bear Pits, this popular, easygoing little local institution is a place to settle in with a newspaper and a *Dezi* (deciliter) of wine. You'll find old-style basics—*Kalbskopf* (chopped veal head) in vinaigrette, pigs' feet, stuffed cabbage—as well as French-accented brasserie fare (lamb with rosemary, for instance) and wonderful pastries. Stick to daily specials and one-plate meals; dining à la carte can be expensive. ⊠ *Muristalden 1,* ☎ *031/3314218. AE, MC, V.*

$$ ✗ **Della Casa.** Affectionately nicknamed "Delli," this favorite has been
★ serving generous platters of local specialties for over 100 years. The waitresses are "wonderfully prickly dragons," according to one Swiss food magazine, but no one seems to mind. The yellowed downstairs Stübli and the wood-panelled upstairs rooms are unofficial Parliament headquarters; they buzz during lunch. ⊠ *Schauplatzg. 16,* ☎ *031/ 3112142. AE, DC, MC, V. Closed Sun. No dinner Sat.*

$$ ✗ **Harmonie.** Run by the same family since 1900, this lively leaded-glass and old-wood café-restaurant is pleasantly dingy, very friendly, and welcoming to foreigners. Expect the basics: sausage and *Rösti* (hash brown potatoes), *Käseschnitte* (cheese toast), *Bauern* omelets (farm style, with bacon, potatoes, onions, and herbs), and fondue. ⊠ *Hotelg. 3,* ☎ *031/3113840. MC, V. No dinner Sat., no lunch Sun. and Mon.*

$$ ✗ **Il Grissino.** In a busy Bernese square, this very popular haunt specializes in pizzas cooked in a wood-fired oven—26 colorful varieties—and such traditional pastas as *fettuccine nere Stefano* (black noodles with salmon and broccoli). Run by a Swiss-Italian family, it has a bright, contemporary interior with curious ceiling lamps dressed up with glass beads and metallic leaves. The wine list is all Italian. ⊠ *Waisenhauspl. 28,* ☎ *031/3110059. AE, DC, MC, V.*

Bern Dining and Lodging

Dining ●
Bellevue-Grill, **15**
Brasserie zum
Bärengraben, **24**
Della Casa, **6**
Harmonie, **14**

Il Grissino, **4**
Jack's Brasserie, **5**
Klötzlikeller, **20**
Kornhauskeller, **11**
Lorenzini, **8**

Menuetto, **16**
Schultheissenstube, **5**
Verdi, **21**
Zimmermania, **17**
Zum Zähringer, **18**

Lodging ○
Bären/Bristol, **7**
Belle Epoque, **22**
Bellevue Palace, **15**
Bern, **9**
Glocke, **12**

Goldener
Schlüssel, **13**
Innere Enge, **2**
Jardin, **25**
Krebs, **1**
Kreuz/Metropole, **10**
Landhaus, **23**

Marthahaus, **3**
Schweizerhof, **5**
Zum Goldenen
Adler, **19**

KEY
—— Rail Lines
✈ American Express
Office

$$ ✕ **Lorenzini.** After a few days of Bern's rib-sticking cooking, authen-
★ tic Italian food may sound more appealing than ever. Delicious home-
made pastas and seasonal specialties representing various Italian
regions, such as fish carpaccio and ravioli filled with fish and herbs,
jostle for attention with the very trendy patrons crowding the coffee
bar. ⊠ *Theaterpl. 5,* ☎ *031/3117850. AE, DC, MC, V. Closed Sun.*

$$ ✕ **Menuetto.** A reaction against meaty Bern cuisine, this refreshing veg-
★ etarian oasis represents the city's Green (also very Germanic) side, cre-
ating sophisticated, imaginative cooking—*rouladen* (roulades) of
spinach and feta with tamari beer sauce, raspberry sorbet with thick
almond milk and chunks of fresh fruit. The sleek, chic, white-on-white
decor is warmed with parquet floors and hanging greens. ⊠ *Münsterg.
47 and Herreng. 22 (2 entrances),* ☎ *031/3111448. AE, DC, MC, V.
Closed Sun.*

$–$$ ✕ **Klötzlikeller.** This cozy wine cellar dates from 1635 and is the old-
★ est in Bern. Since 1885 only unmarried women have been permitted
to own and run the place—a tradition begun by the daughters of Mr.
Klötzli himself. Monthly musical-theater dinner programs and a changing menu featuring foods and wine from selected regions make this place
unique. Or try their satisfying traditional Bernese dishes on the standard menu, like tripe and Rösti. ⊠ *Gerechtigkeitsg. 62,* ☎ *031/
3117456. AE, MC, V. Closed Sun.–Mon.*

LODGING

As a frequent host to conventioneers, tourists, and visiting members
of Parliament, Bern is well equipped with hotels in all price ranges. Rooms
are hard to find when Parliament is in session; this is one town where
you need to book well ahead. All but the bargain hotels are concentrated in the Old Town.

CATEGORY	COST*
$$$$	over 300 SF
$$$	200 SF–300 SF
$$	120 SF–200 SF
$	under 120 SF

*Prices are for a standard double room, including breakfast, sales tax, and
15% service charge.*

$$$$ 🏨 **Bellevue Palace.** At press time, all the guest rooms of this 1865 landmark were about to undergo extensive renovations, which should be
completed by the end of 2000. The excellent Bellevue-Grill (☞ Dining, *above*), however, will remain open. ⊠ *Kocherg. 3–5, CH-3001,*
☎ *031/3204545,* 🗏 *031/3114743. Number of rooms not available at
press time. 3 restaurants, bar. AE, DC, MC, V.*

$$$$ 🏨 **Schweizerhof.** This landmark just across from the Hauptbahnhof
is decidedly nonpalatial: the lobby is on a human scale, though deluxe,
and the broad corridors are lined with the antiques and objets d'art of
the Gauers, the hotel's founding family. Each room's decor is different—you might be assigned to one of four rooms designed by young
Bernese artists representing the ultramodern streak in Swiss design, or
you might find a room drenched in sea-blue toile de Jouy. They're well
equipped for business meetings, but the thoughtful touches—the next
day's weather report on your pillow beside the requisite truffle—keep
it welcoming, not just efficient. And you won't go hungry; there's the
Schultheissenstube (they say the peephole in the door was installed for
a local politician) and Jack's Brasserie (☞ Dining, *above*). ⊠ *Bahnhofpl. 11, CH-3001,* ☎ *031/3268080,* 🗏 *031/3268090. 70 rooms, 15
suites. 2 restaurants, bar, nightclub. AE, DC, MC, V.*

$$$ ⊞ **Bären/Bristol.** These adjoining, connected Best Western properties are the hotel equivalent of Siamese twins; both are dependable business-class hotels, with fresh, modern rooms in blues and yellows and new tile baths. Top-floor rooms on the court side are quietest. ⊠ *Bären: Schauplatzg. 4–10, CH-3011,* ☎ *031/3113367 or 800/528–1234 in the U.S. (both hotels),* 𝔽𝔸𝕏 *031/3116983, 57 rooms; Bristol:* ☎ *031/ 3110101,* 𝔽𝔸𝕏 *031/3119479, 92 rooms. Both hotels: Snack bar, sauna, solarium, bicycles. AE, DC, MC, V.*

$$$ ⊞ **Belle Epoque.** Although it's stationed along a medieval, Old Town
★ street, this hotel draws from a different inspiration. Every inch of the arcaded row house has been filled with authentic Art Nouveau or Jugendstil antiques, from the stylized wooden vines on the reception desk to the vintage posters and stunning light fixtures. The style is suggestive of Gay Paree, but the amenities are up-to-date, with electric blinds and a no-smoking floor. The glowing, snug hotel bar is one of the most beautiful in the city; look for the photo of Henri de Toulouse-Lautrec over the door. ⊠ *Gerechtigkeitsg. 18, CH-3011,* ☎ *031/3114336,* 𝔽𝔸𝕏 *031/ 3113936. 14 rooms, 2 suites. Breakfast room, bar. AE, DC, MC, V.*

$$$ ⊞ **Bern.** Behind a severe and imposing neoclassic facade, this former theater and once-modest hotel has been transformed into a slick, business-class lodging, with air-shaft gardens supplying light to the inner rooms. All the rooms are a bit heavy on the wine-red color scheme, so for the most light, ask for one on the top floors, either facing the back or the traffic-free street. The restaurant, Seven Stuben, consists of seven rooms—each with its own motif—within one restaurant. There is also a separate, chic French restaurant. The bar is cozy and well stocked. ⊠ *Zeughausg. 9, CH-3011,* ☎ *031/3292222,* 𝔽𝔸𝕏 *031/3292299. 98 rooms, 1 suite. 2 restaurants, bar. AE, DC, MC, V.*

$$$ ⊞ **Innere Enge.** Eighteenth-century origins and Jugendstil updates are discreetly discernible in this quiet hotel just outside the city center. The rooms are spacious, light, and airy; generous windows face the Bernese Alps. You'll find exposed wood beams and lots of angles in the top floor rooms, and soothing colors with hints of the Jazz Age throughout. The real thing is to be found downstairs in Marian's Jazzroom, which features top jazz acts Tuesday through Saturday (☞ Nightlife, *below*). Take Bus 21 (marked BREMGARTEN) from the train station. ⊠ *Engestr. 54, CH-3012,* ☎ *031/3096111,* 𝔽𝔸𝕏 *031/3096112. 13 rooms, 15 suites. Restaurant, bar, café. AE, DC, MC, V.*

$$$ ⊞ **Kreuz/Metropole.** Though facing each other across Zeughausgasse, these two standard hotels have joined forces. The Kreuz is the brighter of the two, with clean, simple, rose-hued rooms. Rooms on the upper floors are significantly quieter. The Metropole is slowly shedding a dark 70's decor, but it's worth a look; at press time the rooms varied greatly in quality but not in price, so you could snag a comfortable bargain. Manager Mr. Schüpbach is offering a special rate to Fodor's users, which bumps the price back into the 2$ category—ask about it when making reservations. ⊠ *Kreuz: Zeughausg. 41, CH-3011,* ☎ *031/3111162,* 𝔽𝔸𝕏 *031/3113747. 103 rooms. Bar, restaurant. Metropole: Zeughausg. 28, CH-3011,* ☎ *031/3115021,* 𝔽𝔸𝕏 *031/3121153. 59 rooms. Both hotels: AE, DC, MC, V.*

$$ ⊞ **Krebs.** A small, scrupulously maintained hotel, the Krebs is solid
★ and impeccable, thanks to the ownership's eye for detail. The older rooms are spare but pristine, while the newly renovated, no-smoking rooms are crisp and bright with light wood accents, pastels, and polished granite. The self-service laundry facilities (rare in Switzerland) and Internet access in the rooms prove they've got your interest at heart. ⊠ *Genferg. 8, CH-3001,* ☎ *031/3114942,* 𝔽𝔸𝕏 *031/3111035. 46 rooms, 41 with bath. Breakfast room, café, laundry. AE, DC, MC, V.*

$$ ⚏ **Zum Goldenen Adler.** Built in a magnificent patrician town house
★ in the Old Town, this guest house has been lodging travelers since 1489,
though the current structure dates from 1764. One family has run it
for 100-odd years. Despite the striking exterior with its coat of arms,
the interiors are modest and modern, with linoleum baths and severe
Formica furniture, but the ambience is comfortable and welcoming
nonetheless. ⊠ *Gerechtigkeitsg. 7, CH-3001,* ☎ *031/3111725,* ℻
031/3113761. 16 rooms. Restaurant. AE, DC, MC, V.

$ ⚏ **Glocke.** Although it's very plain, there's a young, friendly manage-
ment here and the spic-and-span rooms are a bargain. Top-floor rooms
with views of the rooftops are best. Downstairs there's Quasimodo, a
popular spot with oldies playing in the background. The upstairs
Bistrorant is a friendly and affordable restaurant. ⊠ *Rathausg. 75, CH-
3011,* ☎ *031/3113771,* ℻ *031/3111008. 26 rooms, 7 with bath.
Restaurant, bar. AE, DC, MC, V.*

$ ⚏ **Goldener Schlüssel.** This bright, tidy little hotel in the heart of the
Old Town has standard-issue rooms with fresh linens and tile baths.
As the building looks over the Rathausgasse, you'll find the back
rooms quieter. The good, inexpensive restaurant serves home-cooked
meat-and-Rösti favorites. The seven rooms without bath are a bargain.
⊠ *Rathausg. 72, CH-3011,* ☎ *031/3110216,* ℻ *031/3115688. 29
rooms, 22 with bath. Restaurant, Stübli. AE, MC, V.*

$ ⚏ **Jardin.** In a commercial neighborhood far above the Old Town, this
is an efficient, straightforward hotel with a welcoming management.
The decor is a bit drab, but the rooms' spaciousness makes up for it.
It's easily reached by Tram 9 to Breitenrainplatz. ⊠ *Militärstr. 38, CH-
3014,* ☎ *031/3330117,* ℻ *031/3330943. 20 rooms. Restaurant, bowl-
ing, free parking. AE, DC, MC, V.*

$ ⚏ **Landhaus.** Just across the river from the Altstadt, this 90-year old
★ apartment building has been freshly renovated into a simple, clean, and
bright hotel/hostel, with natural-wood floors, soothing pastel walls,
and modern, metal-frame beds. Pick anything from a dorm-style cu-
bicle to a double room with shower; value-for-money-wise, it's a great
bargain. Cook for yourself in the community kitchen or dine at the
hotel's trendy restaurant. You can get a modem connection at the
front desk; there's live jazz at the bar on Thursday. ⊠ *Altenbergstr.
46, CH-3013,* ☎ *031/3314166,* ℻ *031/3326904. 4 rooms, plus 3 4-
or 6-bed dormitories. Restaurant, 2 bars, food shop, bicycles, coin laun-
dry. AE, DC, MC, V.*

$ ⚏ **Marthahaus.** This cheap, cheery pension stands at the end of a
★ quiet cul-de-sac in a residential neighborhood north of the Old Town.
All the rooms have been freshly decorated in white, and the squeaky-
clean look is reinforced with hospital-style metal beds. It's an easy ride
via Lorrainebrücke on Bus 20. Ride two stops past the Gewerbeschule
train station. ⊠ *Wyttenbachstr. 22a, CH-3013,* ☎ *031/3324135,* ℻
031/3333386. 38 rooms. Breakfast room. MC, V.

NIGHTLIFE AND THE ARTS

This Week in Bern, issued every week, carries listings of concerts, muse-
ums, and nightlife; it's available at the tourist office (☞ Visitor Information
in Bern A to Z, below) and hotels. *Bern Aktuell,* published every two weeks
and also distributed by the tourist office, has listings in English.

Nightlife

Bars

Arlequin (⊠ Gerechtigkeitsg. 51, ☎ 031/3113946) is a cozy wine bar
where small meals are served. On the ground floor of the little hotel

Belle Epoque (☞ Lodging, *above*) there's a lovely, small bar where you can drink surrounded by Art Nouveau treasures. For a nightcap in a formal hotel venue, go to the **Bellevue Palace** (☞ Lodging, *above*). The chic bar **CoCo** (⊠ Genferg. 10, ☎ 031/3111551) has Gauguin-esque murals on the walls. For history, head for **Klötzlikeller,** said to be the oldest wine bar in Bern (☞ Dining, *above*). The **Schweizerhof** (☞ Lodging, *above*) has a small, American-style bar.

Casino

Bern's **Kursaal** (⊠ Schänzlistr. 71–77, ☎ 031/3331010) has a disco with live music as well as gambling in the **Jackpot Casino,** which stays within the federally mandated 5 SF bet limit.

Dancing

Babalu (⊠ Gurteng. 3, ☎ 031/3110808) draws crowds for dancing with live music. The popular **Mocambo** (⊠ Aarbergerg. 61, ☎ 031/3115041) is lined with lots of mirrors to reflect the Beautiful People. Along with dancing to live and DJ music until 3 AM on weeknights, 3:30 AM on Saturday, it also has a revolving stage and three bars. Do note that places for dancing often also have a separate "cabaret" that is actually a strip club.

Jazz Club

Marian's Jazzroom (⊠ Engestr. 54, ☎ 031/3096111), an intimate, red-velvet club in the cellar of the hotel Innere Enge (☞ Lodging, *above*), offers top live acts nightly. There are shows from Tuesday to Saturday at 7:30 PM and 10:30 PM; Sunday there's a jazz brunch from 10–2. It's closed June through August.

The Arts

Film

Bern's 23 movie theaters show films in their original languages. Current listings can be found in hotels, the daily newspapers *Der Bund* (weekly events supplement "Die Berner Woche") and *Die Berner Zeitung* (weekly events supplement "Die Berner Agende"), and the tourist office (☞ Visitor Information *in* Bern A to Z, *below*).

Music

The **Bern Symphony Orchestra** (☎ 031/3114242 for tickets) is the city's most notable musical institution. Concerts take place at the **Casino** (⊠ Casinopl.) and the **Stadttheater** (⊠ Kornhauspl. 20). There is also a five-day **International Jazz Festival** every April or May, with tickets available at Ticket Corner, at the Schweizerischer Bankverein (Swiss Bank Corporation; ⊠ Bärenpl., ☎ 031/3362539).

Opera

Bern's resident company is famous for its adventurous productions. Performances are at the **Stadttheater** (⊠ Kornhauspl. 20, ☎ 031/3110777); tickets are sold next door (⊠ Kornhauspl. 18) weekdays 10–6:30, Saturday 10–4, and Sunday 10–12:30.

Theater

Although you can see traditional and modern plays at the **Stadttheater** (⊠ Kornhauspl. 20, ☎ 031/3110777), a characteristic of Bern is its range of little theaters, mostly found in the cellars in the Old Town.

The **Berner Puppentheater** (⊠ Gerechtigkeitsg. 31, ☎ 031/3119585) produces funny, action-packed puppet shows—enjoyable even if you don't speak the language. **Kleintheater** (⊠ Kramg. 6, ☎ 031/3113080) has a modern repertoire; buy tickets at the **Müller & Schade** store (⊠ Kramg. 52, ☎ 031/3202626). Avant-garde plays, satires, and burlesques (in Swiss-German), plus pantomime and modern dance, are performed at **Theater am Käfigturm** (⊠ Marktg. 67, ☎ 031/3116100).

OUTDOOR ACTIVITIES AND SPORTS

Bicycling

There are about 300 km (185 mi) of marked trails around Bern; ask for routes at the tourist office. Bikes can be rented at the Hauptbahnhof, the main train station.

Golf

The **Golf and Country Club Blumisberg** (⊠ 18 km/11 mi west of town, ☎ 026/4963438) has 18 holes and a clubhouse with a restaurant, bar, showers, and swimming pool. The club admits visitors weekdays, provided they are members of any golf club with handicaps. Only local members and their guests are admitted on weekends.

Swimming

The beach at **Aarebad Lorraine** (⊠ Uferweg, ☎ 031/3322950) is on the right bank northwest of the Kursaal. Below the Parliament building you can swim in the river at the **Aarebad Marzili** waterfront (⊠ Marzilistr. 29, ☎ 031/3110046). **Hallenbad Hirschengraben** (⊠ Maulbeerstr. 14, ☎ 031/3813656) is an indoor swimming pool.

SHOPPING

Shop hours are generally weekdays 8:15–6:30, Thursday to 9 PM, and Saturday 8:15–4; Sunday most stores are closed, and many remain closed Monday morning.

Department Stores

Globus (⊠ Spitalg. 17–21, ☎ 031/3118811), one of the city's largest department stores, has a wide variety of designer labels. **Loeb** (⊠ Spitalg. 47–57, ☎ 031/3207111) is the good, old-fashioned kind of department store where the owner, Mr. Loeb himself, can sometimes be found greeting his customers.

Markets

Every Tuesday and Saturday morning, colorful farmers' markets (fruits, vegetables, and flowers) take place on the **Bärenplatz,** where buskers perform pantomime and music. There's a meat-and-dairy market on **Münstergasse.** A general market is held on **Waisenhausplatz.** Both are held on Tuesday and Saturday. From May through October, a flea market sets up shop every third Saturday on **Mühleplatz,** behind the cathedral. On the first Saturday of the month, the **Münsterplatz** is the site of an arts-and-crafts fair. Mid-May brings the geranium market (mornings only) to the **Münsterplatz.**

Shopping Streets

The **Old Town** is one big shopping center, and its 6 km (4 mi) of arcades shelter stores of every kind and quality. Many of the modern, mainstream shops are concentrated between the Bahnhof and the Clock Tower, especially on **Spitalgasse** and **Marktgasse.** Beyond, along **Kramgasse** and **Gerechtigkeitsgasse** and, parallel to them on the north, **Postgasse,** are quirkier, artsy spots and excellent antiques stores. Don't overlook the unusual variety of cellar shops, accessible from the street outside the arcades. Good shopping can be had at **Junkerngasse** and **Münstergasse,** especially in art galleries and avant-garde fashion boutiques.

Specialty Stores

Antiques

The best antiques shops line Gerechtigkeitsgasse and Postgasse; their wares range from cluttery *brocante* (collectibles) to good antiques from all over Europe. The **Puppenklinik** (⊠ Gerechtigkeitsg. 36, ☎ 031/3120771) is just this side of a museum, with its shelves and window densely packed with lovely—if slightly eerie—old dolls and toys.

Chocolate

Abegglen (⊠ Spitalg. 36, ☎ 031/3112111) has great chocolate-covered almonds. Don't leave **Beeler's** (⊠ Spitalg. 29, ☎ 031/3112808) without trying their champagne chocolates. **Eichenberger** (⊠ Bahnhofpl. 5, ☎ 031/3113325) is known for its hazelnut *Lebkuchen* (a flat spice cake). **Tschirren** (⊠ Kramg. 73, ☎ 031/3111717) has been making chocolates and sweets for more than 80 years. The mandarin chocolates are divine.

Souvenirs/Gifts

Heimatwerk Bern (⊠ Kramg. 61, ☎ 031/3113000) offers a broad, high-quality range of Swiss-made handicrafts, textiles and ceramics. **Langenthal** (⊠ Marktg. 15, ☎ 031/3118786) is where you'll find fine Swiss embroidery and linens. For the needlepoint enthusiast, stop in the period furniture store **P. Hack** (⊠ Kramg. 11, ☎ 031/3114193) for a wide selection of exquisite motifs to work on.

EXCURSION TO THE EMMENTAL

The great city of Bern stands alone in a large and lovely region tourists usually overlook: the Berner Mittelland, the rural lowlands of the enormous canton Bern. These mist-wrapped, green-velvet foothills lap the base of the Bernese Alps. Driving on back roads, you will see neat, prosperous old towns and farms, a handful of castles, and—most of all—verdant, undulating patchwork countryside.

Its most famous—though as yet unspoiled—region is the **Emmental,** the valley of the River Emme, where Switzerland's trademark cheese is made: Emmentaler, the one with the holes. Here you can visit a cheese factory and admire some of Switzerland's most beautiful farmhouses— plump, broad boxes topped with deep-curving roofs that slope nearly to the ground. In the 19th century, Swiss clergyman Jeremias Gotthelf found the virtues of family life and Christian beliefs in this breathtaking valley to be so inspiring that he turned to writing novels and short stories about the Emmentalers. His efforts revealed a prodigious literary talent, making him one of Switzerland's most famous writers.

Not much has changed in the Emmental since Gotthelf's time. Here, the canton is at its slowest. It isn't rudeness that silences the regulars of a local restaurant and directs their stares when an outsider walks in—it's an age-old wariness of strangers, a "take your time to size 'em up" attitude. Service will be friendly but impossibly slow, so leave your schedules behind and enjoy. Within a half hour of leaving the city of Bern on Highway 10 going toward Worb/Langnau, bedroom communities give way to small farm villages with picturesque curved-roof country inns, their emblems suspended from wrought-iron brackets. After about 10 km (6 mi) you'll be in **Zäziwil.** Follow the signs heading to Langnau, then turn left at Bowil for the small road up the hill to the summit of **Chuderhüsi** (6 km/4 mi). At the top (1,103 m/3,650 ft), the road opens to a panorama of the Bernese Alps in all their glory. There is a restaurant, whose only claim to fame is the view; save your appetite for another local spot.

Heading down on the other side of Chuderhüsi, you'll come to the the the **Würzbrunnen Church,** featured in films made about Jeremias Gotthelf. Take the road down into the valley at Rothenbach and then follow the signs for Eggiwil, where the road meets up with and then follows the Emme, the river from which the valley takes its name. You'll cross or pass seven covered bridges by the time you reach the village of Schüpbach (about 11 km/6½ mi), where you can turn left for a stop in the pretty little village of **Signau** (2 km/1 mi), a good place to see examples of the local architecture, or head right for a side trip to **Langnau** (about 10 km/6 mi) and on to **Trubschachen** (7 km/4½ mi), where you can visit some small local museums and a demonstration pottery studio. From Langnau and Trubschachen, double back to the village of Emmenmat and continue north, following the signs to **Sumiswald.** Take your time—the scenery is nothing short of spectacular.

Here the gentle hills begin to roll out village after beautiful village. The scenery is dotted with many impressive examples of the classic Emmental farmstead. The enormous *Bauernhaus* (main building) shelters the living quarters of the farmer and his family; at the back of the house, built into the central plan, is the cowshed; and grains and feed are stored upstairs, under the deep roof. Next door, in a separate house, lives the older generation: when a farmer retires, he passes the entire farm on to his youngest son and moves into the *Stöckli,* a kind of guest house, conceding the home to the new family. The third building, standing apart, is the *Spycher,* for storing the harvest of food, grains, and in olden days, the family's savings. If the farm caught fire, this building would be saved over the main house.

Continue north in the direction of Huttwil, turning left at Weier (7 km/4½ mi) to visit the cheese museum in **Affoltern**. Follow signs to **Burgdorf** to complete the circuit, where you can pick up the highway back to Bern (about 20 km/13 mi).

TIMING

If you are based in Bern and have a car, a 90-km (56-mi) round-trip begun late morning with lots of stops for photos and lunch can get you back in time for dinner in the city. If you plan to spend some time visiting the cheese factory and museums, get an earlier start.

Numbers in the margin correspond to points of interest on the Emmental map.

Signau

❶ *24 km (15 mi) east of Bern*

Signau is a pretty village typical of the region. There are some impressive examples of the classic Emmental farmstead.

Dining and Lodging

$ ✕ **Zum Wysse Rössli.** In Zäziwil (9 km/6 mi southwest of Signau), this grand old Emmental inn, its roof spreading out like the wings of a mother hen, shelters innumerable halls for local sports clubs and family events, but its main pub and restaurant serve the natives daily. Read a newspaper, meet your card-playing neighbors, and tackle a little local dialect—the menu is in Swiss-German. Rösti, mixed salads, and smoked farm ham are outstanding; heavier meat dishes and meringue with ice cream may do you in (pleasantly). ✉ *Thunstr. 10, Zäziwil,* ☎ *031/ 7111532. AE, DC, MC, V. Closed Tues.*

$ ✕🏨 **Bären.** Look for the enormous bear jutting out above the entrance of this inn on Signau's main street. The restaurant keeps the locals happy with uncompromising Emmental cooking: fluffy cheese tarts, golden Rösti,

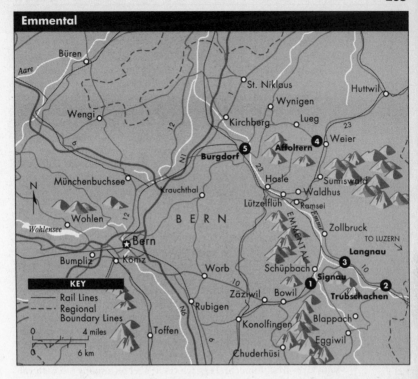

Emmental

enormous mixed salads, local game, and silky wild mushrooms in season. The rooms upstairs offer impeccable modern comfort. ⊠ *Dorfstr. 48, CH-3534 Signau,* ☎ FAX *034/4971364. 4 rooms. MC, V. Closed Mon.*

Trubschachen

2 *13 km (8 mi) east of Schüpbach, 37 km (23 mi) east of Bern.*

Trubschachen, a center for the region's folk-style ceramics, sits in the shadow of the 1,195-m (3,920-ft) ridge Blappach. (If you brave the narrow farm road up the ridge, you'll find more good views toward the Bernese Alps.) There's a **Heimatmuseum** (Local Museum) arranged in the three traditional buildings of a farm, with crafts and household antiques displayed in the *Spycher* and *Stöckli.* If you plan to visit by appointment, call a few days in advance. ⊠ ☎ *034/4956038.* 🖭 *4 SF.* ⊙ *Apr.–Nov., Sun. only 2–4, or by request.*

For a chance to watch local craftspeople at work, visit the *Schautöpferei* (demonstration pottery studio) in the *Bauernhaus* building of the Heimatmuseum. There you'll also find a shop full of local ceramics and a cozy upstairs café. ⊠ ☎ *034/4956029.* 🖭 *Free.* ⊙ *Weekdays 8–noon and 1:30–5:30, Sat. 9–noon and 1:30–5:30.*

Langnau

3 *7 km (4 mi) west of Trubschachen, 30 km (19 mi) east of Bern.*

This graceful old market town serves as capital of the region and clearinghouse for its cheese. Here you will find the **Heimatmuseum Langnau,** a museum of traditional crafts, tools, and furniture as well as military paraphernalia, all in an enormous chalet. ⊠ *Bärenpl. 2a, Langnau,* ☎ *034/4021819.* 🖭 *3 SF.* ⊙ *Tues.–Sun. 1:30–6. Closed Dec.–Mar.*

Affoltern

❹ *30 km (19 mi) northwest of Langnau, 35 km (22 mi) northeast of Bern.*

Affoltern, another small, traditional village, has some strong examples of Emmental architecture. The main attraction is the *Schaukäserei* (demonstration dairy), which allows you to see Swiss cheese in the making. From a glassed-in balcony, you can watch gallons of milk being stirred in copper cauldrons, its curd being separated from its whey in great sieves, with the heavy solids eased into molds to be brine-soaked and then stored. Try to be here between 9 and 11 AM or 2 and 4 PM, when the most active stages of cheese making take place. In a restored *Stöckli* from 1741, old-fashioned ways of cheese making over a wood fire are sometimes demonstrated. ☎ *034/4351611.* ✆ *Free.* ☉ *Daily 8:30–6:30.*

Dining and Lodging

$ ✕ **Emmentaler Schaukäserei.** After you've toured the factory and exhibits on cheese making, you can sate your appetite at the factory's simple restaurant, where the menu covers cheese dishes—fondue, *Käseschnitte*—as well as local cold meats. Special cheese breakfasts are served daily until 11:30. In fine weather, picnic on the self-service terrace. ⊠ *Affoltern,* ☎ *034/4351611. AE, DC, MC, V.*

$$ ✕▦ **Sonne.** This is an archetypal Emmental guest house: weathered but pristine, steeped in tradition but airy and bright, and serving rich, hearty cooking based on ingredients straight off the farm. There are satiny soups, flaky *Pastetli* (puff pastry filled with creamed veal), unusually well-executed veal dishes, and freshwater fish. Make a heroic effort to leave room for the meringue, fluffed to enormous proportions with farm-fresh Emmental egg whites. It's set on a sunny hill with valley views, not far from the demonstration cheese dairy. There are a few simple bedrooms upstairs. The restaurant is closed to nonguests on Thursday and serves no lunch on Friday. ⊠ *CH-3416 Affoltern,* ☎ *034/4358000,* FAX *034/4358019. 12 rooms. AE, DC, MC, V. Closed Jan.*

OFF THE   **LUEG.** From Affoltern, make a side trip northwest to Lueg (887 m/2,909
BEATEN PATH   ft) for views toward the Alps: It's a brief walk uphill to the crest to take in the great panorama and to catch the Alps in a different light from the one seen earlier in the day from Chuderhüsi.

Burgdorf

❺ *12 km (7 mi) west of Affoltern and 25 km (15 mi) north of Bern.*

In Burgdorf there's a sizable Gothic castle built in the 12th century by the Zähringens, the family responsible for the founding of the cities of Bern, Fribourg, Murten, and Burgdorf. The castle was turned into a museum more than 100 years ago: the **Schlossmuseum Burgdorf** (Burgdorf Castle Museum). A walk through the Knights' Hall and the various rooms, towers, and battlements of the original castle introduces you to the history and culture of Burgdorf and the Emmental. Regional costumes, ceramics, and period furniture are displayed along with alternating exhibitions. ☎ *034/4230214.* ✆ *5 SF.* ☉ *Apr. 1–Nov. 1, Mon.– Sat. 2–5, Sun. 11–5.*

The **Kornhaus,** a former granary, now houses the Swiss Center for Folk Culture, a collection of Swiss costumes, phonographs, musical instruments, and a yodeling hall. ⊠ *Kornhausg. 16,* ☎ *034/4231010.* ✆ *10 SF.* ☉ *Tues.–Fri. 10–12:30 and 1:30–5; weekends 10–5.*

Emmental A to Z

Getting Around

BY CAR

Driving is by far the best way to experience this rural region because good, small highways carry you from town to town through countryside often untouched by modern architecture. Highway 10 from Bern is the best way into the region. The small, rural roads are indicated by the names of the towns they connect.

BY TRAIN AND BUS

If you plan your itinerary carefully, you can arrange a comfortable though limited tour of the region combining trains from Bern into Burgdorf, connecting to Hasle; from there you can take a post bus to Affoltern, for instance, to visit the cheese factory. Or stay on the train all the way to Langnau and enjoy the countryside as you travel.

Guided Tours

Badertscher (✉ Freiburgstr. 430, CH-3018 Bern, ☎ 031/9919100) offers coach excursions through the region. **Emmental Tours** (✉ CH-3454 Sumiswald, ☎ 034/4312161) is another resource. Some tours are available in English, but they must be arranged through Pro Emmental (☞ Visitor Information, *below*).

One of the most novel and effective ways to experience the region is by plodding down its back roads behind a team of horses in a Gypsy wagon and lodging in typical Emmentaler inns. You can pack a picnic or stop for lunch at a guest house along the way. Contact **Eurotrek/Unitours** (✉ Freischutzg. 3, CH-8004 Zürich, ☎ 01/2955555).

Visitor Information

Pro Emmental (✉ Schlossstr. 3, CH-3550 Langnau, ☎ 034/4024252, FAX 034/4025667) is extremely helpful; they can supply you with maps and routes for hikes in the region.

BERN A TO Z

Arriving and Departing

By Car

Bern is connected conveniently by expressway to Basel via **A1,** to the Berner Oberland via **A6,** and to Lac Léman and thus Lausanne, Geneva, and the Valais via **A12.**

By Plane

The small airport **Belp** (✉ Belpmoos, 9 km/6 mi south of Bern, ☎ 031/9602111) has flights to Amsterdam, Brussels, Frankfurt, and most other major European airports connecting through **Crossair** (☎ 031/9602121 for reservations), Switzerland's domestic airline. **Air Engiadina** (☎ 061/9601211), a regional airline, offers direct flight connections with Munich and Vienna.

BETWEEN THE AIRPORT AND THE CENTER

A city **bus** runs regularly between Belp and the city's Hauptbahnhof (main train station). The fare each way is 14 SF. A **taxi** from the airport to the Hauptbahnhof costs about 35 SF and takes about 15 minutes.

By Train

Bern is a major link between Geneva, Zürich, and Basel, and **fast trains** run almost every hour from the enormous central station, the **Hauptbahnhof** (☎ 1572222). Bern is the only European capital to have three **high-speed trains**: the ICE, the TGV, and the **Pendolino**. The ICE

from Berlin takes nine hours; the TGV from Paris takes 4½ hours; the
Pendolino from Milan takes 3–4 hours.

Getting Around

The best of Bern is concentrated in a relatively small area, and it's easy
to get around on foot.

By Bus and Tram

Bus and tram services are excellent, with fares ranging from 1.50 SF
to 2.40 SF. Buy individual tickets from the dispenser at the tram or bus
stop: find the name of the stop closest to your destination on the map,
then check to see the fare on the list of stops. There is an unlimited-
travel Visitors Card available—6 SF for 24 hours, 9 SF for 48 hours,
and 12 SF for 72 hours—at the tourist office in the Hauptbahnhof (☞
Visitor Information, *below*) or at the public-transportation ticket office in the passageway leading down to the Hauptbahnhof (take the
escalator in front of Loeb's department store and turn right through
the Christoffel Tower). A Swiss Pass (☞ Train Travel *in* Smart Travel
Tips A to Z) includes free travel in Bern.

By Taxi

Taxis are actually a cumbersome alternative to walking, especially
when streets are dominated by trams. It costs between 12 SF and 15
SF to cross town.

Contacts and Resources

Embassies

United States (✉ Jubiläumsstr. 93, ☎ 031/3577011). **Canada** (✉
Kirchenfeldstr. 88, ☎ 031/3573200). **United Kingdom** (✉ Thunstr. 50,
☎ 031/3597700).

Emergencies

Police (☎ 117). **Ambulance** (☎ 144). **Hospital** (✉ Insel Spital,
Freiburgstr., ☎ 031/6322111). **Medical and dental referrals** (☎ 031/
3112211). **All-night pharmacy referrals** (☎ 031/3112211).

English-Language Bookstore

Stauffacher (✉ Neueng. 25, ☎ 031/3112411) has the broadest selection of books in English. There's a great café-bookshop on its second
floor.

Guided Tours

ORIENTATION TOURS

A two-hour, English-commentary bus tour around the Old Town, covering all the principal sights, is offered for 22 SF by the tourist office,
where you meet.

PERSONAL GUIDES

To arrange for a private guide, contact the tourist office (☞ *below*).

Travel Agency

Carlson Wagonlit Travel (✉ Von Werdt-Passage 5, ☎ 031/3282828).

Visitor Information

Berne Tourismus (✉ Bahnhofpl., at the main train station, CH-3001,
☎ 031/3281212, FAX 031/3121233) has several special services, including
Clock Tower visits, walking tours, and even a city tour by raft on the
Aare.

10 BERNER OBERLAND

Gstaad, Interlaken, Wengen

The Bernese Alps concentrate the very best of rural Switzerland: panoramas of the treble peaks of the Eiger, Mönch, and Jungfrau mountains; crystalline lakes, gorges, and waterfalls; and emerald slopes dotted with gingerbread chalets and cows with bells—not to mention world-class skiing. It's no secret, though: Berner Oberland is the most touristic canton in Switzerland.

Updated by
Susan Tuttle-
Laube

THERE ARE TIMES WHEN THE REALITY OF Switzerland puts postcard idealization to shame, surpassing tinted-indigo skies and advertising-image peaks with its own astonishing vividness. Those times happen often in Berner Oberland. Though the Valais and Graubünden areas offer stiff competition, this rugged region concentrates the very best of rural Switzerland: mountain panoramas that can't be overrated, massive glaciers, crystalline lakes, gorges and waterfalls, chic ski resorts, and emerald slopes scattered with gingerbread chalets.

After contemplating the Staubbach Falls in 1779, the great German writer Johann Wolfgang von Goethe was moved to write one of his most celebrated poems, "Gesang der Geister über den Wassern" ("Song of the Spirits over the Waters"). Rousseau spread word of its astounding natural phenomena to Paris society. Then the Romantics began to beat a path to the awe-inspiring region. Lord Byron came to investigate; it's said he conceived his *Manfred* in barren, windswept Wengernalp. Shelley followed, then William Thackeray, John Ruskin, and Mark Twain; the landscape master painter J. M. W. Turner and the composer Johannes Brahms took in the views; finally, Queen Victoria herself came, beginning a flood of tourism that changed Berner Oberland's—and Switzerland's—profile forever.

Before the onslaught of visitors inspired the locals to switch from farming to innkeeping, agriculture was the prime industry—and is still much in evidence today. As if hired as props to style a photo opportunity, brown cows pepper the hillsides wherever rock gives way to grass, and the mountains echo with their bells. The houses of the Berner Oberland are classics, the definitive Swiss chalets: the broad, low, deep-eaved roofs cover gables that are scalloped, carved, and painted with the family dedication; the wood weathers to dark sienna after generations of harsh cold and clear sun. From early spring through autumn, every window box spills torrents of well-tended scarlet geraniums, and adjacent woodpiles are stacked with mosaiclike precision.

The region is arranged tidily enough for even a brief visit. Its main resort city, Interlaken, lies in green lowlands between the gleaming twin pools of the Brienzersee and the Thunersee, linked by the River Aare. Behind them to the south loom craggy, forested foothills with excellent views, and behind those foothills stand some of Europe's noblest peaks, most notably the snowy crowns of the Eiger (3,970 m/13,022 ft), the Mönch (4,099 m/13,445 ft), and the fiercely beautiful Jungfrau (4,158 m/13,638 ft). Because nature laid it out so conveniently, the region has become far and away the most popular for tourism, with its excursion and transportation systems carrying enormous numbers of visitors to its myriad viewpoints, overlooks, and wonders of the world. The railroad to the Jungfraujoch transports masses of tour groups to its high-altitude attractions, and on a peak-season day its station can resemble the Sistine Chapel in August or the Chicago Board of Trade. But the tourist industry can handle the onslaught, offering such an efficient network of boats, trains, and funiculars; such a variety of activities and attractions; and such a wide range of accommodations, from posh city hotels to rustic mountain lodges, that every visitor can find the most suitable way to take in the marvels of the Bernese Alps.

Pleasures and Pastimes

Dining

Meals in Berner Oberland tend to be down-to-earth, starting with hearty soup or mixed slawlike salads, followed by lake fish or meat and potatoes, and then a sizable dessert. Fried or broiled *Egli* (perch) and *Felchen* (whitefish) are frequently local and lake-fresh; such waterfront resorts as Spiez, Brienz, and Iseltwald specialize in fish. Meat dishes represent Bernese and Zürich cuisines: *Ratsherrentopf* is a mixed grill, *geschnetzeltes Kalbsfleisch* is veal in cream sauce. Colorful mixed salads include crisp shredded celery root, beet, carrot, and cabbage. Because the Alpine experience demands it, the Oberland has adopted the French territories' cheese fondue and raclette (a dish of melted cheese served with potatoes and pickles) as winter-night staples.

The valley town of Meiringen claims to have invented meringue; whether or not this is true, its region consumes enough to corner the culinary market. Enormous, crisp, ivory meringue puffs may be served with or without vanilla ice cream; regardless, they are buried under mounds of heavy piped whipped cream.

CATEGORY	COST*
$$$$	over 70 SF
$$$	40 SF–70 SF
$$	20 SF–40 SF
$	under 20 SF

Prices are per person for a three-course meal (two-course meal in $ category), including sales tax and 15% service charge

Hiking

Partly because of its spectacular ski transport network woven throughout the region, the Berner Oberland offers a wealth of highly developed walking and hiking options. The scenery is magnificent—what can surpass the views from the Mürren plateau toward the Jungfrau, Eiger, and Mönch?—and the options varied, from rough trails toward glaciers to smooth postbus roads. From May through October you'll be unlikely to find yourself alone for long on any given trail; you'll even find company on a snowy trail since nearly one-third of the region's visitors come for winter hiking. A wide variety of topographical maps and suggested itineraries is available at local tourist offices, especially the Jungfrau region central office on the Höheweg in Interlaken.

Lake Cruises

Steamers crisscross the lakes of Brienz and Thun, trailing leisurely across crystal waters past rolling panoramas of forested hills and craggy, snowcapped peaks. They provide an alternative to high-speed car cruises and limited train runs and, with their buslike schedule, allow passengers to step off at any port for a visit; you need only choose the best boat to catch next. Drinks and meals in the glassed-in cafés (both first and second class) offer respite on windy days.

Lodging

Berner Oberland tradition mandates charming chalet-style exteriors replete with scalloped-wood balconies, steeply sloped roofs, and cascades of scarlet geraniums, no matter what architectural era a hotel dates from. But many hotels in the region have interiors that reflect their roots in the '60s ski boom, with their no-nonsense, Scandinavian-spare, avocado-beige and walnut-grain Formica furnishings. Some of the most recently renovated have softened the '60s edge with such folksy touches as carved knotty pine. A few landmarks have preserved interiors that reflect their lovely facades. Although a vast majority of the hotels are still family owned and run, big businesses are creeping in, scooping up properties that private families can no longer carry and creating competition that forces even more family-run places to go under, a sad scenario that is actively being fought in some communities. Small towns may not have street addresses; in those cases, hotels large and small are clearly signposted. Prices below are average for the Berner Oberland; note that such car-free resorts as Wengen and Mürren run well above this curve, especially during ski season. Half-board, or *demipension* (breakfast and one hot meal), and full-board (three meals) plans are often the thrust of regional hotels. Remember that many properties post rates on a per-person basis.

CATEGORY	COST*
$$$$	over 250 SF
$$$	200 SF–250 SF
$$	120 SF–200 SF
$	under 120 SF

Prices are for a standard double room, including breakfast, tax, and service charge.

Skiing

As one of Switzerland's winter-sports capitals, the Berner Oberland provides a dazzling variety of choices to skiers. Each resort offers its own style of transit and its own peculiar terrain, from nursery slopes to the deadly narrow pistes of the Schilthorn. The lift lines are a fair bit more tolerable here, although the region as a whole is not as snow-sure as is, for example, the Engadine.

Exploring Berner Oberland

The central, urban-Victorian resort of Interlaken makes a good base for excursions for visitors who want to experience the entire Jungfrau region, which includes the craggy, bluff-lined Lauterbrunnen Valley and the opposing resorts that perch high above it: Mürren and Wengen. Both busy, sporty Grindelwald, famous for scenic rides and sports, and isolated Kandersteg, ideal for hiking and cross-country skiing, can be visited out of Interlaken, but they also make good home bases themselves; they both lie at the dead end of gorge roads that climb into the heights. Spreading east and west of Interlaken are the Brienz and Thun lakes, both broad, crystalline, and surrounded by forests, castles, and picturesque waterfront resorts, including Brienz and Thun. From Spiez on the Thunersee, you can head west through the forest gorge of the Simmental to the Saanenland and glamorous Gstaad. Connections by rail or car keep most highlights within easy reach.

Numbers in the text correspond to numbers in the margin and on the Berner Oberland map.

Great Itineraries

Ten days in Berner Oberland gives you the luxury of exploring each of the valleys and lakes of this varied region, but you can experience it *en passage* as well, depending on your travel pace.

IF YOU HAVE 3 DAYS

Base yourself in busy ⊠ **Interlaken** ① or the quieter **Bönigen** ②, one day taking a boat trip across the Thunersee to **Thun** ⑫, the next day a driving tour around the Brienzersee to **Brienz** ⑨ and the Freilichtmuseum Ballenberg. The third day (or best-weather day) head up the Lauterbrunnen Valley and take the famous rail trip from **Wengen** ⑥ to the **Jungfraujoch** ⑤, returning via **Grindelwald** ⑦.

Follow the tours above, and while in the Lauterbrunnen Valley, take the cable cars or cogwheel rail up to **Mürren** ④ and the Schilthorn. On day five, drive up to **Kandersteg** ⑮ to hike to the Oeschinensee, or wind through the forest to visit famous 🔝 **Gstaad** ⑯.

Rent an apartment or settle in on a half-board (breakfast and one hot meal) or full-board (three meals) plan in one of the cozier hotels of Interlaken or any crossroads resort (Grindelwald and Lauterbrunnen also offer easy access to sights), taking in the lesser sights as you cruise around the varied region. Visit the Trümmelbach Falls in the Lauterbrunnen Valley, see the castles at **Hilterfingen** ⑬ and **Oberhofen** ⑭ on the Thunersee, and take another high-altitude excursion out of Interlaken to Harder Kulm, Heimwehfluh, or Schynige Platte. You might even hop on a train and make a day trip into the capital city of Bern, only an hour away (☞ Chapter 9).

When to Tour Berner Oberland

In high summer, the Berner Oberland is the most popular tourist area in Switzerland and can feel overrun, so aim for the cusp—mid-June, late September—when the weather still holds but the crowds thin. Ski season begins in mid-December and runs through Easter vacation. May and November are low season, and prices drop—but some hotels and cable cars shut down for maintenance; depending on snow conditions, some excursions may be closed into June or shut down mid-October. But fear not: The Jungfraujoch rail trip (☞ *below*) runs 365 days a year, even in pea-soup fog.

JUNGFRAU REGION

The thriving resort town of Interlaken lies between two spectacularly sited lakes, the Brienzersee (Lake Brienz) and the Thunersee (Lake Thun), and is the gateway to two magnificent mountain valleys, one leading up to the popular sports resort of Grindelwald, the other into Lauterbrunnen and the famous car-free resorts of Wengen and Mürren. Rearing over both valleys, the Jungfrau and its partner peaks, the Eiger and Mönch, can be viewed from various high-altitude overviews.

Interlaken

❶ *58 km (36 mi) southeast of Bern.*

The name *Interlaken* has a Latin source: *interlacus* (between lakes). As a gateway to the Berner Oberland, this bustling Victorian resort town is the obvious home base for travelers planning to visit the region's two lakes and the mountains towering behind them. At 570 m (1,870 ft), Interlaken dominates the Bödeli, the branch of lowland between the lakes that Interlaken shares with the adjoining towns of Unterseen, Wilderswil, Bönigen, and Matten. The town's two train stations, Interlaken East and Interlaken West, are good orientation points; most sights are just a few minutes' walk from one of the stations. There are unlimited excursion options, and it's a pleasant, if urban, place to stay put as well, as its setting is spectacular and its ambience genteel.

The **Höheweg** is the city's main promenade, its tree- and flower-lined walkways cutting through the edge of the broad green parklands of the **Höhematte**. This 35-acre park once pastured the herds of the Augustinian monastery that dominated medieval Interlaken. Cows are still pastured there in fenced-off areas that are moved to different spots on the field daily.

TO
BERN

TO LUZERN

Wiggen

Flühli

SWITZERLAND

TO LUZERN

Marbach

Kleinteil

Oberei

Glaubenbüelenpass

chwarzenegg

Brienzer Rothorn

Lungernsee

Lungern

4

liederhorn

6-11 **Brienz**

9

Freilichtmuseum Ballenberg

10

eatenberg

Harder Kulm

St. Beatushöhlen

Brienzersee

■ Giessbach

Meiringen

nersee

Unterseen

8 **Iseltwald**

Bönigen

1 **Interlaken**
Matten

Heimwehfluh

Wilderswil

Schynige Platte

First

Gündlischwand

Zweilütschinen

Grindelwald

7

6 **Wengen**

Lauberhorn

Lauterbrunnen

3

Staubbachfälle

Kleine Scheidegg

Eiger

Trümmelbachfälle

Mönch

Schilthorn

Mürren

4

OBERER GRINDELWALD GLETSCHER

Mürrenbachfälle

5 **Jungfraujoch**

Jungfrau

BLÜMLISALP

ALETSCH GLACIER

Breithorn

KEY

—— Rail Lines

•••• Funicular/ Cable Car

- - - Regional Boundary Line

🎿 Ski Resort

N

0   6 miles

0   9 km

Mark Twain once sojourned at the **Grand Hotel Victoria-Jungfrau** (☞ Dining and Lodging, *below*), on the Höheweg, conceived to take in the view of the snowy Jungfrau that towers above town. The hotel originated as two humbler inns, the Jungfrau (1864) and the Chalet Victoria (1865); these were merged and expanded in 1895, and the facade redesigned and landmark tower added in 1899.

Between the Höheweg and the River Aare, you'll find the landscaped **Kursaal** (Casino) grounds, complete with a floral clock. Built in 1859 in a dramatic combination of Oberland-chalet and Victorian styles, the Kursaal was renovated in 1968 and has become once again a social focal point for the city. Plays and concerts are presented here, mostly during the high season, and there are folklore evenings in the adjoining *Spycher* (the Swiss name for a farm storage barn). The **casino** here has gambling nightly, including 120 slot machines, but bets are limited by federal law to 5 SF (☞ Nightlife and the Arts, *below*). ⊠ *Off Höheweg,* ☎ *033/8276100.*

The **Schlosskirche** (Castle Church) was once the chapel for the Augustinian monastery. Though founded in 1133, the monastery and the convent that shared its grounds in the 13th century have left only a 14th-century chancel and a wing of the cloister. The rest of the convent was built into a private castle in 1745, which, attached behind the church, is now used as office space. ⊠ *At the end of the Höhematte, south of the Hotel du Nord.*

On the north side of the River Aare is the tiny town of **Unterseen,** with its picturesque Old Town and Marktplatz (Marketplace). Founded in 1279 on land rented from the Augustinians, Unterseen retains some of the region's oldest buildings, including the 17th-century **Stadthaus** (city hall) and the 14th-century **church**, its steeple dating from 1471. The **Schloss Unterseen** (Unterseen Castle), built in 1656 for the reigning Bernese nobleman, stands at the opposite end of the square, near a medieval arched gateway. You can get here via a short (10-minute) bus ride from Interlaken's center, or even by walking; it's near the Interlaken West train station.

Fronting on the Unterseen Marktplatz is the **Touristik-Museum der Jungfrau Region** (Museum of Tourism of the Jungfrau Region), which traces the history of tourism in the Jungfrau region over the last 200 years. Exhibits include models of early transportation and examples of primitive mountain-climbing and skiing equipment. ⊠ *Obereg. 26,* ☎ *033/8229839.* ☎ *5 SF.* ☉ *May–mid-Oct., Tues.–Sun. 2–5.*

OFF THE
BEATEN PATH

HARDER KULM – Take the 12-minute funicular ride up Harder Kulm (1,310 m/4,297 ft); from there, hike uphill to views south over the city, the lakes, and the whole panorama of snowy peaks. A turreted Gothic chalet–style restaurant offers Friday-evening visitors more than food: from mid-June through September, there are folk music and dancing, too, and you're free to join in. The funicular runs every 20 to 30 minutes. ⊠ *Funicular station north of the River Aare near Interlaken East, across the Beaurivagebrücke,* ☎ *033/8287339.* ☎ *Funicular round-trip: 20 SF; music: 4 SF.* ☉ *Funicular: June–Oct., daily 9:10–6:30. Music: departures every 30 minutes 7–8:30, returns at 11, 11:20, and midnight.*

HEIMWEHFLUH – An old-fashioned, red funicular railway leads to the top of this 669-m (2,194-ft) mountain, where you will get views over both lakes and an elevated peek at the Jungfrau, the Eiger, and the Mönch. A restaurant and playground have been built at the top, complete with a 300-m bob-run, and there's a show of model trains every 30 minutes.

The funicular station is a five-minute walk from the Interlaken West station down the Rugenparkstrasse. There's a departure every 15 minutes. If you hike to the top, the train show costs just 6 SF. ☎ *033/8223453.* ☒ *12 SF (includes model train show).* ⊘ *Easter and Apr. weekends; daily May–Oct.*

SCHYNIGE PLATTE – For the most splendid overview in the region, make the ambitious trip to this 1,965-m (6,445-ft) peak for a picnic, a wander down any of numerous footpaths, or a visit to the Alpine Botanical Garden, where more than 500 varieties of mountain flowers grow. You may opt to walk either up or (more comfortably) down: specify when you buy your ticket. Train service runs from approximately 7:40 AM to 6 PM. ☒ *Take 6-min ride on Bernese Oberland Railway from Interlaken East to Wilderswil; take 50-min cogwheel train ride to peak,* ☎ *033/ 8287233.* ☒ *Round-trip 54 SF; one-way 32 SF.* ⊘ *Late May or early June–late Oct., daily, depending on snow conditions.*

Dining and Lodging

$$$–$$$$ ★ ✕ **Alpenblick.** Just 2 km (1 mi) south of Interlaken, in Wilderswil, this hotel restaurant is one of the best in Berner Oberland (competing with Grindelwald's Fiescherblick). It is a carved-wood-and-shingle 17th-century landmark in the quiet old Oberdorf (Upper Village) and serves a varied clientele, among them loyal gastronomes who make a pilgrimage to try chef Richard Stöckli's international cuisine. Locals dine here regularly, too, seeking out old-style classics (Rösti with wild mushrooms) and upscale bistro fare (marinated lake fish tartare, duck liver pâté with onion confit). ☒ *Wilderswil,* ☎ *033/8220707. AE, DC, MC, V.*

$$–$$$ ✕ **Schuh.** With a luxurious shady terrace spilling into the Höhematte in summer and cocktail piano enhancing the dated elegance inside, this sweet shop and café-restaurant serves everything from tea to rich, hot meals. Leave room for the pastries, like the glossy strawberry tarts, which you'll find in the adjoining shop. ☒ *Höheweg 56,* ☎ *033/8229441. AE, DC, MC, V.*

$$–$$$ ★ ✕ **Stellambiente.** For something nicely out of the ordinary, try this restaurant in the Stella Hotel (☞ *below*). The modern, highly flavored cuisine includes several vegetarian options, with locally grown ingredients and an extraordinary variety of salads. Order the "surprise" menu in advance, and you'll be served five courses of unexpected delights on beautiful, individually selected pieces of china. There's an exceptional attention to detail. An attractive terrace, complete with fountain, turns summer dining into a garden idyll. Though it's not absolutely required, try to make reservations in advance. ☒ *Waldeggstr. 10,* ☎ *033/ 8228871. AE, DC, MC, V.*

$$–$$$ ✕ **Zum Bären.** Walk into this restaurant just across the river in Unterseen and you'll feel as though you've entered a model-chalet souvenir piggybank. The building has been a restaurant since 1674 and run by the same family for over 150 years. Standard Swiss dishes are perfectly prepared; for instance, the Rösti are done just right, crisp on the outside and tender within. Piped-in country music (in German) and the occasional yodel from the kitchen round out the experience. ☒ *Seestr. 2, Unterseen,* ☎ *033/8227526. AE, MC, V.*

$$ ★ ✕ **Im Gade.** This welcoming hybrid of carved-wood coziness and sleek formality fills up with appreciative locals who recognize fresh, fine cooking and alert service. Details count here: even that dab of smoky sauerkraut in your crisp mixed salad is homemade. Seasonal specialties (game, mushrooms) stand out. Fondues are available but are not the restaurant's forte: stick to the hearty veal dishes, the lake fish, or the generous daily specials. ☒ *Höheweg 70, Hotel du Nord,* ☎ *033/ 8222631. AE, DC, MC, V. Closed mid-Nov.–mid-Dec.*

\$\$ ✕ **Krebs.** The sunny front-porch serving area looks over the street, but head for the more formal dining room, glassed-in yet still opening onto the main promenade. You may feel you've forgotten your parasol: This is a classic, Old World resort spot and serves its upscale Swiss classics and homey daily plates (look for the fish dishes) with starched-collar style. It has been in Interlaken—and the Krebs family—since 1875. ✉ *Bahnhofstr. 4,* ☎ *033/8227161. AE, DC, MC, V. Closed Nov.–Apr.*

\$–\$\$ ✕ **Laterne.** You'll find this unpretentious local favorite a bit off the tourist
   ★   track, east of the center near the A–8 ring road (a 10-minute walk from Interlaken West). There's a sports-bar ambience, complete with piles of photo albums chronicling what seems to be every party ever held there, and a rustic, woodsy setting. Besides the big meat dinners there are good Swiss specialties: seven kinds of *Rösti* (hash-brown potatoes) served in iron skillets, vegetarian meals, and eight kinds of cheese fondue at reasonable prices. There's also live Swiss folk music every second Friday. ✉ *Obere Bönigstr. 18,* ☎ *033/8221141. AE, DC, MC, V.*

\$\$\$\$ 🛏 **Beau Rivage.** Its atmosphere harkening back more than a few
   ★   decades, this Interlaken old-timer is steeped in intimate, quiet luxury. Rich in brocades, muted tones, and patterned carpets, the rooms have views of either the mountains or the quiet Aare, and the hotel is just a stone's throw from the Interlaken East train station. Set well back from the road and surrounded by gardens, it maintains an unruffled calm. Delicate *cuisine du marché* (based on the freshest ingredients available) is served in the very highly rated hearth-warmed restaurant La Bonne Fourchette. ✉ *Höheweg 211, CH-3800,* ☎ *033/8216272,* 🖷 *033/8232847. 99 rooms. 2 restaurants, 2 bars, indoor pool, sauna, health club, bicycles. AE, DC, MC, V. Closed mid-Nov.–mid-Dec.*

\$\$\$\$ 🛏 **Grand Hotel Victoria-Jungfrau.** Grand says it all. Mark Twain may
   ★   have slept in this 1865 landmark, but its restoration has taken it firmly into the 20th century, with a glitzy postmodern black-and-burled-wood entry and plenty of facilities, including indoor master golf. The rooms are gorgeous, with styles shifting from elegant, fabric-covered walls and marble columns to fresh yellow gingham and waxed wood floors. Nearly all take in the obligatory view. The flashy formal restaurant, La Terrasse, is a vision of marble and glass overlooking the promenade and the Höhematte. A jacket and tie are required at the restaurant. ✉ *Höheweg 41, CH-3800,* ☎ *033/8282828,* 🖷 *033/8282880. 215 rooms. 2 restaurants, 2 bars, indoor pool, outdoor pool, beauty salon, spa, 7 tennis courts, billiards. AE, DC, MC, V.*

\$\$\$\$ 🛏 **Hotel Metropole.** As Berner Oberland's only skyscraper, this 18-story, concrete high-rise gobbles up the scenery and ruins everyone's view but its own—which is spectacular. The rooms have dark furniture, floral drapes, and enormous closets, but nothing can beat those views. The modern decor continues through the green-and-cream atrium lobby. In the rooftop restaurant you can feast your eyes on more staggering views while having a light lunch or snack. ✉ *Höheweg 37, CH-3800,* ☎ *033/8286666,* 🖷 *033/8286633. 97 rooms. Restaurant, indoor pool, massage, sauna. AE, DC, MC, V.*

\$\$\$–\$\$\$\$ 🛏 **Royal–St. Georges.** If you are a fan of Victoriana, this impeccably restored gem is a dream come true, with original moldings, built-in furnishings, and fantastical Art Nouveau bath fixtures. A few rooms were done in ho-hum modern, as some guests object to bathtubs with feet, but you can ask for a period version. The street-side rooms—the ones with Jungfrau views—are noisier. ✉ *Höheweg 139, CH-3800,* ☎ *033/8227575,* 🖷 *033/8233075. 89 rooms, 6 suites. Restaurant, bar, hot tub, sauna, steam rooms. AE, DC, MC, V. Closed Nov.–Jan.*

\$\$\$ 🛏 **Du Lac.** The riverboat docks behind this dependable hotel, with its lovely situation across from a wide, woodsy bank of the Aare. However, the train tracks are nearby and trains run hourly from 5:30 AM until midnight (don't leave your window open). Managed by a single family for more than 100 years, the hotel has been carefully maintained rather than slickly modernized. The high-ceiling rooms have kept their traditional style. ⊠ *Höheweg 225, CH-3800,* ☎ *033/8222922,* FAX *033/ 8222915. 40 rooms. Restaurant, Stübli. AE, DC, MC, V. Closed mid-Nov.–mid-Mar.*

$$$ 🏨 **Stella.** This small, family-run gem defies its outdated '60s exterior
★ and residential neighborhood setting. Inside, you'll find marvelous, friendly service; innovative, cozy rooms; and special, personal touches such as rose petals strewn across your duvet in welcome. This is a small hotel that truly does try harder—and does so successfully. The personal touch carries over to their restaurant, the Stellambiente (☞ *above*). ⊠ *Waldeggstr. 10 CH-3800,* ☎ *033/8228871,* FAX *033/8226671. 29 rooms. Restaurant, indoor pool. AE, DC, MC, V.*

$$ 🏨 **Chalet Oberland.** A vacation-intensive combination of rustic decor and city-crossroads position, this downtown lodge occupies both sides of the street and keeps expanding. The newest rooms (in the building pierced by a life-size cow model) are chic with warm wood tones and funkily designed bathrooms. The rooms in the older wing have a heavy-on-the-browns decor. ⊠ *Postg. 1, CH-3800,* ☎ *033/8278787,* FAX *033/8278770. 148 rooms. Bar, coffee shop, pizzeria. AE, DC, MC, V.*

$$ 🏨 **Splendid.** Location is key here: you can't get more central to shopping and nightlife. It's a modest, family-run, Victorian palace with some woodsy rooms and the occasional spindle bed breaking with the standard beige decor. The back rooms overlook a quiet backstreet; the corner bays are prettiest. The proprietor is a hunter, so game in season is fresh and local. ⊠ *Höheweg 33, CH-3800,* ☎ *033/8227612,* FAX *033/ 8227679. 35 rooms. Restaurant, pub. AE, MC, V. Closed late Oct.–Christmas.*

$$ 🏨 **Toscana.** Well situated in the pedestrian zone, this lodging emphasizes technical perfection: intercom, elevators, cable TVs, indoor parking, angled mountain views. Rooms are spacious, if bland, but the restaurant stands out with its personal touch of good Tuscan cooking, prepared by the Italian owners. ⊠ *Jungfraustr. 19, CH-3800,* ☎ *033/ 8233033,* FAX *033/8233551. 23 rooms. Restaurant, café, free parking. AE, MC, V. Closed Nov.–Christmas.*

$$ 🏨 **Zum Hirschen.** This dark-beam, 17th-century guest house, in one
★ family since 1666, has old, deep-shingle eaves and rooms with fresh knotty-pine walls and built-in furniture. The Stübli, paneled in aged pine, and the highly acclaimed restaurant, scattered with antiques, serve local specialties; veal, beef, cheese, vegetables, and even honey come from the owner's farm. There are a sheltered terrace and balcony overlooking a lovely garden. The hotel's location at an outskirts crossroads makes it convenient for drivers who are covering the region rather than staying in town. ⊠ *Hauptstr. 11, CH-3800,* ☎ *033/8221545,* FAX *033/ 8233745. 20 rooms, 1 suite. Restaurant, Stübli. AE, DC, MC, V. Closed Nov.–mid-Dec.*

$ 🏨 **Alphorn.** Comfortably old-fashioned, this lovely family-run Victo-
★ rian bed and breakfast sits on a quiet side street between Interlaken West and the Heimwehfluh. Some rooms have tapestry wallpaper, waxed parquet floors, and original plaster moldings; florals and other patterns abound. The service is notably warm and welcoming. ⊠ *Rugenaustr. 8, CH-3800,* ☎ *033/8223051,* FAX *033/8233069. 20 rooms. Breakfast room, bar. AE, DC, MC, V.*

$ 🏨 **Balmer's.** This popular private youth hostel offers families and
★ young travelers bare-bones bedrooms at rock-bottom prices. Kitchen access, washers and dryers, videos, two fireplaces, a convenience store, and self-service suppers make you feel at home in this lively, collegiate,

party atmosphere. The English-speaking staff is especially helpful in
finding you the cheapest deals in skiing and other outdoor activities.
Rooms are available with one to five beds, all with sinks. There's even
a massive group tent pitched at the edge of town roughly from June
through September. Check-in is required by 5 PM, checkout by 10 AM;
there are no lockers or day storage. It's a quick bus ride from either
rail station—they even offer a free shuttle bus May–September. ⊠
Hauptstr. 23–25, CH-3800, ☎ *033/8221961,* ⅢX *033/8233261. 50
rooms. Bar, library, coin laundry. AE, MC, V.*

$ ⊞ **Happy Inn Lodge.** Smack in the middle of town, this low-budget,
dorm-style hotel under young management is clean, simple, safe, and
very friendly. The basic rooms have bunk beds, doubles or twins. The
Brasserie 17 (☞ Nightlife, *below*) downstairs is an incredibly popular
nightspot—but since it closes at 12:30 PM you'll still get some sleep.
⊠ *Rosenstr. 17, CH-3800,* ☎ *033/8223225,* ⅢX *033/8223268. 15
rooms. AE, MC, V.*

Nightlife and the Arts

BARS

Buddy's Pub (⊠ Hotel Splendid, ☎ 033/8227612) is a popular conversation spot where locals and visitors actually mingle. **Jones' Blues
Bar** (⊠ Bahnhofstr. 22, ☎ 033/8234863) buzzes with canned blues and
clever drinks. There's a lively, mixed crowd at **Brasserie 17** (Happy
Inn Lodge, Rosenstr. 17, ☎ 033/8223225).

CASINOS

The **Kursaal** (☎ 033/8276140) has *boule* (a type of roulette) and 120
slot machines; it's open from 8 PM till 2:30 AM daily. It's not exactly
Vegas, but there's a friendly atmosphere. Remember there's a 5 SF gambling limit.

DANCING

The disco **Black and White,** in the Hotel Metropole (☎ 033/8236633),
attracts an upscale crowd. **High-life** (⊠ Rugenparkstr. 2, ☎ 033/
8221550), near Interlaken West, brings back easygoing oldies. **Hollywood** (⊠ Hotel Central, ☎ 033/8231033) draws a painfully young
crowd. **Johnny's Club** (⊠ Hotel Carlton, ☎ 033/8223821) has been
the definitive after-hours club for years—it comes alive at midnight.

FOLKLORE

Folklore shows—yodeling and all—are presented at Interlaken's **Folk-
lore-Spycher** in the Kursaal (⊠ Off Höheweg, ☎ 033/8276100), with
admission including meals (44 SF to 54 SF) or not (16 SF), as space
allows. Priority is given to diners. Meals are at 7:30, shows at 9. At
the restaurant at **Harder Kulm** (☎ 033/8223444), reached by funicular, on Friday only from June through September you can hear typical
ländler (traditional dance) music and try a little regional dancing.

THEATER

For a real introduction to the local experience, don't miss the **Tell-
freilichtspiele,** an outdoor pageant play presented in Interlaken every
summer by a cast of Swiss amateurs. Wrapped in a rented blanket—
which you'll need, since evenings can be chilly and the show goes on
regardless of weather June through September—and seated in a 2,200-
seat sheltered amphitheater that opens onto illuminated woods and a
permanent village-set, you'll see 250 players in splendid costume acting out the epic tale of Swiss hero William Tell. The text is Schiller's
famous play, performed in German with the guttural singsong of a
Schwyzerdütsch accent—but don't worry; with galloping horses, flower-
decked cows, bonfires, parades, and, of course, the famous apple-
shooting climax, the operatic story tells itself. Tickets are available

through the **Tellbüro** (✉ Bahnhofstr. 5A, ☎ 033/8223722), travel agents, and some hotel concierges; prices range from 14 SF to 34 SF.

Outdoor Activities and Sports

HORSEBACK RIDING

The area between Lake Thun and Lake Brienz offers a number of scenic marked bridle paths through woods, over fields, and by streams. Guided rides and classes are available from **E. Voegeli** (✉ Scheidg. 66, Unterseen, ☎ 033/8227416 and 079/3545289).

MOUNTAIN CLIMBING

Contact **Alpinzentrum Jungfrau** (✉ CH-3812 Wilderswil, ☎ 033/8235523) for placement with accredited mountain guides. **Adventure World** (✉ CH-3800 Interlaken, ☎ 033/8267711) can also assist you with guides.

SAILING

Lake Thun provides the area's most beautiful sailing. From April through mid-October, Interlaken's **Swiss Sailing School** (☎ 033/8228330) offers courses and boat rental.

TENNIS

In Interlaken, there are four outdoor courts on the **Höhematte** (☎ 033/8221472). Three outdoor and four indoor courts are maintained at **Victoria-Jungfrau Spa Tennis Center** ☎ (033/8282855). Rental equipment is available here.

Bönigen

❷ *2 km (1 mi) east of Interlaken.*

With Interlaken so close, Bönigen never got a fair chance to develop into a resort town. All the better for the tourist who wants to be near the action but not exactly in it. This quiet lakeside village is a leisurely half-hour stroll or five-minute car or bus ride from Interlaken and offers its own picturesque charm. Somehow Bönigen escaped major fires in its 750-year history, so there remains a group of *beschnitzten Häuser*, original wooden houses dating from the 16th to the 18th centuries. The homes are covered with elaborate carvings—curling along posts and window frames, dripping off balconies and underscoring the eaves. Arrowed signs lead you past 18 of the nicest. Many of the sight-seeing boats on the **Brienzersee** start or stop here, and the open expanse of lake is a welcome sight after all the narrow valleys.

Dining and Lodging

$$$$ ✕🏨 **Seiler au Lac.** Give this hotel a point for trying harder. With some
★ heavy competition down the road in Interlaken, this cheerful lakefront hotel makes up for its less prestigious address with wonderful views of the lake and mountains, a genuinely friendly ambience, and individually designed rooms reflecting the rather novel tastes of the owners. A bathroom could have decorative tiles or perhaps a triangular mirror, or draperies could swag the head of your bed. In the same family for more than 100 years, it has kept up with the times while retaining a conservative streak. The rustic pizzeria is very popular and reasonably priced. The classier restaurant specializes in lake fish dishes. ✉ *Am Quai 3, CH-3806,* ☎ *033/8223021,* 🇫🇦🇽 *033/8223001. 45 rooms. Restaurant, bar, grill, pizzeria, lake access. AE, DC, MC, V. Closed late Oct.–Christmas, mid-Jan.–late Feb.*

$ 🏨 **Hotel Oberländerhof.** Comfortably worn at the edges, this century-old, family-run hotel next door to the Seiler au Lac (☞ *above*) is worth a second look. Ignore the need for fresh paint and the worn red linoleum. Instead, notice the carved gargoyles making faces from the woodwork, the angels looking down from the plaster ceilings, the dusty red-velvet curtains, and the central atrium, all recalling a glamorous past. The rooms are clean and up to par, some with lake views; although they don't have bathtubs, they all have showers and toilets. The service is friendly, and the café is filled with locals. ⊠ *Am Quai 1, CH-3806,* ☎ *033/ 8221725.* ℻ *033/8232866. 18 rooms. Breakfast room, café. MC, V.*

Lauterbrunnen

★ ❸ *10 km (6 mi) south of Interlaken.*

Below Interlaken the mountains seem to part like the Red Sea into the awesome, bluff-lined Lauterbrunnen Valley. Around the village of Lauterbrunnen, grassy meadows often lie in shadow, as 460-m (1,508-ft) rocky shoulders rise on either side. This tidy town of weathered chalets serves as a starting point for the region's two most spectacular excursions: to the Schilthorn and to the Jungfraujoch. Lauterbrunnen's airportlike, superefficient parking and rail terminal allows long- and short-term parking for visitors heading for Wengen, Mürren, the Jungfraujoch, or the Schilthorn. Consider choosing this valley as a home base for day trips by train, funicular, or cable, thereby saving considerably on hotel rates.

Magnificent **waterfalls** adorn the length of the Lauterbrunnen Valley, the most famous being the 300-m (984-ft) **Staubbachfälle** (Staubbach Falls) and, just beyond, the spectacular **Trümmelbachfälle** (Trümmelbach Falls), a series of seven cascades hidden deep inside rock walls at the base of the Jungfrau, which you can access by underground funicular. Approach the departure point via a pretty, creek-side walkway and brace yourself for some steep stair climbing. Be sure to bring along a light jacket—the spray can be more than refreshing in the cool Alpine air. ⊠ *Follow signs and walkway,* ☎ *033/8553232.* ▣ *10 SF.* ☉ *Apr.–June and Sept.–Nov., daily 9–5; July–Aug. 8–6.*

Dining and Lodging

$ ✕▥ **Stechelberg.** At the very end of the Lauterbrunnen Valley, where the road peters out into a beautiful foot trail, this isolated old lodging offers unspoiled comforts with a hard-core local touch: heavy smoke, muddy boots, and yodeling on Saturday night. Rooms upstairs are creaky, cozy, and all wood, with balconies that open to the sound of the roaring river. In the restaurant, stick to simple sausage-and-Rösti specials; more ambitious attempts fall short. ⊠ *CH-3824,* ☎ *033/8552921,* ℻ *033/8554438. 16 rooms. Restaurant, café. AE, DC, MC, V. Closed mid-Nov.–mid-Dec.*

$–$$ ▥ **Sternen.** In Lauterbrunnen center, near the parking and rail complex, this century-old, weathered-wood hotel has rooms that show some wear, but clean, sociable public spaces, dramatic views, and low prices should make up for frayed edges. Daily rates go down the longer you stay. ⊠ *CH-3822,* ☎ *033/8551231,* ℻ *033/8554431. 12 rooms, 4 with bath. Restaurant, café. MC, V.*

$ ▥ **Waldrand.** If you really want to get away from it all but still take in Jungfrau/Eiger/Mönch views, drive or take the postbus up a narrow, winding mountain road from Lauterbrunnen to Isenfluh, the poor man's Mürren. Its sole, tiny pension provides big, contemporary, knotty-pine rooms and flower-lined balcony views. The hiking possibilities are endless. On request, the owners will pick you up at the rail station in Lauterbrunnen. ⊠ *CH-3822 Isenfluh,* ☎ *033/8551227,* ℻ *033/8551392. 4 rooms. Restaurant. AE, V.*

Shopping

A good source of Lauterbrunnen *torchon* lace is **Handwärch Lädeli** (⊠ Near the old schoolhouse, ☎ 033/8553551).

Mürren

★ ❹ *7 km (4 mi) southwest of Lauterbrunnen, 16 km (10 mi) south of Interlaken, plus a 5-min cable-car ride from Stechelberg.*

This lofty sports mecca (elevation 1,000 m/3,280 ft) offers panoramic
hiking trails in summer and unrivaled views toward the Jungfrau, the
Mönch, and the Eiger. Skiers may want to settle here for daredevil year-
round skiing at the top; hikers may combine staggering views and bluff-
top trails with extraordinarily peaceful mountain nights. Remember
that this is a car-free resort.

Mürren is one of the stops along the popular cable-car ride up the south
side of the **Schilthorn** (2,970 m/9,742 ft), famed for its role in the
James Bond thriller *On Her Majesty's Secret Service*. The peak of this
icy Goliath is accessed by a four-stage cable-lift ride past bare rock cliffs
and stunning slopes. At each level, you step off the cable car, walk across
the station, and wait briefly for the next cable car up. At the top is a
revolving restaurant, Piz Gloria. The cable-car station that accesses the
Schilthorn actually has its base in nearby Stechelberg, near the site of
the **Mürrenbachfälle** (Mürrenbach Falls), which at 250 m (820 ft) are
among the tallest in Europe. ☎ *033/8562141.* 🚡 *Round-trip cable car
Stechelberg–Schilthorn 85 SF (64 SF between 7:25 AM and 8:55 AM or
after 3:25 PM in May, and mid-Oct.–early Nov.).* ☉ *Departures daily
year-round, twice hourly 6:25 AM–11:25 PM; last departure from the
top 6:03 PM in summer, 5:03 PM in winter.*

If you can't stomach (or afford) the route via cable car, you may approach Mürren by funicular out of Lauterbrunnen's train station, then
connect by cogwheel rail from Grütschalp, following the track along
the run of the cliff and looking toward magnificent views of the Big
Three. The whole trip takes about 30 minutes and drops you at the
Mürren rail station, at the opposite end of town from the cable-car
stop. The trains run every 15–20 minutes, and they're much cheaper
than the cable car. If you're not settling in to stay in a Mürren hotel,
this is an ideal takeoff point for a day hike along the bluff top. Point
your binoculars at the gleaming dome on the Jungfraujoch across the
valley: you can almost hear the winds howling off the Aletsch Glacier.

Skiing

Mürren provides access to the **Schilthorn** (2,970 m/9,742 ft)—the start
of a 15-km (9-mi) run that drops all the way through Mürren to
Lauterbrunnen. At 1,650 m (5,413 ft), the resort has one funicular railway, two cable cars, seven lifts, and 65 km (40 mi) of downhill runs.
A one-day pass covering the Schilthorn region costs 52 SF; a seven-
day pass costs 227 SF.

Lodging

$$ 🏨 **Alpenblick.** This simple, comfortable, modern pension is in a spec-
tacular setting and has balconies with astonishing views. Friendly
owners (and their good home cooking) round out the experience. It's
just beyond the center, near the train (not the cable-car) station, so you
may choose to take the funicular up if you have loads of luggage. ✉
CH-3825, ☎ *033/8551327,* 📠 *033/8551391. 14 rooms. Restaurant,
café. AE, MC, V. Closed mid-Apr.–late May and mid-Oct.–mid-Dec.*

$$ 🏨 **Bellevue-Crystal.** Distinguished from surrounding chalets by its
sturdy, yellow, brick-and-shutter construction, this older landmark
presents itself as a traditional ski lodge with full modern comforts. Each
room has a tiny balcony with fine views, and the decor is fresh pine
and gingham. ✉ *CH-3825,* ☎ *033/8551401,* 📠 *033/8551490. 15
rooms. Restaurant, café, sauna. MC, V.*

Jungfraujoch

★ **⑤** *½-day cog-railway excursion out of Interlaken, Lauterbrunnen, or Grindelwald.*

The granddaddy of all high-altitude excursions, the famous journey to the Jungfraujoch, site of the highest railroad station in the world, is one of the most popular tourist goals in Switzerland. From the station at Lauterbrunnen you take the green cogwheel Wengernalp Railway nearly straight up the wooded mountainside as the valley and the village shrink below. From the hilltop resort of **Wengen** (☞ *below*) the train climbs up steep grassy slopes past the timberline to **Kleine Scheidegg,** a tiny, isolated resort settlement surrounded by vertiginous scenery. Here you change to the **Jungfraubahn**, which tunnels straight into the rock of the Eiger, stopping briefly for views out enormous picture windows blasted through its stony face.

The **Jungfraujoch terminus** stands at an elevation of 3,475 m (11,400 ft); you may feel a bit light-headed from the altitude. Follow signs to the **Top of Europe** restaurant, a gleaming white glass-and-steel pavilion. The expanse of rock and ice you see from here is simply blinding.

If you're not sated with the staggering views from the Jungfraujoch terminus, you can reach yet another height by riding a high-tech 90-second elevator up 111 m (364 ft) to the **Sphinx Terrace**: to the south crawls the vast Aletsch Glacier, to the northeast stand the Mönch and the Eiger, and to the southwest—almost close enough to touch—towers the tip of the Jungfrau herself. Note: even in low season, you may have to wait in long lines for the elevator up.

More than views are offered to the hordes that mount the Jungfraujoch daily. You can take a beginner's **ski lesson** or a **dogsled ride,** or tour the chill blue depths of the **Ice Palace,** a novelty attraction on the order of a wax museum, full of incongruous and slightly soggy ice sculptures. Admission is included in the price of the excursion (the ski lessons and dogsled rides cost extra).

A few things to keep in mind for the Jungfraujoch trip: take sunglasses, warm clothes, and sturdy shoes; even the interior halls can be cold and slippery at the top. Return trains, especially toward the end of the day, can be standing-room only. To save money, take the 6:35 AM train. Guided tours with escort and English commentary (called Jungfrau Tour as opposed to *Jungfrau individuell*) also cost less; these leave once a day from Interlaken East. You can get to Lauterbrunnen or Grindelwald (☞ *below*) on your own steam (or using your Swiss Pass; ☞ Train Travel *in* Smart Travel Tips A to Z) and then buy a ticket to the top; if you've driven, of course, you'll have to return the way you came and miss the full round-trip tour. ☎ *033/8287233, 033/8551022 for Jungfraujoch weather information.* ⊠ *Round-trip Interlaken East–Lauterbrunnen–Wengen–Jungfraujoch (back via Grindelwald) 159 SF; 6:35 AM 120 SF.* ⊙ *Daily June–Sept. 6:35 (first train up)–6:10 (last train down).*

Wengen

⑥ *½-hr cog-railway ride from Lauterbrunnen.*

This south-facing hilltop resort perched on a sunny plateau over the Lauterbrunnen Valley has magnificent panoramas down the valley. It rivals Mürren for its quiet, chic, and challenging skiing, which connects with the trail network at Grindelwald; loyalists prefer Wengen for its memorable sunsets. In summer it is a wonderful place to hike. You can aim for central, upscale hotels, near resort shopping and active bars, or head downhill to pleasant, more isolated lodgings, all artfully skewed toward the view. Most hotels encourage longer stays with reduced rates, and half-board is just short of obligatory. (There are only a few restaurants that are not attached to a hotel.) It's a car-free town; most hotels have porters meeting the trains.

Skiing

Just over the ridge from Grindelwald, the sunny resort of **Wengen** (1,300 m–3,450 m/4,265 ft–11,316 ft) nestles on a sheltered plateau high above the Lauterbrunnen Valley; from there, a complex lift system connects to Grindelwald, Kleine Scheidegg, and Männlichen. Wengen has six funicular railways, one cable car, 31 lifts, and 250 km (155 mi) of downhill runs. The Lauberhorn run is tough; it's used for the World Cup Ski Races in January. One-day lift tickets for Kleine Scheidegg/Männlichen cost 52 SF. A two-day pass costs 95 SF. Lift passes for the Jungfrau/Top-Ski-Region are only available for two days and more; a two-day ticket costs 105 SF, a day ticket 244 SF. For lessons, contact the Swiss Ski and Snowboard School (☎ 033/8552022).

Dining and Lodging

$$$$ ✕⌂ **Regina.** It's all about atmosphere in this genteel Victorian hotel. Between the loyal clientele and the gracious, good-humored owners, a genuinely familial mood is palpable. Most of the large rooms have balconies and are done in mauve and rose; rooms under the eaves have loft beds and a green-and-wood decor. Paintings and local antiques (like a huge wooden sled) are scattered throughout. The emphasis is on half-board, and it's a treat; the dining room shares the chef with the hotel's intimate, à la carte restaurant, Chez Meyer's. There you'll find dark, polished wood wainscoting and old family photos on soothing yellow walls—plus an exceptionally creative seasonal menu which might include lobster ravioli with ginger sauce or veal fillet with chanterelles. Reservations are essential, as are a jacket and tie. ✉ CH-3823, ☎ 033/8551512, ﬀ 033/8551574. 96 rooms. Restaurant, bar, beauty salon, sauna, steam room, exercise room. AE, DC, MC, V. Closed Nov.

$$$$ ⌂ **Park Hotel Beausite.** Grandly situated on the hill above Wengen, this hotel encourages pampering; you can relax with a massage or sauna. Rooms are spacious, some with elegant brass beds, others in a more traditional, rustic style. For a leisurely look at the view, sink into one of the couches in the front lounge off the lobby. The hotel is near the cable-car station, a 10-minute walk from the village. ✉ CH-3823, ☎ 033/8565161, ﬀ 033/8553010. 46 rooms, 7 apartments. Restaurant, piano bar, indoor pool, massage, sauna. AE, DC, MC, V.

$$$$ ⌂ **Silberhorn.** Its 19th-century origins evident only in the roofline, this all-modern resort lodge just across from the cogwheel train station has a young, lively staff and ambience. Bright, generously sized rooms are full of pine and chintz, some with delicate floral and striped wallpaper. The heated floors in the bathrooms are a nice touch. ✉ CH-3823, ☎ 033/8565131, ﬀ 033/8552244. 68 rooms. Restaurant, bar, hot tub, sauna, disco, childrens' playroom. AE, DC, MC, V.

$$–$$$ ⌂ **Alpenrose.** Wengen's first hotel, this welcoming inn has been run
★ by one family for over a century—in tried and true fashion, the owners are there to greet you. The decor is homey with knotty pine, painted wood, and skirted lampshades. Rooms with south-facing balconies are only slightly more expensive and worth it. It's downhill and away from the center, with an emphasis on good half-board food. The restaurant is for guests only. ✉ CH-3823, ☎ 033/8553216, ﬀ 033/8551518. 50 rooms. Restaurant. AE, DC, MC, V. Closed Easter–mid-May, early Oct.–Christmas.

$–$$ ⌂ **Eden/Eddy's Hostel.** A shingled, Victorian jewel box joins forces with an unpretentious crash pad—the Eden Hotel providing marvelous southern views, very comfy rooms with or without bathrooms, and pretty gardens, and Eddy's Hostel providing a no-frills bed, a shower, and a breakfast buffet across the street at the Eden. The proprietress is terrific: she'll help you organize hikes. There are plenty of occasions to mix at barbecues, over aperitifs on the terrace, or at one of many summertime live music events. ⊠ CH-3823, ☎ 033/8551634, FAX 033/8553950. 18 rooms, 6 dorms. Restaurant, café. AE, DC, MC, V. Closed Nov.–mid-Dec.

$–$$ 🏠 **Schweizerheim.** It's worth the hike to this old-fashioned, family-run
★ pension nestled well below the beaten path: the full-valley views are flawless, the gardens pristine, and the terrace picnic tables balance precariously over the Lauterbrunnen Valley. The rooms are a dated mix of wood paneling, Formica, linoleum, and carpet, but the experience is welcoming and fun—and the owner is a Swiss hand-organ celebrity. The restaurant serves pension guests only. ⊠ CH-3823, ☎ 033/8551112, FAX 033/8552327. 24 rooms. Restaurant, bar. MC, V.

$–$$ 🏠 **Zum Bären.** This lodging just below the center is straightforward and bright, with good views and low rates. The rooms are freshly done in blues, yellows, and pale wood; the watercolors are painted by the owner's mother. For extra-cheap sleeps (about 35 SF, including breakfast), you can stay in one of the two scout-camp–style dorm rooms, each with 10 beds. ⊠ CH-3823, ☎ 033/8551419, FAX 033/8551525. 14 rooms. Restaurant, café. AE, DC, MC, V. Closed mid-Oct.–mid-Dec. and for 2 weeks after Easter.

Outdoor Activities and Sports

SKATING

Wengen has a natural **rink** (Natureisbahn) and a partially sheltered indoor rink (Kunsteisbahn); for hours, contact the tourist office (☎ 033/8551414).

TENNIS

Two **public courts** are available for rental through the tourist office (☎ 033/8551414), although equipment is not.

Nightlife and the Arts

DANCING

Hit **Tiffany** (⊠ Hotel Silberhorn, ☎ 033/8565131) for a good mix of locals and tourists.

Grindelwald

❼ 27 km (17 mi) east of Interlaken.

Strung along a mountain highway with two convenient train stations, Grindelwald (1,050 m/3,445 ft) is the most easily accessible of the region's high resorts. It makes an excellent base for skiing and hiking, shopping and dining—if you don't mind a little traffic.

From Grindelwald you can drive, take a postbus, or hike up to the ★**Oberergletscher,** a craggy, steel-blue glacier. You can approach its base along wooded trails, where there's an instrument to measure the glacier's daily movement. Better yet, travel down into the valley to Grund, below Grindelwald, and visit the **Gletscherschlucht** (Glacier Gorge). There you can walk along a trail through tunnels and over bridges about 1 km (1/2 mi) into the gorge itself. Although you can't see the glacier itself while walking along the edges of the spectacular gorge it sculpted, you'll get a powerful sense of its slow-motion, inexorable force. ⊠ Trail: 🎫 5 SF. ☉ Late May–mid-Oct.

Also out of Grindelwald, you can take the **Firstbahn,** a 30-minute gondola ride to the lovely views and pistes of the First ski area (2,163 m/7,095 ft). The **Alpine garden** flourishes within easy walking distance (it's even wheelchair accessible) of the first cable car. Without hiking into the heights, you can see gentians, edelweiss, anemones, and Alpine asters.

Skiing

An ideal base for the Jungfrau ski area, Grindelwald (1,050 m/3,445 ft) provides access to the varied trails of Grindelwald First and Kleine Scheidegg/Männlichen. Grindelwald has eight funicular railways, three cable cars, 22 lifts, and 165 km (103 mi) of downhill runs. Some long runs go right down to the village; there are special areas for snowboarders and beginning skiers. One-day lift tickets for Kleine Scheidegg/ Männlichen and First each cost 52 SF. A two-day pass costs 95 SF.

Dining and Lodging

$$ ✕ **Memory.** A welcoming, no-fuss, family-style chalet restaurant, Memory is well known for its cheese and potato dishes, which extend beyond the seven kinds of Rösti to include gratins with meat and potato-garlic soup. Sunday nights are burger nights. ⊠ *Eiger Hotel,* ☎ *033/8532121. AE, DC, MC, V.*

$ ✕ **Onkel Tom's Hütte.** This tiny, smoke-free pizza parlor, set in a rus-
★ tic A-frame cabin on the main drag, is as cozy as they come. Rough wooden floors accommodate ski boots, and eight wooden tables share space with a huge iron cookstove, where the young owner produces fresh pizzas in three sizes (the smallest of which is plenty!). There are also generous salads, homemade desserts, and a surprisingly large international wine list. Its popularity outstrips its size, so enjoy the good kitchen smells while you wait. ⊠ *Across from the Firstbahn,* ☎ *033/ 8535239. MC, V. Closed Mon. and Nov. and June.*

$$$$ ✕▥ **Belvedere.** As you wind your way into Grindelwald, this large,
★ pink structure, precariously perched above the road, comes into view. Rustic styling has given way to tastefully designed interiors; the Salon Louis Philippe is a particularly pleasant place to relax, with its period furniture and wood-inlay games tables. There are drop-dead views of the Eiger and surrounding peaks from almost every room. The staff and management radiate genuine warmth and absolute professionalism; the owner takes groups of guests skiing, hiking, and golfing weekly. The restaurant offers fresh, creative menus that change according to the delicious whims of their trusted chef. Ask about the terms of their special rates for Fodor's guide users when making reservations. ⊠ *CH-3818,* ☎ *033/8545454,* ℻ *033/8535323. 51 rooms. Restaurant, Stübli, piano bar, indoor pool, hot tub, 2 saunas, exercise room, playroom. AE, DC, MC, V. Closed late Oct.–mid-Dec.*

$$$$ ✕▥ **Schweizerhof.** Behind a dark-wood, Victorian chalet facade dat-
★ ing from 1892, this big, comfortable hotel attracts a loyal clientele. Wingbacks and bookcases in the lobby lounge and dining rooms—of scrubbed pine and hand-painted (and carved) trim—are inviting on rainy days. Rooms are decorated in carved pine and have tile baths, along with luxurious bathrobes. The service is attentive, unhurried, flexible, and extremely friendly. They emphasize half-board, and the menu looks beyond Switzerland—try the duck breast with black currant fig sauce and whole-meal noodles or something from their vegetarian selections. The breakfasts are generously portioned and offered until 11:30 AM (this late schedule is a rarity). In the Stübli you can enjoy Fondue Chinoise (meat cut into paper-thin slices and quickly cooked in a pot of boiling bouillon). ⊠ *CH-3818,* ☎ *033/8532202,* ℻ *033/8532004. 53 rooms. Restaurant, Stübli, indoor pool, beauty salon, sauna, bowling, health club. Closed Easter–late May and Oct.–late Dec.*

$$–$$$ ✕▥ **Fiescherblick.** This is the place to eat in Grindelwald, whether as
★ a pension hotel guest or day-tripper: the serious cuisine in the intimate restaurant continues to draw kudos and devoted food lovers, and the lower-priced Swiss Bistro in the adjoining bar allows casual lunchers

to enjoy the talents of the same chef. The seasonal menu might include wild garlic sausage in fall, freshwater crayfish for a few weeks in spring, or roast lobster with pistachio oil in winter. As for the rooms, try to nab one of the "superior" rooms, which are bright and spacious, if more expensive. The standard rooms tend to the unexciting, functional-brown-decor side. ✉ *CH-3818,* ☎ *033/8534453,* ⅆ *033/ 8534457. 25 rooms. Restaurant, Stübli. AE, DC, MC, V. Closed Easter–mid-May, mid-Oct.–mid-Dec.*

$–$$ ✕⚄ **Hotel Wetterhorn.** Overlooking the magnificent ice-blue upper glacier—as well as the sprawling parking lot where hikers leave their cars—this modest inn offers generous lunches outdoors, with full glacier views, and good regional dining inside its comfortable restaurant. Portions of veal favorites are large and delicious, and there is a good selection of Swiss wines. Everything is homemade, right down to the jam and cheese. The adjoining Gletscherstübli attracts locals as well as the hordes of tourists and hikers who come to marvel at its namesake. Up the creaky old stairs, there are simple, tidy, aged-pine rooms— some have glacier views—with sink and shared bath. They have renovated the neighboring farmhouse and chalet into four vacation apartments. ✉ *CH-3818,* ☎ *033/8531218,* ⅆ *033/8535818. 9 rooms, 4 apartments. Restaurant, café, Stübli. AE, DC, MC, V.*

$$$$ ⚄ **Grand Hotel Regina.** The turreted exterior dates from the turn of the century, but this pricey hotel is hardly a museum. Touches from the past, like antiques and elaborate chairs from the founder's collection, individualize the rooms; a luxurious strain runs throughout, with parquet floors, gold-ceiling baths, and white leather furnishings. The views are flawless, the location central, and the tennis courts may be some of the most spectacularly sited in the world. ✉ *CH-3818,* ☎ *033/ 8545455 or 800/2236800 in the U.S.,* ⅆ *033/8534717. 100 rooms. Restaurant, indoor pool, outdoor pool, beauty salon, massage, sauna, 2 tennis courts, nightclub. AE, DC, MC, V.*

$$$ ⚄ **Gletschergarten.** In the same family for three generations, this atmospheric pension radiates welcome, from the heirloom furniture and paintings (by the grandfather) to the tea roses cut from the owner's garden. There's heraldry in the leaded-glass windows, a ceramic stove with built-in seat warmer, and a cozy lounge paneled in wood taken from an old Grindelwald farmhouse. All rooms have balconies, some with glacier views, others overlooking the emerald green hills. Ask for a corner room, as their angles and view are especially pleasing. ✉ *CH-3818,* ☎ *033/8531721,* ⅆ *033/8532957. 26 rooms. Restaurant, bar, sauna, steam room, Ping-Pong, billiards, coin laundry. AE, MC, V.*

$$–$$$ ⚄ **Alpina.** This chalet has a lofty perch, making for sensational views from its front balconies—and though it's a cement building, the edges are softened inside and out by light wood decor, geraniums below every window, and warm, personal service. The slightly more expensive front rooms are especially cheerful and bright, with lovely new bathrooms. The back rooms saw their heyday in the days of dark, wood-grain Formica. It's a five-minute walk up from the station. ✉ *CH-3818,* ☎ *033/8533333,* ⅆ *033/8533376. 30 rooms. Restaurant. AE, DC, MC, V. Closed just after Easter–early May.*

$$ ⚄ **Gletscherschlucht.** Down below Grindelwald at the entrance to the glacier gorge in Talgrund is this neat, spic-and-span, family-friendly hotel. Bright, sizeable new pine rooms have stained wood furnishings and shiny tile baths. Its quiet valley location is just 2 km (1 mi) below the tourist hubbub. ✉ *CH-3818,* ☎ *033/8536050,* ⅆ *033/8536051. 5 rooms. Restaurant. V.*

$ ⚄ **Mountain Hostel.** It's all uphill from here—this welcoming hostel sits at the foot of the Eiger in Grund, 2 km (1¼ mi) from Grindelwald. The beds, with or without covers, are set up in bunk-bed rooms for 2 to 6 people. Showers and toilets are down the hall. The owners take groups out on hikes and there are grill parties in summer. It's just a couple of minutes by foot from the Grund train station. ✉ *CH-3818,* ☎ *033/8533900,* FAX *033/8534730. 20 rooms. Restaurant. MC, V.*

Nightlife and the Arts

DANCING

Challi Bar (✉ Hotel Kreuz, ☎ 033/8545492) has a DJ who plays requests. The **Gepsi-Bar** (✉ Eiger Hotel, ☎ 033/8532121) is open late; there's a fun crowd and weekly live music. The **Plaza Club** (✉ Sunstar Hotel, ☎ 033/8534240) is a Swiss self-styled "ethno disco" (decorated with cows and alphorns), although the music is strictly modern (no yodeling here). There's also the **Regina Bar-Dancing** with live music nightly (✉ Grand Hotel Regina, ☎ 033/8545455).

Outdoor Activities and Sports

HIKING

Grindelwald is a hiker's paradise, both in summer and winter. Detailed trail maps are available at the tourist office (☞ Visitor Information *in* Berner Oberland A to Z, *below*).

MOUNTAIN CLIMBING

The **Bergsteigerzentrum** (✉ Grindelwald center, ☎ 033/8535200) offers daily and weekly courses to mountain and glacier hikers.

SKATING

The **Sportzentrum Grindelwald** (☎ 033/8541230) has indoor and natural rinks. You can rent skates at the indoor rink.

TENNIS

Grindelwald has six **public courts;** for permits, call the tourist office (☎ 033/8531912).

BRIENZERSEE

Reputedly the cleanest lake in Switzerland—which surely means one of the cleanest in the world—this magnificent bowl of crystal-clear water mirrors the mountain-scape and forests, cliffs, and waterfalls that surround it. You can cruise alongside Lake Brienz at high speed on the A—8 freeway or crawl along its edge on secondary waterfront roads; or you can cut a wake across it on a steamer, exploring each stop on foot, then cruising to your next destination.

Iseltwald

❽ *9 km (6 mi) northeast of Interlaken.*

This isolated peninsula juts out into the lake, its small hotels, cafés, and rental chalets clustered at the water's edge. Every restaurant prides itself on its lake fish, of course. From the village edge, you may want to take off on foot; a lovely forest walk of about 1½ hours brings you to the falls of the **Giessbach** (Giess Brook), which tumbles in several stages down rocky cliffs to the lake. The most scenic route to Iseltwald from Interlaken is via the south-shore road; follow the black-and-white ISELTWALD signs. You can also take the A–8 expressway, following the autoroute signs for Meiringen.

Brienz

★ ❾ *12 km (7 mi) northeast of Iseltwald, 21 km (13 mi) northeast of Interlaken.*

The romantic waterfront village of Brienz, world renowned as a wood-carving center, is a favorite stop for boat tourists as well as drivers.

Several artisan shops display the local wares, which range in quality from the ubiquitous, winningly simple figures of spotted cows to finely modeled nativity figures and Hummel-like portraits of William Tell. Brienz is also a showcase of traditional Oberland architecture, with some of its loveliest houses (at the west end of town, near the church) dating from the 17th century. Once an important stage stop, Brienz hosted Goethe and Byron at its landmark Hotel Weisses Kreuz (☞ Dining and Lodging, *below*); their names, along with the 1688 date of construction, are proudly displayed on the gable.

Switzerland's last steam-driven cogwheel train runs from the center of Brienz, at the waterfront, up to the summit of **Brienzer-Rothorn,** 2,346 m (7,700 ft) above the town. Trains run at least every hour, but to avoid long waits at peak times, purchase your ticket for a particular train in advance on the day you will make the trip; they do not accept reservations. ☎ *033/9522222.* ⊠ *64 SF round-trip.* ☉ *Daily June–Oct. 1st train up 8:30, last train up 4:15, last train down 5:15*

At Brienz you may want to try your own hand at **wood carving**: in one lesson at the atelier of Paul Fuchs you can learn to carve the typical Brienzer cow. Make a reservation through the tourist office in Brienz or directly with Mr. Fuchs. You'll be put in a class of a dozen or more. ⊠ *Scheidweg 19D, in Hofstetten, between Brienz and Ballenberg,* ☎ *033/9511418.* ⊠ *22 SF per person.* ☉ *2-hr workshops Apr.–Oct.*

OFF THE
BEATEN PATH
☙
FREILICHTMUSEUM BALLENBERG – Just east of Brienz, a small road leads to this child-friendly, outdoor museum-park, where 80 characteristic Swiss houses from 18 cantons have been carefully reconstructed. Even the gardens and farm animals are true to type. Old handicrafts and trades like spinning, forging, and lace making are demonstrated using original tools. ☎ *033/9511123.* ⊠ *14 SF.* ☉ *Mid-Apr.–Oct., daily 10–5.*

Dining and Lodging

$–$$
★
✕ **Steinbock.** Whether you dine on the broad, flower-lined terrace or inside the wonderful, old (1787), carved-wood-and-homespun chalet, you'll feel the atmosphere of this proud local institution. Choose from no fewer than nine interpretations of Lake Brienz whitefish, regional pastas, or veal classics. ⊠ *Hauptstr. 123,* ☎ *033/9514055. AE, DC, MC, V. Closed Tues. and Feb.*

$$
✕🏠 **Hotel Weisses Kreuz.** Generic modern improvements have erased some of the fine origins of this structure, built in 1688 and host to Goethe and Byron, but the current version has a tidy, cozy charm of its own. The location is across the highway from the waterfront, close to Rothorn Railway excursion crowds. But if you are a history buff, the idea of its antiquity and the hallowed names on the gable may be allure enough, and the woody Stübli draws loyal locals for a chat and a daily paper. The pine and homespun-linen restaurant offers omelets and *Käseschnitte* (cheese and bread baked in its own whey) as well as lake fish, steaks, and strudel. Some rooms have lake views, and the sunny lake-view terrace café draws locals as well as tourists fresh off the boat. ⊠ *Hauptstr. 143, CH-3855,* ☎ *033/9522020,* ℻ *033/9522021. 14 rooms. Restaurant. AE, DC, MC, V. Closed mid-Nov.–mid-Dec.*

$$
★
✕🏠 **Lindenhof.** In a 1787 lodge high above the touristy lakefront, German and Austrian families settle in for a week or two of evenings by the vast stone fireplace, dinners in the panoramic winter garden (or on the spectacular terrace), and nights in dressed-up theme rooms with such evocative names as Marmot Cave, Venus Room, and Hunter's Hut. The grounds are vast and beautifully manicured, the atmosphere familial and formal at once. Families with small children dine together by the fire, apart from other guests. ⊠ *Lindenhofweg 15, CH-3855,*

☎ *033/9511072,* ℻ *033/9514072. 40 rooms, 4 suites. Restaurant, bar, café, kitchenettes, indoor pool, sauna. AE, MC, V. Closed Jan.–Feb.*

$$ 🏠 **Schönegg und Spycher.** Clinging to a steep, garden-covered hillside
★ over town, this snug pension is run by house-proud Christine Math-
yer, who sees to it that all three small lodgings maintain their old-fash-
ioned charm. There's a 1950s fireplace lounge, with flagstone floors
and wood carvings, and rooms with rustic painted furniture, flower-
sprigged duvets, and chocolates on the pillow at night. Guests can relax
in the sunny garden overlooking the lake, and it's an easy walk up to
the Lindenhof or down to the Steinbock (☞ *above*) for dinner. ⊠ *Tal-
str. 8, CH-3855,* ☎ *033/9511113.* ℻ *033/9513813. 16 rooms. Bar,
breakfast room, Ping-Pong. AE, MC, V.*

$$ 🏠 **Seehotel Bären.** The modern construction and 1960s room decor
are upstaged by the gracious dining room, flower-framed terrace café,
and private waterfront promenade. Lakeside rooms, which have serene
water views, are considerably pricier in high season; back rooms open
over the main road. A small beach gives access to the crystalline water.
⊠ *Hauptstr. 72, CH-3855,* ☎ *033/9512412,* ℻ *033/9514022. 32
rooms. Restaurant, café, lake, beach. AE, DC, MC, V.*

Shopping
Brienz is the place for good selections of local wood carvings—every-
thing from cows to plates to nativity figures. Check out the wares and
get a tour to boot at **Ed Jobin** (⊠ Hauptstr. 111, ☎ 033/9511414) and
Walter Stäheli (⊠ Hauptstr. 41, ☎ 033/9511471). **H. Huggler-Wyss**
(⊠ Fischerbrunnenpl., ☎ 033/9521000) is another worthwhile source.

Meiringen

🔟 *12 km (7 mi) east of Brienz, 35 km (22 mi) northeast of Interlaken.*

Set apart from the twin lakes and saddled between the roads to the
Sustenpass and the Brünigpass, Meiringen is a resort town with 300
km (186 mi) of marked hiking trails and 60 km (37 mi) of ski slopes.
Its real claim to fame, though, are the **Reichenbachfälle** (Reichenbach
Falls), where fictional detective Sherlock Holmes and his archenemy
Professor Moriarty plunged into the "cauldron of swirling water and
seething foam in that bottomless abyss above Meiringen." Visitors can
now view the dramatic fall where Conan Doyle intended to end his series of mysteries. A nearby hotel bears the detective's name, and in the
center of town the **Sherlock Holmes Museum** has created an "authentic" replica of Holmes's front room at 221b Baker Street. ⊠ *Bahnhofstr.
26,* ☎ *033/9714221.* 🎟 *3.80 SF.* ☉ *May–Sept., Tues.–Sun. 1:30–6;
Oct.–Apr., Wed.–Sun. 3–6.*

Dining and Lodging
$$ 🏠 **Sporthotel Sherlock Holmes.** This sports-oriented hotel is ideal for
hikers and skiers. Though the building is modern and unspectacular,
most rooms look out on Reichenbach Falls. Rooms are simple, but wood
cabinetry gives them a cozy, Alpine feel. ⊠ *Alpbachallee 3, CH-3860,*
☎ *033/9729889,* ℻ *033/9729888. 60 rooms. Restaurant, indoor
pool, sauna, health club, Ping-Pong, billiards. AE, MC, V.*

Outdoor Activities and Sports
HIKING
The private, 20-km (12½-mi) **road to Grindelwald** permits no cars but
provides a beautiful, seven-hour Alpine hike. For maps of other local
hiking trails, hit the tourist office (☞ *Visitor Information in* Berner Ober-
land A to Z, *below*).

THUNERSEE

If you like your mountains as a picturesque backdrop and prefer a relaxing waterfront sojourn, take a drive around the Thunersee (Lake Thun)—or crisscross it on a leisurely cruise boat. More populous than Lake Brienz, its allures include the marina town of Spiez and the large market town of Thun, spread at the feet of the spectacular Schloss Zähringen (Zähringen Castle). There are more castles along the lake, and yet another high-altitude excursion for rising above the waterfront to take in Alpine panoramas—a trip up the Niederhorn.

Spiez

⓫ *19 km (11¾ mi) west of Interlaken.*

The town of Spiez is a summer lake resort with marinas for water-sports enthusiasts. Its enormous waterfront castle, **Schloss Spiez,** was home to the family Strättligen and, in the 13th century, its great troubadour, Heinrich. The structure spans four architectural epochs, starting with the 11th-century tower; its halls contain beautiful period furnishings, some from as long ago as Gothic times. The early Norman church on the grounds is over 1,000 years old. ☎ *033/6541506. ☞ 4 SF. ☉ Mid-Apr.–June and Sept.–mid Oct. Mon. 2–5, Tues.–Sun. 10–5; July–Aug. Mon. 2–6, Tues.–Sun. 10–6.*

Dining and Lodging

$$–$$$ ✕🏠 **Seegarten Hotel Marina.** With a pizzeria corner in one wing and two dining rooms that stretch comfortably along the marina front, this is a pleasant, modern family restaurant, and its lake fish specialties are excellent. Spiez Castle looms directly behind you, unfortunately out of sight. The rooms upstairs are spare and modern. ⊠ *Schachenstr. 3, CH-3700,* ☎ *033/6556767,* ℻ *033/6556765. 42 rooms. Restaurant, bar, café, pizzeria. AE, DC, MC, V.*

$$$$ 🏠 **Strandhotel Belvedere.** A member of the Hotel Suisse Silence chain, this graceful, old mansion-hotel has beautiful lawns and gardens, and its manicured waterfront on Lake Thun offers secluded swimming. The decor hearkens back a few decades; rooms are done in blue and old rose, with canopy beds. Corner and lakeside rooms are worth the higher price. Guests have free access to the city's heated outdoor pool, 100 m (328 ft) away. ⊠ *Schachenstr. 39, CH-3700,* ☎ *033/6543333,* ℻ *033/6546633. 30 rooms. Restaurant, beach. AE, DC, MC, V. Closed Oct.–Mar.*

Outdoor Activities and Sports

Spiez has municipal tennis courts at the bay, by the municipal pool (☎ 033/6544917).

Thun

⓬ *10 km (6 mi) north of Spiez, 29 km (18 mi) northwest of Interlaken.*

Built along an island on the River Aare as it leaves Lake Thun, the picturesque market town of Thun is laced with rushing streams crossed by wooden bridges, and its streets are lined with arcades. The main shopping thoroughfare of the Old Town may be unique in the world: pedestrians stroll along flowered terrace sidewalks built on the roofs of the stores' first floors and climb down stone stairs to visit the "sunken" street-level shops.

★   From the charming medieval Rathausplatz (Rathaus Square), a covered stair leads up to the great **Schloss Zähringen** (Zähringen Castle), its broad donjon cornered by four stout turrets. Built in 1191 by Berchtold V, duke of Zähringen, it houses the fine **Schlossmuseum Thun** (Thun Castle Museum) and provides magnificent views from its towers. In the **knights' hall** are a grand fireplace, an intimidating assortment of medieval weapons, and tapestries, one from the tent of Charles the Bold. Other floors display local Steffisburg and Heimberg ceramics, 19th-century uniforms and arms, and Swiss household objects, including charming Victorian toys. ⊠ *Rathauspl.,* ☎ *033/2232001.* ☑ *5 SF.* ☉ *Apr.–May and Oct., daily 10–5; June–Sept., daily 9–6; Feb.–Mar., daily 1–4.*

Dining and Lodging

$$–$$$ ✕☷ **Krone.** Positioned directly on the lovely Rathausplatz in the Old Town, this landmark has some fine, bay-window tower rooms and river views. Despite its historic setting and classic exterior, the slick interior is tile-and-wood modern. The Chinese restaurant, Wong-Kun, has a cross-cultural menu, and an upscale bistro whips up chic versions of regional dishes. ⊠ *Obere Hauptg. 2, CH-3600,* ☎ *033/2278888,* ℻ *033/2278890. 27 rooms. 2 restaurants. AE, MC, V.*

$ ✕☷ **Zu Metzgern.** This grand, old, shuttered and arcaded *Zunfthaus* (guild house), at the base of the castle hill, provides fresh pastel rooms (bathrooms down the hall) with Rathausplatz views. There's atmospheric dining, too, whether in the wood-and-linen restaurant or on the intimate little terrace, tucked behind an ivy-covered trellis. It's ideally placed for a castle climb and Old Town shopping and touring. ⊠ *Untere Hauptg. 2, CH-3600,* ☎ *033/2222141,* ℻ *033/2222182. 8 rooms. Restaurant, café. MC, V.*

Shopping

A good spot for traditional and artisan pottery in Thun is **Töpferhaus** (⊠ Obere Hauptg. 3, ☎ 033/2227065). Just outside Thun in Heimberg, the **Museum Hänn** (Bahnhofstr. 4, ☎ 033/4381242) demonstrates and displays its traditional ceramic work, as it has since 1731.

Hilterfingen

⑬ *4 km (2½ mi) southeast of Thun, 18 km (11 mi) northwest of Interlaken.*

Hilterfingen's castle, **Schloss Hünegg** (Hünegg Castle), was built in 1861 and furnished over the years with a bent toward Jugendstil and Art Nouveau. The stunning interiors have remained unchanged since 1900 and give a good look at how opulent 19th-century castle life was. ⊠ *Staatsstr. 52,* ☎ *033/2431982.* ☑ *4 SF.* ☉ *Mid-May–mid-Oct., Mon.–Sat. 2–5, Sun. 10–noon and 2–5.*

Oberhofen

⑭ *2 km (1 mi) southeast of Hilterfingen, 16 km (10 mi) northwest of Interlaken.*

Oberhofen is topped with its own **Schloss Oberhofen** (Oberhofen Castle), this one a hodgepodge of towers and spires on the waterfront. Begun during the 12th century, it was repeatedly altered over a span of 700 years. Inside, a historical museum has a display on the lifestyles of Bernese nobility. ☎ *033/2431235.* ☑ *4 SF.* ☉ *Mid-May–mid-Oct., Tues.–Sun. 10–noon and 2–5, Mon. 2–5; grounds open 8 AM–dusk.*

....

OFF THE BEATEN PATH | **NIEDERHORN** – Thirteen km (8 mi) east of Oberhofen, the town of Beatenbucht has a shore terminal that sends funiculars to Beatenberg daily in high season. From there you can either walk up a trail or catch a chairlift to the Niederhorn (1,919 m/6,294 ft), from which an astonishing panorama unfolds: Lake Thun and Lake Brienz, the Jungfrau, and even, on a fine day, Mont Blanc.

ST-BEATUSHÖHLEN – Just west of Beatenberg, the illuminated St-Beat-ushöhlen caves have been heavily developed, complete with a wax fig-ure of Irish missionary St. Beatus himself, isolated in his cell as he was in the 6th century. This is less a center for pilgrimage than a simple cave tour with stalactites and stalagmites in dripping grottoes. 🎫 *12 SF.* ☉ *Apr.–Oct., daily 9:30–5:30. Guided tours every 30 mins.*

KANDER VALLEY

Easily reached by car or the Lötschberg rail line from Interlaken via Spiez, the spectacular, high-altitude Kander Valley leads up from Lake Thun toward Kandersteg, an isolated resort strewn across a level plateau. From Kandersteg, you can make a hiker's pilgrimage to the silty blue Oeschinensee. And en route to the lakes below, you may want to visit the touristy but pleasant Blausee.

Kandersteg

⑮ *45 km (28 mi) southwest of Interlaken.*

At 1,176 m (3,858 ft), Kandersteg stands alone, a quiet resort spread across a surprisingly broad, level—and thus walkable—plateau. Lofty bluffs, waterfalls, and peaks—including the **Blümlisalp**, at 3,664 m (12,018 ft), and the **Doldenhorn**, at 3,643 m (11,949 ft)—surround the plateau, and at the end of its 4-km (2½-mi) stretch, the valley road ends abruptly.

Exploration above Kandersteg must be accomplished by cable car or on foot, unless (depending on Swiss army training schedules and weather) you find the tiny paved road into the magnificent **Gastern Val-ley** open: carved into raw rock, portions of the road are so narrow that cars must take turns coming and going. Usually the local tourist office (☞ Visitor Information *in* Berner Oberland A to Z, *below*) knows if the road is passable.

Don't miss the **Oeschinensee,** an isolated, austere bowl of glacial silt at 1,578 m (5,176 ft); from Kandersteg you can walk there in about 1½ hours, and it's also accessible by chairlift to the Oeschinen station, with a downhill walk of approximately 30 minutes through peak-ringed meadowlands. You also may choose to hike back down to Kan-dersteg from the Oeschinensee, but be prepared for the severe downhill grade. Less ambitious hikers can circle back to the chairlift at the end of a relatively level walk.

Although it's a dead-end valley for cars confining themselves to Berner Oberland, Kandersteg is the source of one of Switzerland's more novel modes of transit: the rail-ferry tunnel through the **Lötschenberg.** After driving your car onto a low-slung rail car, you will be swept along pig-gyback through a dark and airless tunnel to Goppenstein, at the east end of the Valais region (☞ Chapter 11). Travel time is 15 minutes; the cost is 25 SF.

Dining and Lodging

$$ ✕🏨 **Ruedihus.** This beautifully, painstakingly restored, all-wood chalet
★ is set in a meadow beyond the village center. With bulging leaded-glass windows, authentically low ceilings and doors (watch your head), and raw, aged woodwork throughout, it re-creates the atmosphere of the 1753 original. Antique beds with bleached, homespun linens are coun-terbalanced by modern baths, and every corner has its waxed cradle, pewter pitcher, or crockery bowl. Upstairs, the Biedermeier restaurant offers excellent meat specialties, but eat downstairs at least once: The

Käse- und Wystuben serves nothing but Swiss products—Vaud and Valais wines, greens, and sausages, and a variety of fondues. (No credit cards are accepted in the restaurants.) As the hotel has only nine rooms, reservations are key. ✉ CH-3718, ☎ 033/6758182, FAX 033/6758185. 9 rooms. 2 restaurants, café. AE, DC, MC, V.

$$–$$$ ⊞ **Waldhotel Doldenhorn.** Nestled into a forest hillside far from the
★ road through the center, this retreat—a member of the Relais du Silence group, inns specializing in peace and quiet—offers several options: large rooms with balconies and mountain views, smaller rooms opening onto the woods, or a separate budget chalet. The rooms gracefully combine modern and rustic styles. A cross-country ski trail starts at the hotel's door. There's a formal Swiss-French restaurant and a casual Stübli, too. For those with a do-it-yourself approach, one apartment has a kitchenette. ✉ CH-3718, ☎ 033/6758181, FAX 033/6758185. 33 rooms, 1 apartment. Restaurant, Stübli. AE, DC, MC, V.

$ ⊞ **Edelweiss.** Built in 1903, this inn has sleek, impeccable rooms and an old-fashioned atmosphere, complete with low ceilings and burnished wood. There's a comfortable, checkered-cloth Stübli for drinks only. The pretty garden makes you forget you're on the main road, five minutes from the train station. ✉ CH-3718, ☎ 033/6751194. 8 rooms. Breakfast room, Stübli. No credit cards.

OFF THE **BLAUSEE (Blue Lake) –** If you're traveling with a family, you may want to
BEATEN PATH visit the much-vaunted Blausee, a naturally blue pool above Frutigen. Be warned: it's privately owned and so developed, with a restaurant, boat rides, and a shop, that you may think the lake itself is artificial. The summer admission price includes a boat ride, a visit to the trout nursery, and use of the picnic grounds. In winter you're free to park and roam the area. ✉ 4 km (2½ mi) north of Kandersteg, above Frutigen, ☎ 033/ 6711641. 🎫 4.50 SF (May–early Nov. only). ☉ Daily 9–6.

SIMMENTAL AND GSTAAD

Separate in spirit and terrain from the rest of the Berner Oberland, this craggy forest gorge follows the Lower Simme into a region as closely allied with French-speaking Vaud as it is with its Germanic brothers. Here the world-famous winter resort of Gstaad has flexed the muscle of its famous name to link up with a handful of neighboring ski resorts, creating the almost limitless sports opportunities of the Gstaad "Super-Ski" region. From Gstaad, it's an easy day trip into the contrasting culture of Lac Léman (Lake Geneva) and the waterfront towns of Montreux and Lausanne.

From Interlaken, take A–8 toward Spiez, then cut west on A–11 toward Gstaad. The forest gorges of the Simmental Valley lead you through Zweisimmen, the area's principal sporting center, to the Saanenland. The total distance from Spiez is about 40 km (25 mi).

Gstaad

🔟 49 km (30 mi) southwest of Spiez, 67 km (42 mi) southwest of Interlaken.

The peak-ringed valley called the Saanenland is anchored by this, the Oberland's most glamorous resort. Linking the Berner Oberland with the French-accented territory of the Pays-d'Enhaut (Highlands) of canton Vaud, Gstaad blends the two regions' natural beauty and their cultures as well, upholding Pays-d'Enhaut folk art traditions such as papier découpé (paper cutouts) as well as decidedly Germanic ones (cowbells, wood carvings). Even Rösti and fondue cohabit comfortably.

But in Gstaad, neither local culture wins the upper hand: the folksy *Gemütlichkeit* (homeyness) of the region gives way to jet-set international style, and although the architecture still tends toward weathered-wood chalets, the main street is lined with designer boutiques that seem oddly out of context. Prince Rainier of Monaco, Julie Andrews, Roger Moore, and Elizabeth Taylor have all owned chalets in Gstaad, rubbing elbows at local watering holes, and the late Yehudi Menuhin founded his annual summer music festival here as well. (The Menuhin festival takes place every August, and hotels fill quickly then—as they do for the Swiss Open Tennis tournament, held here every July.)

This is a see-and-be-seen spot, with less emphasis on its plentiful but moderate skiing than on the scene—après-ski, après-concert, or après-match. The Christmas–New Year's season brings a stampede of glittering socialites to rounds of dinner parties, balls, and elite soirees. Occasionally, the jet-setters even hit the slopes. Despite a few family-style hotels, the number of deluxe lodgings is disproportionate, and prices tend to be high, on the scale of those at St. Moritz. (The village has few street names, but hotels are clearly signposted.) Yet Gstaad's setting defies its socialite pretensions: Richly forested slopes, scenic, year-round trails, and, for the most part, stubbornly authentic chalet architecture keep it firmly anchored in tradition. The village is car-free. You can leave your car at the train station.

Skiing

Gstaad does not hesitate to call itself a "Super-Ski" region, and the claim is not far from the truth. It has become increasingly popular since the beginning of the century, both for its ideal situation at the confluence of several valleys and for the warmth of its slopes, which—at 1,100 m (3,608 ft), stay relatively toasty compared to other resorts.

Skiing in Gstaad is, in terms of numbers, the equivalent of Zermatt: 69 lifts can transport more than 50,000 skiers per hour to its network of 250 km (155 mi) of marked runs. In fact, these lifts are spread across an immense territory, 20 km (12 mi) as the crow flies, from Zweisimmen and Saint-Stefan in the east (where German is spoken, as in Gstaad) to Château-d'Oex, a Vaud town where French is spoken; to understand one another, people sometimes use English.

Gstaad's expansive area means that most of its lifts are not reachable by foot: Since parking is in short supply, public transport is the best option. The flip side is that except in very high seasons (Christmas, February, Easter) and in certain places, such as the lift for the Diablerets Glacier, or the Pillon, the crowds are not heavy, and lift-line waits are tolerable. A one-day ticket costs 50 SF; a six-day pass costs 233 SF. The Gstaad Ski School (☎ 033/7441865) gives lessons in downhill and cross-country skiing and snowboarding.

Dining and Lodging

$$$$ ✕ **Chesery.** This lively late-night dining scene, complete with piano bar, manages to combine the height of upscale chic with summits of culinary excellence—all at 1,100 m (3,608 ft). Chef Robert Speth marries exotic flavors, such as ginger or mango, with market-fresh ingredients: watch for veal and salmon in pastry with spinach, or duck in kumquat sauce. Crowds pack in, ordering dinner until 11:30 PM, so book well ahead in high season. ✉ *Lauenenstr.,* ☎ *033/7442451. AE, DC, MC, V. Closed Mon.*

$$–$$$ ✕🏠 **Posthotel Rössli.** This comfy, modest, pension-style inn, the old-
★   est inn in town, combines down-home, knotty-pine decor with soigné style: Despite the mountain-cabin look, its staff and clientele are young and chic, and the café, a local-landmark watering hole, draws crowds.

The restaurant, full of linens and candlelight, serves simple daily menus at reasonable prices. ⊠ CH-3780, ☎ 033/7484242, FAX 033/7484243. *18 rooms. Restaurant, café. AE, DC, MC, V.*

$–$$ ✕▦ **Gasthof Alte Post/Weissenburg.** This graceful, isolated, old coach
★ stop is on the magnificent forested Simmen Valley road, about halfway between Spiez and Gstaad (roughly a 40-minute drive to Gstaad). Dating from 1808, it has been lovingly restored; you'll find much carved and painted wood, many antiques, and good home cooking. The back rooms look over the Simmen River. ⊠ CH-3764 Weissenburg, ☎ 033/7831515, FAX 033/7831578. *10 rooms. Restaurant. AE, MC, V. Closed Nov.*

$$$$ ▦ **Grand Hotel Park.** A little bit of Vail comes to the Alps in this enormous modern hotel, opened in 1990 to cater to health-conscious socialites unwilling to pay Palace (☞ *below*) prices. The facilities are state of the art, right down to the antistress program and indoor saltwater pool, and treatment weeks offer an irresistible mix of glamour and virtue. The rooms, though, are far from the ultramodern crowd; flowered wallpaper, wooden furniture, and wardrobes painted with folk-arty Swiss scenes keep things down to earth. ⊠ CH-3780, ☎ 033/7489800, FAX 033/7489808. *82 rooms, 11 suites. 5 restaurants, 2 bars, indoor pool, outdoor pool, beauty salon, tennis court, squash. AE, DC, MC, V. Closed late Sept.–mid-Dec. and Apr.–early June.*

$$$$ ▦ **Palace.** Towering over tiny Gstaad like Mad Ludwig's castle, this
★ fantasyland burlesque packs a wallet-wallop. Although it cozily refers to itself as a "family pension" (albeit the largest in Switzerland), it has an indoor swimming pool with underwater music and water-jet massage, chauffeured Rolls-Royces, and oxygen cures, among other amenities. The rooms have rustic touches but are undeniably lavish; you could play hockey in the sprawling tile baths. Be prepared for the steep 15-minute walk uphill. ⊠ CH-3780, ☎ 033/7485000 or 800/2236800 in the U.S., FAX 033/7485001. *111 rooms. 4 restaurants, piano bar, indoor pool, outdoor pool, 2 saunas, steam room, 4 tennis courts, health club, squash, ice-skating. AE, DC, MC, V.*

$$$–$$$$ ▦ **Bernerhof.** The crowds of young people who came during this chalet-style inn's opening season in 1974 are still returning and stay in touch by means of the hotel's newsletter. It's simple, solid, and surprisingly cozy, with tile baths, lots of natural pine, and a balcony for every room. There are good play facilities for children. Though considerably lower than those at the Grand Hotel Park (☞ *above*), prices remain very expensive by Berner Oberland standards. Homemade pasta is the highlight of the restaurant, and local and Asian dishes are served in the café. It's in the center of town a half block from the station. ⊠ CH-3780, ☎ 033/7488844, FAX 033/7488840. *42 rooms. 3 restaurants, café, indoor pool, sauna, health club. AE, DC, MC, V.*

$$$–$$$$ ▦ **Olden.** In the middle of downtown, this charming Victorian inn has
★ artisan woodwork in every niche and an air of cozy-chic. The rooms are folksy and atmospheric but have slick, modern baths. The adjoining chalet wing (slightly pricier) is lovely; the views from the pretty dormer window in Room 39 are worth a special request. See and be seen at the sidewalk café. ⊠ CH-3780, ☎ 033/7443444, FAX 033/7446164. *15 rooms. 2 restaurants, café. AE, DC, MC, V. Closed late Apr.–mid-May, late Oct.–mid-Nov.*

Outdoor Activities and Sports

GOLF

Gstaad-Saanenland (☎ 030/7442636) in Saanenmöser, a little past Schönried on Route 11, has 18 holes in an idyllic setting.

HORSEBACK RIDING

In Gstaad, the **M. J. Lieber Reitzentrum** (☎ 030/7442460) offers guided outings for experienced riders only.

MOUNTAIN CLIMBING

Great day climbs can be had from Gstaad. **Alpinzentrum Gstaad** (☎ 033/7274006) can supply you with mountain guides and snow-sports teachers. **Beats Adventure** (☎ 033/7441521) aims its tough sport excursions at very fit people. **Experience Gstaad** (☎ 033/7448800) is the place to go for guides for off-trail skiing, ice climbing, and snowshoe trekking.

TENNIS

Gstaad Tennishalle (☎ 033/7441090) has three indoor and two outdoor courts. Rental equipment is available.

Nightlife and the Arts

CONCERTS

The **Gstaad Musiksommer,** led for years by the late violinist and conductor Yehudi Menuhin, hosts a series of world-class concerts. Another string of concerts, the **Alpengala,** follows on its heels. For information and advance seat reservations contact **Musiksommer Gstaad Saanenland** (⊠ Chalet Rialto, Postfach 334, CH-3780 Gstaad, ☎ 033/7488338, ℻ 033/7488350). Information on the next summer's programs is generally available in December.

DANCING

The **"Club 95"** disco (☎ 033/7441431) is in the Sporthotel Victoria.

BERNER OBERLAND A TO Z

Arriving and Departing

By Car

There are swift and scenic roads from both Bern and Zürich to Interlaken. From **Bern,** the autoroute A–6 leads to Spiez, then A–8 continues as the highway to Interlaken. From **Zürich,** the planned autoroute link with Luzern (Lucerne) is incomplete; travel by Highway E–41 south, then pick up the autoroutes A–4 and A–14 in the direction of Luzern. From **Geneva,** the autoroute leads through Lausanne and Fribourg to Bern, where you catch A–6 south, toward Thun. A long, leisurely, scenic alternative: leave the autoroute after Montreux, and head northeast on A–11 from Aigle through Château-d'Oex to Gstaad and the Simmental.

By Plane

Belp (Belpmoos, ☎ 031/9613411) Airport in Bern brings you within an hour via train to Interlaken, the hub of Berner Oberland. **EuroAirport** (⊠ Just across the border from Basel in France, ☎ 061/3253111), shared by Basel, Mulhouse, and Freiburg in Germany, is within 2¼ hours by train. The **Zürich-Kloten** (☎ 1571060) airport is within 2½ hours. Geneva's **Cointrin** (☎ 1571500) is just under 3 hours away.

By Train

Trains from **Bern** to Interlaken run once an hour between 6 AM and 11 PM, some requiring a change at Spiez. From **Zürich,** a direct line leads through Bern to Interlaken and takes about 2½ hours, departing hourly; a more scenic trip over the Golden Pass route via Luzern takes about two hours. From **Basel** trains run twice an hour via Olten (approximately a 2½-hour trip). Trains run hourly from **Geneva** (a 2¾-hour ride). Trains stop at the **Interlaken West** (☎ 033/8264750) station first. Next stop is **Interlaken East** (☎ 033/8287333). West is the more central, but check with your hotel if you've booked in advance: some fine hotels are clustered nearer the East station, and all Brienzersee boat excursions leave from the docks nearby. For **train information** in Interlaken, ask at Interlaken West.

Getting Around

By Boat

Round-trip boat cruises around Lake Thun and Lake Brienz provide an ever-changing view of the craggy foothills and peaks. The round-trip from Interlaken to Thun takes about four hours; the trip to Spiez takes about two hours and includes stopovers for visits to the castles of Oberhofen, Spiez, and Thun. A round-trip from Interlaken to Brienz takes around 2½ hours, to Iseltwald about 1¼ hours. These boats are public transportation as well as pleasure cruisers; just disembark whenever you feel like it and check timetables when you want to catch another. Tickets are flexible and coordinate neatly with surface transit: You can cruise across to Thun and then take a train home for variety. Buy tickets and catch boats for Lake Thun at Interlaken West station. For Lake Brienz, go to Interlaken East.

By Bus

Postbuses travel into much of the area not served by trains, including many smaller mountain towns. In addition, a number of private motorcoach tours cover points of interest. Schedules are available from tourist offices or Die Post (the mail, telephone, and telegraph office).

By Cable Car

More than 30 major cableway and lift systems climb Bernese Oberland peaks, including one of the largest cableways in the world, which stretches up to the Schilthorn above Mürren.

By Car

Driving in Berner Oberland allows you the freedom to find your own views and to park at the very edges of civilization before taking off on foot or by train. If you are confining yourself to the lakefronts, valleys, and lower resorts, a car is an asset. But several lovely resorts are beyond the reach of traffic, and train, funicular, and cable-car excursions take you to places ordinary tires can't tread; sooner or later, you'll leave the car behind and resort to public transportation. Remember that Wengen, Mürren, and Gstaad are all car-free. For maximum flexibility, rent a car in Bern if you fly into Belp.

By Train

The Berner Oberland is riddled with federal and private railways, funiculars, cogwheel trains, and cable lifts designed with the sole purpose of getting you closer to its spectacular views. A **Swiss Pass** lets you travel free on federal trains and lake steamers, and it gives reductions on many private excursions (☞ Train Travel *in* Smart Travel Tips A to Z). If you're concentrating only on the Berner Oberland, consider a 15-day **Regional Pass,** which offers 450 km (279 mi) of free rail, bus, and boat travel for any five days of your visit, with half fare for the remaining 10 days, as well as discounts on some of the most spectacular (and pricey) private excursions into the heights. For adults, the price is 235 SF (first class) and 190 SF (second class); children's fares are half those amounts. A seven-day pass allows you three free travel days for 185 SF (first class) and 150 SF (second class) for adults, half-price for children. These regional passes also grant a 50% discount for travel to Luzern, Zermatt, and Brig. With a **Family Card** (20 SF; ☞ Children & Travel *in* Smart Travel Tips A to Z), children up to 16 accompanied by at least one parent travel free. Discount passes pay for themselves only if you're a high-energy traveler; before you buy, compare the price à la carte for the itinerary you have in mind.

On Foot

You can cover a lot of ground without wheels, as this region (like most others in Switzerland) has highly developed, well-groomed walking trails leading away from nearly every intersection. Most are comfortably surfaced and are marked with distances and estimated walking times. Several itineraries are available from the Berner Oberland tourist office; these combine hikes with lodging along the way. The less ambitious walker may take advantage of postbus rides uphill and a leisurely stroll back down—though descents prove more taxing for calf muscles and knees than novice hikers imagine.

Contacts and Resources

Car Rental

Avis (⊠ Waldeggstr. 34a, Interlaken, ☎ 033/8221939). **Hertz** (⊠ Harderstr. 25, Interlaken, ☎ 033/8226172).

Emergencies

Police (☎ 117). **Hospital** (☎ 033/8262626). **Doctor referral** (☎ 033/8232323). **Dentist and pharmacist referral** (☎ 111).

Guided Tours

Auto AG Interlaken offers guided coach tours and escorted excursions within the Berner Oberland. There are **bus** tours to Mürren and the Schilthorn (including **cable car**), to Grindelwald and Trümmelbach Falls, to Kandersteg and the Blausee, and to Ballenberg. Guests are picked up at either the Interlaken West or East stations or at the Metropole or Interlaken hotels (☎ 033/8281717 for reservations). Some tours are available with English commentary. The tourist office (☞ Visitor Information, *below*) is the best source of information.

If you're traveling without either a Swiss Pass or a Regional Pass (☞ By Train, *above*), note that guided tours to the Jungfraujoch or to the Schilthorn, arranged through the railway and cable companies themselves, cost less than independent round-trip tickets.

For a nostalgic tour of the streets of greater Interlaken by **horse-drawn carriage,** line up by the Interlaken West station (⊠ Ernst Voegeli Kutschenbetrieb, ☎ 033/8227416).

Travel Agencies

Kuoni (⊠ Höheweg 3, Interlaken, ☎ 033/8283636). **Jungfrau Tours** (⊠ Strandbadstr. 3, Interlaken, ☎ 033/8283232). **Vaglio** (⊠ Höheweg 72, Interlaken, ☎ 033/8270722).

Visitor Information

Berner Oberland Tourismus dispenses tourist information for the entire region, though it's not oriented toward walk-ins, so write or call (⊠ Jungfraustr. 38, CH-3800 Interlaken, ☎ 033/8230303, FAX 033/8230330). The **Interlaken Tourist Office,** at the foot of the Hotel Metropole (⊠ Höheweg 37, ☎ 033/8222121, FAX 033/8225221) provides information on Interlaken and the Jungfrau region. Arrange your excursions here.

Other tourist offices: **Brienz** (⊠ CH-3855, ☎ 033/9528080). **Grindelwald** (⊠ CH-3818, ☎ 033/8541212). **Gstaad** (⊠ CH-3780, ☎ 033/7488181). **Kandersteg** (⊠ CH-3718, ☎ 033/6758080). **Lauterbrunnen** (⊠ CH-3822, ☎ 033/8551955). **Meiringen** (⊠ Bahnhofstr. 22, CH-3860, ☎ 033/9725050). **Mürren** (⊠ CH-3825, ☎ 033/8568686). **Spiez** (⊠ CH-3700, ☎ 033/6542020). **Thun** (⊠ Bahnhof, CH-3600, ☎ 033/2222340). **Wengen** (⊠ CH-3823, ☎ 033/8551414).

11 VALAIS

Crans, Verbier, Zermatt

Alpine villages, verdant vineyards, world-class resorts, and that rocky celebrity the Matterhorn—all are good reasons to visit the valley (*valais*) of the Rhône. This is wilderness country, where tumbledown huts and state-of-the-art sports facilities share steep green hillsides and forests. Long isolated from the world by mountains, it remains a land apart.

THIS IS THE VALLEY OF THE MIGHTY Rhône, a river born
in the heights above Gletsch (Glacier), channeled into
a broad westward stream between the Bernese and the
Valais Alps, lost in the depths of Lac Léman (Lake Geneva), and then
diverted into France, where it ultimately dissolves in the marshes of
the Camargue. Its broad upper valley forms a region of Switzerland
that is still wild, remote, beautiful, and slightly unruly, its *mazots*
(barns balanced on stone columns to keep mice out of winter food stores)
romantically tumbledown, its highest slopes peopled by nimble farmers who live at vertiginous angles.

Updated by
Ian Plenderleith

The birthplace of Christianity in Switzerland, Valais was never reformed
by Calvin or Zwingli, nor conquered by the ubiquitous Bernese—one
reason, perhaps, that the west end of Valais seems the most intensely
French of the regions of the Suisse Romande.

Its romance appeals to its fellow Swiss, who, longing for rustic atmosphere, build nostalgic Valais-style huts in their modern city centers to
eat raclette under mounted pitchforks, old pewter pitchers, and grape
pickers' baskets. For vacations, the Swiss come here to play: to escape,
to hike, and, above all, to ski. The renowned resorts of Zermatt, Saas-
Fee, Crans-Montana, and Verbier are all in the Valais, some within yodeling distance of villages barely touched by modern technology.

Pleasures and Pastimes

Dining

Though the French influence in the western portion of this region
means a steady diet of cuisine *bourgeoise,* leading newcomers to think
entrecôte with peppercorn sauce is a native dish, the elemental cuisine
of Valais is much simpler. In a word: cheese.

Fondue, of course, is omnipresent. Often it is made with the local Bagnes
or Orsières, mild cheeses from near Martigny. But the best application
for these regional products is raclette (melted cheese with potatoes and
pickles), an exclusive invention of this mountain canton (though the
French of Haute-Savoie embrace it as their own). Ideally, the fresh-cut
face of a half wheel of Orsières is melted before an open wood fire,
the softened cheese scraped onto a plate and eaten with potatoes (always in their skins), pickled onions, and tiny gherkins. Nowadays, even
mountain *carnotzets* (cellar pubs) with roaring fires depend on electric raclette-heaters that grip the cheese in a vise before toasterlike elements. The beverage: a crisp, bubbly, fruity Fendant.

Valais rivals the Graubünden in its production of *viande séchée* (air-
dried beef), a block of meat marinated in herbs, pressed between
planks until it takes on its signature bricklike form, and then dried in
the open air. Shaved into thin, translucent slices, it can be as tender as
a good *prosciutto crudo*—or as tough as leather. The flavor is concentrated, the flesh virtually fat-free.

CATEGORY	COST*
$$$$	over 70 SF
$$$	40 SF–70 SF
$$	20 SF–40 SF
$	under 20 SF

*Prices are per person for a three-course meal (two-course in $ category), in-
cluding sales tax and 15% service charge

Hiking

As skiing is to winter, hiking is to summer in Valais, and the network of valleys that radiate north and south of the Rhône provides almost infinite possibilities. Sociable hikers can join the crowds on trails out of the big resorts—especially outside Saas-Fee and Zermatt, where the mountain peaks and glaciers are within tackling distance—but don't overlook wilder, more isolated alternatives in the less developed Val d'Hérens and Val d'Anniviers. Good maps and suggested itineraries are available through the Valais regional tourist office in Sion (☞ Visitor Information *in* Valais A to Z, *below*).

Lodging

The most appealing hotels in Valais seem to be old. That is, historic sites have maintained their fine Victorian ambience; postwar inns, their lodgelike feel. Most of those built after about 1960 popped up in generic, concrete-slab, balconied rows to accommodate the 1960s ski boom. They are solid enough but, for the most part, anonymous, depending on the personality and dedication of their owners.

Valais is home to some of Switzerland's most famous resorts, and prices vary widely between top-level Zermatt lodgings and those in humbler towns. To indicate the relationship between resort prices and simple, wayside auberges (inns), the price categories below have been equally applied, so remember: the standards in a $$$-rated hotel in expensive Zermatt may be moderate compared to ones in nonresort towns. When you write for information, check prices carefully. *Demipension,* or half board (includes breakfast and a hot meal, either lunch or dinner), is often included in the price, and rates may be listed per person. And when planning a vacation in fall or spring, research your itinerary carefully: many of the resorts shut down altogether during the lulls in May and from November to mid-December and schedule their renovations and construction projects for these periods. That means that while some places offer low-season savings, others simply close their doors. The broad price-category spectrum indicated—sometimes from $ to $$$—shows the sometimes enormous differences between high- and low-season prices.

CATEGORY	COST*
$$$$	over 250 SF
$$$	180 SF–250 SF
$$	120 SF–180 SF
$	under 120 SF

Prices are for a standard double room, including breakfast, tax, and service charge.

Skiing

With plateaus and cavernous gorges branching out from the valley, Valais has nurtured ski resorts for centuries. Zermatt, with its rustic, historic atmosphere, contrasts sharply with its high-tech peers to the west: Verbier, Crans-Montana, and Anzères are virtually purpose-built, with every amenity and connection—and considerably less focus on charm. You can find all ranges of difficulty and all kinds of snow—even, above Crans, in July.

Exploring Valais

Valais is an L-shape valley with Martigny at its angle; the eastern, or long, leg of the L is the most characteristic and imposing. This wide, fertile riverbed is flanked by bluffs and fed from the north and south by remote, narrow valleys that snake into the mountains. Some of these valleys peter out in desolate Alpine wilderness; some lead to its most famous landmarks—including that Swiss superstar, the Matterhorn. Not

Valais

Grindelwald

Lauterbrunnen

Mönch

Handegg

Grimsel Pass

Gletsch

Schilthorn

Jungfrau

19 **20** **Furka Pass**

ER AND

Oberwald

Breithorn

Aletschhorn

Münster

Val de Conches

Grosser Aletschgletscher

Rhône

19

18 **Riederalp**

Mörel

Lonza

nstein

Brig

Rhône

16

mpel

Turtmann

9

Visp

Simplon Tunnel

Stalden

17

Simplon Pass

St-Niklaus

14 **Grächen**

Gondo

Gstein-Gabi

Saas-Grund

Domodossola

15 **Saas-Fee**

Fee-

Alphübel

gletsch

Täsch

Allalinhorn

Mittelhorn

13

Hinterrothorn

ITALY

KEY

——— Rail Lines

•••••• Cable Car/ Funicular

- - - Regional Boundary Lines

⛷ Ski Resort

Breithorn

ROSA

N

0   6 miles

0   9 km

all of Valais covers Alpine terrain, however: the western stretch—between Martigny and Sierre—comprises one of the two chief sources of wine in Switzerland (the other is in Vaud, along Lake Geneva; *see* Chapter 12). Valais wines, dominated by round, fruity Fendant and light or ruby Dôle, come from verdant vineyards that stripe the hillsides flanking the Rhône.

The Val d'Entremont leads southward down an ancient route from Lake Geneva to the Col du Grand St-Bernard (Great St. Bernard Pass), traversing the key Roman crossroads at Martigny. Up the valley, past the isolated eagle's-nest village of Isérables, two magnificent castle-churches loom above the historic Old Town at Sion. From Sion, the Val d'Hérens winds up into the isolated wilderness past the stone Pyramides d'Euseigne and the Brigadoon-like resorts of Évolène and, even more obscure, Les Haudères. The Val d'Anniviers, the valley winding south from Sierre, leads to tiny, isolated skiing and hiking resorts such as Grimentz. The most famous southbound valley, the Mattertal, leads from Visp to the stellar resort of Zermatt and its mascot mountain, the Matterhorn. A fork off that same valley leads to spectacular Saas-Fee, another car-free resort in a magnificent glacier bowl. Back at the Rhône, the valley mounts southward from Brig to the Simplon Pass and Italy or northeastward to the glacier-source Gletsch and the Furka Pass out of the region.

Numbers in the text correspond to numbers in the margin and on the Valais map.

Great Itineraries

It's not necessary to explore every wild valley that ribs out from the Rhône in order to experience Valais; better to choose one region and spend a few days hiking, driving, or skiing. However, you will want to see the sights of the main river valley: Martigny, Sion, and at least one of the great Alpine passes, depending on your next travel goal.

IF YOU HAVE 2 DAYS

If you're using the Rhône Valley Highway as a means to cover ground scenically, enter from Lac Léman and cruise directly to ⌖ **Sion** ⑦, where you'll walk through the Old Town and climb up to the church fortress of Valére. Although you won't have time to cut north or south into a valley, any pass you use to exit the region will cover magnificent terrain: either the climb from **Martigny** ② to the **Col du Grand St-Bernard** ⑤ into Piedmont in Italy, the dramatic ascent from Brig over the **Simplon Pass** ⑰, or the slow, isolated approach to **Gletsch** ⑲ and the **Furka Pass** ⑳. Whenever time and road conditions permit, opt for the slow switchback crawl over the mountain passes rather than more efficient tunnels.

IF YOU HAVE 5 DAYS

Enter from Lac Léman and visit the museums of **Martigny** ②. Spend the night and next day exploring ⌖ **Sion** ⑦, then make your selection: if you have never seen the Matterhorn, head directly for ⌖ **Zermatt** ⑬ and spend three nights shutter-snapping, riding cable cars for better views, and stuffing yourself with fondue. Other Alpine resort options—⌖ **Saas-Fee** ⑮, ⌖ **Verbier** ③, and ⌖ **Crans-Montana** ⑩—are magnificently sited. If you prefer wilderness and old-fashioned retreat, shun the famous spots and head up the Val d'Hérens to pretty little **Évolène** ⑧, up the Val d'Anniviers to **Grimentz** ⑪, or up the Mattertal to charming ⌖ **Grächen** ⑭, teetering on a high plateau.

IF YOU HAVE 10 DAYS

En route to the mountains, take time to visit **St-Maurice** ① and **Martigny** ②, then head up to ⌖ **Verbier** ③ for a couple of days' worth of hiking or skiing. For backcountry exploring, spend a day or two wandering up the Val Hérens to **Évolène** ⑧, with side trips to see the Grande Dixence Dam and the Pyramides d'Euseigne and time for wilderness walks or cross-country skiing. Set aside a full day for the monuments and museums of ⛰ **Sion** ⑦ before heading back into the heights. You'll feel the contrast when you reach highly developed, Germanic ⛰ **Zermatt** ⑬, where another four nights will give you time to exploit its facilities. From Zermatt, you can exit Valais via the **Simplon Pass** ⑰ or the **Furka Pass** ⑳.

When to Tour Valais

Valais is at its sunny best in high summer and mid-winter, with foggy dampness overwhelming the region in late autumn (its low season). Mid-December to Easter is peak ski season in the resorts. As Europeans vacation here for weeks at a time, book well ahead if you want to compete for lodging in August, at Easter time, and at Christmas and New Year's. And remember: May and November to mid-December are renovation and repair time, with many facilities closed.

VAL D'ENTREMONT TO THE COL DU GRAND ST-BERNARD

The Rhône River at Villeneuve broadens deltalike into a flat valley that pours into Lake Geneva. But heading south, up the valley, the mountains already begin to crowd in on either side. Once you cross the Rhône and officially enter the canton of Valais, leaving Vaud behind, the valley and the river begin to change character. The mountains—the Dents du Midi in the west and the Dents de Morcles to the east—come closer; the Rhône no longer flows placidly but gives a foretaste of the mountain torrent it will become as you approach its source. This most ancient of Alpine routes leaves the Rhône at the Martigny elbow and ascends due south to 2,469 m (8,098 ft) at the St-Bernard Pass before descending into Italy's Valle d'Aosta.

St-Maurice

❶ *46 km (28 mi) west of Sion, 56 km (35 mi) southeast of Lausanne.*

The **St-Maurice Abbey** is an important stop on this ancient route to the Great St. Bernard Pass. Here, at the end of the 3rd century, Maurice, leader of the Theban Legion, a band of Christian soldiers, was massacred along with most of his men for refusing to worship the pagan gods of Rome. Christianity was first established in Switzerland here in Valais, and its fierce Catholicism—at both the French and the German ends—reflects this early zeal. The abbey was built in AD 515 to commemorate the martyrdom, and excavations near the baroque *église abbatiale* (abbey church) have revealed the foundations of this original building. The abbey treasury contains an exceptionally precious collection of Romanesque and Gothic objects. ☎ *024/4851181.* 🎟 *Free.* 🕐 *Guided tours July–Aug., Tues.–Sat. 10:30, 2, 3:15, and 4:30, Sun. 2, 3:15, and 4:30; May–June and Sept.–Oct., Tues.–Sat. 10:30, 3, and 4:30, Sun. 3 and 4:30; Nov.–Apr., Tues.–Sun. 3.*

Martigny

❷ *17 km (11 mi) south of St-Maurice, 23 km (14 mi) southwest of Sion.*

This valley crossroads, once used as a Roman camp, is still on the map today thanks to the Foundation Pierre Gianadda, which sponsors a cluster of world-class museums. Its first endeavor: to develop Gallo-Roman ruins discovered during a building project. This became the **Musée Gallo-Romain** (Gallo-Roman Museum), which displays relics excavated from a 1st-century temple: striking bronzes, statuary, pottery, and coins. A marked path leads visitors through the antique village, baths, drainage systems, and foundations to the fully restored 5,000-seat amphitheater, which dates from the 2nd century.

Recent temporary exhibitions have included a Gauguin retrospective and the show "Turner and the Alps." Its permanent collection includes works by Van Gogh, Cézanne, and Picasso. And don't be surprised if you see posters for a concert by an international classical star—the Roman museum not only doubles as an art gallery but also as a concert hall. ⊠ *59 rue de Forum,* ☎ *027/7223978.* 🎫 *12 SF.* ☉ *Mid-June–Oct., daily 9–7; Feb.–June, daily 10–6; Nov.–Jan., daily 10–noon and 1:30–6.*

The Foundation Pierre Gianadda also sponsors a sizable **Musée de l'Automobile** (Automobile Museum), which contains some 50 antique cars, all in working order. They include an 1897 Benz, the Delauneay-Belleville of Czar Nicholas II of Russia, and a handful of Swiss-made models, three of which have horns shaped like menacing serpents' heads. Admission is included in the Gallo-Roman Museum fee. ⊠ *59 rue de Forum,* ☎ *027/7223978.* ☉ *Mid-June–Oct., daily 9–7; Feb.–June, daily 10–6; Nov.–Jan., daily 10–noon and 1:30–6.*

In the gracefully landscaped garden surrounding the Foundation Pierre Gianadda's museums, a wonderful **Parc de Sculptures** (Sculpture Park) displays works by Rodin, Brancusi, Miró, Calder, Moore, Dubuffet, and Max Ernst.

Lodging

$$–$$$ 🏨 **Hotel du Forum.** Martigny is something of a one-street town, but if it suits your itinerary to stop over, then this family-run hotel is a convenient choice. The comfortable rooms are filled with dark pine. The restaurant offers lavish five- or seven-course French-influenced meals, a bigger production than you'll find in the town's usual cafés/bistros. Take the Bus 13 from the railway station to the Le Bourg stop. ⊠ *74 av. de Grand-Saint-Bernard CH-1920,* ☎ *027/7221841,* 📠 *027/ 7227925. 29 rooms. Restaurant. AE, DC, MC, V.*

Verbier

❸ *29 km (18 mi) east of Martigny (exit at Sembrancher), 58 km (36 mi) southwest of Sion.*

It's the skiing, not the social life, that draws committed sports lovers to Verbier, a high-tech, state-of-the-art sports complex that connects to several nearby resorts (including Thyon and Nendaz). Verbier has the biggest aerial cableway in Europe, with two cabins accommodating 150, and some 86 smaller transportation installations. Summer sports are equally serious: hang gliding and its variations compete with golf as the principal sports. Though it's perched on a sunny shelf high above the Val de Bagnes, with the 3,023-m (9,915-ft) Mont Gelé towering behind and wraparound views, Verbier itself is too modern to be picturesque, but thanks to its compact layout and easygoing locals, the town has a friendlier feel to it than the traffic-snarled sprawl of Crans-Montana or hotel-packed Zermatt. You won't have any trouble finding your way around; all hotels are clearly signposted.

Skiing

At 1,500 m (4,921 ft), Verbier is the center of Switzerland's most famous transit network, **Téléverbier**—which consists of 12 gondolas, 8 cable cars, 35 chairlifts, and 47 ski lifts giving access to 410 km (253 mi) of marked pistes. From this resort an immense complex of resorts has developed—some more modest, others more exclusive—covering four valleys in an extended ski area whose extremities are 15 km (9 mi) or so apart as the crow flies and several dozen kilometers apart by way of winding mountain roads.

Les Ruinettes gives access to Verbier's entire upper ski area, which culminates at **Mont-Fort,** at 3,300 m (10,825 ft). This is reached by an aerial tram, *Le Jumbo,* equipped with a cab that accommodates 150. This entire sector is crisscrossed by a dense network of astonishingly varied pistes. There are several strategic passes, including **Les Attelas, Mont-Gelé, Col des Gentianes, Lac des Vaux,** and **Tortin,** whose congestion was tackled with the addition of a new 1,200 person per hour cable-car to Col de Chassoure at the end of 1998. One-day lift tickets cost 56 SF; six-day passes cost 282 SF.

Dining and Lodging

\$\$–\$\$\$ ✕ **Le Bouchon Gourmand.** Away from the main drag of generic fondue cabins and no-surprise pizza houses, this warmly decorated spot serves an excellent range of French-influenced poultry dishes (including gizzard pâté) and tongue-melting desserts. Especially worth sampling are the succulent duck in red wine sauce and for dessert the brandy-inflamed apple tart. ⊠ *rue de la Poste,* ☎ *027/7717296. AE, DC, MC, V.*

\$\$\$\$ ✕🖃 **Rosalp.** The honey-gold pine, rustic-chic decor of the main restau-
★ rant makes a surprisingly warm and comfortable setting for one of Switzerland's great meals. Chef Roland Pierroz continues to earn the highest gastronomic kudos and an international following for his prawn bisque, squab with truffles, and apple tarts, as well as for the variety of fine local cheeses he presents. The other restaurant, the French-influenced La Pinte, is less pricey; the bar is the perfect place to settle into a leather sofa with a cognac. If you plan to stay overnight, ask for one of the newer rooms, which have marble baths. The upper rooms are smaller but quieter, with better views. Reservations are essential at Pierroz's restaurant. ⊠ *rue de Médran, CH-1936,* ☎ *027/ 7716323,* ℻ *027/7711059. 19 rooms, 3 apartments. 2 restaurants, bar, hot tub, exercise room, sauna. AE, DC, MC, V.*

\$\$\$\$ 🖃 **Hotel Vanessa.** This comfortable, quiet, centrally located hotel offers mainly southern views and spacious, pine-decorated rooms complete with balcony, kitchenette (even including a dishwasher), as well as a large number of two- and three-room suites. The questionably decorated but convivial bar features a regular in-house pianist. ⊠ *pl. Centrale, CH-1936,* ☎ *027/7752800,* ℻ *027/7752828. 35 rooms, 21 suites. Restaurant, bar, sauna. AE, DC, MC, V.*

\$\$\$–\$\$\$\$ 🖃 **Golf Hotel.** As modern and central as most other Verbier hotels, the Golf is a bit softer; recent renovations (1998) lightened the rooms with pale pine. Downstairs is the dusky Jacky's Piano Bar, with live piano three nights a week; in summertime, barbecues and raclette dinners promote mingling. The 18-hole golf course offers magnificent views, although even guests will have to pay for the privilege of a round. The hotel runs a private bus to the cable cars. ⊠ *rue de Verbier, CH-1936,* ☎ *027/7716515,* ℻ *027/7711488. 30 rooms. Restaurant, bar, sauna, steam room, 18-hole golf course, exercise room. AE, DC, MC, V.*

\$\$ 🖃 **Ermitage.** The rooms may not quite allow you the space for a vigorous pre-ski stretch, but they are quite comfortable. The hotel is conveniently central; the south-facing rooms are quieter and have better views (though you'll have to gaze over the parking lot and other hotels to the mountains). ⊠ *pl. Centrale, CH-1936,* ☎ *027/7716477,* ℻ *027/7715264. 25 rooms. Restaurant. AE, MC, DC, V.*

\$ 🖃 **Les Touristes.** If you're here for the world-class skiing and want to pass on the pricier comforts, head for this old-style pension. Built in the 1940s in a dark-wood roadhouse style, it's in the village below the

main resort, where a few traditional chalets are still evident. The rooms
are spare, and the bare-bones shower and toilet are down the hall, but
the Stübli-restaurant attracts locals disenchanted with the uptown
scene. Staying here means one more connection to get you to the
slopes—a brief bus ride or a quick ten-minute walk—but it's friendly,
authentic, and you save a bundle. ⊠ CH-1936, ☎ 027/7712147, FAX
027/7712147. 14 rooms. Restaurant, Stübli. AE, MC, V.

Nightlife and the Arts

DANCING

The **Farm Club** (⊠ Rhodania Hotel, rue de Verbier, ☎ 027/7716121)
is the place to be seen in Verbier, with lines often forming in the street
for the privilege of jiving to pop's back catalog while quaffing a bottle of
vodka costing well into three figures in both franc and dollar terms. Apparently it is not the done thing to turn up before 1 AM. The club is closed
Sunday. In the meantime you could head to the less pretentious **Scotch**
(⊠ rue de la Poste, ☎ 027/7711656), whose slogan reads: "We may be
small but we're cheap." **Marshal's** (⊠ Hotel Farinet, pl. Centrale, ☎ 027/
7713572) caters to the techno generation; the popular **Crok** bar (⊠ route
des Creux, ☎ 027/7716934) has live music on weekends.

MUSIC

For more than two weeks overlapping July and August the **Verbier Festival and Academy** hosts an impressive classical music festival; the 1999
festival included pianists Martha Argerich and Evgeny Kissin and conductors Sir Neville Marriner and James Levine. To order tickets, call
☎ 027/7718282 or fax FAX 027/7717057.

Outdoor Activities and Sports

BICYCLING

Jet Sports (☎ 027/7712067) rents mountain bikes.

GOLF

The **Golf Club** (☎ 027/7715314) has two 18-hole courses.

MOUNTAIN CLIMBING

Les Combins (☎ 027/7716825) provides guides and training. **École d'Alpin-
isme de Verbier** (☎ 027/7712212) offers guides and lessons as well.

PARAGLIDING

The **Centre Parapente** (☎ 027/7716818) gives paragliding lessons and
sells equipment. **L'Envol** (☎ 079/4333545) paragliding school offers
training and rentals.

SPORTS CENTERS

Verbier's **Centre Polysportif** (☎ 027/7716601) has indoor skating as
well as a swimming pool, saunas, whirlpools, a solarium, curling, nine
tennis courts, and squash.

Champex

❹ *31 km (19 mi) south of Martigny, 51 km (32 mi) southwest of Sion.*

Clinging high above the Orsières Valley (famous for its raclette cheese),
this delightful little family resort lies wrapped around a tiny mirror of
a lake and surrounded by forested peaks, concentrating some of the
prettiest scenery in the region—including views dominated by the massive Combin (4,314 m/14,150 ft).

Dining and Lodging

$–$$ ✕🏠 **Auberge de la Forêt.** On a quiet street facing the lake, this place
has a few lake-view rooms with a comfortable, modern look. The fireplace and grill turn out authentic raclette. ⊠ CH-1938, ☎ 027/
7831278, FAX 027/7832101. 15 rooms. Restaurant, café. MC, V.

$–$$ ✕⌨ **Belvédère.** This is the prototypical *relais de campagne* (country
★ inn): full of warm wood, cozy rooms with balconies, creaky pine-
panel halls hung with historic photos, and doilies everywhere, crocheted
by the owner herself. Set on a wooded hill above the lake and town,
it offers breathtaking views all the way down to the Val d'Entremont.
The café attracts local workers, and the restaurant serves the owners'
fresh, straightforward *cuisine bourgeoise* as well as a variety of fondues. Watch for garlic-sautéed porcini mushrooms on toast, lamb fillet in sage with *Rösti* (hash brown potatoes), and muscat mousse with
grape compote. Vegetables are local and organically grown. The list
of local wines includes some rare bargains. ✉ *CH-1938,* ☎ *027/
7831114,* 𝔽𝔸𝕏 *027/7832576. 9 rooms. Restaurant, café. MC, V.*

Col du Grand St-Bernard

★ ❺ *40 km (25 mi) south of Martigny, 69 km (43 mi) southwest of Sion.*

The Great St. Bernard Pass, breasting the formidable barrier of the Alps
at 2,469 m (8,101 ft), is the oldest and most famous of the great Alpine
crossings, and the first to join Rome and Byzantium to the wilds of the
north. Used for centuries before the birth of Christ, it has witnessed an
endless stream of emperors, knights, and simple travelers—think of Umberto Eco's *The Name of the Rose,* with its two friars crossing on don-
key back in howling winter winds. Napoléon took an army of 40,000
across it en route to Marengo, where he defeated the Austrians in 1800.

You'll have an easier time crossing today than Napoléon did: if you
simply want to get to Italy quickly, you can take the swift tunnel that
opens out on the other side, above the Valle d'Aosta. But by skipping
the tiny winding road over the top, you'll miss the awe-inspiring,
windswept moonscape at the summit and the hospice that honors its
namesake. In 1038, the story goes, Bernard of Menthon, bishop of Aosta,
came to clear the pass of brigands. When he reached the top, he found
a pagan temple, which he covered with his chasuble. The shrine immediately crumbled to dust and, by the same power, the brigands were
defeated. There Bernard established his hospice.

The **hospice of St. Bernard** served international travelers throughout
the Middle Ages. Kings and princes rewarded the hospice by shower-
ing estates upon the order. By the 12th century, it owned 79 estates in
England alone. Nowadays its residents—Augustinian canons—train as
mountain guides and ski instructors and accommodate young groups.
Behind the hospice, there's a kennel full of the landmark's enormous,
furry namesakes: the famous St. Bernard dogs, who for centuries have
helped the monks find travelers lost in the snow. They supposedly came
to Switzerland with silk caravans from central Asia and were used by
Romans as war dogs; nowadays they're kept more for sentimental than
functional reasons. The most famous was Barry, who saved more than
40 people in the 19th century and today stands stuffed in Bern's
Naturhistorisches Museum (Museum of Natural History; ☞ Chapter
9). Souvenir stands sell plush versions of St. Bernards on either side of
the pass. ☎ *027/7871236.* ⌨ *Kennel: 6 SF.* ☉ *July–Aug. 8 AM–10 PM.*

ISÉRABLES, SJON, AND
THE VAL D'HERENS

The Rhône Valley is most fertile just east of Martigny, its flatlands thick
with orchards and vegetable gardens, its south-facing slopes quilted
with vineyards. The region nurtures a virtual market basket of apples,
pears, carrots, and delicate white asparagus, a specialty of early spring.

The blue-blood crop of the region is grapes: this is one of the primary wine-producing regions in the country, and the fruity Fendant and hearty red Dôle (a blend of pinot noir and gamay grapes) appear on every region's lists, as well as the Dôle Blanche, actually a rosé. Once Valais wines were poured from hinged-lid tin or pewter pitchers called *channes*; reproductions are sold throughout the region. Also from the orchards come potent, intensely perfumed eaux-de-vie (or schnapps), especially *abricotine* (from apricots) and *williamine* (from pears).

This patch of Valais demonstrates the contrasts of this dramatic region: over the fertile farmlands looms the great medieval stronghold of Sion, its fortress towers protecting the gateway to the Alps. Yet jutting sharply up into the bluffs to the south are the isolated mountain villages of Isérables and Évolène.

Isérables

★ ❻ *24 km (15 mi) southwest of Sion.*

This is a rare opportunity to visit one of the scores of eagle's-nest towns you'll glimpse as you pass through the region's valleys. Set on a precarious slope that drops 1,000 m (3,280 ft) into the lowlands, it has narrow streets that weave between crooked old stone-shingle mazots, the typical little Valais barns balanced on stone disks and columns to keep mice out of winter food stores.

Since the arrival of the cable car in recent times, Isérables has prospered and modernized itself considerably. Yet the inhabitants of this village still carry the curious nickname Bedjuis. Some say it is derived from "Bedouins" and that the people are descended from the Saracen hordes who, after the battle of Poitiers in 732, overran some of the high Alpine valleys. Certainly some of the people here—stocky, swarthy, and dark-eyed—seem different from most others in the canton.

Sion

★ ❼ *158 km (98 mi) south of Bern.*

Rearing up spookily in the otherwise deltalike flatlands of the western Valais, two otherworldly twin hills flank the ancient city of Sion. Sion folk are seen as a little "different," not just by the Swiss in general but even by their fellow Valaisans. They are fiercely proud and independent, as reflected in the fanatical support for their soccer team (very rare in a country much keener on winter sports) and their dogged attempts to snatch the Winter Olympics. They failed for 2002 and, in a surprise upset, also lost the bid to host the 2006 Winter Olympics, to Turin, Italy. However, the town is not as hospitable as the tourist-oriented ski resorts around it, since there is a dearth of quality hotels.

Crowning the higher hill, **Tourbillon,** is a ruined château built as a bishop's residence at the end of the 13th century and destroyed by fire in 1788. 🎫 *Free.* ☉ *Mid-Mar.–mid-Nov., Tues.–Sun. 10–6.*

On the other hill, **Valère,** is an 11th-century church. The two hills together are a powerful emblem of the city's 1,500-year history as a bishopric and a Christian stronghold. From the top of either hill, you'll have a dramatic view of the surrounding flatlands and the mountains flanking the valley.

The town itself can be comfortably explored on foot in an afternoon, unless you lose yourself in one of its museums or labyrinthine antiques shops. The **Old Town,** down rue de Lausanne (take a left when leaving the tourist office, map in hand), is a blend of shuttered 16th-century houses and modern shops. The grand old **Maison Supersaxo**

(House of Supersaxo) was built in 1505 by Georges Supersaxo, the local governor, to put his rivals to shame. This extravagantly decorated building includes a Gothic staircase and a grand hall whose painted wood ceiling is a dazzling work of decorative art. ✉ *Tucked into a passageway off rue Supersaxo.* ☎ *Free.* ☉ *Weekdays 8–noon and 2–6.*

The imposing **Hôtel de Ville** (Town Hall) has extraordinary historic roots: though it was built in the 1650s, there are transplanted stones in the entrance bearing Roman inscriptions, including a Christian symbol from the year AD 377. The 17th-century doors are richly carved wood, and the tower displays an astronomical clock. Upstairs, the **Salle du Conseil** (Council Hall) is also adorned with ornate woodwork. ✉ *At the intersection of rue de Conthey and rue du Grand-Pont.* ☎ *Free interior visits only with guided walking tour of the town (8 SF) from the Sion tourist office.* ☉ *Mid-July–Aug., Tues. and Thurs. 4–6.*

The **Musée Cantonal d'Archéologie** (Museum of Archaeology) displays a collection of excavated pieces, including fine Roman works found in Valais. The narrow, cobbled rue des Châteaux leading up toward the twin fortifications passes graceful old patrician houses, among them the museum. ✉ *12 rue des Châteaux,* ☎ *027/6064700.* ☎ *4 SF.* ☉ *Tues.–Sun. 10–noon and 2–6.*

In the ★**Église-Forteresse de Valère** (Church-Fortress of Valère), high above the town, you'll observe a striking example of sacred and secular power combined—as in the church's heyday it often subjugated rather than served its parishioners. Built on Roman foundations, the massive stone walls enclose both the **château** and the 11th-century **Église Notre Dame de Valère** (Church of Our Lady of Valère).

This structure stands in a relatively raw form, rare in Switzerland, where monuments are often restored to Disneyland perfection. Over the engaging Romanesque carvings, 16th-century fresco fragments, and 17th-century stalls painted with scenes of the Passion there hangs a rare **organ** in "swallow's-nest" form, its cabinet painted with two fine medieval Christian scenes. Dating from the 14th century, it is the oldest playable organ in the world, and an organ festival celebrates its musical virtues annually (☞ Nightlife and the Arts, *below*). The church also houses the **Musée d'Histoire** (History Museum), which displays a wide array of medieval chests and sculptures. There are periodic guided tours, but they're not given in English. ☎ *027/6064710.* ☎ *Church 3 SF; museum 5 SF; combination ticket 6 SF.* ☉ *Tues.–Sun. 10–noon and 2–6; guided tours of museum 1st Sat. of the month, 2:30.*

The Cathedral, **Notre-Dame du Glarier** (Our Lady of Glarier), is dominated by its Romanesque tower, built in the Lombard, or Italian, style and dating from the 12th century; the rest of the church is late Gothic in style. ✉ *rue de la Cathédrale.*

Just up from the cathedral grounds, the **Tour des Sorciers** (Sorcerers' Tower) is the last remnant of the walls that once ringed the town. ☎ *3 SF.* ☉ *Tues.–Sun. 2–6.*

Dining and Lodging

$$$$ ✗ **Supersaxo.** One of the few restaurants in Sion enjoying a reputation beyond the city walls, Supersaxo serves excellent cuisine in modern, sleek surroundings. If the elaborate evening menus are beyond your price range, you can always pop in at lunchtime and treat yourself to a *plat du jour* (daily special) for a little over 20 SF. ✉ *Passage Supersaxo,* ☎ *027/3238550. AE, DC, MC, V.*

$$–$$$ ✕ **L'Enclos de Valère.** If you've worked up an appetite climbing the Tour-
billon, you may want to stop here in the Old Town on your way back
down. Unfussy service, fine regional cuisine, and a 15 SF plat du jour
make it a welcome break. In summer you can eat outside on a shady
terrace. ⊠ *18 rue des Châteaux,* ☎ *027/3233230. AE, MC, V. Closed
Jan.–mid-Feb.; closed Sun., Mon. Oct.–Apr.*

$$ 🏨 **Du Rhône.** This spare, cinder-block property could be an American
motel if it weren't for the illuminated antiquities visible from the north
windows. At the edge of the Old Town and handy to the castle walks,
it makes a comfortable, no-frills base for your explorations. ⊠ *10 rue
de Scex, CH-1950,* ☎ *027/3228291,* 🆕 *027/3231188. 45 rooms.
Restaurant. AE, DC, MC, V.*

$ 🏨 **Du Midi.** On the edge of the Old Town, and now absorbed into the
upper floors of a downtown shopping block, this was once a freestanding
roadhouse, a loner in the shadow of the city's twin citadels. Its small
rooms are nothing fancy but are a decent value for the price. ⊠ *29 pl.
du Midi, CH-1950,* ☎ *027/3231331,* 🆕 *027/3236173. 12 rooms.
Restaurant, brasserie. AE, DC, MC, V.*

Nightlife and the Arts

Sion attracts world-class musicians and scholars to its festivals cele-
brating the medieval organ in its church-fortress Valère (☞ Exploring,
above). The **Festival International de l'Orgue Ancien Valère** (Interna-
tional Festival of the Ancient Valère Organ; ☎ 027/3235767) takes
place from July through the beginning of September.

OFF THE   **GRANDE DIXENCE DAM –** Veer right past Vex up the narrow mountain road
BEATEN PATH   that leads about 16 km (10 mi) up the Val d'Hérémence to the Grande
               Dixence Dam, a gargantuan monolith of concrete built in the mid-1960s at
               the improbable altitude of 2,364 m (7,754 ft). Only the Swiss could have
               accomplished such a feat of Alpine engineering—an achievement that
               brings them millions on millions of kilowatt hours every year. The potential
               energy is impressively apparent because the now-vast Lac des Dix backs
               up some 4 km (2½ mi) into the barren, abandoned valley.

En Route   South of Sion, the Val d'Hérens is a valley lined with improbably high
             mountain farms and pastures. Here you will find the **Pyramides d'Eu-
             seigne** (Pyramids of Euseigne), a group of bizarre geological forma-
             tions: stone pillars formed by the debris of glacial moraines and
             protected by peculiar hard-rock caps from the erosion that carved
             away the material around them. The effect is that of enormous, free-
             standing stalagmites wearing hats. A car tunnel has been carved through
             the bases of three of them. Six-day hiking tours of the Val d'Hérens
             (available from mid-June to mid-October) can be booked through the
             Sion tourist office (☞ Visitor Information, *below*).

Évolène

❽ *23 km (14 mi) southeast of Sion, cross the main highway and head
south toward Vex.*

In a broad, fertile valley, Évolène is a town of ramshackle mazots and
wooden houses edged with flower-filled window boxes that provides
a picturesque setting for vacationers—mostly French—and moun-
taineers, who tackle nearby Mont-Collon and the Dent-Blanche. If you're
lucky, you'll see some of the older women villagers in the traditional
dress of kerchiefs and flowered cottons that they still favor.

Les Haudères

❾ *5 km (3 mi) south of Évolène, 28 km (17 mi) southeast of Sion.*

This tiny but popular vacation retreat is little more than a scattering of chalets in a spectacular, isolated mountain valley. Farther on, the little skiing and mountaineering resort of **Arolla** (2,010 m/6,593 ft) is custom-made for those seeking a total retreat in Alpine isolation.

CRANS-MONTANA AND THE VAL D'ANNIVIERS

Spiking north and south of the crossroads of Sierre, you'll find polar extremes: the sunny, open plateau, home to the glamorous resorts of Crans and Montana, and the wild, craggy Val d'Anniviers that leads to the isolated forest retreat of Grimentz.

Crans-Montana

❿ *12 km (7 mi) north of Sierre, 19 km (11¾ mi) northwest of Sion.*

This well-known twin sports center rises above the valley on a steep, sheltered shelf at 1,495 m (4,904 ft) and commands a broad view across the Rhône Valley to the peaks of Valais Alps; its grassy and wooded plateau shares the benefits of Sierre's sunshine. Behind it, the **Rohrbach-stein** (2,953 m/9,686 ft), the **Gletscherhorn** (2,943 m/9,653 ft), and the **Wildstrubel** (3,243 m/10,637 ft) combine to create a complex of challenging ski slopes. Every September, the 18-hole golf course is the site of the annual Swiss Open, a period the locals describe as "party week." The most direct route to Crans-Montana is from Sierre, just southeast, either by car, postbus, or funicular.

The resort towns themselves are highly developed and charmless, lacking the regional color and grace of Zermatt. The streets are lined with modern shops and hotels, and car traffic is almost always heavy. As in Verbier, all hotels are signposted. The crowds are young, wealthy, and international, although only a cynic would go so far as to describe the ambience as overbearingly vacuous.

Skiing

The pearl of the region is the **Plaine Morte,** a flat glacier 5 km–6 km (3 mi–3½ mi) long, perched like a pancake at an elevation of 3,000 m (9,840 ft), which has snow year-round. A cross-country ski trail (watch out for your lungs at this altitude) of 10 km–12 km (6 mi–7½ mi) is open and maintained here seven months of the year. You can also downhill-ski on the gentle slopes in summer; in winter, the descent from the Plaine Morte follows wide and relatively easy pistes as far as one or two chutes. The ascent on the gondola from **Violettes Plaines-Morte,** virtually under assault during the high season and in good weather, will in itself justify your stay in Crans-Montana. Expert skiers may prefer the **Nationale Piste,** site of the 1987 world championships. The incredibly steep-pitched **La Toula** is also a challenge for pros. A one-day lift ticket costs 56 SF; a six-day pass costs 265 SF.

Dining and Lodging

$$$-$$$$ ✕🏨 **Aïda-Castel.** In a resort that mushroomed during the 1960s and
★ seems to be frozen in that decade, this warm and welcoming complex is refreshingly au courant. The public areas have carved or aged wood, terra-cotta, and stucco, and the rooms have hand-painted furniture and some stenciled ceilings. The amenities are all top quality. The very popular public restaurant, La Hotte, serves Italian fare, some prepared on the open grill, as well as raclette made at fireside—so good that reserva-

tions are essential. The hillside location is moderately isolated, with great southern views from nearly every balcony. ⊠ *CH-3962 Montana,* ☏ *027/4854111,* ℻ *027/4817062. 61 rooms. 3 restaurants, pool, hot tub, sauna, exercise room, meeting room. AE, DC, MC, V.*

$$$$ 🏨 **Grand Hôtel du Golf.** This is the blue blood of the lot, a grand, gen-
★   teel, old resort oasis with urbane good taste and every amenity. Built by English golfers in 1907 and owned by the same family since 1914, it's been postmodernized outside and carefully tended within. The perfectly turned-out rooms are done in pastels. In addition to a for-mal restaurant and a homey café, there's a fine bar completely pan-eled in oak. Manicured grounds adjoin the 9- and 18-hole golf courses. ⊠ *CH-3963 Crans,* ☏ *027/4854242,* ℻ *027/4854243. 76 rooms, 8 suites, 2 apartments. Restaurant, bar, café, in-room VCRs, indoor pool, beauty salon, sauna. AE, DC, MC, V.*

$$$–$$$$ 🏨 **Crans-Ambassador.** A stylized château with a three-peak roofline and direct access to the slopes, this dramatic modern structure stands apart from the twin towns and offers some of the resorts' finest views south. Each room has a balcony or terrace, and the back rooms look onto shaggy pine forests. The interiors are anonymously sleek, warmed up by occasional touches of wood; all the baths sparkle. ⊠ *CH-3962 Montana,* ☏ *027/4814811,* ℻ *027/4819155. 60 rooms, 12 suites. 2 restaurants, piano bar, indoor pool, sauna, exercise room, beauty salon. AE, DC, MC, V.*

$$–$$$$ 🏨 **Le Green.** What was once a rustic, welcome alternative to Crans glitz has succumbed: decorated in jazzy, bright *style golf,* this has become another pricey four-star option. Most rooms have a balcony and face south. Facilities include a brasserie, a pine-deck bar, and a sauna-so-larium. ⊠ *CH-3963 Crans,* ☏ *027/4813256,* ℻ *027/4811781. 32 rooms, 2 suites. Restaurant, bar, brasserie, sauna, exercise room. AE, DC, MC, V.*

$$–$$$$ 🏨 **Mirabeau.** Completely done in pastels straight out of suburbia, this attractive midtown property has views of the street—or of other ho-tels. It's at the hub, however, of the downtown dining and shopping scene, and in 1998 opened a new *carnotzet* in addition to its restau-rant. ⊠ *CH-3962 Montana,* ☏ *027/4802151,* ℻ *027/4813912. 45 rooms. Restaurant, bar, exercise room. AE, DC, MC, V.*

$$–$$$ 🏨 **La Prairie.** Wally Cleaver might have stayed here on a school ski trip: there are rough-hewn fireplaces everywhere, and the young, rec-room atmosphere is downright wholesome. Built in the 1930s, the updated rooms glow with pine, and the baths are very modern. The hotel is away from the noisy center but conveniently placed. ⊠ *CH-3962 Montana,* ☏ *027/4814421,* ℻ *027/4818586. 32 rooms. Restaurant, bar, pool. AE, DC, MC, V.*

$–$$ 🏨 **Regina.** On the main shopping street in Montana, this is a spare, tidy city inn with the rare option of inexpensive rooms (bathrooms are down the hall). Although their decor is dated (wood paneling, all-weather carpet), some rooms have balconies that overlook the valley. There's a cozy lounge downstairs as well as a wonderful bakery—so break-fasts are homemade and fresh. ⊠ *CH-3962 Montana,* ☏ *027/4813522,* ℻ *027/4801868. 24 rooms. Breakfast room. AE, DC, MC, V.*

Nightlife

DANCING

If you've ever wondered what Salvador Dali would have produced if he'd illustrated a vodka ad, then head for the **Absolut** (☏ 027/4816596), a nightclub in Crans. At 15 SF for a beer you might find the prices pretty surreal, too. **Pub Georges et Dragon** (☏ 027/4815496) is a lively in-ternational meeting place with a DJ every night of the season. Up in Montana, the small but convivial **Amadeus** (☏ 027/4812495), beneath

In case you want to see the world.

At American Express, we're here to make your journey a smooth one. So we have over 1,700 travel service locations in over 130 countries ready to help. What else would you expect from the world's largest travel agency?

do more

Travel

Call 1 800 AXP-3429 or visit
www.americanexpress.com/travel

In case you want to be welcomed there.

We're here to see that you're always welcomed at establishments everywhere. That's why millions of people carry the American Express® Card — for peace of mind, confidence, and security, around the world or just around the corner.

do more

Cards

To apply, call 1 800 THE-CARD
or visit www.americanexpress.com

In case you're running low.

We're here to help with more than 190,000 Express Cash locations around the world. In order to enroll, just call American Express at 1 800 CASH-NOW before you start your vacation.

do more

AMERICAN EXPRESS

Express Cash

And in case you'd rather be safe than sorry.

We're here with American Express® Travelers Cheques. They're the safe way to carry money on your vacation, because if they're ever lost or stolen you can get a refund, practically anywhere or anytime. To find the nearest place to buy Travelers Cheques, call 1 800 495-1153. Another way we help you do more.

do more

Travelers Cheques

©1999 American Express

the Olympic Hotel, is a popular après-ski venue with the young crowd; the disco **Number Two** (☎ 027/4813615) is comparatively cheap, popular with locals, and described by some as a bit wild.

Outdoor Activities and Sports

BICYCLING

The **Avalanche Pro Shop** (✉ Montana, ☎ 027/4802424) rents mountain bikes at 38 SF per day and 130 SF for six days. A map of possible routes is available at the tourist office (☞ Visitor Information *in* Valais A to Z, *below*).

GOLF

Crans and Montana have one 18-hole **golf course** and two nine-hole courses (☎ 027/4812168).

TENNIS

The **Centre de Tennis Au Lac Moubra** (☎ 027/4815014) has seven indoor courts.

En Route   East of the city limits of Sierre and south of the Rhône, follow signs southward for Vissoie. Here you enter the **Val d'Anniviers,** a wild and craggy valley said to derive its name from its curious and famous (among anthropologists, at least) nomads, known in Latin as *anni viatores* (year-round travelers). Some claim they are descended from the Huns who straggled into the area during the 5th century. Since the development of modern roads, the Anniviards no longer follow their ancient pattern: migrating down into the valley around Niouc in spring, moving to Sierre in summer to cultivate collectively owned vineyards, and returning to their isolated villages to hole up for the winter. The ancient practice disappeared in the 1950s, but many residents are the nomads' descendants.

Grimentz

⑪ *20 km (12½ mi) south of Sierre.*

With a population of 370, this ancient 13th-century village has preserved its weathered-wood houses and mazots in its tiny center, although anonymous hotels have sprung up near the ski facilities above.

Skiing

Grimentz shares transit facilities with **Zinal** (☞ *below*) and **Chandolin** in the Val d'Anniviers. Though they're separated by wilderness, each can provide a day's skiing, with easy access for variety the next day. Grimentz's trails, while limited, should meet everyone's needs. There's a hair-raising expert run from **Pointe de Lona** (at 2,900 m/9,512 ft) all the way back down to the parking lot (at 1,570 m/5,150 ft). Beginners can enjoy equally spectacular sweeps from **Orvizal,** starting at 2,780 m (9,118 ft), back to town. The upper runs are reached by ski tows only; a cable car has been added to the first level. **Grimentz,** at 1,570 m (5,150 ft), has eight tows, one chairlift, one cable car, 50 km (31 mi) of downhill runs, and 22 km (14 mi) of cross-country trails. A ski pass, which costs 36 SF for one day, 172 SF for six days, offers access to all Val d'Anniviers facilities, including 46 lifts and 250 km (155 mi) of downhill runs.

Dining

$ ✕ **Le Mélèze.** Warm your feet by the central fireplace, open on all sides, in the old, all-wood café and restaurant on the edge of Grimentz that serves raclette, crepes, and generous hot meals. ☎ 027/4751287. *AE, DC, MC, V. Closed June and Nov.*

Zinal

⑫ *25 km (16 mi) south of Sierre.*

Summer travelers can veer down a tiny forest road from Grimentz toward Zinal, with the Weisshorn dominating the views. Zinal (1,675 m/5,494 ft) is another isolated mountaineering center with well-preserved wood houses and mazots. It is worth building enough time into your itinerary to stop over in one of these windswept mountain aeries and walk, climb, ski, or relax by the fire.

ZERMATT AND SAAS-FEE

Immediately east of Sierre, you'll notice a sharp change: *vals* become *-tals,* and the sounds you overhear at your next pit stop are no longer the throaty, mellifluous tones of the Suisse Romande but the lilting, guttural Swiss-German dialect called Wallisertiitsch, a local form of Schwyzerdütsch. Welcome to Wallis (*vahl*-is), the Germanic end of Valais.

This sharp demographic frontier can be traced back to the 6th century, when Alemannic tribes poured over the Grimsel Pass and penetrated as far as Sierre. Here the middle-class cuisine changes from *steak-frîtes* (steak with french fries) to veal and Rösti, though the basics—cheese, bread, and wine—are found throughout.

Zermatt

★ **⑬** *29 km (18 mi) south of Visp, plus a 10-km (6-mi) train ride from Täsch.*

Despite its fame—which stems from that mythic mountain, the Matterhorn, and from its excellent ski facilities—Zermatt is a resort with its feet on the ground, protecting its regional quirks along with its wildlife and its tumbledown mazots, which crowd between glass-and-concrete chalets like old tenements between skyscrapers. Streets twist past weathered-wood walls, flower boxes, and haphazard stone roofs until they break into open country that slopes, inevitably, uphill. Despite the crowds, you are never far from the wild roar of the silty river and the peace of a mountain path.

★   Hordes of package-tour sightseers push shoulder to shoulder to get yet another shot of the **Matterhorn** (4,477 m/14,685 ft). Called one of the wonders of the Western world, the mountain deserves the title: though it has become an almost self-parodying icon, like the Eiffel Tower or the Empire State Building, its peculiar snaggle-tooth form, free from competition from other peaks on all sides, rears up over the village, larger than life and genuinely awe-inspiring. Leaving the train station and weaving through the pedestrian crowds, aggressive electric taxi carts, and aromatic horse-drawn carriages along the main street, Bahnhofstrasse, you are assaulted on all sides by Matterhorn images: on postcards, on sweatshirts, on calendars, on beer steins, on candy wrappers, it looms in multiples of a thousand, the original obscured by resort buildings (except from the windows of pricier hotel rooms). But breaking past the shops and hotels onto the main road into the hills, visitors seem to reach the same slightly elevated spot and stop dead in their tracks: There it is at last, up and to the right, its twist of snowy rock blinding in the sun, mink-brown weathered mazots scattered romantically at its base. Surely more pictures are taken from this spot than from anywhere else in Switzerland.

It was Edward Whymper's spectacular—and catastrophic—conquest of the Matterhorn, on July 14, 1865, that made Zermatt a household word. Whymper stayed at the Hotel Monte Rosa (☞ Dining and

Lodging, *below*) the nights before his departure and there named his party of seven for the historic climb: Michel Croz, a French guide; old Peter Taugwalder and his son, young Peter, local guides; Lord Francis Douglas, a 19-year-old Englishman; Douglas Hadow; the Reverend Charles Hudson; and Whymper himself. They climbed together, pairing "tourists," as Whymper called the Englishmen, with experienced locals. They camped at 11,000 ft and by 10 AM had reached the base of the mountain's famous hook. Wrote Whymper of the final moments:

The higher we rose the more intense became the excitement. The slope eased off, at length we could be detached, and Croz and I, dashing away, ran a neck-and-neck race, which ended in a dead heat. At 1:40 PM, the world was at our feet, and the Matterhorn was conquered!

Croz pulled off his shirt and tied it to a stick as a flag, one that was seen in Zermatt below. They stayed at the summit one hour, then prepared for the descent, tying themselves together in an order agreed on by all. Croz led, then Hadow, Hudson, Lord Douglas, the elder Taugwalder, then the younger, and Whymper, who lingered to sketch the summit and leave their names in a bottle.

I suggested to Hudson that we should attach a rope to the rocks on our arrival at the difficult bit, and hold it as we descended, as an additional protection. He approved the idea, but it was not definitely decided that it should be done.

They headed off, "one man moving at a time; when he was firmly planted the next advanced," Whymper recalled.

Croz . . . was in the act of turning around to go down a step or two himself; at this moment Mr. Hadow slipped, fell against him, and knocked him over. I heard one startled exclamation from Croz, then saw him and Mr. Hadow flying downward; in another moment Hudson was dragged from his steps, and Lord Douglas immediately after him. All this was the work of a moment. Immediately we heard Croz's exclamation, old Peter and I planted ourselves as firmly as the rocks would permit; the rope was taut between us, and the jerk came on us both as on one man. We held; but the rope broke midway between Taugwalder and Lord Francis Douglas. For a few seconds we saw our unfortunate companions sliding downward on their backs, and spreading out their hands, endeavoring to save themselves. They passed from our sight uninjured, disappeared one by one, and fell from precipice to precipice on to the Matterhorn glacier below, a distance of nearly 4,000 feet in height. From the moment the rope broke it was impossible to help them. So perished our comrades!

A "sharp-eyed lad" ran into the Hotel Monte Rosa to report an avalanche fallen from the Matterhorn summit; he had witnessed the deaths of the four mountaineers. The body of young Lord Douglas was never recovered, but the others lie in the grim little cemetery behind the Zermatt church, surrounded by scores of other failed mountaineers, including a recent American whose tomb bears the simple epitaph I CHOSE TO CLIMB.

In summer, the streets of Zermatt fill with sturdy, weathered climbers, state-of-the-art ropes and picks hanging at their hips. They continue to tackle the peaks, and climbers have mastered the Matterhorn literally thousands of times since Whymper's disastrous victory.

In Zermatt it's quite simple to gain the broader perspective of high altitudes without risking life or limb; the train trip up the **Gornergrat** on the *Gornergratbahn* functions as an excursion as well as ski transport. Part of its rail system was completed in 1898, and it's the highest open-air rail system in Europe (the tracks to the Jungfraujoch, though higher, bore through the face of the Eiger). It connects out of the main Zermatt train station and heads sharply left, at a right angle to the track that brings you into town. Its first stop is the **Riffelberg,** which, at 2,582 m (8,469 ft), offers wide-open views of the Matterhorn. Farther on, from **Rotenboden,** at 2,819 m (9,246 ft), a short downhill walk leads to the **Riffelsee,** which obligingly provides photographers with a postcard-perfect reflection of the famous peak. At the end of the 9-km (5½-mi) line, the train stops at the summit station of **Gornergrat** (3,130 m/10,266 ft), and passengers pour onto the observation terraces to take in the majestic views of the Matterhorn, Monte Rosa, Gorner Glacier, and an expanse of scores of peaks and 24 other glaciers. If you ski or hike down, the cost of the trip is just 37 SF. ⊠ *Leaves from Zermatt station.* 🚠 *63 SF round-trip.* ☉ *Departures every 24 mins 7–7. Bring warm clothes, sunglasses, and sturdy shoes.*

Zermatt lies in a hollow of meadows and trees ringed by mountains—among them the broad **Monte Rosa** (4,554 m/14,937 ft) and its tallest peak, the **Dufourspitze** (at 4,634 m/15,200 ft, the highest point in Switzerland)—of which visitors hear relatively little, so all-consuming is the cult of the Matterhorn. In the mid-19th century, Zermatt was virtually unheard-of; the few visitors who came to town stayed at the vicarage. It happened, however, that the vicar had a nose for business and a chaplain named Seiler. Joseph Seiler convinced his little brother, Alexander, to start an inn. Opened in 1854 and named the Hotel Monte Rosa, it is still one of five Seiler hotels in Zermatt. In 1891, the cog railway between Visp and Zermatt took its first summer run and began disgorging tourists with profitable regularity—though it didn't plow through in wintertime until 1927.

Skiing

Zermatt's skiable terrain lives up to its reputation: The 74 lift installations are capable of moving well above 50,000 skiers per hour to reach its approximately 245 km (152 mi) of marked pistes—if you count those of Breuil in Italy. Among the lifts are the cable car that carries skiers up to an elevation of 3,820 m (12,532 ft) on the Klein Matterhorn, the small *Gornergratbahn* that creeps up to the Gornergrat (3,100 m/10,170 ft), and a subway through an underground tunnel that gives more pleasure to ecologists than it does to sun-loving skiers.

This royal plateau has several less-than-perfect features, however, not least of which is the separation of the skiable territory into three sectors. **Sunegga-Blauherd-Rothorn** culminates at an elevation of 3,100 m (10,170 ft). **Gornergrat-Stockhorn** (3,400 m/11,155 ft) is the second. The third is the region dominated by the **Klein Matterhorn;** to go from this sector to the others, you must return to the bottom of the valley and lose considerable time crossing town to reach the lifts to the other elevations. The solution is to ski for a whole day in the same area, especially during high season (mid-December to the end of February, or even until Easter if the snow cover is good). On the other hand, thanks to snowmaking machines and the eternal snows of the Klein Matterhorn, Zermatt is said to guarantee skiers 2,200 m (7,216 ft) of vertical drop no matter what the snowfall—an impressive claim. A one-day lift ticket costs 60 SF; a six-day pass costs 296 SF. A ski school (⊠ Skischulbüro, Bahnhofstr., ☎ 027/9662466) operates during the high season, from mid-December until April.

Dining and Lodging

$$-$$$ ✕ **Grill-Room Stockhorn.** The tantalizing aromas of melting, pungent cheese and roasting meat on the open grill should sharpen your appetite the moment you step across the threshold into this low-slung, two-story restaurant. This is a great place to fortify yourself with re-

gional dishes; the service and the clientele are equally lively. ✉ *Hotel Stockhorn,* ☎ *027/9671747. AE, MC, V. Closed May and Oct.*

$$ ✕ **Findlerhof.** Whether for long lunches between sessions on the slopes,
★   for the traditional wind-down après-ski, or for a panoramic meal break on an all-day hike, this mountain restaurant is ideal. It's perched in tiny Findeln, between the Sunnegga and Blauherd ski areas. The Matterhorn views from the wraparound dining porch are astonishing, the winter dining room cozy with pine and stone, and the food surprisingly fresh and creative. Franz and Heidi Schwery tend their own Alpine garden to provide spinach for the bacon-crisped salad and rhubarb and berries for their hot desserts. It's about a 30-minute walk down from the Sunnegga Express stop and another 30 minutes back down to Zermatt. ✉ *Findeln,* ☎ *027/9672588. No credit cards. Closed May–mid-June and mid-Oct.–Nov.*

$$ ✕ **Zum See.** This alternative to Findlerhof, beyond Findeln in a tiny
★   village (little more than a cluster of mazots) of the same name, serves up light meals of a quality and inventiveness that would merit acclaim even if it weren't in the middle of nowhere at 1,766 m (5,792 ft). In summer, its shaded picnic tables draw hikers rewarding themselves at the finish of a day's climb; in winter, its low-ceiling log dining room sets skiers aglow with an impressive assortment of brandies. Regional specialties are prepared with masterly care, from wild mushrooms in pastry shells to rabbit, Rösti, and *foie de veau* (calves' liver). ✉ *Zum See,* ☎ *027/9672045. Reservations essential après-ski. MC, V. Closed mid-Apr.–June and Oct.–mid-Dec.*

$ ✕ **Elsie's Bar.** This tiny log cabin of a ski haunt, directly across from the Zermatt church, draws an international crowd for cocktails American style. Light meals include cheese dishes and escargots. ✉ *Kirchepl.,* ☎ *027/9672431. AE, DC, MC, V.*

$$$$ ✕▥ **Hotel Monte Rosa.** Alexander Seiler founded his first hotel in the
★   core of this historic building, expanding it over the years to its current scale. (This was the home base of Edward Whymper when he conquered the Matterhorn in 1865.) Behind its graceful, shuttered facade you find an ideal balance between modern convenience and history in the burnished pine, flagstone floors, the original ceiling moldings, the fireplaces, and in the Victorian dining hall. The beige-oriented room decor is impeccable; southern views go quickly and cost more. The bar is an après-ski must. ✉ *CH-3920,* ☎ *027/9673333,* ℻ *027/9671160. 44 rooms, 5 suites. Restaurant, bar, sauna (at Mont Cervin). AE, DC, MC, V.*

$$$$ ✕▥ **Mont Cervin.** One of the flagships of the Seiler dynasty, this lux-
★   urious, urbane mountain hotel is never grandiose, in either scale or attitude. Built in 1852, it's unusually low-slung for a grand hotel. Its restaurant was completely rebuilt in 1998—it's now brighter both in decor and tone, with light beams replacing the old dark ones and jacket and tie required only for the Friday gala buffet. The Residence, across the street through a handy tunnel, offers chic, luxurious apartments. ✉ *CH-3920,* ☎ *027/9668888,* ℻ *027/9672878. 101 rooms, 40 suites. 2 restaurants, bar, indoor pool, sauna, beauty salon. AE, DC, MC, V.*

$$$$ ✕▥ **Pollux.** This modern hotel is simple and chic, with its straightforward rooms trimmed in pine and leatherette. It's small-scale, and none of its windows looks onto the Matterhorn, but its position directly on the main pedestrian shopping street puts you in the heart of resort activities. The bathrooms are being renovated in sequence; all are due to be finished in 1999. The restaurant is based on a village square, with garden furniture and a central fountain; an appealing, old-fashioned Stübli draws locals for its low-price lunches, snacks, and Valais cheese dishes. Children in adjoining rooms get a 60% reduction. ✉ *CH-3920,* ☎ *027/9664000,* ℻ *027/9664001. 33 rooms. Restaurant, Stübli, sauna, dance club. AE, DC, MC, V.*

$$$–$$$$ ✕🏨 **Julen.** This hotel's radical 1998 room renovation happily shunned
    ★   regional kitsch. Instead, rooms have a Bavarian-style, century-old
        spruce-wood decor paired with primary-color carpets and silk curtains;
        each suite has a green tiled stove. A new three-floor sports center in-
        cludes an elaborate Roman bath where you can indulge in various ther-
        apies. The main restaurant offers international cuisine, while the
        welcoming Stübli serves unusual dishes prepared with lamb (such as
        lamb's tongue in capers) from local family-owned flocks. ⊠ *CH-3920,*
        ☎ *027/9667600,* FAX *027/9667676. 27 rooms, 5 suites. 2 restaurants,
        café, indoor pool, sauna, exercise room. AE, DC, MC, V.*

$$$$ 🏨 **Zermatterhof.** If you can afford no-limits luxury, then you might as
    ★   well go for the best and indulge in this faultless hotel. As it was built
        in 1879, they have had more than a century to get things exactly right.
        Rooms in multifarious shades and styles of wood have either granite
        or marble bathrooms, where you can lie back and enjoy the ultimate
        in Alpine decadence—nibbling a chocolate Matterhorn while your
        back is massaged by Jacuzzi bubbles. The formal restaurant is for
        guests only, but the quality of its French-Italian-influenced cuisine
        meets the hotel's five-star standard. The glass-dome Rôtisserie La
        Broche is open to nonguests. ⊠ *CH-3920,* ☎ *027/9666600,* FAX *027/
        9666699. 60 rooms, 26 suites. 2 restaurants, bar, indoor pool, hot tub,
        sauna, tennis court, health club. AE, DC, MC, V.*

$$$ 🏨 **Europe.** This tasteful lodging has rooms—many with a Matterhorn
        view—outfitted in cherry wood and, in some cases, dark blue carpets
        and curtains. Over breakfast you can read the hotel's own daily news
        briefing and squeeze your own orange juice. You can also use the ex-
        cellent sports center at the sister property Julen (☞ *above*) just a
        minute's walk away. ⊠ *CH-3920,* ☎ *027/9662700,* FAX *027/9662705.
        22 rooms. Restaurant, bar. AE, DC, MC, V.*

$$–$$$ 🏨 **Alphubel.** Although it's surrounded by other hotels and is close to
        the main street, this modest, comfortable pension built in 1954 feels
        off the beaten track—and it offers large, sunny balconies to lodgers
        on the south side. The interiors are a little institutional, but there's a
        sauna in the basement, available to guests for a small charge. ⊠ *CH-
        3920,* ☎ *027/9673003,* FAX *027/9676684. 31 rooms. Restaurant, sauna.
        AE, MC, V.*

$–$$$ 🏨 **Romantica.** Among the scores of anonymously modern hotels cloned
        all over the Zermatt plain, this modest structure—unremarkable at first
        glance—offers an exceptional location directly above the town center,
        no more than a block up a narrow mazot-lined lane. Its tidy, bright
        gardens and flower boxes, its game trophies, and its old-style granite
        stove give it personality, and the plain rooms—many in pastel colors—
        benefit from big windows and balconies. You can also stay in one of
        the two *Walliserstudel,* 200-year-old, tiny (but charming) huts in the
        hotel's garden. Views take in the mountains, though not the Matter-
        horn, over a graceful clutter of stone roofs. ⊠ *CH-3920,* ☎ *027/
        9662650,* FAX *027/9662655. 13 rooms. AE, DC, MC, V.*

$–$$$ 🏨 **Touring.** Its reassuringly traditional architecture and snug, sunny
        rooms full of pine, combined with an elevated position apart from town
        and excellent Matterhorn views, make this an appealing choice for trav-
        elers who want an informal alternative to the chic downtown scene.
        Hearty daily menus are served to pension guests in the cozy dining room
        (the same menu is available in the Stübli), and a sunny enclosed play-
        ground has lounge chairs for parents. ⊠ *CH-3920,* ☎ *027/9671177,*
        FAX *027/9674601. 21 rooms. Restaurant, Stübli. MC, V.*

$–$$ 🏨 **Mischabel.** One of the least, if not *the* least, expensive hotels in this
        pricey resort town, the Mischabel provides comfort, atmosphere, and
        a central situation few places can match at twice the price: southern
        balconies frame a perfect Matterhorn view—the higher the better.

Creaky, homey, and covered with *Arvenholz* (Alpine pine) aged to the color of toffee, its rooms have sinks only and share the linoleum-lined showers on every floor. A generous daily menu, for guests only, caters to families and young skiers on the cheap. ⊠ *CH-3920,* ☎ *027/ 9671131,* FAX *027/9676507. 28 rooms. Restaurant. MC, V.*

$–$$ 🏨 **Parnass.** Across the street from the roaring river, with views east and south to the Matterhorn, this simple '60s structure offers a cozy, clublike lounge, knotty-pine rooms, and private pension dining with unusually adventurous and successful cooking. In winter, annual regulars rub shoulders by the fireplace in this exceptionally welcoming hotel. ⊠ *CH-3920,* ☎ *027/9671179,* FAX *027/9674557. 32 rooms. Restaurant. MC, V.*

Nightlife

GramPi's Bar (☎ 027/9677788), on the main drag, is a lively young people's bar, where you can get into the mood for dancing downstairs with a Lady Matterhorn cocktail. The newly renovated **T-Bar** (☎ 027/ 9674000), below the Hotel Pollux, plays more varied music then the generic disco-pap of the ski resorts, and its walls and ceilings are interestingly adorned with ancient skiing equipment, which somehow looks more comfortable than the garish space-age wear of today.

Outdoor Activities and Sports

MOUNTAIN BIKING AND CLIMBING

Mountain biking is severely limited by Zermatt authorities to prevent interference with hiking on trails. About 25 km (15 mi) have been set aside, however. A map is available at the tourist office (☞ Visitor Information *in* Valais A to Z, *below*). Bikes can be rented at **Slalomsport** (☎ 027/9671116). For mountain-climbing guides and instruction, contact the **Alpin Center Zermatt** (☎ 027/9662460).

TENNIS

The **Tennisstar/Club** (☎ 027/9663000) has three courts. The **Gemeinde** (☎ 027/9673673) maintains nine courts.

Shopping

Zermatt may be Switzerland's souvenir capital, offering a broad variety of watches, knives, and logo clothing. Popular folk crafts and traditional products include large, grotesque masks of carved wood and lidded *channes* in pewter or tin, molded in graduated sizes; they are sold everywhere, even in the grocery stores of tourist-conscious resorts.

SPORTS EQUIPMENT AND APPAREL

Zermatt's streets are lined with stores offering state-of-the-art sports equipment and apparel, from collapsible grappling hooks for climbers to lightweight hiking boots in psychedelic colors. You'll see plenty of the new must-have walking sticks—pairs of lightweight, spiked ski poles for hikers to add a bit of upper-body workout to their climb. Although prices are consistently high, the selection is dazzling.

Bayard (⊠ Bahnhofpl., ☎ 027/9664950; ⊠ Bahnhofstr., ☎ 027/ 9664960) heads the long list of sporting-goods stores. **Glacier Sport** (☎ 027/9672719) specializes in ski equipment and accessories. **La Cabane** (☎ 027/9672249) is the best source for trendy sports clothing.

Grächen

🔢 *28 km (17 mi) south of Visp.*

From the valley resort village of St. Niklaus, a narrow, winding road crawls up to this small, tame family resort nestled comfortably on a sunny shelf at 1,617 m (5,304 ft). Little more than a picturesque scattering of small hotels, chalets, and mazots, it concentrates its business near a central parking lot and closes the rest of its streets to car traffic. Small and isolated as it is, there are enough shops and cafés to keep visitors occupied on a foggy day. This is a place to escape tourist crowds, hike high trails undisturbed by the traffic you find near the larger resorts, or ski a variety of fine trails on the Hannigalp. Grächen makes a heroic effort to keep families happy, offering a staffed and supervised winter-sports area, with ski and toboggan lifts, playgrounds, and even igloos, free of charge, for children under six years old.

Dining and Lodging

$$ ✕🔲 **Walliserhof.** Directly in the center of town, this eye-catching dark-wood Valais-style chalet is ringed with balconies; in summer, geraniums spill from every window. The interior is bright and elegant, and rooms glow with warm knotty pine. The south-side suites hog the magnificent views. The restaurant, serving basic French fare, has a formal air, with candles and crisp linens. ⊠ *CH-3925,* ☎ *027/9561122,* FAX *027/9562922. 25 rooms. Restaurant, café, dance club. AE, MC, V.*

$-$$ ✕🔲 **Désirée.** Though the rooms are institution-modern, the balconies take in mountain views and the restaurant-Stübli downstairs is rich in smoky, meaty, local atmosphere, serving Valais and Italian specialities. It's in the center but above traffic; access is by electric cart. ⊠ *CH-3925,* ☎ *027/9562255,* FAX *027/9562070. 22 rooms. Restaurant, Stübli, exercise room. AE, DC, MC, V.*

$-$$ ✕🔲 **Hannigalp.** The oldest hotel in town, this welcoming landmark
★ built in 1909 and run by the same family for 90 years has been completely modernized without losing its regional character. The rooms have been updated to spare, blond-wood simplicity; most have balconies. The amenities are remarkable for the price. Headed by the owner himself, the kitchen creates straightforward French and international cuisine for the restaurant and regional specialties to serve in the cozier bar. It is in a quiet, car-free zone. ⊠ *CH-3925,* ☎ *027/9562555,* FAX *027/9562855. 22 rooms. Restaurant, bar, indoor pool, hot tub, sauna, tennis court. MC, V.*

Saas-Fee

⓯ *36 km (22 mi) south of Visp.*

At the end of the switchback road to Saas-Grund (1,559 m/5,114 ft) lies a parking area where visitors must abandon their cars for the length of their stay in Saas-Fee. But even in the parking lot you'll be amazed, for the view on arriving at this lofty (1,790 m/5,871 ft) plateau is humbling. Saas-Fee lies in a deep valley that leaves no doubt about its source: it seems to pour from the vast, intimidating **Fee Glacier,** which oozes like icy lava from the broad spread of peaks above. *Fee* can be translated as "fairy," and although Saas-Fee itself is a tourist-saturated resort, the landscape could illustrate a fairytale. The town is at the heart of a cirque of mountains, 13 of which tower to more than 4,000 m (13,120 ft), among them the **Dom** (4,545 m/14,908 ft), the highest mountain entirely on Swiss soil.

Skiing

The first glacier to be used for skiing here was the **Längfluh** (2,870 m/9,414 ft), accessed by gondola, then cable car. The run is magnificent, sometimes physically demanding, and always varied. From the Längfluh you can take the new ski lift to reach *the* ski area of Saas-Fee, the **Felskinn-Mittelallalin** sector (3,000 m–3,500 m/9,840 ft–11,480 ft). Felskinn harbors its own surprise: in order to preserve the land and landscape, the Valaisans have constructed a subterranean funicular, the Métro Alpin, which climbs through the heart of the mountain to Mittelallalin, that is, halfway up the Allalinhorn (4,027 m/13,210 ft); tourists debark in a rotating restaurant noted more for the austere grandeur of its natural surroundings than for the quality of its food. Felskinn-Mittelallalin's exceptional site, its high elevation, its runs (15 km/9 mi), and its ample facilities (cable car, funicular, and five ski lifts) have made Saas-Fee the number one summer-skiing resort in Switzerland. It is also one of two official European snowboard centers sanctioned by the International Snowboard Federation. A one-day lift ticket costs 58 SF; a six-day pass costs 270 SF.

Dining and Lodging

$$$$ ✕🏨 **Waldhotel Fletschhorn.** High on a forested hillside above the re-
★ sort, this quiet *Landgasthof* (country inn) is a sophisticated retreat for gourmets who like to rest undisturbed after an excellent meal. The baths are sizable, and although the rooms have ultramodern fittings, they're mellowed with pine paneling, antiques, and serene views. Half-board includes innovative French cuisine based on local products: reindeer with wild mushrooms, stuffed quail with polenta in pinot noir. (The chef also runs culinary courses at the hotel.) Reservations are essential at the restaurant. Manager Hansjörg Dütsch provides transportation from town. ⊠ *CH-3906,* ☎ *027/9572131,* ℻ *027/9572187. 15 rooms. Restaurant, sauna. AE, DC, MC, V.*

$$$$ 🏨 **Ferienart Walliserhof.** The slightly battered woodwork of the rooms suggests it may soon be time for renovation, but it is hard to believe you are in the same hotel when you come downstairs and take advantage of the unrivalled facilities this friendly hotel has to offer. The pool with the mock-glacier roof is an unusual in-water experience, and you can peruse the labyrinth of bars and restaurants offering a choice ranging from Thai to Italian cuisine. The hotel's location in the town's very center doesn't deprive it of great panoramas on all sides. ⊠ *CH-3906,* ☎ *027/9581900,* ℻ *027/9581905. 47 rooms, 5 suites. 4 restaurants, café, piano bar, indoor pool, barbershop, beauty salon, massage, sauna, pro shop, nightclub. AE, DC, MC, V.*

$$$–$$$$ 🏨 **Allalin.** Families, especially, will appreciate the flexibility and up-
★ to-date design of the apartment quarters available here, all with kitchen equipment as well as balconies. In high season, guests usually pay half-pension and eat one meal per day in the restaurant—no great punishment, as the kitchen is surprisingly sophisticated—although a breakfast-only arrangement can be made. Built in 1928, the hotel feels warm, bright, and natural. It's on the hill just east of the center and a block from the main parking, and all doubles but one have a spectacular southern or southeastern view. ⊠ *CH-3906,* ☎ *027/9571815,* ℻ *027/9573115. 16 rooms, 11 suites. Restaurant, bar, café, kitchenettes, sauna. AE, DC, MC, V.*

$$$–$$$$ 🏨 **Saaserhof.** What this hotel has going for it is location: it's near the best lift facilities. Rooms are either in generic dark wood or modern pastels; the restaurant, open to non-guests, focuses on French-influenced cuisine. ⊠ *CH-3906,* ☎ *027/9573551,* ℻ *027/9572883. 40 rooms, 5 suites. Restaurant, bar, hot tub, sauna. AE, DC, MC, V.*

$–$$$ 🏨 **Britannia.** Compensating for its brand-new architecture with light carved pine in every corner, this tidy, fresh, simple lodging is in the heart of town, near resort shopping on the main pedestrian street. The best balconies face south and east; the dining room also has a tantalizing view. ⊠ *CH-3906,* ☎ *027/9571616,* ℻ *027/9571942. 19 rooms. Restaurant, bar. AE, MC, V.*

Outdoor Activities and Sports

MOUNTAIN CLIMBING

The **Swiss Mountaineering School** (☎ 027/9574464) conducts daily guided forays.

The **Bielen Recreation Center** (☎ 027/9572475) has a four-lane swimming pool, children's pool, whirlpools, steam baths, sauna, solarium, fitness center, and games.

Kalbermatten Sports Ground (☎ 027/9572454) has two tennis courts available. **Bielen Indoor Tennis Courts** (☎ 027/9572475) also has a pair.

BRIG AND THE ALPINE PASSES

This region is the Grand Central Station of the Alpine region; all mountain passes lead to Brig, and traffic pours in (and through) from Italy, the Ticino, central Switzerland, the Berner Oberland—and, via the latter, from Paris, Brussels, and London and Rome.

Brig

16 *209 km (129 mi) southeast of Bern.*

A rail and road junction joining four cantons, this small but vital town has for centuries been a center of trade with Italy. It guards not only the Simplon route but also the high end of the Rhône Valley, which leads past the Aletsch Glacier to Gletsch and the Grimsel Pass (toward Meiringen and the Berner Oberland) or the Furka Pass (toward Andermatt and central Switzerland). The fantastical **Stockalperschloss,** a massive baroque castle, was built between 1658 and 1678 by Kaspar Jodok von Stockalper, a Swiss tycoon who made his fortune in Italian trade over the Simplon Pass. Topped with three gilt onion domes and containing a courtyard lined by elegant Italianate arcades, it was once Switzerland's largest private home and is now completely restored. Group tours in English are available upon request. ⊠ *Alte Simplonstr., from station walk up Bahnhofstr. to Sebastienpl., turn left onto Alte Simplonstr.,* ☎ *027/9216030.* 🎟 *5 SF.* ⊙ *June–Sept., Tues.–Sun., guided tours at 10, 11, 2, 3, 4, and 5; May and Oct., Tues.–Sun., guided tours at 10, 11, 2, 3, and 4.*

En Route   Above the eastern outskirts of Brig is the entrance to the **Simplon Tunnel,** which carries trains nearly 20 km (12 mi) before emerging into Italian daylight. The first of the twin tunnels—the world's longest railway tunnels—was started in 1898 and took six years to complete.

Simplon Pass

17 *23 km (14 mi) southeast of Brig.*

Beginning just outside Brig, this historic road meanders through deep gorges and wide, barren, rock-strewn pastures to offer increasingly beautiful views back toward Brig. At the summit (2,010 m/6,593 ft), the **Simplon-Kulm Hotel** shares the high meadow with the **Simplon Hospice,** built 150 years ago at Napoléon's request and now owned by the monks of St. Bernard. Just beyond stands the bell-towered **Alt Spital,** a lodging built in the 17th century by Kaspar Jodok von Stockalper.

From the summit you can still see parts of the old road used by traders and Napoléon, and it is easy to imagine the hardships travelers faced at these heights. Look north toward the Bernese Alps and a portion of the massive Aletsch Glacier. Beyond the pass, the road continues through Italy, and it's possible to cut across the Italian upthrust and reenter Switzerland in the Ticino, near Ascona.

Riederalp

18 *13 km (8 mi) north of the Brig.*

The bleak and stony ascent of the Val de Conches follows the increasingly wild, silty Rhône to its source, with mountain resorts threading into the flanking heights. Within the Val de Conches, Riederalp is best known as the home of Art Furrer, who became famous in the United States as one of the pioneers of freestyle skiing. On his return to Switzerland, he came to this resort and established a freestyle ski school available to nearly every good skier.

On a rugged, treeless plateau, the resort is accessible only by cable car from **Mörel,** and its views over the Italian Alps are rivaled only by the staggering views over the Aletsch Glacier on the secondary ascent by cable car up to **Moosfluh.** A swift gondola up to Moosfluh, reputedly the fastest in Europe, holds 12 people. Riederalp borders the preserved pine stands of the **Aletsch Forest,** one of the highest in Europe. From Fiesch, just up the valley from Mörel, you can ascend by cable car all the way to the top of the **Eggishorn** (2,927 m/9,600 ft). This extraordinary vantage point looks over the entire sweep of the Aletsch and its surrounding peaks.

Skiing
At 1,900 m (6,232 ft), with a peak of 2,700 m (8,856 ft), **Riederalp** has seven lifts and 30 km (19 mi) of downhill runs, a third of which are expert. A one-day lift ticket (including access to the whole Aletsch ski area) costs 43 SF; a six-day pass costs 208 SF. Stretching from Münster to Oberwald, the **Val de Conches** offers superior snow conditions and villages straight out of the Middle Ages, as well as the most beautiful cross-country skiing trails in the Alps, with the exception of those in the Upper Engadine (☞ Saint-Moritz *in* Chapter 4) at 1,300 m (4,265 ft), with a peak of 1,450 m (4,757 ft); it has 85 km (53 mi) of trails and an ice-skating rink. Freestyle skier Art Furrer's ski school (Skischule Forum Alpin; ☎ 027/9272121) is still up and running.

Gletsch
19 *48 km (30 mi) northeast of Brig.*

Summer travelers may want to travel the distance to the tiny resort of Gletsch, named for its prime attraction: the glacier that gives birth to the Rhône. The views over the Bernese and Valais Alps are magnificent. From Gletsch, you can drive over the Furka Pass directly or over the scenic Grimsel Pass (2,130 m/7,101 ft) to the Bernese Oberland.

Furka Pass
★ **20** *11 km (7 mi) east of Gletsch, 59 km (37 mi) northeast of Brig.*

Making the final ascent of Valais, drivers arrive at Oberwald, starting point of the train tunnel through the Furka Pass, which cuts over the heights and leads down to central Switzerland. Spectacular views and stark moonscapes are punctuated by the occasional Spielberg-esque military operations—white-clad soldiers melting out of camouflaged hangars carved deep into solid-rock walls. The sleek, broad highway that snakes down toward Andermatt shows Swiss Alpine engineering at its best.

VALAIS A TO Z

Arriving and Departing

By Car
Valais is something of a dead end by nature: a fine expressway (**A9**) carries you in from Lac Léman (Lake Geneva), but to exit—or enter—from the east end, you must park your car on a train and ride through the **Furka Pass** tunnel to go north or take the train through the tunnel

under the **Simplon Pass** to go southeast. (The serpentine roads over these passes are open in summer; weather permitting, the Simplon road stays open all year.) You also may cut through from or to Kandersteg in the Berner Oberland by taking a car train to Goppenstein or Brig. A summer-only road twists over the **Grimsel Pass** as well, heading toward Meiringen and the Berner Oberland or, over the **Brünig Pass**, to Luzern.

By Plane

Geneva's Cointrin (☎ 022/7177111) serves international flights and is nearest the west (French) end of Valais; it's about two hours away by train or car. **Zürich's Kloten** Airport (☎ 1571060) brings you closer to the east (German) side, but the Alps are in the way; you must connect by rail tunnel or drive over one of the passes.

By Train

There are straightforward rail connections to the region by way of Lausanne to the west and Brig/Brigue to the east. The two are connected by one clean rail sweep that runs the length of the valley. For information, call ☎ 1572222.

Getting Around

By Car

If you want to see the tiny back roads—and there's much to be seen off the beaten path—a car is the only solution. The **A9** expressway from Lausanne shrinks, at Sierre, to a well-maintained highway that continues on to Brig. Distances in the north and south valleys can be deceptive: apparently short jogs are full of painfully slow switchbacks and distractingly beautiful views. Both Zermatt and Saas-Fee are car-free resorts, though you can drive all the way to a parking lot at the edge of Saas-Fee's main street. Zermatt must be approached by rail from Täsch, the end of the line for cars. (There is a central, secure, long-term parking lot.) Car trains through tunnels under mountain passes, either to Kandersteg or under Furka Pass, can be claustrophobic and time-consuming: think of them as the world's longest car washes.

By Train

The main rail service covers the length of the valley from Lausanne to Brig. Routes into the tributary valleys are limited, although most resorts are served by cheap and reliable postbuses running directly from train stations. There is a train station in the main tourist magnet, Zermatt (☎ 027/9664711). The **Brig-Visp-Zermatt Railway,** a private narrow-gauge system, runs from Brig to Visp with connections to Zermatt.

On Foot

This is one of the hiking capitals of Switzerland, and it's impossible to overstate the value of setting off on a mountain path through the sweet-scented pine woods and into the wide-open country above timberline. The trails are wild but well maintained here, and the regional tourist office (☞ Visitor Information, *below*) publishes a thorough map with planned and timed walking tours. Ask for *Sentiers valaisans;* it's written in English, French, and German.

Contacts and Resources

Emergencies

Police: Crans-Montana (☎ 027/4866560); **Sion** (☎ 027/6065656); **Verbier** (☎ 027/7656320); **Zermatt** (☎ 027/9666920). **Medical assistance: Crans-Montana** (ambulance, ☎ 144); **Sion** (ambulance, ☎ 144); **Verbier** (☎ 144); **Zermatt** (ambulance, ☎ 027/9672000). **Late-night pharmacies** (☎ 111).

Guided Tours

BUS

Guided coach tours of Valais, including lodging and dining packages, are offered by **Valais Incoming** (✉ 6 rue du Pré-Fleuri, Sion, ☎ 027/3273591).

HELICOPTER

Sion's **Air-Glaciers** (☎ 027/3226464) proposes several itineraries out of Sion for groups of four or six who want a bird's-eye view of Valais—from a helicopter. Prices range from 341 SF for 10 minutes on up into the thousands for personalized itineraries.

VINEYARDS

Wine lovers can trace the best Valais *vignobles* (vineyards) firsthand by following a list provided by the **OPAV** (Office de Promotion des Produits de l'Agriculture Valaisanne; ✉ 5 av. de la Gare, Sion, ☎ 027/3222247), which promotes agriculture in the region; you must arrange the visits yourself.

Visitor Information

The main tourist office for Valais is in **Sion** (✉ 6 rue Pré-Fleuri, CH-1951, ☎ 027/3273570, FAX 027/3273571).

Local offices: **Brig** (✉ Train station CH-3900, ☎ 028/222222). **Crans-sur-Sierres** (✉ CH-3963, ☎ 027/4850800). **Martigny** (✉ 9 pl. Centrale, CH-1920, ☎ 027/7212220). **Montana** (✉ av. de la Gare, CH-3962, ☎ 027/4850404). **Riederalp** (✉ CH-3987, ☎ 027/9271365). **Saas-Fee** (✉ CH-3906, ☎ 027/9581858). **Sion** (✉ pl. de la Planta, CH-1950, ☎ 027/3228586). **Verbier** (✉ CH-1936, ☎ 027/7753888). **Zermatt** (✉ CH-3920, ☎ 027/9670181).

12 VAUD

Lausanne, Montreux, Les Alpes Vaudoises

The verdant vineyards of La Côte and Lavaux, the rugged Alpes Vaudoises, and two graceful waterfront cities—Lausanne and Montreux—comprise one of Switzerland's most diverse regions. Centered around Lac Léman, also known as Lake Geneva, this French-speaking canton harbors some of the country's most famous cathedrals and castles, as well as Alpine retreats, balmy lake resorts, and picturesque wine villages.

Updated by
Kay
Winzenried

IF PRESSED TO SELECT JUST ONE REGION, you can experience a complete cultural, gastronomic, and scenic sweep of Switzerland by choosing Vaud (pronounced Voh). It has a stunning Gothic cathedral (Lausanne) and one of Europe's most evocative châteaux (Chillon), palatial hotels and weathered-wood chalets, sophisticated culture and ancient folk traditions, snowy Alpine slopes and balmy lake resorts, simple fondue and the legerdemain of some of the world's great chefs. Everywhere there are the roadside vineyards that strobe black-green, black-green, as the luxurious rows of vines alternate with rich, black loam.

This is the region of Lac Léman, or Lake Geneva, a grand and romantic body of water crowned by Lausanne's cathedral and the castle of Chillon. Its romance—Savoy Alps looming across the horizon, steamers fanning across its surface, palm trees rustling along its shores—made it a focal point of the budding 19th-century tourist industry, an object of literary fancy, an inspiration to the arts. In a Henry James novella, the imprudent Daisy Miller made waves when she crossed its waters unchaperoned to visit Chillon; Byron's Bonivard languished in chains in the fortress's dungeons. From their homes outside Montreux, Stravinsky wrote *The Rite of Spring* and Strauss his transcendent *Four Last Songs*. Yet at the lake's east end, romance and culture give way to wilderness and farmland, to mountains with some peaks so high they grow grazing grass sweet enough to flavor the cheese. There are resorts, of course—Leysin, Villars-Gryon, Château-d'Oex—but none so famous as to upstage the region itself.

Throughout the canton, French is spoken, and the temperament the Vaudoise inherited from the Romans and Burgundians sets them apart from their Swiss-German countrymen. It's evident in their humor, their style, and—above all—their love of their own good wine.

Pleasures and Pastimes

Châteaux
Home to magnificently restored Chillon, the most visited if not the best château in Switzerland, Vaud offers a variety of smaller draws as well, including Coppet, Nyon, Prangins, Rolle, Allaman, Aubonne, and Rougemont. Most house museums and offer baronial views.

Dining
Because of its fortuitous position, draped along a sloping, sunny shore and facing a sparkling lake backdropped by looming peaks of the French Alps, the Lake Geneva shore draws weekenders and car tourists who speed along the waterfront highway, careening through cobbled wine towns, gastronomy guides on the dashboard, in search of the perfect lunch. As in all great wine regions, *dégustation* and *haute gastronomie* go hand in hand, and in inns and auberges throughout La Côte and Lavaux (the two stretches of vineyard-lined shore) you'll dine beside ascoted oenophiles who lower their half-lenses to study a label and order a multicourse feast to complement their extensive tastings.

With a host of Europe's renowned chefs to please, from the retired Fredy Girardet to the latest Michelin star aspirant, the Vaud table teases and gratifies. The culinary delights of the region range from the *cuisine du marché* (cuisine based on fresh market produce) of top-drawer chefs to the simplest fare: *papet Vaudois*, a straightforward stew of leeks, potatoes, and cream served with superb local sausages; delicate *filets de perche* (local perch fillets, sautéed in butter and served by the dozen); and even *malakoffs*, egg-and-Gruyère fritters, which hark back to soldiers of La Côte fighting in the Crimean Wars.

Though nowadays fondue is de rigueur in any Alpine setting, Vaud is the undisputed capital of the Swiss national dish and one of its most loyal custodians. In the Pays-d'Enhaut (Highlands) and on the slopes of the Jura Mountains, the cattle head uphill every summer, and production of the local cheese soars—the nutty hard cheese known as Gruyère, whether or not it comes from that Fribourgeois village. It is sold at various stages of its production: young and mild, ripe and savory, or aged to a heady tang.

The concept of fondue is elementary: grated cheese (generally a Gruyère and Vacherin blend, perhaps with a handful of Appenzeller) is melted in a pot with white wine, garlic, and a dash of kirsch. Diners sit in a circle around the pot, dipping chunks of bread into the bubbling mixture with long, slender forks. Many restaurants prefer to serve it in an adjoining *carnotzet*, or Stübli (the French and German version of a cozy drinking parlor)—not only to re-create a rustic Alpine experience but also to spare fellow diners the fierce aroma of cheese and garlic as well the smell of the fuel used to keep the pot's mixture warm and liquid.

It is a dish at its best when the windows are thick with frost. To accompany it, you drink fruity white wine or plain black tea—never red wine, beer, or (shudder) cola. And halfway through, you down a stiff shot of kirsch—the reviving blast called the *coup du milieu* (shot in the middle). A mixed salad of winter crudités—grated carrots, celery root, beets, or cabbage—is indispensable to digestion.

To experience Vaud's best cuisine, look for *déjeuners d'affaires* (business lunches), plats du jour, and prix-fixe menus, which can offer considerable savings over à la carte dining.

CATEGORY	COST*
$$$$	over 70 SF
$$$	40 SF–70 SF
$$	20 SF–40 SF
$	under 20 SF

*Prices are per person for a three-course meal (two-course meal in $ category), including sales tax and 15% service charge.

Lodging

It's a pleasure unique to Vaud to wake up, part floor-length sheers, and look out over Lake Geneva to Mont Blanc; a series of 19th-century grand hotels with banks of balconied lake-view rooms were created to offer this luxury to such grand-tourists as Strauss, Twain, Stravinsky, and Henry James. Yet there's no shortage of charming inns offering similar views on an intimate scale. Up another 1,200 m (3,936 ft) you'll find the antithesis to an airy lakefront inn: the cozy, honey-gold Alpine chalet, with down quilts in starched white envelopes, balustrade balconies with potted geraniums, and also panoramic views.

The hotels of Lausanne and Montreux are long on luxury and grace, and low prices are not easy to find. Especially at peak periods—Christmas–New Year's and June–August—it's important to book ahead. Many hotels have been increasing in-room facilities; minibars, direct phone and fax lines, in-room safes, and business centers are now the rule rather than the exception. Small auberges in the villages along the lake and the vineyards offer traditional dishes and simple comforts. Up in the Pays-d'Enhaut and the Alps southeast of the lake, there are comfortable mountain hotels in all price ranges—though rates are naturally higher in the resorts themselves. Charges are generally not as steep as those in the Alpine resorts of Graubünden or Valais.

	COST
$$$$	over 300 SF
$$$	200 SF–300 SF
$$	120 SF–200 SF
$	under 120 SF

*Prices are for a standard double room, including breakfast, tax, and service charge.

Mountain Sports

The Alpes Vaudoises are home to lovely, not overly developed high-altitude resorts—Leysin, Villars-Gryon, Les Diablerets, Château-d'Oex—where you can experience all levels of skiing difficulty and all the Swiss Alps atmosphere you could wish for. Summer opens trails and high altitude passes for hikers and mountain bikers. You could also take on a more unusual activity, such as strenuous river gorge expeditions, breathtaking paragliding and hot air ballooning, even mountain surfing (zipping downhill on a skateboardlike scooter with handlebars).

Museums

Lausanne is a city of museums and galleries, not only covering history, science, and the fine arts, but eclectic subjects as well—the Olympics and *l'art brut* (raw art), for example. And all along the shore you'll find tiny, meticulous museums covering local history, from the strong influence of the Romans to wine making, the military, and, at Nestlé's Alimentarium, the history of food.

Wine

As one of the main wine producing regions in Switzerland, Vaud can't be savored without sampling the local vintages. If you're only tangentially interested, check the blackboard listings in any café for local names of *vins ouvert* (open wines), sold by the deciliter: the fruity whites of Épesses and St-Saphorin of Lavaux (between Lausanne and Montreux); the flinty Luins, Vinzel, and La Côte variations between Lausanne and Geneva. If time allows, plan a drive worthy of Albert Finney and Audrey Hepburn in *Two for the Road,* steering that rental car down narrow, fountain-studded stone streets in tiny wine villages, stopping at inns and *vignobles'* (vineyards') dégustations to compare. (Do designate a driver.) And head for a market Saturday in Vevey, where vendors sell wine wholesale and tasters carry a glass from booth to booth. For a boost in your knowledge of wine cultivation, processing, and labeling, track farther east to the Musée de la Vigne et du Vin (Museum of Viticulture and Wine) in Aigle.

Exploring Vaud

Lac Léman, or Lake Geneva, is a graceful swelling in the Rhône River, which passes through the northern hook of the Valais, channels between the French and Vaudoise Alps, then breaks into the open at Bouveret, west of Villeneuve. Its northern shore hosts three of Switzerland's great French cities, grandes dames of the Suisse Romande: Lausanne, Montreux, and Geneva (☞ Chapter 13). The southern shore lies in France's Haute-Savoie. The north portion of the lake with its green hillsides and the cluster of nearby Alps that loom over its east end make up the canton of Vaud.

Numbers in the text correspond to numbers in the margin and on the Vaud and Lausanne maps.

Great Itineraries

You could easily spend a full Swiss vacation in Vaud, flying directly in and out of Geneva Cointrin. You can move quickly into the heart of the region by car or rail. Visit the shore towns of Coppet, Nyon, and Morges, then dig into Lausanne's urban graces and crawl through delightful wine villages en route to Montreux. After exploring the castles and museums along the lakefront, head straight up into those mountains that have been looking over your shoulder.

IF YOU HAVE 3 DAYS

Drive the shore highway through **Coppet** ① to **Nyon** ② to visit the Roman museum and medieval castle that juts over the lake. Spend a day exploring the lively waterfront city of ⌘ **Lausanne** ⑥–⑱, then set out for the winding road, La Corniche de la Vaud, visiting a vignoble or two at Épesses or St-Saphorin. You'll end up at the lakefront town of ⌘ **Montreux** ㉑, with its fabled **Château de Chillon** ㉒.

IF YOU HAVE 5 DAYS

Begin in ⌘ **Lausanne** ⑥–⑱ and spend two days savoring the Old Town and the hyperactive waterfront. Follow the Corniche route east as it winds its way through the vineyards of Lavaux, stopping as thirst and hunger dictate. The market-centered, harbor-front town of ⌘ **Vevey** ⑳ deserves a leisurely visit. Take in the highlights of the glitzy, Riviera-like city of ⌘ **Montreux** ㉑ before threading your way through the grand halls and cells of **Château de Chillon** ㉒. Hop a late train from Montreux or take the half-hour winding drive for an overnight in the brisk mountain air of ⌘ **Villars-Gryon** ㉔. Break in the new day with an Alpine hike or stroll, before heading back down the steep canyon to main route connections that speed you west for an afternoon among Roman and medieval structures in **Nyon** ②.

IF YOU HAVE 10 DAYS

Expand on the five-day program by spending more time outside the cities in the wine villages and mountain resorts. After launching your tour with a few days in ⌘ **Lausanne** ⑥–⑱, go west along the Route du Vignoble to Rolle, Aubonne, **Allaman** ③, **Morges** ④, and **St-Sulpice** ⑤, overnighting in ⌘ **Nyon** ②. (Lake steamers are an alternative transport for hopping from town to town.) After taking in this section of Vaud, backtrack east past Lausanne. Pick up the Corniche Road for stops in Cully, Épesses, and St-Saphorin to taste the local wines. If you arrive in ⌘ **Vevey** ⑳ on a Saturday, you may need a few extra hours to peruse the market and sample fresh produce, cheese, and local vintages. Next stop: the resort town of ⌘ **Montreux** ㉑ paired with a visit to the **Château de Chillon** ㉒. Leaving the lake behind, zigzag your way into the Alpes Vaudoises. Spend a couple of nights in ⌘ **Villars-Gryon** ㉔ to hike, ski, or bask on a sunny balcony. Cross the Col des Mosses and the Gorges du Pissot into ⌘ **Château-d'Oex** ㉘ for another day or two of hiking and studying the folkloric chalets that link the region culturally to Gstaad and the Berner Oberland (☞ Chapter 10). (In winter the passes are often closed.) Or you could return to Montreux on the Montreux–Oberland–Bernois Railroad (MOB), a spectacularly panoramic train ride.

When to Tour Vaud

The lake sparkles and clouds lift from Mont Blanc from spring to fall; November tends to be drizzly gray, then winter brightens things up above the plain (as they call the flatter terrain surrounding the lake). Crowds monopolize Montreux and Chillon year-round but overwhelm it in July (jazz festival time) and August (Europe-wide vacations). It's worth aiming for concert and dance season in Lausanne: from September through May. Prime ski time in the Alpes Vaudoises is from late December through

Vaud

Rougemont 29

GSTAAD

La Torneresse

Château- 28
d'Oex

L'Étivaz 27

Col des Mosses

Les 25
Diablerets

Villars-Gryon

Grand
Muveran

A11

Col de la
Croix

Villars-Gryon 24

Montbovon

Caux

Leysin 26

Vyorne

Aigle 23

Bex

St-Maurice

TO
MARTIGNY

Les Avants

Glion

Veytaux

A9 Rhône

Chexbres

Vevey 20

Montreux 21
22

Château de
Chillon

Villeneuve

Roche

Monthey

Savigny

St-Saphorin 19

Épesses

Cully

Bouveret

Vouvry

Vionnaz

21

Montpreveyres

Essertes

Pully

Cully

Lausanne
6 — 18

Cheseaux

St-Sulpice 5

Évian-les-Bains

Dent d'Oche

La Dranse

Monthey

A12

A1

Lac Léman

F
R
A
N
C
E

N

Bussy

Vufflens-
le-Château

Morges 4

Allaman 3

La Dranse

8 miles

12 km

Bière

Vinzel

Aubonne

Rolle

Gland

0

0

V A U D

Bursins

Lavins

Begnins

Céligny

Nyon 2

Coppet 1

Mies

Vésenaz

Gingins

St-Cergue

Divonne-les-Bains

A1

F R A N C E

Meyrin

Genève

KEY

Rail Lines

Regional
Boundary Lines

Ski Resort

Easter, and prices go up accordingly. Early spring brings daffodil season in Les Avants and the tulip festival in Morges. Remember that at
these latitudes summer daylight extends until 9 PM, allowing you to
pack a lot into one day; the reverse is true in winter.

LA CÔTE AND LAUSANNE

Just northeast of Geneva, La Côte (the shore) of Lac Léman (Lake
Geneva) has been settled since Roman times, with its south-facing
slopes cultivated for wine. It is thus peppered with ancient waterfront
and hillside towns, castles, and Roman remains. A car is a must if you
want to wind through tiny wine villages, but do get out and walk—if
only to hear the trickling of any number of Romanesque trough fountains. Be willing to traverse a few times from the slopes to the waterfront and back if you're determined to cover all the region's charms;
sticking exclusively to either the diminutive Route du Vignoble or the
shore road deprives you of some wonderful sights. You'll end your rural
tour in the sophisticated city of Lausanne.

Coppet

❶ *9 km (6 mi) south of Nyon, 46 km (28 mi) southwest of Lausanne.*

Its pretty, arcaded main street, with occasional peeks through to the
jettied waterfront, makes Coppet a pleasant stop for a stroll. But it is
★ the **Château de Coppet** that puts this natty lake village on the map. Enclosed within vast iron gates, the château has been kept in its original
18th-century form, with luxurious Louis XVI furnishings arranged in
a convincingly lived-in manner; its grounds, with grand old trees, hidden courtyards, and stone stairs, are equally evocative.

The château, built in the 1300s, was restored when purchased in 1784
by Jacques Necker, a Genevan banker who served as financial minis-
ter to France's Louis XVI. The turmoil of the French Revolution and
Necker's opposition to Napoléon led him into exile in this splendid
structure, where his remarkable daughter, Madame de Staël, created
the most intriguing salon in Europe. Her intellectual sparkle and con-
cern for the fiery issues of the day attracted the giants of the early Romantic period: Lord Byron, the Swiss historian Jean-Charles Sismondi,
the German writer August Wilhelm von Schlegel, and British historian
Edward Gibbon. Part of the château is still occupied by family descendants, but you can see the interior on a guided tour. (The language
of the commentary is generally chosen according to the language of
the tour participants.) ⊠ *3 chemin des Murs, just uphill from the waterfront highway,* ☎ *022/7761028.* 🖼 *9 SF.* ☉ *July–Aug., daily 10–
noon and 2–6; Apr.–June and Sept.–Oct., daily 2–6.*

For the house-tour hound, the small **Musée Régional du Vieux-Cop-
pet** (Regional Museum of Old Coppet), in a 15th-century residence on
the arcaded Grand-rue, displays the restored furnishings of a local 19th-
century bourgeois family. There's a noteworthy instrument in the
music room: part piano, part violin. ⊠ *30 Grand-rue,* ☎ *022/7763688.*
🖼 *3 SF.* ☉ *Apr.–Oct., Tues.–Sat. 2–5. Guided tours by request.*

OFF THE   ★ **CÉLIGNY** – Six kilometers (4 miles) north of Coppet on the shore road,
BEATEN PATH   bear left inland at the first sign for Céligny, where you'll discover the en-
dearing village that was home to Richard Burton during the last years of
his life. With its lakefront, small port, lawns for sunbathing, and a rock-
solid pier, it provides the best swimming opportunities for miles around.
The enclave is endowed with the prerequisites of charm: rows of vineyards, a historic (but private) château and church, a village square

adorned with flowers, a fountain, and its best-kept secret, the wonderfully *sympa* (friendly) Hôtel du Soleil. From there you can walk to the village cemetery, the smaller one hugging the edge of the forest, to visit Burton's simple grave. Rumor has it that Elizabeth Taylor has already purchased the adjacent plot.

Dining and Lodging

$$$$ ✕🏨 **Hôtel du Lac.** First ranked as a *grand logis* in 1628 to distinguish it from a common roadhouse, this historic inn still feels like an exclusive men's club, catering to power-lunchers and well-heeled travelers. It fronts on the main road and is accessible by boat, with a sycamore-shaded terrace; an awning-covered restaurant; and rooms with exposed beams, niches, and antiques. Its inventive restaurant draws a regular clientele for its exquisite open-grill specialities such as sea bass with fennel or veal kidney with mustard sauce. ✉ *51 Grand-rue, CH-1296 Coppet,* ☎ *022/7761521,* ℻ *022/7765346. 12 rooms, 7 suites. Restaurant (reservations essential), bar, free parking. AE, DC, MC, V.*

$–$$ ✕🏨 **Hôtel du Soleil.** Lured by the charm of Céligny and the chance to
★ own a 300-year-old building, Californian chef John Olcott and his German wife, Catrin, have established a wonderful auberge. For years the building lay dormant, until the couple took it over in 1996 and renovated every nook and cranny, including the seven sweet guest rooms up the winding stone staircase. Whether in the café up front or the quieter restaurant in back, the decor is a minimalist showcase for the chef's fetching presentations, such as *mâche* (lamb's lettuce) salad with seared fresh scallops in a blood-orange vinaigrette. Although part of the menu changes frequently, the local standards, which include Rösti (shredded fried potatoes), perch, and fondue, never vary. Be sure to save room for the *tarte crème brûlée.* You'll need a reservation in order to snatch a table from the locals, essential in summer for a table on the terrace. ✉ *10 Rte. des Coudrées, CH-1298 Céligny,* ☎ *022/9609633. AE, DC, MC, V. Restaurant closed Tues. No dinner Mon.*

Nyon

② *9 km (4 mi) north of Coppet, 27 km (17 mi) southwest of Lausanne.*

Lovely Nyon, with its waterfront drive, shops, museums, and a castle dominating its cliff-top Old Town, was founded by Julius Caesar around 45 BC as a camp for war veterans. The Romans called it Noviodunum and developed the entire region for miles around, charting, building, and developing sophisticated systems. Flanked by a statue of Caesar, the ★**Musée Romain** (Roman Museum) contains an attractively mounted collection of sumptuously detailed architectural stonework, fresco fragments, statuary, mosaics, and earthenware. The museum was built atop foundations of a 1st century AD basilica; a pristine miniature model inside and an excellent trompe-l'oeil artist's impression of the palace on the outside wall of the museum make clear the remarkable distinction of the original structure. A complete listing of the exhibits in English is available upon request. ✉ *rue Maupertuis,* ☎ *022/ 3617591.* 🎫 *6 SF; pass for all 3 Nyon museums 12 SF.* ☉ *Apr.–Oct., Tues.–Sat. 10–noon and 2–5, Sun. 10–5; Nov.–Mar., Tues.–Sat. 2–5, Sun. 10–5. Guided tours by request.*

Dominating Nyon's hilltop over the waterfront, the **Château de Nyon** is a magnificent, multispire 12th-century fortress with a terrace that takes in sweeping views of the lake and Mont Blanc. Within its spacious rooms, you can visit the **Musée Historique** (Historical Museum), which covers the history of Nyon and focuses on a fascinating part of its heritage: after the French Revolution, Nyon became a great porcelain center, creating flower-sprigged tea sets, vases, and bowls, of which fine examples are on display. At press time the museum was under renovation, and only one wing was open to the public. ✉ *pl. du Château,* ☎ *022/3615888.* ✉ *6 SF; pass for all 3 Nyon museums 12 SF.* ⊙ *Apr.–Oct., Tues.–Sat. 10–noon and 2–5, Sun. 10–5. Guided tours by request.*

Along with the views from the château-museum's terrace, don't miss the town's waterfront promenade below, where boats and swans bob in the waves. Nestled in a charming floral park that parallels the water, the **Musée du Léman** exhibits models of Lake Geneva steamers, sculling kayaks, and private yachts as well as sizable lake-water aquariums, housed in a shuttered 18th-century hospital. ✉ *8 quai Louis-Bonnard,* ☎ *022/3610949.* ✉ *6 SF; pass for all 3 Nyon museums 12 SF.* ⊙ *Apr.–Oct., Tues.–Sat. 10–noon and 2–5, Sun. 10–5; Nov.–Mar., Tues.–Sat. 2–5, Sun. 10–5.*

The 18th-century **Château de Prangins** was opened in 1998 as the Suisse Romand branch of the **Musée National Suisse** (Swiss National Museum). The château's reincarnation was nearly two decades in the preparation, with its four floors detailing (in four languages, including English) Swiss life and history in the 18th and 19th centuries. For instance an exhibit might describe the country's history of international exports. Surrounded by parks and gardens (the estate once stretched all the way to Rolle), the museum is also a major venue for cultural events and regional celebrations. If you're traveling with kids, you'll get a price break; there's free admission for children up to age 16. ✉ *3 km (2 mi) northeast of Nyon,* ☎ *022/9948890.* ✉ *5 SF.* ⊙ *Tues.–Sun. 10–5.*

OFF THE BEATEN PATH	**ST-CERGUE –** From Nyon you can take a beautiful ride into verdant Jura-range resort country on the private mountain railway Nyon–St-Cergue–La Cure (☎ 022/9942840) up to St-Cergue, 20 km (12 mi) to the north, and beyond. Note the contrast between the old rolling stock, museum pieces in themselves, and the modern, bright red coaches. St-Cergue is a quaint, time-capsule resort that flourishes in both summer and winter—the first hint in Vaud of bigger Alpine sprawls to come—with good ski facilities for children, modest skiing for adults, mushing (dogsled races), and fine cross-country trails. It's also the birthplace of snowshoeing, the hot winter sport that involves lightweight, plastic *raquettes de neige.* If you find yourself here in late September or the first week of October, be sure to take in the annual *Fête Desalpe,* the ritual parade of cows coming down from the mountains. It lasts all of a Saturday morning, allowing hundreds of cows to file through the streets in amazing floral headgear. ✉ *20 km (12 mi) northwest of Nyon.*

ROUTE DU VIGNOBLE – Parallel to the waterfront highway, threading through the steep-sloping vineyards between Nyon and Lausanne, the Route du Vignoble unfolds a rolling green landscape high above the lake, punctuated by noble manors and vineyards. Luins, home of the flinty, fruity white wine of the same name, is a typical pretty village. Just up the road, the village of Vinzel develops its own white wines on sunny slopes and sells them from the wine cellars (*vin-cellier*) that inspired its name. It is also the best source for a very local specialty, the malakoff. These rich, steamy cheese-and-egg beignets have always been a favorite of the Vaudois, but after the Crimean Wars they were renamed after a beloved officer who led his army of Vaud-born mercenaries to victory in the siege of Sebastopol. For a great spot to sample them, head to Au Coeur de la Côte (☞ Dining and Lodging, *below*). The Route du Vignoble continues through Bursins, home of an 11th-century Romanesque church—and of the venerable actor Peter Ustinov. Drivers can choose to follow it all the way to Morges or cross under the autoroute to view lakefront castles and the Swiss National Museum in the Château de Prangins (☞ *above*). ☒ *Route between Nyon and Lausanne, parallel to the shore highway.*

Dining and Lodging

$$ ✕ **Auberge du Château.** This reliable restaurant, just steps from Nyon's château, serves straightforward Swiss fare and plats du jour, including veal five different ways (such as scalloped veal with lime and fresh ginger) and game in autumn. In summer, a big terrace lets diners study the château; in winter, broad windows take in the view. ☒ *8 pl. du Château,* ☎ *022/3616312. AE, DC, MC, V. Closed Wed. Oct.–Apr.*

$ ✕ **Au Coeur de la Côte.** Following ROUTE DU VINOBLE signs on the Jura side of the A1 autoroute after exiting at Gland, head up the vine-lined slopes to Vinzel (wine cellar), where this modest village inn and its flowered terrace overlook the vineyards and the lake beyond. Here you can taste the commune's Vinzel, or fill up on two or three hot, rich, Gruyère-based malakoffs, served with pickles and mustard, any time of day from 11:30 AM to 9:30 PM. ☒ *Vinzel, along Rte. du Vignoble,* ☎ *021/8241141. No reservations. MC, V. Closed Mon.*

$$–$$$ ⊡ **Hôtel Ambassador.** Terra-cotta stucco and peaked dormers set off this petite hotel on Nyon's main thoroughfare. Request one of the "under the roof" rooms; these have hand-hewn, dark wooden beams, floral bedding, and compact modern baths. Stone walls and polished wooden beams lend a sophisticated air to L'Amphithéâtre, the hotel's intimate restaurant, which serves fresh lake fish and tasteful, uncomplicated fare. The quiet garden terrace with its view of the castle (which is illuminated at night) is an exquisite spot for a glass of wine or light meal. Breakfast is included. ☒ *26 rue St-Jean, CH-1260,* ☎ *022/9944848,* FAX *022/994486. 20 rooms. Restaurant. AE, DC, MC, V.*

En Route   Twelve kilometers (7 miles) northeast of Nyon, the lakefront village of **Rolle** merits a detour for a look at its dramatic 13th-century **château**, built at the water's edge by a Savoyard prince. Seek out the Moinat Antiques and Decoration shop in town for a sample of what it takes to furnish a grand country home.

Allaman

③ *17 km (10 mi) northeast of Nyon, 20 km (12 mi) west of Lausanne.*

This village is little more than a cluster of stone and stucco houses and red-tile-roofed barns; the streets are so narrow that two cars can barely pass. The main draw is the stately, 16th-century **Château d'Allaman,** built in the 12th century by the barons of Vaud, then reconstructed by the Bernois after a 1530 fire. It has been converted to a stunning antiques mall, its narrow halls and stairwells lined with beeswaxed armoires and ancestral portraits, all for sale at lofty prices through private entrepreneurs who rent space within. The château's vaulted crypt offers wine déustations for potential buyers as well. For antiques, collectibles, and art at more reasonable prices, head to the annex next door, known as **La Grange,** the château's erstwhile stables and barn. ☒ *Between Aubonne and Allaman, signposted,* ☎ *021/8073805.* ▭ *Free. Shops:* ☉ *Wed.–Sun. 2–6. Wine crypt:* ☎ *021/8088239.* ☉ *Wed.–Fri. 1–8, weekends 11–7.*

Morges

④ *9 km (5 mi) northeast of Allaman, 8 km (5 mi) west of Lausanne.*

On the waterfront just west of the urban sprawl of Lausanne, Morges is a pleasant lake town favored by sailors and devotees of its *Fête de la Tulipe* (Tulip Festival), held annually from mid-April to mid-May. Its château, built by the duke of Savoy around 1286 as a defense against the bishop-princes of Lausanne, now houses the **Musée Militaire Vaudois** (Vaud Military Museum), which displays weapons, uniforms, and a collection of 10,000 miniature lead soldiers. In the Général Henri Guisan Hall, you'll find memorabilia of this World War II general, much honored for keeping both sides happy enough to leave Switzerland safely alone. ⊠ *Le Château,* ☎ *021/8012616.* ⊑ *5 SF.* ☉ *Feb.–mid-Dec., weekdays 10–noon and 1:30–5, weekends 1:30–5.*

One kilometer (½ mile) west of Morges, the tiny village of **Tolochenaz** honors a beloved long-term resident in the **Pavillon de Audrey Hepburn.** Founded in 1996, the contemporary, white, shoeboxlike building is a few minutes' walk from the village cemetery where the star is buried, a bit farther from La Paisable, the gracious, shuttered manor house where she lived for 26 years. Exhibits of photographs, posters, and Academy Awards chronicle her artistic and humanitarian achievements, but equally touching is the sentiment with which the villagers volunteer their time to keep her memory alive. ⊠ *Chemin des Plantées, Tolochenaz,* ☎ *021/8036464.* ⊑ *10 SF.* ☉ *Mid-Mar.–mid-Nov., Tues.–Sun. 10–6; mid-Nov.–mid-Mar., Tues.–Sun. 1:30–5.*

Dining and Lodging

$$$–$$$$ ✕⊞ **Hotel Fleur du Lac.** The sun-splashed Mont Blanc falls into direct view as the draperies are pulled back from south-facing windows. Just out of town, but on the main route to Lausanne, this lakefront oasis is surrounded by abundant seasonal plantings and stately old trees. Innkeepers Elsbeth and Rodolphe Schelbert attend to your every need without hovering. Trained in top starred restaurants, chefs deliver exceptional results to bistro and dining room patrons. Book well in advance, as their guest return rate is unusually high. Reservations are essential for the restaurant. ⊠ *70 rue de Lausanne CH-1110,* ☎ *021/8815811,* ℻ *021/8115888. 31 rooms, 7 suites. Restaurant, bar, free parking. AE, DC, MC, V.*

OFF THE **VUFFLENS-LE-CHÂTEAU** – Two kilometers (1 mile) northwest of Morges,
BEATEN PATH this village is known for its namesake château, a 15th-century Savoyard palace with a massive donjon and four lesser towers, all trimmed in fine Piedmont-style brickwork. It is privately owned, but the grounds are open to the public.

St-Sulpice

⑤ *5 km (3 mi) east of Morges, 3 km (1¾ mi) west of Lausanne.*

Just west of Lausanne, turn right toward the waterfront to visit St-Sulpice, an ancient village and site of one of the best-preserved 12th-century
★ Romanesque churches in Switzerland. The severe but lovely **Église de St-Sulpice** (Church of St. Sulpice) was built by monks from Cluny Abbey in Burgundy; its painted decoration softens the spare purity of its lines. Three original apses remain, although the nave has disappeared; the short bell tower is built of small stone blocks likely brought from the ruined Roman township at nearby Vidy. At one time the home of 40 monks, the adjoining priory was converted into a private residence in the 16th century. Today the church earns new renown as a venue for classical music concerts. ⊠ *chemin du Crêt, at the dock.* ⊑ *Free.*

Lausanne

66 km (41 mi) northeast of Geneva.

"Lausanne is a block of picturesque houses, spilling over two or three gorges, which spread from the same central knot, and are crowned by a cathedral like a tiara. . . . On the esplanade of the church . . . I saw the lake over the roofs, the mountains over the lake, clouds over the mountains, and stars over the clouds. It was like a staircase where my thoughts climbed step by step and broadened at each new height." Such was Victor Hugo's impression of this grand and graceful tiered city. Voltaire, Rousseau, Byron, and Cocteau all waxed equally passionate about Lausanne—and not only for its visual beauty. It has been a cultural center for centuries, the world drawn first to its magnificent Gothic cathedral and the powers it represented, then to its university, and during the 18th and 19th centuries, to its vibrant intellectual and social life. In the 1990s, the Swiss consider Lausanne the most desirable city in which to live.

Lausanne's importance today stems from its several disparate roles in national and world affairs. Politically, it is the site of the Tribunal Fédéral, the highest court of appeals in Switzerland. Commercially, although it is by no means in the same league as Zürich or Bern, it figures as the headquarters for many multinational organizations, corporations, and sports federations. On a major international rail route and a vital national junction, Lausanne serves as a trade center for most of the surrounding agricultural regions and the expanding industrial towns of Vaud. This prosperity spills over into the arts; there's a surprising concentration of dance companies—including that of Maurice Béjart—as well as several theaters, jazz cellars, and a pair of excellent orchestras. Lausanne is also the world's Olympic capital; the International Olympic Committee has been based here since 1915 (its founder, Baron Pierre de Coubertin, is buried nearby at Montoie Cemetery).

The balance of old and new has not always been kept. The first 20 years after World War II saw an immense building boom, with old buildings and whole neighborhoods pulled down to make way for shining new office blocks and apartment buildings—an architectural exuberance that has given Lausanne a rather lopsided air. Rising in tiers from the lakeside at Ouchy (360 m/1,181 ft) to more than 600 m (2,000 ft), the city covers three hills, which are separated by gorges that once channeled rivers; the rivers have been built over, and huge bridges span the gaps across the hilltops. On one hill in particular, modern skyscrapers contrast brutally with the beautiful proportions of the cathedral rising majestically from its crest. For the sake of hygiene, atmospheric alleys and narrow streets have mostly been demolished, yet the Old Town clustered around the cathedral has been painstakingly restored.

For walking in Lausanne you should bring comfortable shoes, as the city's steep inclines and multiple layers add considerable strain to getting around. There are plenty of buses and a Métro (subway system), but to see the concentrated sights of the Old Town, it's best to tackle the hills on foot.

A Good Walk

Begin in the commercial hub of the city, the **place St-François** ⑥ (nicknamed Sainfe by the Lausannois), where you'll see the former Franciscan **Église St-François**. Behind the church, take a near hairpin turn right onto the fashionable main shopping street, the ancient **rue de Bourg** ⑦. At the top of rue de Bourg, rue Caroline leads you left and left again over the **Pont Bessières**, where you can see the city's peculiar design spanning gorges and covered rivers.

Crossing the bridge and bearing right brings you up into the Old Town. On your left, the imposing palace of the Old Bishopric now houses the **Musée Historique de Lausanne** ⑧. Straight ahead, at the top of rue St-Étienne in the place de la Cathedral, towers the tremendous **Cathé-**

Lausanne

KEY

AE American Express Office

── Rail Lines

┅┅ Metro Line

N

0 _____ 200 yards

0 _____ 200 meters

Ancienne-Académie, **13**

Cathédrale de Notre-Dame, **9**

Château St-Maire, **12**

Collection de l'Art Brut, **14**

Débarcadère, **16**

Hôtel de Ville, **10**

Musée Historique de Lausanne, **8**

Musée Olympique, **17**

Musée Romain de Lausanne–Vidy, **18**

Ouchy, **15**

Palais de Rumine, **11**

Place St-François, **6**

Rue de Bourg, **7**

drale de Notre-Dame ⑨, which is on par with some of France's and England's finest churches.

With the cathedral on your left, walk up the narrow passage of rue Cité-Derrière to the place du Château and its namesake monument, the **Château St-Maire** ⑫, a stern, castellated structure. As you face the château, turn left and walk down the rue Cité-Devant. On your right you will see the **Ancienne-Académie** ⑬ halfway between the château and the cathedral. As you pass the cathedral, again on your left, veer right toward a flight of wooden steps that leads down to the second, more dramatic **Escaliers du Marché**, a wood-roof medieval staircase. At the bottom of the 150 covered steps, you'll run into the place de la Palud and the **Hôtel de Ville** ⑩, the seat of the municipal and communal councils. Turning right, just up rue Madeleine from the place de la Palud, you will come upon the place de la Riponne and the imposing **Palais de Rumine** ⑪, which houses a pack of museums covering subjects from archaeology to zoology.

Some of Lausanne's other worthwhile museums take a bit of extra effort to reach. A long hike up avenue Vinet, northwest of the Old Town, will take you to the **Collection de l'Art Brut** ⑭, an unusual museum of fringe art. South of the Old Town, the waterfront community of **Ouchy** ⑮ can be easily reached by the steep funicular Métro; there are stations across from the Gare Centrale (train station) and under the rue du Grand-Chene in the Flon (city center, a bit west of the Old Town). Ouchy's **Débarcadère** ⑯ has all the typical quayside attractions—vendors, people strolling on a promenade, and a relaxed atmosphere. Just east of Ouchy, on a hillside overlooking the lake, the dramatic **Musée Olympique** ⑰ conveys the history and disciplines of the Olympic Games. It's less than half a mile from the Débarcadère along the quai de Belgique, which turns into the quai d'Ouchy. West of Ouchy at Vidy (just off the Lausanne-Maladière exit from E25/A1) is the **Musée Romain de Lausanne–Vidy** ⑱, where you can see a reconstructed private Roman home. Like the Musée Olympique, this is easy to get to on foot; it's just under a mile from the Débarcadère.

TIMING

You can tour the Old Town in a couple of hours following the above route (do not reverse the order unless you're keen to walk up instead of down the Escaliers du Marché). But that's without stopping: if you have time, plan a full day to include visits to at least a few of the museums and the cathedral—not to mention some unique shops off the place du Palud. Or you could spend your afternoon in Ouchy and the nearby museums; getting to Ouchy by car or funicular takes under 10 minutes, while walking down the Avenue d'Ouchy from the Gare Centrale to the Débarcadère takes about 15 minutes. Remember that, except for the Musée Olympique, museums are closed on Monday.

Sights to See

⑬ **Ancienne-Académie** (Old Academy). Originally the first school of Protestant theology in Europe (1536), the edifice later became home of the city's university and is now a secondary school. ⊠ *7 rue Cité-Devant.*

★ ⑨ **Cathédrale de Notre-Dame** (Cathedral of Our Lady). A Burgundian Gothic architectural treasure, this cathedral is Switzerland's largest church—and probably its finest. Begun in the 12th century by Italian, Flemish, and French architects, it was completed in 1275. Pope Gregory X came expressly to perform the historic consecration ceremony—of double importance, as it also served as a coronation service for Rudolf of Hapsburg as the new emperor of the Holy Roman Empire. Rudolf brought his wife, eight children, seven cardinals, five archbishops, 17 bishops, four dukes, 15 counts, and a multitude of lesser lords, who must have crowded the church's exquisitely proportioned nave.

Viollet-le-Duc, a renowned restorer who worked on the cathedrals of Chartres and Notre-Dame-de-Paris, brought portions of the building to Victorian Gothic perfection in the 19th century. His repairs are visible as paler stone contrasting with the weathered local sandstone; his self-portrait appears in the face of King David, harp and scroll in hand, to the right of the main portal. Streamlined to the extreme, without radiating chapels or the excesses of later Gothic trim, the cathedral wasn't always so spare; in fact, there was brilliant painting. Zealous Reformers plastered over the florid colors, but in so doing they unwittingly preserved them, and now you can see portions of these splendid shades restored in the right transept. The dark and delicate choir contains the 14th-century tomb of the crusader Otto I of Grandson and exceptionally fine 13th-century choir stalls, unusual for their age alone, not to mention their beauty. The church's masterpiece, the 13th-century painted portal—considered one of Europe's most beautiful—was reopened in 1997 after more than a decade of restoration.

Protestant services (the cathedral was reformed in the 16th century) exclude non-worshiping visitors on Sunday from 10 to 11:30. You may want to come instead for the evening concerts given on an almost-weekly basis in spring and autumn; call ahead for a precise schedule. ☒ *pl. de la Cathédrale*, ☎ 021/3167161. ☉ *Apr.–Oct., weekdays 7–7, weekends 8–7; Nov.–Mar., weekdays 7–5:30, weekends 8–5:30.*

★ ⑫ **Château St-Maire.** The fortresslike elements of this 15th-century stone cylinder certainly came into play. The castle was built for the bishops of Lausanne; during the 16th century, the citizens wearied of ecclesiastic power and allied themselves with Bern and Fribourg against the bishops protected within. Before long, however, Bern itself marched on Lausanne, put a bailiff in this bishops' castle, and stripped the city fathers of their power. The Bernese imposed Protestantism on the Lausannois, and their Catholic churches and cathedral were ransacked to fill the coffers of Bern. Today the Château St-Maire is the seat of the cantonal government. ☒ *pl. du Château.*

★ ⑭ **Collection de l'Art Brut.** This singular museum focuses on the genre of fringe or "psychopathological" art, dubbed *l'art brut* in the 1940s by French artist Jean Dubuffet. His own collection forms the base of this ensemble of raw material from untrained minds—prisoners, schizophrenics, or the merely obsessed. Strangely enough, the collection is housed in the Château de Beaulieu, a former mansion of Madame de Staël, she of the sophisticated salons. The exhibits range from intricate yarn and textile pieces to a wall full of whimsical seashell masks. One of the most affecting works is a panel of rough carvings made by an asylum patient in solitary confinement; it was shaped with a broken spoon and a chamber pot handle. You can get here by walking up avenue Vinet or by taking Bus 2 from place St-Laurent in the direction of Le Désert. ☒ *11 av. des Bergières*, ☎ 021/6475435. ☒ 6 SF. ☉ *Tues.–Sun. 11–1 and 2–6.*

⑯ **Débarcadère** (Wharf). The main boat traffic comes from the white steamers that land here. In fine weather, the waterfront buzzes with nightlife—strollers, diners, people lingering in outdoor cafés, roller-skaters, artisans selling their wares. It's as if sedate Lausanne lifts her skirts a bit at the shoreline. ☒ *pl. du Port, Ouchy.*

🔟 **Hôtel de Ville** (Town Hall). This building, constructed between the 15th and the 17th centuries, is the seat of municipal and communal councils. A painted, medieval **Fontaine de la Justice** (Justice Fountain) draws strollers to lounge on its heavy rim. Across from the Town Hall, you can watch the **animated clock,** a modern work with moving figures that was donated to the city by local merchants; the figures appear every hour on the hour. A street market is held in the square every Wednesday and Saturday morning. ⊠ *2 pl. de la Palud,* ☎ *021/ 3152223.* 🖘 *Free.*

❽ **Musée Historique de Lausanne** (Lausanne Historical Museum). The Ancien-Évêché (Old Bishopric) holds a wealth of both temporary and permanent historical exhibits about the city. Don't miss the 250-square-ft scale model of 17th-century Lausanne, with its commentary illuminating the neighborhoods' histories; also look for the re-created 19th-century shop windows. ⊠ *4 pl. de la Cathédrale,* ☎ *021/3310353.* 🖘 *4 SF.* ☉ *Tues., Wed., and Fri.–Sun. 11–6, Thurs. 11–8.*

🔟⓱ **Musée Olympique** (Olympic Museum). With high-tech presentation and touching mementos, this complex pays tribute to the athletic tradition in ancient Greece, to the development of the modern Games, to the evolution of the individual sports, and to the athletes themselves. There are art objects—an Etruscan torch from the 6th century BC, Rodin's *American Athlete*—7,000 hours of archival films and videos, interactive displays, photographs, coins and stamps, and medals from various eras throughout Olympic history. You'll even see the running shoes Carl Lewis wore to win the 200-m gold medal at Los Angeles in 1984. A museum shop, a lovely café overlooking the lake and sculpture park, and occasional Sunday-afternoon classical concerts complete this ambitious, world-class endeavor. Brochures and guides are available in English. ⊠ *1 quai d'Ouchy,* ☎ *021/6216511.* 🖘 *14 SF.* ☉ *May–Sept., Mon.–Wed. and Fri.–Sun. 9–7, Thurs. 9–8; Oct.–Apr., Tues., Wed., and Fri.–Sun. 10–6, Thurs. 10–8.*

⓲ **Musée Romain de Lausanne-Vidy** (Lausanne-Vidy Roman Museum). This is the current incarnation of the restored remains of the late Roman communities Lousonna and Vidy, both of which flourished here from 15 BC into the 4th century. A private home, complete with a well and decorative murals, has been reconstructed and used as the centerpiece for a permanent exhibition on the ancient settlements. The displays include a small treasure trove of coins, votive figures, and objects from daily life—carved combs, toga pins, jewelry. You can get guided tours in English of the museum and neighboring archaeological sites on request. The site is west of Ouchy, just off the Lausanne-Maladière exit from E25/A1. ⊠ *24 chemin du Bois-de-Vaux, Vidy,* ☎ *021/6251084.* 🖘 *4 SF.* ☉ *Tues., Wed., and Fri.–Sun. 11–6, Thurs. 11–8.*

⓯ **Ouchy.** Officially a separate township, Ouchy can be easily reached by the steep funicular Métro across from the Gare Centrale (train station) and from the Flon (city center). It serves as Lausanne's port, and it's a fashionable place to live. The resort area is dominated by the **Château d'Ouchy** (Ouchy Castle), now a hotel; its tower dates from the Middle Ages.

⓫ **Palais de Rumine.** Built at the turn of the century, this enormous neo-Renaissance structure houses several museums, all with a local spin. The **Musée Cantonal de Géologie** (Cantonal Geology Museum) has an excellent fossil collection, including a mammoth skeleton. Besides its collection of regional fauna, the **Musée Cantonal de Zoologie** (Cantonal Zoology Museum) has a rare collection of comparative anatomy. The top exhibit at the **Musée Cantonal d'Archéologie et d'Histoire** (Cantonal Archeology and History Museum) is the gold bust of Marcus Aurelius discovered at nearby Avenches in 1939. The **Musée Cantonal des Beaux-Arts** (Cantonal Museum of Fine Arts) has an enlightening collection of Swiss art, not only by the Germanic Hodler and Anker but also by Vaud artists—especially Bocion, whose local landscapes are well worth study during a visit to this region. Each museum has some descriptions or an abbreviated guide in English. ⊠ *6 pl. de la Riponne. Geology Museum:* ☎ *021/6924470.* ☒ *Free.* ☉ *Tues.–Thurs. 11–6, Fri.–Sun. 11–5. Zoology Museum:* ☎ *021/3163460.* ☒ *Free.* ☉ *Tues.–Thurs. 11–6, Fri.–Sun. 11–5. Archaeology and History Museum:* ☎ *021/3163430.* ☒ *Free.* ☉ *Daily 10–noon and 2–5. Museum of Fine Arts:* ☎ *021/3163445.* ☒ *6 SF.* ☉ *Tues.–Wed. 11–6, Thurs. 11–8, Fri.–Sun. 11–5.*

❻ **Place St-François** (St. Francis Square). The brick-paved square is dominated by the massive post office and the former Franciscan **Église St-François** (Church of St. Francis), built during the 13th and 14th centuries. From 1783 to 1793, Gibbon lived in a house on the site of the post office and there finished his work on *The Decline and Fall of the Roman Empire.* In those days, the square, now reserved for pedestrians, was a popular riding circuit.

NEED A BREAK?   An espresso or bite to eat at this see-and-be-seen gathering spot opposite the church is a welcome respite from climbing cobblestone streets. **Restaurant Place Saint François** (⊠ 5 place St-François, ☎ 021/3202751) serves decadent pastries and inventive light meals in a sleek, blond-wood setting. Just behind the restaurant is an epicurean boutique chock full of gourmet items including private-label products from Philippe Rochat (☞ Dining and Lodging, *below*).

❼ **Rue de Bourg.** Once a separate village isolated on this natural ridge, this is now the fashionable main shopping street (☞ Shopping, *below*). Narrow and cobblestoned, it's lined with platinum-card stores like Hermès and Louis Vuitton; boutiques have been built into the centuries-old buildings, though some have added fittingly modern facades. Tony stores notwithstanding, the street has its down-to-earth moments; on weekends a fresh-produce market makes things even more crowded.

Dining and Lodging

$$$$ ✕ **La Grappe d'Or.** In this relaxed but classic firelighted French restau-
★   rant, imaginative modern cooking is prepared by Bavarian chef Peter Baermann and impeccably served under the discreet supervision of his wife, Angelika. Try the fillet of venison with a sauce of figs and red wine, scallops with potato gnocchi, or the hearty *cardons* (cardoons; an artichokelike vegetable cultivated in Geneva and Lyons) in foie gras. Pastries are extraordinary. ⊠ *3 Cheneau de Bourg,* ☎ *021/3230760. Reservations essential. AE, MC, V. Closed Sun. No lunch Sat.*

$$$$ ✕ **Restaurant de l'Hôtel de Ville–Philippe Rochat.** Secure in his posi-
★   tion as heir to the legendary chef Fredy Girardet, Philippe Rochat reigns as culinary don of the region. It's a quick drive east from Lausanne to his understated manse. Service and presentation are spectacular, if a notch less ceremonious than in Girardet's era, and the food remains absolutely stellar. For these finely orchestrated prix-fixe menus and à la carte selections, the ingredients are key—lamb raised in the Pyrénées, cardons grown in the village. Pace yourself, reserving time and room for selections from the immense cheese cart or celestial desserts. Make reservations as far ahead as possible. ⊠ *1 rue d'Yverdon, Crissier, 7 km (4 mi) east of Lausanne,* ☎ *021/6340505. Reservations essential. AE, MC, V. Closed Sun.–Mon., end of July–mid-Aug.*

$$–$$$ ✕ **Café Beau-Rivage.** As if turning its back on the aristocratic Beau-
★ Rivage Palace that shelters it, this young, lively brasserie-café faces the
lake and the Ouchy waterfront scene. Its flashy, brass-and-Biedermeier
dining area and bar fill with smart Lausannois and Grand Tour internationals enjoying trendy cuisine du marché, *bollito misto* (pot-au-feu
with beef, veal, and poultry), and citron risotto. Despite the brasserie
atmosphere, there are no paper place mats: linen, silver, and mono-
grammed damask set the BCBG (*bon chic, bon genre*) tone. In summer, the pillared terrazzo terrace (protected from embarcadero traffic
by rose gardens) is the place to be seen. ✉ *pl. du Général-Guisan, Ouchy,*
☎ *021/6133330. Reservations essential. AE, DC, MC, V.*

$$ ✕ **À la Pomme de Pin.** In the Old Town behind the cathedral, this win-
some *pinte* (wine pub)—one of Lausanne's oldest—produces an eclec-
tic menu ranging from French to Italian to Swiss (rabbit and Rösti,
anyone?) along with reasonable plats du jour, served both in the ca-
sual café and the adjoining linen-decked restaurant. ✉ *11–13 rue Cité-
Derrière,* ☎ *021/3234656. AE, MC, V. Closed Sun. No lunch Sat.*

$$ ✕ **Café du Grütli.** Tucked in between the place de la Palud and the covered stairs to the cathedral, this is a typical old-style Suisse Romand
restaurant, with a bentwood-and-net-curtain café on the ground floor
and a simple, more formal dining room upstairs. There are several fondues as well as brasserie classics—boiled beef vinaigrette, rabbit in mustard sauce, profiteroles, and tarte Tatin (upside-down apple tart). Have
one of several open Vaud wines or a *café pomme* (coffee with a side
shot of apple eau-de-vie) with the locals, who unwind here with the
daily papers. ✉ *4 rue de la Mercerie,* ☎ *021/3129493. DC, MC, V.
Closed Sun. No dinner Sat.*

$ ✕ **Bleu Lézard.** A complete cross-section of Lausanne urbanites—hip
★ artists, yuppies, shoppers, university students—fights for tables at this
laid-back, stylish restaurant. Sample dishes such as aubergine carpaccio, duck breast in violet vinegar sauce, and marrow crisps and grapes,
all for remarkably low prices. A tongue-in-cheek decor of found-ob-
ject art and easygoing waiters dressed in whatever khakis and flannels
they found near the bed that morning add to the New Age ambience.
Mixed drinks along with live jazz, Latino, and disco music draw a nocturnal clientele downstairs in the cellar. ✉ *10 rue Enning,* ☎ *021/
3127190. AE, MC, V.*

$ ✕ **Café Romand.** All the customers seem to know each other at this
★ vast, smoky, parquet dining institution, where shared wooden tables
and clattering china create the perfect ambience for fondue feasts,
smoked fish platters, mussels, *choucroûte* (sauerkraut), or a sausage
plate. Prominent members of Lausanne's arts community swarm here
after rehearsals and concerts and are known to toast each other loudly
across the crowded room. ✉ *2 pl. St-François,* ☎ *021/3126375. MC,
V. Closed Sun.*

$ ✕ **Manora Crocodile.** If you're fed up with heavy Vaud cheese dishes
and local sausage, this cheery self-service chain offers startlingly inexpensive options. Stir-fries sizzle in huge woks under silent no-smoke
hoods; there are also iced pitchers of fresh-squeezed fruit juices, four
sizes of salad, a fruit bar, a pasta station, and a daily risotto. No one
dish costs more than 20 SF, and the no-smoking dining room is a life-
saver in this city of chain-smokers. ✉ *17 pl. St-François,* ☎ *021/
3209293. Reservations not accepted. No credit cards.*

$$$$ 🏨 **Beau-Rivage Palace.** Of the scores of deluxe hotels in Switzerland,
★ this gleaming grande dame stands apart, its neoclassic structure seamlessly restored to period opulence, its vast waterfront grounds manicured like a country manor estate. It opened in 1861 as the Beau-Rivage
(the Palace wing and Renaissance cupola were added in 1908), but every
inch of marble, crystal, and polished mahogany sparkles like new. (In

1999 it was recognized with the prestigious Swiss Historic Hotel Award.) Rooms have plenty of modern touches—remote light controls, maid lights, towel heaters, piped-in music over the tub and walk-in shower, and phones sprouting from every surface—as well as classic comforts such as wing chairs, Asian rugs, and balconies with lake views. Among the facilities is a pair of first-class restaurants: the romantic La Rotonde and the Café Beau-Rivage with up-to-the-minute brasserie fare. Jacket and tie are required at La Rotonde. ⊠ *chemin de Beau-Rivage, CH-1000 Ouchy 6,* ☎ *021/6133333,* FAX *021/6133334. 155 rooms, 15 suites. 3 restaurants, 2 bars, in-room data ports, minibars, in-room safes, indoor-outdoor pool, beauty salon, sauna, 2 tennis courts, exercise room, playground, concierge, meeting rooms, parking (fee). AE, DC, MC, V.*

$$$$ ⊡ **Lausanne Palace & Spa.** This Edwardian landmark—smaller than
★ the Beau-Rivage and distinctly urban in setting and style—stands on a hill high over the lake, with layers of city scenery draped behind. It faces a city street, so to take advantage of its views you need a back room—though three-quarters of the rooms have balconies. The room decor varies from Empire reproduction to cool modern, with period details such as inlaid wood and dramatic, art deco baths. A "Centre de Bein-Être" (Wellness Center) opened in 1998, centered on a sleek, calming Aveda spa. Its stunning indoor pool is flanked by mosaic-like murals; trim white columns reach to an undulating ceiling. Programs include meditation, massage, aromatherapy, yoga, and tai chi. The adjacent restaurant, Côte du Jardin, has a light menu which can be a welcome respite in the land of cheese and Rösti. Another of the hotel's restaurants, the street-side, Parisian-style Brasserie du Grand-Chêne, is decidedly hip and engaging. ⊠ *7–9 rue du Grand Chêne, CH-1002,* ☎ *021/3313131,* FAX *021/3232571. 119 rooms, 31 suites. 3 restaurants, bar, in-room data ports, minibars, in-room safes, indoor pool, beauty salon, spa, massage, sauna, health club, night club, concierge, meeting rooms, parking (fee). AE, DC, MC, V.*

$$$–$$$$ ⊡ **De la Paix.** This turn-of-the-century business-class hotel in the center of town has all the amenities of a Best Western property and wonderful lake views. The rooms facing the lake are done in warm shades of pumpkin and terra-cotta; those on the back street side are considerably humbler. Its bar, Jacky's, is a Lausanne institution. ⊠ *5 av. Benjamin-Constant, CH-1002,* ☎ *021/3107171,* FAX *021/3107172. 111 rooms, 6 suites. Restaurant, bar, café. AE, DC, MC, V.*

$$$–$$$$ ⊡ **Hotel Victoria.** If you need to stay near the train station, try this polished, business-oriented hotel. Though it's on the busy avenue de la Gare, it's well-buffered from noise. Plaid sofas and modern artwork rub elbows with a marble staircase and a 17th-century tapestry. Rooms have plenty of work space and well-lit desks; only 10 are air-conditioned. Since the hotel is geared towards businesspeople, you can often land a reduced weekend or holiday room rate. Although there's no restaurant on the premises, there are plenty of choices in the neighborhood. ⊠ *46 av. de la Gare, CH-1001,* ☎ *021/3420202,* FAX *021/3420222. 51 rooms, 4 suites. Breakfast room, bar, no-smoking floor, fitness center, free parking. AE, DC, MC, V.*

$$$–$$$$ ⊡ **Mövenpick.** This is a business-style chain hotel across the street from a busy marina. One of the nicer of the newest hotels that stretch along the lake in Ouchy, it's a five-minute drive from the city center. Rooms, à la Laura Ashley, are spacious for a European hotel, but those facing the lake can be noisy. ⊠ *4 av. de Rhodanie, CH-1000,* ☎ *021/6127612,* FAX *021/6127611. 258 rooms, 7 suites. 3 restaurants, piano bar, no-smoking rooms, sauna, exercise room, free parking. AE, MC, V.*

$$$-$$$$ 🏨 **La Résidence.** Within four graceful 18th- and 19th-century villas near
★ the waterfront at Ouchy, this polished small hotel complex has been
modernized without ruffling its gentility or disturbing its graceful
stone arches, marble floors, or discreet gardens. The historic Hotel L'An-
gleterre, where Lord Byron penned *The Prisoner of Chillon*, was added
to the complex in 1998. At press time, renovations were planned
through 2000, although the hotel will remain open continually. The
metamorphosis of "Florissant", the building overlooking the pool and
gardens, was completed 1999. All other buildings are slated for over-
hauls to maintain their grand style and sumptuous decor. Personal ser-
vice from the attentive staff makes this the delightful antithesis of a
grand-hotel experience. Best of both worlds: guests may use the facil-
ities of the Beau-Rivage Palace next door. ⊠ *15 pl. du Port, CH-1006,*
☎ *021/6133434,* ⨎ *021/6133435. 60 rooms. 2 restaurants, bar, pool,
concierge, parking (fee). AE, DC, MC, V.*

$$$-$$$$ 🏨 **Royal Savoy.** Here you can not only stay in an enormous Victorian
castle but also enjoy a broad, private landscaped garden and park, with
outdoor swimming pool, terrace restaurant, and strolling musicians.
The rooms themselves are lovely—something more expensive hotels
sometimes seem unable to achieve—with florals and jewel tones, del-
icate period reproduction desks and chairs, and French doors that
open onto balconies over the lawns and lake. ⊠ *40 av. d'Ouchy, CH-
1000,* ☎ *021/6148888,* ⨎ *021/6148878. 99 rooms, 9 suites. 2 restau-
rants, bar, pool, exercise room, sauna. AE, DC, MC, V.*

$$$ 🏨 **Château d'Ouchy.** Here, you pay for the privilege of staying in a 12th-
century castle that was converted into a pseudo-medieval hotel in the
19th century. The interiors are dated-modern and a little faded. If you
really want medieval atmosphere, spring for the deluxe top tower
room ($$$$), which has wraparound views through Romanesque windows. There's a Parisian-style brasserie and a popular waterfront veranda with pasta and pizzas. ⊠ *2 pl. du Port, CH-1006,* ☎ *021/
6167451,* ⨎ *021/6175137. 36 rooms, 3 suites. 2 restaurants, bar, dance
club, free parking. AE, DC, MC, V.*

$$-$$$ 🏨 **Des Voyageurs.** In a narrow town house in the city center, this is a
comfortable, friendly hotel, with pleasant decor and impeccable maintenance. The rooms' modern stamp (modular, dormitory-like furniture
and computer/fax access) is tempered with Victorian details; the oak
stairways, stained glass, and period breakfast room individualize what
could have been an anonymous urban space. ⊠ *19 rue Grand-St-
Jean, CH-1003,* ☎ *021/3199111,* ⨎ *021/3199112. 33 rooms. Breakfast room, no-smoking rooms. AE, DC, MC, V.*

$$-$$$ 🏨 **Elite.** Directly uphill from the train station on a surprisingly quiet
street, this hotel is a tranquil little enclave. Most rooms have a view
of fruit trees and a garden; ask for a fourth-floor room for a spectacular lake view. Although the modular furnishings are standard, they're
warmed by the beige, peach, and rose color scheme. The hotel has been
in one family for 50 years, and it shows—from the solid renovation
and modern touches (electric doors, piped-in music) to the squeaky-
clean maintenance. There are kitchenettes available. ⊠ *1 av. Ste-Luce,
CH-1003,* ☎ *021/3202361,* ⨎ *021/3203963. 33 rooms, 1 suite.
Breakfast room, no-smoking rooms, free parking. AE, DC, MC, V.*

$$ 🏨 **City.** This once-faded urban hotel, at the hub of the downtown
★ crossroads, underwent a profound and daring renovation, transform-
ing itself from a steam-heated dinosaur into a spectacular architectural
showcase with curving chrome planes, a two-way escalator flanked by
a sleek waterfall, and breathtaking views of the city, especially from
the glassed-in breakfast room. Slick and soundproof, with fresh du-
vets, pink-tile baths, videos, hair dryers, and room service, the City is
a value-priced model for its peers. ⊠ *5 rue Caroline, CH-1007,* ☎ *021/*

3202141, FAX 021/3202149. *51 rooms. Breakfast room, in-room VCRs. AE, DC, MC, V.*

$$ 🖬 **Regina.** The best thing about this tiny lodging near the Old Town is the owners' friendly service; the couple spent over a decade in the United States, so the language barrier is nonexistent. The guest rooms are squared away with color-coordinated carpets and upholstery. Those in the back are quiet, with roofline views; although the rooms don't have bathtubs, they all have private bathrooms with showers. ⊠ *18 rue Grand-St-Jean, CH-1003,* ☎ *021/3202441,* FAX *021/3202529. 30 rooms. Breakfast room, free parking. MC, V.*

Nightlife and the Arts

Lausanne is one of the arts capitals of Switzerland, sharing with Geneva the **Orchestre de la Suisse Romande.** It also hosts the great ballet company of **Maurice Béjart** since his exodus from Brussels. The **Opéra de Lausanne** performs in its eponymous hall. The event seasons generally run from September to May; summer brings outdoor concerts and more casual events. For ticket outlets contact the Lausanne Convention and Tourist Office (☞ Visitor Information *in* Vaud A to Z, *below*). The tourist office's calendar of monthly events and the *Reg'art* (published bimonthly in French) give information on upcoming activities. Check out the daily newspaper *24 Heures* for listings as well.

BARS

One of the chicest and liveliest gathering spots in Lausanne is the **Café Beau-Rivage** (☎ 021/6133330), in the luxury hotel of the same name (☞ Dining and Lodging, *above*); there's an American-style bar, the wicker-and-marble decor of a Parisian brasserie, and live music nightly. There's also a tiny wine bar just inside the hotel's lower lobby entrance, where you can sip local or imported vintages. The Lausanne Palace (☞ Dining and Lodging, *above*) serves the after-hours crowd in **Le Bar du Palace** (☎ 021/3313131). The Royal Savoy (☞ Dining and Lodging, *above*) serves drinks at one end of its bowered garden restaurant, **La Terrasse** (☎ 021/6148888), throughout the warm season, with guitarists or small ensembles; its interior bar is an intimate, armchaired lounge.

CLASSICAL MUSIC

The **Opéra de Lausanne** (⊠ 12 av. du Théâtre, ☎ 021/3101600) performs in its eponymous hall. **Théâtre-Municipal Lausanne** (⊠ 12 av. du Théâtre, ☎ 021/3126433), like a tattered bomb shelter deep underground in the heart of Lausanne, is one of the city's central performance venues for concerts, opera, and ballet, including the riveting experiments of Maurice Béjart. The **Théâtre de Beaulieu** (⊠ 10 av. des Bergières, ☎ 021/6432111), right across from the Collection de l'Art Brut (☞ Exploring, *above*), hosts full-scale performances of orchestral music, opera, and dance in its larger hall; this is where the Orchestre de la Suisse Romande performs. The Orchestre de Chambre de Lausanne plays at the **Salle Métropole** (☎ 021/3111122).

DANCING

Since most nighttime activity is centered in the Flon or place St-François neighborhoods, it's easy to sample several hot spots. If you pass a crowded club where the music is to your taste, duck in—it's probably one of the happening locations too new or ephemeral to list. The popular **D Club** (⊠ 4 rue de Grand Pont, ☎ 021/3515142) is decked out with works of contemporary European sculptors. Inside the discotheque **La Griffe** (⊠ 2 pl. de la Gare, ☎ 021/3110262) you'll find a DJ, video screen, and light show. **Le Gibo** (⊠ Galeries St-François, ☎ 021/3120935) offers tropical atmosphere and dance music. The club crowd comes from as far away as Zürich and Basel for techno concerts and live performances at **Le Mad** (⊠ 23 rue de Genève, ☎ 021/3121122).

JAZZ CLUB

Le Chorus (⊠ 3 av. Mon Repos, ☎ 021/3232233) has a renowned jazz cellar and also serves food and drinks. For acoustical jazz, drop in at **Pianissimo** (⊠ Foyer du Théâtr'Onze, 11 rue des Deux-Marchés, ☎ 021/3120043).

NIGHTCLUBS

The Lausanne Palace's upscale **Brummell** (⊠ 7 rue du Grand-Chêne, ☎ 021/3120920) has Las Vegas–type dancing shows and a cabaret.

THEATER

Théâtre Kléber-Méleau (⊠ 9 chemin de l'Usine-à-Gaz, Lausanne-Malley, ☎ 021/6258400), at Vidy, offers a variety of French-language theater, old and new. **Théâtre Vidy-Lausanne** (⊠ 5 av. Émile-Jacques-Dalcroze, ☎ 021/61945445), also west of Lausanne's center, presents classical and contemporary theater in French.

Outdoor Activities and Sports

BIKING

Gare CFF de Lausanne (train station; ⊠ 1 pl. de la Gare, Baggage Service, ☎ 051/2242162) rents bikes; you must make a reservation at least one day in advance; in summer three days is recommended. For a lakefront ride, check out a set of wheels at **Kiosque d'Ouchy** (⊠ 2 pl. de la Navigation, ☎ 021/6162383).

SAILING

La Nautique (⊠ 1 pl. du Vieux-Port, ☎ 021/6160023) has a clubhouse, changing rooms, and a crane. The **École de Voile de Vidy** (⊠ Port de Vidy, ☎ 021/6179000) is a sailing school with rentals.

SKATING

Open-air skating rinks and rollerblade parks in the Lausanne area stay open from October to March. **Patinoire de Montchoisi** (⊠ 30 av. du Servan, ☎ 021/6161062) has 35,000 square ft of surface. **Patinoire de la Pontaise** (⊠ 11 rte. Plaines-du-Loup, ☎ 021/6484142) attracts urban crowds.

SWIMMING

In Lausanne, the pool **Piscine de Montchoisi** (⊠ 20 av. du Servan, ☎ 021/6161062) makes artificial waves; it's open from May through August. **Bellerive Beach** (⊠ 23 av. de Rhodanie, ☎ 021/6178131) has access to the lake and three pools, one Olympic-size, plus generous lawns and a self-service restaurant. The covered pool at **Mon-Repos** (⊠ 4 av. du Tribunal-Fédéral, ☎ 021/3234566) stays open all winter, closing only July–August.

Shopping

The main shopping circle centers on **place St-François, rue St-François, rue de Bourg,** and **rue du Grand-Pont.** Less expensive shopping is along **rue St-Laurent** and **rue de l'Ale.**

BOOKS

Librairie Payot (⊠ 4 pl. Pépinet, ☎ 021/3413331) carries mass-market French books and a good assortment in English.

DEPARTMENT STORES

Bon Génie (⊠ 10 pl. St-François, ☎ 021/3204811) has clusters of designer areas on several levels. The large department store **Globus** (⊠ rue Centrale at rue du Pont, ☎ 021/3429090) has splendid food halls on the basement level.

LINENS

Coupy (⊠ 4 Madeleine, ☎ 021/3127866) has a large selection of duvets, pillows, and linens. **Drafil** (⊠ pl. St-Laurent, ☎ 021/3235044) carries a lovely line of trousseau goods, all made in Suisse Romande. **Langenthal** (⊠ 8 rue de Bourg, ☎ 021/3234402) is the central source for towels, sheets, and embroidered handkerchiefs, mainly Swiss made.

MARKETS
There are fruit and vegetable markets in Lausanne along **rue de l'Ale, rue de Bourg,** and **place de la Riponne** every Wednesday and Saturday mornings. **Place de la Palud** adds a flea market to its Wednesday and Saturday produce market and is the site of a handicrafts market the first Friday of the month from March through December.

TOYS
Davidson Formation (⊠ 20 rue Grand St-Jean, ☎ 021/3232522) has a unique collection of educational toys and English-language books. **Franz Carl Weber** is the main Swiss source for international toys (⊠ 23 rue de Bourg, ☎ 021/3201471).

WATCHES
The place St-François has most of the watch shops. **Bucherer** (⊠ No. 5, ☎ 021/3206354) sells Rolex and Piaget. **Junod** (⊠ No. 8, ☎ 021/3122745) carries Blancpain. **Grumser** (⊠ 10 rue de Bourg, ☎ 021/3124826) specializes in Baume & Mercier. **Roman Mayer** (⊠ No. 12 bis, ☎ 021/3122316) carries Audemars Piguet, Ebel, and Omega.

LAVAUX VIGNOBLES AND MONTREUX

To the east of Lausanne stretches the Lavaux, a remarkably beautiful region of vineyards that rise up the hillsides all the way from Pully, on the outskirts of Lausanne, to Montreux—a distance of 24 km (15 mi). Brown-roof stone villages in the Savoy style, old defense towers, and small baronial castles stud the green-and-black landscape. The vineyards, enclosed within low stone walls, slope so steeply that all the work there has to be done by hand. Insecticides, fungicides, and manure are carried in baskets, and containers are strapped to men's backs. In early October pickers harvest the heavy, round fruit, carrying the loads to the nearest road, emptying them into vats, and driving them by tractor to the nearest press. Some Lavaux vintages are excellent and in great demand, but unfortunately, as with so much of Switzerland's wine, the yield is small, and the product is rarely exported. From May to October, especially on weekends, you'll find a wine-grower's cellar in every village and some of the private châteaux-vignobles open for tastings (and, of course, sales).

Cully

The cluster of businesses, homes, barns, and cellars in Cully epitomizes the Lavaux lifestyle. While it's not as picturesque as some lakeside or hill towns, in this narrow crossroads you can get a sense of what a vintner's life is really like, full of hard work and good eating. There are few reasons to stop, except the paramount one: to pause long enough to absorb the rich seasonality. The town is just off the Corniche Road.

En Route The scenic **Corniche Road** stretches some 17 km (10 mi) through Lavaux, threading above the waterfront from Lausanne to Vevey, between the autoroute and the lakeside Route 9. This is Switzerland at its most Franco-European, reminiscent in its small-scale way of the Riviera or the hill towns of Alsace. You'll career around hairpin turns on narrow cobbled streets, with the Savoy Alps glowing across the sparkling lake and the Dents du Midi looming ahead, hand-painted signs beckoning you to stop and taste the wines from the vineyards on either side of the road. Stop to gaze at roadside overlooks or wander down a side lane into the fields of **Riex, Epesses, Rivaz,** or the **Dézaley,** the sources of some of Switzerland's loveliest white wines and typically magical little Vaudois villages.

Dining and Lodging

$$$$ ✕⊞ **Auberge du Raisin.** Fashionably dressed families, romantic couples, and international business teams gather here to celebrate birthdays, weddings, and deal closings. In the center of the animated room, rotisserie hooks and spits twirl in a raised-hearth grill, as the chef seasons, times, and dispatches meats to the waiters. (Side dishes are synchronized in the kitchen.) The wine list is fittingly thorough with both local and French vintages. After dinner there's no need to budge; you can overnight in the auberge's guest rooms. Checked spreads cover the draped four-posters and the brightly painted armoires and chests are a change from the usual fruitwoods; some of the large baths have skylights. Reservations are essential for the restaurant. ⊠ *1 pl. de l'Ho*Ň*X*tags error: Unexpected end of lineŇ

St-Saphorin

19 *15 km (9 mi) southeast of Lausanne.*

At the end of the Corniche Road, just west of Vevey, St-Saphorin is perched just above the water. With its impossibly narrow, steep cobbled streets and ancient wine-makers' houses crowded around fountains and crooked alleys, this is a village that merits a stop. It lies along the ancient Roman highway, and its small church sits atop Roman foundations. There's a tiny museum of Roman artifacts (including a sizeable millstone) in the church. Go through the low door near the altar; you can see the museum whenever the church is unlocked and services are not being held. The guides are all in French, but even without a guide it's easy to chart the church's expansion through its ruins.

Dining

$$ ✕ **Auberge de l'Onde.** Once the main *relais* (stagecoach stop) between
★ the Simplon Pass and Geneva, this is a vineyard inn out of central casting, groaning with history and heady with atmosphere: Igor Stravinsky and Charlie Chaplin were among the artists loyal to its charms. The ambience is equally seductive in its tiny wood-panel café, where locals read the papers over a chipped pitcher of St-Saph, as they call it, and a plate of butter-fried lake perch, or in its dainty beamed dining room lined with ancient crockery and lighted with grape-wood sconces. Some regulars complain that the kitchen is not quite as good since management passed to the younger generation, but you can still get excellent, silver-platter service (two helpings) of very local *omble chevalier* (salmon trout) in sorrel sauce and bubbling hot fruit gratins. White-bloused waitresses hover with a good bottle of the local *récolte* (vintage) while day-tripping connoisseurs sniff and roll the almond-perfume wine over their tongues. ⊠ *St-Saphorin,* ☎ *021/9213083. AE, V. Closed mid-July–mid-Aug.*

Vevey

★ **20** *2 km (1 mi) east of St-Saphorin, 19 km (12 mi) east of Lausanne.*

This soigné waterfront town was the setting for Anita Brookner's evocative 1985 novel *Hotel du Lac,* about a woman retreating to a lake resort to write; her heroine was attracted to the site, in part, because of its slightly stuffy 19th-century ways. In the 1870s, Henry James captured this mood of prim grace while writing (and setting) *Daisy Miller* in the Hotel des Trois Couronnes. Indeed, despite its virtual twinning with glamorous Montreux, Vevey retains its air of isolation and Old World gentility. Loyal guests have been returning for generations to gaze at the **Dent d'Oche** (2,222 m/7,288 ft) across the water in France and make sedate steamer excursions into Montreux and Lausanne: today there are some who come just to see the bronze statue of Charlie Chaplin in the waterfront Rose Park and to take the funicular or mountain train up to Mont Pèlerin. Yet Vevey is a great walking town, with more character in its shuttered **Old Town,** better museums, landmarks, and shops, and more native activity in its wine market than cosmopolitan Montreux can muster.

Vevey is a marketing center for wines of the region, and the local white is sold in summer at its Saturday market on the waterfront, alongside fruits and vegetables; you buy your own glass and taste *à volonté* (at will). Vevey is also the hometown of Nestlé, the chocolate and milk products giant; its laboratories and world headquarters are based here.

Among the notables who have been drawn to Vevey as a place to live or merely to sojourn are Graham Greene, Victor Hugo, Jean-Jacques Rousseau (who set much of *La Nouvelle Heloise* here), Dostoyevsky, Gustave Courbet, Oskar Kokoschka, Charlie and Oona Chaplin (buried in the cemetery at Corsier), and Swiss native Édouard Jeanneret, known as Le Corbusier. By following an excellent brochure/map published by the tourist office, you can travel "On the Trail of Hemingway"—and to the homes and haunts of some 40 other luminaries.

★ Le Corbusier's **Villa le Lac,** a low-slung, single-story white house built directly on the Vevey waterfront, was constructed for his parents in 1923; it remains unaltered, with his original furnishings and details preserved within. Shingled in corrugated sheet metal, with a white-metal railed balcony looking over the water and a "birdhouse" chimney in molded concrete, it is typically sculptural and, in a modest way, visionary. ⊠ *On the western outskirts of Vevey, just west of the marina, Corseaux,* ☎ *021/9235371.* 🎫 *Free.* ⊙ *Guided tours May–Oct. Wed. 2–5.*

A controlling financial power in the region, Nestlé sponsors an unconventional museum in Vevey, the **Alimentarium.** This well-funded, unusually presented exhibition addresses three aspects of food and food production: science (the food chain), ethnology (food in different world cultures), and history (eating habits through the ages). Displays are in a grand 19th-century mansion; in addition, there are films, computers, and—if the subject matter makes you feel a bit hungry—a snack bar. There is an English-language guide, but most signs and interactive exhibits are in French, German, and Italian. ⊠ *Between quai Perdonnet and rue du Léman,* ☎ *021/9244111.* 🎫 *6 SF.* ⊙ *Tues.–Sun. 10–noon and 2–5.*

The **Musée Jenisch** owes its considerable inventory of the works of the Expressionist Oskar Kokoschka to his retirement on Vevey's shores. If it is strictly the Kokoschkas you want to see, they are not always on display. Advance arrangements can be made to view the holdings in the archives. The museum's partner wing, the **Cabinet Cantonal des Estampes** (Cantonal Print Collection) contains a rich assortment of engravings, including some by Dürer and Rembrandt. ⊠ *2 av. de la Gare,* ☎ *021/9212950,* 🎫 *8 SF–12 SF.* ⊙ *Tues.–Sun. 10:30–noon and 2–5:30.*

The **Musée Historique du Vieux Vevey** (Historical Museum of Old Vevey) occupies a grand 16th-century manor house, briefly home to Charlotte de Lengefeld, wife of Friedrich von Schiller. It retains some original furnishings as well as collections of arms, art, keys, and wine-making paraphernalia. The first floor serves as headquarters for the Brotherhood of Winegrowers, the organization that stages the mammoth Fêtes des Vignerons (Winegrowers' Festival). The festival is held roughly every

25 years; you can get a taste of the most recent celebration (1999) from the costumes, photographs, and memorabilia on display. ⊠ *2 rue du Château,* ☎ *021/9210722.* 🎫 *4 SF.* ☉ *Mar.–Oct., Tues.–Sun. 10:30–noon and 2–5:30; Nov.–Feb., Tues.–Sun. 2–5:30.*

The **Musée Suisse de l'Appareil Photographique** (Swiss Camera Museum) displays an impressive collection of cameras, photographic equipment, and mounted work. It also hosts "Images," a biennial, multimedia show next held in October 2000. ⊠ *6 Anciens-Fossés,* ☎ *021/9219460.* 🎫 *5 SF.* ☉ *Apr.–Oct., Tues.– Sun. 11–5:30; Nov.–Mar., Tues.–Sun., 2–5:30.*

Dining and Lodging

$$$$ ✕ **Restaurant Denis Martin Le Château.** Owner Denis Martin creates a chic, magnetic atmosphere here, attracting well-heeled locals and Nestlé executives. His seven-course "discovery" menu might lead off with duck liver with pineapple chutney and honey vinaigrette, followed by herbsteamed lobster and tomato confit. Only the chef knows what the dessert of the moment might be—no doubt, a splendidly sweet surprise for the palate. ⊠ *2 rue du Château, in cellar of Musée Historique du Vieux Vevey,* ☎ *021/9211210. Reservations essential. AE, DC, MC, V. Closed Sun.–Mon.*

$$–$$$ ✕ **Les Temps Modernes.** This alternative restaurant/club is named after the film starring Vevey's most famous resident, Charlie Chaplin. An artsy crowd mingles with buttoned-down financiers, and Chanel-suited ladies sit next to baggy-clothed skaters. The decor is equally mixed: an industrial space with flea-market-modern furniture. (Since the building is a converted factory it's difficult to heat; wear an extra layer in cold weather.) Menu selections are sophisticated and well-presented: rabbit fillet atop mixed greens with raspberry vinaigrette or breast of guinea hen with fresh lemon thyme definitely merit a try. The easy chairs around the open fireplace invite another round of grappa. The performance space is connected to the dining room by a wide hallway; one evening the beams pulse with hot Latin music, another the familiar rhythms of concert jazz. Open jam sessions and concerts pack the house. Admission to the club ranges from gratis to 20 SF, depending on the performer. ⊠ *6B rue des Deux Gares,* ☎ *021/9223439. No credit cards. Closed July–Aug.*

$–$$ ✕ **Café de La Clef "chez Manu."** Jean-Jacques Rousseau stayed here in 1730, making this café as much a landmark as the pillared marketplace in front of it. No one seems to mind the uninspired decor of tile floors, salmon-pink walls, and the odd potted palm; the locals line up for lunchtime tables to savor such well-prepared traditional specialties as fondue and *filets de perches* (perch fillets—for something different try them curried) along with *julienne de légumes au bouillon safrané* (fresh fish and vegetable soup with saffron). ⊠ *1 rue du Théâtre,* ☎ *021/9212245. MC, V. Closed Sun.*

$$$$ ✕▥ **Le Mirador.** Anchored on a ledge above Vevey, this combination
★ spa resort and elite conference center is set among the meadows and modest villages of Mont Pèlerin. Breathtaking, panoramic views encompass the lake, the Alps, and vineyards—it's easy to spend hours on the terrace absorbing it all. Once in your room, draw back the tasseled drapes for more peaks-and-water views. The luxurious spa has a wide-ranging treatment menu, from jet lag relief to skin care. The exercise facilities are equally extensive, including jogging trails, an indoor-outdoor pool, and a golf simulator. Amusing, lifelike sculptures of everyday people by American artist J. Seward Johnson are scattered around the property, though they seem a bit out of place among the traditional oil paintings and stained-glass windows. Guest privacy is closely guarded; you'll have to guess which celebrity or corporate chief

arrived by helicopter or commandeered the hotel's private yacht. Formal and casual meals with health-conscious options are served in separate, elegantly furnished restaurants or on the terrace. ⊠ *Mont Pèlerin, CH-1801,* ☎ *021/9251111,* FAX *021/9251112. 87 rooms, 15 suites. 2 restaurants, bar, in-room safes, minibars, VCRs, indoor-outdoor pool, beauty salon, spa, 2 tennis courts, health club, volleyball, library, concierge, business services, helipad, free parking. AE, DC, MC, V.*

$$$$ 🏨 **Des Trois Couronnes.** Honeycombed by dramatic atrium stairwells and thick with alabaster and faux marble, this regal landmark was Henry James's home base when he wrote (and set here) the novella *Daisy Miller.* (The antiheroine strayed unchaperoned to Chillon and, having thus flown in the face of Victorian propriety, met a richly deserved demise.) A vast lakefront terrace overlooks the pollards, the promenade, and the steamers that still carry their cargo of headstrong women toward Chillon. A change of ownership may continue the improvements needed to keep the grand old place up-to-date and justify its top-of-the-line rates. ⊠ *49 rue d'Italie, CH-1800,* ☎ *021/9213005,* FAX *021/9227280. 55 rooms, 10 suites. Restaurant, bar, café. AE, DC, MC, V.*

$$$-$$$$ 🏨 **Du Lac.** Anita Brookner set her novel *Hotel du Lac* in this lesser sister of the Trois Couronnes (☞ *above*): its readers may be disappointed to find the hotel lacking the discretion, refinement, and even the stuffiness she so precisely described. Instead, there are plenty of reminders that this is a link in the Best Western chain. Though some rooms are done in prim florals or chic burled wood, others retain the kelly-green carpet and mustard chenille of another era in decorating. Its location is the hotel's main attraction, as there are a sheltered terrace restaurant, garden, and pool all just across the street from the waterfront. ⊠ *1 rue d'Italie, CH-1800,* ☎ *021/9211041,* FAX *021/9217508. 56 rooms. Restaurant, café, pool, parking (fee). AE, DC, MC, V.*

$$$-$$$$ 🏨 **Hotel Pavillon.** The best of old and new can be found here. Nineteen-twenties frescoes of a winegrowers' festival cover the ceiling of La Brasserie, the old-fashioned restaurant, while a new annex of guest rooms is wired with up-to-the-minute technology (ISDN lines, fax connections, and acoustical insulation). The colors are strong—plaid spreads and geometric print draperies in bold orange and red, cherry furniture, carpets dominated by dark green or blue. The fifteen older rooms are comfortably furnished in subdued aqua and pink stripes with multi-colored rattan; they do not have air conditioning. The hotel is adjacent to the train station, making it convenient for early departures. ⊠ *pl. de la Gare, CH-1800,* ☎ *021/9236161,* FAX *021/9211477. 80 rooms, 5 suites. 2 restaurants, bar, snack bar, exercise room, parking (fee). AE, DC, MC, V.*

$-$$ 🏨 **Des Négociants.** Handy to the market, by the lake, this is a comfortable, no-nonsense lodging. Its arcaded, shuttered facade is in sharp contrast to the laminated, foursquare interiors, but the top floor has a dormer room of knotty pine that is suitable for families, and all baths are tiled. ⊠ *27 rue du Conseil, CH-1800,* ☎ *021/9227011,* FAX *021/ 9213424. 23 rooms. Restaurant. AE, DC, MC, V.*

Outdoor Activities and Sports

Interconnected **hiking trails** (signposted in several languages including English with informative tidbits) span the length of the shore from Ouchy to Chillon, traversing vineyards and traffic arteries from the lakefront to hillside villages. Walking the entire 32-km (19-mi) *parcours viticole* takes about eight and a half hours, but you can also break it into smaller segments—and allow time for wine tastings. (If you're doing a portion of the trail, you can easily catch a train back to your starting point, as there are hourly stops in nearly every village.) Speaking of trains, if the distance and grade of the trails seem too much, you can take the bright yellow coaches of the **Train des Vignes** (vineyard train) through the rows of pinot noir, gamay, and chasselas vines. The train starts from Vevey's station near the waterfront and ends more than 2,000 feet above sea level in the village of Puidoux-Chexbres; its timetable is part of the regular CFF schedule.

Montreux

㉑ *4 km (2 mi) southeast of Vevey, 21 km (13 mi) southeast of Lausanne.*

Petite Montreux could be called the Cannes of Lake Geneva—though it might raise an eyebrow at the slur. Spilling down steep hillsides into a sunny south-facing bay, its waterfront thick with magnolias, cypresses, and palm trees, the historic resort earns its reputation as the capital—if not the pearl—of the Swiss Riviera. Unlike the French Riviera, it has managed, despite overwhelming crowds of conventioneers, to keep up appearances. Its Edwardian-French deportment has survived considerable development, and though there are plenty of harsh new high-rises with parking-garage aesthetics, its mansarded landmarks still unfurl orange awnings to shield millionaires from the sun.

The site where Stravinsky composed *Petrouchka* and *Le Sacre du Printemps* and where Vladimir Nabokov resided in splendor, Montreux and its suburbs have attracted artists and literati for 200 years: Byron, Shelley, Tolstoy, Hans Christian Andersen, and Flaubert were drawn to its lush shoreline. When its casino opened in 1883, tourism began in earnest. Today, Montreux is best known for its history-making Montreux Jazz Festival, which takes place each July; with Vevey, it also sponsors a Festival International de Musique (International Festival of Music) in September.

★ ㉒ Certainly the greatest attraction at Montreux and one of Switzerland's must-sees is the **Château de Chillon,** the awe-inspiring 12th-century castle that rears out of the water at Veytaux, just down the road from and within sight of Montreux. Chillon was built on Roman foundations under the direction of Duke Peter of Savoy with the help of military architects from Plantagenet England. For a long period it served as a state prison, and one of its shackled guests was François Bonivard, who supported the Reformation and enraged the Savoyards. He spent six years in this prison, chained most of the time to a pillar in the dungeon, before being released by the Bernese in 1536.

While living near Montreux, Lord Byron visited Chillon and was so transported by its atmosphere and by Bonivard's grim sojourn that he was inspired to write his famous poem *The Prisoner of Chillon.* He charts the prisoner's despair and brief moments of hope, culminating in the realization on release that "These heavy walls to me had grown/A hermitage—and all my own!/ . . .So much a long communion tends/To make us what we are:—even I/Regain'd my freedom with a sigh." Like a true tourist, Byron carved his name on a pillar in Bonivard's still-damp and chilly dungeon; his graffito is now protected under a plaque.

In high season, visitors to Chillon must now file placidly from restored chamber to restored turret, often waiting at doorways for entire busloads of fellow tourists to pass. Yet the restoration is so evocative and so convincing, with its tapestries, carved fireplaces, period ceramics and pewter, and elaborate wooden ceilings, that even the jaded castle hound may become as carried away as Byron was. While you're waiting your turn, you can gaze out the narrow windows over the sparkling, lapping water and remember Mark Twain, who thought Bonivard didn't have it half bad. ⊠ *CH-1820 Veytaux, less than 3 km/2 mi south of Montreux,* ☎ *021/9633912.* ⊒ *7 SF.* ⊙ *Nov.–Feb., daily 10–noon and*

1:30–4; Mar. and Oct., daily 10–noon and 1:30–4:45; Apr.–June and Sept., daily 9–5:45; July–Aug., daily 9–6:15.

NEED A
BREAK?

Follow the lunch crowd that regularly descends on **Zurcher** (⌂ 45 av. du Casino, ☎ 021/9635963), the irresistible *confiserie* on Montreux's main drag. A green salad, the *potage du jour* (soup of the day), and a chocolate-striated torte make a great quick meal. The café is closed on Monday.

Dining and Lodging

$$$$ ✕ **Le Pont de Brent.** Tucked on a hillside next to its namesake bridge
★   in the unassuming Montreux suburb of Brent, this small but elegant establishment ties with Philippe Rochat's restaurant for the honor of the best table in Switzerland. Who would guess that the green-shuttered windows and pale stone exterior of this unassuming building screen showstopping cuisine? Norman chef Gérard Rabaey performs alchemy with local ingredients to turn out dishes almost too pretty to eat: pastry filled with frogs' legs, truffles, and celery root, lobster and scallop lasagne with parsley jus, caramelized pears with honey ice cream. All is warm here, from the ocher walls to the welcome and service. ⌂ *Rte. de Brent, 7 km/4½ mi northwest of Montreux, Brent,* ☎ *021/9645230. Reservations essential. MC, V. Closed Sun. and Mon., last 2 wks of July, late Dec.–early Jan.*

$$ ✕ **Du Pont.** In the Old Town high on the hill over Montreux's waterfront, this bustling, old restaurant-café takes its food and its customers seriously. You can relax in the smoky café (where jeans aren't out of place) or enjoy full service and pink linens in the lovely dining room upstairs. Suit your whim: the menu and the prices are exactly the same, including a cheap daily special—and whether you order them upstairs or down, the German-born chef (who spent years in Italy) will personally grate your white Alba truffle. ⌂ *12 rue du Pont,* ☎ *021/9632249. AE, DC, MC, V.*

$$$$ ✕▥ **L'Ermitage.** Freestanding on its own waterfront-garden grounds,
★   this genteel, intimate retreat offers top-drawer *haute gastronomie* and a few luxurious rooms upstairs. The guest rooms are lightened with fresh flowers, lacquered cane furniture, and lake views; many rooms have balconies. Chef Étienne Krebs's exceptional menu may include cannelloni of rabbit stuffed with foie gras, fillet of veal with turnip tagliatelle and truffles, or pineapple fritters with ginger ice cream. The ultimate splurge: his seven-course "let yourself go" menu, a parade of delicately orchestrated surprises. The main restaurant is closed Sunday and Monday; there's a terrace for alfresco dining open daily in summer. ⌂ *75 rue du Lac, CH-1815,* ☎ *022/9644411,* ℻ *021/9647002. 7 rooms. AE, DC, MC, V. Free parking. Closed late Dec.–late Jan.*

$$$–$$$$ ✕▥ **Hôtel Victoria.** Noël Coward stayed in Room 49 some 40 years
★   ago while his chalet was being renovated in nearby Les Avants (the playwright had a penchant for high places). Since 1869, this superb Relais & Châteaux hotel set in its own park in the heights of Glion above Montreux has drawn its share of celebrities and royalty, who come not to be seen but to see the glories of the lake from this unique vantage point—and to be pampered without pomposity. The current owner oversees every detail from the foot-high down seat cushions in the grand salon to the hand-painted stenciling in the corridors and the freshly cut flowers everywhere. The dining room could be a Coward stage set, its opulence tempered by the occasional eccentric guest. Room decor mixes fine art with soothing pastels, swish amenities, and often a balcony. A lap pool, a lighted tennis court, and a French restaurant serving excellent light cuisine complete this elegant country-house fantasy. ⌂ *CH-1823 Glion,* ☎ *021/9633131,* ℻ *021/9631351. 50 rooms, 9*

suites. Restaurant, bar, breakfast room, minibars, pool, tennis court, sauna, exercise room, piano, library. AE, DC, MC, V.

$$$$ 🏨 **Le Montreux Palace.** Dominating the hillside over the Grand-rue and
★ the waterfront, the silver mansards and yellow awnings of this vast institution flag the Palace as a landmark, though its aristocratic interiors are now filled with cell-phone-chatting travelers. It was first opened in 1906, a colossal Belle Epoque folly of stained glass, frescoes, and flamboyant molded stucco. Author Vladimir Nabokov lived among the furbelows for almost 20 years at the end of his life. Much of that excess has been tempered with age and updated with touches of modern tastefulness, including a grand marble staircase connecting the porte cochere with the upper-level main lobby and a modern shopping arcade. Across the street is the hotel's pavilion (Le Petit Palais) with a large conference center, a British tea room, a nightclub, a cyber-café, and Switzerland's first Harry's New York bar. Lakeside rooms are appropriately posh; mountainside rooms, in the back, miss out on the hotel's raison d'être: a commanding Lake Geneva view. Reservations are recommended in all restaurants; a jacket and tie are required in La Veranda. ⊠ *10 Grand-rue, CH-1820,* ☎ *021/9621212,* ℻ *021/9621717. 210 rooms, 25 suites. 4 restaurants, 2 bars, in-room data ports, in-room safes, no-smoking rooms, pool, beauty salon, tennis court, exercise room, concierge, convention center. AE, DC, MC, V.*

$$$–$$$$ 🏨 **Hotel Righi Vaudois.** Ascend in a funicular from Veytaux for a stay 700 m (2,300 ft) above Montreux. From the wraparound porch of this 1860s country house you'll have a different experience of the often touristy resort town—this is a quiet neighborhood. Ruby Oriental runners on buffed parquet lead through genteel salons with cushiony sofas and marble fireplaces. There are also acres of private gardens to explore. Antiques, botanical prints, and English country–style accents appoint the guest rooms; the spacious, modern baths shine with polished tile. ⊠ *Glion-sur-Montreux, CH-1823,* ☎ *021/9611881,* ℻ *021/9611512. 48 rooms, 10 suites. Restaurant, bar, tennis court, free parking. AE, DC, MC, V.*

$$–$$$ 🏨 **Hôtel Villa Toscane.** Looking out on the sleek, glass-paneled Auditorium Stravinski, this *garni* hotel (without restaurant) stays on the side of homey, not fussy. The building is a turn-of-the-century villa; stained-glass windows filter light into the mahogany stairwell. Sitting areas, fireplaces, and kitchenettes in the larger rooms make longer stays more comfortable. Salmon and gray decor is spruced up with Tiffany lamps and black-accented, burl-wood desks and cabinetry. The portable air-conditioning units look like small jukeboxes. ⊠ *2–8 rue du Lac, CH-1820,* ☎ *021/9638426,* ℻ *021/9638421. 39 rooms, 4 suites, 1 apartment. Breakfast room, bar, sauna, free parking. AE, DC, MC, V.*

$$ 🏨 **Masson.** If you're traveling by car or enjoy being away from the down-
★ town resort scene, look up this demure little inn on a hillside in Veytaux, between Chillon and Montreux. Since it was built in 1829, it's had only four owners, and the current family takes pride in its genteel period decor and up-to-date technology, including color television with remote headphones so one guest won't disturb another. There are floral prints, brass beds, pristine linens, buffed parquet, and expansive lake views from the numerous balconies. The breakfast buffet is generous, with homemade breads and jams. ⊠ *5 rue Bonivard, CH-1820 Veytaux,* ☎ *021/9660044,* ℻ *021/9660036. 35 rooms. Restaurant. AE, MC, V. Closed early Nov.–mid-Mar.*

Nightlife and the Arts

Montreux's famous festivals and arts events are listed in a seasonal booklet published by the tourist office; tickets are sold from its booth at the waterfront. The renowned **Montreux Jazz Festival** takes place every

July in the ultramodern Auditorium Stravinski (⊠ 95 Grand-rue). The more sedate, classical **Festival International de Musique** (International Festival of Music) shares venues with Vevey from August through September; it's also held in the Auditorium Stravinski. For tickets to these popular events, contact their **ticket office** (☎ 021/9622119) as far in advance as possible (although the schedule is not released until May). In summer, Montreux offers a variety of free outdoor concerts from its bandstand on the waterfront near the landing stage.

BARS

The **Montreux Palace** (☞ Dining and Lodging, *above*) has a swank **Harry's New York Bar** with a pianist after 5. The **Royal Plaza** (⊠ 97 Grand-rue, ☎ 021/9635131) has a piano bar with jazz in the summer and an American-style bar in the lobby.

CASINO

The **Casino** (⊠ 9 rue du Théâtre, ☎ 021/9628383) at Montreux, established in 1883, was burned in 1971 and rebuilt in 1975; now you'll find dancing, slot machines, a billiards room, and an ethnic restaurant. A 5 SF gambling limit applies.

DANCING

A DJ spins at the **Backstage Club** (⊠ 100 Grand-rue, ☎ 021/9633444), Montreux's hottest scene for dancing. You can glide along the lake as you dance on the **Bateau Dansant,** (☎ 084/8811848), which departs from the landing stage on Wednesday at 7:25 PM and 9 PM throughout July and August.

Outdoor Activities and Sports

SAILING AND WATER SPORTS

Pedal boats are popular along Montreux-Vevey's waterfront. Rentals are available at **Albert Morisod** (⊠ By the convention center, ☎ 021/9633936). **Jean Morisod** (⊠ At the quai du Casino, ☎ 021/9633160) also rents them.

Cercle de la Voile de Montreux (⊠ Clarens, ☎ 021/9604171) is the local sailing club. Montreux offers guests of its hotels free and supervised use of its waterfront facilities for windsurfing and waterskiing; afternoons, there's a fee at the **Ski-Nautique Club** (☎ 021/9634456).

La Maladaire (☎ 021/9645703) in adjoining Clarens has an Olympic-size indoor pool. The **Casino** (⊠ 9 rue du Théâtre, ☎ 021/9628383) has a pool on an outdoor terrace with a bar.

OFF THE BEATEN PATH

BLONAY–CHAMBY RAILROAD – The allure for travelers to Montreux is not limited to the shoreline scene. Out of Montreux, a number of railways climb into the heights, which, in late spring, are carpeted with an extravagance of wild narcissi. If you like model railroads, you will especially enjoy a trip on the Blonay–Chamby Railroad line, whose real steam-driven trains alternate with electric trains on weekends only between Blonay and Chamby above Montreux, with a stop at a small museum of railroad history in between. You can depart from either end; the trip takes about 20 minutes each way, not including a browse in the museum. ⊠ *Case Postale 366, CH-1001 Lausanne,* ☎ *021/9432121.* 🎫 *Round-trip ticket 12 SF.* 🕙 *Trains run May–Oct., Sun. 9:40–6 and Sat. 2–6.*

LES AVANTS – The Montreux–Oberland–Bernois Railroad (MOB) line leads to the resort village of Les Avants (970 m/3,181 ft)—and then on to Château-d'Oex, Gstaad, and the Simmental. Noël Coward bought his dream home in Les Avants, at No. 8, Route de Sonloup; Ernest Hemingway wrote to his family and friends of its fields of daffodils—and, more in character, of its bobsled track.

LES ALPES VAUDOISES

At the eastern tip of Lake Geneva, the Alps on the French and Swiss sides close in on the Rhône, and the lakefront highways begin a gradual, ear-popping ascent as the scenery looms larger and the mountains rise around you. The high-altitude Alpine resorts of Villars-Gryon, Leysin, and Les Diablerets each have their charms for winter-sports fans and summer hikers; a visit to any one of the three would suffice for a mountain retreat. On the other hand, the Pays-d'Enhaut, over the Col des Mosses, is a rustic, lower-altitude region surrounded by rocky ridges and velvet hillsides sprinkled with ancient carved-wood chalets; either Château-d'Oex or Rougemont would serve well as home base for a sojourn in this gentle resort area. You can make a beeline from one to another, but rail connections are limited and driving often torturous; you'd do well to choose one dreamy spot and stay put—by the fireplace, on the balcony—for as many days as your itinerary allows.

The resorts of the Vaud Alps, although anything but household words to most ski buffs, offer the bonus of a transportation linkup and lift-ticket package with the sprawling Gstaad "Super-Ski" region (☞ Chapter 10). This skiing mecca takes in the entire Saanen Valley from Zweisimmen to Château-d'Oex and even dovetails with the parallel valley resorts of Adelboden and Lenk, justifying a visit for skiers who want to cover a lot of territory during their stay.

Aigle

㉓ *17 km (10 mi) south of Montreux, 38 km (24 mi) southeast of Lausanne.*

On a smooth plain flanked by the sloping vineyards of the region of Le Chablais, Aigle is a scenic wine center. Its spired and turreted **Château de Savoie,** originally built in the 13th century, was almost completely destroyed—and then rebuilt—by the 15th-century Bernese.

The **Musée de la Vigne et du Vin** (Museum of Viticulture and Wine), in the Château d'Aigle, displays casks, bottles, presses, and wine-makers' tools within its wood-beam chambers. Some living quarters are reproduced, and there's even a collection of costumes worn over the centuries at the local Fête des Vignerons. ⊠ *Château d'Aigle,* ☎ *024/4662130.* ⊡ *8 SF, 9 SF combination ticket with International Museum of Wine Labels.* ☉ *Apr.–June and Sept.–Oct., Tues.–Sun. 10–12:30 and 2–6; July–Aug., daily 10–6; Nov.–Mar., tours by appointment.*

A timbered attic in an adjacent warehouse shelters a separate museum, the **International Museum of Wine Labels,** which chronicles a history of prestigious vintages in its collection of labels from more than 50 countries dating back 200 years. ⊠ *Maison de la Dîme,* ☎ *024/4662130.* ⊡ *4 SF, 9 SF combination ticket with Museum of Viticulture and Wine.* ☉ *Apr.–June and Sept.–Oct., Tues.–Fri. 10–12:30 and 2–6, Sat. 9–noon; July–Aug., Tues.–Fri. 10–6, Sat. 9–noon.*

Chasselas grapes are cultivated on the steep shale and sandstone terraces by Aigle and Yvorne; these local wines flare with exuberance. Generations of the Badoux family have tended the land around Aigle held by *murailles* (stone walls), producing a signature wine identified by the lizard on the label. Their **La Boutique des Grands Vins,** a lovely wine shop, is just the place to scout a local find. Browse the shelves for select vintages, etched decanters, and corkscrews. ⊠ *18 av. du Chamossaire,* ☎ *024/4686885.* ☉ *Weekdays 8–noon, 1:30–6; Sat. 8–noon.*

OFF THE   **SWISS VAPEUR PARC** – Where the Rhône empties into Lake Geneva, be-
BEATEN PATH   tween Vaud and France, families may want to visit the Swiss Vapeur
         ☙   Parc (Swiss Steam Park), a miniature railway circuit laid out in a green
                 park. There you can straddle the tiny models and cruise around a re-
                 duced-scale landscape. It also includes a full-blown waterpark. ☒ *CH-
                 1897 Le Bouveret,* ☎ *024/4814410.* ☒ *10 SF. Mid-May–late Sept.,
                 weekdays 1:30–6, weekends 10–6; late Apr.–mid-May and late Sept.–
                 Oct., Wed. and weekends 1:30–6.*

En Route   At **Roche,** on the highway between Villeneuve and Aigle, there's a
            massive 15th-century stone barn that was built by the monks of Grand
            St-Bernard, on a scale as big as an airplane hangar, and divided into
            three great pillared naves. The building itself would be worth the de-
            tour, but today—after extensive restorations—it houses the **Musée Su-
            isse de l'Orgue** (Swiss Organ Museum), a vast collection of instruments
            that had been without the cathedral-scale space required for display
            until it arrived in this gargantuan barn. There's an ornate Louis XVI
            organ case, an 18th-century pedal board, a neo-Gothic harmonium,
            and even an Emmental home organ. The curator leads three one-hour
            tours a day (in French) and demonstrates the instruments. ☎ *021/
            9602200.* ☒ *5 SF.* ☉ *May–Oct., Tues.–Sun. 10–noon and 2–5.*

Villars-Gryon

★ ㉔ *15 km (9 mi) southeast of Aigle, 53 km (33 mi) southeast of Lausanne.*

At 1,300 m (4,264 ft), this welcoming ski center spreads comfortably
along a sunny terrace, the craggy peaks of Les Diablerets (3,210
m/10,528 ft) behind it and before it a sweeping view over the Rhône
Valley all the way to Mont Blanc. Balanced along its ridge and open
to the vast space below, its busy little downtown—sports shops, cafés,
resort hotels—tapers off quickly into open country. Though it's thriving with new construction, Villars retains a sense of coziness and tradition, and some of its family-owned hotels have preserved the feel of
mountain lodges that's rare these days in Switzerland. What Villars lacks
in glitz, it amply compensates for with unpretentious good cheer. A network of lifts connecting with Les Diablerets make this a good choice
for skiers or hikers who want to experience Suisse Romande relatively
unspoiled. The boarding schools headquartered in the area keep the
town animated with teen adrenaline, backing sports like snowboarding, mountain biking, in-line skating, and rock climbing.

Skiing

For serious skiers, Villars itself nicely balances sophistication and
Alpine isolation, offering some of the best-developed options and including a new and very accessible link to **Les Diablerets Glacier.** The
main ski area over the village can be reached easily either by cable car
to **Roc d'Orsay** (2,000 m/6,560 ft) or by cog railway from the center
to **Bretaye;** either site allows access to the lifts that fan out over a sunny
bowl riddled with intermediate runs and off-trail challenges. From Bretaye, you can also take lifts up to **Grand Chamossaire** (2,120 m/6,954
ft) for gentle, open runs. Trails from **Chaux Ronde** and **Chaux de
Conches** are easy enough for beginners, but the more advanced can
find jumps and trees enough to keep them more than alert. Just beyond Villars, the linking resort of **Gryon** presents a few more options
and a change of scenery, again with trails for all levels of skill. **Villars**
itself has 45 lifts, 120 km (75 mi) of downhill runs (including the Diablerets Glacier), and 44 km (27 mi) of cross-country trails.

Dining and Lodging

$–$$ ✕ **Le Refuge de Frience.** A few scenic kilometers from Villars en route
★ to Gryon, this 18th-century Heidi-esque chalet combines the grist of
Alpine legend with good, honest food. Three cheery rooms glowing
with log fires under low, beamed ceilings give way to unfettered views
of the mountains and, in summer, of cows roaming the slopes. You won't
see tourists here; it's a word-of-mouth place that packs in locals and
weekend expats in the know. They go for the fondue and raclette, river
trout, and plates of fresh regional mushrooms—and wine spouting from
an old *fontaine,* a wrought-iron contraption rarely seen in restaurants.
⊠ *Alpe des Chaux, 4½ km (3 mi) from Villars,* ☎ *024/4981426. MC,
V. Closed Tues. and Apr.–May.*

$$$–$$$$ ☒ **Le Bristol.** This resort hotel, the poshest in town, rose from the ashes
of an older landmark and—despite the Colorado-condo exterior and
the jutting balcony for every room—is now furnished with a light, bright,
and convincingly regional touch. The interiors are mostly white with
mauve touches and carved blond pine, and picture windows are an-
gled to take in the views. There are good health facilities and a choice
of attractive restaurants, including a terrace above the valley. ⊠ *av.
Centrale, CH-1884,* ☎ *024/4963636,* FAX *024/4963637. 87 rooms, 23
suites. 2 restaurants, bar, indoor pool, hot tub, sauna, exercise room,
squash. AE, DC, MC, V.*

$$ ☒ **Alpe Fleurie.** From the minute you check in, you'll know this is a
family-run, family-oriented hotel: there are faded snapshots of children
and dogs over the reception desk. Launched in 1946, this chalet-hotel
has been updated steadily, and the rooms show a thoughtful mix of
modern textures and classic pine. It stands on the valley side of the main
street, and south-facing rooms have terrific views. Local residents hit
the restaurant for their favorite Vaudoise specialties. ⊠ *av. Centrale,
CH-1884,* ☎ *024/4953464,* FAX *024/4963077. 17 rooms, 2 suites.
Restaurant, bar, café. AE, DC, MC, V.*

$$ ☒ **La Renardière.** This group of three classic chalets, set back from the
resort center and surrounded by tall firs, hasn't budged from its '50s
mountain lodge identity; it's still got its golden pine, plaid curtains, and
log bar. The lounges and sitting areas have fireplaces; the rooms are
simple, done in pine and chenille, with the customary color scheme of
orange and brown. In the traditional restaurant, linens, crystal, and
fresh flowers soften the rustic edges, and there's an agreeable terrace
café that serves good lunches under the firs. ⊠ *rte. des Liyeux, CH-
1884,* ☎ *024/4952592,* FAX *024/4953915. 20 rooms, 5 suites. Restau-
rant, bar, café. AE, DC, MC, V.*

$ ☒ **Écureuil.** Although there's a restaurant downstairs and a carnotzet
for fondue, nearly every room in this warm, family-run inn has a
kitchenette, so you can make yourself at home, mountain cabin–style.
Opened in 1947 and now run by the son of the founder, the hotel has
lots of homey touches: books and magazines, swing sets, and a piano
parlor. An older, stone-base chalet on the grounds offers bigger rooms;
both buildings stand across the street from the Bristol and therefore
don't have direct access to those Villars views. ⊠ *av. Centrale, CH-
1884,* ☎ *024/4952795,* FAX *024/4954205. 27 rooms. Restaurant, café,
Ping-Pong, free parking. MC, V.*

Outdoor Activities and Sports

GOLF
Precipitously sited, the **Golf Club Villars,** open June to October, (⊠ av.
Central, ☎ 024/4954214) has 18 holes.

SKATING
Nonskiers can amuse themselves at a centrally located indoor **skating
rink** (⊠ Chemin de la Gare, ☎ 024/4951221).

SWIMMING

In the same building as the skating rink in Villars, there's an **indoor pool** (☎ 024/4951221). There's an outdoor pool at **New Sporting Club** (⊠ Rte. du Col de la Croix, ☎ 024/4953030).

OFF THE BEATEN PATH

MINE DU SEL – Children inured to the thrill of cable cars, narrow-gauge railroads, and steam trains might brighten at a journey to the center of the earth in the Mine du Sel (Salt Mine) at Bex, just off the south-bound Route 9. First dug in 1684, this ancient underground complex bores into the mountain as far as Villars and covers some 50 subterranean km (30 mi). After an introductory audiovisual show, you ride a narrow-gauge train into the depths and take a guided walk through the works. Wear sturdy shoes and warm clothing as the temperature stays at 63°F (17°C) year-round. ⊠ CH-1880 Bex, ☎ 024/4630330. *15 SF. Prior booking essential, even for individuals.* ☉ Apr.–mid-Nov., with 2¼-hr-long tours leaving daily at 10, 2, and 3.

Les Diablerets

㉕ *19 km (12 mi) northeast of Aigle, 59 km (37 mi) southwest of Lausanne.*

In summer, car travelers can cut along spectacular heights on a tiny 13%-grade road over the Col de la Croix (1,778 m/5,832 ft) to get from Villars to the small neighboring resort of Les Diablerets (1,160 m/3,806 ft). Train travelers will have to descend to Bex and backtrack to Aigle. Les Diablerets lies at the base of the 3,209-m (10,525-ft) peak of the same name—which sheds the dramatic namesake 3,000-m (9,840-ft) glacier. The village was named after the folklore tale of devils that played skittle among the desolate glacier peaks. The compact handful of hotels, shops, and steep-roofed chalets is strung along a winding road. The valley brightens only when sun finds its way over crags and crests, which may be why skiing is guaranteed year round and the Swiss team trains here in summer.

Skiing

The connection of Les Diableret's ski facilities with those of Villars adds considerably to ski options—including summer skiing on the glacier itself and some dramatic intermediate peak-top runs at **Quille du Diable** and **Scex Rouge.** There's one gravity-defying expert slope, directly under the gondola, from **Pierre-Pointes** back to the valley. From Scex Rouge, a popular run carries you around the top of the **Oldenhorn** and down to **Oldenegg,** a wide-open intermediate run through a sheltered valley. At 1,250 m (4,100 ft), **Les Diablerets** has six cable cars, 18 lifts, 120 km (75 mi) of downhill runs, 30 km (19 mi) of cross-country trails, and 6 km (4 mi) of prepared tobogganing trails. Lift tickets cost 49 SF for a one-day pass, 233 SF for a six-day pass. (Reduced family prices are available.)

Dining and Lodging

$$–$$$ ✕⊞ **Grand-Hôtel.** Carved wooden eaves and ornate balconies frame this chalet-style hotel. It practically breathes Alpine ambience, from the heavy, carved, blonde-wood furniture to the starched, white, mile-high duvets. The café and brasserie are true to type, serving traditional cheese dishes. The hotel is just minutes from the lifts—and it has outstanding, inspiring views. ⊠ *chemin du Vernex, CH-1865,* ☎ *024/4923551,* FAX *024/4922391. 60 rooms, 4 suites. Restaurant, café, bar, minibars, indoor pool, parking (fee). AE, DC, MC, V. Closed late Apr.–Jun., Oct.–Nov.*

Leysin

㉖ *16 km (10 mi) northeast of Aigle, 54 km (33 mi) southeast of Lausanne.*

From the switchback highway A11, a small mountain road leads up to this family resort, which has easy skiing and a spectacular, sunny plateau setting and looks directly onto the Dents du Midi.

Skiing

Small-scale and cozy, Leysin offers a widespread network of lifts that allows you to cover a lot of varied ground on easy-to-medium slopes. From Berneuse, a peak 6,720 ft above Leysin, you can muster up your courage in the revolving restaurant and head for the **Chaux de Mont** (2,200 m/7,216 ft), where an expert run winds along a razorback ridge and through the forests to town. At 1,250 m (4,100 ft), Leysin has two cable cars, 18 lifts, a shuttle train, and 60 km (37 mi) of ski runs, as well as skating, curling, ski bob, and 36 km (22 mi) of cross-country trails. Snowboarding hotshots swarm the slopes; Leysin is home to the European championships.

PAYS-D'ENHAUT

Separated from the high-altitude Alpine resorts by the modest Col des Mosses (1,445 m/4,740 ft) and isolated, high-altitude family ski centers (Les Mosses, La Lécherette), the Pays-d'Enhaut (Highlands) offers an entirely different culture from that of its Vaud cousins. Here the architecture begins to resemble that of the Berner Oberland, which it borders: deep-eaved wooden chalets replace the Edwardian structures of the lakelands, and the atmosphere takes on a mountain-farm air. The Pays-d'Enhaut once belonged to Gruyères, then was seized by Bern; when Vaud was declared a canton, the Pays-d'Enhaut went with it. A stone's throw up the valley, you cross the Sarine/Saanen and the so-called Rösti Border, where the culture and language switch to Bernese German. This is still Gruyère cheese country and also the source of one of Switzerland's most familiar decorative arts: *papier découpé*, delicate, symmetrical paper cutouts. They are cut in black, often with simple imagery of cattle and farmers, and fixed on white paper for contrast. The real thing is a refined craft and is priced accordingly, but attractive prints reproducing the look are on sale at reduced prices throughout the region.

L'Etivaz

27 *21 km (13 mi) northeast of Aigle, 59 km (37 mi) southeast of Lausanne.*

Visitors to the Pays-d'Enhaut who cross the Col des Mosses first pass through the village of L'Etivaz, where a Gruyère-style cheese is made from milk drawn exclusively from cows grazed on pastures of elevations between 1,000 m and 2,200 m (3,280 ft and 7,216 ft). The sweet, late-blooming flowers they eat impart a flavor that lowland cheeses can't approach. The very best L'Etivaz cheese—*Rebibes*—is aged for three years in the cooperative here until it dries and hardens to a Parmesan-like texture; then it's shaved into curls and eaten by hand. Feel free to stop in at the **cooperative**; one of the workers in rubber boots will be happy to sell you brick-size chunks of both young and old cheeses at prices well below those at resort groceries.

Dining and Lodging

$ ✕🏨 **Du Chamois.** For four generations, a single family has coddled guests
★ in this weathered-wood chalet. Its bookcases are full of rainy-day reading, and its meals simple, impeccable presentations of trout, cheese, omelets, and steaks. Warm gold pine planking covers nearly every surface, and historic photos, lace curtains, and local paper cutouts add the grace notes. The baths are up to date, while the rooms are simple

and genuinely homey. ⊠ CH-1831, ☎ 026/9246266, 𝔽𝔸𝕏 026/9246016.
15 rooms. Restaurant, café, tennis court, playground. V.

En Route   Clinging to a precarious cliff-side road between L'Etivaz and Château-
d'Oex, drivers penetrate the canyon wilderness of the **Gorges du Pissot,** where sports lovers in wet suits "canyon"—literally, hike the river
bottom—under the white waters of the Torneresse River (☞ Outdoor
Activities and Sports *in* Château d'Oex, *below*).

Château-d'Oex

㉘   *33 km (20 mi) northeast of Aigle, 64 km (40 mi) east of Lausanne.*

At the crossroads between the Col des Mosses highway to Aigle and
the Valais and the route to the Berner Oberland lies Château-d'Oex
(pronounced *day*), a popular sports resort that connects, in these days
of sophisticated ski transit, with the greater Gstaad ski region. Its perhaps even greater claim to fame these days is ballooning, with periodic hot-air-balloon competitions that draw mobs of international
enthusiasts and fill hotels throughout the region. In spring 1999, the
Breitling *Orbiter 3* balloon launched from the valley floor for its
record-breaking nonstop trip around the world. The town itself is a
mix of Edwardian architecture with weathered-wood chalets, spreading over a green, forest-top hillside above the highway. It heads the French
end of the valley of the Sarine River—also known, in the Berner Oberland, as Saanenland.

★   In Château-d'Oex's small center, the **★Musée Artisanal du Vieux
Pays-d'Enhaut** (Artisan and Folklore Museum of the Old Highlands)
gives you insight into life in these isolated parts. Complete interiors
are evocatively reproduced: two kitchens, a farmer's home, a cheese
maker's house, and a carpenter's studio. Marvelous wood carving and
ironwork, a variety of ceramics, plus displays of old papier découpé,
furniture, and popular art round out the collection. ⊠ *Grand-rue, CH-
1837,* ☎ *026/9246520.* ⛛ *5 SF.* ☻ *Tues., Thurs., and Fri. 10–noon
and 2–4:30, weekends 2–4:30.*

Le Chalet is a reproduction of a mountain cheese maker's home, with
afternoon demonstrations over an open fire. Visitors sit at café tables
(and are sold drinks or cheese dishes) while they watch the hot labor
of stirring milk in a vast copper vat. Regional crafts and dairy products are on sale downstairs. ⊠ *CH-1837,* ☎ *026/9246677.* ⛛ *Free (a
purchase or consumption is expected).* ☻ *Sat.–Thurs. 9–6, Fri. 9 AM–
11 PM. Demonstrations Tues.–Sun. 9:30–11:30 and 2–4; July–Aug.,
Tues.–Sun. 2–4*

Skiing

Château-d'Oex has cable-car links to **La Braye** and the expert and intermediate trails that wind back down. At 1,000 m (3,280 ft), it has
one cable car, two chairlifts, 10 lifts, 50 km (31 mi) of downhill runs,
and 30 km (19 mi) of cross-country trails. A one-day lift ticket costs
33 SF; a six-day pass costs 166 SF. La Braye also has an equipment
test center where you can try out the latest snowboards and skis.

Dining and Lodging

$ ✕ **Buffet de la Gare.** Though you'd be better off driving five minutes
up to L'Etivaz for equivalent (but better prepared and served) middle-
class cuisine, this easygoing and convenient train-station café draws a regular local crowd for light meals and a dependable plat du jour. Stick with
croûtes (rich, toasted-cheese sandwiches) and salads, and opt for the casual—and smoky—café rather than the more formal restaurant, though
it's fun to watch the trains roll by the latter. ☎ *026/9247717. MC, V.*

$$–$$$ ✕🏠 **Bon Accueil.** Occupying a beautifully proportioned, weathered-
★ wood, 18th-century chalet, this is the quintessential French-Swiss
country inn. The rooms mix aged pine planking, spindle furniture, and
antiques, and under the old low-beam ceilings the floors creak agree-
ably. If you prefer quieter though smaller accommodations, take a
room—perhaps with a sun terrace—in the new building (connected by
lawn and tunnel to the old). Up-to-date amenities, immaculate appointments, pastel accents, and fresh flowers—inside and out—keep
standards at a well-above-rustic level. The restaurant (reservations are
essential) is even more civilized, and the menu offers a range of specialties, from simple lake fish to such intricate creations as freshwater
fish roasted in pinot noir accompanied by *choucroûte* (sauerkraut) and
fried leeks. Meals are served in a warm dining room with a brick fireplace, much waxed wood, and pewter accents. For winter nights,
there's a firelit stone cellar bar with low-key jazz. ✉ *CH-1837*, ☎ *026/
9246320*, 🖷 *026/9245126. 20 rooms. Restaurant, bar, sauna. AE, DC,
MC, V. Closed mid-Oct.–mid-Dec.*

$$ 🏠 **Ermitage.** Hoteliers Fabio and Françoise Piazza spent nearly a
decade converting this once-ordinary mountain hotel into a unique,
cozy inn. Timbered ceilings and stenciled detailing warm up the amply
sized rooms, which are furnished with traditional, blond-wood armoires
and fluffy, cotton-encased duvets. The terrace is the perfect perch for
watching balloon takeoffs—it overlooks the launch field. The carnotzet's
meals—cassoulet, coq au vin, and other heartwarming dishes—are
drawn from Piazza's grandmother's recipes. An excellent five-course
prix-fixe meal (and at 85 SF, a great value) has faithfuls driving up from
glitzy Gstaad. ✉ *CH-1837*, ☎ *026/9246003*, 🖷 *026/9245076. 16
rooms, 4 suites. Restaurant, café, minibars, playground, free parking.
AE, DC, MC, V.*

$$ 🏠 **Richmont.** The exterior is authentic (weather-blackened wood,
flower boxes on the balconies), but the interior is a study in florid Vic-
torian excess—the colors intense, the upholstery heavy, and the half-
timbering an apparent afterthought. ✉ *CH-1837*, ☎ *026/9245252*,
🖷 *026/9245384. 10 rooms. Restaurant, bar, café, pizzeria. AE, DC,
MC, V.*

Outdoor Activities and Sports

In summer the slopes turn into "mountain-surfing" runs. Mountain-
bike shops rent big-wheeled scooters on which you can race downhill.

BALLOONING

The hot-air-ballooning center in Château-d'Oex offers accompanied
flights. To arrange one, contact the tourist office (☞ Visitor Information *in* Vaud A to Z, *below*). An annual festival gets off the ground in
January. On the Friday night before the festival, a *night glow* is held.
Scramble to the top of the hill behind the church (look for the steeple)
for a stunning view of brilliantly colored, back-lit balloons choreographed to music.

BICYCLING

In this graceful region of rolling hills and steep climbs, mountain bikes
can be rented at **Planète Sports** (☎ 026/9244464). Also try **Palaz Bike**
(☎ 026/9244251).

RAFTING, HYDROSPEED, AND CANYONING

Several gorges near Château-d'Oex offer excellent rafting, as well as
two unusual white-water sports: Hydrospeed involves floating the waters in flippers and wet suit; canyoning has you hiking the river bottom clad in wet suit, life jacket, and helmet. **Rivières et Aventures** (✉
Case Postale 68, CH-1837, ☎ 026/9243424) organizes hiking, rafting, and kayaking excursions to the Gorges du Pissot (☞ *above*). You

can also arrange supervised initiations into these sports through the tourist office (☞ Visitor Information *in* Vaud A to Z, *below*).

SKATING
There's an outdoor rink at the **Parc des Sports** (☎ 026/9246700).

SWIMMING
In summer, **Château-d'Oex** opens a heated, 50-m open-air pool with restaurant (☎ 026/9246234).

Rougemont

⑳ *40 km (25 mi) northeast of Aigle, 71 km (44 mi) east of Lausanne.*

Though this historic village is now being encroached on by sporty Gstaad—its beautiful wooden barns and ornately decorated chalets crowded out by modern resort lodgings—it retains its ancient monuments. The striking Romanesque **church,** with its deeply raked roof and needle-sharp spire, was built between 1073 and 1085. The exterior wall of the 16th-century **château** behind the church is emblazoned with the *grue* (crane) of Gruyères, harking back to the Pays-d'Enhaut's earliest loyalties. (The château is privately owned and closed to the public.)

Skiing

Rougemont has **La Videmanette,** a cable run that drops you off for leisurely, moderate skiing back to the village, or on up to trails that wind over toward Gstaad, the glamour resort across the invisible German-language frontier. From the second stop up the Videmanette, there's also a 4½-km (3-mi) sledding run. A regional ski pass permits access to lifts, rail lines, and buses in all ski villages at a reduced rate.

VAUD A TO Z

Arriving and Departing

By Car

There are two major arteries leading to Lac Léman (Lake Geneva), one entering from the north via Bern and Fribourg (**A12**), the other arcing over the north shore of Lake Geneva from Geneva to Lausanne (**A1**), then to Montreux and on south through the Alpes Vaudoises toward the Grand St. Bernard Pass (**A9**) in canton Valais. They are swift and often scenic expressways, and the north-shore artery (A1 and A9) traces a route that has been followed since before Roman times. Secondary highways parallel the expressways, but this is one case where, as the larger road sits higher on the lakeside slopes, the views from the expressway are often better than those from the highway. Be sure, however, to detour for the Corniche Road views between Lausanne and Montreux.

By Plane

Geneva's **Cointrin** (⊠ 55 km/34 mi southwest of Lausanne, ☎ 022/7177111) is the second-busiest international airport in Switzerland, servicing frequent flights from the United States and the United Kingdom on **Swissair** as well as other international carriers. From Cointrin, **Crossair** (☎ 061/3253636 for central reservations; ☎ 1553636 toll free within), Switzerland's domestic line, connects to secondary airports throughout the country.

By Train

Lausanne lies on a major train route between Bern and Geneva, with express trains connecting from Basel and Zürich. From Geneva, trains take about 30 minutes and arrive in Lausanne up to four times an hour;

from Bern, they take a little more than an hour and arrive twice an hour. TGVs (high-speed trains) run from Paris four times a day and take 3 hours and 40 minutes. The Pendolino train has two departures a day between October and May: one to Milan and one to Venice. From June to September two more departures are added. A daily ICE, the German high-speed train, goes directly to Cologne, other hourly departures head to Germany with a change in Basel or Bern.

Getting Around

By Boat
Like all fair-size Swiss lakes, Lake Geneva is crisscrossed with comfortable and reasonably swift **steamers.** They carry you scenically from port to port and sometimes run more often than the trains that parallel their routes. With a Swiss Pass (☞ Train Travel *in* Smart Travel Tips A to Z) you travel free. For boat schedule and docking information contact **Compagnie Générale de Navigation** (☎ 084/8811848) or pick up a timetable in any tourist office.

By Bus
A useful network of **postbus** routes covers the region for the resourceful traveler with plenty of time; some routes are covered only once or twice a day. Schedules are available from tourist offices (☞ Visitor Information, *below*) and rail stations. In smaller towns you can also check with the post office. Lausanne has a good bus network; if you have a Swiss Pass, you can travel free on city buses in Montreux, Vevey, and Lausanne.

By Car
A web of **secondary highways** cuts north into the hills then winds east of the southbound expressway into the Alpine resorts, giving the driver maximum flexibility.

By Train
Trains along the waterfront, connecting major Lake Geneva towns, are swift and frequent. There are also several **private rail systems** leading into small villages and rural regions, including the **Montreux–Oberland–Bernois Railroad Line** (MOB; ☎ 021/9898181), which climbs sharply behind Montreux and cuts straight over the pre-Alps toward Château-d'Oex and the Berner Oberland. There is also the **Blonay–Chamby Railroad Line** (✉ Case Postale 366, CH-1001, Lausanne, ☎ 021/9432121). The Swiss Pass is accepted on these private lines, but there may be an additional fee for panoramic excursions. Inquire at local tourist offices or train stations about a regional pass that combines rail, boat, bus, and cable car excursions on these private lines at a reduced fee. It can be used for unlimited travel for three out of seven days and discounts on the other four days.

Lausanne itself has a tiny but essential **Métro** that every seven minutes connects the waterfront at Ouchy to the train station and the place St-François above. It runs until midnight; tickets are less than 3 SF and a day pass costs 6.50 SF.

Contacts and Resources

Emergencies
Vaud (☎ 117). **Police: Château-d'Oex** (☎ 026/9244421); **Montreux** (☎ 021/9632121); **Villars** (☎ 024/4955321). **Ambulance: Château-d'Oex** (☎ 026/9247593); **Montreux** (☎ 144); **Villars** (☎ 024/4951537). **Hospitals: Aigle** (☎ 024/4688688); **Lausanne Centre Hospitalier Universitaire Vaudois** (emergency services; ☎ 021/3141111); **Montreux** (☎ 021/9666666). **Medical and dental referrals: Lausanne** (☎ 021/

6529932). **Late-night pharmacies:** (☎ 111). **Auto breakdown: Touring Club of Switzerland** (☎ 140).

Guided Tours

ORIENTATION

The **Lausanne tourist office** runs a daily, two-hour coach trip into the Old Town, including a visit to the cathedral and an extended city coach tour that takes in the Lavaux vineyards. Walking tours led by local historians are increasing in popularity. They are also organized by the tourist office and are given at 10 AM and 3 PM between May and September. There are three daily general tours during the summer: one to Gruyères; one to Chamonix and Mont Blanc; and one to the Alps by coach and the Montreux–Oberland–Bernois Railroad Line *Panoramic Train* to Les Diablerets and Château-d'Oex (☞ Getting Around, *above*). To ensure a tour with English commentary, reserve in advance.

VINEYARD TOURS

The **Office des Vins Vaudois** (⊠ 6 ch. de la Vuachère, CH-1005 Lausanne, ☎ 021/7296161) offers carefully marked walks—not personally guided—through the vineyards, passing production centers, winegrowers' homes, and *pintes* (pubs) for tasting along the way. Write for the *Guide du Vignoble Vaudois* for itineraries, hours, and addresses of suggested stops. Vevey's **Le Train des Vignes** (vineyard train) runs through the area's vineyards; some outings include tastings and cellar tours. Inquire at Vevey's tourist office (☞ Visitor Information, *below*).

Visitor Information

The **Office du Tourisme du Canton de Vaud** (⊠ 60 av. d'Ouchy, CH-1006 Lausanne, ☎ 021/6177202, FAX 021/6177240) has general information on the region.

Regional offices: **Château-d'Oex** (⊠ CH-1837, ☎ 026/9242525). **Les Diablerets** (⊠ CH-1865, ☎ 024/4923358). **Lausanne** (⊠ 2 av. de Rhodanie, CH-1000, ☎ 021/6137321). **Leysin** (⊠ CH-1854, ☎ 024/4942244). **Nyon** (⊠ 7 av. Viollier, CH-1260, ☎ 022/3616261). **Montreux** (⊠ 5 rue du Thêâtre, CH-1820, ☎ 021/9628484). **Vevey** (⊠ Case Postale 27, CH-1800, ☎ 021/9222020). **Villars-Gryon** (⊠ CH-1884, ☎ 0953232).

13 GENEVA

As the headquarters of the United Nations, the World Health Organization, and the International Red Cross; the birthplace of Calvinism; and a stronghold of luxurious stores and fine restaurants, Geneva is, in many ways, a paradox. It is also Switzerland's most cosmopolitan city; a high-profile crossroads of wealth, influence, and cultures from around the world.

Updated by
Jennifer
McDermott

NESTLED BETWEEN THE JURA AND THE ALPS at the southwestern tip of Lac Léman (Lake Geneva), Geneva is the cosmopolitan, graceful soul of Switzerland's French-speaking territory. Surrounded by France but for a four-kilometer corridor along the northern shore of the lake—to the north and west is the Pays de Gex, to the south and east the Haute-Savoie—the city exudes a Gallic hauteur. Grand, mansarded mansions stand guard beside the Rhône river, yachts bob, gulls dive, and Rolls-Royces purr past manicured promenades. The combination of Swiss efficiency and French savoir faire gives Geneva a chic polish; the infusion of international blood from the UN adds a heterogeneity rare in a city of only 180,000. The canton has a population of 400,000, 38% of which is not Swiss.

Foreigners are now drawn by the city's many international organizations, but Geneva has long been known for enlightened tolerance. It gave refuge to the writers Voltaire, Victor Hugo, Alexandre Dumas, Honoré de Balzac, and Stendhal, as well as the religious reformers John Calvin and John Knox. Lord Byron, Percy Bysshe and Mary Shelley, Richard Wagner, and Franz Liszt all fled from scandals elsewhere into Geneva's sheltering arms.

The narrow austerity and bigotry of 16th-century Calvinism—whose namesake reformed the city that sheltered him, preaching fire and brimstone and stripping the cathedral of its papist icons—did, however, cause non-believers to leave Geneva even as masses of Protestants fled *to* it. The English fled Bloody Mary, Protestant Italians the wrath of the pope, Spaniards the Inquisition, French Huguenots the oppressive French monarchy—and Geneva flourished. Philosopher (and Geneva native) Jean-Jacques Rousseau first left the country as a Roman Catholic convert, then returned years later to reenter the Protestant church.

To this day the conservative Genevois seem to hear Calvin tsk-tsking in their ears as they hurry by some of the world's most expensive stores and palatial hotels; it is the urbane foreigners who seem to indulge themselves the most. Some say that in the 1970s there was more Middle Eastern oil money in Geneva than in the Middle East, and stories abound of sheikhs taking over whole hotels for monthlong shopping sprees.

But Geneva does let down her discreet chignon twice a year. Every August the city organizes an enormous week-long party, *Les Fêtes de Genève,* for the sole purpose of blowing off summer steam. The grande finale—a waterfront fireworks display choreographed to music—sends residents scrambling for vantage points. And in December the Genevois celebrate their independence during the *Fête de l'Escalade* (Festival of the Escalade). Under cover of night on December 11–12, 1602, the duke of Savoy—coveting Geneva and hoping to restore it to Catholicism—sent his men to scale the city walls with ladders. An alert sentry sounded the alarm, however, and the entire population turned out to fight. The most original defense was mounted by a housewife, who emptied a *marmite* (pot) of hot soup over the Savoyards scaling her walls. During the commemorative celebration, chocolate marmites are filled with marzipan vegetables, the 18 Genevois dead are remembered, and throughout the city the usually decorous Genevois take to the streets in costume.

Pleasures and Pastimes

Antiquing
Catering to a public that follows the auctions at Sotheby's and Christie's, Geneva's Old Town bulges with shops full of gilt and leatherbound books, ancient engravings, beautifully restored furniture, and fine old silver.

Churches
The Gothic and neoclassical Cathédrale St-Pierre, its early Christian excavations, and the Auditoire de Calvin, where John Calvin lectured to his disciples, offer an illuminating overview of Geneva's Catholic and Reformed personae.

Dining
Geneva is a true gastronomic crossroads. The city has more restaurants per capita than New York City, ranging from elite French dining rooms to traditional Genevois bistros to trendy, creative, international restaurants.

The international community palpably marks the city's eating habits, and the French influence leads the pack. With only 150 km (94 mi) separating Geneva and Lyons, the two cities are blood brothers. Geneva's traditional cuisine emphasizes *abats* (organ meats), *andouillettes* (chitterling sausages), potatoes, and onions. And like that of Lyon, its haute cuisine rivals the best in the world.

Genevois regional cuisine is seasonal, with some dishes to be had only at specific times of year. *Cardon* (cardoon, a locally grown, artichoke-like vegetable available in winter) is baked with cream and Gruyère. Lac Léman yields its abundant fish—perch, trout, *féra* (a rare fish related to salmon), and *omble* (char)—during summer months. *Pieds de cochon* (pigs' feet), fricasée of pork (pork simmered in wine), and *longeole* (unsmoked sausage of pork by-products, cabbage, and fennel) may be had year round; *petit salé* (salt pork), tripe, and *boudin noir* (rich, rosy-brown blood pudding) also have their place on traditional menus. *La chasse* (wild game) turns up between late September and mid-December.

Prices at the elite gastronomic meccas can be dry-mouth high, but—as in most Swiss cities—you'll save considerably by choosing a prix-fixe menu or a lunchtime *plat du jour*. It is possible to eat well at even the plainest corner bistro but, if you want to splurge, starting with tiers of briny oysters, ending with good *poire William* (a pear-based eau-de-vie), and plumbing the depths of great French-Swiss wine lists, there's no limit to what you can spend (and enjoy) here.

Museums
Privately sponsored, eclectic collections of contemporary sculpture, French painting, primitive art, and Asian ceramics complement Geneva's impressive (and free) public art and history museums. The Palais des Nations, although 100% functional as the European seat of the UN, serves as a living museum of 20th-century history, radio-age translation devices, and socialist-realist murals. The Musée International de la Croix-Rouge (International Red Cross Museum) puts the horrors of modern conflict into uncomfortable perspective.

Neighborhoods
The well-preserved, evocative *Vieille Ville* (Old Town) is undeniably captivating, but many of the city's various residential and commercial areas on both sides of the lake have strong personalities as well: the scruffy area behind the *gare;* the honky-tonk sleaze along rue des Pâquis; the stately homes above Parc des Bastions; the artists' work-

shops of Carouge, to the south; the glittering shops on the rue du Rhône; and the university centers near the Plaine de Plainpalais.

EXPLORING GENEVA

The canton of Geneva pads the southwestern tip of Lac Léman, then bulges farther west into France. The city itself follows the lake as it funnels into the Rhône river. The tightest bottleneck for both traffic and water is between the Pont du Mont-Blanc and the pont de la Coulouvrenière. Geneva is both a river town and a lake town, and its Rive Droite (Right Bank, on the north side) and Rive Gauche (Left Bank, on the south side) have distinct personalities. Most of the central city's best is concentrated on the Rive Gauche, but the Rive Droite includes the International Area and many handsome hotels.

Numbers in the text correspond to numbers in the margin and on the Geneva map.

Great Itineraries

IF YOU HAVE 2 DAYS

Allow yourself an hour to stroll the Right Bank quays, then cross to the Left Bank and enter the Old Town. Save time for the hybrid Gothic-neoclassical Cathédrale St-Pierre. Then window-shop your way through ancient streets to the Musée d'Art et d'Histoire, where works by Swiss masters such as Ferdinand Hodler complement fine archaeological and applied art collections. The next day, head for the International Area and spend the morning at the Palais des Nations, the afternoon at the Musée International de la Croix-Rouge. Nights are for outdoor concerts (in summer) and hearty dinners with a glass or two of Genevois wine.

IF YOU HAVE 3 DAYS

Start your first day with a brief stroll along the Right Bank, then head for the Musée Rath; its temporary exhibits lure even heads of state to fit in a quick tour. Stop at the Monument de la Réformation, then climb up into the Old Town to visit the cathedral and its excavations. The Auditoire de Calvin, the 14th-century Maison Tavel, and any number of bookstores and antiques shops will easily fill the afternoon. The next day, concentrate on the museums behind the Old Town—the Collections Baur or the Musée d'Histoire Naturelle. On your third day, head north to the International Area. Spend the morning at the Palais des Nations, the afternoon at the Musée International de la Croix-Rouge. If time remains, explore the Musée Ariana.

IF YOU HAVE 4 DAYS

With a fourth day, you can absorb even more of the city's museums—spend a morning at the Musée Barbier-Mueller studying primitive and tribal art from around the world; follow it up with an afternoon at the cutting-edge Musée d'Art Moderne et Contemporain.

Right Bank, Left Bank, and Old Town

Geneva is centered on water. Grand hotels line the Right Bank, the Left Bank bristles with prestigious shops, and monuments, parks, and fountains relieve the big-city modernity on both sides. Climb into the ancient, peaceful heights of the *Vieille Ville* (Old Town), and you'll find high-caliber museums, boutiques, and sidewalk cafés.

A Good Walk

Begin your walk from Cornavin, the main train station. It can be awkward to dodge traffic on the **place de Cornavin** ①, so take the pedestrian underpass through the shopping center below the station. You'll emerge at the top of rue du Mont-Blanc, a partially pedestrian shopping street that slopes down to the lake. When rue de Mont-Blanc reaches the lake, it becomes the Pont du Mont-Blanc, a wide bridge that spans the last gasp of Lac Léman as it narrows into the Rhône. From the bridge you can see the snowy peak of Mont Blanc itself, and from March to October there's a fine view of the **Jet d'Eau** ②.

Retrace your steps to the Right Bank, turn right onto quai du Mont-Blanc, and follow the plane trees toward the *débarcadères,* the docks used by Swissboat, Les Mouettes Genevoises, and the CGN steamers. On your left you'll pass the elaborate neo-Gothic **Monument Brunswick** ③, the tomb of Charles II, Duke of Brunswick, who left his fortune to the city. Just beyond, at the Hôtel Beau-Rivage, you'll see the discreet sign for Sotheby's auction house (☞ Shopping, *below*). Follow the string of luxury hotels along the quay until it veers due north; out on the jetty to your right are **Les Bains des Pâquis**, public beaches with a sauna, changing rooms, restaurants, and protected space to swim and sunbathe.

Head back to the Pont du Mont-Blanc and cross the street to the quai des Bergues. In the center of the river, off the pedestrian-only Pont des Bergues, the romantic **Ile Rousseau** ④ harbors a statue of its namesake and an 18th century style pavilion.

Continue down quai des Bergues and cross the river at the Pont de l'Ile, until 1834 the only bridge spanning the Rhône. Look back to see the **Tour de l'Ile** ⑤, all that remains of the island's early 13th-century château.

On the Left Bank, cross place Bel-Air, the center of the banking district and a major hub for the city's buses, and cut right to rue de la Corraterie. Follow it south past city walls that bore the brunt of the 1602 Savoyard attack to **place Neuve** ⑥, Geneva's focal point for the arts. To your immediate right is the **Musée Rath** ⑦. The **Grand Théâtre**, to its right, resembles the Palais Garnier in Paris. At the far end of the square is the graceful Conservatoire de Musique.

Go through the gates of the historic Parc des Bastions—setting of the **Université de Genève**, which Calvin founded in 1559 as an academy—and keep to your left. At the foot of the ramparts you will see the imposing **Monument de la Réformation** ⑧, erected in 1909; sit down on the terrace steps—made of Mont Blanc granite—to take it all in. Then keep walking toward the back of the park, exit, and turn left onto rue St-Léger.

As you pass under an ivy-hung bridge and begin to climb, the present falls away and 16th-century houses with weathered shutters ease you into the picturesque *Vieille Ville* (Old Town). When you reach the bottom of the tiered plateau and medieval marketplace known as **place du Bourg-de-Four** ⑨, climb the steps and angle uphill to the left on rue de l'Hôtel-de-Ville. Cut right into place de la Taconnerie, where you'll see Christie's auction house (☞ Shopping, *below*) on your left. Literally across the street, if symbolically miles away, is the small Gothic **Auditoire de Calvin** ⑩, where Calvin and his successors taught missionaries his doctrines of reform.

To the left of the Auditoire rises the magnificent mongrel **Cathédrale St-Pierre** ⑪, which Calvin stripped of its Catholic trappings. After exploring its austere interior and the ornate Chapel of the Maccabees, take the stairs to the left of the main doors down to the *site archéologique* ⑫; you can tour what remains of earlier churches built on the site. From there, head straight to the rue du Puits-St-Pierre and the city's oldest house, the **Maison Tavel** ⑬.

Geneva (Genève)

Les Bains des Pâquis

↑ **Area of Inset**

Rue de Berne

Rue Rossi

Rue de Monthoux

Rue des Pâquis

Rue Sismondi

Rue Ph.-Plantamour

Rue des Alpes

Rue Ami Lévrier

Rue Adhémar-Fabri

3

24 **23**

Place des Alpes

Place Dorcière

Chemin de l'Impératrice

Route de Pregny

Musée Internationale de la Croix-Rouge

25

Avenue de la Paix

Rue de Lausanne

Square du Mont-Blanc

22

21

Palais des Nations

26

Jardin Botanique

Quai du Mont-Blanc

AE

i

Kléberg

Place des Bergues

Place des Nations

Avenue de la Paix

Chemin de Vidollet

Chemin des Mines

bergues

Pont des Bergues

Pont du Mont-Blanc

4

Ile Rousseau

Avenue de France

Parc Mon Repos

27

2

uai du Rhône

Pl. du Rhône

Pl. de la Fusterie

Général-Guisan

Rue du Rhône

Promenade du Lac

Quai Gustave-Ador

R. de la Scie

Rue Muzy

Quai du Lac

Rue du 31 Décembre

Pl. du Port

Jardin Anglais

Quai du Général-Guisan

R. des Eaux-Vives

Pl. du Molard

R. Neuve-du-Molard

R. du Marché

Pl. Longemalle

Rue du Rhône

Rue Versonnex

Av. Pictet-de-Rochemont

Rue de la Rôtisserie

Rue de la Croix-d'Or

Rue de Rive

Rue d'Italie

R. P.-Fatio

Rue P.-Fatio

Pl. des Eaux Vives

Av. de Frontenex

R. Calvin

14

13

R. du Puits St-Pierre

Rue de la Fontaine

Rue de Rive

Blvd. Helvétique

R. de la Terrassière

12 **11**

Rue Verdaine

Rond-Point de Rive

Cours de Rive

Carrefour de Rive

15

R. de l'Hôtel-de-Ville

10

9

Rue des Chaudronniers

R. Théodore-de-Bèze

Rue Ferdinand-Hodler

Glacis-de-Rive

R. A.-Lachenal

Rue de Villereuse

Croix-Rouge

Pl. de la Taconnerie

Promenade St-Antoine

Rue Etienne-Dumont

Blvd. Jacques-Dalcroze

17

Rue Charles-Galland

Rue Toepffer

R. Lefort

R. Sturm

Place Émile-Guyénot

20

19

Malagnou

R. de l'Athénée

Rue St-Léger

Cours des Bastions

Promenade du Pin

Blvd. Helvétique

16

Rue St-Victor

R. F. Lefort

18

R. Munier-Romilly

Blvd. des Tranchées

Once you've scoured the historical museum from Roman cistern to 19th-century attic, turn left onto rue Calvin. No. 11, now a stately neoclassical facade, was the address of John Calvin himself. Across the street, the **Musée Barbier-Mueller** ⑭ keeps its private collection of African and Southeast Asian tribal art in permanent rotation.

Continue down rue Calvin and turn left onto rue de la Pélisserie at the plaque commemorating author George Eliot's five-month visit to the city in 1849. Turn left again onto the Grand-Rue and walk past gorgeous antique stores, the birthplace of Jean-Jacques Rousseau (No. 40), and painter Ferdinand Hodler's atelier at No. 33. You come out at the city's Old Arsenal, stocked with ancient cannons, and the imposing facade of the **Hôtel de Ville** ⑮, home of today's cantonal government.

Follow the rue de l'Hôtel-de-Ville back to place du Bourg-de-Four, cross the square, and dip down rue Etienne-Dumont. Curve left across the promenade du Pin and continue along rue St-Victor to the **Petit Palais** ⑯, a statue-framed mansion that houses the **Musée d'Art Moderne**'s private collection of French art.

On leaving the Petit Palais, return to the promenade du Pin and veer to the right. The promenade St.-Antoine takes you over a parking garage built carefully around the massive remnants of Geneva's medieval ramparts—take the elevator down and back for a quick tour. Follow this with a visit to the vast **Musée d'Art et d'Histoire** ⑰, across the rue Charles-Galland. Its holdings range from archaeological treasures to Hodler landscapes. Turn right outside the museum and follow rue Charles-Galland until you see the gilt cupolas of the 19th-century Église Russe, completely decorated within in neo-Byzantine styles. Turn right on rue François-Lefort, left on rue Munier-Romilly. At the end of the block on the right is the **Collections Baur** ⑱, an elegantly mounted collection of Asian decorative art objects.

Return to rue Charles-Galland and follow it right to boulevard des Tranchées; turn left and head for place Émile Guyénot. To your right is the modern, black-and-white **Musée d'Histoire Naturelle** ⑲. Behind it, set back from the route de Malagnou, is the **Musée de l'Horlogerie et de l'Émaillerie** ⑳. It's a quick walk down rue Ferdinand-Hodler back to the Old Town from here, or you can catch Bus 8 for the Right Bank.

TIMING

There's an embarrassment of sightseeing riches in these neighborhoods; doing the walk in one day will give you a good orientation but not leave much time for prowling the museums or shops. If you have time, stretch it out over a couple of afternoons. Keep in mind that several museums are closed Monday.

Sights to See

❿ **Auditoire de Calvin** (Protestant Lecture Hall). John Calvin taught missionaries his doctrines of radical, puritanical reform in this Gothic structure built on the foundations of a 5th-century Catholic chapel. From 1556 to 1559, the Scots reformer John Knox also preached here. As Reformation gathered speed, the Auditoire became a haven of worship for Protestant refugees, encouraged by Calvin to hold services in their native English, Italian, Spanish, German, and Dutch. Today it is still a multilingual center of worship, used by the Church of Scotland, the Dutch Reformed Community, and the Waldensian Church of Italy for Sunday services. The austerity of the building is striking, the period furniture still in use. The Church of Scotland's Sunday morning service at 11 is open to visitors. ⊠ *pl. de la Taconnerie,* ☎ *022/ 3118533.* ▭ *Free.* ◎ *Weekdays 2–5.*

★ ⑪ **Cathédrale St-Pierre** (St. Peter's Cathedral). Construction began in 1160, but this towering Gothic cathedral lost its aesthetic balance and some of its grandeur when a massive, sternly beautiful, neoclassical facade was added in the 18th century. The interior remains wholly Romanesque, its austerity reflecting the building's change from a Catholic cathedral to a Protestant church. (Calvin's faithful obliterated the original colorful frescoes and shimmering stained glass.) The flamboyant, 15th-century **Chapel of the Maccabees,** to the right of the main entrance, contrasts greatly with the austerity of the nave, as it was left untouched by the Calvinists. Don't forget to climb the **north tower** (to the left of the far end of the nave) for a magnificent view of Geneva. ⊠ *cour Saint-Pierre,* ☎ *022/3117575.* ⚏ *North tower 3 SF.* ⊙ *Oct.–May, Mon.–Sat. 10–noon and 2–5, Sun. 11–12:30 and 1:30–5; June–Sept., Mon.–Sat. 9–7, Sun. 11–7.*

★ ⑱ **Collections Baur.** A broad and exquisite array of art objects from the Far East fill this graceful private mansion. Businessman Alfred Baur's impeccably displayed collection of rose and celadon porcelains from China, medieval Japanese stoneware, Samurai swords, jade, and Chinese lacquer boxes spans more than ten centuries of Asian art. ⊠ *8 rue Munier-Romilly,* ☎ *022/3461729.* ⚏ *5 SF.* ⊙ *Tues.–Sun. 2–6.*

⑮ **Hôtel de Ville** (Town Hall). The oldest part of this past and present seat of political power is the **Tour Baudet** (Baudet Tower; 1455), and the 16th century cobbled ramp gave riders on horseback unusually direct access to the third floor. But the real star is the **Alabama Hall.** Named after the ship at the center of a British-American dispute settled here in 1872, the hall witnessed the signing of the Geneva Convention and the birth of the International Red Cross on August 22, 1864; on November 15, 1920, the League of Nations convened its first Assembly here. The building is now used by the cantonal government, but you can visit the courtyard. ⊠ *2 rue de l'Hôtel-de-Ville.*

❹ **Ile Rousseau.** Geneva-born French philosopher Jean-Jacques Rousseau drew favorable attention to the city in his 18th-century writings on liberalism, education, and politics—but the conservative city didn't take kindly to his views. His statue on this former city bastion was effectively hidden, positioned facing out to the lake and surrounded by trees, until the 1861 construction of the pont du Mont-Blanc provided the perfect sight line. ⊠ *Off pont des Bergues.*

❷ **Jet d'Eau.** Originally a safety valve for Geneva's water supply system, Europe's tallest fountain gushes 140 m (460 ft) into the air between March and October. ⊠ *Lake Geneva.*

★ ⑬ **Maison Tavel** (Tavel House). Geneva's oldest house (14th century) traces the development of the city's urban life from the 14th to the 19th centuries. The cellars and the ground-floor kitchens display historical objects ranging from medieval graffiti to a guillotine and a miter worn by convicted pimps in Calvin's day. The first floor exhibits ironwork, doors, and other fragments of long-demolished Genevois houses, while the second floor recreates a 17th–19th century bourgeois home interior, complete with period wallpaper. In the attic you'll find the Magnin Model, an enormous replica of Geneva as it looked in 1850 before the medieval ramparts that surrounded the city came down. ⊠ *6 rue du Puits-St-Pierre,* ☎ *022/3102900.* ⚏ *Free.* ⊙ *Tues.–Sun. 10–5.*

❸ **Monument Brunswick.** Charles II, the famously eccentric Duke of Brunswick, died in Geneva in 1873 and left his fortune to the city with instructions that his tomb be given prominence and modeled on the Scaglieri monument in Verona. ⊠ *Bounded by rue des Alpes, quai du Mont-Blanc, and rue Adhémar-Fabri.*

★ ❽ **Monument de la Réformation** (Reformation Monument). This granite and quartz monument is as impressive for its simplicity and clean lines as for its size; it measures 100 m (325 ft) long and 10 m (30 ft) high. A central group of 15-ft-tall statues depicts the great leaders of the Reformation—Bèze, Calvin, Farel, and Knox. On either side of these giants are smaller statues of major Protestant figures; the bas-reliefs and inscriptions around them relate important events connected with the Reformation. Bas-reliefs of the 1689 presentation of the Bill of Rights to King William III by the English Houses of Parliament and of the Pilgrim fathers praying on the deck of the *Mayflower* surround the figure of Oliver Cromwell. A third relief shows John Knox preaching with obvious passion. The monument is flanked by memorials to Martin Luther and Ulrich Zwingli. ⊠ *Parc des Bastions.*

OFF THE
BEATEN PATH

MUSÉE D'ART MODERNE ET CONTEMPORAIN (Museum of Modern and Contemporary Art; MAMCO). Original concrete factory floors and fluorescent lighting frame this gritty collection of stark, profound, mind-stretching artworks, none dating from before 1965. The building's spare, bleak lines serve as a foil for the often overscaled pieces: paintings, sculptures, and structures by Gordon Matta-Clark, Jenny Holzer, Sol Le Witt, Nam June Paik, Dennis Oppenheim, and Jean-Michel Basquiat, among others. Take Bus 1 (direction Rive) and get off at École de Médécine. Walk back one block and turn left down rue des Vieux-Grenadiers. The entrance is the last doorway on the right. Descriptive materials are available only in French. ⊠ *10 rue des Vieux-Grenadiers,* ☎ *022/3206122.* ▨ *9 SF.* ☉ *Wed.–Sun. noon–6, Tues. noon–9.*

CENTRE D'ART CONTEMPORAIN (Center for Contemporary Art). Geneva's *Kunsthalle* (art gallery) has been encouraging new work and organizing exhibits by cutting-edge, international contemporary artists since it opened in 1974. Its shows have included work by Cindy Sherman, Kiki Smith, Robert Mapplethorpe, Nan Goldin, and Tony Oursler. It shares the former factory with MAMCO (☞ *above*). Descriptive material is available only in French. ⊠ *10 rue des Vieux-Grenadiers,* ☎ *022/ 3291842.* ▨ *4 SF.* ☉ *Tues.–Sun. 11–6.*

★ ⓱ **Musée d'Art et d'Histoire** (Museum of Art and History). Archaeology, fine arts, and applied arts are featured in this mother lode of world culture, which was built in 1910 to house the overflow from the Musée Rath. Its collection of Egyptian art is the largest in Switzerland, and artifacts from Greece, Rome, and the Middle East give way to a hall of Escalade-era Genevois weapons. The enormous painting collection includes the 15th-century *Miracle of the Fishes,* by Swiss painter Konrad Witz, in which Christ paces the waters of a recognizable Lac Léman, and a room of Alpine landscapes by Swiss post-impressionist Ferdinand Hodler. There are no guides in English. ⊠ *2 rue Charles-Galland,* ☎ *022/4182600.* ▨ *Free.* ☉ *Tues.–Sun. 10–5.*

★ ⓮ **Musée Barbier-Mueller.** Josef Mueller began collecting primitive art in 1907, and by now his family has amassed a staggering quantity of fine pieces from Africa, Oceania, Southeast Asia, and the Americas. Only a small selection is on view at any given time, but each item is exquisitely lighted, framed, and juxtaposed with similar and contrasting works. Labels in English guide you past ivory fly-whisk handles from Zaire, massive carved masks from New Ireland, and jewelry from the South Seas. The museum building, a restored Old Town vault of scrubbed terra-cotta and halogen-lighted stone, is a work of art itself. ⊠ *10 rue Calvin,* ☎ *022/3120270.* ▨ *5 SF.* ☉ *Daily 11–5.*

WITHOUT KODAK MAX
photos taken on 100 speed film

TAKE PICTURES. FURTHER.™

© Eastman Kodak Company, 1999. Kodak, Max and Take Pictures. Further. are trademarks.

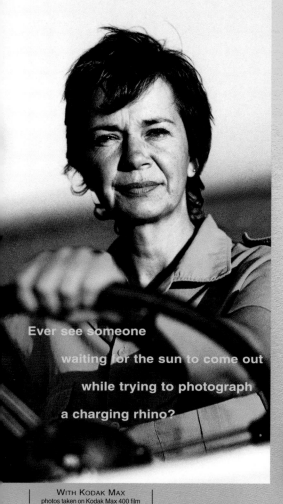

Ever see someone

waiting for the sun to come out

while trying to photograph

a charging rhino?

WITH KODAK MAX
photos taken on Kodak Max 400 film

New!
Kodak Max film:

Now with better color, Kodak's maximum versatility film gives you great pictures in sunlight, low light, action or still.

It's all you need to know about film.

www.kodak.com

Distinctive guides packed with up-to-date expert advice
and smart choices for every type of traveler.

Fodor's. For the world of ways you travel.

Musée d'Histoire Naturelle (Museum of Natural History). Local schools enthusiastically support this museum, so it's normally overrun with kids. Large, evocative wildlife dioramas complete with sound effects are the biggest draw for young children. You can also study exhibits on the evolution of man, local flora and fauna, Swiss geology, exotic birds, and the history of the solar system. There are gigantic crystals, a case full of polyhedrons, beehives, Tyrannosaurus Rex footprints, and a multimedia display on plate tectonics. All labels are in French. ⊠ *1 rte. de Malagnou,* ☎ *022/4186300.* 🖾 *Free.* ⊙ *Tues.–Sun. 9:30–5.*

Musée de l'Horlogerie et de l'Émaillerie (Museum of Watchmaking and Enameling). The permanent collections here include timepieces large and small from as far back as 1550—many of them crafted in Geneva— as well as music boxes and intricate enameled watchcases. There's also a reproduction of a watchmaker's workshop. To put it all in perspective, check out the display that traces the history of timekeeping from the sundial to the wristwatch. Try to be there on the hour for the chiming of the clocks. ⊠ *15 rte. de Malagnou,* ☎ *022/4186470.* 🖾 *Free.* ⊙ *Wed.–Mon. 10–5.*

★ ❼ **Musée Rath.** Switzerland's first fine-arts museum opened in 1826, a gift to the city from the Rath sisters in memory of their brother Simon. Originally home to his prodigious collections, it now hosts three major temporary exhibitions of archaeology and contemporary art each year. Upcoming shows include an exhibit on Belle Epoque paintings, posters, and caricatures by Théophile Alexandre Steinlen and his contemporaries (fall 1999–January 2000), and a major archaeological exhibit on Ostia, the Roman port (fall 2000 to January 2001). There are no descriptive materials available in English. ⊠ *pl. Neuve,* ☎ *022/ 4183340.* 🖾 *Up to 10 SF, depending on the exhibit.* ⊙ *Tues. and Thurs.– Sun. 10–5, Wed. noon–9.*

❶ **Petit Palais–Musée d'Art Moderne** (Museum of Modern Art). You can approach this private, personal mansion-gallery in two ways: either you'll see the collection of French art from 1870 to 1930 as a dilute gathering of school-of-Seurats, also-ran Renoirs, and wannabe Braques. . . or as a rare illustration of the evolution of French modernism, laced with works of unknown female artists and pillared by a few masters' experiments—some, as in the three-dimensional Gauguins, unexpected joys. ⊠ *2 terrasse St-Victor,* ☎ *022/3461433.* 🖾 *10 SF.* ⊙ *Weekdays 10–6, weekends 10–5.*

❶ **Place de Cornavin.** Streets radiate from this Right Bank hub into Geneva's key neighborhoods and across the lake to the Left Bank. Here you can catch a bus to the airport, Carouge, and the International Area (☞ *below*).

★ ❾ **Place du Bourg-de-Four.** In this layered Old Town square, you can still make out vestiges of the ancient roads that led south to Annecy and Lyon and east to Italy and the Chablais. Once a Roman cattle market, later flooded by Protestant refugees, it is still the quintessential Genevois crossroads; shoppers, lawyers, workers, and students meet for drinks around the 18th-century fountain, striking a delicate, charming balance between scruffy bohemia, genteel tradition, and slick gentrification. ⊠ *Intersection of rue Verdaine, rue des Chaudronniers, rue Etienne-Dumont, and rue de l'Hôtel-de-Ville.*

| NEED A BREAK? | Have a coffee or *apero* (aperitif) at the lively **La Clémence** (⊠ 20 pl. du Bourg-de-Four, ☎ 022/3122498), an old and much-loved sidewalk café spilling out into the middle of the place du Bourg-de-Four. |

★ ❻ **Place Neuve.** The city walls defended so vigorously in 1602 stand guard over this lyrical square and its proud statue of General Guillaume-Henri Dufour, four-time leader of Switzerland's federal army and a key figure in the 1847 Sonderbund separatist conflict. The stately houses above the ramparts belong to some of Geneva's wealthiest families. ⊠ *Intersection of bd. du Théâtre, rue de la Corraterie, rue de la Croix-Rouge, and rue Bartholoni.*

★ ⓬ **Site archéologique.** Archaeologists found layer upon layer of ancient debris when they tunneled under St. Peter's Cathedral (☞ *above*) in 1976, and excavations continue to this day. Meanwhile, careful lighting, models, audiovisual displays, and walkways guide visitors through ruins that include a Christian sanctuary from 350 AD, ornate 5th-century mosaics, and the remains of several early churches and baptisteries. The first Romanesque cathedral on this site dated from 1000. Its ruins—notably an unusual circular crypt—serve as the foundation for today's cathedral. There is also a collection of sculptures from the site. ⊠ *6 cour Saint-Pierre,* ☎ *022/3117575.* ▣ *5 SF.* ☾ *June–Sept., Tues.–Sun. 11–5:30; Oct.–May, Tues.–Sat. 2–5, Sun. 10–noon and 2–5.*

❺ **Tour de l'Ile.** The lone surviving fragment of Bishop Aymon de Grandson's 13th-century fortified château served as a prison during the Reformation. It is not open to the public. ⊠ *Pont de l'Ile.*

International Area

Ten minutes by car or bus north of the city center, open grassland and hills are scattered with modern office buildings, a handful of museums, embassies, and 19th-century villas. The serene botanical garden is an especially good place to digest the heavy historical and political fare you will find inside them.

A Good Walk

From the Gare Cornavin, take Bus 8 (direction OMS) to the place des Nations. Get off here and take in the impressive **Palais des Nations** ㉑, the European headquarters of the United Nations. Then walk up avenue de la Paix to the visitors' entrance. To save time, stay on the bus until the next stop (closer to the entrance), getting off at Appia. From the Appia stop you can also visit the palatial, Italianate **Musée Ariana** ㉒, which houses the **Musée Suisse de la Céramique et du Verre.**

Continue up avenue de la Paix, which becomes route de Pregny, past one of the three campuses of the International School of Geneva, on the right, and the American Mission to the UN, on the left. Turn right on chemin de l'Impératrice to the Château de Penthes. The lovely grounds of this 19th-century mansion are open to the public, while the building itself houses the **Musée des Suisses à l'Étranger** ㉓, a permanent exhibit addressing the relations of the Swiss people with the outside world. The much smaller **Musée Militaire Genevois** ㉔, set in one of the Château's former stables, focuses exclusively on local military history.

Retrace your steps down route de Pregny and turn right into a cut in the hill to find the **Musée International de la Croix-Rouge** ㉕, a fiercely moving museum that traces the history of humanitarian assistance. You may want to follow this with a 20-minute contemplative stroll down the length of avenue de la Paix. You'll pass the peaceful, leafy **Jardin Botanique** ㉖ on your way to the lake.

Leave the botanical gardens by the gate at place Alfred-Thomas, turn right on the rue de Lausanne, and enter the Parc Mon Repos through the gate to the left of the Perle du Lac restaurant. The **Musée d'His-**

toire des Sciences ㉗, a stunning museum in the neoclassical Villa Bartholoni, is surrounded by gardens and breathtaking views. Bus 4-44 will take you back to the city center.

TIMING

You can easily devote a full day to this part of town. But pace yourself: the International Area covers the equivalent of many city blocks. Wear your walking shoes, check opening times in advance, and balance the museum shuffle with brisk strides through the area's parkland.

Sights to See

㉖ **Jardin Botanique** (Botanical Garden). These 69 restful acres are a legacy of the city's 19th century fascination with botany. The arboretum harbors trees that pre-date 1700; there's also an aviary, a deer park, exotic hothouses, and a rose garden, plus lots of alpine rock plants. There's even an area devoted to scent and touch. ⊠ *1 chemin de l'Impératrice,* ☎ *022/4185100.* ☞ *Free.* ☉ *Apr.–Sept., daily 8–7:30; Oct.–Mar., daily 9:30–5.*

★ ㉒ **Musée Ariana.** This superb Italianate palace, built in 1884, is now home to the **Musée Suisse de la Céramique et du Verre** (Swiss Museum of Ceramics and Glass). Its enormous permanent collections of pottery, porcelain, and faience span seven centuries, emphasizing the exchange of styles and techniques between East and West. Head down to the basement to see temporary exhibits on contemporary ceramics. A gallery devoted to glass is planned for fall 2000. There are no descriptive materials in English. ⊠ *10 av. de la Paix,* ☎ *022/4185450.* ☞ *Free.* ☉ *Wed.–Mon. 10–5.*

★ ㉗ **Musée d'Histoire des Sciences** (Museum of the History of Science). Age-old sun dials, astrolabes, microscopes, globes, and barometers, many of them wonderfully crafted, are displayed like jewels in walk-around glass cases. This is Switzerland's only museum to document the evolution of the modern scientific method. The exquisite building, the Villa Bartholoni, dates from the late 1700s. ⊠ *128 rue de Lausanne,* ☎ *022/7316985.* ☞ *Free.* ☉ *Wed.–Mon. 1–5.*

★ ㉕ **Musée International de la Croix-Rouge** (International Red Cross Museum). From a country armed to the teeth despite over 700 years of neutrality, this painstakingly nonjudgmental museum sends a different message to the world. Set in a grim glass-and-concrete structure punctuated by powerful statues of bound, hooded figures, the exhibits use state-of-the-art technology to illuminate human kindness in the face of disaster.

Audiovisuals show the postbattle horrors at Solferino that moved Henri Dunant to form the Red Cross. Good deeds are dramatized, from the proverbial Samaritan's to Clara Barton's. There are endless aisles of file boxes filled with records of World War I prisoners, and a reconstruction of a 3 m-by-2 m (10 ft-by-6½ ft) concrete cell that once contained 17 political prisoners—34 footprints make the conditions poignantly clear. And you'll learn what people did to help: the Red Cross provided information to the families of the World War I prisoners, and its formal protests led to improved conditions for the cell's captives.

The museum's masterpiece is the **Mur du Temps** (Wall of Time), a simple time line that traces, year by year, wars and natural disasters that killed 100,000 or more people. Earthquakes, volcanic eruptions, and plagues dominate the early years; in the modern age, the lists stretch long and heavy with ever-deadlier wars. Tours are given with English commentary, and English-language museum literature is also available.

✉ *17 av. de la Paix,* ☎ *022/7489511 or 022/7489506 for tour reservations.* 🎫 *10 SF.* ☉ *Wed.–Mon. 10–5.*

㉔ Musée Militaire Genevois (Geneva Military Museum). Switzerland may not have waged war outside its borders since 1292, but it has always maintained its military preparations. The arms, uniforms, flags, and documents on display here present the colorful story of Genevois soldiers from 1813 to the present, highlighting the great generals Guillaume-Henri Dufour and Henri Guisan. ✉ *18 chemin de l'Impératrice,* ☎ *022/7349021.* 🎫 *Free.* ☉ *Apr.–early Dec., Wed.–Fri. 2–5, Sat. 2–6, Sun. 10–noon and 2–6; late Dec.–Mar., Wed.–Sun. 2–5.*

㉓ Musée des Suisses à l'Étranger (Museum of Swiss Citizens Abroad). Inside the ivy-covered **Château de Penthes,** a series of exhibits outlines Switzerland's relations with the outside world from the Middle Ages to the present. Displays of documents, models, and paintings (with the occasional audiovisual aid) are set in ornate, perfectly restored rooms with period furnishings; many have a military bent. Climb to the third floor for displays on nonmilitary topics, from Swiss artists to Swiss participation in the California gold rush. There are no English-language descriptive materials available. ✉ *18 chemin de l'Impératrice,* ☎ *022/7349021.* 🎫 *5 SF.* ☉ *Apr.–Dec., Tues.–Sun. 10–noon and 2–6; Jan.–Mar., Tues.–Sun. 2–5.*

NEED A
BREAK?

Have a generous plat du jour or a slice of homemade fruit tart on the summer terrace at **Cent Suisses** (✉ 18 chemin de l'Impératrice, ☎ 022/7344865), a lunch-only spot on the grounds of the Château de Penthes.

★ **㉑ Palais des Nations** (Palace of Nations). Originally intended for the League of Nations, the Palais was built between 1929 and 1936. The League foundered during World War II and the Palais took on the European branch of the newly formed United Nations in 1946. Today it is the largest center for multilateral diplomacy in the world—host to some 7,000 conferences and 25,000 delegates each year—and the largest nexus for United Nations operational activities after New York. The design of the building's original wing was determined by an architectural competition in 1926; the group of five architects who won followed a style that has, ironically, come to be known as fascist. The building remains a superb example of the severe blend of Art Deco and stylized classicism that Mussolini and Hitler idealized. Its details—bronze torchères, gleaming marble—and many of its decorations and monuments from the interwar period have been preserved practically untouched.

High points include the **Assembly Hall,** the largest of the Palais' 34 conference rooms, which has hosted the Security Council and scores of world leaders. The ornate **Council Chamber,** which is regularly used by the Council on Disarmament, glows with splendid allegorical murals by Catalan artist José Maria Sert. Out in the corridors, rows of delegates' overcoats hang trustingly under signs marked VESTIAIRE NON GARDÉ (coatrack unsupervised). You'll need to join a tour to visit the Palais. Tours last about an hour and are given in English. You'll need your passport and there are no set starting times.

The Palais also runs temporary exhibitions and film screenings. The Museum of the League of Nations and the United Nations Philatelic Museum are quartered here as well. (Admission to the philatelic museum is included in the Palais entrance fee, but there's an additional charge for the Museum of the League of Nations, and it requires an appointment as well. Hours for all museums are the same.) The literature in the U.N. bookshop covers everything from world hunger to peacekeeping. ✉ *14 av. de la Paix,* ☎ *022/9074896.* 🎫 *8.50 SF.* ☉

Apr.–June and Sept.–Oct., daily 10–noon and 2–4; July–Aug., daily 9–6; Nov.–Mar., weekdays 10–noon and 2–4.

DINING

Geneva's restaurants, regardless of their cultural leanings, take advantage of seasonal produce; menus change three or four times a year. Most restaurants offer lunchtime plats du jour that allow you to dine for a reasonable price even at expensive establishments. It's a good idea to make reservations wherever you go, as even more casual spots quickly fill up.

CATEGORY	COST*
$$$$	over 90 SF
$$$	60 SF–90 SF
$$	30 SF–60 SF
$	under 30 SF

Prices are per person for a three-course meal (two-course meal in $ category), excluding drinks, sales tax, and 15% service charge.

$$$$ ✕ **Le Béarn.** French chef Jean-Paul Goddard's elegant, intimate restaurant features modern, light, and creative seasonal cuisine: duck-breast carpaccio with apricot chutney, rabbit with sage and nettles, subtle but sweet tarragon sorbet, and a spectacular truffle soufflé. Both the dessert cart and the French-Swiss wine list are remarkable. The only somber notes in the Empire-style dining room are struck by civil-service and diplomatic guests. ⊠ 4 quai de la Poste, ☎ 022/3210028. AE, DC, MC, V. Oct.–Apr., closed Sun., no lunch Sat. May–Sept., closed weekends.

$$$$ ✕ **Le Chat Botté.** Richard Cressac's kitchen is as silent and concentrated as an operating theater. Menus mix local specialties with the best of French cuisine, and the seafood challenges that of top coastal establishments. Savor such dishes as warm lobster salad with eggplant caviar, pan-crisped cod on a bed of peppers, baked sea bass with olive oil and fresh coriander, and toasted figs with iced nougat and quince jelly. The wine cellar is exceptional, the dining room aristocratic and graceful. The flower-decked lakefront balcony-terrace offers the ultimate summer dining experience. ⊠ Hotel Beau-Rivage, 13 quai du Mont-Blanc, ☎ 022/7166920. Reservations essential. AE, DC, MC, V.

$$$$ ✕ **Les Continents.** Chef Patrick Domon apprenticed with Fredy Girardet ★ and earned his wings in London, Hong Kong, and Singapore. The golden touch and Asian influences come through in ever-changing dishes such as coriander-creamed coconut and langoustines, chilled breast of pigeon in lemon, filet mignon with truffles and candied onions, and pineapple soufflé with rum and tropical fruit. Although the flavors reach abroad, the dining room remains classic with Victorian wood panels, creamy linen, and chandeliers. ⊠ Hotel Intercontinental, 7–9 chemin du Petit-Saconnex, ☎ 022/9193350. Reservations essential. AE, DC, MC, V. Closed weekends.

$$$$ ✕ **Le Cygne.** Splendid views of the Jet d'Eau and Mont Blanc accompany ★ Parisian chef Philippe Jourdin's soigné, if conservative, menu at the Noga-Hilton's handsome restaurant. Smoked sea bass with truffle vinaigrette is a perennial favorite, or try the lobster salad with truffles and mâche (lamb's lettuce). There's a fabulous cellar of French and Swiss wines, but the real show is the caravan of ever-changing dessert carts—crêpes flambées are particularly exciting. ⊠ 19 quai du Mont-Blanc, ☎ 022/9089085. AE, DC, MC, V.

$$$$ ✕ **Le Lion d'Or.** Cologny is Geneva's Beverly Hills with a view, and this ★ culinary landmark takes full advantage of its real estate—the summer terrace overlooks the city, the lake, and the Jura. Local celebrity chefs Gilles Dupont and Tommy Byrne give seafood and seasonal menus a

356

Geneva Dining and Lodging

light, sophisticated edge; duck wings with foie gras and fricassée of lobster with lemon and endive are among the highlights, as are warm soufflés from the dessert cart. The wood-paneled bistro next door shares the restaurant's kitchen but not its prices—grab a cab and come for lunch. ✉ *5 pl. Pierre-Gautier, Cologny,* ☎ *022/7364432. AE, DC, MC, V. Closed weekends.*

$$$ ✕ **L'Ange du Dix Vins/Le Dix Vins.** Chef Réné Fracheboud's innova-
★   tive kitchen serves two crowds—one in the main restaurant, the other in the cozy, antiques-cluttered bistro next door. (Guests are welcome to flow from one to the other.) The seasonal menu is marked by original, vivid dishes flavored with curry oil, cocoa, and even coffee, served in a warm Mediterranean decor of gold and ocher. The list of bottled wines is impressive and there's a good lineup of lesser-known wines by the glass. Prices between the two restaurants are comparable. ✉ *31–29 rue Jacques Dalphin, Carouge,* ☎ *022/3420318. AE, MC, V. Jan.–Aug., closed weekends; Sept.–Dec., closed Sun., no lunch Sat.*

$$$ ✕ **La Favola.** Run by a Ticinese chef from Locarno, this quirky little
★   restaurant may be the town's most picturesque. The tiny dining room, at the top of a vertiginous spiral staircase, strikes a delicate balance between rustic and fussy, with lace window panels, embroidered tablecloths, polished parquet, and a rough-beam ceiling sponge-painted in shades of ocher and rust. The food echoes this orientation: part country-simple and part city-chic. Homemade pastas melt on the tongue, the carpaccio is paper-thin, and the tiramisu is divine. Lunch menus offer excellent value. ✉ *15 rue Calvin,* ☎ *022/3117437. No credit cards. Closed Sun. No lunch Sat.*

$$$ ✕ **La Glycine/Chez Jipek'à.** You'll enter through the kitchen at this classic *caboulot* (downscale cabaret-bistro) where waiters recite the menu and music is played outside under the *glycine* (hanging wisteria) in summer. Jipek'à—a Czech turned Swiss—is the soul of the place, which is always smoky, noisy, and full to bursting. The food is only average, but you come here for the ambience, to sing or laugh with the pianist, and to mix with *les bohèmes* who frequent the place. People have been known to dance between tables. ✉ *21 rue de Montbrillant,* ☎ *022/ 7336285. MC, V. Closed Sun.*

$$$ ✕ **La Perle du Lac.** This grand wooden chalet, set along the most romantic stretch of Geneva's Right Bank park-promenade, has a lovely summer terrace as well as an intimate dining room, L'Orangerie, that looks straight out over the water at Mont Blanc. The French-accented, seasonal menu focuses on fish such as *rouget barbet* (red mullet), *dorade* (dorado), and salmon. The list of French wines is exhaustive. ✉ *126 rue de Lausanne,* ☎ *022/7317935. AE, DC, MC, V. Closed Mon.*

$$$ ✕ **Roberto.** Roberto Carugati and his daughter, Marietta, have made
★   this spot the meeting point for businesspeople, chic Italians, and political bigwigs. Parmesan cheese arrives to whet your appetite (in lieu of bread); then choose from dishes such as eggplant carpaccio with coriander, pasta in saffron sauce, buttery sole with tarragon, and risotto served from shining copper and silver pots. Try to leave room for the delicious raspberry mousse. Unusual and rare Italian wines loosen the elegance as the night wears on. ✉ *10 rue Pierre-Fatio,* ☎ *022/3118033. AE, MC, V. Closed Sun. No dinner Sat.*

$$ ✕ **Les Armures.** Everyone from workers to politicians comes to this Old Town institution next to the Maison Tavel. The dining rooms have old beams, heavy wrought iron, and authentic medieval arms. This is not the place to come for light or nuanced cooking; robust Swiss specialties include fondue, raclette, *filets de perches* (perch fillets), *schübling* (sausage), and *Rösti* (hash browns). It serves until midnight—unusually late for Geneva. ✉ *1 rue du Puits-St-Pierre,* ☎ *022/3103442. AE, DC, MC, V.*

$$ ✕ **Au Pied-de-Cochon.** Crowded, noisy, smoky, and packed shoulder to shoulder with hip young legals spilling over from the Palais de Justice, this is the real article—an authentic Genevois bistro in all its gruff, clattering glory. White tiles, wood panelling, ancient beams, and a worn zinc bar make a perfect background for simple regional cuisine: grilled andouillettes, boudin noir, longeole with lentils, and the namesake pigs' feet, served grilled, poached, or boned with pork knuckles. ✉ *4 pl. du Bourg-de-Four,* ☎ *022/3104797. AE, DC, MC, V.*

$$ ✕ **Boeuf Rouge.** This send-up of a Lyonnais bistro, packed with kitschy
★ ceramics and Art Nouveau posters, delivers the real thing: rich bacon-egg-and-greens *salade Lyonnaise,* hand-stuffed, pistachio-studded sausage, *boudin noir* (blood sausage) with apples, and tender quenelles *de brochet* (of pike). The ambiance is relaxed, the service brisk and flamboyant: all dishes are presented on flower-crowded trays for your inspection, then served with a flourish. Dessert includes an unusual selection of smooth chestnut and citrus mousses. ✉ *17 rue Alfred-Vincent,* ☎ *022/7327537. AE, DC, MC, V. Closed weekends.*

$$ ✕ **Brasserie Lipp.** Green and white tiles, mustard-yellow ceilings, warm wood, and bustling waiters in ankle-length white aprons bring this Parisian clone to life. Genevois intellectuals of all stripes gather over classic brasserie fare, including good *choucroûte* (sauerkraut) and heaping platters of seafood. (You can choose between small and large portions.) The odd location, on the third floor of a slick shopping center, is made up for in summer by a spectacular terrace at the foot of the Old Town. ✉ *Confédération-Centre, 8 rue de la Confédération,* ☎ *022/3111011. AE, DC, MC, V.*

$$ ✕ **L'Entrecôte Couronnée.** Exclusive and clubbish, this little bistro isn't exactly gentrified—it's at the edge of the Pâquis quarter near the red-light district, and it's run by a retired chanteuse. The entrecôte is excellent, which is a blessing: it's the house specialty and the only thing on the menu save for a delicious green salad. The bistro's name means "the Crowned Steak," but it's not just the steaks that are crowned—prominent guests have included a Hapsburg archduke and Marie-Astrid de Luxembourg. ✉ *5 rue des Pâquis,* ☎ *022/7328445. MC, V. Closed weekends.*

$$ ✕ **Les Fous de la Place.** This chic spot next to the Musée Rath pulls in an arty, young-pro crowd for ever-changing, creative cuisine at reasonable prices. The mock-gilt-framed menus reveal Asian and Middle Eastern influences. The decor leans to the ornate, with candelabras just inside the door, slim red settees, saffron tasseled drapes, and scarlet cone lamps. ✉ *21 rue de la Corraterie,* ☎ *022/3105340. AE, DC, MC, V. Closed Sun. and Mon. No lunch Sat.*

$$ ✕ **Hôtel-de-Ville.** Behind its somewhat bedraggled lace curtains, this steamy, clattering brasserie packs in civil servants and art dealers, who settle onto wooden banquettes for typical Genevois *filets de perches* (perch), longeole, mussels, and beautifully garnished game platters in season. Don't let the brusque service deter you; they're like that to everyone. It serves until midnight. ✉ *39 Grand-Rue,* ☎ *022/3117030. AE, DC, MC, V.*

$$ ✕ **Jeck's Place.** Even by Geneva's cosmopolitan standards, this halo-
★ gen-lit, peach-accented restaurant offers a staggering mix of cultures. Owner Jeck Tan, a native of Singapore and a graduate of the Swiss Hotel School, greets you warmly in English at the door and presents a menu written in Malay, Chinese, Thai, and French. The food, whether it's smooth, deep fried bean curd with peanut sauce, chicken in delicate green curry, fried Mee Hoon vermicelli, or spicy roast duck *au diable,* is finely nuanced. The service is irreproachable. ✉ *14 rue de Neuchâtel,* ☎ *022/7313303. AE, DC, MC, V. No lunch Sat.*

$$ ✗ **Le Lyrique.** Black and white floor tiles offset warm yellow walls and
★ high wedding-cake ceilings in this relaxed café-brasserie in the heart
of Geneva's musical quarter. Portraits of Beethoven, Verdi, Strauss, and
Liszt watch over pre-theater diners as they choose homemade pasta
with scampi, summer gazpacho, or steak tartare. The dessert cart in-
cludes a succulent *crème caramel*. While the Lyrique is generally closed
on weekends, it makes an exception and stays open on performance
dates at the Grand Théâtre across the street. ⊠ *12 bd. du Théâtre,* ☎
022/3280095. AE, DC, MC, V.

$$ ✗ **L'Opera Bouffe.** This extremely popular spot serves almost-classic
★ Geneva bistro fare—many with a unusual twist courtesy of the Syrian
chef, who overhauls the menu every month. The setting is chic and relaxed, with opera music in the background and wine stacked floor to
ceiling. Don't pass up the warm *tarte Tatin* (caramelized, upside-down
apple tart) with Gruyère cream. ⊠ *5 av. de Frontenex,* ☎ *022/7366300.
AE, DC, MC, V. Closed Sun. and Mon. No lunch Sat.*

$$ ✗ **Le Relais de l'Entrecôte.** *Steak frîtes* is a perennial French favorite,
★ but the standard cut of beef and pat of herb butter are easily eclipsed
by the perfectly spiced *sauce maison* and tender morsels you will find
here. The accompaniments—crisp green salads sprinkled with walnuts,
thin, golden fries, and a robust house wine—more than make the
grade. The smoky, popular restaurant is wedged between haute cou-
ture emporia and decorated with gigantic Belle Epoque posters. ⊠ *49
rue du Rhône,* ☎ *022/3106004. MC, V.*

$ ✗ **Café du Grütli.** Black-clad filmmakers, actors, photographers,
dancers, and students from the nearby Université de Genève congre-
gate in this sun-soaked, smoky lunch spot inside the postmodernized
Grütli arts center. Choose from unfussy, satisfying dishes such as
salmon carpaccio with lime or fettucine with tuna and black olives.
Finish with chocolate mousse with pistachio sauce. There are un-
dubbed classic film screenings in the basement. ⊠ *16 rue du Général-
Dufour,* ☎ *022/3294495. AE, DC, MC, V.*

$ ✗ **Chez Léo.** This tiny corner bistro hard by Roberto (☞ *above*) pre-
sents the simple Italian cuisine of Roberto's son, Léo. Here you'll find
veal piccata in raspberry vinegar, homemade tortellini, and a batch of
intense locals in an old-fashioned bentwood-and-posters setting. ⊠ *12
rue Pierre-Fatio,* ☎ *022/3115307. MC, V. Closed Sun. No dinner Sat.*

$ ✗ **L'Echalotte.** Polished wood banquettes, good food, and low prices
★ draw local artists and journalists to this comfortable spot. The menu
stretches from vegetarian options to abats, and such dishes as buttery
crème de courge (pumpkin soup) and grilled shrimp with fresh thyme
arrive piping hot. The chocolate terrine is sinful. ⊠ *17 rue des Rois,*
☎ *022/3205999. MC, V. Closed weekends.*

$ ✗ **Taverne de la Madeleine.** Tucked almost out of sight behind l'Église
de la Madeleine at the foot of the Old Town, this big, local, friendly
Swiss café claims to be the oldest in Geneva. Run by the city's tem-
perance league, it serves no alcoholic beverages and thus loses the busi-
ness-lunch crowd, who miss out on homemade choucroûte and petit
salée in winter, generous salads and *filets de perches* in summer, and
fresh-baked fruit tarts all year round. The kitchen closes at 9 in sum-
mer, at 4 on Saturdays and in winter. ⊠ *20 rue Toutes-âmes,* ☎ *022/
3106070. MC, V. Closed Sun.*

$ ✗ **Le Thé** A three-course meal at this tiny, hole-in-the-wall Chinese tea
★ room costs less than an appetizer of similar quality anywhere else. The
choices are all *à la vapeur* (steamed), including succulent rice-flour crepes
stuffed with shrimp, dim sum, and steamed bread. There are 20 dif-
ferent kinds of green tea alone; appropriately enough, delicate red
clay teapots (for sale) line the walls. The six tables fill up fast—call

ahead or drop by after 1:30 for lunch. ⊠ *65 rue des Bains,* ☎ *079/ 4367718. No credit cards. Closed Sun.*

LODGING

Spending the night in Geneva can be financially taxing—rates are comparable to those in most European capitals—but you'll limit the damage by taking advantage of weekend or other special rates. One side effect of Geneva's popularity as a convention city is the hotels' willingness to drop rates for groups or during nonpeak times. (Prices plummet most dramatically at luxury hotels.) Book well in advance: whole blocks of rooms or entire hotels can fill up during major conferences.

CATEGORY	COST*
$$$$	over 300 SF
$$$	200 SF–300 SF
$$	130 SF–200 SF
$	under 130 SF

Prices are for a standard double room, including breakfast, tax, and service charge.

$$$$ 🏨 **D'Angleterre.** In an impeccable balancing act, this hotel evinces ★ both Victorian and modern leanings. Broad satin pinstripes cover walls and settees throughout; each hallway stocks leather-bound books in several languages. Rooms have fine British antiques, dark green and pale yellow accents, and wood-edged baths—and, from some rooms, wrought-iron café tables on balconies with views of Mont Blanc and the Jet d'Eau. The Library bar has a working fireplace and live jazz Thursday through Saturday; the winter-garden restaurant is nothing short of spectacular. ⊠ *17 quai du Mont-Blanc, CH-1201,* ☎ *022/ 9065555,* ℻ *022/9065556. 39 rooms, 6 suites. Restaurant, bar, sauna, exercise room, 2 meeting rooms. AE, DC, MC, V.*

$$$$ 🏨 **Les Armures.** This hotel in the heart of the Vieille Ville is steeped in ★ history. Original 17th century stonework, frescoes, painted beams, and tapestries adorn the lobby and some rooms. All rooms have somber antiques, marble baths, and thick bathrobes; the casual restaurant is an Old Town must (☞ Dining, *above*). Two very quiet rooms give onto a tiny inner courtyard; those overlooking rue du Perron have picturesque cobblestone views. ⊠ *1 rue du Puits-St-Pierre, CH-1204,* ☎ *022/3109172,* ℻ *022/3109846. 24 rooms, 4 suites. Restaurant, bar. AE, DC, MC, V.*

$$$$ 🏨 **Beau-Rivage.** Hushed and genteel, this grand old Victorian palace ★ maintains much of its original 1865 splendor. The building centers on a four-story atrium with a murmuring fountain. Rooms are decorated with period furniture and dramatic swagged fabrics and have enormous baths; many retain fine old architectural details, and those in front overlook the Jet d'Eau. The opposite of Hilton-slick, this discreet landmark banks on the Mayer family's warm hospitality; since the hotel's founding they have hosted Richard Wagner, Jean Cocteau, and Sissi, the Empress Elizabeth of Austria, who died here after being stabbed only 100 m (328 ft) away. ⊠ *13 quai du Mont-Blanc, CH-1201,* ☎ *022/ 7166666,* ℻ *022/7166060. 91 rooms, 6 suites. Restaurant, piano bar, café, 6 meeting rooms. AE, DC, MC, V.*

$$$$ 🏨 **Des Bergues.** The oldest, most discreet, and least self-conscious of ★ Geneva's grand hotels is also, not coincidentally, among its most expensive. However, friendly service and a graceful interior keep it unpretentious. It's been thoroughly renovated from the roots up over the past sixteen years. Now the Louis-Philippe elegance—crystal chandeliers, 1834 architectural details, luxurious marble bathrooms—is

matched by modern conveniences like individual fax machines and modems in all rooms. The sunny Le Pavillon restaurant serves a extraordinary afternoon tea. ⊠ *33 quai des Bergues, CH-1201,* ☎ *022/ 7315050,* FAX *022/7321989. 104 rooms, 14 suites. 2 restaurants, bar, 6 meeting rooms. AE, DC, MC, V.*

$$$$ 🖭 **De la Cigogne.** Every room here showcases a different decorative style, but the overall feel is neo-medieval. It's a great place to enjoy antiques, tapestries, working fireplaces, and an easy mix of atmosphere and modern comforts. The location, in the heart of the Left Bank shopping area in the shadow of the Old Town, can't be beat. ⊠ *17 pl. Longemalle, CH-1204,* ☎ *022/8184040,* FAX *022/8184050. 35 rooms, 15 suites. Restaurant, meeting room. AE, DC, MC, V.*

$$$$ 🖭 **Intercontinental.** Perhaps it's the airport terminal–sized lobby, the ultra-flexible conference rooms, or the multitude of world figures that draw so many media folks and government officials here. Regardless, the status of this 1960s high-rise as a virtual branch of the United Nations is clear. It is also, however, a luxury hotel: plants soften the hard lines of anonymous paneling and Oriental rugs, pastel fabrics, and brass accents warm the rooms. The panoramic views of Geneva and Mont Blanc are spectacular—it's like looking at a map. ⊠ *7–9 chemin du Petit-Saconnex, CH-1211,* ☎ *022/9193939,* FAX *022/9193838. 278 rooms, 67 suites. 2 restaurants, bar, pool, beauty salon, health club, 14 meeting rooms, free parking. AE, DC, MC, V.*

$$$$ 🖭 **Métropole.** Swissôtel manages this imposing 1855 Left Bank palace, now separated by six lanes of traffic from its former estate; it's a favorite with businesspeople thanks to well lighted modern conference facilities and close ties to Swissair. The ambience is relaxed and unfussy despite the grand scale; hunter green, yellow, and salmon are the colors of choice, and all windows are triple-glazed to ensure silence. High-voltage rue du Rhône shopping is literally just outside, and the wraparound view from the roof is the envy of the city during Fêtes de Genève fireworks. ⊠ *34 quai Général-Guisan, CH-1204,* ☎ *022/ 3183200,* FAX *022/3183300. 115 rooms, 13 suites. Restaurant, piano bar, 7 meeting rooms. AE, DC, MC, V.*

$$$$ 🖭 **Le Richemond.** Crimson satin and velvet, fringed braid, moiré, lush floral carpets, pastel silks, and 18th-century antiques—once inside this opulent, slightly stuffy 1875 landmark you might feel as though you're on a movie or theater set. This place is for real, though, and it's not completely stuck in the past: the luxurious rooms all have modems and voice mail. Individual balconies overlook the Brunswick Monument, while Rolls Royces angle for space outside. ⊠ *Jardin Brunswick, CH-1201,* ☎ *022/7311400,* FAX *022/7316709. 67 rooms, 31 suites. Restaurant, piano bar, beauty salon, exercise room, 7 meeting rooms. AE, DC, MC, V.*

$$$ 🖭 **Ambassador.** Don't let the airport lounge–style lobby fool you—
★   even rooms on the first floor of this just-renovated (1999) Right Bank hotel are smartly decorated and flooded with light. Many of the huge doubles would be called suites elsewhere, and bathrooms gleam with white tile. Although you'll pay more for a room with a view, it's worth it to see the sun rise over the Old Town across the river. ⊠ *21 quai des Bergues, CH-1211,* ☎ *022/7317200,* FAX *022/7389080. 83 rooms. Restaurant, meeting room. AE, DC, MC, V.*

$$$ 🖭 **De Berne.** Most of the edges in this solid, spacious, well-maintained, business-class hotel have been softened with polished wood, touches of brass, and warm colors. Mont Blanc is visible from the deluxe fifth floor, and double-glazed windows keep the noise of unruly 24-hour street activity at bay. (The hotel is on a street considered red-light by the Genevois, but this is relative. The kebab stands and cheap shoe stores may seem scruffy in comparison to the rest of the city, but it is not a dangerous area.) Breakfast options are unusually rich. ✉ *26 rue de Berne, CH-1201,* ☎ *022/7316000,* ⒻⒶⓍ *022/7311173. 81 rooms, 8 suites. Restaurant, bar, 2 meeting rooms. AE, DC, MC, V.*

\$\$–\$\$\$ 🏨 **Le Montbrillant.** Nineteenth-century stone walls and beams accent the clean lines, rose fabrics, and blue-gray trim of this family-run hotel less than 50 m (150 ft) from the Gare Cornavin. (Double-glazed windows keep it quiet.) If you'll be in town for a while, request one of the fifth-floor studios, let on a weekly or monthly basis—these have kitchenettes, dormer windows, cathedral ceilings, and plenty of space. The third floor is a no-smoking floor. ✉ *2 rue de Montbrillant, CH-1201,* ☎ *022/7337784,* ⒻⒶⓍ *022/7332511. 58 rooms, 24 studios. 2 restaurants, bar, meeting room, free parking. AE, DC, MC, V.*

\$\$ 🏨 **D'Allèves.** There may not be a view from this quiet, somewhat musty hotel on a secluded square, but there are unusual architectural details. The cavernous rooms are filled with the owner's collection of art and antiques and exude an elegant heaviness no longer in vogue. One of the suites has a grand piano. Suites on the seventh floor have lofts. ✉ *13 rue Kléberg, CH-1211,* ☎ *022/7321530,* ⒻⒶⓍ *022/7383266. 36 rooms, 6 suites. 2 restaurants. AE, DC, MC, V.*

\$\$ 🏨 **Montana.** The warm welcome from the multilingual staff sets this spot well above its neighbors. Two rooms still have two-way shoe-shine doors from 1957—but the property is up-to-date with in-room cable TV, white tiled bathrooms, and modems. Windows on all but the top floor are soundproof. The hotel is just a block from the train station. ✉ *23 rue des Alpes, CH-1201,* ☎ *022/7320840,* ⒻⒶⓍ *022/7382511. 40 rooms. Breakfast room, laundry service. AE, DC, MC, V.*

\$\$ 🏨 **Suisse.** In spite of its name, the narrow, cheerful, sponge-painted
★ lobby of this corner hotel facing the train station feels positively Parisian. Colorful trompe l'oeil scenes decorate the elevator doors; a model tall ship or clipper greets you on the landing of each floor. The large, bright rooms are soundproof; they also have generously sized, impeccable bathrooms. ✉ *10 pl. de Cornavin, CH-1201,* ☎ *022/7326630,* ⒻⒶⓍ *022/7326239. 57 rooms. Restaurant, bar. AE, DC, MC, V.*

\$–\$\$ 🏨 **Bernina.** Duvets are starched and puffed to Germanic perfection in this 19th-century building—perhaps due to the antique laundry press still in use. The overall atmosphere is mildly gloomy, but you're not paying for personality. There are several options to suit your budget, from cheap double beds with sink to full doubles with the works. Windows are double-glazed throughout. It's a convenient choice if you've got an early train to catch—the hotel is directly across from the station. ✉ *22 pl. de Cornavin, CH-1201,* ☎ *022/9084950,* ⒻⒶⓍ *022/ 9084951. 80 rooms. Breakfast room. AE, MC, V.*

\$–\$\$ 🏨 **International et Terminus.** This modest, comfortable hotel is a sure sell-out when there's a conference in town. Its airy rooms were recently overhauled (1999), painted in pastel colors and equipped with amenities such as minibars, safes, and cable TV. The hotel is just down the block from the train station. ✉ *20 rue des Alpes, CH-1201,* ☎ *022/ 7328095,* ⒻⒶⓍ *022/7321843. 60 rooms. Restaurant. AE, DC, MC, V.*

\$ 🏨 **Bel'Espérance.** The Salvation Army owns this former *foyer pour dames*
★ (ladies' boarding house) tucked away near place du Bourg-de-Four. Its conference facilities, bright yellow and blue rooms (all with tiled bath), and graceful, Louis-Philippe style breakfast room put it on a par with much pricier hotels. Monthly rates, no-smoking rooms, and communal kitchen space are available; each studio has a kitchenette. The hotel serves no alcohol. ✉ *1 rue de la Vallée, CH-1204,* ☎ *022/8183737,* ⒻⒶⓍ *022/8183773. 38 rooms, 2 studios. Breakfast room, meeting room. AE, DC, MC, V.*

$ 🏨 **Central.** Once you've found this bargain hotel threaded between offices at the top of an anonymous building on a back Left Bank shopping street, the worst is over. The rooms are functional if a bit scuffed, the welcome is cordial, and prices are the lowest in town for rooms with bath. The ownership changed in 1999—a slow but steady overhaul is taking place room by room. ⊠ *2 rue de la Rôtisserie, CH-1204,* 🕾 *022/8188100,* FAX *022/8188101. 30 rooms. AE, DC, MC, V.*

$ 🏨 **De la Cloche.** Christian Chabbey and his mother Esther keep friendly,
★ eager watch over their guests in this once-luxurious first floor apartment. It has been carved into eight bedrooms with toilets down the hall, and the homey decor (flocked wallpaper, crowded bookcases, creaky parquet floors) matches the spirit of the place. You won't find a more central location with breakfast in bed in Geneva for this price. Half of the rooms have their own toilet and shower, and showers are being added room by room to the rest. (All have sinks.) ⊠ *6 rue de la Cloche, CH-1201,* 🕾 *022/7329481,* FAX *022/7381612. 8 rooms. AE, DC, MC, V.*

$ 🏨 **St-Gervais.** Red tartan carpeting underfoot and fresh, creamy linen
★ warm the garretlike rooms in this old, Right Bank inn. The tiny, wood-panelled café on the ground floor doubles as a breakfast room. Most major bus lines stop right around the corner. ⊠ *20 rue des Corps-Saints, CH-1201,* 🕾 *022/7324572,* FAX *022/7324572. 21 rooms, 1 with bath, 1 with shower. Breakfast room/café. AE, MC, V.*

$ 🏨 **Des Tourelles.** Once worthy of a czar, now host to summer backpackers, this imposing, stripped-down Victorian town house has enormous bay-window corner rooms, marble fireplaces, tiled stoves, balconies, and spectacular river views. The furnishings are strictly functional and the hallways a bit scuffed, but all rooms have complete modular bathrooms and the staff is young and friendly. Bring earplugs if you like your windows open: there is plenty of noise from both the river and traffic. ⊠ *2 bd. James-Fazy, CH-1201,* 🕾 *022/7324423,* FAX *022/7327620. 23 rooms. Breakfast room. AE, DC, MC, V.*

NIGHTLIFE AND THE ARTS

Geneva Agenda, a bilingual (English and French) weekly publication, lists concerts, exhibitions, performances, and other events. It is available free from tourist information booths and most hotels. The monthly *Genève Le Guide,* also available free in information booths and hotels, or for 3 SF from any kiosk, has film synopses and a detailed city map in addition to events listings. It's bilingual (French and English) as well.

Nightlife

Genevois nightlife can be chic and exclusive, centered on trendy cafés and bistros, or linked to a lively pub circuit lifted whole from the British Isles. Virtually wherever you go you'll find someone who speaks English—the international crowd likes to party.

Bars and Pubs

Le Baroque (⊠ 12 pl. de la Fusterie, 🕾 022/3110515) combines Baroque opulence and a tailored, young-pro, cell-phone-brandishing crowd. Many of the luxury hotel bars offer piano music and cocktails; the **Beau-Rivage** (☞ Lodging, *above*) bar is particularly genteel. In summer, **La Clémence** (⊠ 20 pl. du Bourg-de-Four, 🕾 022/3122498) fills with university students and explodes into the street. **Flanagan's** (⊠ 4 rue du Cheval-Blanc, 🕾 022/3101314) marks the start of Geneva's thriving pub circuit. **Mr. Pickwick's Pub** (⊠ 80 rue de Lausanne, 🕾 022/7316797) serves fish-and-chips, shows English football, and staves off homesickness in British expats. You'll find Guinness on tap, Kilkenny beer, and Irish accents at **Mulligan's** (⊠ 14 rue Grenus, 🕾 022/

7328576), on the Right Bank. The **Roi Ubu** (⊠ 30 Grand-Rue, ☎ 022/
3107398) is a haunt for younger drinkers in the Old Town.

Casinos

The **Casino de Genève Les Boucaniers** (⊠ 19 quai du Mont-Blanc,
☎ 022/7326320), has a range of slot machines and a 25 SF
gambling limit. Big money changes hands on the blackjack tables of
the **Casino de Divonne,** in France (⊠ Divonne, ☎ 059/450403437).
Take the Geneva-Lausanne autoroute 15 minutes north to Coppet-
Divonne (☞ Arriving and Departing *in* Geneva A to Z, *below*)

Dancing

Arthur's (⊠ 20 rte. de Pré-Bois, ☎ 022/7917700) plays house music
and packs some 1,500 guests into multi-layered dance areas and several bars. **Griffin's** (⊠ 36 bd. Helvétique, ☎ 022/7351218) has live
rhythm and blues during the week and a yuppie-chic, black-tie crowd
studded with famous names. **L'Interdit** (⊠ 18 quai du Seujet, ☎ 022/
7389091) blasts deafening techno and classic disco music in a flamboyantly extravagant space. **Macumba** (⊠ rte. d'Annecy, St. Julien, ☎
059/450492350), across the French border to the south, grooves to '80s
music, salsa, and classic rock. **Le Petit Palace** (⊠ 6 rue de la Tour-de-
Boël, ☎ 022/3110 033) fills up on weekends with techno music, jazzy
style, and energetic young people. **Shakers** (⊠ 3 rue de la Boulangerie,
☎ 022/3104198) is an Old Town hole-in-the-wall with stone walls,
cheap drinks, and a DJ who plays anything but techno. **L'Usine** (⊠ 4
pl. des Volontaires, ☎ 022/7813490) favors funk, hard rock, punk,
grunge music, and the occasional live band.

Jazz Clubs

AMR–Sud des Alpes (⊠ 10 rue des Alpes, ☎ 022/7165630) fosters musical improvisation and contemporary jazz; it also draws a hip young
crowd. **Au Chat Noir** (⊠ 13 rue Vautier, Carouge, ☎ 022/3434998)
has a program that cycles through musical styles. It draws an international group to its casual bar. The restaurant **Aux Halles de l'Ile** (⊠
1 pl. de l'Ile, ☎ 022/3115221) spices up its languid river views with
classic New Orleans jazz on Friday and Saturday nights.

The Arts

Geneva supports an unusually rich arts scene for its size. The city's mix
of cultures all but guarantees a steady influx of foreign artists and influences, who mesh seamlessly with Swiss performers in the city's theaters and concert halls. You can nab tickets to most performances just
a day or two ahead of time, or even on the day of performance. Buying tickets directly from the theater is a reliable option, and Globus
Grand Passage (⊠ 50 rue du Rhone, ☎ 022/3109193) is another
source.

Film

Most movies are dubbed, but English-language films are shown in English, usually in the late afternoon and after 10 PM. Check local newspaper listings for the initials *v.o.,* short for *version originale.* The **CAC
Voltaire** (⊠ 6 rue du Général-Dufour, ☎ 022/3207878) shows classic
films in their original languages. From early July to mid-August the
outdoor **Cinélac** (Port-Noir, Cologny) screens films at sunset against
the magnificent backdrop of the lake and the Jura. The films are un-
dubbed (the majority are in English) and they change every night.

Music and Dance

The **Bâtiment des Forces Motrices** (⊠ 2 pl. des Volontaires, ☎ 022/
3221220) presents a varied program of classical music, modern dance,

and musical theater. The 1886 building originally funneled drinking water to the city, and it retains two of its original turbines. Recitals, chamber music concerts, and a major annual solo competition take place at the **Conservatoire de Musique** (✉ pl. Neuve, ☎ 022/3196060). The **Grand Théâtre** (✉ pl. Neuve, ☎ 022/4183000) ranks among the best opera houses in the world and stages a full-scale production about once a month between September and June. Its luscious red velvet and cutting-edge technical facilities date from 1998, when the theater was fully overhauled and restored. The list of artists who have performed with L'Orchestre de la Suisse Romande since 1918 in the gilt-and-velvet bijou **Victoria Hall** (✉ 14 rue du Général-Dufour, ☎ 022/8070017) reads like a who's who of classical music.

Theater

Am Stram Gram (✉ 56 rte. de Frontenex, ☎ 022/7357924) makes magic with every production of its childrens' theater, whether based on obscure myth, lyric poetry, or contemporary sources. These creative performances are completely enjoyable even if you don't speak French. The **Comédie de Genève** (✉ 6 bd. des Philosophes, ☎ 022/3205001) stages classic French comedy and drama, but change is in the air; a vigorous new artistic director arrived in mid-1999. The program at the **Théâtre du Grütli** (✉ 16 rue du Général-Dufour, ☎ 022/3289878) mixes contemporary experimental theater and foreign plays in translation (into French) in a flexible blackbox setting.

OUTDOOR ACTIVITIES AND SPORTS

Golf

The **Golf Club de Genève** (✉ 70 rte. de la Capite, Cologny, ☎ 022/7074800) welcomes visitors March to November and rents equipment.

Sailing

The **École Club Migros** (✉ 3 rue du Prince, ☎ 022/3196161) offers sailing courses between April and October. **Les Corsaires** (✉ 33 quai Gustave-Ador, ☎ 022/7354300) rents boats and holds classes.

Ice Skating

Bring your skates to the outdoor **Patinoire de Meyrin** (✉ chemin Louis Rendu, ☎ 022/7821300), which is open daily from October to March. The **Patinoire des Vernets** (✉ 4–6 rue Hans-Wilsdorf, Acacias, ☎ 022/4184022) has indoor skating Tuesday through Sunday during the same period. Rental skates are available.

Skiing

Geneva itself is not a ski destination, but the French Alps are close by. From early December until mid-April ski buses depart daily from the **Gare Routière de Genève** (✉ pl. Dorcière, ☎ 022/7320230) for Chamonix, Les Contamines, and Morzine-Avoriaz, all major resorts in France. Trips take 1–1½ hours, and the 50 SF fare includes a ski-lift pass.

Swimming

The skating rinks at Meyrin and Les Vernets (☞ *above*) become outdoor pools in summer. Some Genevois still swear that you'll catch an impressive array of diseases from swimming in the cleaned-up waters of Lake Geneva, but the city's beaches are crowded from the moment they open in April until closing time in October. Take Bus 2 to the end of the line for the outdoor pool, lake access, and water slide at **Genève-Plage** (✉ Port-Noir, Cologny, ☎ 022/7362482). The popular sauna and restaurant at **Les Bains des Pâquis** (✉ 30 quai du Mont-Blanc, ☎ 022/7322974) stay open through the winter while the beach is closed.

Tennis

Visitors are welcome at the **Open Club** (⌧ 51 rte. de Collex, Bellevue, ☎ 022/7741514) during off-peak hours. The **Tennis Club du Bois Carré** (⌧ 14 chemin des Bûcherons, Vessy, ☎ 022/7843006) also offers badminton and squash. The **Tennis Club de Champel** (⌧ 41 route de Vessy, ☎ 022/7842566) accepts visitors year round. You can rent equipment from local sports stores.

SHOPPING

Auctions

As a jewelry capital rivaled only by New York and an international center for Swiss watchmakers, Geneva regularly hosts high-profile auctions by the major houses. **Antiquorum** (⌧ 2 rue du Mont-Blanc, ☎ 022/9092850) deals exclusively in contemporary and antique watches. **Christie's** (⌧ 8 pl. de la Taconnerie, ☎ 022/3191766) adds wine to its glamorous jewelry sales in the equally swank Hotel Le Richemond. **Sotheby's** (⌧ 13 quai du Mont-Blanc, ☎ 022/7328585) holds previews at the Hôtel Beau-Rivage before each sale.

Department Stores

Globus Grand Passage (⌧ 48 rue du Rhône, ☎ 022/3195050) links the main Left Bank shopping streets. Its kitchen goods, mens' clothing, and fresh food sections are exceptional. **Bon Génie** (⌧ 34 rue du Marché, ☎ 022/8181111) sells high-profile designer clothing and cosmetics on floor after hushed floor.

Markets

Halle de Rive (⌧ 29 blvd. Helvétique, ☎ 022/4186230) sells fresh cheeses, meats, and pasta Monday through Saturday. It is augmented every Wednesday and Saturday morning by a large outdoor fruit and vegetable market on the **Boulevard Helvétique.** Place de la Fusterie has an arts-and-crafts market every Thursday. On Wednesdays and Saturdays you'll find antiques and knickknacks (*brocante*) at the flea market on the Plaine de Plainpalais.

Shopping Streets and Malls

Geneva's two principal shopping streets run parallel along the Left Bank. Closest to the river is the the epicenter of luxury shopping, **rue du Rhône.** One block toward the Old Town is the less-expensive but still posh street known variously as: **rue de la Confédération, rue du Marché, rue de la Croix-d'Or,** and **rue de Rive.** The **Grand-Rue** in the Old Town is lined with galleries, antiques shops, bookstores, and cafés. Streets radiating from **place du Bourg-de-Four** are full of boutiques. **Rue du Mont-Blanc,** on the Right Bank close to the train station, has less expensive watch and souvenir shops. The **Confédération Centre** is a glitzy, three-story shopping center that opens at the bottom onto rue de la Confédération and leads from the top into the Old Town. **Les Cygnes,** a small, glossy urban mall near the train station on rue de Lausanne, has everything from shoes to gourmet food.

Specialty Stores

Antiques

Antiquités Scientifiques (⌧ 19 rue du Perron, ☎ 022/3100706) sells and restores old brass telescopes, barometers, and other scientific instruments. **Au Vieux Canon** (⌧ 40 Grand-Rue, ☎ 022/3105758) deals in extravagant English silver. **Buchs** (✉ 36 Grand-Rue, ☎ 022/3117485) sells antique frames of Old Master vintage and quality. The showroom at **Galerie 5** (✉ 5 pl. du Bourg-de-Four, ☎ 022/3107824) is full of well-polished old English furniture. Head to **Librairie Ancienne** (✉ 20 Grand-Rue, ☎ 022/3102050) for leather-bound and gilt first editions. **Rue des Belles Filles** (✉ 6 bis rue Étienne-Dumont, ☎ 022/3103131) is a crowded treasure trove of vintage clothing, jewelry, and knickknacks.

Books

À Montparnasse (✉ 37 Grand-Rue, ☎ 022/3116719) deals in unusual old books and prints. **Elm Books** (✉ 3 rue Versonnex, ☎ 022/7360945) stocks current and classic English-language titles for all ages. **Galerie Bernard Letu** (✉ 2 rue Calvin, ☎ 022/3104757) carries an inspired collection of art and photography books. **La Joie de Lire** (✉ 38 pl. du Bourg-de-Four, ☎ 022/3113565) has a full, colorful range of children's books in French. **Librairie Archigraphy** (✉ 1 pl. de l'Ile, ☎ 022/3116008) presents art and architecture books in a setting worthy of its subjects. **Librairie Jullien** (✉ 32 pl. du Bourg-de-Four, ☎ 022/3103670) has sold books old and new since 1839. **L'Oreille Cassée** (✉ 9 quai des Bergues, ☎ 022/7324080) captures the market for hardcover *bandes dessinées* (comic books). The commercial chain **Payot** (✉ 5 rue de Chantepoulet, ☎ 022/7318950; ✉ 16 rue du Marché, ☎ 022/3197940) serves French, English, and German readers.

Chocolate

Silky, handmade, white chocolate truffles top the selection at **Arn** (✉ 12 pl. du Bourg-de-Four, ☎ 022/3104094). The dark chocolate at **Le Comptoir du Chocolat** (✉ 19 pl. du Bourg-de-Four, ☎ 022/3109910) is pure and lightly spiced. **Du Rhône** (✉ 3 rue de la Confédération, ☎ 022/3115614) has sold refined, cinnamon-dusted morsels since 1875. **Merkur** (✉ 13 rue du Mont-Blanc, ☎ 022/7322719; ✉ 32 rue du Marché, ☎ 022/3102221) has Swiss-themed gift boxes, individual bars, and huge champagne truffles. The house speciality at **Rohr** (✉ 3 pl. du Molard, ☎ 022/3116303; ✉ 42 rue du Rhône, ☎ 022/3116876) is chocolate truffles shaped like Geneva garbage cans.

Jewelry

There's no ceiling on the price of precious baubles in Geneva. **Bucherer** (✉ 26 quai Général Guisan, ☎ 022/3196266) sells diamonds of all sizes and luminous pearls. **Bulgari** (✉ 30 rue du Rhône, ☎ 022/3177070) favors heavy gold necklaces and rings crusted with jewels; some pieces incorporate ancient coins. You can wrap your wrist with a diamond-studded watch at **Chopard** (✉ 8 rue de la Confédération, ☎ 022/3113728; ✉ 27 rue du Rhône, ☎ 022/3107050). **Cartier** (✉ 35 rue du Rhône, ☎ 022/8185454; ✉ 90 rue du Rhône, ☎ 022/3102040) displays rubies, emeralds, and diamonds set in a variation on the trademark panther and a series of interlocked rolling rings.

L'Arcade (✉ 20 rue de la Corraterie, ☎ 022/3111554) showcases Edith Moldaschl's unique line of "real" costume jewelry from 1930 to 1960. **Ludwig Muller** (✉ 5 rue des Chaudronniers, ☎ 022/3102930) finds inspiration in the commedia dell'arte and uses rare blue gold.

Watches

Geneva's watchmakers are known for unparalleled excellence. **Bucherer** (✉ 45 rue du Rhône, ☎ 022/3196266) carries 2,000 prestigious, indestructible Rolex models. **Franck Muller** (✉ 1 rue de la Tour de l'Ile, ☎ 022/8180030) creates refined, complicated timepieces in the best Swiss tradition. **Patek Philippe** (✉ 41 rue du Rhône, ☎ 022/7812448) still occupies the building where it was founded in 1839 and where the winding mechanism behind all watches was invented. **Piaget** (✉

40 rue du Rhône, ☎ 022/8170200) wraps its ultra-flat watch movements in platinum and gold. **Vacheron-Constantin** (⌧ 1 rue des Moulins, ☎ 022/3103227) is the oldest manufacturer of watches in the world. The first of its sober, exclusive designs appeared in 1755.

GENEVA A TO Z

Arriving and Departing

By Bus

Long-haul bus lines arrive from and depart for points across Europe at the **Gare Routière de Genève** (bus station; ⌧ pl. Dorcière, ☎ 022/7320230), off the rue du Mont-Blanc in the city center.

By Car

Approaching Geneva by car is straightforward. A major expressway (**A1**) follows the northern shore of Lac Léman and connects the city to the rest of Switzerland through Lausanne, where autoroute links with Bern (**A12**) and Martigny (**A9**) join. The scenic southern shore of the lake connects Geneva with the Valais via Évian-les-Bains, in France. Geneva is surrounded almost completely by France and border controls are minimal. Grenoble (to the south), Lyons (to the southwest), and Chamonix (in the French Alps to the southeast) are all between 1 to 2 hours away on the French A40 (*l'Autoroute Blanche*). No matter how brief your foray onto any expressway in Switzerland, you will need a *vignette* or Swiss road-tax sticker (☞ Car Travel *in* the Gold Guide).

By Plane

Cointrin (⌧ 5 km/3 mi northwest of city center, ☎ 022/7177111) is Geneva's airport and the second-largest international airport in Switzerland. Several airlines fly directly to Cointrin from New York City and London, and **Swissair** (☎ 800/221–4750 in the U.S.; 0171/434–7300 in London; 022/7993111 in Geneva) operates hourly connector flights to its hub in Zürich. **Crossair** (☎ 0171/434–7300 in London, 022/7995200 in Geneva), Switzerland's domestic airline, connects Geneva with Basel, Zürich, Lugano, and most major European cities.

BETWEEN THE AIRPORT AND THE CITY CENTER

By Bus. Regular bus service (Bus 10) runs between the airport and downtown Geneva. The ride is about 20 minutes, the fare 2.20 SF. Some hotels have their own shuttles.

By Limousine. Globe (☎ 022/7310750) limousines are manned by multilingual drivers. **Privilege** (☎ 022/7383366) rents chauffeur-driven Mercedes and stretch Rolls Royces.

By Taxi. Taxis are plentiful but expensive. You'll have to pay about 25 SF to reach the city center and there is a 1 SF surcharge per bag.

By Train. Cointrin has a direct rail link with the **Gare Cornavin** (⌧ pl. Cornavin, ☎ 1572222), Geneva's main train station. Trains run about every 15 minutes from 5:45 AM to midnight; the six-minute trip costs 5 SF each way.

By Train

The **Gare Cornavin** (⌧ pl. Cornavin, ☎ 022/1572222) is an important terminus for the Swiss Federal Railways. Direct express trains arrive from most Swiss cities every hour and the French TGV provides a fast link to Paris.

Getting Around

By Bicycle

Geneva has an excellent network of well-maintained bike paths and marked itineraries, both in town and throughout the canton. **Genèv'Roule** (⊠ 17 pl. Montbrillant and Les Bains des Pâquis, ☎ 022/7401343) rents bicycles for 5 SF per day between May and October.

By Boat

The **Compagnie Générale de Navigation** (CGN; ⊠ Jardin Anglais, ☎ 022/3125223) provides steamer transportation between the larger lakeside towns, including Lausanne, Montreux, and Vevey, as well as to Thonon and Évian-les-Bains in France. Holders of the Swiss Pass (☞ Train Travel *in* the Gold Guide) travel free, those with a Swiss Boat Pass (☞ Boat Travel *in* the Gold Guide) for half price.

Smaller-scale lake connections are covered by the **Mouettes Genevoises** (⊠ 8 quai du Mont-Blanc, ☎ 022/7322944) and by **Swissboat** (⊠ 4 quai du Mont-Blanc, ☎ 022/7324747).

By Taxi

Taxis (☎ 022/3314133) are immaculate, and the drivers are polite, but do expect a 6.30 SF minimum charge plus 2.70 SF per km (about ½ mi). In the evening and on Sundays, this rate rises to 3.30 SF per km.

By Tram and Bus

Geneva's public transportation network is cheap, comprehensive, clearly marked, and efficient. Every bus stop has a machine selling tickets, and for 2.20 SF you can use the system for one hour, changing as often as you like between buses, trams and the Mouettes Genevoises, which serve as ferries across the harbor. If you plan to travel frequently, buy a *carte journalière,* which provides one day of unlimited travel within the city center for 5 SF; it's available at most newsstands and from the TRANSPORTS PUBLICS GENEVOIS (TPG) booths at the train station and Cours de Rive. Holders of the Swiss Pass travel free on Geneva public transport.

Contacts and Resources

Consulates

Australia (⊠ 2 chemin des Fins, ☎ 022/7999100). **Canada** (⊠ 1 rue du Pré de la Bichette, ☎ 022/9199200). **New Zealand** (⊠ 28A chemin du Petit-Saconnex, ☎ 022/7349530). **United Kingdom** (⊠ 37-39 rue de Vermont, ☎ 022/9182400). **United States** (⊠ 29 rte. de Pré-Bois, ☎ 022/7981615).

Emergencies

Police (☎ 117). **Ambulance** (☎ 144). **Hospital** (⊠ Hôpital Cantonal, 24 rue Micheli-du-Crest, ☎ 022/3723311). **Doctor referral** (☎ 022/3202511); emergency house calls (☎ 022/7484950). **Pharmacies** (☎ 111).

English-Language Bookstores

Titles sold at **Elm Books** (⊠ 3 rue Versonnex, ☎ 022/7360945) come directly from Britain and the States. **Payot** (⊠ 5 rue de Chantepoulet, ☎ 022/7318950; ⊠ 16 rue du Marché, ☎ 022/3197940) tucks English-language best-sellers in with French books.

Guided Tours

BOAT

Swissboat (⊠ 4 quai du Mont-Blanc, ☎ 022/7324747) operates guided excursions with recorded commentary in English along the shores of Lac Léman from March to November. You'll glimpse grand homes and châteaux. Daily departures are from the quai du Mont-Blanc. The **Mouettes Genevoises** (⊠ 8 quai du Mont-Blanc, ☎ 022/7322944) also provide tours of the lake and the Rhône. You're given a printed text (ask for the English version) and a map when you board at the quai du Mont-Blanc. Boats departing from the place de l'Ile near place Bel-Air have recorded commentary in English.

ORIENTATION

Bus tours of Geneva, operated by **Key Tours** (☎ 022/7314140), leave from the Gare Routière de Genève (⊠ pl. Dorcière), behind the English church off of rue du Mont-Blanc, at 10 AM and 2 PM daily during high season (May–October) and at 2 daily during low season. Each tour costs 35 SF and lasts approximately two hours. Commentary is in English. Tours include an overview of the International Area and a minitrain ride from place Neuve up the steep, narrow streets into the Old Town. In high season you can catch the minitrain independent of the bus tour; it departs from the entrance to the Parc des Bastions at place Neuve. Each loop lasts about 30 minutes, and the cost is 5.90 SF.

Key Tours also offers bus excursions into the Geneva countryside and the Jura, up the lake to Montreux/Chillon, and all-day trips farther afield to Gruyères, the Jungfraujoch, Zermatt, Interlaken, and Chamonix, in France.

SPECIAL INTEREST

The **United Nations** organizes lecture tours of the Palais des Nations. Enter by the Pregny Gate on avenue de la Paix. If you take Bus 8 from Cornavin, don't get off at the Palais de Nations: wait for the smaller Appia stop. Tours last about an hour and cost 8.50 SF; they're offered in English, but there are no set starting times.

WALKING

Geneva's **tourist office** (☞ Visitor Information, *below*) offers private guided tours of the city for fees starting at 35 SF; there's a minimum of two people. The tourist office also provides an English-language audioguide tour of the Old Town that covers 26 points of interest. Rental for the map, cassette, and player costs 10 SF, plus a deposit of 50 SF.

Travel Agencies

American Express (⊠ 7 rue du Mont-Blanc, ☎ 022/7317600). **Carlson Wagonlit Travel** (⊠ 5 rue du Nant, ☎ 022/7372230).**Touring Club Suisse** (⊠ 8 Cours de Rive, ☎ 022/4172040).

Visitor Information

The city's tourist office, the **Office du Tourisme de Genève,** is well organized. You'll find **tourist information booths** at the airport (⊠ Cointrin arrivals, ☎ 022/7178083), on the Right Bank (⊠ 18 rue du Mont-Blanc, ☎ 022/9097000, FAX 022/9097011), at the train station (⊠ Gare Cornavin, ☎ 022/9097045), and even in the middle of the river (⊠ pont de la Machine, ☎ 022/3119827). For information **by mail,** contact the administration (⊠ Case Postale 1602, CH-1212, Genève 1, ☎ 022/9297000, FAX 022/9297011).

14 PORTRAITS OF SWITZERLAND

SKIING SWITZERLAND

TWO CABLE-CAR RIDES and thousands of feet above the resort village of Verbier, we sit in a mountain restaurant. On the table in front of us are one *café renversé*, two cups of hot chocolate, one tiny glass of bubbly white *Fendant* wine from Sion. Our legs tired from a long day of skiing, we catch our breath before the evening run, while the slopes and pistes below empty themselves of skiers and fill up with evening light. Outside, the sun hovers only inches above the horizon. Mont Blanc is an island of ice rising out of a sea of summits along the Franco-Swiss border. Peaks and passes stretch as far as the eye can see, an art director's Alpine fantasy in late light.

Verbier skiing is one reason I've returned to Switzerland in winter, faithfully, for the past 25 years. This is a giant of a ski area in a region of giant ski areas, perched high in the French-speaking, southwest corner of Switzerland, draped over four mountain valleys, embracing six villages, a labyrinth of interconnected lifts (more than 100), interlaced slopes (too many to count)—a ski area you can't explore in a week or even exhaust in a season.

For passionate skiers every trip to Switzerland is a homecoming. All our skiing archetypes originate here. White sawtooth horizons point to the sky, picture-postcard chalet roofs poke up under great white hats of snow, necklaces of lifts and cable cars drape themselves over the white shoulders of fairy-tale mountains, and runs go on forever.

These are big mountains, with vertical drops twice the length of those of the Rockies. In the Alps you can often drop four, five, or six thousand vertical feet in one run. Here runs are so long that halfway down you need a break—which you'll find at a little chalet restaurant in the middle of nowhere, where the views are as exhilarating as the schnapps that's so often the drink of choice.

These are pure white mountains, too, whiter than we're used to. In the Alps, the tree line is low, often only 1,000 m (3,000 ft) above sea level, and ski areas stretch upward from there. The skier's playing field is white on white; marked pistes are white rivers of groomed snow snaking down equally white but ungroomed flanks of Alpine peaks. There are more treeless bowls than you can count, than you can hope to ski in several skiers' lifetimes.

When European skiers tell you that the western Alps are higher and more glaciated, more likely to have good snow in a dry year, and that the eastern Alps are lower in elevation but full of charm, with more intimate, more richly decorated villages, they are usually referring to the difference between the French Alps and Austria. In fact, they could just as well be talking about the mountains and ski resorts of southwest Switzerland versus those of eastern Switzerland, Graubünden, and the Engadine; for Switzerland, with its many cantons, is a microcosm that mirrors the diversity of skiing all across the greater Alps. You can test your credit-card limits at the Palace Hotel in worldly Saint-Moritz, hear the Latin echoes of Romansh as you ride the cog railways of modest Kleine Scheidegg, or ponder the hearty existence of hearty mountain farmers among the peaks of French-speaking Valais—but always, the local mountain culture will be part of your ski experience.

As varied as the regions are the people who ski them. Depending on which canton you ski, you may hear the lilting singsong French of Vaud and the western Valais, the incomprehensible Swiss German of the Berner Oberland and eastern Wallis, or the haunting Latin echoes of Romansh in the high valleys of Graubünden. The ski pistes of Switzerland are the polyglot crossroads of Europe, where stylish Parisians in neon outfits rub elbows with Brits in navy blue, Munich businessmen in Bogner suits, and Swedish students with punk haircuts. And yet, when you're surrounded by mountains that will outlast fashions, lifetimes, and languages, such differences fade, and the mountains are all you can see.

We walk uphill through knee-deep powder toward the summit of the Allalinhorn—the friendliest of Canton Wallis's many 4,000-m (13,120-ft) peaks. Early morning sunshine rakes the corniced ridges around us; the village of Saas-Fee still hides in shadow below. With climbing skins glued to the bottom of our skis, we've shuffled up the Feegletscher to earn a morning's bliss in deep untracked snow. This glacier highway is taking us above the domain of passes and ski lifts and groomed slopes, into a world of icy north walls, pure knife-edge ridges, undulating mile-long coverlets of fresh powder, summits of whipped meringue, and snow crystals sparkling at our feet. Munching cheese and chocolate as we climb, thinking that we must look like silhouettes in one of Herbert Matter's prewar Swiss travel posters, breathing deeply, climbing slowly, we daydream our way to the top. Our tracks, like zippers in the snow, stretch up to a vanishing point in the midnight-blue sky above.

IT'S A SOFT APRIL morning at Les Diablerets, a ski area on the frontier between francophone Vaud and the German canton of Bern. It's already 11 AM and the frozen corn snow is only now softening up on the wide glacier beneath the dark, thumblike peak of the Oldenhorn. From the topmost lift we can see west toward Lake Geneva, south toward the giant peaks of the Valais, and east toward the dark brooding peaks of the Berner Oberland. An observation deck on the roof of the Alps reveals mountains filling space to its farthest corners, to the hazy horizon, waves on a wind-tossed sea, frozen white, as far as one can see. On the deep valley flanks below Les Diablerets, winding west toward the Rhône Valley, another winter's worth of cow manure has performed its annual alchemy: the slopes are greening up with no respect for common-sense color—pastures of eye-dazzling kelly green under dark forests and crags. Only a few miles away, down the eastern German-speaking side of the mountains, the chic resort of Gstaad seems deserted; its jet-set winter guests have already hung up their skis and headed for the Mediterranean. The mountains are ours for a day.

At the top of the lift we break through the clouds. A sea of fog fills the Rhône Valley below us, a fluffy false plain, punctured only by snowy peaks, stretching to the horizon. Somewhere under these clouds is Lake Geneva, and far across, Les Dents du Midi ("The Teeth of Noon") rise out of the clouds like ice-sheathed knuckles. Villars-Gryon is a ski resort so small most American skiers have never heard of it, even though it's bigger than half the ski areas in Colorado. Alone, we ski along the edge of the piste, where the slope steepens and drops away in a succession of rocky ledges. Just over the border that separates the skier's world from the mountaineer's, we see a lone ibex, posing on a rock outcrop against the clouds, scimitar-shape horns swept back in wide twin arcs. We christie to a stop, stand in awe wishing we had cameras, and realize eventually that the ibex is not going to bolt. These are its Alps, its domain; we are the newcomers, birds of passage, intruders. It feels like a privilege to share the roof of Europe with this ibex, a privilege that our Swiss hosts have slowly earned over 700 years by farming basically unfarmable mountainsides, by making this land their domain. We push off, the cold winter snow squeaking under our skis. Behind our backs the ibex still stares off into the distance.

These images stay with me, indelible as the Alps themselves. Say the word *Switzerland* and I see the gentle slopes of the Plateau Rosa above Zermatt, perforated by the dotted lines of T-bars, peppered with tiny, bright-color skiers, slopes lapping in white waves against the base of the Matterhorn. Near Saint-Moritz, I see the blue-green crevasses of the Morteratsch Glacier, a frozen white-water rapid spilling down from the Diavolezza ski area: ice walls, blue ice caves, a labyrinth of ice. I see the three giants of the Berner Oberland, the Eiger, the Mönch, and the Jungfrau—the Ogre, the Monk, and the Virgin—shadowy 13,000-ft-high northern faces that loom above the toy skiers and runs of Grindelwald and Wengen.

That Switzerland has some of the best skiing in the world goes without saying. In the end, though, it's not the skiing I remember, or the runs, or the trails, or my turns. It's the mountains I remember. And so will you.

—Lito Tejada-Flores

BOOKS AND VIDEOS

Books

Wilhelm Tell, by Friedrich von Schiller, is the definitive stage version of the dramatic legend. *The Prisoner of Chillon,* by Lord Byron, is an epic poem inspired by the sojourn of François Bonivard in the dungeon of Chillon. *A Tramp Abroad,* by Mark Twain, includes the author's personal impressions—and tall tales—derived from travels in Switzerland. *Arms and the Man,* by G. B. Shaw, was the source of Oscar Straus's Viennese operetta *The Chocolate Soldier;* both are about a Swiss mercenary with a sweet tooth.

Novels set at least partially in Switzerland include *Daisy Miller,* by Henry James (Lac Léman, Chillon); *Tender Is the Night,* by F. Scott Fitzgerald; *A Farewell to Arms,* by Ernest Hemingway; Thomas Mann's *The Magic Mountain,* (Davos); Albert Cohen's *Belle du seigneur* (Geneva); and *Hotel du Lac,* by Anita Brookner (Vevey). The best-known children's book set in Switzerland is, of course, *Heidi,* by Johanna Spyri (Maienfeld). *Banner in the Sky,* by James Ramsey Ullman, is a powerful children's book about a boy's attempt to climb Switzerland's most challenging mountain.

La Place de la Concorde Suisse, by John McPhee, was developed from a series of *New Yorker* pieces the author wrote after traveling with members of the Swiss army. *Heidi's Alp,* by Christine Hardyment, a first-person account of a family traveling in a camper-van in search of the Europe of fairy tales, includes an adventure with a latter-day alm-uncle in a cabin above Maienfeld. *A Guide to Zermatt and the Matterhorn,* Edward Whymper's memoirs of his disastrous climb up the Matterhorn, is now out of print, but it may be available in a library (excerpts appear in Chapter 11, Valais). In *The Climb Up to Hell,* Jack Olsen details the dramatic 1957 Eiger expedition. *Terminal,* by Colin Forbes, is a murder-mystery tale containing fantastic descriptions of Swiss cities. There have been several books published on the recent findings of the Swiss banks' handling of Jewish and Nazi funds during and after World War II. Among these are *Nazi Gold: The Full Story of the Fifty-Year Swiss-Nazi Conspiracy to Steal Billions from Europe's Jews and Holocaust Survivors,* by Tom Bower, and *Hitler's Silent Partners: Swiss Banks, Nazi Gold, and the Pursuit of Justice,* by Isabel Vincent.

Videos

Heidi is undoubtedly the best-known film to be shot in Switzerland. Make sure you see the 1937 version directed by Allan Dulan, starring Shirley Temple. Swiss air must agree with James Bond; several films have Swiss scenes in them, including 1995's *GoldenEye* and *Goldfinger* (1964); *On Her Majesty's Secret Service* (1969) shows dazzling ski scenes of the Schilthorn in central Switzerland. You can also get glimpses of Swiss scenery in the 1994 version of *Frankenstein. Trois Couleurs Rouge (Three Colors Red),* the last in director Krzysztof Kieslowski's trilogy, and a big hit in Europe, is set in Geneva's Old Town, while Peter Greenaway's 1993 *Stairs* shows Geneva through the director's unique artistic vision. *The Unbearable Lightness of Being* follows a couple fleeing from the 1968 Russian invasion of Czechoslovakia. The moving *Reise der Hoffnung (Journey of Hope),* directed by Xavier Koller in 1990, centers on a Kurdish family fleeing Turkish persecution to seek sanctuary in Switzerland. In French director Claude Chabrol's *Rien Ne Va Plus (The Swindle;* 1997), Isabelle Huppert and Michel Serrault play a pair of con artists who attempt an out-of-their-league scam; a section was shot in Sils-Maria, and a Swiss Army knife comes into play.

376

Winter Activities of the Resorts

Resort	Lift-Ticket Cost (SF) * (one day/six day)	Elevation (m/ft)	Number of Lifts	Lift Capacity (number of riders per hour, in thousands)	Maintained Trails (km/mi)†	Snowmaking
Arosa	49/219	1,800–2,650 m 5,900–8,700 ft	16	21.7	70/43	❄
Crans-Montana	54/255	1,500–3,000 m 4,920–9,843 ft	42	41.0	160/100	❄
Davos-Klosters	52/259	1,560–2,844 m 5,118–9,330 ft	55	55.0	344/197	❄
Flims-Laax	56/280	1,160–3,292 m 3,808–10,798 ft	32	41.2	220/140	❄
Gstaad-Saanenland	50/233	1,100–3,000 m 3,600–9,843 ft	69	50.0	250/160	❄
La Vallée de Conches (cross-country)	n/a	1,300–1,450 m 4,265–4,757 ft	n/a	n/a	n/a	❄
Le Val D'Anniviers	38/200	1,350–3,000 m 4,430–9,843 ft	45	25.0	250/155	❄
Les Portes du Soleil (Champery and 14 linked Swiss and French areas)	48/219	1,000–2,500 m 3,280–8,200 ft	219	228.8	650/400	❄
Verbier (including 6 linked areas of Quatre-Vallées)	56/282	820–3,330 m 2,690–10,925 ft	100	72.7	400/248	❄
Saas-Fee	56/260	1,800–3,600 m 5,900–11,800 ft	26	26.4	100/50	❄
St. Moritz	54/258	1,856–3,060 m 6,100–10,000 ft	55	65.0	350/34	❄
Grindelwald-Wengen	52/232	1,300–3,450 m 4,265–11,300 ft	45	37.0	188/113	❄
Zermatt	60/296	1,260–3,820 m 4,132–12,530 ft	73	70.7	245/152	❄

*varies according to extent of areas selected to ski in
†depending on type and quality of snow, as well as grooming of slopes

Average Annual Snowfall (cm/in)	Difficulty of Terrain: % Beg/Int/Exp	Cross-Country (km/mi of trails)	Glacier Skiing	Heli-Skiing	Para/Hang Gliding	Ice-Skating	Luge Runs	Skibob Runs	Ballooning	Accommodations (bed in hotels, chalets, and apartments)
692/272	31/57/12	26/16			❄	❄	❄		❄	8,000
518/204	38/50/12	48/31	❄	❄	❄	❄	❄	❄	❄	40,000
427/168	30/40/30	75/46			❄	❄	❄	❄		24,000
440/173	50/30/20	60/37	❄	❄	❄	❄	❄		❄	10,800
627/247	40/40/20	127/75	❄	❄	❄	❄	❄	❄	❄	12,500
522/206	n/a	180/53				❄				20,000
348/137	30/40/30	82/51		❄	❄	❄	❄	❄		20,000
619/244	25/40/35	250/155		❄	❄	❄				93,000
491/193	32/42/26	42/33	❄	❄	❄	❄	❄	❄		25,000
357/141	25/25/50	8/4	❄		❄	❄		❄		7,500
368/145	10/70/20	150/93	❄	❄	❄	❄	❄	❄	❄	12,000
389/153	30/50/20	17/10		❄	❄	❄	❄	❄		10,000
434/131	30/40/30	10/6	❄	❄	❄	❄				13,500

WORDS AND PHRASES

	English	French	French Pronunciation
Basics			
	Yes/no	Oui/non	wee/no
	Please	S'il vous plaît	seel voo **play**
	Thank you	Merci	mare-**see**
	You're welcome	De rien	deh ree-**enh**
	Excuse me	Pardon	pahr-**doan**
	Hello	Bonjour	bone-**zhoor**
	Goodbye	Au revoir	o ruh-**vwahr**
Numbers			
	One	Un	un
	Two	Deux	deuh
	Three	Trois	twa
	Four	Quatre	**cat**-ruh
	Five	Cinq	sank
	Six	Six	seess
	Seven	Sept	set
	Eight	Huit	weat
	Nine	Neuf	nuf
	Ten	Dix	deess
Days			
	Today	Aujourd'hui	o-zhoor-**dwee**
	Tomorrow	Demain	deh-**menh**
	Yesterday	Hier	yair
	Morning	Matin	ma-**tenh**
	Afternoon	Après-midi	ah-pray-mee-**dee**
	Night	Nuit	nwee
	Monday	Lundi	**lahn**-dee
	Tuesday	Mardi	**mahr**-dee
	Wednesday	Mercredi	**mare**-kruh-dee
	Thursday	Jeudi	**juh**-dee
	Friday	Vendredi	**vawn**-dra-dee
	Saturday	Samedi	**sam**-dee
	Sunday	Dimanche	**dee**-mawnsh

*Prevalent Swiss-German dialect

German	German Pronunciation	Italian	Italian Pronunciation
Ja/nein	yah/nine	Sí/No	see/no
Bitte	**bit**-uh	Per favore	pear fa-**voh**-reh
Danke	**dahn**-kuh	Grazie	**grah**-tsee-ay
Bitte schön	**bit**-h **shern**	Prego	**pray**-go
Entschuldigen Sie *Äxgüsi	ent-**shool**-de-gen-zee **ax**-scu-see	Scusi	**skoo**-zee
Guten Tag *Grüezi *Grüss Gott	**goot**-en **tahk** **grit**-zee groos got	Buon giorno	bwohn **jyohr**-noh
Auf Widersehen *Ufwiederluege *Tschüss (*familiar*)	Auf **vee-der**-zane oof-**vee-der**-lawgah choohs	Arrivederci	a-ree-vah-**dare**-chee
Eins	eints	Uno	**oo**-no
Zwei	tsvai	Due	**doo**-ay
Drei	dry	Tre	tray
Vier	fear	Quattro	**kwah**-troh
Fünf	fumph	Cinque	**cheen**-kway
Sechs	zex	Sei	say
Sieben	**zee**-ben	Sette	**set**-ay
Acht	ahkt	Otto	**oh**-to
Neun	noyn	Nove	**no**-vay
Zehn	tsane	Dieci	dee-**eh**-chee
Huete	**hoi**-tah	Oggi	**oh**-jee
Morgen	**more**-gehn	Domani	do-**mah**-nee
Gestern	geh-**shtairn**	Ieri	ee-veh-ree
Morgen	**more**-gehn	Mattina	ma-**tee**-na
Nachmittag	nahkt-**mit**-ahk	Pomeriggio	po-mer-**ee**-jo
Nacht	nahkt	Notte	Noh-teh
Montag	**moan**-tahk	Lunedì	**loo**-neh-dee
Dienstag	**deens**-tahk	Martedì	**mahr**-teh-dee
Mittwoch	**mit**-voahk	Mercoledì	**mare**-co-leh-dee
Donnerstag	**doe**-ners-tahk	Giovedì	**jo**-veh-dee
Freitag	**fry**-tahk	Venerdì	**ven**-air-dee
Samstag	**zahm**-stahk	Sabato	**sah**-ba-toe
Sonntag	**zone**-tahk	La Domenica	lah doe-**men**-ee-ca

	English	French	French Pronunciation

Useful Phrases

	Do you speak English?	Parlez-vous anglais?	par-lay-vooz awng-**gleh**
	I don't speak French/German/ Italian.	Je ne parle pas français.	juh nuh parl pah fraun-**seh**
	I don't understand.	Je ne comprends pas.	juh nuh kohm-prawhn **pah**
	I don't know.	Je ne sais pas.	juh nuh say **pah**
	I am American/British.	Je suis américain/ anglais	jhu sweez a-may-ree-**can**/awn-**glay**
	I am sick.	Je suis malade.	juh swee ma-**lahd**
	Please call a doctor.	Appelez un docteur s'il vous plâit.	a-pe-lay un dohk-**tore** seel voo **play**
	Have you any rooms?	Est-ce que vous avez une chambre?	**es**-seh-kuh vooz ah-vay-oon **shahm**-br
	How much does it cost?	C'est combien?	say comb-bee-**enh**
	Do you accept . . . (credit card)	Est-ce que vous acceptez . . .	Ehskuh voo zahksehptay . . .
	Too expensive	Trop cher	troh **shehr**
	It's beautiful.	C'est très beau.	say tray boh
	Help!	Au secours!	o say-**koor**
	Stop!	Arrêtez!	a-ruh-**tay**

Getting Around

	Where is . . .	C'est où . . .	say oo
	The train station?	la gare?	la gahr
	The post office?	la poste?	la pohst
	The hospital?	l'hôpital?	lo-pee-**tahl**
	Where are the rest rooms?	Où sont les toilettes?	oo sohn lay **twah**-let
	Left	A gauche	a **gohsh**
	Right	À droite	a **drwat**
	Straight ahead	Tout droit	**too drwat**

Dining Out

	Waiter/Waitress	Monsieur/ Mademoiselle	muh-**syuh**/ mad-mwa-**zel**
	Please give me . . .	S'il vous plait, donnez-moi . . .	see voo **play** doh nay **mwah**

*Prevalent Swiss-German dialect

German	German Pronunciation	Italian	Italian Pronunciation
Sprechen Sie Englisch?	**Shprek**-hun zee **eng**-glish	Parla inglese?	**par**-la een **glay**-zay
Ich sprech kein Deutsch.	ihkh **shprek**-uh kine doych	Non parlo italiano.	non **par**-lo ee-tal-**yah**-no
Ich kahn nicht ferstehen.	ihkh cahn nicht fair-**shtay**-en	Non capisco.	non ka-**peess**-ko
Ich habe keine Ahnung.	ihkh hah-beh kine-eh **ah**-nung	Non lo so.	non lo **so**
Ich bin Amerikaner(in). Engländer(in).	ihkh bin a-mer-i **so**-no-er(in)/**eng**-glan-der(in)	Sono americano(a)/ Sono inglese.	**so**-no a-may-ree-**kah**-no(a)/**so**-no een-**glay**-zay
Ich bin krank.	ihkh bin **krahnk**	Sto male.	sto **ma**-lay
Bitte rufen einen Arzt.	**bit**-uh **roof**-en ine-en **ahrtst**	Chiami un dottore per favore.	kee-**ah**-mee oon doe-**toe**-ray pear fah-**voh**-reh
Haben sie ein Zimmer?	**Ha**-ben zee ine **tsimmer**	C'e una camera libera?	chay **oo**-nah **cam**-er-ah **lee**-ber-eh
Wieviel kostet das?	**vee**-feel **cost**-et dahs	Quanto costa?	**kwahn**-toe-**coast**-a
Nehmen Sie . . .	**nay**-men zee . . .	Posso pagare . . .	**pohs**-soh pah-**gah**-reh . . .
Es kostet zu viel.	es **cost**-et tsu feel	Troppo caro	**troh**-poh **cah**-roh
Das ist schön.	dahs is **shern**	É bello(a).	eh **bell**-oh
Hilfe!	**hilf**-uh	Aiuto!	a-**yoo**-toe
Halt!	hahlt	Alt!	ahlt
Wo ist . . . Der Bahnhof? Die Post?	**vo** ist dare **bahn**-hof dee **post**	Dov'è . . . la stazione? l'ufficio postale?	doe-**veh** la sta-tsee-**oh**-nay loo-**fee**-cho po-**sta**-lay
Das Krankenhaus? *Das Spital?	dahs **krahnk**-en-house dahs shpee-**tahl**	l'ospedale?	lo-spay-**dah**-lay
Wo ist die Toilette?	vo ist dee twah-**let**-uh	Dov'è il bagno?	doe-**vay** eel **bahn**-yo
Links	links	a sinistra	a see-**neess**-tra
Rechts	rechts	a destra	a-**des**-tra
geradeaus	geh-**rod**-uh ouse	Avanti dritto	a-**vahn**-tee **dree**-to
Herr Ober/ Fraülein	hehr **oh**-ber **froy**-line	Cameriere(a)	kah-meh-**ryeh**-reh(rah)
Bitte geben sie mir . . .	**bit**-uh gay behn zee-**meer**	Mi dia pear-fah-**voh**-reh . . .	mee **dee**-a

English	French	French Pronunciation
The menu	La carte	la cart
The bill/check	L'addition	la-dee-see-**ohn**
A fork	Une fourchette	ewn four-**shet**
A knife	Un couteau	uhn koo-**toe**
A spoon	Une cuillère	ewn kwee-**air**
A napkin	Une serviette	ewn sair-vee-**et**
Bread	Du pain	due penh
Butter	Du beurre	due bur
Milk	Du lait	due lay
Pepper	Du poivre	due **pwah**-vruh
Salt	Du sel	due sell
Sugar	Du sucre	due **sook**-ruh
Coffee	Un café	uh(n) kahfay
Tea	Un thé	uh(n) tay
Mineral water *carbonated/still*	De l'eau minéral *gazeuse/non gazeuse*	duh loh meenehrahl gahzuhz/noh(n) gahzuhz
Wine	Vin	venh
Cheers!	A votre santé!	ah vo-truh sahn-**tay**

German	German Pronunciation	Italian	Italian Pronunciation
Die speisekarte	dee **shpie**-zeh-car-tuh	Il menù	eel may-**noo**
Die Rechnung	dee **rekh**-nung	Il conto	eel **cone**-toe
Ein Gabel	I-nuh-**gah**-buhl	Una forchetta	oona for-**ket**-a
Ein messer	I-nuh-**mess**-ehr	Un coltello	oon kol-**tel**-o
Einen Löffel	I-nen **ler**-fuhl	Un cucchiaio	oon koo-kee-**ah-yo**
Die Serviette	dee zair-vee-**eh**-tuh	Il tovagliolo	eel toe-va-lee-**oh-lo**
Brot	broht	Il pane	eel **pa**-nay
Butter	**boo**-tehr	Il burro	eel **boo**-roh
Milch	meelch	Il latte	eel **lot**-ay
Pfeffer	**fef**-fehr	Il pepe	eel **pay**-pay
Salz	zahlts	Il sale	eel **sah**-lay
Zucker	**tsoo**-kher	Lo zucchero	loh **tsoo**-ker-o
eine Kaffee	**ine**-eh kah-feh	un caffè	oon kahf-**feh**
einen Tee	**ine**-en tay	un tè	oon teh
Mineral wasser	mi-neh-**raal**-**vahs**-sehr	L'acqua minerale	l'ah kwa mee-neh-**rah**-leh
mit gas/ohne gas	mit gahz/**oh**-nuh gahz	_gassata/naturale_	gahs-**sah**-tah/ nah-too-**rah**-leh
Wein	vine	Il vino	eel **vee**-noh
Zum Wohl! *Proscht	zoom vole prosht	Salute!	sah-**loo**-teh

INDEX

NOTES

NOTES

NOTES

Looking for a different kind of vacation?

Fodor's makes it easy with a full line of specialty guidebooks to suit a variety of interests—from adventure to romance to language help.

Fodor's. For the world of ways you travel.

L@@king FOR A great place to go?

We know just the place. In fact, it attracts more than 125,000 visitors a day, making it one of the world's most popular travel destinations. It's previewtravel.com, the Web's comprehensive resource for travelers. It gives you access to over 500 airlines, 25,000 hotels, rental cars, cruises, vacation packages and support from travel experts 24 hours a day. Plus great information from Fodor's travel guides and travelers just like you. All of which makes previewtravel.com quite a find.

Preview Travel has everything you need to plan & book your next trip.

© 1999 Preview Travel, Inc. Visitors estimated from Media Metrix 3/99 Key Measures Web Report.
CST #2022036-40

air, car & hotel reservations

vacation packages & cruises

destination planning & travel tips

24-hour customer service

previewtravel.com

preview travel

aol keyword: previewtravel
www.previewtravel.com